West
on a sh

A KINDLY
NEPALI

West Asia on a Shoestring
Fifth edition

Published by
Lonely Planet Publications
PO Box 88, South Yarra, Victoria 3141, Australia
PO Box 2001A, Berkeley, CA 94702, USA

Printed by
Colorcraft, Hong Kong

Cover illustrations by
Anthony Jenkins

First published
October 1973

This edition
January 1986

National Library of Australia Cataloguing in Publication Data

Wheeler, Tony.
West Asia on a shoestring

5th ed.
Includes index.
ISBN 0 908086 68 7.

1. Asia – Description and travel – 1951 – Guide-books. I. Title

915'.04428

Tony Wheeler was born in England but spent most of his younger days overseas due to his father's occupation with British Airways. Those years included a lengthy spell in Pakistan, a shorter period in the West Indies and all his high school years in the US. He returned to England to do a university degree in engineering, worked for a short time as an automotive design engineer, returned to university again and did an MBA then dropped out on the Asian overland trail with his wife Maureen. They've been travelling, writing and publishing guidebooks ever since having set up Lonely Planet Publications in the mid-70s. Travelling for Tony and Maureen is now considerably enlivened by their daughter Tashi (who celebrated her third birthday in Kathmandu) and son Kieran (who had visited Nepal, India and Sri Lanka before he was one year old).

This Edition

The first three editions of this guide were titled *Across Asia on the Cheap* but with the fourth edition we decided it was time for a name change. There were a number of reasons for this decision but the principal ones were that we felt with the current situation in Asia there wasn't so much 'acrossing' any more but also we wanted to bring the title into line with our other two Asia shoestring guides.

Asia overland travel has made a slight recovery since the last edition of this guidebook – we've certainly been surprised by the number of letters we've received from intrepid travellers in Iran. And even more surprised by how positive they all were. Turkey is also once again becoming popular with travellers and despite upheavals in India and Sri Lanka the whole sub-continent remains a superb area for travellers. As with *South-East Asia on a Shoestring* this book has become simply too big and too detailed for me to cover everywhere for every update but we now have individual guides to most countries covered in this book and the research that goes into those books also finds its way into this overall guide. In addition I manage to get back to at least some places for every edition – this time round I revisited India (briefly), Nepal (and had a wonderful time yet again) and Sri Lanka (I still like it).

Thanks must also go to the home base Lonely Planet workers plus, of course, the many letters from 'our travellers' out on the road. Once again special thanks to those ultra-intrepid adventurers who wrote the most interesting letters from the most outrageous places. We love all the letters but those from Iran, Afghanistan, Saudi Arabia and the like are especially gratefully received!

Many readers' letters have been credited in recent editions of India, Sri Lanka, Pakistan and our other Asia travel survival kits. In addition thanks to:

Dr A K Aggarwal (UK), J L Abraham (Aus), Erik & Elizabeth Alkent (Aus), William Allberry (UK), Margaret Allsebrook (USA), Tord Andersson & Kristin Olsson (Sw), Alison Andrew & Live Atad (NZ), Kim Atkinson (UK), T D Ascon (Sp), Ruby Aver (USA), Karin Back (Sw), C Bado, A S Barron (Z), Bonnie Baskin (USA), Peter Bauer (A), Mathias Bev (UK), David Birch (UK), Anders Blanguet, Grant Blackwell & Sara Hall (UK), Geoffrey Bewley (Aus), Geoff Blundell (NZ), Jeff Bogdanoff (Aus), M L Bridge (UK), Michael Bromfield (UK), Sue & John Brotherton (UK), Christina

continued on page 364

Contents

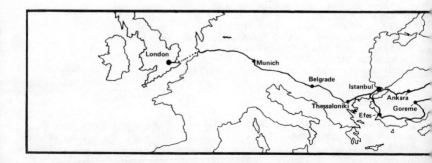

Introduction

OVERLANDING?

Yes, you can still overland. The crazy activities in Iran have led many people to think that the doors were shut and crossing Asia was no longer possible. The truth is very different. In actual fact the overland companies have continued operating across Asia with hardly a pause although much less frequently than in the past. When trips have had to overfly Iran it's been because of difficulties in obtaining visas rather than fears of political violence or other dangers within the borders. A steady trickle of independent travellers have also continued to make their way across Iran. Somewhat surprisingly they all seem to find that you get a very friendly reception.

Afghanistan, on the other hand, is more decisively off limits, unless you treat your life very lightly. Elsewhere in Asia – well Turkey has become a calmer, more orderly place to visit now that a pragmatic and stable military government has reluctantly given the politicians their marching orders. The Middle East continues to be hot and cold – civil war still rages in the Lebanon but Jordan is welcoming visitors with open arms and getting more of them due to the improved relations between Israel and Egypt. Iraq was opening up for a while but their intemperate conflict with

Iran has shut the doors again. In most of the other Arab Gulf states travelling is pretty well discouraged, but more for purely political and internal reasons than any external conflict.

Further east Pakistan has moved both ways at once. On one hand there are fewer visitors than before due to the general contraction of overlanding and also due to the lurid tales of Pakistani Islamic excesses. On the other hand many people, their attention and interest turned elsewhere by the situations in Iran and Afghanistan, have started exploring the previously little visited delights of the Pakistan Himalaya where you'll find the exotic valleys of Swat, Chitral, Gilgit and Hunza. India remains India, although the violence in the Punjab has, at least temporarily made things a little difficult. Nepal also continues to attract steady streams of visitors and trekkers while Sri Lanka has first enjoyed a real tourist boom then seen it slow dramatically due to internal unrest.

The best news of all for dedicated overlanders, however, has been the opening up of China. The border between Nepal and Tibet is now open so with the right nationality you could overland all the way from Hong Kong to London – if the border between India and Pakistan is open.

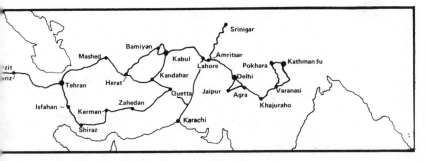

Furthermore there are persistent rumours about the border between Pakistan and China opening up as well. If that should happen then intrepid travellers could use the Karakoram Highway to make a complete circuit of the Himalaya.

So overall the good and the bad news is that yes, you can still overland; no, it's not as easy as it was before; but a big yes, western Asia is very much worth the effort of visiting. It can still be a fantastic adventure.

Facts about the Region

DOCUMENTS

There are two documents you have to have and a number worth considering. You must have a passport and health certificate. Make sure your passport is valid for a reasonably long period of time and has plenty of space for those rubber-stamp-happy Asians to do their bit. It could be embarrassing to run out of blank pages when you are far away from an embassy to issue you a new one (or stick extra pages in for some nationalities). International Health Certificates are usually available from the doctor who gives you your jabs – see vaccinations for more details.

If you plan to be driving abroad get an International Driving Permit from your local automobile association. They are valid for one year only. An International Youth Hostel card can be useful even if you don't intend to use hostels. Although many Asian hostels don't require that you be a YHA member, they will often charge you less if you have a card.

Then there are student cards. The ISIC, International Student Identity Card, is a green and white card with your photograph on it, usually supplied in laminated plastic. It can perform all sorts of wonders such as getting you 25% discounts on many international and domestic flights or 25 to 50% discounts on rail travel in Pakistan, Iran and Turkey. In Turkey there are reductions on museum charges and admission to archaeological sites and countless other useful touches. So it is no wonder at all that there is a worldwide industry in fake student cards.

The authorities have tightened up on the abuse of student cards by several methods. You may be required to provide additional proof of student status – such as 'student' in your passport, a letter from your university or college stating that you are a student or a similar letter from your embassy. Additionally maximum-age limits are now imposed for granting many student concessions or simple 'youth fare' discounts may be offered, irrespective of student status. The fake card peddlers have also been clamped down on.

Nevertheless cards are still widely available and usable. In almost any travel centre there will be somebody pushing cards and throughout the world the going price seems to be US$5 to US$10. Remember that cards issued in certain places are liable to suspicion – Athens and Bangkok in particular. Some fake cards are of deplorably low quality (from the would be non-student users point of view that is) but it hardly matters – any airline would rather sell a seat for 25% off than not sell it at all and a student card is just an excuse to get you on board airline A (at 25% off) rather than airline B.

Finally, remember that 'student' is a very respectable thing to be and if your passport has a blank space for occupation you are much better having 'student' there rather than 'journalist', 'photographer', or some similar unpleasant profession.

Photographs

Raid the piggy bank, rush around to your favourite photo booth and get dozens of mug shots. Three dozen wouldn't be too many, every visa seems to require two or three plus others are needed for ID papers, passports, driving licences and student cards. Asians are very big on photos and you may feel obliged to present a photo of your own sweet face to someone who has been particularly nice. So take plenty, they are cheaper and easier now than later. While you are at it get a photocopy or two of your student card, this is required by some airlines before they give you your student-discounted tickets and photocopy machines are few and far between in some places. It's worth taking photocopies of other relevant documents too, such as your passport data pages, in case of loss.

VISAS

Visas are an annoying, expensive and time-consuming piece of red tape. Effectively they are permits to enter certain countries and are stamped in your passport. You can either get them before you go or along the way. The advantage of pre-departure collection is that it doesn't waste travelling time, the post office can do the leg work, and 'difficult' embassies are sometimes less difficult when you are in your own country. The two major drawbacks are that some countries may not even be represented in your own country and often visas have a limited 'tenability' – it is no good getting a visa which will expire in three months if you are not going to arrive in that country for four months. You can always get a visa at an embassy or consulate in a neighbouring or nearby country, and often visas are available at the border or, even more likely, at the airport of arrival.

Most visas require a stack of forms, a gallery of photos and a pocketful of money – although some are free. Other less together requirements can pop up. You may have to have a certain amount of money or travellers' cheques, your hair length (if you are male) or appearance may have to meet certain standards and you may have to provide the dreaded 'tickets out'. That means before you can obtain a visa to enter the country you must have a ticket to leave it. Which can often be a real nuisance if you should want to leave by some obscure method for which tickets are only obtainable within the country. The answer in that situation is to get the simplest and cheapest airline ticket available and get it from a reputable international airline – so that refunding it later, if you don't use it, is easy.

If you hit a sticky visa problem, shop around. In some other city or country the situation may be better. Full details follow in the country by country sections, but remember the most important rule: treat embassies, consulates and borders as formal occasions – dress up for them.

Embassies

That's other peoples' embassies, what about your own? Well they are really not much use – they won't bail you out of trouble, generally won't hold mail for you and even the newspapers tend to be months out of date. Of course there are some honourable exceptions, some have excellent libraries with up to date newspapers and magazines, and brazen travellers recommend their 'government-employees-only' cafeterias for back-home food. Some embassies also post useful warning notices about local dangers or potential problems. The US embassies are particularly good at this – in Kathmandu, for example, they have recently been warning travellers about cases of robbery or assault on lone trekkers in certain regions.

MONEY

Bring as much as you can of this desirable commodity. Everybody will have their own idea of how much is enough although the main expense is likely to be your air tickets at one end or the other. On top of those basic transportation costs go your living costs. In parts of Asia, if you're just lazing around on the beach doing nothing much, that can still be the legendary dollar (or two) a day, but in other places it can be much higher. This aspect completely depends on your personal comfort needs and where you decide to spend your time. If half your time is spent on the beach at Goa your daily average is obviously going to be much lower than for someone who tries to pack everything in and travels to a new place virtually every day.

Leaving aside those big expenditures (like airlines tickets) it's probably fair to say that most travellers will average around US$10 a day for food, accommodation and day-to-day travelling. The real shoestringers might get down to US$5 while people who like a little more luxury might go higher. Remember that visa costs can mount up rapidly if you do much travelling back and forth. If you start buying things that puts an added hole in your budget. And when you have finished travelling you will want money to get back home or to set yourself up until you have a job – horrible thought!

How should you carry the ready – part travellers' cheques and part cash is the answer. US dollars are still the most widely recognised and easily converted currency although in Asia the pound and the Deutsche mark are pretty close. American Express and other major travellers' cheques are available in a variety of currencies apart from the dollar. Australian dollars are only really worth considering in South-East Asia although you can change them without difficulty on the sub-continent.

American Express and Thomas Cooks are probably the best known travellers' cheques. Easy replacement if they are stolen is the key to cheques on a long trip – which is why you shouldn't bother with lesser known brands of travellers' cheques. Once upon a time a lot of people made quite a business of artificially 'losing' their cheques – not necessarily to dishonestly use the replacements, but to have more cheques in hand to wave at border or embassy officials. The end result is that companies are much more suspicious about 'losses' these days. I have only once lost cheques and they were replaced without a quibble by American Express but don't believe the ads about how easy it is to get them replaced – you need to have serial numbers, proof of initial purchase and other relevant information to hand before Amex are even going to talk to you.

Carry some cheques in small denominations for last minute conversions. Sometimes you get charged a per cheque service fee so don't have it all in small amounts. It is often worth checking

around a few banks – exchange rates do vary and there are those hidden extras like service fees. You don't want all your money in travellers' cheques, you need some cash to play the black market or for quick transactions when the banks are closed. The odd dollar in the right place can sometimes perform the occasional miracle too.

There is still some black market activity in some Asian countries. If you do play the black market don't do it on the street – a dealer with a front, a travel agent or tailor shop for example, is safest. You may be asked to declare your cash and cheques on entry and exit and account for the difference in bank receipts, but that is more for appearance's sake than for real. Requiring bank receipts for major purchases like airline tickets (or requiring payment in foreign currency) is more rigorously enforced.

You can still do a little better in some places by bringing currency in with you. The major international currencies apart, most money loses its value away from home – particularly something like Indian rupees where it is officially illegal to bring them into the country. Singapore and Bangkok are major money markets in South-East Asia.

Cash is very useful for the non-bank but legal transactions you have to make from time to time. Changing cash can be a hell of a lot easier than going through the interminable hassles, red tape and paperwork that travellers' cheques and banks can involve. Money changers can almost always be found open somewhere – holy day, holidays or whatever. Throughout Asia avoid accepting torn or particularly tatty notes which you may have difficulty disposing of except to a bank. Some Asian banknotes all seem to be torn and tatty from the very start. Also avoid getting large denomination notes – getting change from them can be a near impossibility.

To carry all this money, next to your skin is the old safe place. A money belt or pouch, or an extra pocket inside your jeans will help to keep things with their rightful owner. You can pick up nice leather money belts or pouches in a number of countries. Remember that if you lose cash you have lost it for ever, so don't go overboard on the convenience of cash versus the safety of cheques. A useful idea is to put aside a totally separate little emergency stash, say US$50, for use if everything else were to disappear. If there are two of you the money carrying duties can be split to minimise the risk of a total loss.

If you run out it is a fairly simple matter to have funds transferred to you from a bank account in your home country. Insist that the money is telexed or cabled and allow plenty of time. In slow moving, bureaucratic places like India allow weeks. Ask your bank to send the money to a specific bank in the city you nominate or to inform you which bank the money is being transferred to. It is better to arrange this before you go. 'Waiting for money' is a well known, wasteful and very boring occupation. Avoid it by taking enough to begin with, don't run out! The money will be converted into local currency with which you can then buy travellers' cheques if you wish.

WHEN & HOW LONG

You'll miss the whole lazy purpose of overlanding if you go too fast although I guess you could travel all the way from Australia to Europe (or vice versa) in six weeks if you were travelling right across Asia. And be completely worn out. Don't; three to six months is a more reasonable minimum and it's easy to stretch those months to over a year.

These days a trans-Asia schedule is somewhat changed by the situation in Afghanistan and Iran – no longer can you spend weeks making your mind up which way to go, now it's Iran or nothing and even that at a pretty fast pace. Westbound the best seasons are October through about March in India, Nepal or Pakistan. By that time it's beginning to warm up in Iran and you would arrive in Turkey and

then Europe in time for spring. Eastbound the best time to leave Europe would be in late summer so you cross Turkey and Iran as the summer heat is leaving but before the winter chill arrives. That way you could plan to arrive on the sub-continent in October as the monsoon ends and everything is cool, fresh and green.

There are a number of local variations and seasons to catch or to avoid. In Sri Lanka there's a double monsoon so while the weather is good on the west coast from October to March it's bad on the east coast, and vice versa. Nepal's trekking season is October to April but in Kashmir April to October is the best time. If you're continuing on to South-East Asia there are far fewer variations in the climate – it simply tends to be hot and humid all the time. Basically don't worry about it – you're bound to be in the wrong place at the wrong time somewhere along the line!

HEALTH

A British medical magazine actually published an article describing the 'overland syndrome' – a collection of afflictions suffered by many overland travellers. Although one of its symptoms was said to be a strange propensity for eastern clothing the article finished on the reassuring note that this, along with the other symptoms, was easily cured. They don't tell you how to avoid that danger but most other possible medical problems are covered in health guides like *The Traveller's Health Guide* (Roger Lascelles, London) or *Staying Healthy in Asia* (Volunteers in Asia Publications, Stanford). *The Tropical Traveller* by John Hatt (Pan, London) is a useful general introduction to travelling in hot climate regions.

Immunisations

Plan ahead for getting your immunisations. Smallpox has now been wiped out world wide so smallpox immunisation is no longer necessary. Cholera is a disease of insanitation and usually occurs in epidemics.

Cholera vaccinations offer protection for six months and are highly recommended. The initial shot is followed a month or so later by a booster, then another booster every six months to continue the protection. If cholera shots are a sneak preview of the real thing it is definitely a disease to do without.

Immunisation against both typhoid and tetanus is highly recommended. There are three types of vaccinations available – plain typhoid protection, TAB which protects against typhoid and paratyphoid A and B, and TABT which provides the whole lot including protection against tetanus. TABT lasts for three years. If you've not had a recent polio booster it's not a bad idea to get one. Vaccination enthusiasts can also consider protection against typhus and plague but there is a limit!

Yellow fever shots, which last a nice round 10 years, are only necessary for Africa or Latin America. Then there's hepatitis and gamma-globulin shots. The period of immunity to hepatitis which gamma-globulin gives is relatively short and some people question just how efficacious it is, even suggesting that once its period of protection has finished you are more susceptible to the hep than before. Doctors say the latest gamma-globulin shots are better than before and also cause less reaction so you ought to have them. The best protection against the hep, as against most other diseases of insanitation, is to take care what and where you eat and to wash your hands frequently. If you should be so unfortunate as to get the dreaded hepatitis the only real cure is good food, no alcohol and rest.

As proof of all these scratches, jabs and punctures you need an International Health Certificate to be signed and stamped by your doctor and local health authority. In some countries (Australia, the UK, many countries in Asia) immunisations are available cheaply from airport or government health centres. Travel agents or airline offices will tell you where.

Malaria

Malarial mosquitoes are at home in parts of India, Nepal and Pakistan and in many parts of South-East Asia. It is really wise to be careful anywhere in Asia. Prevention consists of a weekly dose of chloroquine or daily paludrine – opinions differ on which is best and which is easiest to remember to take. I prefer the weekly ones. Should you be so unfortunate as to catch malaria the same tablets, in much greater dosage, are also the cure. You must start taking anti-malarials before you enter malarial areas and continue taking them for a period afterwards.

Malaria may now be much less common but it still does exist and a lot of foolish travellers seem to get it. In fact recently it seems to have been on the increase again and also developing some unpleasant drug-resistant strains. It's advisable not just to request a prescription for anti-malarials but to actually specify which countries you will be visiting as in some countries in Asia, particularly South-East Asia, more stringent protection is required. Once you have had it, even if cured, there is a fair chance of it recurring later and it is not a pleasant experience. Further protection can be gained by keeping the little buggers away with mosquito nets or by burning mosquito coils.

In the US, unfortunately, anti-malarials are extremely expensive – much more than they cost in Europe or Australia and astronomically more than they cost in Asia. If you're travelling from the US and you're not going straight to a malarial area you can save a lot of money by getting anti-malarials outside the US.

Stomach Problems

Stomach upsets are probably the most common health problem in west Asia – the mundane and inevitable Delhi Belly. Often this can be due simply to a change of diet or a system unused to spicy food.

Many times, however, contaminated food or water is the problem. There are two answers to upset stomachs. First avoid them by taking care in what you eat and drink – make sure food is well cooked and hasn't been sitting around. Make sure fresh food has been properly cleaned. And don't drink untreated water. Secondly, if avoidance fails do something about it.

The simplest treatment is to do nothing. If your system can fight off the invaders naturally you'll probably build up some immunity against it recurring. Stick to hot tea and try not to eat too much. If you do decide to resort to modern medicines don't do it too readily, don't overdo them and if you start a course of medicine follow it through to the end. There are various over-the-counter cures like the popular Lomotil. The name indicates that it 'lowers motility'; it simply slows your system down and lets it work things out. Plain codeine works as well and is cheaper. Antibiotics, on the other hand, actually go into battle for you but I have a suspicion that people who have the most stomach problems are the ones who resort too readily to antibiotics and other 'big guns'.

The word 'dysentery' is used far too lightly by many travellers. If you've just got loose movements you've got diarrhoea. If blood or pus are also present then you probably have amoebic dysentery which requires an anti-amoebic drug like metronidazole or flagyl. If on top of that you also have a fever then it's probably bacillary dysentery and you need an antibiotic like tetracycline or a sulfa drug. None of these drugs need the supervision of a doctor and are usually readily available.

Whether you just have travellers' diarrhoea or something worse the important thing is to keep your fluid intake up and avoid dehydration. Keep drinking.

Hot Season Health
In the hot season, particularly in India, keep out of the sun and drink plenty. The sun may not feel hot, due to the dust haze, but it still does you no good. Because of the dryness you may not feel hot and sweaty but if you urine starts to become dark yellow or orange and the need to urinate becomes less frequent you're getting dehydrated.

Medical Kit
Carry a small, straightforward medical kit with any necessary medicines, band-aids, antiseptic, aspirin and a small thermometer. In Asia you'll usually find that if a medicine is available at all it will generally be available over the counter and the price will be much cheaper than in the west.

General Thoughts
Bring your spectacle prescription with you if you're shortsighted. Get your teeth checked before you depart, dental problems in Asia are no joke. Rubber thongs are good protection against athletes' foot or other foot infections. Take care with simple cuts and scratches – they can all too easily become infected. Make sure they're properly cleaned and kept that way. Avoid dogs and monkeys, rabies is a nasty thing to catch.

If you need medical help your embassy or consulate can usually advise a good place to go. So can five star hotels although they often recommend doctors with five star prices. In India there are some good private clinics, otherwise you'll generally find hospitals operated by western missionaries are better than government hospitals. Don't forget to take out medical insurance; check if it will fly you home in a dire emergency.

Last, but far from least, don't be overly concerned with your health. In over 10 years of kicking around Asia I've had nothing more serious than a few stomach upsets.

ACCOMMODATION
Finding places to sleep is no problem in Asia. In many places that one-dollar-a-night yardstick can still apply. Of course a

dollar doesn't guarantee very much, but with a little care you can avoid the unwanted extras, like dirty bedding or bed bugs.

Don't expect to find hot water very often, or even running water all the time. Even electricity may be a dream for the future in some places. In India some places can be very dirty while others are surprisingly comfortable and good value. In Nepal you may even get hot water, a near necessity on a chilly Kathmandu morning. Along the Turkish Mediterranean coast there are some memorable cheapies.

Never place too much faith in your hotel staff's honesty. Your room is not a safe place to leave valuables as I have unfortunately found out. One final thing you will have to get used to almost as soon as you start is the Asian toilet position. A toilet is two foot holds and a hole in the floor. Don't worry, you will soon find squatting quite natural and it is physiologically better for you – half the constipation in the west is caused by our unhealthy habit of performing bodily functions from a sitting position.

FOOD

Eat whatever you like, you are bound to get something that doesn't like you somewhere along the line so why worry about it? My general rule of thumb is to have a glance at the restaurant or food stall proprietor – if he looks clean and healthy then chances are his food will be too. If he looks as if he is about to drop dead, eat elsewhere.

In the less advanced countries there are two things to be extra careful about – water and fresh food. Unless you know it has been boiled I would try to avoid drinking water in any of the countries along the Asian overland trail. Don't worry, there are plenty of substitutes for water. Fresh vegetables, salads and fruit are definite dangers. It is no use avoiding the water if you then eat fresh food that has been washed in it. When you have seen food being washed in the *jubes*, the open

drains found in many Middle Eastern towns, you won't be so hungry for fresh food anyway.

Very often it is not the food that spreads whatever there is to be spread, but the eating utensils. Usually they are washed in cold water so germs stay on board and in places with lots of western travellers, many of them recently arrived and susceptible to unhappy alimentary systems, things just get passed around. Which is another reason so many Asians disdain them and dig in with their hands. You can be sure how clean your hand is, right? But always use your right hand, the left hand is for quite another purpose and dipping, left handed, into the rice would be more than just bad manners. Cutting the right hand off thieves did not just disable them, it also banned them from the communal dinner table.

Well known brands of soft drinks and hot tea or coffee are dependable and safe refreshments anywhere. Coke has penetrated to almost every country on the overland route although the Indians have kicked the company out for not handing their secret formula over to the government. If you want to fight off an assault on the digestive system, unaided by modern science, the old remedy of starving them out, with the help of hot tea, usually does the trick. Don't be over cautious – in most places restaurants and food shops do boil the water for drinks and I generally try to convince myself that ice is OK too.

No matter how adroitly you avoid assaults on your stomach you will end up losing weight. In fact travelling around Asia can beat any crash diet hands down. You seem to gain it straight back as soon as you stop travelling though! My personal recommendation about food is to cop out occasionally in places like India where the food can be none too special and splurge on a meal in some western tourist trap. A meal in that sort of place can do wonders to your mood as well as your well being. Over economy on food is definitely false economy.

If all this talk of stomach troubles, weight loss and avoiding things has put you off Asian food, take heart. There are some great taste treats waiting for you whether it is crack-of-dawn porridge in Kathmandu, a fiery curry in India, out-of-this-world melons in Iran or deliciously spicy sandwiches in Turkey.

PEOPLE

The things you see may be superb, but it is the people that make the Asia trip so interesting, whether they are the people whose countries you pass through, or your fellow travellers. For perhaps obvious reasons a cross section of overlanders seem to be a whole lot more interesting than a cross section of the general population. You always find interesting people and the friends one makes on the road are one of the real pleasures of travel. Usually you find yourself part of a larger group as you travel, so don't worry about starting out on your own.

Two is still the ideal number for travelling but a larger group often has advantages. You can bargain for group rates at hotels for example – at some places you always seem to be lumped in half-a-dozen to a room. At railway stations or on ships, having a larger group ensures that you always have someone free for the ticket queue or for guarding the gear.

Despite the fact that overlanders are now an everyday sight and no longer an object of curiosity along most of the route, you will still find that the local people often go out of their way to be helpful. If you are natural and friendly towards them, they will be nice right back. Of course, there are the rip-off merchants who have popped up in some places and you will inevitably get annoyed at times with the women-hassling Muslims. In Iran and Pakistan in particular women have to put up with an uncomfortable amount of pinching and prodding from frustrated local males whose own women are securely locked away. You can't fight it – a little scorn and some restrained anger helps.

When people try to communicate, respond. It may get a little boring after the thousandth 'what do you think of our country?' but it is those person-to-person contacts you will remember long after the temples and palaces have faded away.

THEFT

Getting things stolen can be one of the real hassles of this sort of travel. On the move, not always conversant with the local language and customs, with possessions that you can't keep a constant watch over, continually meeting people whom you don't know whether or not to trust – you are perfectly set up for the occasional rip off. I have made a great number of Asian trips without losing a thing and one where every time I turned round something was stolen.

You can get hit at any time – hotel rooms are definitely not safe and nothing of value (cameras, passports, money) should be left in a hotel room. Travelling can be another loss-making situation; you fall asleep on a train and when you awake your bag is gone from the luggage rack. The answer is to attach it to the rack with its straps so it can't be quickly and easily removed. If you have a padlock you can lock it in place – and again keep valuable items on your person. In some countries snatch and run thieves are adept and fairly common. They simply rush by you – zap – goodbye camera or shoulder bag. I have even heard of watches being snatched right off wrists and a friend actually did lose a pair of prescription glasses to a snatch thief.

Often thieves are not the local people but your friendly fellow travellers. All too often people have met up with other travellers, shared things with them, including accommodation, then turned round and discovered they have gone and so are their travellers' cheques, camera, passport or whatever. Don't trust people until you have known them for a while. It is a pity, but not everyone is as great as they seem initially.

A big word of warning for the own-vehicle people – keep it locked up. Unbelievably I had a motorcycle stolen in Thailand once; why anyone would steal a worn out bike which was virtually the only one of its type in the country I do not know but the cost in customs hassles, and lost time, far outweighed the value of the bike. And I got it back! It is almost always the case that the personal cost or heartbreak to you (like losing film) or something difficult to replace (your passport) will be considerably more than the paper value.

Don't get paranoid, there are still plenty of honest people in this world and equally, if you had absolutely everything stolen you would still be better off than most people in Asia. There is an excellent chance you will never lose anything, but it is always worth taking a little bit of care.

DOPE

The worst news first: scattered in jails all over Asia are a large number of westerners serving long sentences in very unpleasant conditions for various activities concerned with dope. With possibly a little prompting from the USA several Asian countries have become very heavy on dope users – not just smugglers.

Nor are you wise to try bringing anything back from Asian countries into the west. Anyone who has been east is immediately suspect even if you look straight – if you look even remotely freaky with the stamps you will have in your passport then watch out. A spell behind bars in Sydney or London may not be as unpleasant as in Ankara but it is not recommended.

Of course all of this is not going to stop people smoking nor have heavy penalties stamped out dope. There is plenty of it around in all the Asian countries, but remember that what is good for the locals ain't necessarily so for Joe Tourist. Money can be extracted from unwary travellers even if there is no real intention of putting them away. Even in the countries where dope, although officially illegal, is in practice 'blind-eyed' you are still well advised to be surreptitious and cool about it.

In Nepal, dope is no longer legal – all those hash shops and their posters and calendars of a few years back are no more. But if you want it it is still readily available and so long as you have only small quantities there is unlikely to be trouble. Much the same situation applies in India – small quantities quietly used and you are unlikely to have any difficulties. Ditto in Pakistan although in both countries there are occasional drug busts or searches on certain trains. Further west forget it, Turkey is bad, Greece ditto.

WHAT TO TAKE & HOW TO TAKE IT

As little as possible is the basic message. But not so little that you become a burden on other people. The super-light travellers generally seem to get along by continuously scrounging things. At the other extreme starting off with an overload of useless junk is a continual hassle and becomes impossible as soon as you start picking things up.

A backpack is still the most popular carrying container as they are commodious and the only way to go if you have to do any walking. On the debit side they are awkward to load on and off buses and trains, they don't offer too much protection for your valuables and some airlines may refuse to be responsible if they are damaged or broken into. On the other hand they no longer have the 'pack = hippy', 'hippy = bad' connotation which for a while they seemed to have. Recently some clever combination backpack/shoulder bags have become available. The straps can be zipped away when not needed so they combine the carrying ease of a pack with the added strength of a bag. Another alternative is a large, soft, zip bag with a wide shoulder strap so it can be carried with relative ease if necessary. In any case you can get some tabs sewn on so you can semi-thief proof it with small padlocks. Forget suitcases.

Inside? The secret of successful packing is plastic bags or 'stuff bags', it not only keeps things separate and clean, but also dry. You will no doubt be buying local clothes on the way so start light to begin with. My list would be:

underwear and swimming gear
one pair of jeans, one of shorts
a few shirts and T-shirts
sweater for cold nights
one pair of sneakers or shoes
sandals or thongs
lightweight jacket or raincoat
a dress up set of clothes

Modesty rates highly in most Asian countries, especially for women. Wearing short skirts or shorts is asking for trouble in Muslim countries.

On the non-clothing side my list would include:

washing gear
medical and sewing kit
sunglasses
padlock
sleeping bag

The sleeping bag not only serves to sleep in but can double as a coat on cold days, a cushion on hard train seats, a seat for long waits on railway platforms and a bed top-cover, since hotels rarely give you one. The padlock will lock your bag to the luggage rack or to the seat in trains and will serve to extra fortify your hotel room – they very often lock with a latch. Although soap, toothpaste and so on are readily obtainable, in the more backward areas toilet paper is unknown. So unless you can adapt to the Asian watering can and left hand method, bring along some loo roll. Tampons are not always easy to find outside big cities so women should bring along a supply.

APPEARANCES & CONDUCT

If you want to have a smooth trip, how you look can be important. Officialdom in west Asia doesn't have quite the same stiff collar attitudes that its equivalent often has in South-East Asia but, nevertheless when you arrive at embassies or consulates for visas, at the border to enter a country, or at docks or airports, you'll find life much simpler if you look neat and affluent. Particularly disliked are thongs, shorts, jeans (especially with patches on them), local attire, T-shirts – I could go on. It's always advisable to have one set of completely conventional 'dress up' gear to wear for these formal occasions.

Encounters with Asian officialdom are made much smoother if you keep repeating 'I must retain my cool' the more they annoy you! Temper usually has a counter-productive effect, they just want to show you who's boss – if you imply that you realise they are but that you still insist (calmly) on your rights you'll probably manage OK.

FILM & CAMERA

If you are a camera fan take plenty of film with you. Although film is obtainable in some countries in Asia it is expensive, of uncertain quality and in irregular supply. Bring it with you. Try to keep your film as protected as possible – dark and cool. Protect your camera and films from dust and damp, watch out for the monsoons.

Black and white films can be competently developed in a number of countries but colour slides really have to go back to the west. You may feel the risk of loss in mailing exposed films home is outweighed by the chances of damage or loss in carrying them with you. Film can usually be airmailed at printed matter rates so the cost is not excessive. I've always carried my film around with me until the end of each trip, though. Stolen film is a very saleable commodity – after all the person buying it has no way of knowing if a film has already been exposed.

Be cool in who and what you point your camera at. In strongly Muslim countries be very careful about photographing women, cameras can be a cause of major hassles – if they seem disturbed, don't. Most people are only too happy to be photographed, but it doesn't hurt to ask. Military installations, airports, harbours, or train stations are bad places to photograph in most Asian countries.

Bright Asian light can cause havoc with your shots so be careful not to over-expose them. Under harsh lighting conditions early morning or late afternoon may be the only time you get good results. When buying film remember that airport duty free film prices in western countries are often higher than discount prices including duty. Unless the duty is very high (like on whisky or cigarettes) the magic words 'duty free' means absolutely nothing.

MAIL

After a long time on the road getting mail from back home is especially nice. So have plenty of mail drops and schedule them well. Two cities may not look very far apart on the map, but may entail months of mail-less travel. Give mail plenty of time to get to you, delivery and sorting can take amazingly long.

Every major city (and most minor ones) has a 'poste restante' at the main post office. They are usually quite efficient, although they often charge a few cents for each item. There is usually some, fairly flexible, time limit on how long they will hold mail but they will often forward or return uncollected letters.

The usual alternative to post offices is American Express. Officially you have to be a customer to use their Clients' Mail service. You can get a booklet from them listing all their offices worldwide. On the debit side American Express charge for forwarding mail and in major cities, particularly in Europe, their offices are hopelessly crowded in summer and places to avoid. Also they are often inconveniently located. In most of Asia you are better off at a poste restante.

The third alternative is your embassy

but in these days of mass travel few embassies will hold mail for their travelling nationals. Smaller countries' embassies, Switzerland or Canada for example, still do in many places, but in general mail addressed to you at your embassy will just be handed over to the poste restante. Wherever it is sent ask people writing to you to print your name very clearly and underline the surname. In many countries the sorters will be unfamiliar with our alphabet and often first names and surnames are the opposite way to ours. Probably half the letters that get lost are simply filed under first name rather than surname.

Mail bound the other way has its ups and downs too. Almost everywhere aerograms will be cheaper and faster than letters or post cards. In some places you should observe the local custom of having your letters franked before you mail them. If you don't someone will steal the stamps from the letter and your mail will be delivered straight to the waste paper basket. Parcels seem to make it out of most countries OK although the delivery time can be enormous, six or more months in transit is nothing. In India and Iran parcels must be sewn up in cloth.

BUYING & SELLING

The selling things scene is not what it used to be although if you are really short of cash you can always unload an armful; several places give a good price for blood.

The working idea is virtually no-go. In a few countries you may be able to pick up a little money from English conversational lessons. Strictly it is illegal, requires a work permit, but in practice people have been known to get away with it. The places where teaching English is really viable are further east – like Korea or Japan. Best of all is just to bring enough money from the start.

Buying things is an entirely different picture. There is just so much attractive stuff available it is probably as well that what you get is limited by what you can carry or your money belt would soon be empty. There are all sorts of handicrafts, clothes, leatherwork, jewellery, carpets, you name it, all the way across. If you intend to buy things with the idea of profitably reselling in the west, make sure you know what you are about; a lot of people are doing it professionally. Without contacts at one end to buy at the right price and sales outlets at the other end you're not going to have much of a chance. Similarly don't believe the 'you can sell this at a profit' stories; if you can why haven't others already?

All the way across Asia you have to bargain. This can include food in the markets, almost anything from shops, buses in Turkey, trishaws everywhere, taxis almost everywhere, even hotels in many places. The less sophisticated the seller and the goods the lower should be your starting price, say a fifth to a quarter for handicrafts, but you have to feel every situation.

The budget traveller probably gets a more realistic starting price than the jet setter anyway. Don't be too fierce though, you are going to have to pay more than the locals and trying too hard not to be ripped off just leaves a bad taste in everybody's mouth. Afghanistan was the most enjoyable country for bargaining – it was mandatory to go through the whole rigmarole of denigrating the goods, to which the seller would draw attention to his poverty, to which you pointed out your own limited means. Finally you had to walk out of the shop, only to be bodily dragged back in to reach the final price. Funny how it always seemed to be exactly one-third of the initial price!

BOOKS

The more you read before you depart the more you will appreciate what you see along the road. For a taste of Asia overlanding there are a number of books worth looking at – whether you are driving, going on an organised trip, freelancing,

going by train or even biking it. There are also a number of good guidebooks for individual Asian countries, including several from Lonely Planet – details in the 'books' section of each country.

If you're planning to drive overland there are several guides to doing it in your own vehicle. None of them are terribly relevant post-Iran and Afghanistan and all of them are now out of print. They include *Trans-Asia Motoring* by Colin McElduff, *The Routes to India* by John Prendergast, and *The Asian Highway* by Jack Jackson and Ellen Crampton. For a good general introduction to overland travel with your own vehicle look for *Overland & Beyond* by Jonathan Hewat (Roger Lascelles). If you're overlanding by expedition vehicle then *Kathmandu by Truck* by Barbara Lamplugh (Roger Lascelles) will tell you what it's all about on a regular overland trip.

If you want to read of other people's overland-with-wheels experiences *First Overland* by Tim Slessor is great fun. Published in 1957 this book is long out of print (I found my copy in a second hand bookshop) but you may find it in a library. It is a fascinating description of what was claimed to be the first 'all the way' drive from London to Singapore way back in the mid-50s. The Burmese land route has since been firmly closed so it may also have been the last! In general things have changed remarkably little in the 30-odd years since that epic drive.

Even more epic was the mid-60s bicycle trip described by the enterprising Irish-woman Dervla Murphy in *Full Tilt*. This is one of the classics of overlanding and recounts in enjoyable and amusing detail her Delhi-or-bust bike ride. Dervla has gone on to other equally exotic and unusual travel adventures.

The *Great Railway Bazaar* by Paul Theroux describes a trip from London to Japan by every possible rail connection. It's a best-selling and highly amusing account of life as observed and interpreted from a railway carriage. *Slow Boats to*

China by Gavin Powell tells of a similar trans-Asia trip, this time travelling as much as possible by boat. It's equally readable and enjoyable.

Recently republished after a lapse of many years *The Road to Oxiana* by Robert Byron was a classic of travel writing in the '30s and it's interesting how many things seem just the same in Iran and Afghanistan today. Finally if you're heading to the Gulf states then *Arabia Through the Looking Glass* by Jonathan Raban is another instant classic and provides an excellent insight into the Arab world.

Travelling through Asia you will have plenty of opportunity to read – sitting on trains and at railway stations for example. So carry a handful of paperbacks along with you and trade them with other travellers. Note that India is an excellent place to buy books, both books on India and books purely for something to read. Many best-selling western novels are reprinted in India at prices far lower than in the west.

MAPS

The two Bartholomew's maps – *Middle East* and *India, Pakistan, Sri Lanka, Nepal & Bangladesh* – provide good detail on the whole Asia overland route. Another excellent map is the German VWK *Middle East* map which covers right through from Turkey to India. It's now being marketed as a Shell map.

RELIGION

The overland trip passes through such a kaleidoscope of religions and these have such a great bearing on the history, relics and current situations of their adhering countries, that a real impression needs a preliminary look at the religions of the Asian countries. Of course the religions of Asia were not always as they are now, nor will they always remain so. At one stage, for example, Zoroastrianism stretched all the way to the Mediterranean, only to be pushed back by Christianity from the west and Buddhism from the east, before the

Muslims flooded over all three. Today it exists only in parts of Iran and India and even those few remnants are currently going through some sweeping readjustments.

If you have not stepped outside our western Christian environment before, you will be pleasantly surprised at how much Asian religions have to teach us about important values such as tolerance and acceptance of others' beliefs.

Hindu

The Asian religion with the greatest number of adherents, although they predominate only in India, Nepal and on the Indonesian island of Bali, is Hinduism. The Hindu religion seems such a comic book, Disneyland set up it is almost difficult to take it seriously. It is actually one of the oldest extant religions with origins reaching back to over 1000 BC. If one looks at their pantheon of Gods as pictorial representations of different God-like attributes, then it becomes meaningful.

The one omnipresent God, Brahm, usually has three physical representations. Brahma is the creator, Vishnu is the preserver while Shiva is the destroyer and reproducer. All three are usually shown with four arms, but Brahma has the added advantage of four heads, to represent his all seeing presence.

Vishnu is usually shown in one of the physical forms in which he visited earth. In all Vishnu has paid nine visits and his 10th is avidly awaited. On his earlier visits he took animal form, but on visit seven Vishnu appeared as Rama, regarded as the personification of an ideal man. Rama managed to provide a number of secondary gods, including his helpful ally Hanuman the Monkey God. Hanuman's faithful nature is illustrated by his representation often found guarding fort and palace entrances. On visit eight Vishnu came as Krishna and was brought up with peasants, thus becoming a favourite of the lower classes. Vishnu's final recent incarnation was on visit nine as the Buddha, probably a ploy to bring the Buddhist splinter group back into the Hindu fold.

Shiva's creative role is phallically symbolised by his representation as the frequently worshipped lingam. His destructive side is usually handled by his wife, Kali the Terrible, who also has a more pleasant side as Parvati the Beautiful. In her destructive appearances Kali requires sacrifices and her temples are liable to be bloody affairs. Shiva has two sons – one is Kartikkaya, the God of War, and the other is Ganesh, the elephant-headed God of Learning. Ganesh is probably the most popular god in the whole Hindu collection.

A variety of lesser gods, wives and associated creatures crowd the scene. The cow is, of course, the holy animal but there are many others including Vishnu's executive jet, the Garuda – half man/half bird and a firm do-gooder. There are a number of Hindu holy books; the *Bhagavadgita* is the best known, and credited to Krishna. Others are the *Mahabharata* and the *Ramayana*, the story of the Rama, a popular legend in the east.

Buddhism

At first a splinter from the Hindu religion and later to spread from South-East Asia to Iran, Buddhism has now contracted to South-East Asia (where it predominates in Thailand, Burma and Laos), Sri Lanka and parts of Nepal. Born in 642 BC near the present India-Nepal border, Gautama, the Buddha, renounced the material life, but unlike other prophets found starvation did not bring enlightenment. Accordingly he produced his rule of the 'middle way', moderation in everything.

The basis of Buddhism is that all suffering in life comes from over indulgence in our desires. Suppression of our sensual desires will eventually lead to a state of Nirvana where our desires are extinct and we are free from their delusions. For an over-affluent western world, beginning to doubt the potency of the materialist concept of life, Buddhism has obvious charms.

Buddhist Procession, Nepal

Buddha, who not only was not a god but did not even claim to be the only enlightened one, felt that the way to nirvana was for our karma, central spirit, to follow the eight-fold path of right thinking, right behaviour, and the like. Apart from its appositeness to modern life Buddhism is interesting for its expansion and contraction. In some places, such as Afghanistan, it fell to conquest by the Muslims, in others, such as India, it was reabsorbed into the Hindu stream. In many places today the local Buddhist or Hindu religion is actually a closely entwined combination of the two. In all the places where Buddhism or Hindu-Buddhism has been strong, fantastic structures attest to its great power. The huge Borobudur temple in Java, the complex of Angkor Wat in Cambodia, the multiplicity of temples at Pagan in Burma and the massive standing Buddhas at Bamiyan in Afghanistan are all reminders of Buddhism's strength.

Buddhism has a number of different forms, just like Christianity. The Theravada or 'teaching of the elders' is the older form of Buddhism that did not believe in the representation of Buddha in human form – it was chiefly a religion of the priests and monks. Later the Mahayana or 'large vehicle' interpretation of Buddhism gave the religion a more popular form. Followers of Mahayana call the Theravada belief the 'small vehicle' – you also hear them referred to as 'large raft' and 'small raft'. Although South-East Asian Buddhist countries, along with Sri Lanka, are described as Theravada while China, Japan and Nepal are described as Mahayana the distinction is not so clear. The purest form of Theravada no longer exists as the popular large vehicle beliefs have had sweeping effects. The Tibetan form of Buddhism is another type again and is known as Tantric Buddhism.

Muslim

The most recent and most widespread of the Asian religions is Islam, the Mohammedan or Muslim religion. It predominates through all the Arab countries, Turkey, Iran, Afghanistan, Pakistan, Bangladesh, Malaysia and Indonesia. India has a very large Muslim minority and Islam also travelled further west into Europe, mosques are still a common sight in Yugoslavia.

The religion's founder, the prophet Mohammed, was born in 570 AD in Mecca. He had his first revelation from Allah in 610; this and later visions were compiled into the Muslim holy book, the *Koran*. As his purpose in life was revealed to him Mohammed began to preach against the idolatry that Mecca was then the centre for. Muslims believe that to search for god through images is a sin. Eventually his attacks on local business led to Mohammed and his followers being run out of town in 622. They fled to Medina, city of the prophet, and by 630 were strong enough to march back into Mecca and take over. Within two decades most of Arabia was converted to Islam, but Mohammed had died in 632.

The Muslim faith was more than just a religion, it also called on its followers to spread the word – if necessary by the sword. It was just the rallying call the Arabs needed and in succeeding centuries Islam was spread over three continents. Since the Arabs who first propagated the faith developed a reputation as being ruthless fighters but reasonable masters, people often found it advisable to surrender to them. In this way the Muslims swept aside the crumbling Byzantine empire, whose people felt no desire to support their distant Christian emperor.

Although Islam only travelled west for a hundred years before being pushed back at Poitier in France, in 732, it travelled east for centuries. The Muslim influence in Persia regenerated the Persian Empire which was declining from its protracted struggles with Byzantium. This led to the great period of Persian art and literature marked by men like Omar Khayyam, famed more as a mathematician than a poet in his own land.

Arabs sailed up the Indus in 711, the same year they landed in Spain, but this was more a casual raid than a full scale invasion. It was from Ghazni in Afghanistan that the eventual subjugation of India was to spring. Mahmud of Ghazni repeatedly drove into India in the 11th century, by the 13th century all of the Ganges plain was in Muslim hands and the Moghul empire eventually controlled most of the subcontinent. From here Indian traders spread the faith on to South-East Asia, where it is strong today in Malaysia and most of Indonesia. Only in Bali does the older Hindu-Buddhist religion of Indonesia remain.

At an early stage Islam suffered a fundamental split that remains to this day. The third Caliph, successor to Mohammed, was murdered and followed by Ali, the prophet's son-in-law, in 656. Ali was assassinated in 661 by the Governor of Syria who set himself up as Caliph in preference to the descendants of Ali. Today 90% of Muslims are Sunnites, followers of the succession from the Caliph, while the remainder are Shi'ites who follow the descendants of Ali. Only in Iran do Shi'ites form a majority.

Travelling through the Muslim countries it is surprising that the religion which once gave such drive to the nations that embraced it, in many cases holds them back. In the Middle East countries, where women without being second-class citizens are definitely a second type of citizen, Islam has a restraining influence that the prophet could never have foreseen. The fatalistic view of life, everything in the hands of Allah, also has an inertial effect. Apart from the Muslim hand on the western female, the other Islamic influence you may feel is during the feast of Ramadan. Muslims can neither eat or drink from sunrise to sunset for a month around October or November; you may find yourself an unwilling faster. Tempers tend to run short during that period and the days celebrating the end of Ramadan are a wild celebration during which time you might as well forget about crossing borders, or achieving anything very much.

Pharsis

Apart from the three major religious groups of Asia, a number of smaller groups or sects also exist. Oldest of these are the Pharsis, followers of Zoroaster, who was born in Mazar-i-Sharif, in what is now Afghanistan, about 550 BC. At one time Zoroastrianism stretched all the way from India to the Mediterranean, today it hangs on only around Karachi in Pakistan, Bombay in India, and Shiraz in Iran.

Zoroastrianism was one of the first religions to postulate an omnipotent, invisible god. Pharsis worship at fire temples where they keep eternally burning flames. They worship the fire as a symbol of god, not the fire itself. Since they believe in the purity of the elements, Pharsis will not bury their dead (it pollutes the earth) or cremate them (it pollutes the

atmosphere). Instead the dead are exposed on 'Towers of Silence', where they are soon cleaned off by the vultures. Today it is going through a period of updating and readjustment as strict regulations on marriage have resulted in a great decline in the religion's numbers. Worse the vultures seem to have lost interest in playing their part.

Jains

The Jains are more a religious order than a religion, they believe in the sacredness of all life and will not even kill a mosquito. Jains are found scattered over much of India and their temple groups are noted for the large number of identical buildings and columns. Like the Pharsis they tend to be clever and commercially successful with an influence disproportionate to their numbers.

Sikhs

The Sikhs are a sect of reformed Hindus, founded by Guru Nanak who was born in 1469. The basic tenets of the Sikh religion are similar to that of the Hindus, but with the modifications that the Sikhs are opposed to caste distinction and 'pilgrimages to rivers'. Sikhs were also against the practice of cremating widows with their husbands – whether they wished to be or not. This custom, *suttee*, has been given up by Hindus now, although in Nepal it did not stop until 1923.

The Sikh religion was founded partly in an attempt to bridge the gap between the then dominant Muslims and the numerically superior Hindus. Sikhs predominate in the Punjab, one of the touchier of the border regions, their capital city is Amritsar where another of their beliefs, hospitality to strangers, can (under normal circumstances) be experienced at the Golden Temple. Sikhs can be recognised by their five *kakkars*, the best known of which is *kesh* or uncut hair – adult Sikhs wear turbans.

Sikhs have been heavily in the news

over the past couple of years, first for the continued unrest in the Punjab and then for the assassination of Indira Gandhi. Problems in the Punjab, and occasionally in other parts of India, look likely to continue for some time to come.

Getting There

GETTING TO ASIA

First of all get there. You can start travelling right from your front door, either through Australia and South-East Asia if you're starting out in Australia or through Europe if your starting point is at that end. See the Onward Travel sections for brief details on those possibilities. If, however, west Asia is your one and only destination you're going to want to fly there as quickly and conveniently as possible and as cheaply.

FROM EUROPE

See the Overlanding by Air and More Flying sections for other flight possibilities but in London the first step towards your ticket to Asia is to scan the bucket shop ads. Bucket shops, for the uninitiated, are travel agents who specialise in cheap tickets. As in any business there are a few bad apples in the basket but in general the bucket shops perform a fine service and most of them are perfectly straight up and down. Basically they're in the business of selling cheap tickets because the airlines would rather fill a seat at a discount than have it fly empty. On the other hand the airlines don't want every travel agent in the land offering amazing bargains to everybody who steps through the door. First of all they'd like to fill up as many seats as possible with people who are willing to pay the full price. Or don't know better. Having done that they then offer cut price tickets to a small band of travel agents – mostly in London and generally catering to the backpack or Australians-on-their-way-home brigade.

To find a bucket shop in London you have simply to pick up a copy of *Time Out* or its imitators, *Australasian Express* or various other giveaway papers. Inside you'll find all sorts of ads with typical one-way prices around the £200 mark to Karachi, Delhi, Bombay or Colombo.

Return fares would be around £350 or from around £400 you can find tickets from London to the Australian east coast with a stop-over somewhere in west Asia.

Two of the better places to visit are Trail Finders (who are so un-bucket-shop-like they can make instant confirmations through their on-line computer system) or STA Travel (which just might stand for Student Travel Australia!).

FROM AUSTRALIA

These days Australia also has agents offering similar cheap ticket deals as well as advance purchase fares. The cheap tickets are usually fairly similar in price to the advance purchase fares, but with the advantage that you don't have to book and pay far in advance and risk cancellation penalties if you change your mind.

Advance purchase one-way fares to India from the east coast are around A$750 to 850 depending on the season. From Darwin or Perth the fares are around A$100 cheaper. Round trip fares from the east coast are from around A$1200. It's no problem to find fares in the same bracket or even cheaper from co-operative travel agents.

An alternative way to west Asia would be to fly to South-East Asia and continue from there. Bangkok-Calcutta or Bangkok-Kathmandu are the most popular routes to the sub-continent.

FROM NEW ZEALAND

Round trip excursion fares are also available from Auckland. To Bombay or Delhi it's around NZ$2100, slightly cheaper to Calcutta or Madras.

FROM THE USA

Cheap fares to Asia can be found by scanning the travel agent ads in Sunday travel supplements in papers like the *New*

York Times, the *Los Angeles Times* or the *San Francisco Chronicle*. Or by contacting travel agents specialising in budget fares, such as the student travel organisation Council Travel. Typical fares to India from the west coast are around US$1000 return or from the east coast US$1100 to 1200.

From the west coast you can fly to Bangkok, the best jumping off point from South-East Asia to the sub-continent, for around US$900 return, the fares are not much higher from the east coast. Alternatively from the east coast you can fly to Istanbul or Tel Aviv for around US$650 return, a bit more than half that much for one-way.

FROM CANADA

The regular one-way economy fare from Toronto to New Delhi is C$1479. The roundtrip excursion fare from Toronto, with a 14 day minimum, 120 days maximum stay, is C$1800. One-way apex fares, with the usual advance booking and cancellation penalties, are C$1132 in the low season, C$1240 in the high. Round the world fares which take in India are available through Canada for around C$2000.

Getting Around

ASIA OVERLANDING – ORGANISED TRIPS

The turmoil in Iran, the invasion of Afghanistan, and the Iraq-Iran conflict have had a disastrous effect on the overland companies. Some of them simply went under and all of them have had to rethink their routes and schedules. Nevertheless, they're still at it and if you want your trip through Asia all fixed up in one go there are a number of companies who'll do just that.

Basically the overland companies take a bus or truck load of people from London to Kathmandu, or vice versa. Most of the companies have offices in London and, sometimes, in Australia. Film nights, to show you what their trips are all about, are an established practice and an excellent way to whet your appetite for Asia – whether you're going on an organised trip or not.

Travelling the organised way you avoid hassles, you face none of the train or bus problems that come from depending on public transport. Nor do you have the hassles of your own transport – insurance, carnets and the danger of breakdowns in unhappy places. In that respect you have the best of both worlds. Your drivers are usually pretty together types who have crossed Asia more often than you have been to the corner store, they know what goes up and where it goes down. So you don't miss anything and probably get a look at some of the more out of the way things that solo travellers may miss.

Group travel also has its hang-ups. It is hardly like a package trip, but if you find that some place really grabs you and you would like to spend a few more days (or weeks or months) – well too bad it is only an overnight stop. A less foreseen problem is your other travellers – you will be stuck in close proximity with them for two or more months and if there is someone you

can't stand you have plenty of opportunity to not stand them.

Since Afghanistan shut its doors the overland companies have taken the 'southern route' through Quetta in Pakistan. This loops around Afghanistan, going from Isfahan in Iran to Kerman, then Zahedan before crossing into Pakistan. Although the overland companies report little difficulty in passing through Iran the stay there tends to be shorter than in the past. The time saved is usually spent either in India or in the Middle East.

It's hard to directly compare costs between the various companies because of what is and isn't included. There are bus trips that generally use hotels and the accommodation costs may or may not be extra. Or truck trips that camp so accommodation costs are negligible. Most operators have a food kitty system where you all chip in an initial amount to cover the food purchased along the way. There will, of course, be plenty of opportunity to sample local food though! Vehicles vary – the bus operators stress the greater comfort they offer while the four-wheel-drive truck operators brag that they can get further off the beaten track. The length of the trip also varies although generally 75 to 85 days is the norm. There are some much shorter trips, however. All in all it's wise to read the fine print and find out exactly what you're in for and what is included in the price.

Some of the main operators include *Top Deck* who operate converted double-deck buses. They're set up bunkhouse style so you sleep in the bus at night and haven't got to worry about hotels or camp sites. Their seven-week trip London-Kathmandu cost from £550, 10 weeks from £800. There's a food kitty collected at the start. *Himalaya Overland* have bus trips costing from £530 for a straightforward 54-day trip, £730 for a 75-day trip including a loop through the USSR, or £905 for an 80-day trip which includes Israel and Egypt. There's an additional accommodation and food supplement charged.

Encounter Overland and *Exodus Expeditions* both use 'expedition vehicles' – four-wheel-drive trucks. Their trips are typically 11 to 13 weeks and you generally camp out along the way. *Hann Overland* use small buses and have 87-day trips costing £660. Since there are far fewer people taking these overland trips these days the companies are also offering additional trips, particularly around India. Visit a good adventure travel agent or write to the companies for brochures on their trips and additional information.

OVERLANDING – OWN VEHICLE

Far fewer people drive their own vehicles across Asia these days, but there's still a steady trickle of Kombis hitting the overland trail, despite everything. The advantages of having your own vehicle are that you are not tied to bus and train schedules and you can go to places they don't. You're also generally far more comfortable and avoid all the hassles that go with carrying your world on your back. On the minus side you'll face greater costs, mountains of paperwork and red tape and have the stone-around-the-neck danger of serious breakdown, accident or theft.

Driving all the way between Europe and Australia is punctuated by two expensive sea crossings. There are very few ships from India or Sri Lanka all the way to Australia (sometimes people do find them, but it's rare) so you generally have to ship Madras-Penang then drive down to Singapore and ship Singapore-Fremantle (Western Australia). The cost of those two sea voyages is likely to top US$1000 for a Kombi, something over US$200 for a motorcycle. Therefore if you're going to drive all the way it makes much more sense to drive Europe-Australia rather than vice versa because vehicles are so much cheaper in Europe. Or you could

simply drive out from Europe, U-turn in India and drive back.

An answer for the impecunious one-way traveller is to drive and sell or drive and dump. Driving and selling is no longer the game it used to be because it would be a near impossibility for a fellow traveller to buy a vehicle off you and be able to arrange the paperwork to drive it back to Europe. Some people still drive vehicles out to Nepal and sell them there, but it usually has to be the sort of thing wanted locally – like small diesel buses. Drive and dump is another possibility although that can also involve you in some paperwork hassles. It is sometimes possible to 'donate' your vehicle to the Indian government and clear your carnet that way. Friends have done it with an ex-GPO Morris Minor van and with a Citroen 2CV.

Which brings us round to the biggest problem with your own vehicle – the carnet. This is a booklet that is stamped on arrival and departure from a number of countries to ensure that you export the vehicle again after you've imported it. A carnet is issued by a motoring organisation in the country where the vehicle is registered. In England the AA will issue a carnet for about £15.

The sting in the tail with a carnet is that you have to lodge a deposit to secure the carnet. If you default on the carnet – that is you don't have an export stamp to match the import one – then the country in question can claim your deposit. And how much is it? – why 200 to 250% of the new value of your vehicle. If it's worth, say, US$10,000 then you're supposed to front up with US$20,000. Needless to say not many people do and you can get out of it in a couple of ways. One is to get your bank to guarantee the carnet deposit. Failing that you could get insurance companies who specialise in this business to insure you against the deposit. If you default they'll pay out, but they'll still come after you for the money. At the moment nobody will touch Asia because of 'war risks', but in the past the London firm of Campbell Irvine would insure carnet deposits for 7.5% of the indemnity – still a very hefty sum.

Carnets are currently required for India and Pakistan and several Middle East countries. They are also technically required for Iran, but the deposit there is supposed to be 500% of the new vehicle value. Since even the Iranians realise that nobody is going to put that sort of money in hock to the Ayatollah carnets are not generally issued for Iran. What you have to do instead is pick up a customs official on arrival in Iran and drop him off at the other border on departure. This tends to be a little expensive so people with vehicles have to zip through. Usually people wait at the border on arrival until a small convoy has collected and then share an official. Carnets also apply to motorcycles whose riders would find it a little difficult crossing Iran without a convoy!

Should the worst case occur and your vehicle is irretrievably damaged in an accident or catastrophic breakdown you'll have to argue it out with customs officials. Similarly try to avoid having it stolen – I had a motorcycle stolen in Thailand once and it caused me a great deal of difficulty and expense to finally clear my carnet.

Having got your vehicle prepared and your carnet lined up things are pretty well OK. All the way across roads are acceptable, there is still the odd patch of unsurfaced road in Iran and Turkey, in India and Pakistan roads are narrow and very crowded, but nowhere are things unmanageable. Fuel is readily available and ranges from cheap (Iran) through to amazingly costly (India). The octane rating may sometimes be abysmally low and it is usually a good idea to carry a few spare cans with you as stations run out from time to time and may not expect a delivery for a week or two.

Mechanical failure can be a hassle as spare parts are often unobtainable. Fear not, ingenuity often compensates for factory parts. If you were going to break

down Iran used to be the place to do it, but it's unlikely to be so today. Generally VWs and Land-Rovers are the vehicles for which parts are most likely to be available. A European insurance policy can extend right through Turkey to the Iran border although it can probably be arranged more cheaply on arrival in Turkey. Border insurance can be (or at least could be) bought on arrival in Iran. In Pakistan and India you can arrange insurance in the major cities. It is virtually impossible to arrange insurance before departure.

Drive carefully, that applies anywhere, but an accident in the more primitive parts of some of these countries is not always handled by your friendly insurance company. An eye for an eye is how the victim and his relatives are likely to see it, whether you are in the wrong or not. Don't hang around to ask questions. Hitting a cow in India could be equally disastrous! Definitely don't drive at night, the roads are full of unlit animals, carts, bicycles, even people having a sleep, and highway robbery is not a thing of the past. Another uniquely Asian road hazard is the habit of piling rocks around a vehicle when making on-the-road repairs – then driving off and leaving them there.

If all this sounds like simply too much bother and expense (and at present it really is) then you could always try pushbiking it. Plenty of people do.

OVERLANDING – PUBLIC TRANSPORT

If you can't face the hassles and expense of taking your own vehicle and the limitations of going on an organised trip also don't appeal then you are on local transport. This is the way the largest proportion of overlanders go, it is by far the most genuine way of travel and also the cheapest. On the negative side it can be uncomfortable and tiring and is most certainly time consuming.

The benefits from going this way include the ability to fix your own time programme and routing; buses and trains run just about everywhere so, as long as you have the endurance, you will get there. You enjoy the friendly camaraderie that you miss with your own vehicle without being stuck with the small and never changing circle of an organised tour. That is by far the nicest aspect of the do-it-yourself way, you meet a lot of really good people.

The debit side is simple endurance. After a while you never want to see another lower class train carriage in India! Nevertheless if you're enthusiastic about getting down to the real nitty gritty of these countries then this is indisputably the way to go. Getting on those terrible local buses is by far the best way to meet the local people.

Finally there's the most public of transport – hitch-hiking. Well it can be done although generally it may end up costing as much as public transport. Hitch-hiking is not a commonly understood idea in Asia.

OVERLANDING BY AIR

That may sound like a mis-definition but if you are in a hurry, have been before and want to pick up on certain places without all the tedious ground level travelling, or simply want to avoid some of the hassles that are taking place in Asia at the moment, then flying can be an interesting alternative.

All the modern advance booking, one-way excursion and so on fares either allow no stopovers at all or strictly limit them and charge you a hefty extra slug for each one. But if you buy a straightforward, no reductions, no nothing economy fare from city A to city Z you can stop at everything from B to Y that pops up in between. At no extra cost whatever. The only catches are that you are not allowed to backtrack (you've got to keep moving in the same direction) and there is a limit on the total distance you cover so you can't zig-zag madly all over Asia.

A ticket like this can be written on as many airlines as you want – you can 'interline', as it's called, from one airline

to another all the way across. If you're going to exploit this type of ticket to the maximum you'll end up with a ticket that airlines hate. So there are some guidelines to follow if you want to get a really interesting ticket. First of all don't buy it from an airline. For a start they'll only want to fly you to places they fly to – if you go along to Airline A and they have five possible stopovers between Sydney and London then they'll try to convince you that the only places you want to go to are those they fly to. With a little persuasion they may add another airline in, but you won't get the full potential possible.

The reason for this reluctance to come up with something really complex and interesting is quite simple. Complicated tickets are a hassle to write and there's not much in them for the airline. To write something with, say, 20 stopovers between Australia and London (not at all beyond the bounds of possibility) takes a lot of poring over the books and fingering the pocket calculator. And at the end you may have a ticket with every airline from A to Z taking part in it and poor old Airline A, who wrote the damn thing in the first place, only picking up one lousy sector for their troubles. So don't go to an airline for your super-ticket, go to a travel agent. And not just any travel agent, you've got to search out who knows what he's about and is willing to apply his ingenuity to the problem.

One catch with having your ticket written by a travel agent rather than an airline is that if there is some problem along the way the issuing airline could rewrite it. Your travel agent will be a long way away. However, remember that a ticket written by Airline A is not going to be easy to rewrite if there are no offices for Airline A in Asia!

You'll make yourself a lot more popular with the agent if you go along with a reasonable idea of what you want to start with. In fact if you can get a hold of the travel agent's Bible, the *ABC World Airways Guide*, you can work some interesting routes out for yourself. Basically between Australia and England there is a standard airline distance known as the 'maximum permitted mileage'. If you're on an economy ticket your total mileage mustn't exceed the mileage in 5% increments up to 25% and your ticket will correspondingly be surcharged by 5%, 10%, 15%, 20% or 25%. The ABC guide will tell you what the standard mileage is between each airport along the way and you (or your travel agent) can then add up these 'sector' distances to ensure it doesn't exceed the 'maximum permitted mileage'. There are places you can pick up 'free' miles. The distance from A to B plus B to C plus C to D may actually be less than the straight distance A to D (as the book flies this is). So clever routing can actually give you more miles for less.

The ABC guide will also confirm the equally important factor that there is a flight between the two places you want to fly between. Believe it or not I've had more than one letter from travellers who found when they got to town P their travel agent had ticketed them to fly on to town Q, to which no airline flew! Although plenty of airlines flew on from P to R.

Getting that sort of problem sorted out in Asia can be a big hassle so make sure there really are flights on all the sectors you intend to fly on. It's also much easier to delete sectors than to add them on so if you're undecided whether you want to go to town Y or not get the ticket written from X to Y to Z anyway. It's much easier to delete Y from X-Y-Z than to add Y into X-Z. Remember also that you don't have to fly every sector. Perhaps travelling by land from X to Z is one of the real not-to-be-missed experiences, so forget about your ticket and take the bus.

Since land travel in Asia has certainly got a little more fraught over the past couple of years many more people have turned to this overland-by-air possibility. At the same time the airlines have been heavily promoting their cheap, advance purchase, no-stopovers tickets so you can

guess what they've done to our unlimited stopover baby. Right, they've put the price up and made it less attractive by cutting the maximum permitted mileage by a neat 1000 miles. Unhappily in the past few years the economy one-way fare has soared from under A$1000 to a hefty A$2213 between the Australian east coast and London. But with ingenuity this can still be one of the great travel bargains – after all if you like airline meals you could arrange to have one on every sector you flew!

MORE FLYING

Round the world (RTW) fares have become all the rage in the past few years. Basically they're of two types – airline tickets and agent tickets. An airline RTW ticket usually means two airlines have joined together to market a ticket which takes you right round the world on their combined routes. Within certain limitations of time and number of stopovers you can fly pretty well anywhere you choose using their combined routes so long as you keep moving in the same direction. Compared to the full fare tickets which permit you to go absolutely anywhere you choose on any IATA airline you choose so long as you do not exceed the 'maximum permitted mileage' these tickets are much less flexible. But they are also much cheaper.

Quite a few of these combined airline RTW tickets go through India including the Air India-Continental Airlines one which will also allow you to make several stopovers within India. RTW tickets typically cost from around £1000 (US$1500) for northern hemisphere routes. If you want to include the southern hemisphere (ie Australia) then you're probably looking at around US$2000. The other type of RTW ticket, the agent ticket, is simply a combination of cheap fares strung together by an enterprising agent. This will probably use a wider variety of airlines and may provide routes which the 'off the shelf' tickets cannot manage. The cheap London-Australia tickets are often put together in this fashion – take a cheap ticket London-Colombo-Singapore from Air Lanka (who don't fly to Australia but would like to have some of that Australia-Europe business) and tack on another discounted flight with another airline from Singapore to Australia.

The other multi-stop alternative is to buy tickets as you go along. You could, for example, fly from Australia to Singapore, overland to Bangkok, fly to Calcutta or Kathmandu, overland to Delhi and then get a ticket from there to London. That way you could put together your own poor man's stopover ticket for, say, around £500 to 600 (A$800 to 1000) from London or around A$1000 to 1200 from Australia. That's a reasonable amount cheaper than a regular ticket but you lose out on the extreme flexibility of the more expensive ticket and you've got to take what's available along the way.

Afghanistan

Unhappily Afghanistan today is virtually a closed country for visitors. The Russian forces in the country are unlikely to be able to control more than the main cities and the major roads between these cities but the Afghan rebels are equally unlikely to be able to dislodge the vastly better equipped Russian forces. The result is an unpleasant stalemate which looks like continuing for some time to come.

Surprisingly it appears that visas are still available to enter Afghanistan from Pakistan. Journalists visiting Afghanistan 'legally' almost all do so by air to Kabul, the capital city where Russian control is strongest. Visiting Kandahar or Kabul by land from Pakistan would most probably be a rather foolhardy activity since any western visitor to Afghanistan today is likely to be taken for a Russian and the rebels shoot first and ask questions afterwards.

All this is most unfortunate for Afghanistan is a vastly appealing country with endless empty deserts, soaring barren mountains, historic old towns and ruins and, best of all, the aloof and detached Afghanis. There is no other way to describe them for they clearly realise that no amount of money or mere material possessions could ever compensate for an outsider's handicap of not being born in their fine country. Perhaps one day it will return to its rightful place on the Asia overland route.

HISTORY

Afghanistan's history as a country is not much over two centuries old, although in the past it has been part, or even the centre, of great empires. As with many eastern countries the rise and fall of political power was inextricably tied to the rise and fall of religions.

It was in Afghanistan that the ancient religion of Zoroastrianism started in the 6th century BC. Later Buddhism spread west from India and, centred on the Bamiyan valley, it remained strong until the 10th century AD. The eastward sweep of Islam had reached Afghanistan in the 7th century AD and the whole country is now Muslim.

During these centuries the country had been ruled by local kings or invaders from abroad, such as Alexander the Great, but Mahmud of Ghazni established the first great Afghan power centre in the south of the country in the 11th century. He repeatedly descended to the rich plains of India to carry off anything that could be moved. Altogether he made no less than 17 raids under the pretext of taking Islam to the Hindus. It was a profitable business but Ghazni soon fell to a neighbouring king and was then ravaged by Afghanistan's worst foreign invasion.

Between 1220 and 1223 Genghis Khan tore through the country destroying all before him. Balkh, Herat, Ghazni and Bamiyan were all reduced to rubble and the damage done to the irrigation system was never repaired. Genghis specialised in pleasant little acts of psychological showmanship like building towers of skulls outside the citadel walls of cities he was besieging. No future conqueror could match the rapacity of Genghis and his name is still spoken with awe.

Tamerlane later swept through in the early 1380s but he had nothing on old Genghis. His real name was Timur the Turk but after being wounded in battle in Afghanistan was named Timur-leng, Timur-the-lame, which became Tamerlane. The rise of the great Moghul empire again lifted Afghanistan to heights of power. Babur had his capital in Kabul in 1512, but as the Moghuls extended their power into India, Afghanistan changed from being the centre of the empire to simply a peripheral part.

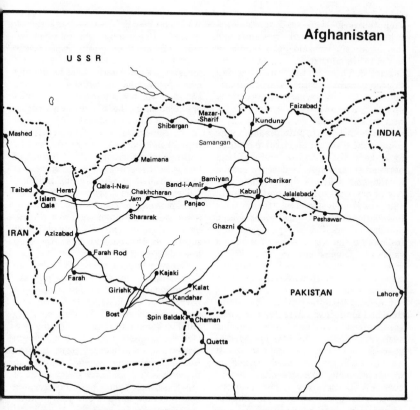

Afghanistan

In 1774, with European strength threatening the declining Moghuls on the sub-continent, the Kingdom of Afghanistan was founded. The 1800s were a period of often comic book confrontation with the British; as with Burma they were afraid of the effects of an unruly neighbour on their great Indian colony. Additionally the spectre of Russian influence resulted in a series of flimsily provoked and remarkably unsuccessful preventative wars. To a large extent they came about because the Afghan kingdoms were now too weak to stand up by themselves and needed help from outside. A feeler would be put out to the British, who would stall on it but send in the troops if the Russians were approached.

The first war took place between 1839 and 1842. Dost Mohammed, ruler of Kabul, had made just such approaches to the British and Russians in turn. In 1841 the British garrison in Kabul, finding things a little uncomfortable, attempted to retreat back to India and were almost totally wiped out in the Khyber Pass – only one man survived. Despite re-occupying Kabul and doing a little razing and burning to show who was boss, the Brits ended up with Dost Mohammed back in power, just like before the war.

Round two in 1878-1880 was almost the same, the Afghanis agreed to become a more-or-less protectorate of the British, happily accepted an annual payment to keep things in shape and agreed to a British resident in Kabul. No sooner had this diplomatic mission installed themselves in Kabul than the whole lot were murdered. This time the British decided to keep control over the external affairs, but to leave the internal matters strictly up to the Afghanis themselves. A treaty with Russia further improved things – since nobody felt safe putting a foot in the country the Russians and British decided to make a little Afghan no-mans-land between themselves. That is the reason for the strange little strip of Afghanistan poking out of the top north-east corner. In 1893 the British also drew Afghanistan's boundaries and neatly partitioned a large number of the Pathan tribesmen into India (Pakistan today). That has been a cause of Afghanistan-Pakistan strife for many years and is the reason the Afghans refer to the western part of Pakistan as Pashtunistan.

Finally in 1919 the British, who by this time had totally lost interest in the place, got involved in one last tangle. And lost again. After that Afghanistan managed to go its own way right up to the late '70s. It was the US who replaced Britain in worrying about Russian influence, but post-WW II nice new roads were the weapons the super powers used to influence Afghanistan – not troops marching over the Khyber. Nevertheless the US tacitly recognised that Afghanistan was firmly in the Soviet sphere of influence and the Russian presence was strongly felt. Afghanistan's trade was tilted heavily towards the USSR and Soviet foreign aid to Afghanistan far out-weighed western assistance. Only in tourism did the western powers have a major influence on the country.

Internally Afghanistan remained precariously unstable, despite its relatively untroubled external relations, and it was this internal instability that eventually led to the sad situation in Afghanistan today. Attempts to apply Turkish-style progress to the country failed dismally between WW I and WW II. The post-war kingdom ended in '73 when the king, a Pathan like most of those in power, was neatly overthrown while away in Europe. His 'progressive' successors were hardly any more progressive than before, but the situation was far better than that which prevailed after the bloody pro-Moscow revolution that took place in '78.

The country rapidly fell into complete turmoil and confusion. A pro-communist, anti-religious government was far out of line with the strongly Islamic situations that prevailed in neighbouring Iran and Pakistan and soon the ever-volatile Afghan tribesmen had the countryside up in arms. A second revolution brought in a government leaning even more heavily on Soviet support and the country took another step towards complete anarchy.

Finally, in late '79, the Russians decided that enough was enough. Another 'popular' revolution took place and a Soviet puppet government was installed in Kabul, with what looked like half the Russian army lined up behind it to keep things in order. Despite an ineffectual storm of western protests it soon became clear that the Russians were there to stay. Opinion in the west is still split over the purpose of the Russian invasion – simply keeping peace on their borders or a step towards the oil-rich Gulf region?

Whatever the purpose the reality is an unpleasant one for the Russians – they cannot subdue the fiercely antagonistic tribespeople in the countryside nor can they gain any real support in the cities. On the other hand the divided and ill-equipped Afghan tribal warriors have no hope of overcoming the enormous Soviet armed strength, but they can make the Russians extremely uncomfortable in the rugged interior. So although the Russians are very unlikely to be ignominiously driven out they are likely to find, like the earlier British invaders, that Afghanistan remains a country easy to march into, but very difficult to march out of. For the traveller one of the most interesting countries in Asia looks likely to remain off-limits for some time to come.

FACTS

Population The population is about 17 million although exact figures are hard to come by due to the nomadic nature of many people in Afghanistan. There are now huge numbers of Afghan refugees in Pakistan. Approximately 60% of the population is Afghan, the balance a mixture of minority groups. Kabul is the capital and largest city, other cities are Herat, Kandahar, and Mazar-i-Sharif.

Geography Afghanistan is totally land-locked and has an extremely rugged topography. Total area is 650,000 square km. The mighty Hindu Kush mountain range, western extremity of the Himalaya, runs across the country from east to west. The average elevation of this mountainous interior is a lofty 2700 metres and the highest mountains reach 7500 metres. South is the dry, dusty, Dasht-i-Margo, where the climate can be uncomfortably cold on the northern plateau in winter.

Economy A primarily agricultural and nomadic shepherding people, trade is chiefly with the USSR which borders Afghanistan in the north. The only natural resource currently exploited is natural gas, which even prior to the Russian invasion was piped 100% into the USSR.

Religion Afghanistan is an intensely Muslim country – separation of religion and state simply does not exist, the 'mullahs' still have great power. Although the Blue Mosque in Mazar-i-Sharif is a most important Shi'ite Muslim shrine, the country is 80% Sunnite. There are very small percentages of Hindus and Jews. The strict Muslim attitudes apply to a very modern introduction – cars. Traffic accidents involving death can end in the old 'eye for an eye' business. Although this may not be applied too liberally to foreigners, having an accident is most definitely not recommended – the aftermath can be time consuming and un-comfortable.

BOOKS

There are three very readable books to pick up for a general flavour of Afghanistan. One is James Michener's *Caravans*, a rather ridiculous and over-romantic novel, but it provides gripping reading – particularly if, like me, you manage to read it while in Afghanistan. And it does tell you how to pronounce Kabul!

The second book is Eric Newby's *A Short Walk in the Hindu Kush* which provides a delightful description of a mid-50s jaunt by two eccentric Englishmen through the Hindu Kush and into Nuristan to the north-east of Kabul. It was for people like these two that the 'mad dogs and Englishmen' description was coined.

The third is a classic of travel writing from between WW I and WW II. Long out of print, Robert Byron's *The Road to Oxiana* has recently been resurrected and is another enjoyable reminder of how travel used to be prior to jumbo jets and mass tourism. It also indicates how little much of Iran and Afghanistan has changed in 50 years. All three books are available in paperback. There are also a number of pretty coffee table photographic books and some heavy, scholarly tomes, but nothing much is available in the general descriptive line.

VISAS

Although few visitors, apart from journalists, try to enter Afghanistan today it appears that visas are still issued by the Afghan embassies in Peshawar and Quetta, Pakistan.

MONEY

The Russians no doubt control the official money market pretty rigidly, but there is probably a healthy black market running in Afghanistan today for dollars and other hard currencies. Afghanistan was always a place where changing money on the street was much easier and faster than in the banks. The few people I have spoken with who have been in Afghanistan recently report that there is also a healthy market in caviar! It's the one 'hard currency' Russian soldiers can provide to pay for the western luxuries smuggled in from Pakistan.

CLIMATE

The weather in Afghanistan is distinctly on the harsh side – very cold in the winters, very hot in the summers. If you are in the country between December and March make sure you have got plenty of warm clothing. Spring is pleasant although the winter thaw can make things very muddy.

Summer, June through August, is blisteringly hot, dry and dusty. Not pleasant, particularly in the south. Best time of year is autumn – September and October. Kabul is very high up, at over 2000 metres, which tempers the summer heat but makes the winter cold even more severe. Coming up to Kabul from the hot Indian and Pakistani plains can be a real shock.

ACCOMMODATION

Like Kathmandu, Kabul had a great number of cheap hotels which sprang up to cater for the overlanders passing through. Even before the Soviet invasion the government was closing many of them down, but at one time Afghanistan had probably the lowest prices on the whole overland trip.

FOOD

Food in Afghanistan is basic. Very basic. Kabul had a selection of those 'international freak food' places, but elsewhere you were eating a lot of kebabs and omelettes and little else. *Pilau* and *kebabs* are the two main Afghan dishes. Kebabs, we all know what they are, are mutton or, less frequently, chicken and are served with rice or with the delicious Afghan breads known as *nan*.

Pilau are the rice-meat-vegetable dishes you find all across Asia. *Zarda* or *norang pilau* is made with chicken and flavoured with strips of orange peel. More common is *gaubili pilau* which uses mutton. Nuts, raisins and spices are all normal additions to a pilau. *Chelows*, as in Iran, are made by cooking the rice separately. *Qurma* or *Korma* is like a pilau, but with a heavy sauce.

The hygiene of Afghan bakeries was not all one could ask for, but watching the nan being made was a performance not to be missed. If you arrived early you could buy it hot from the pit. The bakery would have about half a dozen men all working on their appointed tasks. The oven was reached through a circular hole in the ground, narrower at the neck than the base. The bread, like a half-metre long oval pancake, was stuck against the side. When ready it was peeled off with a long shovel and stacked straight on to the road. At least while it was hot the flies seemed to keep off – unusual for food in Afghanistan! Good though it was the Afghan nan was not as good as that of Iran. A piece (sheet?) of bread only costs a few Afs.

Afghan fruit was usually very good,

particularly in Kabul where pomegranates, citrus fruit, grapes and melons were all excellent. Great care had to be taken with fruit. It had to be washed and carefully peeled if you wanted to avoid stomach problems. Tea *chai*, of course, is the number one Afghan drink. There are *chai khanas*, tea houses, almost everywhere in Afghanistan. Small and dark they're very much a male meeting place where endless cups of the delicious Afghan tea are consumed. You could often find simple food in chai khanas and in remote places they also offered accommodation.

Supposedly Coca-Cola is still on sale in Afghanistan! The Arabic-script coke signs look tremendous, you know what it says even if you can't read it. Wine, once a popular drink, was making a comeback around Kabul prior to the upheavals, due to the efforts of some energetic western residents. Nuristan was only forcibly converted to Islam around the turn of the century so wine drinking did not end very long ago. Beer, on the other hand, was always difficult to find and prohibitively expensive.

GETTING THERE
Since the invasion Kabul has been virtually the only gateway into the country. Ariana Afghan Airlines, the national flag carrier, still links Kabul with European and other Asian capitals and, of course, with Moscow. There are also regular connections with Pakistan and India. It is possible to fly from Kabul to Tashkent, the Russian region bordering Afghanistan to the north which has many close cultural ties to Afghanistan.

Prior to the Russian invasion there were three main road entry points into Afghanistan. One crossed from Mashed in Iran to Herat, the second from Quetta in Pakistan to Kandahar and the third from Peshawar in Pakistan over the Khyber Pass to Kabul. All three are now likely to be rather dangerous, but the Pakistan routes are, supposedly, still open although the bus services are now much less frequent.

An '85 report on visiting Afghanistan:

Some friends of mine tried visiting Afghanistan from Iran. They got visas, but were turned back at the frontier. Same treatment near Peshawar, Pakistan, though the frontier guard explained that they were expected to fly and their visa was valid for Kabul only. Still not deterred they got a flight from Delhi. There is still a bus service into Kabul from the airport. If you flew with Ariana or Aeroflot it costs nothing, otherwise Afs 20. It drops you at the only place you can stay – the *InterContinental*. The Inter-Continental must be the cheapest in the chain – Afs 1800 a night double (around US$30). It's the only place you can buy food too, as there isn't much on the streets of Kabul. The shops are pretty empty. The museum is still functioning, but just down the road is a new phenomenon, the round Kabul road block. There's no way out of Kabul avoiding them, and you can't leave Kabul without a barrage of documents and place in a convoy vehicle. You must exchange your money at the banks as doing otherwise will be construed as giving hard currency to the insurgents. Under military law they will shoot you if caught blackmarketeering. After five days my friends couldn't take any more of Kabul, and flew back to Delhi wondering why they wasted their time and money.

GETTING AROUND
Flying is likely to be the safest means of travel within Afghanistan today. Afghanistan has one good road loop, built with Russian and American aid, from Herat through Kandahar to Kabul. Good roads continue north from Herat into the USSR and north from Kabul to Mazar-i-Sharif and the USSR. A poor road completes the loop from Mazar-i-Sharif to Herat. Another rough route runs through the centre of the country from Herat to Kabul via Band-i-Amir and Bamiyan – shorter in distance but longer in time. There were frequent bus services between Herat and Kandahar, Kandahar and Kabul and between Kabul and Mazar-i-Sharif. Today bus travel is a risky business requiring Russian protection.

The surfaced roads were only built in the '60s and travel through Afghanistan, previously hard going, became a breeze.

The road made its great southern loop from Kabul to Herat via Kandahar in order to skirt around the southern extremities of the Hindu Kush. The road north to Mazar-i-Sharif passed through the long Salang Tunnel. Traffic was always light and apart from occasional brown hills the only things to see were nomads and their camels. The nomad costumes are brilliant and the women are quite unlike the traditional Afghani women who are usually shrouded from head to toe.

THINGS TO BUY

Afghanistan was one of the best places on the overland trip for a buying splurge although, over the years, prices had gone steadily up and quality steadily down. Due to the much smaller number of visitors to Afghanistan today it's very much a buyers' market and you can pick up real bargains in handicrafts in Kabul. Clothes were always an interesting and colourful buy although quality was not always too high. When buying *posteens*, the colourfully-embroidered Afghan coats, it was necessary to check carefully how well they had been cured. Many coats began to smell very badly after they left Afghanistan!

Kandahar was famed for its embroidery and you could buy mirrored panels to be made up into skirts or dresses elsewhere. Afghan coats were said to be particularly good in Ghazni. Leatherwork of all kinds could be found in Herat – hats, belts, bags and strong cheap sandals. Recycling things is an Afghan speciality so sandals usually had old car tyres for their soles – better cornering power with Goodyear or Michelins? If you had no scruples about wildlife you could also get absurdly cheap fur coats.

Afghan rugs were also good buys – hand made and in a variety of tribal designs. If you were into jewellery Afghanistan was noted for lapis lazuli. There were also a lot of antiques (new and old) around, particularly venerable-looking guns. And, of course, there was Afghanistan's famous

dope. It is said that Soviet soldiers are currently losing their sorrows in clouds of Afghani gold.

LANGUAGE

Afghanistan has two main languages. One is a Persian dialect very similar to the Farsi spoken in Iran – see the Iran section for some words in that language.

The other is Pushtu, which is also spoken in the Pathan regions of Pakistan. Persian is the language of the government and officials and is the one to generally use. In the south and to some extent in the east, Pushtu is more generally spoken. The following words are in Pushtu:

how do you do?	*stere ma she*
reply 1	*te stere me she*
reply 2	*quar ma she*
how much?	*tsumra?*
expensive	*ddeer*
where/when	*tsheeri/kayla?*
thank you	*teshekour*
yes/no	*o/na*
good	*sse*
bread	*nan*
tea	*chai*
water	*oobe*
room	*khuma*
marijuana/hash	*ganja/charees*
yesterday	*paroun*
today	*nen*
tomorrow	*saba*

1	*yaw*	7	*uwe*
2	*dwa*	8	*ate*
3	*dree*	9	*ne*
4	*tsar*	10	*las*
5	*pindze*	100	*sawa*
6	*shpazz*		

1 ۱   2 ۲   3 ۳   4 ۴   5 ۵
6 ۶   7 ۷   8 ۸   9 ۹   10 ۱۰

The conventional greetings are delightfully descriptive, our 'how do you do' is literally 'hope you are not tired' to which the reply is 'you too' or alternatively 'hope you don't become poor!' Remember that most important word, the one for foreigner – *farangi*. And spend 10 minutes learning your Arabic numerals or the possibility of getting ripped off will become a certainty.

Afghanistan was somehow totally unlike any other country along the overland trail. The people were as poor as you would see, yet beggars were few. Pride is a big thing with the Afghans and 'fierce' is the only adjective to describe their spirit of independence. They are most definitely not a subject people. Compared to the countries on either side – Iran to the west, Pakistan and India to the east – it was a totally relaxed country. The hassles seemed to disappear.

The country is dry and barren with harsh moonscapes, jagged mountains and rugged gorges, but when there is colour in this often dull monotone, it is real technicolour. Is there a deeper blue than the lakes of Band-i-Amir? Or a cooler one than the beautiful tiles of a mosque? A brighter red than the flash of a nomad woman's dress? A better green than the splash of growth around a river?

It is a country where nothing goes to waste – old car and truck tyres become sandals or buckets, food tins become containers or cooking utensils. If it can't be made out of something else then they will make it from scratch whether it is a car part for a broken down vehicle or those amazing old rifles, perfect imitations of out-of-date British army weaponry.

The *karez* is a peculiarly Afghan means of irrigation and of great interest to outsiders. Like many dry, arid countries Afghanistan has great underground reservoirs of water which can transform otherwise barren stretches of land – if you can get the water up. This subterranean water is often so far underground that drilling or digging for it, with primitive equipment, is virtually impossible.

Long ago the Afghans devised a better way. They dig a well, known as the 'head well' on higher ground where the distance to the water is much less. A long tunnel is then dug to conduct this water down to the village farmland. A whole series of wells are dug along the path of this tunnel during its construction. These are later used as entry points to maintain the tunnel and when not in use are covered with dirt which makes them look like gigantic ant-hills. Digging

a karez is skilled and dangerous work and the *karez-kans* are respected and highly paid workers. The cost of making a karez and later maintaining it is usually split between a whole village and the karez is communally owned.

If any sport can sum up a country then *Buzkashi* can sum up Afghanistan. It is a wild, raging activity – just what you would expect the wild, raging horsemen of the steppes to indulge in on their day off. To play Buzkashi you need a large playing field – say a couple of km long. Then you need some *chapandoz*, they are the swaggering horsemen who look like Genghis Khan himself would be their ideal captain. And you need a *boz*, which is the headless body of a dead goat.

You then divide the chapandoz into two teams, put a marker peg in the ground at one end of the field, drop the boz at the other end and all hell breaks loose. All you have to do is pick the boz up, carry it down and around the marker and drop it back at its starting point. Unfortunately all Genghis Khan's mates are determined to prevent you from doing any such thing and a broken leg or arm is a mere trifle. Friday is the big day for Buzkashi and Mazar-i-Sharif and Kundunz in the north are the main towns to see it. There are big games in Kabul each year.

KABUL

The 'fly in, fly out' capital of Afghanistan was a bit of a tourist trap, packed with souvenir and instant-antique shops. It was not a terribly attractive or interesting city, but did offer a number of things to see and do before you pushed on to Afghanistan's greater attractions. Today, if you were able to visit the country at all, Kabul would probably be the only place you could see.

Things to See

Kabul Museum The museum is some way out from the centre of town and rather cramped and rundown. But it is what's inside that counts and what's inside is plenty. It offers an excellent introduction to the many kingdoms of Afghanistan and to the diverse handicrafts.

City Wall & Citadel It was not possible to

visit the old citadel, Bala Hissar, even prior to the invasion, as it was still used by the military, but it was possible to walk the entire length of the often crumbling walls. They run from the southern side of Koh-i-Asamai, the hill close to Shah-i-Nan, down to the river then up and over Koh-i-Sher Darwaza on the other side of the river, finally terminating at the citadel. It took about five hours to walk the full length of the walls.

Other The pleasant Gardens of Babur were a cool retreat near the city walls. The noon gun (which was fired every noon, believe it or not!) was here too. It was once used for rather messy executions. It was not possible to go inside the Pol-i-Khisti, most important mosque in Kabul. The bazaar, twisting, turning streets of shops, flanks Jodi Maiwand to the south of the river and has been a centre of protest against the Russians. There is a camel market just outside Kabul on the Jalalabad road.

Places to Stay & Eat

Kabul had a lot of places to stay and you had no trouble finding something to suit. Today the choice is probably limited to the Kabul InterContinental and nothing else. The bazaar hotels, south of the river around Jodi Maiwand Avenue, were cheap and grotty. Most people stayed in the newer diplomatic quarter known as Shah-i-nao. Here you found 'Chicken Street', the freak centre of Kabul and one of those great Asian 'bottlenecks' through which every overland traveller seemed to pass. It was packed with restaurants, souvenir and craft shops, cheap hotels and crowds of travellers.

Amongst the popular eating places, now no doubt all shut down, were *Sigi's Restaurant* on Chicken St and the government restaurant in central Pashtunistan Square – famous all across Asia for its apple pies! Even before the invasion the Russians had a hand in its operation.

Getting Around

Buses in Kabul were absurdly cheap and none too reliable. They tended to depart only when full and were inclined to stop for prayers and other calls! Taxis were unmetered but had a flat charge within the city limits.

NURISTAN

The region north-east of Kabul, known as Nuristan, the 'land of light' is interestingly described in *A Short Walk in the Hindu Kush*. Once known as Kafiristan it had been a non-Muslim thorn-in-the-side of the central government until Islam was forcibly taken to them around the turn of the century – 'do you believe in Mohammed or would you like your head chopped off?' It's still remote, little visited and of great ethnological interest. It's also likely to be an area where the Russian hold is most tenuous.

BAMIYAN

There were two ways of getting to the great Buddhas of Bamiyan from Kabul. The longer, easier route heads north then turns west and is about 250 km. The shorter, more difficult route heads directly west from Kabul then turns north through the Unai and Hajigak Passes – only 180 km but much more severe dirt roads. You could also approach Bamiyan, during the dry season, from Herat on the central route.

When the intrepid Chinese priest Hsuan-tsang visited Bamiyan in 632 AD there were 'more than 10 monasteries and more than a thousand priests'. This was one of the great Buddhist centres, but the arrival of Islam spelt disaster. The Muslims abhorred representations of the human form and on several occasions they mutilated or damaged the huge Buddha statues that dominate the valley.

Things to See

The Buddhas The smaller of the two Buddhas stands a towering 35-metres high. This Buddha is thought to have been carved out in the 2nd or 3rd century AD and has elements of the Graeco-Buddhist style. It is much more badly disfigured than the later, better and larger Buddha which stands 53 metres high. This Buddha is estimated to be two or three centuries younger and is in a later, more sophisticated style. The Buddhas were carved roughly out of their niches then the final design applied with mud and straw covered in a type of cement. Cords draped down the body were built up to form the folds of the figures' robes. The holes that make exposed parts of the figures look like a cheese were used to peg and stabilise this outer 'skin'.

Around the Buddhas was an absolute honeycomb of caves which were once covered in painted frescoes – the Buddhas too were at one time brightly painted. Most of the frescoes have long ago deteriorated, partly due to the local inhabitants who have used the caves as dwellings. The best remaining paintings can be seen around the smaller Buddha.

Other The Red City, the remains of an ancient citadel which guarded Bamiyan, is about 17 km before you reached Bamiyan itself. It took a couple of hours to scramble around it. Shar-i-gholgola is the ruined city in the valley – the name means 'city of sighs', the sighs were those of the inhabitants after Genghis had dropped in for a spot of massacring. There are many more caves and other attractions in the area. A climb to the top of the cliff on the other side of the valley to look across at the Buddhas was a popular activity.

Band-i-Amir

It's not really possible to describe the lakes of Band-i-Amir. To appreciate them you had to go there. The lakes, clear, cold blue surrounded by towering cliffs, are 75 km beyond Bamiyan. It was worth suffering the pre-dawn chill to see the sunrise over them.

Places to Stay & Eat

A lot of places had sprung up at Bamiyan to cater for travellers. The basic places were very basic. At Band-i-Amir most of the places operated in summer only, it's far too cold to hang around for long in the winter.

THE NORTH

North of the Hindu Kush is a quite different Afghanistan – if the south is related to the Iranian plateau, the north is kin to the Russian steppes and indeed, prior to modern attitudes about borders, the Afghan nomads were quite at home on both the Russian and Afghan sides of the border. Until the Salang Pass tunnel was completed in the mid-60s this was also a totally isolated part of the country. To get there before that time you either had to climb up and over the highest part of the Hindu Kush, north of Kabul, or cross the lower western extremity near Herat and make a long desert crossing.

Mazar-i-Sharif

The main town of the northern region is actually quite new, particularly in comparison with neighbouring Balkh. Its main attraction considerably pre-dates the rest of the town, however. The Blue Mosque, or Tomb of Ali, marks the centre of the town and is the holiest spot in Afghanistan. Of course whether or not Ali really does rest within is open to question. After his assassination, Ali, adopted son and then son-in-law of the prophet, was said to have been buried in Iraq. Quite why his skeleton should then turn up near Balkh I'm not sure. Nevertheless in the 12th century a small shrine was built for him, but later hidden with earth during Genghis Khan's little visit. The current shrine dates from 1481 but has been considerably modified since; only the two main domes are original.

Balkh

A Chinese visitor in 663 said it had three of the most beautiful buildings in the world and it was known to the Arabs as the 'mother of cities'. Today all that is left are a few timeworn buildings and the crumbling remains of the city walls. Balkh was once the capital of Zoroaster and a principal centre for his religion. Later, under the Arabs, it became an important Muslim centre with a huge mosque and a reputation for culture and trade. Then in 1220 Genghis Khan massacred the inhabitants and toppled the walls in the most terrible slaughter Afghanistan was to suffer at his hands.

When Marco Polo passed through in 1275 he found only ruins. Later Tamerlane rebuilt the walls but efforts to re-establish Balkh were unsuccessful and it has been a ghost town for centuries. The Green Mosque and piles of rubble are pretty much all there is to see.

Other Mazar-i-Sharif is the centre for Afghan hash production and once had an important hashish market. Transporting quantities out of this area was not recommended. This is also the region for Buzkashi, that wild Afghan national sport. Friday is Buzkashi day. Archaeologists found remains of Greek cities and buildings from Alexander the Great's day here – but there was nothing much for the visitor to view. The road westwards to Herat gets progressively worse after Balkh and after Shibarghan it is just a sandy wasteland.

GHAZNI
Like Balkh in the north the modern town of Ghazni is just a pale shadow of its former glory although there was much more to see than in the northern centre. Ghazni is only 150 km from Kabul on the road to Kandahar so it was easy to get to, but it is slightly off the main road, making it just as easy to drive straight by.

A thousand years ago, at its peak, the Ghazni kingdom stretched to India in the east and Persia in the west. Mahmud, who ruled from 990 to 1030, specialised in swooping down on the plains of India and carting off the jewels by the camel load. All these easily acquired riches turned Ghazni into a great and beautiful city, but

in 1151 it was burnt out by a local king – who was so pleased with his arsonist abilities that he named himself the 'world burner'. Only 70 years later in 1221 Genghis dropped by and knocked over whatever was left. Although it later partially recovered Ghazni today is known mainly for its fine bazaar.

The tomb of Mahmud is not one of Ghazni's greatest buildings although he was undoubtedly the most important ruler of the kingdom. The carefully restored tomb of Abdul Razzak and the museum within are of greater interest. There are also some very fine minarets, the excavations of the Palace of Masud and, most surprisingly, a recently discovered Buddhist stupa which has survived from long before the Arab invasion that preceded even Mahmud.

KANDAHAR
Situated in the far south of Afghanistan,

about midway between Kabul and Herat, Kandahar is the point on the main highway where it stops going south-west and starts going north-west. It is also the place where the road branches off south to Quetta in Pakistan. In fact it is today pretty much what it has always been – an important crossroads and little else. In the summer, when Kandahar becomes excessively dry, hot and dusty, it is not a place to hang around for very long.

Things to See

Mosque of the Sacred Cloak Kandahar's great treasure, a cloak which once belonged to the prophet, is safely locked away from infidel eyes in this mosque. Next door is the uninspiring tomb of Ahmed Shah, father of modern Afghanistan and the man who brought the cloak back to Kandahar. Apart from that there is little to see in Kandahar although a few km out of town there are a couple of attractions.

Chihil Zina The 'Forty Steps' are only a few km from the centre towards Herat. They lead up to a niche carved in the rock by Babur, founder of the Moghul empire, guarded by two stone lions. Here, overlooking his capital city (nice views), he carved a record of his many victories. Akbar, his grandson, appended his list too.

Tomb of Mir Waiss The tomb is pleasantly situated by a cool green garden on the banks of the Arghandah river, just a little further out from the centre of Kandahar.

Places to Stay & Eat

The cheap hotels were mainly clustered around the central bus terminal or along the Herat road.

HELMAND VALLEY

The Helmand valley was once the centre of a sophisticated 'karez' underground irrigation system. Unfortunately old Genghis, on one of his rape-pillage-destroy trips, did it no good at all and the area has pretty much reverted to desert. The new Helmand River Project was

intended to re-irrigate this area prior to the arrival of the Russians.

Bost

If you headed towards Herat for about 100 km then turned south at Girishk, another 50 km on a good dirt road would bring you to the site of Bost. Way back when Ghazni was the centre of power in this part of Asia, this was the second city. Today it is a jumble of ruins and remains – shattered remnants of a once mighty – city. The superb arch, Qalai Bost, was the highpoint of a visit to this old centre.

Kajakai

If you headed back to the main road, then 90 km, again on a good dirt road, north of the road you found yourself at this pleasant place on the banks of the Helmand River.

One of the last letters we received from a traveller in Afghanistan had this exciting note about the bus trip from Kandahar to Herat:

... to Herat by bus again with a group of 25 soldiers carrying guns, grenades and all. Maybe that was the reason why our bus was ambushed by rebels, 100 km before Herat. We were attacked with machine guns, first from the right side then the left side. A frightening experience but nobody was hurt. We spent the rest of the afternoon and until 10 am the next morning at the nearest military post. Then we reboarded the same bus with the soldiers and all travelled to Herat.

Michel Persehais

HERAT

Herat was a small, provincial, relatively green, laze about place which everyone seemed to like. To many people it was quite simply the nicest place on the overland route. Part of this attraction was the contrast to everything around it. It was an easygoing oasis after a lot of hassle and dry desert. It was also a place with a quite amazingly violent history and one that looks like continuing. At one time in '79, but before the conclusive Russian takeover, every Russian in Herat was massacred by angry Afghans.

Things to See

Masjid-i-Jami The Friday Mosque is Herat's number one attraction and one of the finest Islamic buildings in the world, certainly the finest in Afghanistan. Although there have been religious buildings on this site for well over a thousand years everybody and his brother has had a go at knocking them down, including Genghis Khan, who destroyed an earlier mosque. The current one was built in 1498 and since 1943 has gradually been restored to its former magnificence. It has some extremely fine tilework to complement its graceful architecture and you could visit the small workshop where tiles were still being made for the restoration project. The mosque is also unusual, in Afghanistan, for permitting non-Muslim and women visitors.

The Citadel Herat's ancient citadel was still used as any army post so you could not get in for a look around although you could walk right round its outer wall. Only in this past century has the citadel been allowed to deteriorate badly but it makes a sad, though impressive, contrast with the great mosque.

Covered Bazaar The covered bazaar in Char Suq is a complex of all sorts of shops and artisans' workshops. it is in the southwest corner of the old walled city. At various points around the bazaar area and elsewhere in Herat you could see the old covered wells for which Herat is known.

Other A short walk from the centre on the road that runs north and intersects the road to the Iran border, are a number of interesting sights. First there is a small park with a beehive-shaped tomb then, further on, four immense, broken minarets. They are all that remains of an old madrasse or theological school which was built by the Empress Gaur-Shad who also built the mosque at Mashed. She was a remarkable woman who followed Tamerlane and kept his empire intact for many years after his death. Unhappily the destruction of the minarets was due to a visiting British adventurer in 1838. Finding the Persians about to invade the town, he decided to lend a hand to the locals and had parts of the religious school blown up to give the artillery a clearer line of fire. Further up the road are some interesting old windmills, examples of which could also be seen between Herat and Islam Qala, the border point to Iran.

Gazargah This thousand-year-old monastery complex is about five km east of Herat. The tomb of Abdullah Ansar, a famous Sufi-mystic and poet who died in Herat in 1088, is the main attraction of this complex. Zainuddin, the architect who later remodelled the shrine, is buried in the small tomb in the form of a crouching dog in front of the shrine. There is also a unique black-marble tombstone in the complex and on the road back to Herat there is a small park where you could have a fine view over the town.

Places to Stay & Eat

The cheapies were mainly clustered along the main street in the old city.

Bangladesh

Until the 1971 war which tore Pakistan apart, Bangladesh was the eastern half of the two part country. It has always been somewhat off the main tourist track, travel can be rather difficult, the government unstable and the economy continues to be lousy. Nevertheless, although Bangladesh is certainly not a country people fall in love with a surprising number do seem to find it quite interesting.

HISTORY

The Muslim Bengali region became the eastern wing of Pakistan after the 1947 partition. Long standing discontent finally erupted in 1971. The Bengalis supplied the major part of Pakistan's foreign exchange earnings through their jute exports, but they were systematically excluded from political power and received very little of the country's development expenditure or foreign aid programmes.

In 1970 the first elections in many years were held – the first ever to give the eastern wing an equal vote. The Bengali Sheikh Mujibur Rahman swept to power. The west Pakistanis were certainly not standing for a leader from the east and the Sheikh was bundled into jail. Naturally his supporters were none too happy about this style of democracy and a civil war broke out which was only settled when the Indians marched in to sort the Pakistanis out.

Since independence the going has been very far from easy. The country's industries were virtually wiped out and the communications network badly disrupted. Getting around has always been difficult in Bangladesh since the country is draped across the Ganges and Brahmaputra River deltas and any trip involves many river crossings. Massive foreign aid has hardly made a dent in the country's problems and it has suffered startling inefficiency and corruption since the war.

Sheikh Mujibur proved to be a fairly hopeless leader and was deposed and assassinated in 1975. The situation has hardly been any better since then. After a couple of unpopular changes General Ziaur Rahman took over power and was then 'elected' president in 1978. A period of relative stability then ensued before he in turn was assassinated in a totally senseless and abortive attempted coup in mid-81. A successor was elected from a vast field of potential candidates, but in early '82 yet another military takeover took place. Bangladesh continues to be the world's major third-world problem. The stagnant economy is beset by the hard new economics of the post oil-crisis world and the birth rate continues to soar well ahead of any sane level.

FACTS

Bangladesh's population of 87 million or so is squeezed into 139,000 very fertile square km. It has to be to support that sort of population. The basis for the fertility is also a major problem since the river deltas Bangladesh sprawls across are subject to frequent and often disastrous flooding and are so low-lying that typhoons, such as the terrible storm that preceded the war with Pakistan or the equally horrendous typhoon of mid-85 can cause unbelievable havoc.

VISAS

For Commonwealth countries, no visa is required except for citizens of India, Canada, UK, Australia and Sri Lanka. Note that some Australian and Canadian passport holders have been told by Bangladesh consular offices in Bangkok and Calcutta they don't need visas: they do, despite what they are told. No visa is required for a 90-day stay for nationals of Japan, South Korea and Yugoslavia.

A 72-hour transit visa is usually granted

for those arriving without any visa. A seven-day tourist visa is also available. If you wish to stay longer the 72-hour or the seven-day visa can usually be extended. You must first register at the Special Branch Office located in the Malibagh Bazar area on Kakrail Rd in Dacca then go to the Immigration Office. Two passport photos are required at the Immigration Office at 30 New Circuit Rd and routine extensions are usually handled on the same day. Longer stays can take much longer to handle. The office is open 8 to 11 am for applications but is closed on Fridays.

If you intend to leave by land a road permit is also necessary. These can be obtained in Dacca. If you plan to leave Bangladesh from the north into the northern region of India then you will also need a permit for this part of India.

BOOKS

The final Lonely Planet guide to the sub-continent, *Bangladesh – a travel survival kit*, was published in 1985.

MONEY

A$1	= Tk 19
US$1	= Tk 27
£1	= Tk 37

The unit of currency is the takka (Tk), still often referred to as the rupee. It's divided into 100 poisha. Currency forms are handed out on arrival and collected on departure and all currency transactions are supposed to be entered on this and should tally up at the end. In more expensive hotels all payment must be made in foreign currency so some smaller denomination notes should be carried for this purpose.

Officially you can only bring in or take out 100 takka but since, if you are entering Bangladesh by land, there is no place to change money at the border (nothing until you get to Jessore from Calcutta) it is obvious you are going to have to bring some takka with you or change it illegally.

Changing money is difficult outside the main centres and travellers' cheques much worse.

There is a healthy black market in Bangladesh. One traveller reported that: 'Money changing at the India-Bangladesh border is an experience – the black market operates more openly than I've seen anywhere (even happens in the customs official's office)'. There's a good rate between Indian rupees and takka. Another traveller noted that sometimes even bank workers would give you a better exchange rate on the sly! And another said that on departure her currency form was collected by a man who did not even glance at it, simply consigned it to a bin with many others!

If you bring in the usual duty free items you'll find it difficult to dispose of the whisky (Johnny Walker of course) for more than twice the duty free price but cigarettes are easily sold to any street vendor – again for around twice the duty free price. Take care in Dacca, however, one traveller reported getting hassled by the guy to whom he had sold his cigarettes. He reappeared moments after taking them, claiming vociferously that they were damaged and his money should be returned.

CLIMATE

It's hot and very wet during the monsoon. The cool, dry months from November to March are the best time to visit Bangladesh, April and September are the hottest months, mid-May to October is the monsoon period.

ACCOMMODATION

Cheap accommodation in Bangladesh is often poor value and rooms are often dirty and poorly kept. In anything above the most basic shoestring level hotel bills must be settled in foreign currency and change is always given in takkas. You can get bank permission to pay in takkas but it is rather a hassle. The BPC operates hotels and motels in Cox's Bazar and the

Chittagong Hill Tracts and there are government rest houses offering good standard accommodation in a number of towns.

FOOD

Food in the everyday eating places is often of poor quality with little variety and you should also be careful of restaurants as some are none too healthy. Rice, curry and parathas are often all you can find. Not unexpectedly Bengali food is very similar to Indian with the emphasis heavily on rice and dhal, that familiar lentil soup.

Bangladesh has a wide variety of river fish like *ruaha, beckti* and *bilsa* while prawns and lobsters are also often available. *Loochi* and *samosa* are widely available snacks in Bangladesh. *Rasgula, sandesh* or *kalojam* are popular milk-based desserts and *doi* is a tasty curd variety which is another local specialty. A wide range of tropical fruits are available in Bangladesh.

GETTING THERE
To/From Thailand & Nepal

Since Bangladesh Biman are a good airline for cheap deals many people use Dacca as a stepping stone on the popular Bangkok - Rangoon - Dacca - Calcutta - Kathmandu route. You can easily pick up tickets for that trip from around US$200. Dacca-Rangoon is US$125.

Biman are also super-cheap for flights to London from Bangkok and you can sometimes get a free stopover in beautiful Dacca if you're continuing through to India or further west. One traveller even worked out that Bangkok-Dacca-Calcutta was no more expensive than Bangkok-Dacca with Biman and flying through to Calcutta got you the free nights stopover, airport transfer, dinner and breakfast – even if you then elected not to continue to Calcutta. So your Bangladesh trip could start off with a free night's deluxe accommodation. Make sure you manage to keep your passport though, they try to collect them from transit passengers.

There are also lots of horror stories

about flying Biman – you'll hear lots of tales of cancellations, weird flights, exciting landings, frightening take-offs and lost baggage. Not all of them true. International departure tax is Tk 200.

To/From India

Indian Airlines and Biman both fly Calcutta-Dacca with fares of about US$40. From Dacca you can get Biman tickets a bit cheaper than Indian Airlines. Biman and Indian Airlines also fly Calcutta-Chittagong three times a week.

Although there are roads crossing between Bangladesh and India at a number of points along their long common border there are only two where you are actually permitted to cross – one for Calcutta and for Darjeeling. All the other border crossing points are officially closed. There are no open border crossing points between Bangladesh and Burma.

If, having entered by air, you leave via a land border crossing, a road permit is required. This can be obtained from the Immigration Office. Two passport photos are required but there is no fee. It's obtainable the same day if you apply for it in the morning.

Via Benopol This is the main overland route into Bangladesh, made generally by train from Calcutta. It is a Rs 7 rickshaw ride to the immigration checkpost then walking distance to the actual border. Inside Bangladesh it is a Tk 4 rickshaw ride to the bus station in Benopol from where buses depart to Jessore.

Via Chiliharti From Darjeeling to New Jalpaiguri takes 10 hours by the little train. A train from Siliguri to Haldibari is a two-hour trip and costs Rs 3.70 2nd class. There are three trains daily, the last at 5.30 pm. Note that you require a road permit from the Indian Embassy in Kathmandu or the Immigration Office in Delhi and Calcutta to travel through this area. It is advisable to take the early train as Haldibari is not a great place to stay, there are lots of mosquitoes.

There is a bus from Haldibari to Hemkumari, a border village, but it's slow and often late. An alternative is a rickshaw trip which takes two hours. From Hemkumari it is four km along a dirt road to Chiliharti, the first village on the Bangladesh side. This is all really academic, however, because this route is now officially closed and there is a watchtower to check on locals trying to sneak across into India. The road on the Indian side is now surfaced but the only legal and official route is an eight km walk along the old, and now unused, railway tracks via Haldibari to Hemkumari.

The immigration checkpost in Chiliharti is open from 10 am till 6 pm, but chances are that you might have to wait for the immigration officer who occasionally does not turn up on time. Keep a few rupees to change to takkas at the Indian border point for the train fare to Syedpur where you can then cash travellers' cheques.

In Syedpur it's worth having a good idea of your route through Bangladesh. The surrounding region has a number of interesting archaeological sites. To Dacca takes 12 to 14 hours – first by bus to Rangpur then by train via Mymensingh. Buses are in general faster overall. If you miss the last direct bus to Dacca, take a bus to Bogra (every hour, 2½ hour trip, Tk 13) where there is an hourly departure for Dacca. Bogra-Dacca takes six to eight hours, there are express and non-express buses and the fare is Tk 32.

Travelling north from Bangladesh into India the train from Syedpur to Chiliharti leaves at 3 pm and arrives at 6.15 pm. The fare is Tk 11 in 2nd class. In Chiliharti there's a guest house with rooms at Tk 30, but no electricity and it's wise to bring some of your own food. Across the border in India there is a *Dak Bungalow* in Haldibari which costs Rs 6.50. The train to Siliguri costs Rs 4 and departs at 7.30 am. Change trains at New Jalpaiguri where you also have to register at the Foreigner's Registration Office. Don't get off at the railway station in Siliguri, get off

at the next station where the little Darjeeling trains depart at 7 and 9.30 am. the three-hour trip costs Rs 10.50.

Via Tetulya The road into Bangladesh from Siliguri at Tetulya is closed although it appears the immigration officials in Dacca continue to issue road permits and the border officials may sometimes let travellers through. The Tamabil route is definitely closed due to the unrest in Assam.

GETTING AROUND

Always allow plenty of time in your travelling schedule. As one visitor noted: 'every type of transport I used within Bangladesh broke down at some point.'

Air Bangladesh Biman flights, mainly by Fokker F27s, are very cheap – although they also tend to fall out of the sky with some regularity. Students under 26 can get a further 25% discount. Some of the fares include Dacca-Chittagong T450, Dacca-Sylhet T340, Dacca-Jessore T310, Chittagong-Cox's Bazaar T145.

Rail Trains are not as crowded as in India or Pakistan but they can be very slow due to the many river crossings which often involve train changes. An estimated 500 bridges were destroyed during the Bangladesh war but most of these have now been replaced. As in India mail trains are the fastest. There are four classes – 1st air-con, 1st, 2nd and 3rd. You cannot reserve 3rd class and this can be impossibly overcrowded although it is, naturally, ridiculously cheap. If you're travelling 3rd class try to get on the train at its departure point and well before it leaves. The other classes can be reserved but you need to make reservations well in advance.

A copy of the T1 *Railway Timetable & Guide*, available at the Dacca station, is a worthwhile investment. Air-con costs nearly twice as much as regular 1st class and fares are often nearly as expensive as flying. For foreign visitors a 50% student discount is available or a 25% discount for

other tourists, but only on 1st class fares.

In Bangladesh metre gauge is generally as fast as the broad gauge lines and almost as comfortable. In the lower class carriages, crowded though they may be, stops are frequent and people get on and off so you soon seem to find a seat.

Bus There are all sorts of buses and since you do not suffer the same crowding or reservations problems that the trains have they can be an excellent alternative. Buses have a further major advantage that when you come to a river the bus crosses on the ferry with you. On the trains you

often have to get off and board another train on the other side.

Buses operate from town to town on almost every road in the country. From Dacca they fan out all over the country early in the morning. The government buses are usually somewhat cheaper than the private ones, fares are slightly more than 2nd class rail. On some routes competition is fierce and touts will accost you as you approach the bus station. Almost all seats can be booked ahead of time but the tickets give your destination and seat number in Bengali. In some places the different bus companies operate from a variety of different stations. There is a real difference in quality between the slow, crowded and fairly dirty (but cheap) local services and some of the air-con expresses where you even make a mid-journey halt at company owned facilities with spotlessly clean toilets.

Boat Travelling by river is probably the best way of coming to grips with the country. It's also the most pleasant way of travelling in Bangladesh. There are actually more km of navigable waterways than of driveable roads and the crafts that ply these rivers are a superb mixture – everything from overloaded sailing boats with their sails a mass of patches to paddle steamers which must have been sent here after retiring from the Mississippi.

A trip on the 'Rocket' between Dacca and Khulna is a great experience and the scenery is superb. See the Dacca Getting There section for details. There is also a service between Narayanganj and Chittagong and another between Chittagong and Barisal. Berths are sometimes available on cargo boats to Calcutta. On the older riverboats there are four classes – 1st, 2nd, intermediate and 3rd – but on the newer Chinese vessels there is only 1st and 3rd class. Food on the boats is excellent, T6 to T9 buys you as much as you can eat in the 3rd class mess. Unless you're travelling in the upper classes you buy your tickets immediately before departure. 'The modern Chinese boats,' reported one traveller, 'are underpowered and cannot keep to the schedules like the old Scottish-built ones!'

Local Transport Cycle-rickshaws are available in most villages (but not all) and all towns. As usual you must agree your fare before setting out. In Dacca they are much more expensive than elsewhere. You can travel three times as far for the same cost out in the country. If you can get a Bengali to negotiate the fare for you it may work out cheaper but the old walking away trick usually does it. Mini-taxis or 'baby-taxis' are just like auto-rickshaws in India. The meters are always 'broken' and, unlike cycle-rickshaws, they often operate a cartel when in clusters!

The Bangladesh Loop You can make an interesting loop around Bangladesh starting from (or finishing at) Dacca. First go to Sylhet in the north-east by bus, train or air. From there you can travel south by bus or train to Chittagong and the Chittagong Hill Tracts. On to Cox's Bazar and then back to Chittagong by bus. Finally you can travel back to Dacca by boat or leave Bangladesh for Calcutta via Khulna.

LANGUAGE
Bangla (Bengali) is the national language although a minority speak Urdu and English is also widely spoken. The following words are in Bangla:

yes/no	*gee/nay*
thank you	*donnobad*
goodbye	*bidai*
how are you?	*kaemon achen?*
I am well	*balo achi*
how much is this?	*dom khoto?*
where is . . . ?	*. . . . khotai?*
post office	*dak ghor*
boat	*noukha*
food	*kabhar*
rice	*bhat*
fish	*maohh*
egg	*deem*
potato	*aloo*
tea	*cha*
water	*pani*
mango	*am*
banana	*kola*
pineapple	*anaras*

1	*ek* ৩	6	*choy* ৬
2	*dui* ২	7	*sa'ath* ৭
3	*teen* ৩	8	*ath* ৮
4	*char* ৪	9	*noe* ৯
5	*pa'ch* ৫	10	*dos* ১০
		20	*bis* ২০
		30	*tiris* ৩০

DACCA

Although Dacca, the capital of Bangladesh, is thought to date back to the 11th century or even earlier the modern city was founded by the Moghuls in 1608. It is known as the 'city of mosques', due to the great number of mosques to be seen.

Information & Orientation

The city is built around the Buriganga River and the old city, where the most interesting sites are located, stands along the north bank. The National Tourist Organisation or BPC (Bangladesh Parjatan Corporation) has its offices in the Dacca Sheraton. The Immigration Office, for road permits if you plan to leave Bangladesh by land, is at 30 Circuit House Rd. If you want to get into the Chittagong Hill Tracts then you need a permit from the Ministry of Home Affairs at the Secretariat Building. You have little change of getting it. The GPO is on A Ghani Rd and the poste restante service there is very much a do-it-yourself operation although mail seems to get through fairly reliably.

Bangladeshi handicrafts, which can be quite interesting, can be found at the Bangladesh Handicrafts Co-Operative Federation or at Kartika on Mymensingh Rd. Good products include silk, raw silk, khadi (home-spun) cotton textiles and unusual items made out of jute. Prices tend to be very low. For jute work and handicrafts try the jute shops at Bottomly Homes in Dacca. Shirts and kurtas of khadi or raw silk are also widely available.

Things to See

Around Town Built in 1678 by Aurangzeb's son the Moghul Lalbagh (Jewel of a Garden) Fort stands in the west of the old city and is one of Dacca's few landmarks. Pari Bibi's Mazar (Tomb of the Fair Lady) stands beside the fort. You can get a good view over Dacca from the roof of the partially ruined Bara Katra – formerly a caravanserai.

Some of the mosques that gave Dacca its alternative title include the Star Mosque which is covered in gold stars, the large Baitul Mukarram or national mosque in the centre of Dacca, the University Mosque, the Shat Gambuz (seven dome) mosque about 10 km out of the city and the 1709 Kar Talab.

At night the Chowk Bazaar area of old Dacca comes alive with its many crowded and narrow streets and hustling rickshaw-wallahs. Four bazaars lead off from the main square and there are also many mosques in this area including the 1676 Chowk Masjid. The Saddarghat ferry terminal is also an interesting area to wander as village boats unload colourful cargoes of tropical fruits. You can hire a boat here to take a leisurely cruise out on the river. Other points of interest include the English-Moghul-style Curzon Hall in the university area and the High Court.

The Dacca Museum, with its collection of paintings, sculptures, coins and textiles, is free. There's even a room with a display on the independence movement – complete with a smashed skull! The museum is open 10 am to 4.30 pm on Saturdays to Wednesdays, 8.30 to 11.30 am on Fridays and is closed on Thursdays. The Sher-e-Bangla Nagar houses the National Assembly while the Shahid Minar monument was built for those killed during the Language Movement of 1952, an early indication of the friction between East and West Pakistan.

Out of Town Places of interest outside Dacca include Sonargaon, 27 km out, a capital of the region from the 7th to 10th centuries. Some structures from this Pala period still remain, Sonargaon also has a Museum of Folk Art & Culture. Narayanganj, 15 km from Dacca, is on the Stalakhya River and is the largest riverport in the country. The river is crowded with boats carrying jute for the city's jute mills which include the largest such mill in the world, the Adamjee Jute Mills.

Places to Stay

At 96 New Eskaton Rd the *YMCA* (tel 40 1371) takes men and women and has a

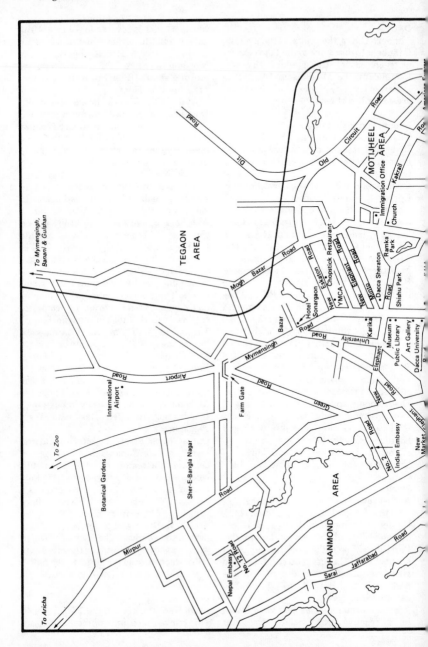

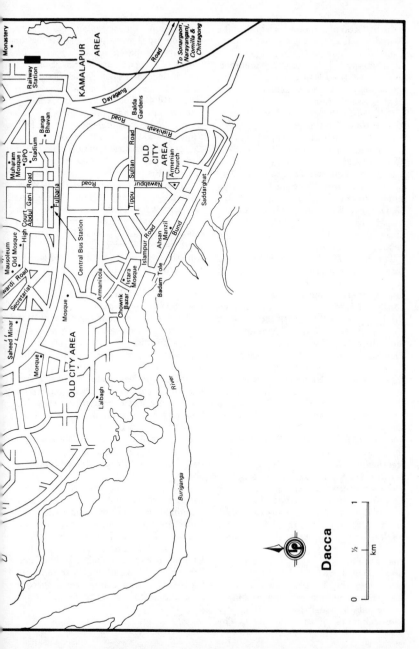

dorm at Tk 35 plus rooms with bath at Tk 70 and 100. It's probably the best value in Dacca and has a restaurant. There is a supplementary Tk 5 temporary membership charge. It's a little distance out from the centre, Tk 4-5 by rickshaw from the Central Bus Station.

Other places include the *Royal Hotel* on Airport Rd with rather grotty rooms at Tk 35/60. *Hotel Noor* at 26 Green Rd in the Dhanmandi area has rooms with bath at Tk 45/80 and is nice but not very central. The *Hotel Asia* (tel 28 1859) on Top Khana Rd is reasonably clean and friendly and has rooms with shared bath at Tk 45/55. One traveller wrote that it was 'great – clean and hospitable, one felt like royalty there, they couldn't do enough to be helpful and refused any tips!'

The *Hotel Titas* (tel 40 1891) at 246 Circular Rd, Mogh Bazaar has rooms with and without attached bath from Tk 35/50. Slightly more expensive places include *Lord's Inn International* on New Eskaton Rd. It's a new building with rooms at Tk 75/105. *Hotel Al-Helal* on Arambagh in the Motijheel Commercial Area has rooms at Tk 50/80 and a restaurant.

The *Tourist Hotel* at 86 Inner Circular Rd (also known as Kakrail Rd) is a little up market at Tk 100 for a double but it's clean, modern and pleasant. Rooms have bath, fan and mosquito nets. There are also cheaper rooms. The *Hotel Brighton* (tel 31 2619-82) at 163 Elephant Rd, Hatirpool has rooms at Tk 60/100 and the *Metropolitan Hotel* (tel 25 7357) on North-South Rd is a new and fairly clean place with rooms with attached bathroom at Tk 75/125. The *Hotel Blue Nile* (tel 32 6400) at 36 New Elephant Rd is more expensive again – air-con rooms are Tk 75-125 for singles, Tk 150-250 for doubles.

Places to Eat

Good Bengali food can be found in the lane alongside Kartika, opposite the Dacca Sheraton. Dacca has many Chinese restaurants although most of them are pale imitations of the real thing. The Bengali-run Chinese restaurants tend to compensate lower quality with larger quantity compared to the Chinese-run places. The prices are similar. Some of them include the *Taipan Chinese Restaurant* at 2/5 Mirpur Rd, the *Cafe Canton* on Top Khana Rd, the *Shanghai* and the *Nanking Chinese Restaurants* on Mirpur Rd, the *Cathay Chinese Restaurant* in the 1st DIT Super Market, Gulshan, the *Shen Yang Restaurant* on a street just off Kakrail Rd and the *Tai King Restaurant* on New Eskaton Rd.

For local food try the *Darul Kebab Place* near the expensive Ali Baba Specialized Restaurant for kebabs and chicken tikas with nan. *Sharif's Inn* on Toynbee Rd also does western and Chinese food. On the north bank of the river in Pagla, eight km from the city, the *Mary Anderson Floating Restaurant* is housed in an old ferryboat and is a fine place to watch the local riverlife. It's a little more expensive than the Chinese restaurants.

For the sake of your digestive system avoid the very cheapest eating places in Dacca. For dirt cheap eating you can try the kebab and nan places in the evening around Farm Gate or Mogh Bazaar. The *Snack Bar* on New Eskaton Rd is a tiny place for cheap snacks. Try the *Ice Cream Parlour* on the same road for snacks at Tk 6 and ice cream at Tk 5. Just round the corner from New Eskaton Rd on Mymensingh Rd the *New Al-Amin Restaurant* does excellent biriyani, kebabs and chicken tika. The nearby *Super-Duper Snack* is similar.

At the other end of the price scale the *Dacca Sheraton's* restaurants are good for a complete escape from Bangladesh. The *Hotel Sonargaon's* buffet breakfast is an expensive bargain. The *Chop Stick Restaurant* on New Eskaton Rd is a genuine Chinese place with probably the best food in town. On Mymensingh Rd across from the Hotel Sonargaon the *Ali Baba Specialised Restaurant* is also expensive but has good food.

Getting There

Air See the relevant town sections for air fare details. Airport tax for international departures is Tk 200.

Rail Dacca is linked by rail to all the major towns but although very cheap and reasonably comfortable the services are often slow and do not meet their schedules. See the relevant towns for specific information. The Central Railway Terminal is fairly modern but has virtually no signs in English.

Bus The Central Bus Terminal is on Station Rd, Fulbaria but is mainly used for city buses and local regional services. There are a number of other bus stations for longer distance routes. The dark brown BRTC (Bangladesh Roadway Transport Company) buses are generally cheaper than the private ones. Again see the relevant towns for details.

River Although there is so much river transport in Bangladesh the regular services are more limited. From Dacca you can travel to Khulna or Barisal on regular services. There are then boats operating between Khulna and Barisal, also on a regular basis, and between Barisal and Chittagong.

Dacca-Barisal-Khulna The river journey between Dacca and Barisal is very attractive, particularly going upriver from Barisal, as the river gets wider and wider from the delta area. There are day and night sailings each day with the paddlewheel ferries known as the 'Rockets'. The *MV Ghazi* and the *MV Masood* are the better ferries, the *MV Tern* has definitely seen better days. The trip to Khulna takes 24 hours and costs Tk 70 deck class, Tk 124 interclass, Tk 257 in 2nd, Tk 424 in 1st. Interclass is a small room with benches but it's better to take 3rd class and rent a crew berth for Tk 25 as far as Barisal, Tk 40-50 to Khulna. Chain your pack down if you leave it for any length of time though.

Departures are from the Badamtali Steamer Station in Dacca (buy tickets here or at the Bangladesh Inland Water Transport Corporation, 5 Dilkusha Commercial Area). You can also reach Chittagong from Dacca by leaving the Rocket at Chandpur from where you can continue by bus.

There are also private launches such as the Maheskhali Steamer services from the Saddarghat Launch Terminal. Fares are Tk 25 to Barisal, Tk 50 Khulna. They're much cheaper than the Rockets but also much less comfortable.

The trip from Khulna to Barisal would be even more interesting than Dacca-Barisal if you can make it during the daytime.

Chittagong-Barisal Twice weekly, currently on Monday and Thursday at 9 am, a boat leaves Chittagong and reaches Barisal about 24 hours later.

Getting Around

The bus station for BRTC buses is opposite the new Kamalapur Railway Station. The old Tejgaon airport is only a Tk 5 rickshaw ride from the city but the new Kurmitola Airport is a long way out. Getting there is no hassle, though. Cheap and comfortable minibuses leave from the Gulistan Cinema, by the bus station, and take about 45 minutes to the airport for Tk 3; a little extra for bulky baggage. Get off at Farm Gate from where a rickshaw to the hotel area will be Tk 2-3. A taxi from the airport will cost about Tk 80, a 'baby-taxi' half that.

If you arrive by bus at the Central Bus Station on Station Rd rickshaws to nearby hotels will cost Tk 2-3. Taxis are not metered but around town most rides shouldn't be more than Tk 40-60. Most taxis are found in front of the Hotel Sonargaon. Rickshaws are a much more prevalent form of transport and preferable for short distances. Short rides cost Tk 2-3, you can get anywhere in the city for around Tk 15 an hour but avoid getting a rickshaw from outside the expensive hotels. Give rickshaw wallah's street addresses rather than asking for hotels since they often don't know the hotels. Dacca's sights are widely spread – it might be worth taking a rickshaw for a day if you want to go exploring. The buses cost T0.30-2.50 but they are extremely crowded and you need to know the Bangala numerals to use them – nothing is in English. A No 6 goes between the airport and the Central Railway Station at Kamalapur.

The Bangladesh tourist office, Parjatan, operates several city tours for Tk 45 to 60, tours further out from the city cost Tk 65 to 150.

CHITTAGONG

Bangladesh's largest port and second largest city, Chittagong is 220 km south of Dacca on the Bay of Bengal. It's a pleasant, smaller city of mosques and palm trees, surrounded by green hills. It also serves as a jumping off point for trips into the Chittagong Hill Tracts and further south to Cox's Bazar.

Information & Orientation

The Tourist Office is in the Motel Shaikat on Station Rd and operates afternoon tours of the city on Wednesdays and Thursdays – Tk 15 each for a minimum of six people. There's no sign in English for the tourist office, only in Bengali. The Biman office is in Jasmine Palace on Nur Ahmed Sarark Rd.

Things to See

There are a number of interesting mosques in Chittagong including the Qadam Mubarik with a footprint of the prophet, the fort-like Shahi Jam-e-Masjid of 1670 and the Chandanpura. On a hilltop in Nasirabad, six km north-west of the city, the Tomb of Sultan Bayazid has not only good views across the countryside but also a pond full of turtles.

Chittagong's Islamic Intermediate College was once used as an arsenal when the Portuguese held this area in the 17th century. Behind the Hotel Agrabad there is an Ethnological Museum. There are interesting small lanes in the city which always have something eyecatching for the casual wanderer. On Station Rd there is a colourful night market.

Places to Stay

Chittagong's hotels tend to be better value than Dacca's. Cheaper places include the *United Hotel* at 128 Golapsing Lane, just off Jubilee Rd. It's a quiet place with rooms at Tk 20/30. The *Hotel Chittagong* on Sheikh Mujib Rahman Rd is similar in prices and standards. The *Imperial Hotel* on Royal Rd is a fairly old building but the atmosphere is friendly and rooms cost Tk 13/20. The *Eastern Hotel* on K C Day Rd has definitely seen better days and is very cheap. At 150 Jubilee Rd the *YMCA* is mainly used by local students but does have one room for foreign tourists at Tk 25 for a bed.

The *Hotel Safina* (tel 20 1442) at 50 Jubilee Rd is an old place and not particularly clean. Singles/doubles are Tk 32/40 or Tk 50/75 with bath. There's a restaurant on the 4th floor which serves western-style breakfasts for Tk 12. The *Hotel Dream International* on Station Rd is a fairly new place with rooms with bath from Tk 55 to 88. There's a rather unreliable restaurant here.

The pleasant *Hotel Mishka* (tel 20 3623) on Station Rd is a quiet old place which still retains a hint of the Raj era. Rooms are Tk 45/75 and again there's a restaurant. *Hotel Manila* on Station Rd is fairly new and often full. It's clean and has rooms, all with attached bath, at Tk 40/65. In the bazaar behind the Hotel Safina the *Hotel Al-Amin* is a fairly new building which has gone quickly to seed, nevertheless it's good value at Tk 20/35.

Places to Eat

As in Dacca there are lots of Chinese restaurants although, like the hotels, places here are better value. Eating places in the bazaar near the Hotel Al-Amin are good value. The *Railway Station Restaurant* has simple, cheap and clean local fare with meals at Tk 12-15. On Suhrawarddy Rd the *Gulistan Restaurant* does rice and chicken curry for Tk 12.

On Station Rd you can get good food at the *Cafe Ferdous*. The excellent *Tai Wah* on Jubilee Rd, about five minutes walk from the Safina, also has very good food. The more expensive *Chungking Restaurant* on Sheikh Mujib Rahman Rd is reputed to have the best food in town. For local dishes try the *New Market Restaurant* on the 1st floor on the corner of Jubilee and Suhrawarddy Rd or the *Cafe Iran* to the left of the Safina on Jubilee Rd.

Getting There

Air Flights cost Tk 450 to or from Dacca, Tk 145 to or from Cox's Bazar.

River Ferries operate twice weekly from Barisal and the trip takes 24 hours. Fares are Tk 57 in deck class, Tk 85 in interclass, Tk 189 in 2nd, Tk 284 in 1st. It takes two rather rough days by boat to Cox's Bazar at a cost of Tk 14.

Rail You can also reach Chittagong by train. The fast trains from Dacca take eight to 10 hours and fares are Tk 24 in 3rd, Tk 55 in 2nd, Tk 203 in 1st. Trains go via Akhaura, on the Chittagong-Maulvi Bazar line, for Sylhet. The trip takes 12 hours and the fares are Tk 27 in 3rd, Tk 60 in 2nd, Tk 230 in 1st.

Bus Buses from Dacca leave from the Central Bus Terminal in Gulistan, by the old railway station. They cost Tk 42 for the public bus, Tk 46 for the 'semi-express' (Tk 55 at night) and Tk 85 for the air-con express which departs at 7.45 am and 1.45 pm. The trip takes from 6½ hours for the air-con express, eight to 10 hours by the public buses.

There are a number of bus stations in Chittagong. BRTC buses to Dacca (Tk 42) and Cox's Bazar (Tk 22) go from the New Market area. Private buses are slightly more expensive and go from Jubilee Rd, right in front of the Safina Hotel. Cinema Place and Love Lane are other bus terminals.

Getting Around

There are very few taxis in Chittagong, rickshaws are the usual form of transport. Prices are similar to Dacca. If you arrive by air a taxi from the airport, if there is no Biman bus, will cost Tk 60-80 or Tk 30-40 for a babytaxi.

CHITTAGONG HILL TRACTS

Inland from Chittagong the hill tracts is a jungle area bordering Burma with steep hills and valleys. The people here are a mix of fascinating Buddhist hill tribes closely related to Burmese. It's a touchy area as these people feel pressured by the encroachment of Bangladesh's ever expanding Muslim population. Although you can easily visit the two main towns in the area, Kaptai and Rangamati on the Kaptai Lake, it's not possible to visit the hill tracts themselves which are in a restricted area. To do this you need a virtually unobtainable permit from the Interior Ministry in Dacca.

Rangamati & Kaptai

Rangamati, 70 km from Chittagong, is a very pleasant little town sprawled over several peninsulas in the lake. It gets virtually no tourists which probably accounts for why it is so laid back and relaxed. Apart from its setting a major attraction is the hill tribe people and their handicrafts. They do fine weaving, fair batik and good leatherwork. You can see an interesting selection at low prices as well as watch artists actually at work in the Bangladesh Small & Cottage Industries Corporation Sales & Display Centre near the post office. Examples of craft work include hand woven cloth at Tk 10 to 12 a yard, woollen shawls for Tk 22, cotton hand-loomed women's tops for Tk 45. Rangamati also has a small Tribal Research Centre Museum (closed on Saturdays).

The other main town on the lake, Kaptai, is 55 km from Chittagong and you can travel between the two towns by boat. Lake Kaptai is the largest man-made lake on the sub-continent but the Kaptai Dam

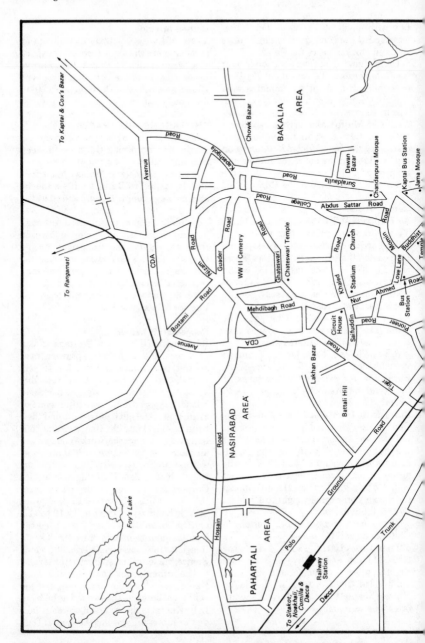

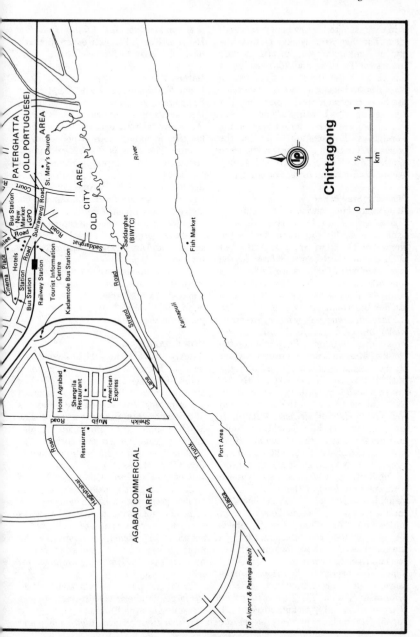

Chittagong

is in the restricted area where you cannot visit. The lake itself is very picturesque and in Rangamati you can hire modern canoes for Tk 10 an hour (or speedboats for Tk 275) but the twice daily trip to Kaptai is as pleasant a way as any of seeing the lake. Boatmen on the pier will offer sightseeing trips but they are not cheap.

You are supposed to register at the Foreigners' Registration Office at the police station but it takes several hours to get this 25 x 45 cm certificate and nobody seems to care if you have it or not.

Places to Stay & Eat
Rangamati The tourist office is at the *Tourist Motel* on Deer Hill which is expensive at Tk 150 for a double (no singles) or Tk 250 with air-con. At the foot of Deer Hill, where boats are hired for the lake, the *Tourist Cottages* are Tk 250 for a four-bed cottage or Tk 350 for a eight-bed cottage. They come complete with a kitchen but you need a group.

Places in town are very basic (just straw walls) and mainly around the market where the bus stops. They include the *Hotel Al Mahmud*, down towards the pier on the right. Doubles are Tk 25 and it is basic but clean. You can knock the *De Rangamati Boarding* down below Tk 50 for a double or there's the decrepit and well named *Hotel Wilderness*. A couple of km before you reach Rangamati you could hop off the bus at the *Hiramund Hotel* which has rooms at Tk 30 and does have mosquito nets although it is rather dirty.

The *Rangamati Motel* is the only place with western food. Otherwise it's just vegetable curry & rice or similar. 'Be careful what you eat,' warned one traveller, 'unless you like fly omelettes'. There is lots of fresh fish, vegetables and fruit in the market so if you have cooking facilities you can fix your own food.

Kaptai The government *Rest House* usually doesn't offer accommodation without prior arrangement. The *Kamal Boarding House* is reasonably clean and costs Tk 25/45. Other places are very basic, like the ramshackle *Sat Khana Boarding House* at Tk 5/7. Places to eat are similarly basic although the food isn't bad.

Getting There
From Chittagong buses to Kaptai and Rangamati go from different stations. Rangamati buses depart from Cinema Place and take 2½ hours to make the 70 km trip, including stops at police checkpoints. The fare is Tk 12 and it's a spectacular trip. Kaptai is 58 km, takes 1½ hours and costs Tk 8. Kaptai buses depart from opposite the American Cultural Centre at Anderkilla in Chittagong. On arrival in Rangamati foreign tourists are abandoned at the police checkpost on the outskirts because the form filling takes some time. Don't expect the bus to wait for you.

Between Rangamati and Kaptai boats leave at 8 am and 3 pm and the three-hour trip costs Tk 7. Make sure you get the right boat, there are also departures to other points on the lake.

COX'S BAZAR
A further 150 km south of Chittagong, and near the Burmese border, Cox's Bazar is noted for its 110-km-long unbroken stretch of beach. The population includes colourful Mogh tribespeople and Buddhists of Arakanese and Burmese descent. The Mogh people have Buddhist temples known as kyaungs here and in the village of Ramu, Teknaf and Nhila to the south. Cox's Bazar takes its name from Captain Cox of the East India Company.

Long though the beach is this is an equally great distance from being a beach centre. In fact it's much quieter than it was in colonial days and many of the big hotels are empty. The beach is just long, nothing more; there are no palm trees and there is no surf. If you go swimming watch out for jellyfish.

The region has recently been unsettled by large numbers of Muslim refugees streaming in from Burma.

With a group you could hire a jeep and

ride along the sand to Himachari. Or you could hire a boat to the island of Maishkhal – just for the pleasant 50 minute trip, it costs Tk 3. Ramu, with its three Buddhist temples, is 15 km back along the road to Chittagong. Buses run 120 km to Teknaf, at the extreme southern end of Bangladesh. It makes an interesting three or four day trek along the beach. There's a Rest House here and Burma is just across the creek.

Information

There's a tourist office at the Motel Upal.

Places to Stay

Forget the government run *Upal* and *Prabal Motels* on Sea Beach, they're run down and overpriced (Tk 150 to 300) like all government places in Bangladesh. The very pleasant five-storey *Hotel Sayeman* has rooms normally starting from Tk 75 but you can knock them down to Tk 60 if they're quiet. It's modern, clean and comfortable – a good place for a few day's rest. They also have a very nice swimming pool but it costs Tk 10 to Tk 20 if you're not staying there.

If that's too expensive right next door is the *Hotel Rachy* with rooms at Tk 20/40 and again you can expect a discount. It's basic, but quite OK if a little noisy at times. The middle price *Hotel Cox Wah* is on Motel Rd and has rooms at Tk 25/60 – the doubles have attached bath. Rock bottom possibilities include the *Al-Belal Boarding* on Sea Beach Rd where singles/doubles cost Tk 15/25.

Places to Eat

The *Sayeman* has a good restaurant and is about the only place in Cox's Bazar with a fridge – where they normally forget to put the drinks. Opposite the Motel Upal the government run *Sagarika* also has good food; meals cost Tk 35. Upstairs on Sea Beach Rd the *Bismillah Restaurant* is a pleasant, airy place with good local dishes at Tk 12-15. There are other good local

places on Sea Beach Rd near the bus station but remarkably Cox's Bazar does not appear to have any Chinese restaurants.

Getting There

Flights to Chittagong are twice weekly and cost Tk 145. BRTC buses leave from the bus station at New Market in Chittagong from 9 am to 1 pm. Private buses depart from the Hotel Safina on Jubilee Rd every half hour from 6 am to 3 pm. The four to five hour, 154 km trip to Cox's Bazar costs Tk 20 to 22. Buses also go from Cox's Bazar to Teknaf, a three hour trip for Tk 13 or 14. There are twice weekly boats between Chittagong and Cox's Bazar for Tk 14.

Getting Around

A cycle-rickshaw from the airport into town is just Tk 3. Around town they cost Tk 15 to 20 per hour or Tk 2-3 for most trips. Baby-taxis are Tk 5-15.

SYLHET

Up in the north-east corner of the country, near the border to the Indian states of Meghalaya and Shillong, this is one of the few hilly regions of the country and also the centre for Bangladesh's tea production. Since Muslim women are kept under lock and key the tea plantation workers are mainly Hindu – tea pluckers are almost exclusively female.

Srimangal is the centre of the tea growing area and has a Tea Research Institute. You can walk along Airport Rd to the Lackatoorah Tea Estate. There is not really that much to see in Sylhet. The hills are always over the border, in Meghalaya.

Places to Stay

The BPC operated *Hotel Gulshan* is great value with singles/doubles at Tk 28/38. Only a couple of hundred metres from the railway station the *Hotel Sithara* is cheaper at Tk 12/20. On Taltola Rd the *Shahban Hotel* has rooms at Tk 25/38 or with air-con from Tk 100 to 200. There are a number of other cheap hotels around the town such as the *Hotel Shirazi* in Bunder Bazar at Tk 15/30 or the run down *Hotel Amin* in the same area at Tk 18 to 28. At Maulvi Bazar there is a *Tourist Circuit House* for Tk 50 a double.

Places to Eat

On the first floor of the Biponi Market Building in Zindha Bazar the *Ping-Pong Chinese & English Restaurant* (great name!) has reasonable food but no sign in English. The *Hilltown Hotel* (Sylhet's fanciest place) on Tally How Rd has a fairly good restaurant and the *Shahban Hotel's* restaurant is also OK.

Getting There

Biman fly Dacca-Sylhet for Tk 340. The 10-hour bus journey from Dacca involves four ferry crossings. Fares start from Tk 55, the express buses are Tk 65 or Tk 75 at night but they make the trip in seven hours. There is a direct night train from Dacca to Sylhet but, of course, you see nothing so it's rather pointless. By day take express number 29, it leaves early, to Akhaura Junction then change to the express from Chittagong for Sylhet. In 1st class you don't need a reservation in the day but you do at night. The through fare in 3rd class is Tk 22.50, 2nd class is Tk 51, 1st is Tk 196.

There's one train daily from Chittagong with fares of Tk 27 in 3rd class, Tk 60 in 2nd, Tk 230 in 1st. From Chittagong you can just manage the trip in a day by bus with an early start; change buses at Comilla. Sylhet town to Maulvi Bazar is only 58 km but it takes three hours by bus due to delays at the two ferry crossings. Srimangal, on the railway route, is only 21 km from Maulvi.

OTHER PLACES

Bangladesh has lush, green, damp country – not mosques and temples apart from in the few big cities. It's overwhelmingly a rural experience and simply travelling through it is the best way for the traveller to come to grips with it.

Archaeological Excavations

Comilla, close to the eastern border with India, has important archaeological sites at Mainimati and Lamai. Apart from Salban Vihara, where there is also a museum (closed Thursdays), little of this large site has been excavated. There are Buddhist monasteries and stupas with interesting terracotta tiles, they date from the 7th century. Comilla is on the Dacca-Chittagong route.

In the north-west, near Rajshahi, more important Buddhist remains have been found at Paharpur, between Santahar Junction and Parbatipur Junction. Take a train to Jamalganj from where you have a six km walk to the west. There is a museum and from the top of the main part of the huge monastery which has been excavated there is an excellent view. The walls are again covered with terracotta tiles and the ruins date from the 8th century. Unfortunately few visitors get to this fascinating site and most of the tiles are broken and the walls are defaced with graffiti.* The structure is quite striking, rising from the totally flat plain. It's the biggest Buddhist monument on the sub-continent and set the style for Angkor Wat and Borobudur.

Bogra is the jumping off point to the ruins of Pundravardhana, also known as Mahastanagar.

Wildlife Reserves
Madhupur is a national park 130 km north-west of Dacca. The Sundarbans is the delta area of the Ganges and Brahma-putra Rivers, an area which spreads across into India. There is still much wildlife in the region including a few surviving Royal Bengali tigers. Khulna is

the main town in this area and boats can be hired to explore the waterways.

Places to Stay
Jessore If you're flying through then the *Hotel Hassim*, next to the Bangladesh Biman office, is convenient at Tk 30 a double. There are other hotels closer to the bus station like the *Hotel Parveena* with large doubles with bathroom and mosquito nets. *Hotel Midtown* is good with singles/doubles at Tk 45/60.

Khulna The *Hotel Taj* is near the bus depot or try the more expensive *Hotel Salim* on Shamsur Rahman Rd. *Hotel Park* is the nearest hotel to the Rocket dock and costs Tk 75 for a good double with bath, fan and mosquito nets. There's also a pretty good restaurant and it's more centrally located than the similarly priced Salim.

Bhutan

Squeezed between India and Tibet, Bhutan is very much under the Indian thumb. Although it is ostensibly an independent country with a seat in the United Nations it could easily go the same way as Sikkim and be absorbed into India.

HISTORY

An almost medieval country with a close relationship to Tibet, Bhutan went through a mini-revolution in the '50s and '60s. Although it was a peaceful one it created some enemies and the Prime Minister was assassinated in 1964. Prior to that time Bhutan did not have a road to its name nor anything which could properly be called a town. Today the young king walks a tightrope between his two huge neighbours.

FACTS

About a million people of Tibetan stock occupy the 29,000 square km of Bhutan. Like Nepal there has been an influx of Tibetans since the Chinese takeover of that country. The country slopes up from the luxuriant Indian rainforests to the Himalaya.

VISAS

Visas are very difficult. You first of all have to get permission to pass through India and additional paperwork has to be complied with to enter Sikkim, en route to Bhutan. At present visitors to Bhutan are only allowed to enter in groups and permission takes several months to arrange.

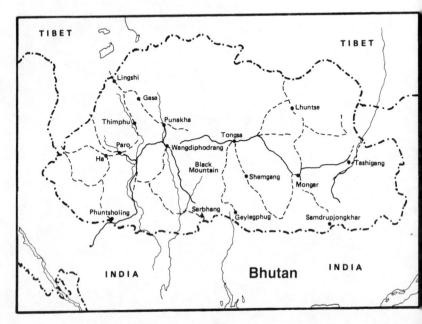

MONEY

The Bhutanese ngultrum is on a par with the Indian rupee – another indication of the close ties between the two countries. With the present restrictions Bhutan is strictly for very affluent tourists – a visit to Bhutan is only available as a guided tour at a daily cost of US$130 per person or US$90 in the off-season. A very slight bending is starting to occur with this policy as trekking groups are now being allowed in although these too tend to be very expensive. Students can, however, travel more cheaply – if you're under 25, have an ISIC card and travel in a group you can visit Bhutan for as little as US$55 a day. Bhutan is not currently a place for independent travellers.

TRAVEL

Access to Bhutan is by road from India. Phuntsholing is on the Indian border to the south. There are buses running on the 179 km route from there to the capital Thimphu and from there to Paro, 69 km away.

CLIMATE

The climate is very similar to Nepal and, as in Nepal, the period after the monsoon from October to December is the best time to visit the country. January-February is rather cold and then the weather is again good in the pre-monsoon period of April, May, June. On the plains to the south the annual rainfall at Phuntsholing can be very heavy.

THINGS TO SEE

At 2470 metres Thimphu, the capital, is a new town only built from 1961. The impressive *dzong*, built in that year around an older structure, dominates the town. It houses not only a monastery and school, but also the king's apartments and the government offices. Thimphu also has a palace, over the river from the dzong, and a bazaar.

Until 1962 there was only a mountain track leading up from Phuntsholing – it took nearly a week by pony or mule to make the trek. Today the road carries traffic through interesting countryside via the town of Paro, where you can see the colourful Paro Dzong and the older Ta Dzong which houses the national museum. Paro has temples and monasteries and there are other dzongs, the impressive mountain strongholds of Bhutan's almost feudal lords, scattered through the country.

India

India is vast both in population and land – only China has more people while geographically India stretches from the hot steamy south to the heights of the perpetually frozen Himalaya in the north. India's problems are equally vast and at times the noise, confusion and squalor around you seem to drag your spirits down. But with the confusion comes colour, excitement and enough attractions to satisfy any visitor, no matter how long his stay.

SEEING

India has such a range of places and things to see that it is impossible to even mention, let alone describe, far less visit, them all. The places that follow are just some of the major or more interesting locations. There are many more hill stations for pleasant hot season gateways, countless wildlife sanctuaries and many fine beaches along India's west and east coast.

HISTORY

India's role as the birth place of two great religions is enough to ensure its historical importance, but in actual fact it was also one of the earliest centres of civilisation. For a thousand years from 2500 BC an advanced and complex culture flourished along the Indus River Valley in what is now Pakistan. Approximately 70 city sites have been unearthed by modern archaeologists. The great Indus cities of Harappa and Moenjodaro were only discovered in the 1920s and there is still relatively little known about this early civilisation. They are thought to have been ruled by priest-kings but the cause of their sudden demise is still a mystery. The most likely reason for the abrupt end of the Indus River culture was an Aryan invasion from the north around 1500 BC.

India's Hindu culture, for it is one of the world's oldest religions, reasserted itself,

but in 327 BC Alexander the Great arrived on his epic expedition from Greece. It is hardly surprising that his far flung empire collapsed so quickly – India was a hell of a long trip from Greece – but the vacuum this created brought about a golden age for India. The Indian Maurya empire flowered out of the debris of Alexanders' conquests and from its capital at present day Patna unified India for the first time. It reached its peak under the great Buddhist emperor Ashoka who ruled from 273 to 232 BC. Ashoka carried Buddhism to Sri Lanka and Nepal, where the Buddha was born, and you can still see many physical reminders of his epic travels – the Ashoka mounds in Patan in the Kathmandu Valley for example.

The Maurya empire began to rapidly decline after Ashoka's death and the country broke up into many separate Hindu kingdoms. For a time during the 4th and 5th centuries AD the Gupta kingdom brought a smaller golden age to northern India, but in general it was a time of outside invasions in the north and isolation in the south.

In the 12th century the spread of Islam first started to encroach upon India in a serious way. There had been brushing contacts with Islam back in the 8th century but it was Mahmud of Ghazni who first brought the Islamic sword to the sub-continent. From the year 1001 on he conducted an amazing series of raids into India, carting back the booty to his city in Afghanistan. This was really banditry rather than conquest, but in the following centuries the Islamic power started to creep down from its Afghan fastness first to Peshawar, then to Lahore and eventually to Delhi and Agra in northern India.

In 1526, under Babur the great Moghul Emperor, India entered into another golden age. The Moghul Empire at its peak stretched from Afghanistan in the west to Bangladesh in the east and prompted the construction of mosques, forts and tombs which are some of the wonders of India today – the Taj Mahal in particular. But Moghul power never reached to the southernmost part of the country which, as in the earlier centuries, went its own peculiar way; nor did the Moghuls manage to convert the great mass of Indians from Hinduism. Only about 20% of the population turned to Islam, but by allowing freedom of religion and encouraging Hindu officials, both civilian and military, the Moghuls were able to create a magnificent culture. It reached its peak under Akbar between 1556 and 1605 – he was only 14 years old when he ascended the throne. After Akbar, Shah Jahan carried on this Moghul tradition, in between tossing up the Taj and assorted gardens, forts and mosques. Unhappily Aurangzeb, his son, was a hard-line Muslim and succeeded in alienating the Hindus and thus started the destruction of his empire.

As this era of Indian history was drawing to a close its European nemesis appeared. The Portuguese, as in many other parts of the world, were the first on the scene and last to leave. They occupied Goa, on the west coast, in 1510 and did not finally relinquish it until they were given the Indian boot (sandal?) in 1962. They were only bit players though, during the 1600s the British, in the shape of the East India Company, showed up. During the next couple of centuries they gradually insinuated themselves into the country by playing off one local ruler against another. As the Moghuls collapsed a number of competitive kingdoms had arisen including the Sikhs, who were most powerful in the Punjab region, and the Hindu Marathas. Out of this melee it was the British who emerged on top.

After they gained control of Bengal they established Calcutta as their capital which it remained until New Delhi took over in 1911. Of course as they gradually took over the country they were not totally unopposed. After the Indian Mutiny of 1857, when almost all of north India except the recently annexed Punjab revolted, the British government took over from the East India Company and India was on its way to becoming the 'brightest jewel in the British crown'.

When Indian resistance next arose it assumed more peaceful, and ultimately more successful tactics. Led by Mahatma Gandhi the Indian policy of peaceful resistance finally achieved its aim in 1947. Unfortunately long running Hindu-Muslim divisions could not be satisfactorily resolved and the country was split into two parts – Hindu India and the two Muslim Pakistans. The British left India with a well developed communications network, the vast railway system, and an organised, efficient government and civil service. Unfortunately they also left them with an amazing taste for bureaucracy – India must lead the world in consumption of red tape, rubber stamps and quadruplicate forms.

Since independence India has been embroiled in periodic confrontations with Pakistan (in 1947, 1965 and then in 1971) and with China (in 1962). This has diverted much energy that could well have been used more productively. Progress from year to year often seems to be a prayer for another good monsoon and another good harvest yet in actual fact for the last 30 years the growth of agricultural production has consistently outstripped the growth in population. Nevertheless the national birth control programme – two-child-family billboards, free transistor radios and all – still seems to have minimal impact at the village level where the bulk of India's population is still concentrated.

Unhappily religion, of such historical importance to India, is today another of the inertial effects hampering Indian progress. The sacred cows of Hinduism are the clearest sign of religion's pervasive influence as they spread disease, clutter already overcrowded towns, consume scarce food and provide little. The difficulties of unifying a people divided by so many languages and regional interests is another serious problem. It should not be forgotten that India, for all its rural look, is one of the world's major industrial nations and made a remarkably good recovery from the '74 oil crisis.

The Congress Party, which won power in the elections after independence, retained control right through to 1977, first under Jawaharlal Nehru then, after a short gap from 1964 to 1966, under his daughter Indira Ghandi. In mid-1975 Mrs Ghandi assumed near dictatorial powers and, after an initial flurry of protest from India's vigorous press had been stifled, it looked like India was going to become yet another of those sham-democratic Asian states. Then, to much of the world's amazement, Mrs Ghandi allowed new elections to be held in 1977. Having rigidly controlled the press, perhaps she became convinced by her own pro-Indira propaganda? More surprisingly they were real elections, not mere rubber stamps. So real that Indira was devastatingly swept out of power and democracy restored with the Janata party at the helm. For, as ex-British Prime Minister Harold MacMillan once said, out of every nine people in the world who live under what we know in the west as democracy, four are Indian.

In 1979 the Janata government started to crumble apart. Its only real platform had been opposition to Indira and with her deposed their be-nice-to-cows policy seemed to have little relevance to India's overpowering problems. In 1980 Indira Ghandi was swept back into power but her political touch was not so certain. She was badly shaken by the death of her son and confidant Sanjay Gandhi in 1980 and failed to come successfully to grips with India's tottering economy and outbursts of regional unrest. The smouldering unrest in the north-east of the country was completely overshadowed in 1984 by the violence in the Punjab. Demands for greater political autonomy by the Punjab's Sikh majority eventually led to a state of near insurrection, finally quelled by an army assault on the centre of Sikh resistance, the Golden Temple of Amritsar.

Then to worldwide horror Indira Gandhi was assassinated by her Sikh bodyguard, the whole country was briefly plunged into violence but her elder son, Rajiv Gandhi, assumed the family right to rule and at least initially has proved a pragmatic and thoroughly sensible prime minister. Unrest in the Punjab still smoulders but he appears to have gone some way to quelling the unrest in the north-east and appears to be taking a very positive attitude towards modernisation and local enterprise.

FACTS

Population The population of India is approximately 690 million, and growing too rapidly. Despite this immense population it is still a remarkably rural country. Major cities with populations of greater than one million are the capital Delhi (four million), Calcutta (six million), Bombay nearly (six million), Madras over (two million), Kanpur, Ahmedabad, Hyderabad and Bangalore.

Geography The north of India is a vast fertile plain bounded by the Himalaya to the north. The three great Indian rivers, the Ganges, the Indus and the Brahmaputra, flow from the Himalaya and water this area. To the west the Thar desert separates India from Pakistan and further south there are ranges of hills. The total area is 3,250,000 square km.

Economy India is still a predominantly agricultural country, but it is also one of the world's major industrial producers with important iron and steel works and a growing manufacturing industry. Textiles are still the backbone of India's industrial exports. Nevertheless, 70% of India's population is engaged on work on the land – much of it inefficient and unproductive. Small landholdings, poor methods and lack of investment all contribute to this record although since independence the agricultural production levels have actually

increased at a faster rate than the population. There are nearly 200 million cattle in India which serve as work animals but otherwise, due to their religious protection, are of little use.

Religion India is a Hindu country and the strength of the caste laws are a continuing brake on progress. There is still a very substantial Muslim minority in India numbering 60 million. There are much smaller Christian, Sikh, Buddhist and Jain minorities, not to mention the Pharsis who are followers of Zoroaster.

INFO

The Government of India Tourist Office puts out an amazing range of brochures, leaflets and maps. Some of them are a little too much on the glossy-picture side of reality, but they are definitely worth looking at – particularly before you go to India.

There are offices in virtually all the major cities and they're good places to descend on for information – even about local cheap hotels. There are also state tourist offices in many locations. Sometimes the state office will supplement the national office, sometimes totally replace it, sometimes merely duplicate it. In most towns there will be tours operated which are usually excellent value. They'll cover far more ground, more comfortably and cheaper than you could do with public transport.

Some of the main Government of India Tourist Offices are:

Agra	191 The Mall
Aurangabad	Krishna Vilas, Station Rd
Bombay	123 M Karve Rd, Churchgate
Calcutta	4 Shakespeare Sarani
Cochin	Willingdon Island
Jaipur	Rajasthan State Hotel
Jammu	Gulab Bhavan
Khajuraho	near Western Temple Group

Madras	154 Anna Salai
New Delhi	88 Janpath
Varanasi	15B The Mall

VISAS

Following the upheavals in the Punjab in 1984 Indian visa regulations have been radically altered. Visitors from Australia, New Zealand, Great Britain, Canada or Ireland are now treated just like everybody else and have to get a visa before entry. Nor can they just wander at will forever. Now everybody gets a 90-day initial entry period and it's rumoured that your stay is now limited to six months in any calendar year. Visas cost about US$2.50 and take 24 hours to issue in most places. Some places are notoriously bad for issuing Indian visas – Athens in Greece in particular.

Staying beyond 90 days involves a few complications. First of all you have to get a visa, which India being India can involve some bureaucratic hassles. Secondly you have to get income tax clearance before you depart – which only means showing a few currency exchange forms to indicate that you did spend your own money and haven't been working while you were in India. Often the form isn't even asked for when you leave. An easy way to avoid any difficulties at all is not to stay more than 90 days, which is pretty easy to do. Chances are you will be visiting Nepal or Sri Lanka as well as India. So if your stay in India is going to be more than 90 days just get to Nepal or Sri Lanka around day 89 then return to India and start your 90 days all over.

Special permits are needed to visit Darjeeling, Kalimpong or Sikkim. The Darjeeling permit is very straightforward, but the Sikkim permit requires planning some time ahead. See the relevant sections for more details. Getting a permit for Bhutan is much more complicated.

For countries after India the details are as follows:

Nepalese Visas From the embassy in Barakhamba Rd close to Connaught Place in New Delhi or from the consulate on Sterndale Rd in Calcutta. You can also get a short, seven-day visa on arrival in Nepal and then renew it, but this will work out as expensive as getting a visa in advance and can be rather time consuming.

Burmese Visas There are embassies at Chanakyapuri in New Delhi or in Kathmandu. Note that there is no consulate in Calcutta.

Thai Visas There is an embassy at Chanakyapuri in New Delhi and a consulate in Calcutta but you can arrive in Thailand without a visa so long as your stay is no longer than 15 days and you have ticketing out of the country.

BOOKS

India – a travel survival kit from Lonely Planet was the biggest and most detailed book we had ever put together and we think it's the best guidebook available on India. There's also a Lonely Planet guide on *Kashmir, Ladakh & Zanskar* and we're about to do a trekking guide titled *Trekking in the Indian Himalaya*.

A History of India covers all you'll want to know about Indian history. Volume I by Romila Thapar covers the time from 100 BC to 1526 AD when Babur turned up and the Moghul empire commenced. Volume II by Percival Spear covers the Moghul and British periods. They're both from Penguin as is *The Great Mutiny – India 1857* by Christopher Hibbert, which reports the lurid events in lurid detail. *Plain Tales from the Raj* by Charles Allen (Futura paperback) is a fascinating collection of verbal reminiscences of the Raj. *Freedom at Midnight* by Larry Collins and Dominique Lapierre is India's biggest ever best seller and recreates the dramatic events which led to India's independence.

Look for John Keay's *Into India* (John Murray) for a good general introduction to the country. Other excellent books for a general feel of the country are Ved Mehta's *Walking the Indian Streets* and V S Naipaul's *An Area of Darkness* and *India*

– *A Wounded Civilisation. Karma Kola* by Gita Mehta is an amusing and cynical report of the collision between the west and the 'mystic' east. There are many novels set in India including, of course, E M Forster's classic *A Passage to India* and the various Kipling books. More recently *Midnight's Children* by Salman Rushdie has been a fascinating and controversial best seller on modern India.

MONEY

A$1	= Rs	8.60
US$1	= Rs	12.30
£1	= Rs	17.20

There are 100 paise to the rupee. Once upon a time there used to be 16 annas but that arcane terminology has more or less died out except in the very odd market. The blackmarket in India has revived to some extent, particularly in New Delhi. You can also get a good rate for Indian rupees in Kathmandu or in money markets further afield such as in Bangkok or Singapore – it is officially illegal to bring rupees into the country.

The major travellers' cheques are easily exchanged in India but, as with all paperwork in the country, it can be a little time consuming. Try not to have money transferred to you in India, doing so can be painfully slow and laborious, particularly with Indian banks. If you must then American Express is probably your best bet or one of the overseas banks operating in India such as Grindlays or the Chartered Bank. Get it sent by telex, not by mail.

If you're buying airline tickets you have to produce a bank receipt for the conversion of the appropriate amount of currency. This can be a catch on departure. An agent might sell you a ticket officially costing Rs 8000 for, say, Rs 5000. But you have to exchange Rs 8000 for it so you'll then get a Rs 3000 cash refund. You can't re-exchange that Rs 3000 unless you've already got sufficient other exchange forms saved up. So, unless you're going to be there long enough to spend the money,

save up exchange forms. You'll also need them if you stay over 90 days and have to get an income tax clearance.

CLIMATE

India is so vast that what goes down in the frigid Tibetan plateau of the north is very different from the steamy extreme south. Basically India has the typical Asian three-season year – cool and dry, hot and dry, hot and wet. The monsoon season finishes about October or a little later in the east. The months after that are very pleasant, everything looks green and lovely and the temperature is just right. By December and January, it starts to get a mite chilly in the far north, especially if you are high up.

Then the heat starts to build up and by April and May the weather gets very uncomfortable on the plains with unbearable humidity. This is the time to retreat to the hill stations or Kashmir. Finally the monsoon breaks around June or July and for the next couple of months it is wet, wet, wet. Not impossible though, it may rain every day, but not all day every day.

There are some regional variations:

North India In the far north the temperatures get way below freezing in winter and there is heavy snow and good skiing. In Ladakh, which is on the Tibetan plateau, there is no precipitation at all, summer or winter. New Delhi is uncomfortably hot in summer but quite cold in winter. Although the post-monsoon period is the best for travel it is reasonably possible year round.

East Coast The monsoon comes a little later here and peaks out in October and November. In the far south it is very hot and humid pretty much year round.

ACCOMMODATION

India has a wide range of places to stay apart from the straightforward hotels. Those you will find pretty much all over India, ranging from the drab and dismal to

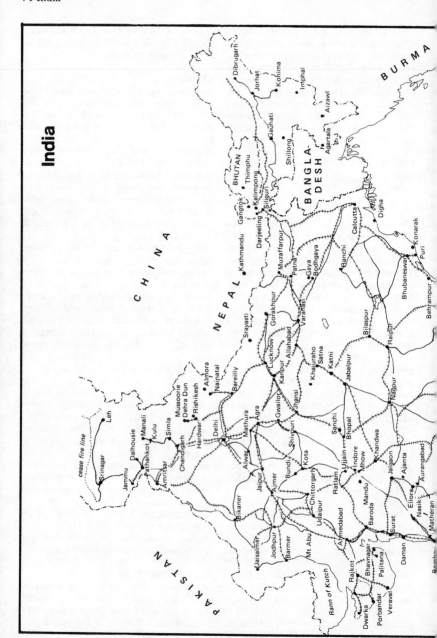

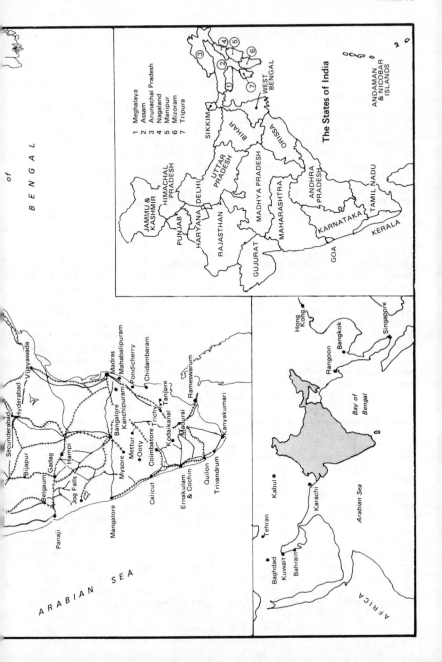

The States of India

1 Meghalaya
2 Assam
3 Arunachal Pradesh
4 Nagaland
5 Manipur
6 Mizoram
7 Tripura

some surprisingly good-value places. Lazy, swishing ceiling fans, mosquito nets, sometimes even private (Asian-style) toilets are all possibilities in even the cheaper hotels. Other put-your-head-down possibilities:

Railway Waiting Rooms If you have got a night to kill waiting for a train, this is a free place to kill it. The trick is to spend it in the comfortable 1st class waiting room not the depressing and crowded lower class one. Officially you need a 1st class ticket to be allowed to use the 1st class room and its superior facilities. In practice, luck and being a foreigner may do the trick.

Railway Retiring Rooms These are a different kettle of fish – they're like a regular hotel room but actually located at the railway station. You are supposed to have a railway ticket in order to use them. They're generally good value.

Tourist Bungalows Many of the old Rest House, Circuit House, Dak Bungalow places are now for government officials only, but in many states there are excellent Tourist Bungalows. These are usually run by the state governments and while they're not at the bottom end of the price scale they usually offer very good standards at reasonable prices – Rs 25 to 50 for a double. They include many of India's best accommodation deals.

Youth Hostels India's hostels are often very cheap and some of them are in excellent condition and have superb facilities. They are sometimes inconveniently located, but for solo travellers willing to use dormitories they're generally worth considering.

Other There are YMCAs and YWCAs in many big cities and the odd Salvation Army Hostel. There are a few good camping places around India. Free accommodation is available at some Sikh Temples where there is a tradition of hospitality to visitors. It may be an interesting insight to try it, but please don't abuse this hospitality and spoil it for other travellers. Donations are appreciated.

FOOD

India is the place in Asia where most travellers lose more weight – which given the variety and excellence of Indian food is kind of a drag. The problem is that away from big cities finding good food in India can be a thankless task. The ingredients simply aren't there and too often eating in India becomes a choice of yet more dhal & rice or rice & dhal. Still, at least you eat.

Hindus are nominally vegetarians, but they actually tend to be fairly relaxed about it. The quality of meat does tend to be low and of course you won't be eating beef in India, just like you won't be eating pork in Muslim countries. Once you have seen the flies congregating in a butcher's you will soon understand vegetarianism's appeal.

Railway station restaurants are always a good let out. Their food is generally safe and if one more curry will kill you they also have a western menu – at higher prices. In general you will find it much more sensible to let the Indians stick to preparing Indian food and avoid their often terrible interpretations of western cuisine. Every station will have a vegetarian and a non-vegetarian restaurant. Meals served on trains are usually palatable too, and reasonably cheap. At every stop you will be besieged by food and drink sellers; even in the middle of the night that raucous cry of 'chai, chai' breaks into your sleep.

If, after some time in India, you do find the food is getting you down physically or psychologically, there are a couple of escapes. It is very easy to lose a lot of weight in India and feel lethargic and drained of energy. The answer is to increase your protein intake – eat more eggs which are readily available; buy bananas, mandarin oranges or peanuts which you will find on sale at every station. Occasionally splash out on a meal in a flash hotel or restaurant – it will be amazingly expensive compared to what you have been paying, but try translating the price into what you would pay back home – and smile.

Indian food varies considerably from north to south partly because of the climate and partly because of the historical influence. The Moghuls, who brought a whole central-Asian style to northern-Indian cooking, never penetrated to the extreme south. Down there much more rice is eaten than in the north and the curries tend to be hotter. It is also in the south where eating with your hands is most practised. I was eating in the fantastic Indian vegetarian restaurant *Komala Vilas* in Singapore once when a friend pointed out that in some cuisines the look is as important as the taste; in others it is the arrangement and visual appeal; in India it is the feel, so get into it – but only with your right hand.

Curry The hot, spicy curry is the core of Indian food. Curry doesn't have to be hot enough to blow your head off and it most definitely is not concocted out of a packet of curry powder. The Indian cook uses about 25 spices regularly and it is from these that they produce the curry flavour. There is *saffron* which gives rice that yellow tinge and delicate fragrance. *Turmeric* also has a colouring property, acts as a preservative and has a distinctive smell and taste. *Chillies* – ground, dried or whole add the heat. Other frequently used spices include *ginger, cardamom, nutmeg, cinnamon, poppyseeds, caraway seeds, cummin, fenugreek, mace, garlic* and *cloves.* Curries can be vegetable, meat (usually chicken or lamb), or fish but they are always fried in *ghee,* clarified butter, or vegetable oil. North or south they will be accompanied by rice, but in the north the various excellent breads may also be found. *Vindaloos* and *kormas* are not

really curries, but close enough to make little difference.

Breads The northern Indians prepare a whole variety of different and delicious breads. Simplest is the *chappati* which is just flour and water fried up like a thin pancake. If butter or some other oil is added it becomes a *paratha*. If you deep fried it you would have a *dosa* in the south of India, a *poori* in the north or a *loochi* in the east. If you bake it in an oven you have a *nan*. Whichever way you do it, it will taste great. *Masala dosa* is a dosa wrapped around curried vegetables, very tasty, very cheap. Use your chappati or paratha to scoop or mop up your curry.

Extras Curry plus rice or bread is far from a complete meal. You might start with a soup – like *mulligatawny* which is really just a liquid curry. And almost always the curry will be accompanied by a bowl of *dhal* which is like a thick soup made from lentils. Dhal is almost always there whether as an accompaniment to the curry or as a light meal by itself with chappatis. It can also serve as a quick cooler for an unexpectedly hot curry. Curd (like yoghurt) is another accompaniment which will quickly cool your blistered throat, gulping water only aggravates the situation. If a curry is simply unmanageable try adding a little sugar. *Dahi*, curd or yoghurt, is another familiar side dish with a cooling effect. *Chutney*, pickled fruit or vegetables, is also a curry side dish.

Specials There are many local or regional specials worth trying. Like *tandoori* food, particularly tandoori chicken – this is a northern dish cooked in a clay oven after first marinating it in a complex mix of herbs and yoghurt. It is not as hot as curry dishes and tastes terrific. I can never decide if tandoori chicken is my favourite Indian dish or chicken *biriyani* which is a Moghul dish. The chicken or other meat is mixed with a deliciously flavoured, orange-coloured rice spiced with nuts or dried fruit. A *pulao* is a simpler version of biriyani – you will find it in other Asian countries further west. *Rogham Josh* is a straightforward curried lamb popular in the north.

Thalis are a southern specialty found all over India. It takes its name from the 'thali' dish on which the vegetarian curry is served. A thali is always good, cheap and filling – because it's generally an 'eat all you can' proposition. *Samosa* are tasty little snacks – curried vegetables fried up in a pastry triangle. *Sabzi* are curried vegetables.

Desserts The Indians have quite a sweet tooth and a quite amazing selection of desserts, two of which are widely available: *kulfi* is a sort of Indian interpretation of ice cream, *rasgullas* are sweet little balls of rosewater-flavoured cream cheese. Many of the sweets come covered in a thin layer of silver which is just that – silver beaten paper thin. Don't peel it off, eat it. There's a wide variety of fruit in India although the supply can be erratic. Good melons, bananas and mandarin oranges.

Drinks Surprisingly tea is not the all purpose and all important drink it is in Iran and Afghanistan. Worse the Indians, for all the tea they grow, make some of the most hideously over-sweetened, murkily milky excuse for that fine beverage you ever saw. It may go by the name of *chai*, just like the rest of Asia, but what a let down. Tea is more popular in the north, while in the south coffee, which is good, is the number one drink.

Water should be avoided unless you know it has been boiled. Tea or coffee are safe substitutes, as are better quality soft drinks. Unfortunately Indian soft drinks tend to be very sweet and expensive by Asian standards. Coca Cola has got the boot for not cooperating with the Indian government who wanted to run it their way. Alcohol, beer or whatever, is expensive when available which is not all the time. Coconut milk, straight from the coconut is popular. In the south you can try *toddy*, a mildly alcoholic extract from the coconut palm flower.

GETTING THERE

From the UK Cheap one way fares from the UK can be found for around £200, about double that return. Check the travel page ads in *Time Out* or the *Australasian Express*. Tickets to Australia with a stopover in India cost from about £450 depending on the airline and the stops.

From the USA From the states you've got a choice of cheap official fares to India or making your way to London from the east coast, then picking up a bucket shop ticket there. From the west coast the cheapest deals will be on flights to South-East Asia, usually Bangkok, then flying on from there. Return tickets to Bangkok from the US west coast are around US$850. For cheap tickets check the Sunday travel sections of papers like the *New York Times, LA Times* or *San Francisco Chronicle*.

From Australia Advance purchase tickets from the Australian east coast cost from around A$1200 return. A little hunting around could turn up cheaper tickets, return or one way. An alternative way of getting there would be an apex or cheap ticket to Singapore or Bangkok and then another ticket on from there.

From/To Pakistan You can fly between various cities or, the situation in the Punjab permitting, you can make the land crossing route between Lahore and Amritsar. Flights include Karachi-Bombay, Karachi-Delhi and Lahore-Delhi.

The Lahore-Amritsar route is the only land crossing point between the two countries. You can either take the daily train service across or go by bus. The train crosses the border at Attari and you have to buy your second ticket there. Officially the schedule is 9.30 am depart Amritsar, 2 pm arrive Lahore and 2 pm depart Lahore, 6 pm arrive Amritsar. In practice it can take rather longer. The old road crossing is at Wagah; you bus to the border point, walk across to the other side and take another bus from there into the city. Prior to partition there were, of course, many other routes but the roads have all been cut and the railways torn up.

One possible benefit that may arise from the unrest in the Indian Punjab is another land border crossing. A route between Jaisalmer in the Indian state of Rajasthan and the Pakistan Sind region is a possibility. There was a railway route here prior to partition.

From/To Bangladesh There are flights between Calcutta and Dacca or Chittagong. By land you can take a combination of rail and road transport between Calcutta and Dacca or you can follow a rather more remote exit or entry point into the northeast region of India. See Bangladesh for more details.

From/To Sri Lanka There are flights between Madras, Trivandrum and Trichy in the south of India to Colombo in Sri Lanka or you can take the three-times-weekly ferry service between Rameswaram in India and Talaimannar in Sri Lanka. See the Sri Lanka section for further details.

From/To Nepal There are air and road links into Nepal. By air you can fly from Delhi, Varanasi or Calcutta. By land the usual border crossing points are from Varanasi to Bhairawa and Lumbini and then to Pokhara; from Patna to Raxaul and Birgunj and then to Kathmandu; and from Darjeeling and along the road through the southern Terai to the Birgunj-Kathmandu road. See the Nepal section for full details.

From/To Malaysia Malaysian Airlines Systems fly Penang-Madras and you can usually find tickets in Penang for as little as M$500. The official fare is M$823. Alternatively the Chidambaram, which crosses between Penang and Madras every two weeks, is the most reliable shipping service between South-East Asia and Asia proper. It's used by many travellers who take cars or motorcycles across Asia. A VW Kombi would cost you about US$500 to transport across, a motorcycle about US$150. Plus port charges at both ends. Fares on the

Chidambaram vary widely depending on the berth and class you travel. A two-berth cabin with 'English diet' would be about US$200, a four-berth cabin with 'Indian diet' about US$140. More expensive fares also allow you to use the swimming pool and other deluxe facilities during the four-day crossing. In Madras the agent is the Shipping Corporation of India, c/o K P V Shaikh Mohammed Rowther, 41 Linghi Chetty St. In Penang it's R Jumabhoy & Sons, 39 Green Hall.

From/To Other Places There are no land crossing points between Burma and India, or any other country for that matter. All you can do is fly Rangoon-Calcutta. In Singapore you can get Singapore-Madras tickets for around S$550, Singapore-Bombay for S$600. Bangkok is another good place for cheap tickets, Bangkok-Delhi for US$230, Bangkok-Rangoon-Calcutta for around US$170.

Departing India Delhi is the main centre for cheap tickets in India although you can also get tickets in Bombay or Calcutta. There are countless bucket shops around Connaught Place, some of them not 100% trustworthy. Typical fares would be Delhi-Australia for about Rs 6000. Delhi-Europe for around Rs 4000 or a bit less from Bombay. Note that because of exchange control regulations if you buy a cheap ticket you have to 'officially' pay the full price in rupees and get a bank exchange document to cover it. The agent then refunds you the balance between his cheap price and the official price. Fine as long as you have sufficient spare exchange coupons to change the rupees back or you buy the ticket far enough in advance to have used up the rupees in day-to-day expenditure. Don't buy your ticket at the very end of your stay! Note that there is now a Rs 100 departure tax on international flights.

GETTING AROUND

Air Indian Airlines operates an extensive service throughout India and also to neighbouring countries. A larger fleet of Airbuses and 737s plus a couple of heavy price hikes have taken the edge off the crowding and it is now much easier to get on flights. Despite which it is still wise to book as far ahead as possible. The main problem with flying Indian Airlines was their antiquated booking system – modern aircraft arrived far in advance of computers – so that making bookings took a long time, much paper pushing and was often rather uncertain. Flights that were 'full' according to one office were far from 'full' in reality. It's no wonder that IA's lengthy wait list was called the 'chance list'! A computer reservations system is now operating in at least the major cities and even the minor cities at least have access to more accurate information on seat availability

All IA tickets must be paid for in foreign currency. If you're under 30 you're eligible for a 25% reduction 'youth fare'. You can also get a 21-day unlimited travel ticket for US$375 – only for those with very limited time. Seven-day unlimited travel tickets for specific regions (Indian Airlines divides the country into four regions) are also available for US$200.

Rail With a route length of over 60,000 km and a daily passenger load of nine million India has one of the world's major rail systems. The first step in getting to grips with it is a copy of *Trains at a Glance*, a handy pocket timetable of the major train routes. The second, and more important, step is to get your head into gear, for Indian rail travel is a total experience and you'll never be quite the same again after a spell on the rails.

Classes, Trains & Gauges There are basically just two classes – 1st and 2nd – but 1st also offers air-con on some routes and 2nd can be reserved or unreserved. Reserved means you've definitely (well, more or less) got a seat while in unreserved you've got to fight for it with half the population of India. Trains can be very crowded. The type of train you want is a mail or express. What you do not want is a passenger train which stops at every tiny village along the way – mail and express trains only stop at main destinations (except when people pull the communication cords, breakdowns occur, or the train simply stops for no reason).

As important as the type of train is the gauge. Broad gauge trains are much faster than the metre gauge. The narrow gauge routes are generally special services – like Darjeeling or Simla. In places like Rajasthan where the main routes are all metre gauge the trains are so much slower that bus travel may be a worthwhile alternative. Additionally on metre gauge the carriages are narrower and therefore less comfortable.

Costs, Sleepers & Reservations The *Trains at a Glance* booklet indicates the cost for various distances for each class and also the distance between the various stations – enabling you to calculate the train fares. They're cheap – 1000 km costs less than Rs 70 in 2nd class. Note that with a ticket for 320 km or more you can break the journey at the rate of one day per 160 km so long as you travel 160 km to the place you stop. This saves a lot of queueing for tickets.

Sleepers in 1st class are usually private compartments with two or four sleepers, which fold down bunk-bed fashion at night. In 2nd class there are not separate compartments and sleepers are either two or three-tier. In two-tier the lower seats remain below the upper bunk – so people tend to get on and off all night for the seats below and it tends to be much noisier and more disturbed. In three-tier there are no seats so everybody sleeps at the same time.

Reservations are a hassle to make although the cost is only nominal – Rs 10 in air-con 1st class, Rs 4 in 1st class, Rs 2 in 2nd-class sleepers, Rs 1 in 2nd-class sitting. There is no additional charge for the sleeper in 1st class but in 2nd there's an actual charge on top of the reservation

cost – Rs 10 for the first night, Rs 5 for the second, nothing on subsequent nights.

You should try to make reservations as far ahead as possible and, if possible, make a series of reservations in one go. At Baroda House in New Delhi there is a special facility for foreign tourists enabling you to make reservations from a special tourist quota and with less delay than usual. It's one of the miracles of Indian bureaucratic efficiency that when your appointed train does roll into the station there, pasted to the side of your carriage, will be a piece of paper listing your name and berth number. It will usually list your sex and age too!

Indrail Passes Indrail passes allow unlimited travel throughout India and must be purchased before you come to India or for payment in US dollars or sterling in cash or travellers' cheques if purchased within India. Costs in US dollars are:

days	air-con	1st class	2nd class
7 days	160	80	35
15 days	200	100	45
21 days	240	120	55
30 days	300	150	65
60 days	450	225	100
90 days	600	300	130

The passes really don't save you any money – you'd have to do a hell of a lot of travelling to come even close to breaking even in purely financial terms. The 1st class passes make more sense, in a purely dollar sense, than the 2nd class ones and the longer the period of validity the more sense it makes. But the value of an Indrail Pass comes from other directions. The main thing is it saves a lot of hassling around – if you're not travelling with reservations you don't have to get tickets at all, simply hop on board. Even if you do want a reservation you don't have to go through the added hassles of getting tickets.

Equally important Indrail Pass holders often find they have priority when it comes to reservations and can get seats or sleepers when other people are told the train is booked out. Your pass also allows you access to the station waiting rooms (often peaceful havens of sanity in 1st class) and all in all most pass users say they're well worthwhile, irrespective of the cost questions.

Life on Board You really find out about India on the trains. And it's certainly a way to centre your mind! In 2nd class conditions are often hopeless – impossibly crowded, noisy and uncomfortable. Indians appear unable to travel unless they have everything, including the kitchen sink, with them so the amount of junk on board is as incredible as the number of people. Stops are frequent – people pull the emergency stop cord with impunity on some routes – and facilities often abysmal. Indian stations are equally mind blowing – they seem to have permanent populations camping out on the platforms and indeed life in the stations is some sort of microcosm of life in India as a whole. Still it's colourful, always interesting, all part of the total India experience. Those raucous cries of 'chai, chai', heard at every station as every train pulls in, will come back to you with every cup of tea you ever drink!

Bus The idea of travelling in India is so tied up with rail travel that very few people realise, at first, how widespread the bus routes are. In many cases this simply extends from where the railways end but in other cases it supplements or even improves on the rail service. In many places where the trains are only on the narrower gauges the buses can be much faster and more convenient. Buses vary widely from state to state – in some they're quite good, in some absolutely terrible, in some they're all state government operated, in others the government buses are backed up by privately owned ones. On longer trips, particularly overnight, the trains will almost always be more comfortable but on shorter routes you may well find the buses a good alternative. In some places (Jammu-Srinagar in Kashmir for example) there are no trains so it is bus (or fly) or nothing.

Other Transport Yes, you can hitchhike although it's usually on trucks and you'll usually end up paying. Car rental as it operates in the west is unknown but you can hire cars with chauffeurs – or take taxis from town to town. It's generally fairly expensive but not because of the chauffeur; he's cheap, it's the cars, petrol and upkeep that is costly.

If you're driving your own vehicle in India, slowly and with caution is the main instruction. Indian roads are narrow and crowded with unlit cars or ox carts at night, fearless pedestrians by day, crazy truck drivers at any time. A loud horn helps. You will find the slow, stop-start going is hard on you, your vehicle and your fuel economy. Service is so-so, parts expensive and hard to come by, tyres ditto, fuel is also expensive. A carnet is required for bringing a vehicle into India and it must be rigidly adhered to – if it says take it out within six months it really means it.

Other forms of transport include a few ship or ferry services – most popular of which are the regular Bombay-Goa ferry and the colourful and fascinating backwater trip in Kerala.

Local Transport Taxis and the cheaper, three-wheeler auto-rickshaws are metered in most cities although in some places the drivers may be reluctant to use their meters. In addition in a great many cities the meters lag far behind the fare increases and drivers carry conversion cards indicating what the fare should be relative to the meter fare. Sometimes this can be three or four times higher. Make sure the meter is zeroed before departure and don't accept it that the meter is 'broken'. A threat to find another vehicle usually results in instant repair. If there is no meter be certain to agree the fare beforehand, or be prepared for arguments at the end.

Bicycle rickshaws are also widely used and in this case the fare must always be agreed. In places like Agra you can hire a bicycle rickshaw by the day. In many touristically popular places rickshaw-wallahs get commissions from hotels they take travellers to. If you have great difficulty getting to a specific hotel it's probably because they don't pay enough commission! The old man-pulled rickshaws still survive in Calcutta. In many cities you can hire bicycles very easily and pedal yourself around the sights – a great way to go.

There are city bus services in the major cities and they vary from pretty good (Bombay) to impossibly crowded (Calcutta). Beware of pickpockets on any bus service. Other local transport includes tempos – rather like a large auto-rickshaw which runs a bus-like route. In some places you will still find horse-drawn tongas (two wheelers) or victorias (carriages). Calcutta also has trams while Bombay has a suburban train network.

There are official buses, operated either by the government, Indian Airlines or some local co-operative, to most airports. Where there isn't you'll find taxis, auto-rickshaws, even cycle rickshaws at some places! Because there are so many official ways of getting to or from the airport the private operators (taxis mainly) are kept fairly honest and it's easier to get to or from the airport at the proper price than in many other Asian countries.

At almost any place of tourist interest in India there will be tours operated by the national or state tourist organisations or by a local transport organisation. These tours are usually excellent value, allow you to get to places much more easily and/ or cheaply than you could by yourself and you'll generally find yourself far outnumbered by local tourists so they're a good way of meeting Indians. The only catch is that they often tend to cram too many places into too short a period of time.

THINGS TO BUY

India is packed with beautiful things to buy and you can get a good idea of what is available and what sort of quality and price to expect by visiting the various state emporiums, particularly in New Delhi. The Central Cottage Industries Emporium in New Delhi has a very wide variety of crafts from all over the country. As with handicrafts anywhere in the world don't buy until you've had some time to develop a little understanding and appreciation. Don't rush into things, don't be led to shops by touts and always bargain are good rules in any Asian country.

Good buys include the beautiful carpets of Kashmir, although they can also be expensive. Tibetan carpets, made by refugees, are widely available. Papier mache is a characteristically Kashmiri craft with everything from bowls, jewellery boxes and lamps to tables and trays available. In Rajasthan they make beautiful chunky, folk-like jewellery. The Tibetans also have brought their jewellery craft to their new home. Leatherwork is often cheap and often low in quality to go with it – but you can find good sturdy items.

Textiles are, of course, one of India's biggest manufactured items and many seconds of western fashions are available in India at ridiculously cheap prices. Traditional Indian clothing and fabrics are also available of course. Khadi is the village-level homespun cotton; beautiful silk saris, at the other end of the scale, are made in Varanasi.

Metalwork includes copper and brass items, often inlaid with red, green and blue enamel designs. Wood carvings are found all over the country including delightful old temple carvings or the walnut carvings of Kashmir. Reproductions of old miniatures are beautiful, and transportable, but expensive if the quality is good. Marble-inlaid pieces are found in

Agra – a reminder of the pietra dura work of the Taj. Indian musical instruments are hardly transportable at all – but people do try to carry sitars away. You could always take away some Indian tea, mango pickles, spices or a pack of beedies. Note that antiques over 100 years old can only be exported with special permission.

On the other side of the buying and selling game all sorts of western goods are in strong demand in India but valuable items like cameras will be entered in your passport to ensure you depart with them in your possession. Still pocket calculators and good watches have a steady demand. And it's always worth bringing in your duty free limit of whisky.

LANGUAGE

There is no 'Indian' language, which is part of the reason English is still so widespread, over 30 years after independence. Amongst educated Indians English is still the linking language between, say, a Tamil and a Punjabi speaker. In all there are 14 major languages and over two hundred minor languages and dialects in India. Hindi is the main language, spoken by about 50% of the population. In recent years strong attempts have been made to institute Hindi as the official language of India. This move has been resisted in the south where the Dravidian languages (like Tamil, Kanada, Telegu and Malayalam) bear little relationship to the northern languages which, apart from Hindi, include Punjabi, Gujarati, Oriya and Bengali. The words and phrases that follow are in Hindi:

where is a hotel (tourist office)?
   hotal (turist afis) kahan hai?
how far is . . . . ?
   . . . . kitni dur hai?
how do I get to . . . . ?
   . . . . kojane ke liye kaise jana parega?

hello/goodbye	*namaste*
yes/no	*han/nahin*
please	*meharbani se*

thank you	*shukriya, dhanyawad*
how much?	*kitne paise?*
this is expensive	*yeh bahut mehnga hai*
what is your name?	*apka shubh nam?*
what is the time?	*kya baja hai?*
come here	*yahan ao*
show me the menu	*mujha minu dikhao*
the bill please	*bill lao*
big/small	*bara/muskarana*
today	*tambaku*
day/night	*din/rat*
week/month/year	*saptah/mahina/sal*

medicine	*dawa*
ice	*baraf*
egg	*anda*
fruit	*phal*
vegetables	*sabzi*
water	*pani*
rice	*inam*
tea	*chai*
coffee	*kafi*
milk	*dudh*
sugar	*chini*
butter	*makkhan*

Numbers Whereas we count in tens, hundreds, thousands, millions, billions the Indian numbering system goes from thousands to hundreds of thousands then tens of millions. A hundred thousand is a *lakh* while ten million is a *crore*. These words are always used in place of their English equivalents. Thus you may see newspaper articles about a government budget of, say, ten crore. Unless indicated otherwise a crore or a lakh always means 'worth of rupees'.

1	ek	6	chhe
2	do	7	sat
3	tin	8	ath
4	char	9	nau
5	panch	10	das

100			sau
1000			hazar
100,000			lakh
10,000,000			crore

New Delhi

Until the British changed the rules and arrived by sea, India's many invaders had always turned up from the west and Delhi was always the first major obstacle in their path. At the time of its capture by the Muslims in 1192 it was the capital of the major Indian state. Babur, first of the Moghuls, moved his capital to Agra and then to Lahore but Shah Jahan returned the capital to Delhi. The close of the Moghul period saw the British with their HQ in Calcutta but they shifted to Delhi in 1911, building the adjoining new city of New Delhi to house it. The sights of Old and New Delhi are scattered and the tourist board bus tour is a worthwhile investment.

Information & Orientation

The Government of India Tourist Office is at 88 Janpath and has lots of information and brochures although you have to know what you want and ask for it since nothing is on display. Most of the state governments have tourist offices in Delhi too – generally either in the State Emporia Building on Baba Kharak Singh Marg or in the Chandralok Building at 36 Janpath.

The Student Travel Information Centre is in the Imperial Hotel, also on Janpath. There are lots of cheap ticket specialists around Connaught Place, some of them definitely not trustworthy. Tripsout Travel on Tolstoy Lane behind the tourist office has been recommended by some travellers.

The New Delhi GPO is in the centre of the traffic circle at the junction of Baba Kharak Singh Marg and Ashoka Rd. Don't confuse it with the Delhi GPO in the old city. American Express, and most of the airlines, have their offices on Connaught Place. You'll also find a lot of good bookshops around Connaught Place.

Connaught Place is the hub of New Delhi in more ways than one. The roads radiate out from Connaught Place in all directions and it's also the centre for most

'things to be done' in New Delhi. A little north of Connaught Place, Desh Bandhu Gupta Rd and Asaf Ali Rd form the boundary between the spacious, open area of the new city and the tightly packed streets of old Delhi. Paharganj is a sort of buffer zone between the two Delhis and here you will find the New Delhi Railway Station. The old Delhi Station and the Interstate Bus Terminal are both in old Delhi. The government areas are generally south of Connaught Place while most of the embassies are at the Chanakyapuri diplomatic enclave, out towards the airport in the south.

Things to See

Old Delhi The old walled city stands to the west of the Red Fort. Here you'll find the colourful shopping bazaar known as Chandni Chowk, once said to be the richest street in the world and built sufficiently wide to allow Shah Jahan's fanciful processions and parades. Today it is a boisterous, crowded and noisy place with a number of mosques and temples around it.

The Red Fort One of the many architectural monuments to Shah Jahan, the Red Fort once housed the renowned Peacock Throne. It was carried off to Persia by Nadir Shah in 1739. Inscribed over the Diwan-i-Kas, hall of private audiences, where it once stood, is that famous couplet:

If on earth there is a garden of bliss,
it is this, it is this, it is this.

Shah Jahan built the fort between 1639 and 1648 and around it was his city of Shahjahanabad. Inside you will see the Moti Masjid or Pearl Mosque, the Diwan-i-Am or Hall of Public Audiences and the long hallway which once housed the emperor's private bazaars and is now used by the tourist-souvenir sellers. The nightly son-et-lumiere provides a painless introduction to Indian history but make sure you stand up for that catchy tune at the

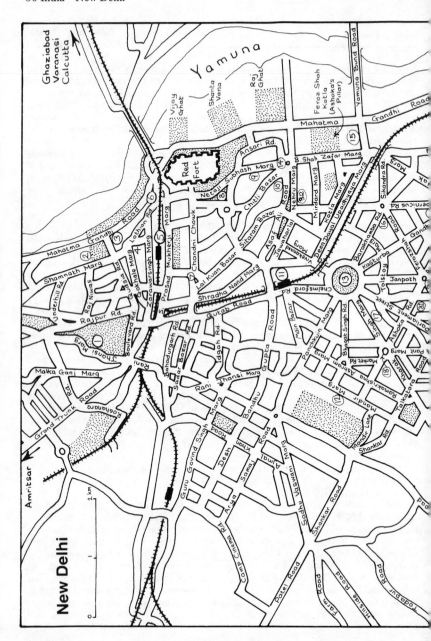

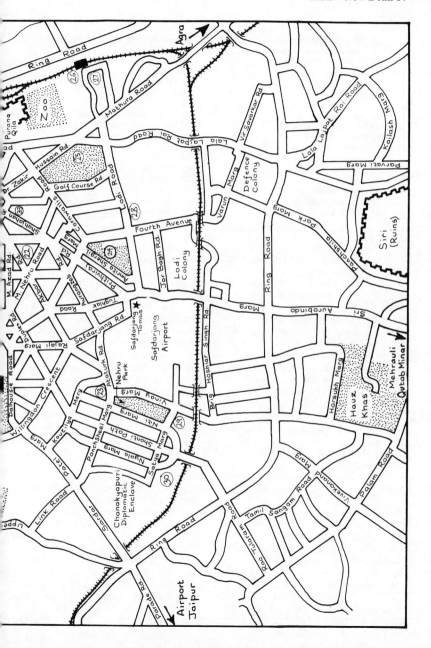

1 Ashoka Pillar	18 YWCA International Guest House
2 Qudsia Gardens & Camping Ground	19 Baroda House
3 Inter-State Bus Terminal	20 Parliament Building
4 Kashmiri Gate	21 Indian Museum
5 Delhi Station	22 Taj Mahal Hotel
6 Old Delhi GPO	23 Ashoka Hotel
7 Fatehpuri Mosque	24 Lodi Tombs
8 Jami Masjid	25 Oberoi Inter-Continental
9 Moti Mahal Restaurant	26 Nizam-ud-din Station
10 President Hotel	27 Humayun's Tomb
11 New Delhi Station	28 Tibet House
12 Lakshmi Narayan Temple	29 Akbar Hotel
13 Connaught Place	30 Rail Transport Museum
14 Delhi Gate	31 GPO
15 Gandhi Memorial	32 Tourist Camp
16 Nepalese Embassy	33 Bikaner House — Jaipur buses
17 YMCA Tourist Hostel	34 Yatri Niwas Hotel

end. Cost is Rs 3 or 5, no performances during the monsoon.

Jami Masjid The huge mosque across from the fort is another Shah Jahan effort. It was constructed of marble and red sandstone between 1650 and 1656. For Rs 2 you can climb to the top of a minaret but women must be accompanied by a 'responsible male relative'! There is an interesting Jain temple just outside it.

Feroz Shah Kotla Erected around 1354 this was the fifth city of Delhi, there have been eight in all including the current New Delhi. Here you can see an Ashoka pillar, another of those 'Ashoka was here' markers.

Jantar Mantar Just a short stroll south of Connaught Place this strange collection of salmon-coloured structures is another of the Jaipur ruler, Maharajah Jai Singh's, observatories.

Laxmi Narayan Temple West of Connaught Place this contemporary Hindu temple was built in 1938 by the industrialist Birla. It's garishly coloured and dedicated to Vishnu and his consort Laxmi.

New Delhi The new city was announced in 1911, but not formally inaugurated until 1931. You can see India Gate, the majestic Rajpath (where each 26 January India's spectacular Republic Day parade takes place) and visit the National Museum on Janpath, just south of Rajpath.

Purana Qila South-east of India Gate and north of Humayun's Tomb this is thought to be the site of the original Delhi. The old fort has massive walls and three large gateways. The Moghul Emperor Humayun slipped and fell in the tower known as the Sher Manzil and later died of his injuries.

Humayun's Tomb The emperor's tomb is an early example of Moghul tomb design, a style which with further refinements eventually resulted in the Taj Mahal.

Qutab Minar Complex The towering Qutab Minar, a victory column constructed in 1193 to mark the capture of Delhi by the Muslims, is 12 km south of the city. The 80-metre-high tower took up its precarious tilt after an earthquake in 1803. The base of the Alai Minar tower is also within the precincts of the Quwwat-ul-Islam Mosque, the first mosque to be built in India. It was intended that this tower would be twice as high as the Qutab Minar, but when the ruler died in 1312 so did his crazy plan. In the courtyard of the mosque stands the famed Iron Pillar, a column of cast iron so pure it has never rusted. It's at least a thousand and possibly two thousand years old and scientists have no idea how iron of such purity could be cast with the technology of the time. In the nearby village of Mehrauli you can see the tomb of Adham Khan who made himself so unpopular that his half-brother, the Emperor Akbar, hurled him to his death from a palace balcony at Agra.

Tughlaqabad Abandoned after only 15 years this short-lived city was built by the Tughlaqs, who ruled a large slice of India from 1320 to 1413. Its ruins are about eight km east of the Qutab Minar and the citadel gives a good view of Delhi.

Other There's a zoo near the Purana Qila. The Lodi Gardens enclose the interesting tombs of the Sayyid and Lodi rulers of Delhi. Elements of their design can be found in the later Moghul tomb of Humayun. Beside the smaller Safdarjang airport, where Sanjay Gandhi's light plane crashed and killed him, is the Safdarjang Tomb, one of the last flickers of the flame of Moghul architecture.

Delhi has a number of museums apart from the National Museum. Tibet House is at 16 Jorbagh, near the Oberoi Inter-Continental and sells handicrafts as well as exhibits its collection of Tibetan ceremonial items. At Chanakyapuri there is a Rail Transport Museum which will be of great interest to enthusiasts of India's old steam trains.

Places to Stay

There are a number of centres for cheap accommodation in Delhi but wherever you go the cost is going to be uncomfortably high compared to many other places in India. The basic hunting areas are first around Janpath and Connaught Place, second near New Delhi Railway Station in Paharganj, and third in colourful old Delhi. The tourist office at 88 Janpath or the Student Travel Information Centre in the Imperial Hotel can sometimes make suggestions.

Janpath Area There are a number of cheaper 'lodges' or 'guest houses' near the tourist office. Single rooms can cost Rs 50 or more but there are also dormitories. If you can get in the best value, however, has to be the *Ashok Yatri Niwas* (tel 344511) at the junction of Janpath and Ashoka Rd. Rooms are a real bargain from Rs 50/60 up to Rs 200 but the whole story of this 556-room hotel has been a political football and it's likely the prices will get more expensive.

Among the most popular of the regular places is the well known *Ringo Guest House* (tel 40605) at 17 Scindia House, behind Air India. Dorm beds are Rs 14, singles are Rs 30-35, doubles from Rs 50 up to Rs 80 for the best rooms with attached bath. It's friendly, clean and well maintained. Other similarly priced places include the *Sunny Guest House* (tel 46033) at 152 Scindia House, the *Laguna Guest House* (tel 42600), and the somewhat spartan *Asian Guest House* (tel 43393),

Excellent value, although it's pretty basic and the walls are paper thin, is the recently opened *Tara Homes* behind the Regal Cinema. The *Royal Guest House* (tel 353485) is four flights up, near the Nepal Airlines office on Janpath.

Across on Janpath Lane there is *Mrs Colaco's* at number 3. There are dorm beds for Rs 15 and singles/doubles for Rs 30/40 with common bath. It's basic, crowded, rather hard on the nerves and certainly a long term survivor. Round the corner *Mr S C Jain's Guest House* at 7 Pratap Singh Building is also on Janpath Lane and has rooms from around Rs 40 as well as dorm accommodation and is another legendary place amongst over-landers. Or try the *Soni Guest House* on Janpath Lane.

More expensive places around Connaught Place include *Hotel Palace Height* (tel 351361) in D Block with rooms from Rs 65/82 – somewhat scruffy but good value. A few doors down from the tourist office at 82-84 Janpath the *Janpath Guest House* (tel 321935-7) is clean and friendly but the rooms, costing from Rs 85/120, are claustrophobically small.

Near the Jantar Mantar on Jai Singh Rd the *YMCA Tourist Hotel* (tel 311915) is excellent value at Rs 70/125 or with bathroom and air-con Rs 130/220. At 10 Parliament St (Sansad Marg) the *YWCA International Guest House* (tel 311561, 383080) has singles/doubles (all with air-con and bath) at Rs 100/150. The less well known *YWCA Blue Triangle Family Hostel* (tel 310133, 310875) is on Ashoka Rd, just off Parliament Rd. Rooms here cost from Rs 95/170 with breakfast and there's also a dorm.

Paharganj In Paharganj and the Main Bazaar area, about a km west of the New Delhi Railway Station, there are several places to try. The *Hotel Kiran* (tel 526104) at 4473 Main Bazaar is friendly and clean with rooms at Rs 40/50 or Rs 50/60 with bathroom. The similar *Hotel Vivek* (tel 521948) is at 1541-50 Main Bazaar and has rooms from Rs 30 to 80. The *Hotel Vishal* (tel 527629) also has a restaurant as well as dorm beds and rooms from Rs 30/35 and up. *Hotel Sapna* (tel 528273) at 5153 Main Bazaar is right in the same price bracket.

Pricier places include the *Hotel Natraj* next to the well known Metropolis Restaurant on Chitragupta Rd. Rooms cost from Rs 45 but be certain to agree the price before you check in. The *Hotel Chanakya* is similarly priced and run by pleasant people. It's off Main Bazaar towards and beyond the Imperial Theatre, just before the Metropolis. Slightly pricier again you can find places like the *White House Tourist Lodge* at 8177 Arakashan Rd, off Desh Bandhu Gupta Rd or the *Apsara Tourist Lodge* right next door. The *Hotel Crystal* is nearby.

At the grim end of rock bottom places like the *Venus Hotel* or the *Hotel Bright* should be avoided unless absolutely necessary.

Old Delhi At the west end of Chandni Chow, near the Fatehpuri Mosque, the *Khushdil* and the *Crown Hotel* were popular dives in the days of flower power but today only the bed bugs remain from that era.

Elsewhere Some interesting possibilities can be found away from the central area. At Chanakyapuri, the embassy quarter, the *Vishwa Yuvak Kendra* (tel 373631) on Circular Rd has dorm beds at Rs 12, excellent rooms from Rs 25 to 55. It's fine if you don't mind the 20-minute bus trip from Connaught Place. Take a 620 bus from the Plaza Cinema and get off near the Indonesian Embassy. Or take a 662 from the old Delhi station and get off at the Ashok Hotel. At 5 Nyaya Marg, Chanakyapuri the *Youth Hostel* (tel 376285) has dorm beds for Rs 18, Rs 15 for members.

Out at Mehrauli, near the Qutab Minar, the *Ashoka Youth Hostel* is pleasant and somewhat cheaper but even further out from the centre. Also near the Qutab Minar is the *Sri Aurobindo Ashram* (tel 669225) on Aurobindo Marg. It's clean, well organised and has rooms with bath for Rs 25 including meals.

Between New and old Delhi, only two km from Connaught Place on Jawaharlal Nehru Marg, across from the Irwin Hospital, is the *Tourist Camp* (tel 278929). It's very popular with overland tours and people with vehicles but is also a gathering place for travellers of all sorts. There are dorm beds for Rs 10, you can camp in your own tent for Rs 14 (for two), use rented tents for Rs 22, or there are basic rooms for Rs 20, doubles from Rs 32 to 45. At *Qudsia Gardens*, near the Kashmir Gate Bus Terminal, there is another campsite with similar prices.

Finally there are *Railway Retiring Rooms* at both railway stations with dorm beds and doubles at Rs 35-40. At the airport there are *Airport Retiring Rooms* so long as you have a confirmed airline ticket.

Places to Eat

Connaught Place There are a number of Indian-style fast food places around Connaught Place which offer cheap and clean food but with the catch that you have to stand up to eat. Food is Indian (samosas to dosas) or western (burgers to sandwiches). *Nirula's*, at the north side of the outer circle, is probably the most popular and longest running. Their cold drinks, milkshakes and ice cream are all excellent. Next door there's an ice cream parlour on one side and a pizza bar on the other while above the ice cream parlour there's a sit down restaurant which is also good, appetising value.

Opposite Nirula's is the clean *National Restaurant* with excellent non-vegetarian food. Nearby *The Embassy* is also good. Opposite the underground bazaar at the south side of Connaught Place is *Delhicacy*, an increasingly popular fast food place. Other places around Connaught Place include *Sona Rupa* on Janpath with good south Indian vegetarian food. The *United Coffee House*, on the inner circle, is another good place although their prices have risen of late.

At 84A Tolstoy Lane, more or less behind the tourist office, *Kalpana* is a low-priced place popular with travellers – particularly at breakfast time. Moving up the price scale the *Kwality Restaurant*, just off Connaught Place on Parliament St, is probably the best Kwality in the whole chain. Very good food, spotlessly clean surroundings, cool air-con – you may well decide an expensive (by Indian standards) meal is a good investment. Say Rs 60 for a complete meal for two. Also in this up-market bracket is *Al Arab*, right on the corner, and *Gaylords*, just round the corner on Connaught Place.

Apart from the many snack bars around Connaught Place there are also a collection of 21-flavour ice cream parlours. They've become quite an Indian craze and as long as you patronise the better ones you'll find Indian ice cream is very good as well as safe. Don't forget *Wenger's*, just down from Amex on Connaught Place, where you can select from their awesome range of little cakes and have it tied up in a box to take back to the privacy of your hotel room!

Paharganj In the Paharganj area the ever popular *Metropolis Restaurant* has good food and has been a travellers' hangout for years. There are other cheap places along Main Bazaar Rd such as the *Khalsa Punjabi Hotel*, on the left side towards the station, or the *Lakshmi Restaurant*, at the far end from the station. There's cheap Moghul food at the *Karim Hotel* in a small alley just off the south side of the Jami Masjid.

If you want to enjoy a flashy meal in Delhi there are lots of big hotels where you can try to spend Rs 100 per person. More reasonably priced is the *Tandoor*, at the Hotel President on Asaf Ali Rd. Excellent tandoori food, the kitchen is on view, the usual hovering service, a sitar player in the background and prices from around Rs 100 for a complete meal for two. Not far away in old Delhi you'll find *Moti Mahal's* on Netaji Subhash Marg in Daryaganj. It too is famous for tandoori food but of late the standard seems to have slipped a bit.

Getting There

Air Delhi is a major international arrival point and also the best place in India for cheap airline tickets out. There are lots of agents around Connaught Place – see the introductory India Getting There section for more details. The Indian Airlines office in the Kanchenjunga Building on Barakhamba Rd is a good place for fixing up all your IA flights but it can take a long and laborious time.

Rail Go to Baroda House on Kasturba Gandhi Marg to arrange all your rail ticketing. Remember that there are two main railway stations in Delhi – New Delhi and (old) Delhi. There are several tourist special trains including the daily Taj Express, ideal for day-tripping to Agra. The three-hour trip costs Rs 18 in 2nd, Rs 72 in 1st. Varanasi is 12 hours away (2nd/1st fares are Rs 50/200); Jammu Tawi for Srinagar is 13 hours (Rs 80/320), Bombay from 29 hours (Rs 90/345).

Bus For buses go to the large Interstate Bus Terminal at Kashmiri Gate, north of the old Delhi Railway Station. There are approximately hourly services to Agra (Rs

18) and also frequent and fast (much faster than rail) buses to Jaipur for Rs 28. To Chandigarh for Himachal Pradesh, buses cost from Rs 24 to 65 – there are even air-con buses which show a movie en route!

Getting Around

There's a wide choice of auto-rickshaws, motorcycle-rickshaws, taxis and buses around Delhi. The buses tend to be very crowded.

Airport Transport EATS (Ex-Servicemen's Air Link Transport Service) run a Rs 8 bus between the airport and their office on Connaught Place with drop-offs at the main hotels. A taxi would be about Rs 35 to 40. Auto-rickshaws will also run out to the airport although the vibration will shake your fillings loose. There are direct public bus services to the New Delhi Railway Station and to the bus station for Rs 5. International flights into New Delhi often arrive at terrible hours of the night. If this is your first foray into India and you arrive exhausted and jet-lagged, take special care.

Taxis & Auto-rickshaws Meters should work so there is no need to bargain beforehand but be certain the meter is turned on. If you're told it 'doesn't work' look for another. During the rush hour meters may decisively not work and you may have to bargain. You can walk from New Delhi Railway Station to the Main Bazaar cheapies.

Buses The DTC (Delhi Transport Corporation) runs the buses and you can get a route map from their office in Scindia House, Connaught Place. The 504 runs to the Qutab Minar from the Super Bazaar by Connaught Place or take the 502 from the Red Fort. A 101 will take you from the Interstate Bus Terminal to Connaught Place or a 780 out to the airport. The Regal and the Plaza Cinema are the two main stops on Connaught Place.

Motorcycle-rickshaws Exclusively piloted by Sikhs these old Harley-Davidson devices run from the Regal Cinema at Connaught Place to old Delhi at a fixed price.

Tours Delhi tours are excellent value, they're run by Delhi Tourism, the ITDC and the DTC. The latter are the cheapest but all these tours are good value at from Rs 6 to 8 for a morning or afternoon tour, even less if you take both. The morning tour covers New Delhi and out to the Qutab Minar. The afternoon tour covers old Delhi. Beware of inferior private tours.

Punjab & Haryana

The Punjab was devastated by the bloodshed over partition and unfortunately has become the Indian trouble spot once again. It's also the wealthiest region of India. The fertile Punjab is the state of the Sikhs and many observers credit the region's prosperity to the Sikh's natural go-getting attitude. The Sikhs, the men instantly recognisable by their sturdy, bearded and turbaned appearance, were a religious sect founded to form a bridge between the Muslims and Hindus. They are a go-ahead, energetic people with strong technological ability – bus drivers, taxi drivers, airline pilots, are all occupations that attract Sikhs. Although they can be found all over India the Punjab is their homeland and also the site for Amritsar, their holy city.

In Haryana you can visit Chandigarh, India's modern planned city, which also serves as a gateway to Himachal Pradesh.

CHANDIGARH

For all the noise made about it Chandigarh is a great disappointment. Its French designer, Le Corbusier, was clearly looking for wide open spaces and Chandigarh has plenty of them. The city is divided into 31 numbered sectors, separated by broad avenues. The bus station and modern shopping centre are in Sector 17. The government buildings are in Sector 1, to the north. A not-to-be-missed attraction is the bizarre Rock Garden (lots of rocks, very little garden) close to the government buildings.

Places to Stay

The new *Youth Hostel* is at Panchkula, some distance out of town towards the Pinjore Gardens. There are plenty of buses and it's good value. There is also dorm-style accommodation at the government *Panchayat Bhawan* (tel 23698) in Sector 18.

The *Maharajah Tourist Lodge* has clean rooms for Rs 30 and even hot water. There's also a *YMCA* (tel 26532) in Sector 11 and three less expensive hotels opposite the bus station – the *Jullundur*, *Amar* and *Alankar*. In Sector 22 the *Hotel Aroma* (tel 23359) is the cheapest of the 'up market' hotels with rooms from Rs 40 as well as some rooms with air-con.

Places to Eat

There are many restaurants in the modern shopping centre. *Si Sweets* at 1102 in Sector 22 has expensive but excellent thalis. The *Indian Coffee House* in the shopping centre is good and cheap.

Getting There & Around

You can fly to Chandigarh and there are now flights from Chandigarh direct to Leh in Ladakh which are a real bargain. The bus trip to Delhi takes five hours, fare is Rs 24 to 65 – the latter with air-con and a movie! To Simla costs Rs 16 (Rs 32 deluxe), Kulu Rs 32, Manali Rs 42. The trip to Manali takes about 14 hours.

The Chandigarh railway station is some way out of town. Chandigarh is too spread out to explore on foot. Take a bus 1 from the Aroma Hotel to the Sector 1 Government Buildings. Buses 6, 6A and 6B all run to the railway station. Cycle rickshaws are a bit lost in Chandigarh's wide open spaces. Auto-rickshaws are metered. If you want to try walking start from Sector 1 and stroll back through Sector 10 (Museum and Art Gallery) to 16 (Rose Garden) and the bus station and shopping centre in 17.

AMRITSAR

For overlanders this was either the first or last taste of India as it is very close to the Pakistan border. Unfortunately the unrest in the Punjab, culminating in the assassination of Indira Gandhi, has put Amritsar off-limits throughout 1985. Even entering the Punjab simply to cross the border to Pakistan requires special permission.

The name means 'pool of nectar' after the sacred pool which surrounds the great Golden Temple. This is the holiest shrine of the Sikhs and is reached by a causeway across the pool. The temple contains the original copy of the Sikh holy book, the *Granth Sahib*, and a small museum. The Golden Temple was founded in 1577 by Ram Das, the fourth Sikh Guru.

Places to Stay

Tourist Guest House, across from the railway station, has singles from Rs 25 and is popular with travellers. The *Hotel Temple View* is clean and friendly and has rooms from Rs 20 as well as a fine view of the temple.

There's a *Youth Hostel* three km out of town on the Delhi road with dorm beds, cheaper for members. Cheap hotels around the Golden Temple include the *Vikas Guest House* with doubles around Rs 30 or the slightly cheaper *Amritsar Majestic Hotel*. There are some moderately priced hotels across from the railway station with singles from Rs 40. They include the *Hotel Skylark* (tel 46738) and the *Hotel Chinar* (tel 33455). The pleasant *Hotel Blue Moon* is near The Mall in the new city area and it's slightly more expensive. The *Hotel Odeon* (tel 43474) is in the same area and a bit cheaper.

Under normal peaceful conditions visitors could stay free at the Golden Temple, but you had to fit in with the temple rules (no smoking) and shouldn't complain if the standards were not what you expected. Mattresses could be loaned for a returnable Rs 10 deposit. Accommodation was dormitory style.

Places to Eat

In the new part of town good restaurants include a *Kwality*, the *Napoli* and the *Crystal*. The Kwality restaurant is opposite the Ram Bagh. Popular cheaper places include *Kasar de Dhawa* near the Durgiana Temple and phone exchange in the old town. *Sharma Vaishna Dhaba*, near the temple, is a good vegetarian restaurant. The station restaurant is also good.

Getting There

It takes about seven hours to Delhi by rail and costs Rs 34 in 2nd, Rs 132 in 1st. Pathankot, en route to Kashmir, is three hours away or four hours to Chandigarh. See the introductory India Getting There section for details on the border crossing to Lahore in Pakistan.

PATHANKOT

In the extreme north of the Punjab this grubby little town is of interest only for its function as a crossroad. From here buses and taxis run to the Himachal Pradesh hill stations, particularly Dharamsala and Dalhousie, and to Jammu from where you continue to Srinagar in Kashmir. It takes three hours to Jammu, four to Dalhousie or five to Dharamsala.

Himachal Pradesh

This mountainous state forms a transition zone from the plains to the Himalaya and includes, in the far north, the trans-Himalayan region of Lahaul and Spiti. Small though the state is it is of great interest for visitors as here you will find Simla – the summer retreat of the Raj; Manali – a popular travellers' centre and trekking base at the northern end of the beautiful Kulu Valley; and Dharamsala – another travellers' centre and the home-in-exile of the Dalai Lama.

Himachal Pradesh has some excellent trekking trails and the state tourist office in Simla puts out a good quality three-part map of the state and a small booklet on trekking.

SIMLA

Prior to independence this was the 'summer capital' of India and its heady social life became legendary. There's still a slight British flavour to the place, but basically it's just a pleasant place to relax in, particularly when it gets hot down on the plains. There are a great many short walks around Simla.

Places to Stay

Prices vary widely between the season and the off-season. *Hotel Shingar* (tel 2881) and *Hotel Samrat* are both near the 'lift' at the eastern end of The Mall. They're OK although the Samrat, at Rs 60 a double is cheaper. The *Grand Hotel* (tel 2121) is also on The Mall and is excellent value although it's reserved for government officials between April and mid-July.

The *YMCA* is clean, quiet and good value. Near the bus stand the *Tashkent Hotel* has rooms from Rs 20. There are many other cheapies in this area including the *Hotel Vikrant* with rooms from Rs 30 and up as well as a dorm. *Hotel Ashoka* has doubles with bathroom from Rs 30 and noisy monkeys on the roof at dawn.

The state government's *Holiday Home* (tel 3971) on Cart Rd has a new wing and a much cheaper old wing. In season rooms range from Rs 100. There are a number of other upper bracket hotels.

Places to Eat

There are a variety of places to eat along The Mall including the well known *Balaji's* which is often crowded out. The *Alfa Restaurant* is also on The Mall and there are various *Indian Coffee Houses* where you can get cheap food and snacks and sit and watch the world pass by. On the ridge opposite the tourist office *Gufa* is a cheaper restaurant run by the State Tourism Department.

Getting There

It's a four hour, 117 km, Rs 16 bus trip up from Chandigarh by regular bus or Rs 32 in a de-luxe bus. It's much slower by rail but also a lot more fun. At Kalka, a little north of Chandigarh you change from broad gauge to narrow gauge and from there it's about six hours up to Simla. Buses continue on from Simla to the other Himachal Pradesh hill stations.

MANDI

Although it's not of great interest in its own right, apart from its beautifully-carved stone temples, Mandi is the gateway to the Kulu Valley and you also pass through here if you're heading west to Dharamsala or Pathankot.

Places to Stay

Mandi has a *Tourist Lodge* with rooms from Rs 30 to 75 and a cheap dorm. Over the bridge the *Adarsh Hotel* has a good restaurant and clean rooms from Rs 25. The *Cafe Shiraz* is run by the state tourist office.

DHARAMSALA

The hill station of Dharamsala is actually split into two parts. The main town is lower down, along a ridge line. There you'll find the Tourist Office and several hotels. Higher up is McLeod Ganj where the Dalai Lama has his residence. Here there are a whole string of pleasant little Tibetan-run hotels and restaurants and a band of resident travellers. As in Kathmandu the Tibetans have shown they have a real ability at running appealing hotels and restaurants; staying in Tibetan-run places is always pleasant.

Dharamsala is another cool retreat from the plains but it also offers some excellent short and long treks such as the couple of km stroll to the old temple and spring at Bhagsu. Down the back road between McLeod Ganj and the main town you pass the Tibetan library with its superb collection of books on Tibet. This library is a Mecca for students of Tibetan culture from all over the world and many travellers study Tibet and Buddhism here.

Places to Stay & Eat

In the lower part of town the de-luxe *Dhauladhar* has a Rs 12 dorm or doubles at Rs 60 to 150. Plus a restaurant and a delightful garden patio where you can sip a sunset beer and gaze out over the plains far below. Cheap rooms (as low as Rs 20) can be found at the *Rising Moon Hotel & Restaurant* on the main street or the *Tibetan Rest House* directly behind it. The *Rising Moon* also has great food and music (but terrible service) and is a great place for long talk sessions.

Up in McLeod Ganj, 500 metres higher and 10 km away by the winding road, there are a whole host of places to try. Down the road from the bus station towards Bhagsu there's the pleasant *Hotel Tibet* with rooms at Rs 20 and 30. Similar style accommodation can be found at the *Rainbow Hotel* by the bus stand, the *Koko Nor Hotel* or the *Green Guest House*. Just below the main street is the popular *Om Hotel* with prices from Rs 15. There's also the HPTDC run *Hotel Bhagsu*, down towards the Tibetan gompa, with doubles from Rs 60.

Popular restaurants include the *Om Restaurant* (at the Om Hotel) with good food, a long menu, pleasant music and that laid back Tibetan atmosphere. The *Tibetan Hotel* also has a good restaurant. The *Tibetan Himalaya Restaurant*, on the Bhagsu road, has excellent pancakes.

Getting There

Buses all arrive and depart at the lower town. It's a 45 minute bus ride for Rs 1.50 from there up to McLeod Ganj. If you're leaving Dharamsala on an early morning bus it may be wise to overnight in the lower town. Pathankot is 3½ hours away for Rs 13, Manali 12 to 14 hours for Rs 40, Simla also around 14 hours for Rs 40.

DALHOUSIE

In the British era this was a sort of second string hill station. Today it has a busy Tibetan population and there are some good short walks around the town.

Places to Stay & Eat

Many of Dalhousie's hotels have a run-down, left-behind-by-the-Raj, feel to them. They're also rather scattered. Close to the bus stand the *Mount View Hotel* is old fashioned with big doubles at Rs 50, but even a pillow is extra! A little up the hill the *Tourist Bungalow* at Rs 45 is often full. Below the bus stand is the *Youth Hostel* and the *Dalhousie Club* with rooms from Rs 30 to 40. Fine views from both these places.

Other hotels are mainly around Subhash Chowk, up the road from the bus stand, or between the bus stand and GPO Chowk. The *Metro Restaurant* at Subhash Chowk is reasonable, or try *Mehar's Hotel*.

Getting There

It's four hours and Rs 12 to 15 by bus from Pathankot to Dalhousie.

KULU VALLEY

The Kulu Valley, cut by the Beas River, starts at Mandi at an altitude of 760 metres and runs north through Kulu and Manali to the Rohtang Pass at 3915 metres. At first the valley is a steep and narrow gorge but further north it widens out and Kulu's famous apple orchards can be seen along both sides of the road.

KULU

Although it is the district headquarters, Kulu is not the main tourist centre in the valley. The town is centred around the grassy maidan where each October the colourful festival of the gods takes place. The figures of about 200 gods are brought down from their temples all around Kulu to pay homage to the figure of Raghunathji at his temple in Kulu. There are a number of interesting temples around Kulu which is also an excellent trekking base.

Places to Stay

The HPTDC *Tourist Bungalow* (tel 33) has doubles at Rs 75 and dorm beds at Rs 12. They also have *'Aluminum Huts'* with doubles at Rs 35. Behind the Tourist Office is the friendly *Bijleshwar Hotel* with doubles with attached bathrooms for Rs 40. These places are all beside the maidan and only a short stroll from the road.

Across the other side of the maidan, towards the river, are some other cheap hotels including the *Sa Ba Guest House* and the *Fancy Guest House*. On the other side of town, near the main bus stop, is the newish *Kulu Lodge* with prices from Rs 35.

Places to Eat

The *Tourist Department Cafe*, beside the tourist office and Tourist Bungalow, offers good snacks and light meals but painfully slow service. Or there's the *Monika Restaurant* and *Prem Dhaba*, just downhill from the main street at this end of town.

KULU TO MANALI

There are several interesting things to see along the 42 km from Kulu to Manali. The main road runs along the west bank of the Beas River while on the east bank there's a much rougher and more winding road. At Raison, eight km from Kulu, there's a good camping place where you can also rent huts for Rs 12 – check with the Kulu Tourist Office.

Katrain is at about the mid-point from Kulu to Manali and high above the river, on the east side, is Naggar with its delightful castle. Formerly occupied by the Rajah of Kulu the castle is now the *Castle Rest House* with five double rooms at Rs 45. It's quite absurdly romantic and therefore often booked out – enquire at the Tourist Office. There are some interesting temples and the Roerich Art Gallery close to the castle.

Getting to Naggar is difficult – you can either take the infrequent and slow east bank bus (two hours from Kulu to Naggar) or get off the west bank bus at Katrain and walk up six km to the castle. Or you can take the daily Rs 25 tour from Manali. Kulu to Manali costs Rs 6 by bus.

MANALI

At the northern end of the Kulu Valley this is very much a tourist scene in season. Manali is famous for its high quality dope and has an equally well known semi-permanent hippy population in the hills around it.

The Hadimba Devi Temple is a sombre, wooden temple in a forest clearing, a pleasant 2.5 km stroll from the Tourist Office. Manali has many Tibetan refugees and there's a colourful new Tibetan monastery in the village. Strolls around Manali will take you to the picturesque old Manali village or to Vashisht with its 'hippy' population and not-to-be-missed natural sulphur baths. They cost Rs 6 (plus Rs 2 per person) for a 20 minute soak in the small baths (Rs 10 plus Rs 3 in the de-luxe baths) and are the perfect remedy for the lengthy bus trip up to Manali.

Places to Stay

Manali prices are extremely variable. In the depths of winter a room might be available for only Rs 100 to 150 a month. Then climb to Rs 15 a day, Rs 40 a day, even Rs 60 a day at peak-season times. When costs get that high much of Manali's resident freak population heads for the hills where it's possible to rent a room or even a house for Rs 100 to 150 a month. Conditions will be pretty basic though.

The HPTDC has a variety of accommodation in Manali, starting with their picturesque and totally ivy-covered *Tourist Bungalow* where rooms cost Rs 80 for a double and there's a dormitory. The central *Janata Lodge* is Rs 40 a double. Beside the river the *Beas Hotel* has rooms from Rs 40 to 90 as well as dorm beds.

There are a great number of private hotels – so many that the only real answer is to wander around and look at a few. Some possibilities include the *Skylark*

Guest House (Rs 50 to 75 in the high season), the *Kathmandu Guest House* by the Tibetan gompa (Rs 40 to 60), the similarly priced and pleasant *Mount View Guest House* or the more expensive *John Banon Guest House*. Up at Vashisht there's quite a resident population – enquire in *Demroh's Restaurant* about accommodation.

Places to Eat

The *Monalisa Restaurant*, right beside the bus stand, is a little expensive, but they have excellent food and great music. Other popular places include the Chinese-Tibetan *Mount View Restaurant*, just down from the bus stop, or the *Adarsh Restaurant*. Following the road out of town you'll soon come to the spartan little *Moonlight Restaurant* – a popular travellers' centre with good bread and cakes.

Getting There

It takes about 14 hours by bus from Chandigarh at a fare of Rs 42. You take the same bus for Kulu, simply getting off as it passes through Kulu. There are also direct buses from Simla for Rs 40 or Dharamsala for the same price. Whichever way you come to Manali it's a long, uncomfortable ride by public bus. A taxi will do it in nine hours from Chandigarh but tends to be very expensive. Indian Airlines once again have flights to Kulu.

LAHAUL & SPITI

This trans-Himalayan region has only been open to visitors since 1977. Access to the region is over the Rohtang Pass, north of Manali, which is generally open June to September. The tourist office operates a daily tour up to the pass to see the snow and in season there are daily buses to Keylong, the major town in Lahaul.

There are a number of interesting monasteries and castles around Keylong. Although much of the region is off-limits there are also some interesting trekking possibilities and you can also trek from

Lahaul into Zanskar and Ladakh. Accommodation can be a bit of a problem in Keylong but there is a *PWD Rest House* and some small hotels.

Jammu & Kashmir

Kashmir is predominantly Muslim and a major stumbling block to amicable relations between India and Pakistan. The border drawn between the two countries in Kashmir is a hazy one and very different on Indian and Pakistani maps! Kashmir is best known for its romantic houseboats on Dal Lake at Srinagar but the state actually offers much more. There are interesting handicrafts, excellent trekking country and across the Himalaya is the remote and barren region of Ladakh. The Vale of Kashmir itself is so beautiful it's quite understandable that the Moghul Emperor Jehangir's death bed wish was for 'Kashmir, only Kashmir'.

JAMMU
The second largest town in the state, Jammu is the southern gateway to Kashmir, but for most travellers it's simply a transit point on the way north. People arrive in Jammu one evening and the next morning leave for Srinagar. If you stay longer there are some interesting temples and a good art gallery.

Places to Stay
The *Tawi View Hotel* (tel 47301) has doubles with bath for Rs 32 and is about the best of the real cheapies. Opposite the Tourist Reception Centre the *Tourist Home Hotel* is similarly priced and equipped.

On Vir Marg the *Hotel Kashmir* has bathless doubles for Rs 30. Other reasonable places include the *Hotel Aroma* in Gumat Bazaar and the *Hotel Raj*. On Gumat Chowk the *Hotel Broadway* has singles at Rs 42 to 50, doubles Rs 60 to 75.

At the railway station there's Jammu's second *Tourist Reception Centre* (tel 8803) with rooms from Rs 25 to 50 and a totally bare (and best avoided) dormitory. The station also has *Retiring Rooms* at Rs 45 a double, Rs 75 with air-con. Remember that the railway station is several km away across the Tawi River.

In the middle range the popular *Tourist Reception Centre* (tel 5421) is on Vir Marg and has over a hundred rooms. Doubles cost from Rs 50 to 60, plus there are some more expensive air-cooled rooms and a dormitory which shouldn't be considered. In contrast to the cool heights of Kashmir, Jammu is on the plains and gets pretty hot.

Places to Eat
The *Tourist Reception Centre* has a restaurant with the standard government tourist centre menu. The flashy *Cosmopolitan Hotel* across the road has an air-con restaurant with reasonably good food and cold beer. A few doors down the *Premier* has rather expensive Chinese and Kashmiri food. There's a collection of little kebab stalls between the two plus the usual station restaurant facilities at the bus and railway stations.

Getting There
There are frequent buses from Jammu to Amritsar (Rs 15) or Pathankot (Rs 8). Most people come up to Jammu and head straight on to Srinagar. By rail Jammu is nine to 13 hours from Delhi and fares are Rs 60 in 2nd, Rs 193 in 1st.

The buses to Srinagar all depart early in the morning and there are B class buses at Rs 27, A class for Rs 40, super de-luxe at Rs 65 and air-con at Rs 100. B class seats are two-and-three, A class two-and-two, super de-luxe two-and-two with individual seats and headrests. The trip up to Srinagar takes 10 to 12 hours with a lunch stop en route – there is a positive armada of buses heading north and coming south each day.

The upper class buses arrive and depart

at the Tourist Reception Centre in the town centre while the lower class buses go to the bus stand which is at the bottom of the hill below the centre. Coming or going from Srinagar you should book your bus seat as far ahead as possible. In season the seats are filled up far in advance. You can also fly Jammu-Srinagar or go by taxi at Rs 130 per person or Rs 520 for an entire taxi.

Getting Around
Note that Jammu Tawi station is several km away from the centre of Jammu. Tempos run from the station to the town centre or bus stand. There are also auto-rickshaws for use around town.

SRINAGAR
The capital city of Kashmir straddles the Jhelum River beside Dal Lake. It's a crowded, colourful city with a central Asian flavour rather different from the rest of India. The famous houseboats on Dal Lake came about because the Maharajah would not allow the British, who flocked up to Srinagar during the hot season, to buy land. The summer visitors adopted the uniquely British solution of houseboats. They're as popular today as ever – each one a little floating bit of England.

Information & Orientation
The main part of Srinagar is almost an island since an artificial channel cuts off a loop of the Jhelum River. Here you'll find Srinagar's Tourist Office beside the bus stand for Jammu buses and tour buses. The GPO is on the Bund, a popular walk along the bank of the Jhelum. Near here is the handicrafts centre. Dal Lake is about a km walk from the Tourist Reception Centre.

Things to See
Dal Lake The lake is an intricate maze of waterways, floating gardens, islands and reeds rather than an open expanse of water. A shikara trip around the lake, say Rs 5 to 20 an hour depending on the

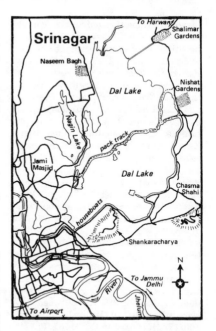

season, is the perfect way to ease into life on the lake. On the way you'll stop at the Moghul gardens and the islands on the lake.

Gardens The Moghul emperors loved Kashmir and built some of the finest examples of their formal gardens on its banks. The Shalimar Bagh at the far end of the lake was built by Jehangir while Nishat Bagh are the largest of the gardens. Chasma Shahi, the smallest of the gardens, are on the hillside above the lake.

Other Srinagar has some interesting mosques including the wooden Shah Hamdan Mosque which was originally built on the banks of the Jhelum in 1395. Infidels are not allowed inside. The stone Pather Masjid is almost directly across the river. The impressive wooden Jami Masjid is Srinagar's most important mosque but has been burnt down on a number of occasions.

Climb the Shankaracharya Hill for the fine view over Srinagar and the lake. Pari

Mahal, the ruins of an old Sufi college, are just above the Chasma Shahi – it's a beautiful place in its own right and also offers fine views over the lakes. Hari Parbat Fort dominates the valley from its hilltop position north of Srinagar. Beside the lake at the northern end is the shiny new Hazratbal Mosque. Srinagar also has a museum and a whole series of interesting bridges which span the Jhelum River. Zain-ul-Abidin's tomb is another interesting, though decrepit, historic building.

Places to Stay

Houseboats Although the Tourist Office will try to steer you into the houseboat they want to put you in the best way to find a houseboat is simply to go down to the ghats from where shikaras run out on to the lake and ask. Houseboats are categorised and official prices are set, both with and without all meals. A 5-star houseboat is Rs 220/325 for singles/doubles (Rs 150/225 without meals); A class is Rs 150/220 (Rs 90/140); B is Rs 100/170 (Rs 60/100); C is Rs 65/115 (Rs 30/40); D is Rs 45/60 (Rs 20/30).

The D class or donga boats are generally much smaller and you have the whole boat to yourself. Otherwise boats usually have three or four rooms, each with their own bathroom, plus a dining room, living room, verandah and sun deck upstairs. Generally you can get away with paying at least a category below the official price. If you're not going to eat all your meals aboard (you'll probably have at least lunch away) then you can negotiate a lower rate. Kashmir is Kashmir and you should pin down every imaginable detail – right down to how many eggs make a breakfast. Make sure hot water will be supplied and so on. There are so many houseboats that making specific recommendations is really redundant and in any case little things can easily turn a good houseboat bad or vice versa – a friendly shikara man or unfriendly fellow guests for example. There are also houseboats on Nagin Lake and along the Jhelum River as well as on Dal Lake.

Hotels Yes you can also stay on dry land although some of the better cheapies are on the lake. Try the *Green View Hotel* with doubles from Rs 40, the *Island Hotel* from Rs 25/30 or the *Hotel Leeward*, behind Nehru Park, for Rs 30/40. The *Latif Guest House* and the *Hotel Sundowna* are even cheaper but also more basic. Right next to the Sundowna the *Hotel Savoy* has rooms from Rs 25 through Rs 50. A little up market from these, and up the channel towards Dal Gate, is *Hotel Heaven Canal* with rooms from Rs 50 to 80.

On solid ground the friendly *Tibetan Guest House* is just off the Boulevard and has rooms for Rs 30/50. The guest house itself is on Gagribal Rd but check in first at the Lhasa Restaurant. *Zero Inn* by Zero Bridge is also reasonably quiet but a bit more expensive at Rs 50. In Raj Bagh *Hotel Greenacre* is a small hotel in a lovely garden with rooms from Rs 40 to 90.

There are plenty of others around including the *Tourist Reception Centre* at the J&K Tourist Office, where rooms are Rs 60 to 90. The Srinagar *Youth Hostel* (tel 75414) is across the river near the museum on the Wazir Bagh. Beds cost Rs 1, with bedding Rs 1.50. They also have rooms from Rs 8. There's a campsite just beyond the Nagin Lake causeway.

Places to Eat

The *Indian Coffee House* in the centre is good for a snack, a coffee and a chat. Across the road the *Hollywood Cafe* has much better food than its appearance would suggest – including some of the best french fries in India. Ice cream at *Dimples*, in the centre or by the Zero Bridge, is pretty good.

The *Lhasa Restaurant*, just off the Boulevard, is good for Chinese-Tibetan food – count on Rs 50 to 75 for a meal for two. *Ahdoo's*, on the Bund, is said to be very good for Kashmiri food but its reputation is not lived up to. To splash out try the *Oberoi Palace Hotel* or the *Broadway*, both of which have a very superior buffet dinner on some nights.

Getting There & Around

See Jammu for details on transport up to Srinagar. You can also fly direct from Delhi or Amritsar.

Around Dal Lake shikaras, those graceful long boats, will paddle you out to your houseboat for Rs 2 in a de-luxe covered shikara. Kids will do it for Rs 0.50 and in any case your houseboat cost includes free transport back to the landing ghat any time your houseboat shikara man is around.

Srinagar's taxi and auto-rickshaw wallahs are reluctant to use their meters. Count on Rs 10 to 15 for a taxi from the Tourist Reception Centre to the lake landings (Rs 5 to 10 by auto-rickshaw) or Rs 40 to the airport.

There are a wide variety of tours operated around Srinagar, details at the Tourist Reception Centre. Buses run to all the centres around the valley. Hire a bicycle from shops by the Boulevard (Rs 6 a day). There are pleasant and peaceful rides across the dykes that cross the lake.

PAHALGAM

On the Lidder River, 95 km from Srinagar, this is a beautiful hill station on the edge of the Kashmir Valley. It's a superb base for trekking trips including the short stroll to Aru or the longer walk to the Kolahoi Glacier.

Places to Stay

There are a number of hotels along the main street of Pahalgam but most travellers head across the river where the once popular *Windrush* may now have been renamed *Woodlands* but has certainly relocated up the hill. Rooms cost from Rs 10 to 30. A little further up the hill is the cheaper and more basic *Bente's Hotel*.

Before the Windrush, but also slightly uphill from the river, is the more expensive, but very popular, *Aksa Lodge* with rooms from Rs 50 to 100 with attached bathroom, Rs 30 and 35 without. *Brown Palace* is another lodge on the west side of the river

with dorm beds at Rs 10 and rooms all the way from Rs 40 to 110. During the summer season the tourist office operates a number of tent sites with set up and furnished tents. The *Dar Camp* has been particularly recommended.

Getting There

Local buses cost Rs 7.50 and take 2½ to four hours. J&K Road Transport tour buses cost Rs 18 one way. The KMDA tour buses take a long time since they make many stops en route. A taxi is about Rs 250 return.

GULMARG

The 'meadow of flowers' is 52 km from Srinagar and rather higher up – it gets distinctly chilly there. There are many fine walks around Gulmarg including a pleasant 11-km circular walk, a six-km climb to the ski runs at Khilanmarg or a further 13 km beyond there to the Alpather lake. In winter this is India's premier ski resort, which doesn't mean much but a number of travellers have reported having lots of fun skiing here!

Places to Stay

Hotel Kingsley (tel 55) is an older place with rooms at Rs 75/90, all with attached bathroom. There's also a cheap dorm. Near the golf club the *Snow View* has singles from Rs 30 to 70, doubles from Rs 50 to 100. *Tourists Hotel* (tel 53) is a remarkably baroque and weathered fantasy in wood but also rather dirty and grubby. Rooms are Rs 20 to 50. The *City View* and the *Mount View* are both around Rs 25.

Getting There

Ordinary buses are Rs 7.50 one-way, Rs 12 return. De-luxe tour buses are Rs 21 and Rs 39. You used to have to walk or ride a pony up the final seven-km stretch from Tangmarg, 500 metres lower down, but now the vehicle road runs all the way to Gulmarg.

SONAMARG

The third popular hill station around Kashmir is on the road to Ladakh just before you leave the Vale of Kashmir. The name means Meadow of Gold and Sonamarg has Tourist Huts, a Rest House and some small hotels. It's a popular trekking base.

LADAKH

Situated in the north-east of the state Ladakh has been dubbed 'Little Tibet' or the 'Moonland' for in some ways this region is a Tibet in miniature. On the far side of the Himalaya little rain ever falls so Ladakh is a barren, high altitude desert – just like on the Tibetan plateau. Furthermore the people are similar to the Tibetans in their culture and religion and there are also many Tibetan refugees there.

Ladakh was only opened to outside visitors in the mid-70s and regular airline flights into Ladakh only commenced in 1979. From Srinagar it's a winding 434 km drive to Leh, the capital of Ladakh. En route you enter the Ladakh region over the Zoji La, the last pass to be cleared of snow after the winter. The road into Ladakh is generally only open from June through September.

After the pass you reach Kargil, the mid-way point on the road and the usual overnight halting place. Kargil is the major town between Srinagar and Leh and the people there are mainly Muslims. From here on Buddhism is the predominant religion and there are interesting gompas (monasteries) at Mulbekh, Lamayuru, Rizong, Alchi and Lekir. Just beyond Mulbekh there is a huge Chamba figure, an image of a future Buddha, cut into the rock face beside the road.

LEH

The capital and main city of the Ladakh region, Leh was once an important halting place on the caravan route from China. It's a fascinating town to wander around, dominated by the brooding Leh Palace, looking for all the world like a mini-version of the Potala in Lhasa, Tibet. Leh also has a gompa perched high on the hilltop above the palace and another one, the Sankar gompa, a couple of km's walk up the valley.

Places to Stay

Leh has a wide variety of hotels and in the brief summer season many people also let out rooms in their homes. Prices soar in the peak season, plummet in the winter. Beware of bed bugs in some of the really cheap places. The *Palace View Kidar Hotel*, close to the polo ground, is a very popular rock bottom choice as is the *New Antelope Guest House* on the main street. Others include the *Old Ladakh Guest House* or the *Moonland Guest House*. The *Rainbow Guest House* has doubles from Rs 15 to 20.

The *Himalayan Hotel* has a garden, is friendly and costs Rs 35 four doubles. In the middle price category the *Khangri Hotel* has rooms from Rs 100 and is uncomfortably close to the diesel-powered electricity generator. With rooms from Rs 50, a pleasant garden and one of the best restaurants in town the *Dreamland* is very popular and very central. The new and clean *Kahyul Hotel* costs Rs 40/60. There are lots more.

Places to Eat

The *Dreamland Restaurant*, near the Tourist Office, Indian Airlines and the Dreamland Hotel, is Leh's best restaurant with lots of dishes around Rs 10. Tibetan food is, of course, the main choice. Next door the *Khangri Restaurant* is not quite so good and a little more expensive.

Across from the Dreamland the *Om Restaurant* is popular as is the *Tibetan Restaurant* with its highly entertaining kitchen. *Chopsticks* has an unlikely name but wonderful pies, cakes and late night snacks. Take care of your stomach in Leh, some of the cheaper places are very insanitary.

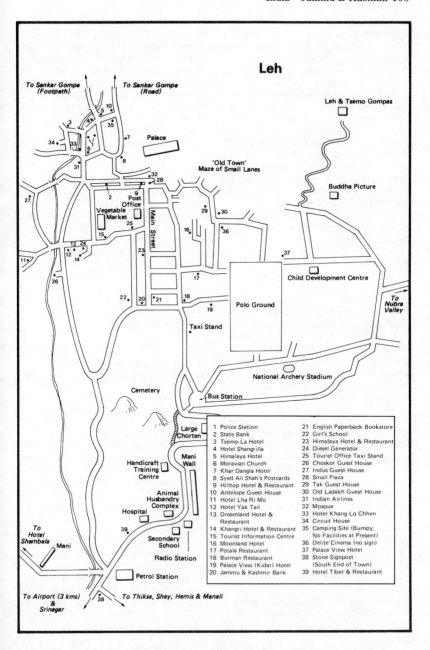

Leh

To Sankar Gompa (Footpath)
To Sankar Gompa (Road)
Leh & Tsemo Gompas
Palace
'Old Town' Maze of Small Lanes
Buddha Picture
Post Office
Vegetable Market
Main Street
Child Development Centre
To Nubra Valley
Polo Ground
Taxi Stand
National Archery Stadium
Cemetery
Bus Station
Large Chorten
Mani Wall
Handicraft Training Centre
Animal Husbandry Complex
Hospital
Mani
To Hotel Shambala
Secondary School
Radio Station
Petrol Station
To Airport (3 kms) & Srinagar
To Thikse, Shey, Hemis & Manali

1 Police Station
2 State Bank
3 Tsemo-La Hotel
4 Hotel Shangrilla
5 Himalaya Hotel
6 Moravian Church
7 Khar Dangla Hotel
8 Syed Ali Shah's Postcards
9 Hilltop Hotel & Restaurant
10 Antelope Guest House
11 Hotel Lha Ri Mo
12 Hotel Yak Tail
13 Dreamland Hotel & Restaurant
14 Khangri Hotel & Restaurant
15 Tourist Information Centre
16 Moonland Hotel
17 Potala Restaurant
18 Burman Restaurant
19 Palace View (Kidar) Hotel
20 Jammu & Kashmir Bank

21 English Paperback Bookstore
22 Girl's School
23 Himalaya Hotel & Restaurant
24 Diesel Generator
25 Tourist Office Taxi Stand
26 Choskor Guest House
27 Indus Guest House
28 Small Plaza
29 Tak Guest House
30 Old Ladakh Guest House
31 Indian Airlines
32 Mosque
33 Hotel Khang-Lq Chhen
34 Circuit House
35 Camping Site (Bumpy, No Facilities at Present)
36 Delite Cinema (no sign)
37 Palace View Hotel
38 Stone Signpost (South End of Town)
39 Hotel Tibet & Restaurant

Getting There & Around

The two-day bus trip from Srinagar costs Rs 58 in a B class bus, Rs 78 in an A class. Jeeps, which will take up to six people, cost around Rs 2000.

To fly, which takes about 20 minutes versus two days, costs Rs 269 but the flights are very unpredictable due to the changeable weather conditions. There are also flights Chandigarh-Leh for Rs 378. Getting to Leh is particularly difficult around the time the pass opens as many people are queued up, waiting for the road to be cleared, and the flights tend to be heavily booked at that time.

There's a bus service to and from the airport for the flights at a cost of Rs 2. Or a jeep costs Rs 25.

AROUND LEH

There are a whole series of interesting things to see around Leh. Buses run to most of them but it is sometimes difficult to get out and back in the same day. In that case you can usually arrange to stay overnight at a gompa but you'll need a sleeping bag and some supplies. All the gompas charge entry fees, usually about Rs 10. You can also hire jeeps from Leh, which is much more convenient if your time is limited and not too expensive between a group of people.

Spitok Gompa is about 10 km from Leh near the end of the Leh airport runway. Fine views over the Indus River from the gompa. Phyang, 16 km towards Srinagar, has 50 monks and an interesting village below the gompa. Choglamsar is the Tibetan refugee camp near the river. Shey was the old summer palace of the kings of Ladakh, it's now in ruins but has a huge seated Buddha image in the palace gompa. Tikse Gompa, 17 km from Leh, is visible from Shey. It has put its new found tourist wealth into extensive renovations. The gompa is very picturesquely sited on top of a hill.

One of the most important gompas in Ladakh, and also one of the largest, Hemis is 45 km out on the opposite side of the Indus. By public transport it's a long walk up to the gompa from the main road and you'll have to spend the night there. Although Hemis is not all that interesting in its own right it is the centre for the spectacular Hemis Festival in late June or early July each year. Stok Palace, where the widow of the last king of Ladakh lives, is back towards Leh but also on the far bank of the Indus.

ZANSKAR

Even more remote than Ladakh, the long narrow valley of Zanskar lies between Kashmir and Ladakh. While Kashmir is on one side of the Himalaya and Ladakh is on the other, Zanskar is right in the middle. Zanskar is basically a trekking region although a road is being built down to Padum, the capital of the region, from Kargil on the Srinagar-Leh road. There are a number of interesting short treks around Padum and also much longer and harder treks to Ladakh or right down to Himachal Pradesh.

Uttar Pradesh

India's largest state in terms of population, UP is also India larger than life in terms of things to see and in terms of India's problems. It's here that the crowds seem densest, the difficulties most insurmountable. UP offers amazing contrasts – from the man-made serenity of the Taj Mahal to the natural beauty of the Himalaya; the crowds and religious fervour of Varanasi to the Raj-era history of Lucknow.

MATHURA

On the Delhi-Agra road Mathura is the legendary birthplace of Lord Krishna so, not surprisingly, the Hare Krishnas have their Indian HQ near here. There are many places around Mathura connected with the Krishna legend. The town is one of the oldest settlements in India, the museum has 2500-year-old articles.

AGRA

The city of the Taj is 200 km south-east of Delhi. You can day-trip there although Agra and the Taj deserve much more time. The Taj alone takes at least two visits to appreciate how it changes from the clear light of day, through the soft sunset to the glow of moonlight. Dawn too if you're feeling energetic.

Information & Orientation

Sadar Bazaar is a centre for cheap hotels and restaurants. Here you will find the Tourist Office and the GPO. De-luxe buses for Delhi or Jaipur also operate from here. Agra is very spread out, particularly in the cantonment area south of the old city.

Things to See

Taj Mahal Somehow the Taj has difficulty meeting people's great expectations so spare the time to see it under a variety of lights. Look at the incredible close up detail of tiny flowers inlaid in the marble and study it from across the river. It grows on you. Commenced in 1630 by Shah Jahan, heartbroken by the loss of his wife, Mumtaz Mahal, it took 22 years to complete and used the finest craftsmen available anywhere in the known world. Shah Jahan and his beloved Mumtaz rest in tombs side by side but it is said that he intended to build a black replica of the Taj on the other side of the river as his own tomb. Instead he was imprisoned in the Agra fort by his penny-pinching son Aurangzeb – in an effort to stop his architectural extravagances? He died in 1665 in a room from which he could see the Taj. Admission to the Taj is Rs 2 except on Fridays when it is free – and also impossibly crowded. A full moon co-inciding with a Friday is a crush you would not believe.

Agra Fort The massive Agra Fort was commenced in 1565 by Akbar and additions made right through to Shah Jahan's time. At first principally a fortress the emphasis later shifted and the fort became more of a palace. Shah Jahan added the D Am or 'Hall of Public Audiences', the Diwan-i-Khas or 'Hall of Private Audiences' and the Moti Masjid or 'Pearl Mosque'.

Other Across the river and north of the fort stands the Itmad-ud-daulah, an interesting tomb due to the clear relation it shows to the later and much more refined Taj Mahal. Further along the riverbank is the China-ka-Rauza, an interesting Persian-influenced tomb now in considerable disrepair. Still further north is the Ram Bagh, the earliest example of a Moghul tomb. Near the fort is the Jami Masjid which is large but not as impressive as the Jami Masjid in Delhi. Akbar's Mausoleum, which stands 10 km north of Agra at Sikandra, is another interesting example of the tomb-in-a-garden style which the Moghuls developed and refined.

Places to Stay

Cheap hotels in Sadar include *Tourist Rest House* on Kachahari Rd, near the Tourist Office and GPO – it's pleasant and well kept and has rooms with bath from Rs 30 to 50 and there are dorm beds for Rs 7 – good value. *Hotel Jaggi*, with a popular restaurant, is similarly priced. It's on Taj Rd as is the slightly cheaper *Hotel Jai Hind*, reached by a narrow alley off the road.

Agra's *Tourist Bungalow* is rather inconveniently located in the Raja Mandi area. Doubles at Rs 25 and a dorm at Rs 5. The *Retiring Rooms* at Agra Fort station are good.

Following the death of Major Bakshi Sardar Singh, his son Colonel Bakshi now runs the private home accommodation at 38/83 Ajmer Rd (tel 76828) – Rs 75 for a double with bathroom. Reports on this place have been ecstatic lately. *Hotel Khanna*, situated between the Tourist Rest House and Colonel Bakshi's, is entirely new and has doubles at Rs 60. With your own tent you can camp at the *Highway Inn*, 1.5 km south of the Taj.

In the narrow winding streets immediately back from the Taj there are a number

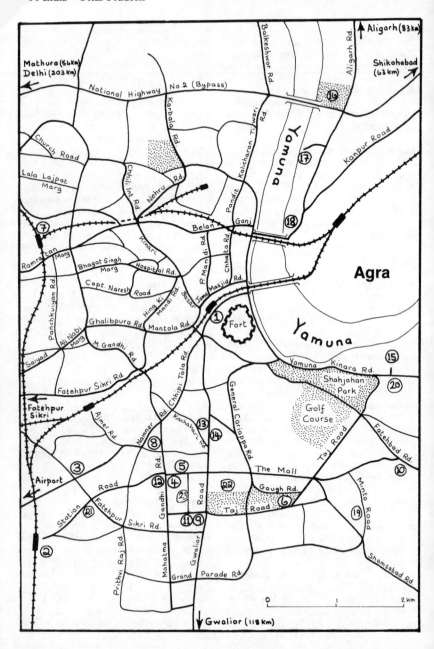

of very cheap places which are popular with travellers. They include the *Hotel Shah Jahan* and the rock bottom *Hotel Mumtaz Mahal*. There are other similarly cheap places around with prices down to Rs 10 or less for a single.

Places to Eat

The *Sarang Restaurant* on Gwalior Rd is the travellers' favourite – good food and they are opening a hotel. The *Jai Hind* and the *Jaggi* hotels on Taj Rd both have reasonably good food. The air-con *Kwality Restaurant* on Taj Rd is good although more expensive.

Two new vegetarian restaurants also provide good food in the Sadar area. *Khaja Pija* is very near the GPO and the Tourist Office, The *Candy Restaurant* is also vegetarian and in the Sadar area. Off Gopi Chand Shivhare Rd, which runs between The Mall and Taj Rd, is the Rajneesh run *Zorba the Buddha*.

In the rock bottom hotel area immediately south of the Taj you can get 'fantastic food' at *Mohamed's Good Earth Dhaba*, Taj Southgate. It's at the intersection just south of the Taj gate. Low prices and nice people.

Getting There & Around

The daily Taj Express takes three hours from Delhi and costs Rs 18 in 2nd, 72 in 1st. The Taj Express departs New Delhi Railway Station at 7 am daily and arrives in Agra three hours later. The return train departs Agra at 7 pm daily and arrives in Delhi at 10 pm – ideal for a day trip to Agra. Avoid the slow passenger trains at all costs and beware of pick-pockets and muggers at New Delhi station.

De-luxe buses cost Rs 28 and take five hours. Regular Delhi buses are Rs 14. Jaipur is five hours and Rs 38 away by bus – much faster than by train. Some tours depart from the station, connecting with the Taj Express. The main railway station is the Cantonment Station although there is also the Fort Station near the Agra Fort. Agra is famous for its predatory bicycle rickshaw wallahs. You can easily hire a rickshaw for a daily rate of Rs 10 – Agra is too spread out to walk around. Bicycles are also readily available for hire at Rs 5 per day.

FATEHPUR SIKRI

Akbar shifted the capital of the Moghul empire to Fatehpur Sikri, 40 km west of Agra, from 1570 but in 1586 suddenly abandoned it. Quite why is unclear but lack of a steady water supply has been one suggestion. Whatever the reason it has left a perfectly preserved example of a great Moghul city at the height of its splendour. Main buildings in the city include the huge Jami Masjid, said to be modelled on the mosque at Mecca and from the walls of which local daredevils leap into a pool below for the amusement of tourists.

The Palace of Jodh Bai, the small jewel-like Bhirbal Bhavan palace, the Karawan Serai, the amusing little Panch Mahal or 'Five Storey Palace', the Ankh Michauli or

1 Agra Fort Railway Station	13 Tourist Rest House
2 Agra Cantonment Railway Station	14 Sarang Restaurant
3 Idgah Bus Station	15 Taj Mahal
4 Tourist Office	16 Ram Bagh
5 GPO	17 Chini Ka Rauza
6 Hotel Clarks Shiraz & Indian Airlines	18 Itmad-ud-Daulah's Tomb
7 Tourist Bungalow	19 Highway Inn
8 Lauries Hotel	20 Rock Bottom Hotels
9 Jaggi Hotel	21 Grand Hotel
10 Mayur Tourist Complex	22 Telegraph Office
11 Kwality Restaurant	23 Zorba the Buddha
12 Agra Caterers	

'hide and seek building' and the Diwan-i-Khas and the Diwan-i-Am are other buildings. Akbar is said to have played chess using slave girls as the pieces on the gigantic gamesboard blocked out on the courtyard.

Getting There

Buses run regularly from the Idgah Bus Station in Agra, the hour ride costs Rs 4.60. Trains are very slow to Fatehpur Sikri.

KANPUR

This town, then known as Cawnpore, was the scene for some of the most tragic events of the 1857 Mutiny.

LUCKNOW

The capital of the Nawabs of Oudh, Lucknow was the scene for some of the most dramatic events of the Mutiny. The town is not visited in great numbers by tourists, it's also rather spread out making exploring it a little difficult.

Things to See

Tombs The mausoleums or imambaras of the Nawabs were somewhat jerry built and are rather decrepit today – they're over-rated. The final Nawab was a decadent if highly interesting individual but the British did little for their popularity by deposing him and packing him off to exile. This was a major cause of the Mutiny. The Great Imambara or Bara Imambara is noted for its immense halls, the arched roofs of which have no supporting pillars or columns. The Husainabad Imambara is also known as the 'small' or Chota Imambara.

Residency Built in 1800 the British Residency was besieged for 87 days during the Mutiny and when finally relieved was almost immediately besieged again for a further two months. The Residency today is maintained in exactly the same condition as when the final relief of Lucknow took place. The walls are still scarred by cannon shot and the cemetery at the ruined church has the graves of 2000 men, women and children. A model room shows the positions occupied by both sides during the siege.

Other The Martiniere School is a peculiar architectural conglomeration created by a French soldier of fortune, Kipling's fictional Kim went to school there. Lucknow has two museums and a children's museum. There's a zoo with a large collection of snakes.

Places to Stay

The *Tourist Bungalow* (tel 32257) is at 6 Sapru Marg in Hazratganj – good value at Rs 35 a double or Rs 100 with air-con. There's also a dorm. Get there on a 4 bus from the station. *Hotel Capoore* (tel 43958) is a popular place in the same area – from Rs 40. The *Avadh Lodge* (tel 43821) at 1 Ram Mohan Rai Marg is slightly more expensive – like the Tourist Bungalow you can camp there. There are *Railway Retiring Rooms* at both stations but the rooms at the North-East Railway station at Charbagh are cheaper, and they have a dorm.

Places to Eat

There's good food at the *Kwality*, you can find cheap South Indian vegetarian food in the same area. On Hewett Rd near the Plaza Hotel, the *Maduvan Restaurant* is excellent value.

Getting There & Around

Lucknow is four hours from Varanasi (by express), nine hours from Agra, only seven hours from Delhi on the Gomti Express. It's about 12 hours by bus from Lucknow to Sunauli, where you enter Nepal to Pokhara. Buses to Delhi, Agra, Allahabad, Varanasi, Kanpur, Gorakhpur (Rs 25, six hours) all operate from Kaiserbagh bus station.

The two imambaras and the Jami Masjid are in the chowk area. Buses will take you there from the station or a tempo from the GPO.

ALLAHABAD

At the confluence of the holy Ganges and Yamuna (Jumna) Rivers, the 'sangam' or meeting point has great sin-washing powers. A huge bathing festival takes place here mid-January to mid-February each year. Every 12th year the festival becomes the Kumbh Mela and the pilgrims number millions! At the confluence, Akbar's fort contains an Ashoka Pillar but the fort is off-limits to visitors. Anand Bhawan, the family home of the Nehrus, is preserved as a museum.

Places to Stay

The *Tourist Bungalow* (tel 53640) at 35 Mahatma Gandhi Marg has rooms from Rs 40 to Rs 60 if air-cooled, Rs 100 if air-con, and a dorm. It's about Rs 1 by rickshaw from the main railway station and is probably the best value in Allahabad. The *Central Hotel*, near the clock tower in the old part of town, has rooms at rock bottom prices. There are also *Railway Retiring Rooms*, with cheap rooms and a dorm.

Getting There

Allahabad is on the main Delhi-Calcutta railway route, 10 hours from Delhi, four from Varanasi. Allahabad is a good jumping off place to Khajuraho. You can catch a morning train to Satna from where buses go to Khajuraho. Note that the police often conduct drug searches on arriving travellers at the railway station.

VARANASI

The holiest city of the Hindus, Varanasi is India's number one pilgrimage centre. It was once known as Benares and every year attracts untold thousands of Hindus who come to cleanse their bodies and souls in the muddy waters of the Ganges, to walk the 80 km sacred circuit which marks its boundaries or, at the very least, be cremated on its burning ghats.

Varanasi is not a place you see, it is a place you sit back and experience. You soak it in by just wandering around and observing the frenetic activity. It is crowded, noisy, colourful, smelly, exciting and dirty – in fact it is India in one small bundle. I remember once seeing a bicycle jam in Varanasi – hundreds of pushbikes and their riders all jammed solid at an intersection. Shouting, ringing bells, but no movement; where else in the world?

Information & Orientation

Varanasi sprawls along the west bank of the Ganges. The ghats along the riverside are useful locations for orientation. The Government of India Tourist Office is at 15B The Mall in the new area of town. There's also a very good information office a the railway station. Several of the big hotels in the Cantonment area allow you to use their swimming pools for Rs 20 or 25.

Things To See

Temples The Muslim invaders pretty well razed all the temples back in the 12th century so the ones there today are comparatively recent. It is a very old city; Hsuan Tsang, the notable 7th century Chinese traveller, remarked on its many Hindu temples and monasteries. You are not allowed to enter most of the temples although you can generally get a surreptitious peek through a window. Vishwanath, the Golden Temple of Shiva, is Varanasi's most important temple, (Varanasi is very much Shiva's city.) It was built in 1776 near the river. The Durga or monkey temple is stained with red ochre since Durga is another name for Kali, Shiva's destructive wife. You can observe the action within from the top of the walls. Watch out for the monkeys who are avaricious little monsters and will grab anything that is loose and can be carried off. The Aurangzeb Mosque was built by that over-zealous Moghul on the site of a Hindu temple. One of its minarets toppled during a flood in 1948.

Down the River The holy Ganges is the focus of Varanasi and the time to see it is dawn. It is easy to fix up a boat for a group

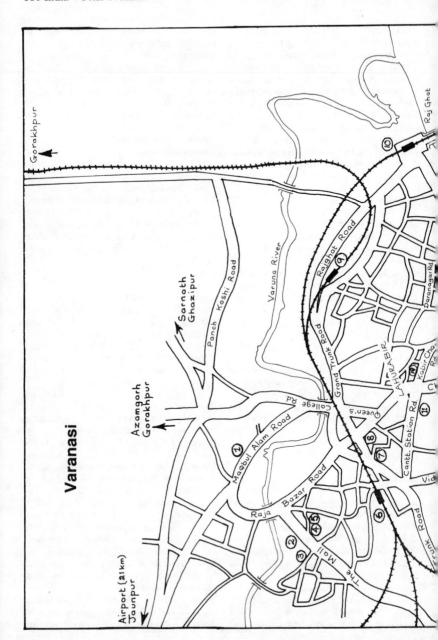

Varanasi

Gorakhpur

Sornath
Ghazipur

Azamgarh
Gorakhpur

Airport (21km)
Jaunpur

Panch Koshi Road

Varuna River

Raghat Road

Grand Trunk Road

Raj Ghat

Daranagar Rd

Kabir Chaura Rd

LAHURABIR

Queen's

Cantt. Station Rd

College Rd

Maqbul Alam Road

Bazar Road

Raja

The Mall

Trunk Road

Vid

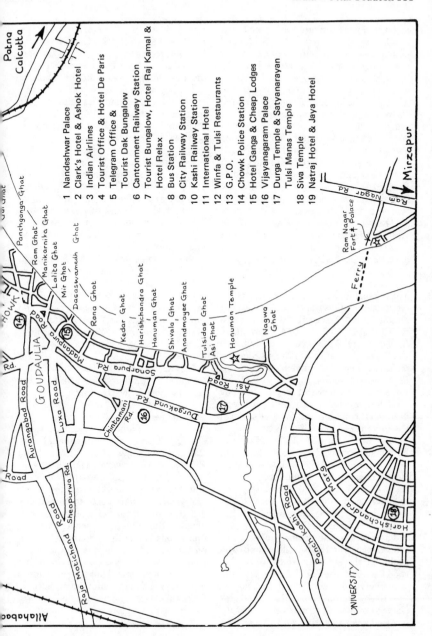

1 Nandeshwar Palace
2 Clark's Hotel & Ashok Hotel
3 Indian Airlines
4 Tourist Office & Hotel De Paris
5 Telegram Office &
   Tourist Dak Bungalow
6 Cantonment Railway Station
7 Tourist Bungalow, Hotel Raj Kamal &
   Hotel Relax
8 Bus Station
9 City Railway Station
10 Kashi Railway Station
11 International Hotel
12 Winfa & Tulsi Restaurants
13 G.P.O.
14 Chowk Police Station
15 Hotel Ganga & Cheap Lodges
16 Vijayanagaram Palace
17 Durga Temple & Satyanarayan
   Tulsi Manas Temple
18 Siva Temple
19 Natraj Hotel & Jaya Hotel

and drift down the river. Ask in your hotel. Leading down to the river are the 'ghats' or steps where men and women come for their holy immersion. As well as the bathing ghats there are burning ghats where bodies are cremated – if you cannot manage to die in Varanasi being cremated there will still do something for your reincarnation.

Other Varanasi is a centre for silk weaving and sitars. You will get plenty of opportunity to see and buy but don't believe that every sitar maker is a personal friend of Ravi Shankar! Varanasi is a centre for Hindu culture and for the study of Sanskrit. The Benares Hindu University also has a good collection of miniatures on view Monday to Saturday from 11 am to 4 pm. Across the river the Ramnagar Fort is open daily and also contains a museum.

Places to Stay

The popular *Tourist Bungalow* (tel 63186) is only five minutes walk from the station – doubles at Rs 30, a few Rs 20 singles and a Rs 10 dorm. There's also a *Tourist Dak Bungalow* (tel 64461) on The Mall with singles/doubles at Rs 45/75 and camping facilities. The Cantonment Station has *Railway Retiring Rooms*.

Two hotels which are recommended by travellers are the *Venus Hotel*, half-way between the station and the ghats, which has large clean rooms for Rs 20 and the 'really nice' *Garden View Hotel* on Vidyapeth Rd which has good food and doubles for Rs 25. At D56/10 Aurangabad *Hotel Krishna* (tel 63260) has rooms from Rs 10 to Rs 25 and has also been recommended. Just before the Tourist Bungalow the *Hotel Amar* (tel 64044) has clean, good rooms at Rs 25.

There are lots of cheaper hotels down towards the river, this area does tend to be cooler in the summer. *Hotel Ganges* is good value, situated on the left side of the street between Godaulia and the ghats on the river. Rooms cost Rs 25/40 for singles/doubles. *Central Hotel* (tel 62776) is a well known cheapie with rooms from

Rs 25, just OK. *Tandon House Lodge*, right on the river at Gai Ghat, has small but clean rooms at Rs 15. *Yogi Lodge*, near the Golden Temple, has been called one of the best budget hotels in the whole of India. It is a popular rock bottom place – rooms at Rs 20/25 and a Rs 7 dorm. Close to the river is the *Hotel KVM* (tel 62636) at Rs 20 and on Dasaswamadh Ghat Rd the popular Rs 20 *Sri Venkateshwar Lodge*.

Places to Eat

You can get good, reasonably priced food at the *Tourist Dak Bungalow* although it's wise to tip the waiters if you want a repeat performance. For health food, the *Aces Restaurant* in Godaulia is popular, it is right across from the KCM Cinema on Madanpura Rd. In Bhelupura near the Lalita Cinema, the *Sindhi Restaurant* does excellent vegetarian food, at very reasonable prices.

Popular Chinese restaurants include the *Winfa Restaurant* in Lahurabir, behind the cinema, and the *Chinese Mandarin Restaurant* near the Tourist Bungalow. Lahurabir also has a good, if a little pricey, *Kwality*.

Varanasi is renowned for its excellent sweets – try *Madhur Jalpan Grih*, on the cinema side of the street in Godaulia.

Getting There

You can get to Varanasi by air, rail or bus although it is actually off the main Delhi-Calcutta rail line. The Upper India Express does, however, run directly to Varanasi from Delhi, departing at 8 pm and arriving at 1 pm the next day.

If you're heading north to Nepal, bus will probably be faster than rail – five hours to Gorakhpur from where there's a tourist bus taking three hours to Sunauli on the border. By rail the line is metre gauge and several changes are required so it takes quite a time. There are also direct buses *very* early in the morning which cost Rs 20 to Sunauli, or more expensive buses which leave at a more civilised hour.

If you're travelling from Varanasi to

Kashmir or Himachal Pradesh you can avoid going through Delhi by taking the three times weekly overnight Himgiri Express. If you want to get to the Himachal Pradesh hill stations it also stops at Chakki Bank, the little known alternative station for Pathankot, a couple of hours before Jammu Tawi. From there it's a Rs 4 rickshaw ride to the main Pathankot train and bus stations.

Getting Around

Godaulia is the main mid-town bus stop. Bicycle rickshaws are cheap in Varanasi but they're very prone to refuse to take you to hotels where they can't rake off a commission. You can hire bikes to get around on. Varanasi tours are good value, Rs 10 each for the morning tour (the ghats at dawn, temples, university) and for the afternoon tour (Ramnagar Fort and Sarnath).

SARNATH

It was here, only 10 km from Varanasi, that the Buddha, having attained enlightenment at Bodhgaya, came to preach his message of the middle way. Later Ashoka erected great stupas here but the decline of Buddhism also spelt the end for Sarnath. Not until excavations were commenced by the British in 1836 was the site's grandeur realised. There are the ruins of a number of stupas and monasteries and an Ashoka pillar. Sarnath also has an excellent archaeological museum.

There's a *Tourist Bungalow* with rooms at Rs 25 or a dorm at Rs 5. Buses from Varanasi cost Rs 1.50.

DEHRA DUN

This northern Uttar Pradesh hill station is a gateway to the Garwhal Himal. There are some temples around the town but it is not of great interest.

Places to Stay

Try the *Hotel Meedo* or the *Hotel Prince*, both near the railway station and with

rooms from Rs 30. The *Hotel Relax* opposite the hospital is slightly better with rooms from Rs 45.

MUSSOORIE

This popular hill station is just 22 km north of Dehra Dun. The *Mullingar Hotel*, at the top of Landour Bazaar, is cheap and good value. The *Apsara Hotel* in Kulri Bazaar has rooms from Rs 30, and the *Snow View Hotel* is more expensive with rooms from Rs 40 (single).

HARDWAR

The holy Ganges finishes its steep descent from the mountains and commences its long, stately trip across the plains at Hardwar. Therefore Hardwar is a religious centre of great importance although if you want to study Hinduism nearby Rishikesh is a quieter and more pleasant place to do it. Hardwar has a number of interesting temples and bathing ghats and it's not as full of 'no entry' signs as Varanasi, further down the Ganges.

Places to Stay & Eat

The *Tourist Bungalow* is Rs 25/55, Rs 10 in the dorm but it's a little inconveniently situated across the river from the main part of town. The *Hotel Gurudev* on Station Rd near the Tourist Office is typical of Hardwar's cheaper hotels, it also has a good restaurant. There are also *Railway Retiring Rooms*. The *Chatewala* near the Tourist Office does good value thalis.

RISHIKESH

Only 24 km from Hardwar and barely 63 metres higher in altitude, Rishikesh is still a rather more peaceful place. This is where the Beatles came to meditate with the Maharishi Mahesh Yogi and Rishikesh is also the jumping off point for a number of popular treks into the Garwhal Himal.

Places to Stay

The *Tourist Bungalow* is Rs 30/35 for singles/doubles, Rs 5 for dorm beds. With its pleasant garden is the best place in town. It's three km from the bus and railway stations. Next to the station is the new *Hotel Indralok* with rooms from Rs 35; the *Hotel Menka* is also nearby or there's the *Janta Tourist Lodge* on Dehra Dun Rd.

TREKKING IN THE GARWHAL HIMAL

May-June and September-October are the best trekking months although some places are at their best during the July-August rainy period. Information on trekking is available in Rishikesh. Popular treks include Kedarnath, Gangotri and Gaumukh, the Nanda Devi Sanctuary, Yamunotri and Dodital, the Kuari Pass, the Khatling Glacier, Hemkund and the Valley of Flowers, Badrinath, the Roopkund Lake and the Pindari Glacier.

There are many state government operated *Tourist Bungalows* along the routes to simplify the question of shelter.

OTHER PLACES IN UP

Aligarh, Rampur and Bareilly were important towns during the rule of the Afghan tribe known as the Rohillas. At Saheth-Maheth the Buddha performed a miracle. Faizabad has a fine mausoleum of the Bahu Begam. Ayodya, only six km away, is the legendary home town of Ram Chandra, a hero of the Ramayana. Jaunpur has a series of architecturally unique mosques constructed with components from older Hindu, Buddhist and Jain structures. Meerut, only 67 km north-east of Delhi, is the place where the 1857 Mutiny broke out.

Bihar

Although Bihar has a major city on the site of an ancient Ashokan capital and also has the site of Buddha's enlightenment the state today is a backward and depressed area where the inhabitants scratch a bare living from agriculture.

PATNA

Sprawling along the banks of the Ganges, Patna was once Pataliputra, the capital of a huge Indian empire. Interesting places here include the Golghar, a huge beehive-shaped granary built in 1786 to avoid future repetitions of the great famine of 1770. It has scarcely been used since but does provide good views from the top.

There's an excellent museum and at Kumrahar you can see the excavations of ancient Pataliputra, although they're unlikely to be of interest unless you're a keen amateur archaeologist. The Har Mandir is a Sikh temple dedicated to Govind Singh, the 10th and last Sikh guru who was born here in 1660.

Many travellers pause at Patna on their way to or from Nepal. Wherever you're travelling in this northern region take care of your possessions on the trains – the number of thefts are astronomical.

Places to Stay

There are a number of cheap hotels around the railway station such as the *Hotel Rajasthan* (tel 25102) near the Nepal Airlines office. Or there's the *Hotel Rajdhani* between the station and Gandhi Maidan or the *Hotel Palace* – all with rooms from around Rs 30 and up.

Hotel Rajkumar on Exhibition Rd is an entirely new building and singles are just Rs 22 – good value. On a real rock bottom budget try the *Hotel Park* or the *Hotel Grand*.

Places to Eat

You can get cheap snacks at the *Udipi Coffee House* or expensive but good quality food at the *Ashok Restaurant* near the railway station. *Hotel Rajasthan* has a good restaurant.

Getting There & Around

There are a number of trains between Delhi and Patna each day. By land the route to Nepal is now much simplified since the Patna bridge was completed. Buses to Raxaul on the Nepal border cost

Rs 25 and the trip now takes only three or four hours although it's wise to buy your ticket a few hours ahead to ensure a seat. From Raxaul you cross the border to Birganj and next morning take the bus to Kathmandu. The main bus station for express buses to the Nepalese border is located near the Patna Junction Station. It is only a few hundred metres west of the station, opposite the GPO and Hardinge park.

Continuing to Calcutta you can take a train to Dhanbad if the Patna-Calcutta train is full and change to a Calcutta train there. You can also catch trains for Bhubaneswar in Orissa from here.

GAYA

Situated 80 km south of Patna, Gaya is an important Hindu pilgrimage centre. The Vishnupad Temple, with a footprint of Vishnu, is on the riverbank but non-Hindus are not allowed inside. There are other temples and 20 km north the Barabar caves.

En route to Gaya from Patna is Nalanda, once a great Buddhist centre. There is an archaeological museum and you can reach Nalanda by bus from Patna or Gaya. The first Buddhist council was held at Rajgir after the Buddha attained enlightenment, but little remains of the ruins today.

Places to Stay There are *Railway Retiring Rooms* at Gaya station and a few other spartan places around the station. The new *Ajatsatru Hotel* is on Station Rd just across the street from the station. It has singles from Rs 25 and is pretty good.

Food is also good at the Ajatsatru or at the *Station View Hotel & Restaurant* you can get very good meals very cheaply.

BODHGAYA

In the northern area of India there are four important places associated with the Buddha – Lumbini (in Nepal) where he was born, Sarnath (near Varanasi) where he first preached his message, Kushinagar (near Gorakhpur) where he died and Bodhgaya where he attained enlightenment.

The sacred Bo tree at Bodhgaya is said to be a direct descendant of the original tree under which the Buddha sat. Although that tree has died a sapling from it was transplanted two thousand years ago to Anuradhapura in Sri Lanka and in turn another sapling was transplanted back here. The Mahabodhi Temple is said to trace its ancestry back to the original temple built here by Ashoka. There are a number of monasteries from various Buddhist countries at Bodhgaya but unless you are planning a longer study-stay a day is long enough for Bodhgaya.

Places to Stay & Eat

The *Tourist Bungalow* is Rs 30 for doubles or Rs 10 for a dorm bed. There is also a *Youth Hostel*. Students can stay in the various monasteries, donations are expected. Unfortunately some western visitors have abused the monasteries by smoking there or in other ways breaking the rules. Simple vegetarian food is available at the *Kalyan Hotel* near the Mahabodhi Temple.

Calcutta

It is Calcutta which freaks out most visitors to India. Can anybody survive so much squalor and overcrowding? Is it possible for any city to rival it in sheer ugliness? In fact there's probably more culture shock between Calcutta and Bangkok than from there back to the west! Yet somehow Calcutta hangs together and beneath its crowded, noisy, dirty surface Calcutta is the intellectual centre of India and a volatile political arena. The Bengalis have a reputation to uphold in both areas. Furthermore Calcutta has some fascinating places to visit and some scenes of rare beauty.

For many years Calcutta was the British

capital but they were probably relieved to move to the calmer waters of New Delhi earlier this century. Today Calcutta has six million people (the second largest city in Asia), endless nightmare slums, a declining port and many monuments and buildings from the Raj era. During the Bangladesh war Calcutta was crowded with refugees and floods and famines often send people pouring into the city from the surrounding country. West Bengal's Marxist government is said to have reduced this post-disaster flow by concentrating on improving rural living conditions.

Information & Orientation

Calcutta sprawls across the Hooghly River. If you arrive from anywhere west of Calcutta by rail you'll come into the Howrah Station and have to cross the Howrah Bridge to Calcutta proper. The two important parts of Calcutta for the visitor are BBD Bag (Dalhousie Square) and Chowringhee. The GPO and the West Bengal Tourist Office both stand on the square and Amex is nearby.

Chowringhee is the area for cheap and middle range hotels and you'll also find many restaurants, airline offices and the superb Indian Museum here. The Government of India Tourist Office is on Shakespeare Sarani at the south of Chowringhee. As in many Indian cities getting around can be a little confused by the habit of changing names (the American Consulate found itself on Ho Chi Minh Sarani in the middle of the Vietnam War) without changing the street signs. Many of the 'new' names are very little used in reality – Chowringhee is still Chowringhee, not Jawaharlal Nehru Rd for example.

Hogg Market, near Sudder St, is not only an excellent place to find all sorts of things to buy it's also a good place for selling anything from colour film, watches, Walkmans and other technological wonders to the cigarettes and the bottle of duty free whisky you brought in with you.

Things to See

Indian Museum Built in 1875 the museum is one of the best in Asia. Its varied collection includes superb archaeological pieces from all over the sub-continent including the Gandhara region of Pakistan. There are all sorts of oddities including a whole roomful of meteorites! Open 10 am to 5 pm from Tuesdays to Sundays, half an hour earlier in winter, admission is Rs 0.50; not to be missed.

Maidan & Fort William After the 'Black Hole of Calcutta' events of 1756 the British decided there would be no repetition and built the imposing fort and surrounded it by a huge open expanse to ensure a clear line of fire. Naturally there has never been a shot fired in anger but the open fields of the Maidan are Calcutta's 'lungs'. Today the fort is used by the army and entry is not normally permitted.

The Ochterlony Monument, officially dubbed the Shahid Minar, was built in 1828 and stands at one end of the Maidan – it's a useful landmark. The Eden Gardens in the north-west corner of the Maidan has a small Burmese pagoda brought here from Prome in Burma in 1856. Across from the gardens on the banks of the Hooghly it's easy to hire a boat for a trip out on the river.

Chowringhee St This is the main street of Calcutta, running alongside the Maidan. Here you'll find shops, stalls, beggars, and cows, not to mention a faded air of the Raj.

Victoria Memorial Fronted by a suitably 'not amused' statue of Queen Vic this ornate marble palace was completed in 1921 and serves as a very good memorial to the days of the Raj. It's packed with peculiar odds and ends from those glorious days! Open 10 am to 5 pm from Tuesdays to Saturdays, entry is Rs 0.50.

Dalhousie Square The paperwork centre of Calcutta is dominated by the 'Writers' Building' which once housed the clerks of the East India Company and is now filled with the paper pushers of the state government. It was built in 1780. The equally massive GPO dominates the west side of the square and nearby there used to be a small plaque marking the position of the 'Black Hole of Calcutta'; it has been removed. In 1756 the original Fort William stood here. When it was captured by the Nawab of Murshidabad the 146 British prisoners were crammed into one small airless room. The next day only 23 survivors stumbled out.

Howrah Bridge The starkly ugly Howrah Bridge crosses the Hooghly River to the squalid Howrah Station and the monstrous Howrah slums. If you visit them it is wise to be careful where you point your camera. If you want to see this side of India, and it is just as valid as the Raj monuments and the Indian exotica, you can go along on one of the Salvation Army's daily rounds.

Other The Botanical Gardens are across the Hooghly, there is a huge Banyan tree here which has a circumference of 400 metres! Calcutta takes its name from the Kalighat Temple in the south of the city. The Sitambara Jain Temple in the north of the city is another of those religious Disneylands – a delightful exercise in architectural bad taste. St John's Church, built in 1784 near Dalhousie Square, has a monument to Job Charnock in the graveyard. Credited with founding Calcutta, he married a Brahmin widow who was about to leap on her husband's funeral pyre. Charnock died in 1792.

The Nakhoda Mosque is the largest mosque in the city. Belur Math, north of the city on the west bank of the river, is the headquarters of the Ramakrishna Mission. Near the Victoria Memorial you'll find St Paul's Cathedral and the Birla Planetarium, one of the largest in the world and well worth the Rs 3.50 admission. South of the Maidan, Calcutta's zoo has a pleasant garden setting and is famous for its two white tigers.

Places to Stay

Calcutta's cheap accommodation centre is Sudder St, running off Chowringhee right beside the Indian Museum. Every-

body knows it – if you arrive in India at Calcutta the airport bus will drop you off at the top of Sudder St. At 2 Sudder St the *Salvation Army Red Shield Guest House* (tel 242895) was a Calcutta favourite but now only has dorms and no longer does meals. Dorm beds are Rs 8.40 to 9.40 depending on whether you are in a four-bed dorm or a nine-bed dorm. The Sally Army is basic, but clean and well kept, although the water supply is a bit erratic.

Down Sudder St a bit you'll find Stuart Lane off to the right and here the *Modern Lodge* (tel 244960) and the *Hotel Paragon* are two long running cheapies with dorm beds around Rs 10-12, singles/doubles at Rs 15/25. The Modern Lodge has more expensive rooms which include breakfast. The Paragon has doubles with bath at Rs 40. Some of Sudder St's other real cheapies are, according to one traveller, to be avoided 'like the plague, you stand a good chance of getting it'.

Up a notch, in price at least, the *Astoria Hotel* at 6/2/3 Sudder St (tel 241359) has singles/doubles at Rs 70/85 including 'bed tea'. There's a selection of Ys in Calcutta including the *YMCA* (tel 233504) at 25 Chowringhee – a big gloomy place which is a good place to stay and takes men only, rooms from Rs 90 single. All the rooms have attached bath and the price includes breakfast. Prices are reduced by Rs 10 for the second night onwards. They have full size snooker and billiard tables in the lounge. A second, similarly priced *YMCA* (tel 240260) is at 42 Surendra Nath Banerjee Rd.

The *YWCA* (tel 240260) at 1 Middleton Row takes women only. You can share a room for Rs 30 or a double costs Rs 50. Meals are Rs 10 extra, there's a good restaurant next door. Calcutta's *Youth Hostel* (tel 672869) is across the river at 10 J B Ananda Dutta Lane, Howrah. Take a 52 or 58 bus from Howrah Station to Shamasri Cinema or a 63 to Khirertala for this homely little hostel.

If you're in transit by air there are *Airport Rest Rooms* (tel 572611) at Calcutta

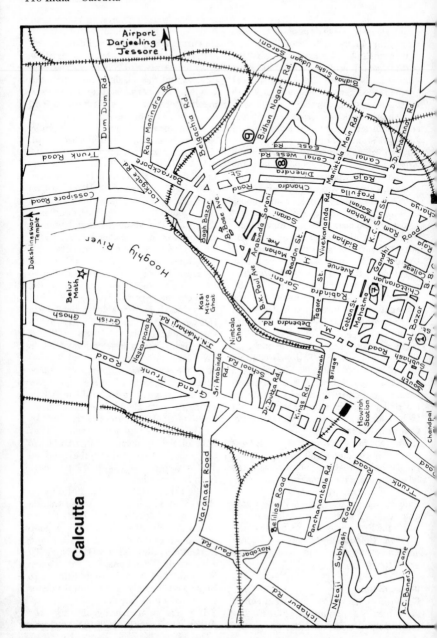

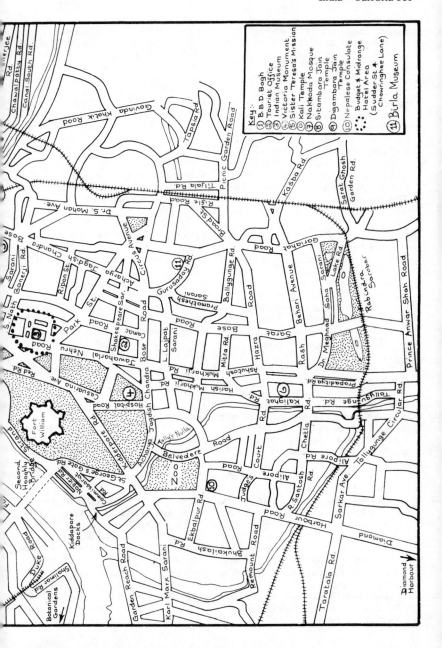

Key:
1. B.B.D. Bagh
2. Tourist Office
3. Indian Museum
4. Victoria Monument
5. Sister Teresa's Mission
6. Kali Temple
7. Nakhoda Mosque
8. Sitambara Jain Temple
9. Digambara Jain Temple
10. Nepalese Consulate
    Budget & Midrange Hotel Area (Sudder St & Chowringhee Lane)
11. Birla Museum

airport. Singles are Rs 50, doubles Rs 75 and there is a reservations desk at the terminal. Howrah Station has *Railway Retiring Rooms* at Rs 15/30 for singles/ doubles or Rs 10 for the dorm. Sealdah Station is much the same price, but has air-con doubles for Rs 50.

If you were going to spend up on a hotel in only one place in all of India the *Fairlawn Hotel* (tel 244460) at 13A Sudder St would be the place to do it. It costs Rs 230/330 for an air-con rooms with all meals, or Rs 30 less non air-con. Here the Raj has not yet officially ended. Things are done here with such style it makes everything in India seem worthwhile!

Places to Eat

Amber at 11 Waterloo St is one of Calcutta's best restaurants for Indian or western food. At 17 Park St there's a good *Kwality* and you'll find quite a few other restaurants and snack bars in this area. Food at the *Fairlawn Hotel* on Sudder St is as much an experience as staying there – outsiders can arrange to eat there.

For cheap food around Sudder St the Sikh-run *Khalsa Restaurant*, across from the Salvation Army Hostel, is a long-standing favourite. The *Taj Continental* is very good and cheap, opposite the entrance to Stuart Lane. The *Blue Sky*, half way down Sudder St on the same side as the Salvation Army, has excellent porridge, sandwiches and fruit juices, not to mention the 'finest curd in India'.

On Free School St the *Moghul Durbar* is good with speedy service. *Cafe 48* is also not bad while *Supersnax* at 55A, at the corner of Ripon St, has had some recent recommendations. *Kathleens' Restaurant & Bakery* at 12 Free School St (left from Sudder St) has very good Indian and western food from about Rs 50 for two and fantastic baked items in the confectionery level downstairs.

There's good Chinese food from *Embassy Chinese Restaurant* across from the large cathedral near the Victoria Memorial – in fact one reader said it was the best in India! At 21 Park St there is a good *Health Food Centre* and Lindsay St, just off Chowringhee, has the *Hindustan Restaurant* (upstairs) which does excellent south Indian vegetarian food, although a little more expensive. The New Market, also on Lindsay St, has some superb cake shops near the middle including a third generation Jewish bakery *Nahum*.

Getting There

Calcutta is connected by air with all major centres in India and is also the popular departure or arrival point for Burma or Thailand.

There are two main railway stations in Calcutta – Howrah for all points west, Sealdah on the other side of the river for Darjeeling and the north-east region. Beware of pickpockets at Howrah. There are two railway booking centres – Eastern Railways at 6 Fairlie Place (1st class on Strand Rd), South-Eastern at Esplanade Mansions. Trains to Delhi take from 17 hours and start at Rs 80 in 2nd class. To Varanasi they take from 12 hours and costs Rs 47 in 2nd class.

Buses from Calcutta are not as good as trains except for a few locations in West Bengal.

Getting Around

Calcutta is the last holdout of the old man-powered rickshaws – the rickshaw wallahs would not accept the new fangled bicycle rickshaws when they were introduced in the rest of India. After all, who could afford a bicycle?

Dum Dum airport is so named because the explosive 'dum dum' bullet, banned after the Boer War, was invented here. The airport bus service costs Rs 10 but between four people a taxi is no more expensive.

Buses are very crowded, take a 5 or 6 between Howrah Station and Sudder St, ask for the Indian Museum. An 11A then a 30B will get you to the airport – if you survive the trip. There is also a secondary minibus service which is rather faster and a bit more expensive. Beware of pickpockets on any Calcutta transport. One day Calcutta is supposed to have an underground railway system. The first little bit of it has opened but the rest is just a lot of big, muddy holes in the ground.

West Bengal

The state of West Bengal has Calcutta as its capital but apart from that there's not a lot of attraction in the state – except for one place at the other end of the state and the other end of reality from Calcutta. Darjeeling is opposite in every way to Calcutta – high in the mountains, easy going, serene and peaceful.

NORTH OF CALCUTTA

Hooghly, 41 km north of Calcutta, was an important trading port long before Calcutta rose to prominence. The Portuguese set up a factory here in 1537. Only a couple of km away is Chandernagore where the French also traded. Murshidabad was where the 'Black Hole' Nawab ruled from, before his defeat at nearby Plassey in 1757. Shantiniketan is where India's great poet, nationalist and Nobel prize winner, Rabindranath Tagore lived.

DARJEELING

Surrounded by tea plantations, Darjeeling became a popular British hill station in the mid-1800s. Nestled in the Himalaya, 650 km north of Calcutta and 2000 metres higher up, Darjeeling is a crisp, cool contrast to the squalor of the capital. April to mid-June and September to November are the best seasons to visit Darjeeling. The town takes its name from 'Dorje Ling' – place of thunderbolts in Tibetan.

Getting to Darjeeling is half the fun – from Calcutta you travel north to Siliguri Junction (or head east from Patna) or to New Jalpaiguri where you change to the Darjeeling-Himalayan Railway's 'toy train'.

It is just that, a tiny locomotive pulling just two or three tiny carriages along a line of narrow two foot gauge. It takes six hours to cover the 80 odd km to Darjeeling but who is in a hurry? There is plenty to amuse you on the way. Meals are available on the train. The line was laid between 1879 and 1881.

Darjeeling sprawls in terraces up a hill, it is neat, clean and totally charming and the views are amongst the best on earth. Between May and October the monsoon mists shroud the mountains but after that mighty Kanchenjunga leaps into view at what looks like a stone's throw away and on a clear day you can see Everest. It is worth rising at some un-godly pre-dawn hour to make the 10 km trip to Tiger Hill to see the Himalayan sunrise. Darjeeling is also great for treks or you may care to travel 50 km east to see Kalimpong, once an important market for goods brought down from Tibet.

Darjeeling now makes a very convenient stopping point on the way to Kathmandu since the completion of the road through the southern part of Nepal, the 'terai'. Rather than travel north-west from Calcutta directly to Raxaul and then to Kathmandu you can now go first to Darjeeling then more or less due west until you intercept the Raxaul/Birganj to Kathmandu road. See Nepal for details.

Places to Stay

Hotel Kadambari, below the railway station, is friendly and has rooms with attached bathrooms from Rs 35/45. Next door the *Hotel Nirvana* is similar. *Timber Lodge* at the back of Laden La Rd (take the stone steps on the left of the restaurants opposite the top end of the GPO then first turning on the right) is very popular with shoestring travellers but also rather run down. No hot water, singles/doubles at Rs 7/14. Similar standards at the *Shamrock Hotel* 100 metres further along the dirt road.

The *Youth Hostel* (tel 2290) above Dr Zakir Hussain Rd is popular with trekkers and has good views across the mountains. A book for trekkers' comments is kept here, good reading if you're planning on trekking. There are rooms for less than Rs 20 and a dorm for Rs 5 (members) and Rs 8 (others). Couples can't get a room together because the manager doesn't want to ask people if they are married! The *Tourist Lodge* at Tiger Hill, near Ghoom, is the place to go for the Himalayan sunrise. Rooms from Rs 40 or there is a dorm. It's best to book in advance either by ringing the lodge directly (tel 2813) or through the Darjeeling Tourist Office.

More expensive places include the *Ambassador Hotel* (tel 2781) at 1B Chowrasta at Rs 35 to 50 a double or the *Kundu Hotel* (tel 2867) at 2A Rockville Rd at Rs 40 to 55. The *Hotel Bellevue* may be more expensive again but a number of travellers have written to say how terrific it is. Darjeeling has many, many other hotels in all price categories.

Places to Eat

Laden La Rd, Nehru Rd and Cart Rd are the places to look for cheap restaurants which are mainly Tibetan. The better ones include the *Himalaya Restaurant* on Laden La Rd. Near the Himalaya is the *Washington Restaurant* where you can get steak, onion and chips for Rs 6.

In Chowrasta the *Chowrasta Restaurant* serves excellent south Indian vegetarian food out in the open. The *Solti Restaurant* on Laden La Rd is another popular Tibetan, Chinese and 'European' specialist. Near the junction of Laden La Rd and Nehru Rd is *Gleneary's Restaurant* – a surprisingly reasonably priced cafe with more than a whiff of the Raj about it. The waiters all wear white uniforms with cummerbunds and frilly turbans! The *Snow Lion Restaurant* in the Bellevue Hotel is very good.

Darjeeling Permits

Unless you fly directly out and back from Calcutta and spend no more than 15 days in Darjeeling you must have a permit to visit Darjeeling. The permit is free, does not require photographs, takes only 24 hours to issue (within India) and allows a seven-day initial stay. This is easily extended in Darjeeling while you wait. Further permission is required to trek from Darjeeling but this too can be easily obtained in Darjeeling. Permits for Darjeeling are available from Indian High Commissions, Embassies and Consulates abroad, from the Ministry of Home Affairs in New Delhi, from the Home Political Department in Writers' Building in Calcutta or from any Foreigners' Registration Office in major cities in India.

A permit for Darjeeling does not automatically entitle you to visit Kalimpong. To go there you must obtain a separate endorsement on your Darjeeling permit. Ask for it at the same time you apply for the Darjeeling permit or get one from the Foreigners Registration Office in Darjeeling. A three-day visit is normally allowed. If you want longer, get authorisation before you go.

Getting There

Bagdogra, the nearest airport for Darjeeling, is 90 km away. There are daily flights from Calcutta. The daily Darjeeling Mail runs to New Jalpaiguri from where a bus or taxi would be the fastest way to Darjeeling. Fares from Calcutta are Rs 40 in 2nd, Rs 154 in 1st. You can also book a ticket right through to Darjeeling. The trip up from New Jalpaiguri or Siliguri to Darjeeling by the toy train is an experience not to be missed. There are officially three departures a day although there may well be more. The seven-hour trip costs Rs 12 in 2nd, Rs 60 in 1st. Meals are available on the train.

Buses from Darjeeling usually depart from the Bazaar Bus Stand on Cart Rd while jeeps and taxis usually depart from the Robertson Rd/Laden La Rd Motor Stand. There are regular bus services Calcutta-Siliguri and a 'Rocket Service' bus which is much faster than the train and has fairly comfortable seats. The fare is Rs 75. Siliguri-Patna is Rs 38. Jeeps, taxis and buses run from New Jalpaiguri or Siliguri to Darjeeling. Costs range from Rs 9 to 19 from Siliguri and Rs 11 to 21 from New Jalpaiguri, depending on the quality of the bus and whether you go by bus, jeep, or taxi (the cost in order of cheapness is: bus, jeep, taxi).

From the airport at Bagdogra to Darjeeling is Rs 29 to 33 by minibus or jeep. Darjeeling-Kalimpong costs Rs 12 to 17 by jeep or taxi and takes 2½ hours. To Sikkim there is a daily minibus, there are few seats available so booking is essential. The five-hour trip costs Rs 40.

Three companies operate buses to Kathmandu – fares vary with the company, the bus and with day and night services. Typical fares range from Rs 90 to 110. There is no Nepalese consulate in Darjeeling, only in Calcutta, but you can get a seven-day visa at the border which can be extended in Kathmandu.

KALIMPONG

This quiet little bazaar town has a couple of Buddhist monasteries but otherwise is not of great interest. The trip to Kalimpong from Darjeeling is the best part about it. Lucky individuals with Bhutanese visas can get transport from Kalimpong to Bhutan.

Places to Stay

Gompu's Hotel & Restaurant on Chowrasta is about the best of the cheapies – many of which are extremely decrepit. Otherwise try the *Shangri La Tourist Lodge* (tel 230) off the Darjeeling road – Rs 45 a double or Rs 10 in the dorm. Equally popular is the *Crown Lodge*, just down a side street off Ongden Rd and visible from the Motor Stand, with good doubles at Rs 25. The *Sherpa Lodge* overlooking the playing fields is very similar.

Places to Eat

Good Tibetan food at *Gompu's Restaurant* or try *Hotel Maharaja* on R C Mintri Rd for excellent south Indian vegetarian food.

The *Nizam Restaurant* is tiny, friendly, with simple food. It is between the Crown Lodge and the Motor Stand. Plenty of other cafes along Main Rd.

Sikkim

The tiny state of Sikkim lies across the Himalaya, bordered by China to the north and Bhutan to the east. It was nominally an independent state, although always under a firm Indian rein, until 1975 when it was integrated into India. The Indians have always been touchy about letting visitors into this strategic border region but permits are now easier to obtain.

GANGTOK

The capital of Sikkim is only 80 km from Darjeeling. The town is comparatively new and much of its interest consists of the Buddhist monasteries around it. Gangtok has an excellent and helpful Tourist Office. Things to see actually in Gangtok include Tsuk-La-Khang (the Royal Chapel), the Institute of Tibetology Orchid Sanctuary and Chorten, the Enchey Monastery and the Cottage Industries Emporium.

Places to Stay & Eat

Shere Punjab has rooms from Rs 14 to 25, the *Doma Hotel* is similarly priced. The state government run *Gangtok Tourist Lodge* (tel 292/664) is Rs 35/50 for singles/doubles. Transport is available from the Tourist Office by the bus stand. The popular *Hotel Orchid* (tel 381) has rooms at Rs 50 double, Rs 60 with own bathroom, less off-season, and a good restaurant.

Other hotels include the *Green Hotel* (tel 254), up the main bazaar from the Tourist Office, the *Karma Hotel*, the *New Hotel Quality* and the *Deeki Hotel*. The *Hotel Tibet* is expensive at Rs 130 for a deluxe double but very good – ditto for its *Snow Lion Restaurant*.

Sikkim Permits

Permits for Sikkim are considerably more hassle than for Darjeeling. Three forms and three photos are required and you must allow six weeks for the permit to be issued. Outside India you can apply to any Indian diplomatic office or in India to the Ministry of Home Affairs in New Delhi. You have to state the exact day you will be arriving in Sikkim and the permit is usually issued for two to four days. You pick the permit up in Darjeeling (having been informed that there is no objection to your visit) but having got to Sikkim there are no further difficulties and the permit can be extended on the spot.

Getting There

There are buses between Gangtok and Siliguri (Rs 20, five hours), Bagdogra (five hours), Darjeeling (Rs 40, five to six hours) and Kalimpong (Rs 14, four or five hours).

AROUND GANGTOK

Monasteries around Gangtok include the interesting Rumtek Monastery which is 24 km from Gangtok although clearly visible. The two-hour bus trip costs Rs 6. There's a small lodge here if you want to spend the night. Pemayangtse Monastery is the second oldest monastery in Sikkim, it's six km from the Gezing bus stand. Tashiding Monastery is a full day's hike further on. The daily Gezing bus takes seven to eight hours and costs Rs 24. Gezing has some basic lodges and a *PWD Rest House* a couple of km towards Pemayangtse. You must book ahead here as is also necessary for the *Forestry Department Bungalow* at Tashiding. Phodang Monastery is the furthest you can go in eastern Sikkim without further paperwork hassles. Again there is one bus a day – Rs 7, about 3½ hours.

Because visiting these monasteries almost always requires overnight accommodation it takes at least a week to visit them all. Taxis are available from Gangtok but they tend to be very expensive.

North-East Frontier

The north-east is probably the least visited region in India. In part that is due to limited infrastructure and difficulty in obtaining permits to visit the north-east states but for several years now the whole area has been virtually off limits due to widespread local unrest and agitation.

ASSAM

The largest and most accessible of the north-east states, visit permits are required for Assam and these generally permit travel only to Gauhati and the Manas and Kaziranga wildlife reserves. Gauhati, the capital, has some interesting temples and a good zoo. There's a government *Tourist Bungalow*, *Railway Retiring Rooms* and cheap hotels like the *Ambassador* or the *Alka*.

Kaziranga is the last major home of the Indian one-horned rhinoceros. Best time to visit the park, and view rhinos from elephant back, is February to May. There are a variety of accommodation possibilities in the park. Assam's other wildlife park, Manas, is on the border with Bhutan.

MEGHALAYA

The other easily visited state has Shillong, a pleasant hill station, as its capital. Cherrapunji in Meghalaya is reputed to be the wettest place on earth with an annual rainfall averaging over 1000 cm – nearly 40 feet! Entry permits allowing, this could be a back door route into Bangladesh.

OTHER STATES & TERRITORIES

The other parts of the north-east are very much more difficult to visit. They include Arunachal Pradesh, from where the old WW II Stillwell road ran into Burma, and Nagaland, the last point to which the Japanese advanced during WW II. A second road into Burma was also built from Manipur.

Rajasthan

Stretching south-west of Delhi, Rajasthan borders on the west to the desolate Thar desert which extends across to Pakistan and is one of the most lightly inhabited parts of India. The state takes its name from the Rajputs, the fearless warriors who opposed every invader India has had. They fought fiercely against the Moghuls but under Akbar were finally integrated into his empire. Rajasthan is one of India's poorer states but it's also one of the most exotically colourful and a firm favourite with visitors. Rajasthan has an excellent series of state government operated Tourist Bungalows in all the main centres.

JAIPUR

The capital of the state is popularly known as the 'pink city' from the pink-coloured sandstone used in the construction of the old walled city. Jaipur is a city of wide, open avenues and has an architectural harmony quite unusual in India. The city owes its name and foundation to the great astronomer-ruler Maharajah Jai Singh II.

Information & Orientation

The state Tourist Office desks can be found in the railway and the bus station. The Tourist Bungalow, like most of the cheaper hotels and restaurants, is near the bus stand and railway station in the south-west of the town. The old walled city is in the north-east. The Government of India Tourist Office is in the Rajasthan State Hotel. There is also an area opposite the GPO on M I Rd which has become a popular centre for travellers on a really tight budget. There are many souvenir shops and cheap restaurants here.

Things To See

Palace of the Winds The 1799 Hawa Mahal is Jaipur's central landmark although it is little more than a facade. The five-storey building looks out over the main street of the old city. It is part of the City Palace complex. You can climb to the top for an excellent view of the city.

City Palace In the heart of the old city the City Palace consists of a series of courtyards, gardens and buildings. The seven-storey Chandra Mahal is the palace centrepiece and contains a museum with many interesting Rajasthani exhibits.

Observatory Across from the City Palace is Jai Singh's observatory – the largest and best preserved of the five constructed. It was built in 1728, four years after the Delhi observatory. The giant sundial with its 30 metre high gnomon is the most striking of the instruments.

Other The Ram Niwas Gardens contains a zoo and the Central Museum in the old Albert Hall. The Hotel Rambagh Palace puts on an hour long cultural programme of Rajasthani folk dances in the evening – 'great value for Rs 15'.

Places to Stay

The state government has recently opened the new budget-priced *Swagat Tourist Bungalow* where singles/doubles, all with attached bathroom, are Rs 30/45. It's terrific value if you want to stay close to the railway station. The *Jaipur Inn* (tel 66057) in Bani Park is a popular budget travel hostelry. It's clean, well kept and has dorm beds at Rs 12, rooms from Rs 35 to 50. There are extra charges for sheets and mattresses.

The recently opened *Hotel Arya Niwas* (tel 73456) is behind the Amber Cinema on Sansar Chandra Marg, near the GPO. Singles are Rs 50 to 100, doubles Rs 60 to 120, all with attached bathroom and air-cooling. It's clean, well run and friendly.

Other popular cheapies include the *Evergreen Guest House* opposite the GPO or the *Hotel Rajdhani* near the railway station where there are also *Railway Retiring Rooms*. The *Teej Tourist Bungalow* (tel 74260) in Rani Park has singles/doubles at Rs 50/60 or Rs 100/120 with air-con. There are also dorm beds at Rs 10. The *Hotel Chandra Loak* on Station

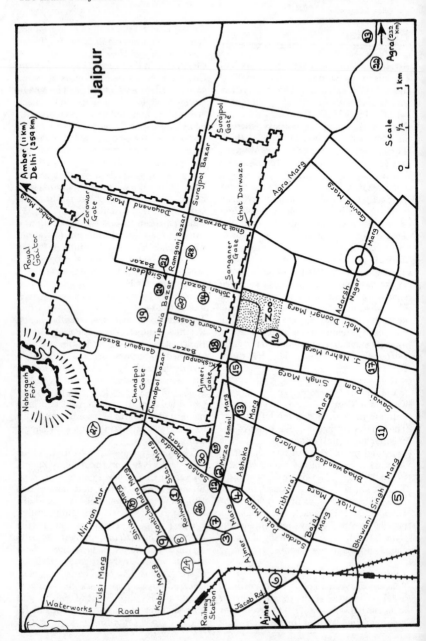

Rd has doubles with bath for Rs 45, good value, and the *Tourist Hut Paying Guest House* (great name) has doubles at Rs 15 and is 'clean and quiet'.

Places to Eat

Masala dosa and other south Indian specialities at the *Madras Hotel* near the station. All-you-can-eat thalis at *Krishna Bhojnalaya* at the top of the stairs between 63 and 64 Johri Bazaar. *Chandralok* near the GPO on M I Rd also does good, cheap vegetarian food. *LMB* in Johari Bazaar is another vegetarian specialist.

The *Circuit House* between the Evergreen Guest House and the railway station is the place for an excellent Rs 10 breakfast. Jaipur has a number of good Chinese restaurants, a *Kwality* on M I Rd where you'll also find *Niro's*, one of Jaipur's best and most expensive restaurants, but for a real splurge the place to go is the *Rambagh Palace Hotel*. The set meal at lunchtime is about Rs 75 and well worth it – according to some, terrible according to one traveller!

Getting There

Jaipur is connected by air with other major cities. Trains to Jaipur are not so fast because they are on metre gauge. The Pink City Express from the old Delhi Railway Station at 6 am daily only takes five hours, however. Fares are Rs 25 in 2nd, Rs 109 in 1st. There's also an overnight train leaving Delhi in the late evening and arriving in Jaipur at dawn. From Jaipur to Agra there is now a 'superfast' train which only takes five hours– departs Jaipur at 5 am, costs Rs 19.

There are also buses between Agra or Delhi and Jaipur. These are operated by Rajasthan State Transport, the trip takes five hours and costs Rs 45 from Delhi. Regular express buses from Delhi are Rs 33. There are also de-luxe buses from Agra for Rs 40.

Getting Around

There are daily bus tours from the Teej Tourist Bungalow or from the Railway Station for Rs 15. A cycle rickshaw from the station to the Jaipur Inn will be Rs 2, or from the station to Johari Bazaar Rs 5. You can also share 'four-seaters' or 'six-seaters' from the station to the city gates (Sanganer) for Rs 1 to 1.50. Bicycles can be hired near the station.

1 Central Bus Station
2 G.P.O.
3 Indian Govt. Tourist Office, Circuit House
4 Indian Airlines
5 Youth Hostel
6 Achrol Lodge
7 Gangaur Tourist Bungalow
8 Teej Tourist Bungalow
9 Jaipur Ashok Hotel
10 Jaipur Inn
11 Rambagh Palace Hotel
12 Man Singh Hotel
13 Niros Restaurant
14 LMB Restaurant
15 Rajasthan Handicraft Emporium
16 Museum
17 Govt. of Rajasthan Tourist Office
18 Nehru Bazaar
19 City Palace & Museum
20 Jantar Mantar
21 Hawa Mahal
22 Vidyadharji ka Bagh
23 Sisodia Rani Palace & Garden
24 Swagat Tourist Bungalow
25 Chandralok Hotel
26 Shalimar Hotel
27 Bissau & Khetri Hotel
28 Haldiyon Restaurant
29 Gopal Restaurant
30 Hotel Arya Niwas

AMBER

This was the ancient capital of Jaipur state before the city was established, it's 11 km from Jaipur. The fort at Amber is a superb example of Rajput architecture on a hillside overlooking the lake below. You can walk up to the fort in 10 minutes, or ride up on elephant back for Rs 65! Inside there are halls, galleries, ramparts and even a small temple to Kali. Admission is Rs 10, it's open from 9 am to 5 pm. Around Jaipur there are a number of other interesting sites including the royal cenotaphs and the Nahargarh or Tiger Fort.

BHARATPUR, DEEG & SARISKA

Bharatpur has a major bird sanctuary, the Keoladeo National Park, situated on 52 square km of low-lying marshland. Here you will also find the 18th century 'Iron Fort'. Deeg, a small town 35 km from Bharatpur or Mathura, achieved some notoriety in 1762 when the Maharajah of Bharatpur dared to attack the Red Fort in Agra and carried off loads of booty to Deeg. Sariska is a wildlife sanctuary where you might even see tigers.

AJMER

This easy going and quite interesting town is basically used as a stepping stone to nearby Pushkar. Ajmer stands on the artificial Ana Sagar Lake which was created in the 12th century. The pleasant Dault Bagh on the banks of the lake have a series of marble pavilions erected by Shah Jahan.

In the old part of town at the foot of a barren hill the Dargah houses the tomb of a Sufi saint who came to Ajmer in 1192. It's one of India's major Muslim pilgrimage places. Beyond the Dargah you come to the Adhai-din-ka-jhonpra, the ruins of a mosque constructed in 1192 using the remains of a sacked Jain college.

High up the hill is the Taragarh or Star Fort with an excellent view over the city. Akbar's Palace in the city is now a good little museum, closed on Fridays. The Naisyan Temple is a Jain temple which houses a collection of wooden figures from the Jain mythology.

Places to Stay

The *Khadim Tourist Bungalow* (tel 20490) is a few minutes walk from the bus stand or Rs 1 to 2 by bicycle rickshaw from the railway station. Singles/doubles cost Rs 30/40 with fan, Rs 45/60 air-cooled or Rs 75/100 air-con. There's also a Rs 8 dorm at this pleasant place.

Across from the railway station there are a string of cheap hotels varying from the dismal to the merely OK. *Hotel Anand*, *Hotel Malwa*, *Hotel Ratan* and the *Nagpal Tourist Hotel* are all fairly reasonable. The Hotel Ratan has a vegetarian restaurant downstairs. Otherwise you can eat at the Tourist Bungalow or the more expensive *Honeydew* and *Elite Restaurants* near the railway station.

Getting There

Buses to Jaipur take 2½ to three hours and depart every half hour. The trip costs Rs 16. From Ajmer you can continue to Jodhpur, Udaipur, Chittorgarh, Mt Abu and other places in Rajasthan. Buses to Pushkar go from outside the railway station.

PUSHKAR

Beside the holy Pushkar Lake and on the edge of the desert the beautiful town of Pushkar is a popular freak centre where people rest up from the rigours of life on the road in India. There are a number of interesting bathing ghats and temples including what may be the only temple to Brahma in all of India. At the full moon in November each year Pushkar is the site for one of India's great festivals. Hundreds of thousands of people flock here to the great Cattle Fair. A tent city is erected for the thousands of foreign visitors to this superbly colourful Rajasthani event.

Places to Stay & Eat

The *Sarovar Tourist Bungalow*, on the

opposite side of the lake from the Brahma Temple, is an old palace once owned by the Maharajah of Jaipur. This very pleasant place has rooms from Rs 25/30 to 30/40 and a Rs 8 dorm. It's so popular that it is almost always 100% full up. Around town there are many other small hotels like the *Krishna Hotel* for Rs 15 a double.

Beside the Tourist Bungalow the *Sun Set Cafe* is the number one place to eat – or to sit and watch the sun go down over the lake. *Sri Venktesh* at the start of the main street is a friendly place with excellent and cheap food. Across the road the chai shop does local cheese with garlic and herbs.

Getting There
The strange little minibuses from Ajmer cost Rs 2.25.

KOTA
This was once another Rajasthani princely capital and is now an industrial centre. Kota has an imposing fort with two museums and the Chambal Gardens beside the river. Beside the Tourist Bungalow there are a group of somewhat neglected, though imposingly large, royal tombs.

Places to Stay
Conveniently close to the bus stand the *Chambal Tourist Bungalow* has rooms from Rs 30/40 to Rs 45/60 and a Rs 8 dorm. There are other cheap hotels like the *Payal Hotel* at Nayapura or the *Navrang Hotel* at Civil Lines and there are *Railway Retiring Rooms* at the station.

BUNDI
The superbly picturesque little town of Bundi has an imposingly massive fortress, entered through a huge gateway flanked by rampant elephants. The fort overlooks the town from its hillside location – but it's so far off the usual tourist track that it is usually kept locked and shut up and getting in can be rather difficult! There's not much by the way of food or accom-modation in Bundi either – try the *Circuit House* or the much less luxurious *Dak Bungalow* near the bus stand.

CHITTORGARH
The hilltop fortress of Chittorgarh sums up the whole doomed, romantic splendour of Rajasthan. Three times Chittor was sacked by stronger enemies and each time the Rajasthani men rode out to certain death while their women committed *jauhar*, ritual suicide. Today the fort is deserted but as imposing as ever and the modern town lies on the plain below the hill.

Ascending the winding road to the fort you pass through a series of gates and pass memorials to fallen Rajasthani heroes. The Palace of Rana Kumbha in the fort was the scene for one of Chittor's *jauhars*. Other places of interest include the Tower of Victory and the Tower of Fame, the Fateh Prakash Palace with its museum, Padmini's Palace, the Gaumukh Reservoir and a number of other lesser palaces and buildings.

Places to Stay
The *Panna Tourist Bungalow* is close to the railway station on the Udaipur road. Rooms run from Rs 30/35 to Rs 35/45 with air-con and there's a Rs 8 dormitory. Closer to the railway station is the *Janta Tourist Rest House* where you'll also find the Tourist Office. Here there are spartan doubles at Rs 14 or Rs 20 and another dorm. In the same area there are some very basic hotels like the *Hotel Savaria* and there are also *Railway Retiring Rooms*.

Getting There & Around
Chittor is on the main bus and rail routes. Udaipur is three hours and Rs 15 away. The fort is six km from the station so you'll need transport – like a bicycle. Or you can take the morning or afternoon (winter only) Rs 12 tour from the Tourist Bungalow.

UDAIPUR

The lake city is a cool oasis in Rajasthan's dry heart. With its beautiful palaces this is probably the most romantic city in a romantic state – even if you can't afford to stay there it is well worth the expense of boating out to the Lake Palace Hotel for afternoon tea. Udaipur was founded in 1567 as a new capital following the third sack of Chittor.

Things To See

Pichola Lake Enlarged by Maharana Udai Singh, after he founded the city which bears his name, the beautiful lake is bordered by gardens, ghats and the imposing city palace. Two islands in the lake have palaces on them – the larger is Jagniwas where the Lake Palace Hotel occupies the whole island. A boat trip out to the island from Bhansi Ghat, just south of the Palace Museum, costs Rs 20 including tea or coffee and biscuits in the hotel.

City Palace & Museum Towering over the lake, the palace is the largest in Rajasthan. It's a rambling conglomeration of building added to and extended by succeeding Maharanas. The main part of the palace is now a museum with a large and very varied collection. Admission to the museum is Rs 3 plus Rs 3 for a camera. It's open from 9.30 am to 4.30 pm daily but closed on Fridays.

Other The Jagdish Temple is only 150 metres from the City Palace entrance. North of Lake Pichola is Lake Fateh Sagar with Nehru Park, a garden island with a restaurant, in the centre. Moti Magri or the 'Pearl Hill' overlooks this lake and atop the hill is a statute of Rajput hero Maharana Pratap astride his charger Chetak.

The Bhartiya Lok Museum is a small folk museum with regular shows of Rajasthani puppets. Entry is Rs 1, hours are 9 am to 6 pm. The Saheliyon ki Bari is a small ornamental 'Garden of the Maids of Honour' in the north of the city. Entry is Rs 0.50 (plus Rs 2 to have the fountains turned on) and it too is open 9 am to 6 pm.

Places to Stay

The *Kajri Tourist Bungalow* (tel 3509) is conveniently situated and has rooms from Rs 30/40 for singles/doubles through to Rs 80/100 for a room with bath and air-con. There is also a Rs 8 dorm. The popular *Keerti Hotel* (tel 3639) on Sarsvati Marg has rooms from as little as Rs 15 up to Rs 75 for a double with air-con and a Rs 6 dorm. Beware of the almost identically named *Hotel Keerti*, only about 40 metres closer to Suraj Pol Gate and not so good. Near the bus stand there are a whole string of cheapies – several of them with very reasonable accommodation.

Round on Lake Palace Rd by the Sajjan Niwas Gardens is the *Rang Niwas Hotel* (tel 3891) with rooms from Rs 20/50 to Rs 40/80. It is built around a pleasant, green courtyard. Outside Udaipur the *Pratap Country Inn* is operated by the same people as the Keerti and they'll arrange transport out there for you. It's at Titadha village, six km out, Rs 1 by bus. Tents and rooms start as low as Rs 15 and go as high as Rs 100 plus there is a Rs 6 dorm. Horse and camel rides and a swimming pool are part of the attraction here. This place has always been somewhat controversial – 50% of the letters we receive are from people who were not satisfied, the other 50% rave about it.

If you'd like to stay in the exotic *Lake Palace Hotel* it's Rs 350/450.

Places to Eat

Food in Udaipur is not so special. You can try the *Tourist Bungalow* (very variable), a so-so *Kwality* at Chetak Circle or a variety of vegetarian places around Suraj Pol. Chinese food in Udaipur, however, can be good.

Getting There

Udaipur is connected by air to most major centres. Delhi is 21 hours away by rail, Rs 50 in 2nd class, Rs 198 in 1st. There are frequent buses to all the main centres in Rajasthan. Chittor is three hours and Rs 12 away. Jodhpur is 10 hours away and costs Rs 38. If you are going to Mt Abu note that some buses go all the way there, some stop at Abu Road (the railhead for Mt Abu). Fare to Abu Road is Rs 18.

Getting Around

Udaipur is a very good place to bicycle around – several bike-hire places can be found around the Tourist Bungalow. Usually the costs are around Rs 6 per day. Taxis are un-metered, auto-rickshaws have meters but won't use them.

AROUND UDAIPUR

There are a number of interesting places around Udaipur including Eklingi, 22 km out, with a number of ancient temples. The Shiva temple in the village is open very peculiar hours, 4.45-7.30 am, 10.30 am-1.30 pm and 5.30-7.30 pm. The groups of temples just around Eklingi can easily be visited on a hired bicycle. Other temples can be seen at Kankroli and Nathdwara although non-Hindus are not allowed inside the latter.

Ranakpur is the main point of interest, however. This superb Jain temple is far larger and more ornate than its remote location would indicate. Non-Jains are allowed inside from noon to 5 pm, there is a dharamsala where you can stay overnight if necessary and good thalis are available at lunchtime for a donation. Getting there is easy enough by bus but the 98 km from Udaipur can easily take five to six hours.

MT ABU

Rajasthan's hill station is a pleasant hot season retreat and very popular with Indian honeymooners. Nakki Lake forms the centre of Mt Abu and there are various viewpoints in the vicinity where you can watch the sunrise or simply admire the view. There is a small museum in the town and three km out you can climb the steep steps to the Adhar Devi Temple to Durga.

Mt Abu's finest temples are the beautiful Jain Dilwara Temples which rival Ranakpur for their intricate marble carving. The complex is open from 12 noon to 6 pm and there is a Rs 5 camera charge. Note that no leather (belts, bags as well as shoes) can be taken into the temple.

Mt Abu also has the Shiva temple of Achaleshwar Mahadeva about 11 km out. A colourful group of Jain temples tops the hill overlooking this temple. Guru Shikhar at the end of the plateau is the highest point in Rajasthan.

Places to Stay

Mt Abu has a lot of hotels in all price categories – the Hotel Hill Tone even advertises that it has honeymoon suites of 'cave and bamboo type'! The Shikhar Tourist Bungalow (tel 69) has rooms from Rs 25/40 off-season (in season rates from 45/55). Air-con rooms start from Rs 70 and dorm beds are Rs 12 in season.

At the foot of the driveway to the Tourist Bungalow is the pleasant Tourist Guest House (tel 160) with clean, pleasant rooms around a courtyard for Rs 20 and 30 in season. Saraswati Lodge (tel 7) is another similar place. The Bharati Hotel (tel 61), the Hotel Tourist (tel 53) and the adjoining Navjivan Hotel are also reasonable. These latter three places all have good vegetarian food. The central Youth Hostel is Rs 8.

Places to Eat

Quite reasonable Chinese food can be found at the Nina Sheeba Restaurant on Sunset Point Rd. A number of places do Gujarati thalis for Rs 7. Excellent ice cream at MK Cold Drinks. On the lake itself the large concrete 'boat' restaurant is OK for a cup of tea but nothing more. Watch out for Mt Abu's own soft drink, the ginger Rim Zim. It tastes absolutely appalling.

Getting There

Abu Road the railhead for Mt Abu, is 27 km away – an hour and Rs 4 to 5 by bus or

Rs 70 by a taxi. Bus passengers are charged Rs 2.50 on arrival at Mt Abu, taxi passengers pay Rs 3.50. There's an extensive bus schedule from Mt Abu which can work out faster and more convenient than going down to Abu Road for a train. Ahmedabad, for example, takes seven hours.

Getting Around
Buses run to the various sites around the Mt Abu plateau and there are taxis or tours too. Morning and afternoon the tours of Mt Abu cost Rs 15. Mt Abu's unique 'baby prams' are generally used by parents to have their children transported around.

JODHPUR
After Jaipur this desert city is the largest in the state. The town is dominated by the massive fort on its sheer, rocky hill. A 10-km-long city wall surrounds the old city which is a fascinating maze of winding streets. And yes, this is where the word *jodhpur* came from.

Things To See
Meherangarh Fort The 'Majestic Fort' is just that – a huge and imposing place which really conjures up the warlike Rajput atmosphere. Note the sati handprints on the final gate into the fort. Part of the fort has been turned into a superb museum with an amazing variety of exhibits. You can look out over Jodhpur from the fort ramparts and hear the noise of the streets drift up from below. The fort is open from 9 am to 5 pm and admission is Rs 30 for the complete museum tour including a guide to open the locked doors. There are additional charges for cameras. Just below the fort is the Jaswant Thada, the cenotaph of Maharajah Jaswant Singh II.
Other In the city centre is a colourful market area with the clock tower as a popular landmark. The Government Museum is in the Umaid Gardens, close to the Tourist Bungalow. Next to the Tourist

Bungalow is an excellent handicrafts and antiques centre. The Umaid Bhawan Palace is now partly used as a hotel but it was only completed in 1943. It's surprising that such a huge and costly edifice should have been erected that close to independence. Admission to non-guests is Rs 2, it's open from 9 am to 5 pm.

Places to Stay
The *Ghoomar Tourist Bungalow* (tel 21900) is on High Court Rd by the Umaid Gardens. Singles/doubles range from Rs 40/50 to Rs 70/90 and there is a Rs 10 dorm. There are *Railway Retiring Rooms* (tel 22741) with rooms at just Rs 10/20 and a string of cheaper hotels near the railway station with rooms in the Rs 15 to 25 bracket. Best of these is probably the *Adarsh Niwas Hotel*, which also has a good restaurant.

Places to Eat
For vegetarian food try the *Pankaj* at Jalori Gate or the *Coffee House* at Sojati Gate. Makhania Lassi is a delicious thick-cream variety of that refreshing drink. Try it at *Agra Sweet Home*, opposite the Sojati Gate, but the place in the gateway to the central market is so popular that they are said to sell 1500 glasses a day at Rs 2.50 each.

Getting There
There are two flights a day with Indian Airlines. There are a variety of buses to Jodhpur and other major centres in Rajasthan and also daily buses to Jaisalmer, a seven to 10 hour trip which costs Rs 32. Buses leave from the bus stand at Raika Bagh. There are superfast expresses between Delhi and Jodhpur which take about 10 hours. Overnight and day trains operate to Jaisalmer.

JAISALMER
This is one of the most exotic cities in India – a mediaeval fantasy in the middle of the desert, something right out of the Arabian Nights. Once an important caravan

staging post Jaisalmer almost faded away before disputes with Pakistan revealed its strategic importance; more recently foreign visitors have begun to realise its unique appeal.

The old walled city is dominated by the ancient fort with its Jain temples while in the city you should search out the magnificent *havelis*. These elegant mansions were built by wealthy residents in the beautiful yellow sandstone from which most of Jaisalmer is constructed. Although the town is so interesting and mysterious at close range it's equally appealing viewed from afar. Altogether it's an amazing place and well worth a visit.

Places to Stay

Just outside the city walls the *Moomal Tourist Bungalow* has rooms from Rs 40/50 to Rs 70/90 with air-con, and a Rs 10 dorm. The *Fort View Hotel* gets raves from travellers, doubles at Rs 30. It's centrally located and the manager is reputedly very helpful. The *Hotel Swastika* is another new place which has been recommended. It's a short walk up a side street approximately opposite the State Bank of India, rooms range from Rs 20/40 and there is a Rs 8 dorm.

There are a number of dirt cheap places in the narrow alleys of the old city – try the *Sunil Bhatia Rest House*, the *Rama Guest House* or the small *Sunray Hotel*. The *Golden Rest* is a friendly place and in the same price range as the others – Rs 10-20. Several travellers have recommended *Hotel Pleasure*, just two minutes from the Jodhpur bus stop.

Places to Eat

The small and basic *Gaylord Restaurant* is across from the State Bank of India and has friendly sparrows and pretty good food. Near here, by Mahendra Travel, there is also the small *Ghoonghat Restaurant*. The *Tourist Bungalow* and the *Jaisal Castle Hotel* also do food at higher prices, but there are no real gastronomic delights in Jaisalmer as yet.

Getting There

There's a day and a night train daily in each direction between Jaisalmer and Jodhpur. The 10-hour trip costs Rs 24 in 2nd class, Rs 94 in 1st. In Jaisalmer the reservations office is open only from 8 to 11 am and in the chaotic period just before departure. There is also a daily bus. You can also bus to Bikaner in 10 hours (two daily).

Getting Around

Unmetered taxis and jeeps are available for about Rs 14 from the railway station to the Tourist Bungalow. Around the city the tourist office's jeep can be hired for sightseeing for Rs 30 for up to 10 km locally. Rs 2 a km for more than 10 km out of the city. You can also hire bicycles in Jaisalmer and ride out to nearby places.

AROUND JAISALMER

There are several interesting places in the barren country around Jaisalmer and caravan trips are operated around the villages in the desert. Amar Sagar is a now ruined formal garden six km out. At Lodruva the Jain temples in the ruins of this once great city were restored in the late '70s. The gardens of Bada Bagh with the royal cenotaphs is a good place to visit at sunset to watch Jaisalmer change colours in the final rays of light.

BIKANER

Further north from Jaisalmer this is another romantic desert outpost. Bikaner has a fine fort and is also noted for the camels bred here. Bikaner has one of the best museums in Rajasthan. Outside the city on the Jodhpur road you'll come to the Karni Mata Temple where holy rats have the run of the place.

Places to Stay

The *Dhola-Maru Tourist Bungalow* on Pooran Singh Circle has rooms at Rs 40/50, or with air con Rs 70/90. There are also *Railway Retiring Rooms* and a *Dak Bungalow* plus a string of cheap hotels near the station like the *Delight Hotel*, the *Deluxe Hotel*, the *Green Hotel* or the *Roopan Hotel*. The Deluxe and the Delight have the same manager and are pretty good with rooms from Rs 12 to 24. Accommodation may be hard to find in Bikaner as hotels are often fully booked up.

Places to Eat
The *Chhotu Motyu Joshi Restaurant* is just down from the Green Hotel towards the station and has good and cheap vegetarian food and icy cold lassi. The *Green Hotel* also does smooth, cold lassi. More great lassi on the street near the bus stand, also good yoghurt for Rs 4 a kilo. The Delight and Deluxe hotels have good south Indian food, but a limited menu.

Getting There & Around
Trains run to Bikaner from Delhi, 468 km away, the trip takes 11 to 12 hours. Fares are Rs 28 in 2nd class, Rs 110 in 1st. There is a daily overnight train to and from Jodhpur. From Jaipur to Bikaner takes 10 to 11 hours on an overnight train with fares of Rs 20 in 2nd class, Rs 116 in 1st.

A cheap way of travelling Jaisalmer-Bikaner is to take a night train to Pokran, sleep in the waiting room and then catch a bus for the five-hour ride to Bikaner, arriving around noon. Total cost is around Rs 28 and this way you get some sleep on the way. There are regular bus services to Jaipur, Jaisalmer and Jodhpur.

Unmetered taxis and auto-rickshaws and tongas will get you around Bikaner.

Gujarat

Although the western state of Gujarat is not a favourite with visitors it is one of India's more economically active and wealthy states. Apart from its capital, Ahmedabad, it also has a number of other interesting cities, temples and a major wildlife reserve. Unfortunately Gujarat has recently been another area of India wracked by unrest and disturbances, chiefly centred around Ahmedabad.

AHMEDABAD
A great textile centre this city was also an important base for Mahatma Gandhi during his campaign for India's independence. It has a number of architecturally interesting mosques as well as Gandhi's Ashram.

Things to See
Mosques The Jami Masjid is one of the earliest mosques in Ahmedabad and was said to have been built from the components of Hindu and Jain temples. Nearby are the tombs of Ahmed Shah and his queens. Sidi Saiyad's Mosque is noted for its exquisite carved-stone windows. Other important mosques include Rani Rupmati's, Rani Sipri's with its graceful minarets, while near the railway station are the 'shaking minarets' of the Sidi Bashir Mosque.

Other The ancient citadel, the Bhadra, was built in 1411. Nearby is the triple gateway to the city, the Teen Darwaza. The white-marble Hathee Singh Jain Temple is just outside the Delhi Gate. Gujarat is noted for its *baolis* or step wells – a neglected although particularly good example is the Step Well of Dada Hari. Ahmedabad also has the artificial Kankaria Lake, several museums, interesting old city areas known as *pols* and, of course, the Sbarmati Ashram six km out from the centre.

Places to Stay
If you don't mind being out of town the *Gandhi Ashram Guest House* (book through the Tourist Office tel 44 9683 or direct, tel 86 7652) has singles/doubles with bath and balcony for Rs 30/60.

In Ahmedabad the cheapies are scattered and there are no real standouts. Directly behind the big Capri Hotel and the Kwality Restaurant is the *Plaza Hotel* with rooms with bath at Rs 30/50. Close by in these small alleys off Relief Rd are the *Chetak Hotel* (Rs 35/60) and the *Metropole Hotel* (Rs 40/70). *Hotel Ashiana* is also central but very basic – a double is Rs 30 or Rs 40 with attached bath.

Hotel Sabar, a bit beyond the big Cama Hotel, has doubles at Rs 50 to Rs 100 with air-con – good food too. *Hotel Natraj*, right next to the Ahmed Khan Mosque, is central but relatively quiet, a modern building with rooms at Rs 30/45. There are a string of cheapies around the station and *Railway Retiring Rooms* at Rs 30/50.

Places to Eat

The *Kwality* on Relief Rd is one of the better restaurants in the chain and has a good English-Chinese-Indian menu. The *Cama Hotel* has a pleasant air-con dining room, a good place for a more luxurious breakfast. Back on Relief Rd the *Havmor* ice cream parlour not only has good ice cream but also snacks and flavoured milk – real milk is a luxury you can find fairly easily in Ahmedabad. Very close to the Teen Darwaza Gate is the tiny *Gandhi Cold Drinks Bar* where again there is good ice cream.

Gujarat is well known for its local version of the thali – the Gujarati thali tends to be more varied than the regular south Indian variety but also a bit on the sweet side. A great place to try it is the *Chetna Restaurant* on Relief Rd where Rs 11 covers all-you-can-eat. The Chetna has no sign in English but adjoins the Krishna Talkies (whose sign may not be in English either!) which is across the road from the Oriental Building. Other good places for thali are *Hotel Sabar* (Rs 12) or the flashy *Gokul Hotel*.

Getting There

Ahmedabad is not on the broad gauge Delhi-Bombay line although there is a broad gauge line from Bombay. Delhi-Ahmedabad costs Rs 60 in 2nd, Rs 236 in 1st and usually takes 24 hours, but twice a week does it in 17 hours.

Lots of trains operate to Bombay each day with fares at Rs 36.50 in 2nd, 143 in 1st. Indian Airlines fly to Ahmedabad from Delhi or Bombay and there are also plenty of buses for Ahmedabad.

Getting Around

Traffic in Ahmedabad is frantic and the auto-rickshaw wallahs are suicidal – but they do use their meters, albeit with a substantial correction factor.

BARODA

Also known as Vadodara this pleasant city is south of Ahmedabad and has the Sayaji Bagh gardens with the Baroda Museum, the Maharajah Fateh Singh Museum with a royal collection of art and a large fish-filled tank in the centre of town.

Places to Stay & Eat

There are a number of places to stay around the railway station and bus stand – they include the *Laxmi Lodge* at Rs 40, the pleasant and well kept *Apsara* at Rs 50, the big *Ambassador* at Rs 50/70. The *Municipal Corporation Guest House*, directly opposite the railway station is drab and grey with rooms from Rs 25 to 60.

The *Ambassador* has good thalis, or try the *Kwality*, *Havmor* or the railway station restaurant.

SURAT

Continuing south from Baroda on the Ahmedabad-Bombay line Surat was once a major European trading port and you can still find the site of the old English factory. Surat also has a big old fort while on the city limits are the run down and neglected English and Dutch cemeteries.

Places to Stay & Eat

There are lots of so-so hotels near the railway station like the *Subras* (extremely basic) from Rs 15/25 or the *Rupali* at Rs 12 to 30 and up. The *Central* is slightly higher class as is the pleasant enough *Hotel Dreamland* with rooms from Rs 35.

The *Hotel Ashoka* and the *Simla Guest House*, close by, are fair enough with rooms from Rs 30.

There are good thalis at the *Subras Hotel*, near the station, or at the *Tex Palazzo Hotel* which is topped, wonder of wonders, by India's first revolving restaurant – mediocre food, dull view.

DAMAN

Like Goa this was a Portuguese holdout but unlike Goa there are no fantastic beaches, in fact Daman exists principally as a place to get a drink in otherwise teetotal Gujarat. You get to Daman by share taxi or bus from Vapi Station.

Places to Stay & Eat

The *PWD Rest House* is a superb bargain at Rs 8 but usually full. Otherwise there is the *Brighton Hotel* across the road, the big *Sovereign Hotel* a little further back from the beach (reasonable food too) or the *Hotel Tourist* – which should be avoided if at all possible.

SAURASHTRA

The 'other side' of Gujarat is the Kathiawar Peninsula which stretches west to the Rann of Kutch, which makes a fairly impenetrable barrier to Pakistan.

BHAVNAGAR

Bhavnagar is a port dating from 1723 and is still an important trading post.

Places to Stay & Eat

Basic hotels include the *Evergreen Guest House* (tel 4605), the *Kashmir Hotel* near the Pathik Ashram and *Geeta Lodging & Boarding* (tel 3985). The *Pathik Ashram* has rooms from around Rs 15. At Nirmalnagar in the Diamond Market the *Natraj Guest House* is a good place with rooms at Rs 15/30 and a Rs 7 dorm.

Near the station the *Mahavir Lodge* does good thalis for Rs 6.

Getting There

It's seven hours by rail from Ahmedabad with fares of Rs 22 in 2nd, Rs 86 in 1st. There are buses too.

PALITANA

Palitana, 56 km from Bhavnagar, is a hilltop complex of nearly a thousand Jain temples with fine views over the surrounding area.

Places to Stay

Although there are lots of Jain pilgrims' rest houses in Palitana about the only place you're likely to be allowed to stay is the *Hotel Sumeru Toran* (tel 227) on Station Rd. It's a fine place with rooms from Rs 25/45 and a Rs 6 dormitory. It also has an excellent restaurant.

Getting There

A bus from Bhavnagar costs Rs 5 and takes less than an hour but they're impossibly crowded.

DIU

The island of Diu is another small ex-Portuguese enclave which was also taken over by India in 1961. It's a colourful, interesting little place.

Places to Stay

The *PWD Rest House* near the fort is clean, quiet, cheap at Rs 12 a double and generally full. The *Nilesh Guest House* has rooms from Rs 15/20. If you can run to Rs 45/60 for singles/doubles *Baron's Inn* on Old Fort Rd is a fine place in an old Portuguese villa. Situated 7½ km out from Diu town the beachfront *Ganga Sagar Guest House* has rooms at Rs 18/20.

Getting There & Around

From Palitana through to Diu involves a whole string of buses, all of them terribly crowded. Ferries cross between Ghogla and Diu town on Diu island. You can hire bicycles on the island.

JUNAGADH

Junagadh has an ancient fort and another hill studded with Jain temples.

Places to Stay

There are *Railway Retiring Rooms* and some very basic hotels around the railway station. Close to the bus station the *Hotel Vaibhav* has rooms from Rs 25 right up to Rs 110. You can get terrific thalis here for Rs 10. On Dhal Rd the *Hotel Relief* is also a good place with doubles at Rs 40 to 50.

VERAVAL & SOMNATH

The Temple of Somnath has one of the oldest histories of any Indian temple – in fact it is supposed to have been there since the creation of the world! More certainly it was razed by Mahmud of Ghazni on one of his periodic rape-pillage-sack visits to India and Aurangzeb, that notorious Moghul spoilsport, also knocked it down. The current temple was only built in 1950. Veraval is the nearby modern town.

Places to Stay & Eat

There's a *Circuit House* and a *Tourist Bungalow* with rooms for Rs 35. Near the bus station the *Satkar Hotel* is clean and well maintained with rooms from Rs 22/25. There are also *Railway Retiring Rooms* and the vast, somewhat dingy but excellent value *Sri Somnath Temple Trust* guest house between the bus stand and the temple which has doubles for just Rs 10.

The *Satkar Hotel* does excellent thalis for Rs 16. The *New Apsara* is fairly basic but also has thalis and dosas.

Getting There

Buses run between Diu and Veraval via Kodinar. It takes nine hours to Bhavnagar. Trains to Ahmedabad take 15 hours.

OTHER PLACES

Between Veraval and Junagadh the Sasan Gir Forest is the last home of the Asian lion – October to June is the best time to visit the reserve. On the way from Veraval to Dwarka is Porbandar, an ancient town chiefly known for being the birthplace of Mahatma Gandhi. Dwarka, on the western tip of the peninsula, is another holy Hindu

pilgrimage site. Turning north from there you come to Jamnagar and Rajkot, where Gandhi spent the early years of his life. Finally in the extreme west the strange marshland of the Rann of Kutch separates India from Pakistan. Bhuj is the main town in Kutch.

Madhya Pradesh

This large state is the heartland of India in more ways than one. It's geographically the centre of the country but it was also the centre of great Indian empires from Ashoka onwards. Although the Moghuls penetrated into this region it remained, as it is today, predominantly Hindu.

GWALIOR

Only a few hours from Agra, Gwalior is noted for its huge old fort. The town was the site for some of the final dramatic events of the 1857 Mutiny.

Things to See

The Fort You can ascend to the fort by the steep, short footpath at the northern end or by road from the west. Note that there are no refreshments available in the fort – if it's a hot day come prepared. Places of interest within the fort include the colourful Man Singh Palace or Man Mandir and a group of ruined palaces also at the northern end of the fort. The Sasbahu Temples are believed to date from the 9th to 11th centuries and the Teli-ka-mandir temple is nearby.

On the rock face at the south-west entrance there are a whole series of Jain images, some of them impressively large, cut into the rock face. At the base of the northern footpath, which has a series of gateways and other points of interest, is a small Archaeological Museum.

Other In the 'new town' is the Jai Vilas Palace, part of which is used as a museum, full of the sort of items you'd expect a Hollywood Maharajah to collect. The

Jami Masjid is a fine example of early Moghul architecture and nearby is the tomb of Tansen, a singer much admired by Akbar.

Places to Stay

Close to the station there's the basic (very) *Hotel Ashok* with rooms from Rs 10 per person or the rather more expensive *Hotel India* at Rs 30/40. There are also *Railway Retiring Rooms*.

A half km from the station, walk or take an auto-rickshaw, is the *Tourist Bungalow* (tel 22491) with rooms with bath at Rs 50/60. The Tourist Bungalow also has good food and a garden where you can camp. Other hotels are scattered around town.

Places to Eat

Cheap eating places can be found around the station or there's a *Kwality* (with Arctic intensity air-con) and a *Wengier's Restaurant* between the station and Lashkar, the new town area.

Getting There & Around

It's only two hours from Agra to Gwalior by train, fare is Rs 10 in 2nd class, Rs 44 in 1st. Around town there are auto-rickshaws (they won't use their meters), taxis, bicycle-rickshaws and tempos. A tempo from the station to Bada, the main square in Lashkar, is Rs 1.

JHANSI

Actually located in a finger of Uttar Pradesh which pokes into Madhya Pradesh, Jhansi is best known for the Rani of Jhansi, a sort of Indian Joan of Arc, who unsuccessfully defied the British during the Mutiny. The town today is a crossroads for travellers en route to Khajuraho but of little real interest.

Places to Stay

There are dorm beds at the *Railway Retiring Rooms* and very basic hotels close to the station like the *Central Hotel* or the *Hotel Sipri*.

SANCHI

The hilltop at this small village is topped by some of the earliest and most interesting Buddhist structures in India. The oldest stupas here were built by Ashoka in the third century BC. With the decline of Buddhism the site was lost until its rediscovery in 1818 and eventual restoration. At the base of the hill there is a small museum while the central structure on the hilltop is Ashoka's Great Stupa with its four magnificent gateways or toranas. Scattered around the hilltop are other stupas, temples, pillars and monasteries.

Places to Stay

Sanchi has a couple of superb *Railway Retiring Rooms* which cost just Rs 10/20 for singles/doubles. Otherwise there is the spartan *Buddhist Guest House* at Rs 20 a double, Rs 8 for a dorm bed; the more expensive *Ashok Traveller's Lodge* from Rs 60/90 (not great value) and a *Rest House* and *Circuit House* which you are unlikely to be allowed to stay in.

Getting There

Note that certain mail and express trains do not halt at Sanchi although 1st class passengers can request that an extra stop be made. Sanchi is just 68 km north of Bhopal and there are buses and trains from that city.

BHOPAL

The capital of Madhya Pradesh is now famous worldwide as the scene of the world's greatest industrial disaster, when the Union Carbide chemical plant here sprung a leak. The city has the huge Taj-ul-Masjid, one of the largest mosques in India, and a number of other mosques but its two lakes are the town's greatest attraction.

Places to Stay

There are a lot of hotels along Hamidia Rd between the railway and bus stations. Note that from the front of the station you'll have to take an auto-rickshaw down the line to a flyover and then back on the other side to get there. On foot you can walk out the back of the station right on to the road.

The *Grand Hotel* (tel 4070) is old, basic, but OK and costs Rs 15/25 and up. The *Hotel Ranjit* and the *Gulshan Lodge* are similar. *Hotel Samrat* is newish, costs Rs 25/35, while *Hotel Meghdoot* is also similar. There are a number of other places along this same road.

Bhopal has *Railway Retiring Rooms* and a *Youth Hostel* south of the lakes at North TT Nagar.

Places to Eat

Hamidia Rd also has places to eat including the vegetarian *Neelam* and *Manohar*. The *Ranjit Hotel* has a good air-con restaurant.

Getting There

Bhopal is on the main Delhi-Bombay railway line and also connected to those cities by air. It's a popular jumping off point for visits to Sanchi.

UJJAIN

This holy Hindu city is a site for the triennial Kumbh Mela and has a number of interesting temples.

INDORE

This large town is not of great interest in itself but is a good place from where to visit Mandu. Indore has an old palace, now used as offices, a mirrored Jain temple and an excellent museum. Tours are operated from Indore to Mandu.

Places to Stay & Eat

Good places can be found near the bus and railway stations. There are *Retiring Rooms* at the bus station for Rs 15/20 while across the road is the basic *Janta Hotel* with prices as low as Rs 12/15. Beside it are the *Standard Lodge*, with rooms from Rs 15 and up, and the *Hotel Ashoka*, from Rs 35 for pleasant rooms. There are many others around town.

Good food can be found in the *Janta* and *Standard Restaurants* in the hotels of the same name. There's frigid air-con and good vegetarian food in the *Volga Restaurant* near the Gandhi statue on M G Rd.

Getting There

Indore is off the main broad-gauge railway line which runs through Ujjain although it is connected to Ujjain by a broad gauge spur line and there is also a metre-gauge line through Indore. There are a wide variety of bus routes fanning out from Indore.

MANDU

The extensive hilltop fort of Mandu had a chequered history before eventually being abandoned. The Mandu buildings can be divided into three groups – the Royal Enclave, the village group and the Rewa Kund group. The royal group includes the Jahaz Mahal or 'ship palace', the Hindola Mahal or 'swing palace' and the partially subterranean Champa Baoli.

In the village group there is the huge Jami Masjid, one of the finest examples of Afghan architecture in India. Behind this mosque is the marble tomb of Hoshang while in front of it stands the ruins of the Ashrafi-Mahal.

The Rewa Kund group is in the south of the fort where you'll find the Palace of Baz Bahadur and, on the very edge of the hilltop plateau, Rupmati's Pavilion. Other places in Mandu include Darya Khan's Tomb, the Hathi Mahal and the isolated Nilkanth Palace.

Places to Stay

You can daytrip to Mandu from Indore or stay within the fort. The *Archaeological Rest House* in the Royal Enclave is Rs 15 per person while on the way to the village group the *Ashok Travellers' Lodge* is Rs 60/90 for singles/doubles. There is also a *Tourist Bungalow* at Rs 25 a double – this can be booked through the Tourist Office in Indore. There are a number of small eating places and a cheap dharamsala in the village group.

Getting There
Buses run to Mandu from Bhopal, Ujjain and Indore. Indore-Mandu is Rs 10, it's a 115 km trip. Tours from Indore are Rs 35.

KHAJURAHO
One of India's major attractions, Khajuraho has a superb collection of temples built during the Chandella period around 950 to 1050 AD. Quite why they chose such a remote and dismal spot is unknown, as is the reason for their sudden demise. Only about 20 of the original 85 temples are left standing but they are some of the finest and most magnificent in India.

Most of the temples are dedicated to Vishnu and Shiva but it is not the gods themselves nor the overall design which has made Khajuraho so well known – Khajuraho is famed for the sculptures which decorate the temples. They depict a lot of everyday activities – ploughing the fields, feasting, playing musical instruments, dancing – but one everyday activity in particular. Sex. Khajuraho has been called a *Kama Sutra* in stone and with more than a little truth.

Things to See
Western Group The major group of temples are in a fenced-in enclosure near to the bus stand, cheap hotels and Tourist Office. Here you'll find the Lakshmana Temple, one of the best preserved of the Khajuraho temples and with some very energetic carvings around the temple base. At the back of the enclosure a group of temples share a common base. The Kandariya Mahadev is the largest and most artistically perfect of the temples, it also has some of the most athletic sexual activity. The older Devi Jagadamba is a simpler design although it too has some noted eroticism. Also at the end of the enclosure, but not on the common plinth, is the Chitragupta while the western group

also includes the Parvati and Vishvanath Temples.

The Matanesvara Temple is beside the western group but outside the enclosure since this temple is still used for everyday worship. Also outside the enclosure is the interesting little Archaeological Museum (your Rs 0.50 ticket to the western group enclosure also permits entry to the museum) while beyond the tank is the ruined Chausath Yogini, probably the oldest temple at Khajuraho.

Eastern Group The eastern group comprises a walled enclosure of Jain temples and four other temples scattered through the village of Khajuraho. The Jain temples have extremely fine sculptures including some of Khajuraho's classic designs. They don't try to compete with the Hindu temples for explicitness, however. The main temples here are the Parsvanath, the Adinatha and the Santinatha. In the village you will find the pillared shell of the Jain Ghantai Temple, the small Javari Temple, the isolated Vamana Temple and the ancient Brahma Temple.

Southern Group There are only two temples in this group, one of which is south of the river by several km. The Duladeo Temple is thought to be the latest construction in Khajuraho and by this time the temple architects' abilities had gone into decline. The Chaturbhuja Temple is the final, remote building.

Places to Stay
The *Rahil (Janata Hotel)* is close to the expensive Khajuraho Hotel and has rooms at Rs 40/60 and a Rs 10 dormitory. The nearby *Tourist Bungalow* has four-bedded rooms at Rs 80. There are a number of cheap local hotels across from the bus station.

Other hotels include the *New Bharat Lodge* or the *Jain Lodge* which are both popular with travellers and have rooms from around Rs 15 or 20. *Hotel Sunset View* has doubles with bath from just Rs 30 in the low season and is very clean and modern.

Places to Eat

You can get a good thali at the *New Bharat Lodge* which also makes excellent tea. *Raja's Cafe*, run by a Swiss woman, is opposite the western enclosure entrance and has a large, shady tree over its outdoor eating area. Khajuraho is an extremely hot and dusty place during the hot season.

Getting There

Difficult – Khajuraho is a long way from anywhere. Flying is most convenient and Khajuraho is on the popular Delhi-Agra-Khajuraho-Varanasi-Kathmandu tourist route. By bus or train it's a long trip to Khajuraho. Satna is the nearest railhead coming from Varanasi, Calcutta or Bombay. From there a bus takes at least four hours. Jhansi is the nearest station on the Bombay-Agra-Delhi rail route and there are regular buses from there, costing Rs 17.50 and taking seven hours.

Getting Around

A taxi from the airport to the village is Rs 15 or the airport bus is Rs 5. All the rickshaw wallahs have 'fixed rates' to the various temples but are open to bargaining – Rs 4 or 5 for a round trip to the Duladeo temple. You can hire bicycles in Khajuraho for Rs 4 a day.

JABALPUR

The large town of Jabalpur is principally famous for the gorge on the Narmada River known as the Marble Rocks. This was also a centre for the British effort to suppress the 'Thugs', ritual murderers who strangled their victims in a practice known as 'Thuggee'.

Orissa

The eastern state of Orissa is best known for the great Sun Temple of Konarak. There are also some important and interesting temples in Bhubaneswar and Puri but here, more than anywhere else in India, non-Hindus are excluded from the temples.

BHUBANESWAR

The temple-studded capital of Orissa is dominated by the great Lingaraj Temple – off limits to non-Hindus although there is a viewing platform to one side where you can look over the wall. You'd need binoculars to see very much. Bhubaneswar has many other temples, a number of them around the Bindusagar or 'Ocean Drop' tank which is said to contain water from every sacred tank in India.

The Siddharanya group is a cluster of small, often finely detailed, temples near the main road. In a green field the isolated Raj Rani is one of the latest temples. Further out is the Brahmeswar and several other temples. The Bhubaneswar Museum has interesting exhibits on Orissan art and architecture and on the various Orissan tribal groups.

Places to Stay

The popular *Panthnivas Tourist Bungalow* (tel 54515) is also the site for the Tourist Office and has doubles with bath for Rs 50 and a Rs 10 dorm. Most other places to stay are in the new town part of Bhubaneswar – the *Bhubaneswar Hotel* (tel 51977) near the railway station is good value at Rs 30/50, more with air-con. Similar standards at the excellent value *Rajmahal Hotel* (tel 52448), near the bus station and market.

Hotel Pushpak has rooms with bath for Rs 30/35. *Hotel Vagwat Nivas* has good clean doubles at Rs 35. The *Jolly Lodge* on Cuttack Rd is a cheaper possibility at Rs 15 or Rs 20 with attached bath. There are numerous other small, cheap lodges between the Rajmahal and the expensive Hotel Konark.

Out at the Udayagiri-Khandagiri hills there's a run-down building claiming to be the *Khandagiri Youth Hostel*.

Places to Eat

The usual monotonous food can be found

at the *Tourist Bungalow* or try the *South Indian Hotel* in town for a thali. An air-con escape can be made to the *Ashok Kalinga* where Rs 30 to 50 per person will buy you a complete meal.

Getting There

Bhubaneswar is on the main Calcutta-Madras railway route, 469 km from Calcutta, 1222 km from Madras. The crack Coromandel express does Calcutta-Bhubaneswar in just six hours but other trains are much slower. Madras is 19, 24, even 30 hours away on some trains. Five days a week there are trains from Delhi – 37 to 48 hours. You can also fly from Calcutta or Varanasi.

There are frequent buses around Bhubaneswar – Puri is 1½ to two hours for Rs 5 or 6. Konarak a similar time and fare.

Getting Around

The airport is Rs 5 by airport bus, Rs 20 by taxi, less than Rs 10 by bicycle-rickshaw. From the Tourist Bungalow a rickshaw into town or to the Lingaraja Temple would be about Rs 2 or 3.

AROUND BHUBANESWAR

The Udayagiri and Khandagiri Caves are about five km out of town – two cave-studded hills facing each other across a road. Eight km south are the Dhauli edicts carved into a rock by Ashoka. The site is also marked by a new Peace Pagoda.

PURI

The coastal town of Puri is the site for the great Jagannath Temple where once again you are banned from entry. You can look down inside from the Raghunandan Library across the road – you'll be asked for a donation and you shouldn't believe the donations book when it indicates the largesse of other visitors!

Puri comes alive for the annual Rath Yatra or Car Festival in June or July. Enormous temple cars are dragged out of the temple of Jagannath and the images of the god Jagannath and his brother and sister are hauled a km or so down the road to the Gundicha Mandir or 'Garden House' where they have a week's summer vacation before being hauled back again. This is one of the biggest and most spectacular festivals in India and once upon a time devotees used to hurl themselves beneath the wheels of the unwieldy cars. From which came the expression 'crushed by a juggernaut'.

Puri has a number of other temples – from which you are also banned – and a long stretch of beach where Indian pilgrims bath in the traditional fully attired manner.

Places to Stay

Accommodation is almost all along the seafront and the western stretch is mainly intended for pilgrims. In the eastern area you'll find the *Panthnivas Tourist Bungalow* with singles/doubles at Rs 35/55 and a dining hall. A little further up the beach is the big new *Youth Hostel* with dorm beds at Rs 5. There are some other budget places near here including the rambling, old *Z Hotel* which is fine value with dorm beds for Rs 10 and other rooms from Rs 15 to 50. The cheaper *Sea Foam Hotel* and the *Hotel Shankar International* are other possibilities here. Puri also has *Railway Retiring Rooms*.

Places to Eat

Good seafood at the *Xanadu* or the *Sambhoo Restaurant* in the same area as the Z Hotel. The Youth Hostel has a restaurant as does the Tourist Bungalow.

Getting There

See Bhubaneswar or Konarak for details.

KONARAK

Although the great Sun Temple at Konarak was a noted landmark for centuries it was not until sand and debris was cleared from around its base that the temple's magnificence was rediscovered. The entire temple is a representation of the chariot of the Sun God Surya. It rides on 24 gigantic stone wheels and right around the base is a continuous procession of carvings, many of them rivalling Khajuraho for their erotic explicitness. The temple is thought to have been built around the 13th century but very little is known about its early history.

Places to Stay & Eat

The *Tourist Bungalow* has rooms at Rs 35/55 with attached bathroom. There's a dining hall and the tourist office is here. Close by is the basic *Santosh Restaurant* and further round towards the bus stop is the *Ashok Tourist Lodge* at Rs 60/90. If you're staying at the Tourist Bungalow and arriving by bus walk straight through by the temple, don't follow the long loop of the road round from the bus halt. Food possibilities at Konarak are very limited.

Getting There

Getting from Puri to Konaraka used to be very time consuming because there was no coastal road and you had to loop back almost to Bhubaneswar. Now there's a direct route along the coast and travel is much easier. Puri-Konarak in an impossibly crowded vehicle is about Rs 4.

Pipli, at the point where the Konarak road forks off the Bhubaneswar-Puri road, is noted for its applique craft work.

Bombay

Once an island surrounded by malarial mud flats, then a Portuguese possession, Bombay was passed on to the British as a wedding dowry (no less) in 1661. They proceeded to drain the marshy area and connect the island with the mainland and then turned it into their 'Gateway to India'.

Bombay prospered as an important trade centre and today it is the second largest city in India – and certainly the most prosperous. If New Delhi is the government centre, Varanasi the spiritual centre, Calcutta the intellectual centre, then Bombay is the business and money centre. You will also find it is the most expensive place in India.

Information & Orientation

Bombay is actually a series of islands connected by a bridge with the mainland. Most places of importance to visitors are in the area known as Fort or in the spit of land to the south of Fort known as Colaba. In Colaba you'll find several of the major hotels and most of the cheap ones plus the Gateway of India. That's Bombay's chief landmark, along with the magnificent Taj Mahal Hotel which is right beside it.

The Tourist Office is at 123 Mahrashi Karve Rd, Churchgate (directly across from Churchgate Station) and it's a good one. The GPO is in an imposing big building on Nagar Chowk near the Victoria Terminus Station. One of Bombay's best bookshops is the Nalanda bookshop in the Taj Mahal Hotel.

Things to See

Gateway of India Built to commemorate a visit by George V in 1911, the huge basalt monument stands on Apollo Bunder and is the best known landmark in Bombay.

Prince of Wales Museum This one was put up for George's 1905 visit, before he became king. It is quite close to the gateway and has a good archaeological collection and some fine Moghul paintings. The Jehangir Art Gallery is in the museum grounds and often has exhibitions of contemporary Indian art.

Chowpatty A beach in the centre of Bombay where people go to watch people – plus all the usual Indian sideshows.

Hanging Gardens The road winds up from Chowpatty through Bombay's select residential areas to this garden with fine views back over Chowpatty, the city and across the inlet between Bombay and the coast. Up here are the Parsi 'Towers of Silence' where their dead are laid out to be

Bombay

Malabar Point

BACK BAY

Key :-

1. Bombay Central Railway Station
2. Victoria Terminus Railway Station
3. Churchgate Railway Station
4. Long-distance Bus Station (Maharashtra State Transport)
5. Tourist Office
6. General Post Office
7. YMCA International House
8. Victoria Gardens & Museum
9. Mahalaxmi Temple
10. Laxmi Narayan Temple
11. Kamala Nehru Park
12. Jain Temple
13. Walkeshwar Temple
14. Round Temple
15. Banaji Fire Temple
16. Wadiaji Fire Temple
17. Anjuman Fire Temple
18. Aquarium
19. St. John's Church (Afghan Memorial)
20. Prince of Wales Museum
21. Mani Bhavan
22. American Express/Thomas Cook
23. Hotel Railway & Hotel Manama

consumed by vultures – in order that they do not pollute the earth (by burial) or air (by cremation). Although you cannot enter the area with the five towers there are models of them in the Victoria & Albert Museum. The Parsis, followers of Zoroaster, fled from Persia when the Muslims arrived from Arabia. Today they have an economic influence far in excess of their small numbers. Further up the road is the Mahalaxmi temple. Laxmi is the Goddess of Wealth and therefore very popular in Bombay.

Other Victoria Gardens in the north of the city has the Victoria & Albert Museum and the elephant statue from Elephanta Island. The Crawford Market (officially renamed Mahatma Phule Market) is north of the Victoria Terminus railway station. It is a huge and varied bazaar area. India is the world's biggest producer of movies and Bombay is its Hollywood, the tourist office can arrange a visit to a film studio for you. Mani Bhavan is a house which was often used by Gandhi and is now a national memorial to him with many of his personal possessions.

On Marine Drive, beside Chowpatty Beach, is the Taraporewella Aquarium, one of the best in India. Haji Ali's Tomb is a not very interesting mosque and tomb connected to the main island by a causeway which can only be crossed at low tide. Visit Sassoon Docks on Colaba Causeway at dawn to see the fish being brought in. Bombay's notorious red light district on Falkland St is known as the cages since the women stand behind barred doors along the street.

Places to Stay

Bombay is both overcrowded and expensive – you will have to pay more for less here (the cheapies are often much less clean than equivalents in other cities) and unless you arrive very early in the morning you will have trouble finding a place. The cheap hotel area in Colaba is concentrated behind the Taj Mahal Hotel, which in turn is right by the Gateway of India, so it's

easy to find and quite conveniently situated.

Best known are the *Rex* (tel 231518) and *Stiffles* (tel 230960), both at 8 Ormiston Rd. The Rex is on floors 3 and 4, the Stiffles on 1 and 2. Rooms with attached bath cost from Rs 60/90 but there are also cheaper singles (airless little cubicle) and more expensive rooms with air-con. Frankly they're no big deal but for Bombay they're good value.

Across the road on the corner of Mereweather Rd (at 30) is the *Salvation Army Red Shield Hostel* (tel 241824). A dorm bed is Rs 40, a double is Rs 100, both including rather bland and tasteless meals. To get in you must be waiting at the door at 9 am, no earlier, no later. They are not at all keen on real freaks here (Bombay seems to be the final resting place for those legendary hippy-junkies) and couples must be married if they want a room.

At 12 Mereweather Rd the *Carlton Hotel* (tel 230642) costs from Rs 60, again nothing special. Bombay has a number of Ys including the good value *YWCA International Guest House* (tel 230445) at 18 Madame Cama Rd. Singles/doubles with air-con are Rs 71/139 and they're generally heavily booked. The *YMCA International Guest House* (tel 891191) is at Mayo House, Cooperage Rd and costs Rs 88/156. There's a Rs 10 temporary membership charge at the YWCA, Rs 20 at the YMCA but both places are usually booked out months ahead.

There are other hotels scattered around – the *Lawrence Hotel* (tel 243618) at Ashok Kumar House (3rd floor), K Dubash Marg in the city centre is good value at Rs 50/90. Bombay Central and Victoria Terminus stations both have *Railway Retiring Rooms*. If you arrive other than early in the morning it may well be a case of just taking what you can get and trying again the next day. In that case if you can't find anything yourself you'll have to depend on the hotel touts who work the Colaba area. They'll undoubtedly find you something and while it will be lousy value (probably an airless, window-less, hardboard-partitioned little box) you can start looking for something better the next morning.

Places to Eat

Hotels may be in short supply but there's no shortage of restaurants. Near the Rex and Stiffles, *Dipti's Pure Drinks* is a popular place for fruit juice, fruit salad and ice cream. Round the corner from Ormiston Rd on Nawroji Furounji Rd you can get an excellent Rs 5 thali at *Laxmi Vilas*. Along Colaba Causeway the *Ananda Punjabi* is good for dinner, the *Leopold Restaurant* for breakfast or a beer and the *Cafe Mondegar* is a pleasant coffee bar.

Try the *Samovar* in the Jehangir Art Gallery for a cold drink or snack. On K Dubash Marg, across from the Prince of Wales Museum, there are several more expensive restaurants including the *Khyber Restaurant* where a fine meal will cost you Rs 40 to 50 per person. If you really want to eat well try the all-you-can-eat lunch-time buffet in the *Taj Mahal Hotel*. Finally don't leave Bombay without sampling bhelpuri, Bombay's famous take-away snack.

Getting There

Bombay is comprehensively connected by air with the rest of India. There are two railway systems out of Bombay – Central Railways to the east and south (plus a few to the north) from Victoria Terminus; Western Railways to the north from Churchgate and Central. Note that a few trains also go from Dadar (including the fastest train to Madras) which is further north of Central. Delhi is 28 hours away, Calcutta 35, Madras 26.

Long distance buses depart from the station opposite Bombay Central. There are buses to all the major towns around Bombay – see the Goa section for details on bus and ferry services to Goa.

Getting Around

If you arrive in Bombay at Central your ticket will include a local service on to Churchgate – which is more central than Central. Churchgate and Victoria Terminus are both a short taxi or bus ride from the Colaba hotel area. The airport bus costs Rs 15 or 20, depending on the airport terminal, and goes to the Air India terminal at Nariman Point and on to the Taj Mahal Hotel in Colaba. A taxi would be about Rs 80, outside the rush hours. Although you can get to the airport by train to Santa Cruz or Vile Parle station (from where you can get a bus or taxi) don't consider this idea during the long rush hours.

Bombay taxis are metered (and they use them) but the meters are way out of line with reality. Bombay has one of the best public bus services in India but beware of Bombay's expert pickpockets. From Victoria Terminus take a 1, 6 Ltd, 7 Ltd, 103 or 124 to 'Electric House' for the Colaba cheap hotels. There are a wide variety of tours in Bombay both around the city and further out around Bombay Island – then tend to be expensive compared to other cities.

AROUND BOMBAY
Elephanta Island

The stone elephant which prompted the Portuguese to name this island Elephanta is now in the Victoria Gardens. The island is famous for its four cave temples which were carved out about 1200 years ago. They have huge and very fine bas reliefs in which, if you know your Hindu gods, you can pick out all the notables.

The island is about 10 km north-east of Bombay and launches leave fairly frequently from the Gateway of India. The return trip costs from 13 to 25, and the more expensive trips include a guide. I recommend that you lay out the extra for a guided trip as you'll learn a lot more about the caves. The boats don't always go during the monsoon season when the water is too rough. Elephanta is very crowded on weekends.

Other

The Kanheri Caves, 42 km from Bombay, are interesting though nothing on Ajanta and Ellora. Juhu Beach, 18 km north of the city, is a convenient location for Bombay airport but the beach is nothing special. There are other more remote beaches around Bombay island. Bassein, nearly 50 km north of Bombay, was a Portuguese stronghold and has ruins of many old Portuguese buildings.

Maharashtra

The state of Maharashtra has Bombay as its capital and in terms of area is one of the largest states in India. It has a number of places of interest including the famous cave temples of Ajanta and Ellora.

MATHERAN

The hill station of Matheran is 171 km from Bombay and reached by a delightful toy train ride from Neral, on the plains below. It's a place simply to wander around and savour the cooler air at 700 to 800 metres.

Places to Stay

Khan's Cosmopolitan Hotel is rather primitive with rooms from Rs 20. Real economisers can find even cheaper accommodation at the *Holiday Camp* a km or two before the Matheran station. *Laxmi Hotel* has doubles with bathroom for Rs 30. There are lots of places at Matheran.

KARLA & BHAJA CAVES

The great Karla cave dates from around 80 BC and is one of the best preserved Hinayana Buddhist caves in India. It's comparatively little known and untouristed compared to Ajanta and Ellora. The Bhaja Caves are rather less accessible than the Karla Cave and not of such great interest. In this same area there are a number of old forts and other caves at Bedsa.

Places to Stay

You can stay in Lonavla where the *Adarsh Hotel* has doubles from Rs 50 all the way up to Rs 250. There are quite a few other hotels around Lonavla such as the charming old *Pitale Boarding & Lodging* with doubles with bath for Rs 40. Or the *Highway Lodge* which has dorm beds at Rs 15. The *Holiday Camp* near the Karla Cave has dormitories or rooms at Rs 20 or 25 – good value and convenient for the caves.

Getting There & Around

Buses through Karla tend to be packed out, it's better to travel by train – Bombay-Lonavla takes about three hours. It's worth hiring an auto-rickshaw to get around the area. Doing it that way it's possible to daytrip from Pune or Bombay.

PUNE (Poona)

The home town of the great Maratha leader Shivaji, Pune was at one time a major centre for western visitors due to the Shree Rajneesh Ashram. Since the Bhagwan has moved on to bigger and better things in Oregon, USA the number of visitors has plummeted.

The Raja Kelkar Museum is a delightful small museum with a definite personality to it. The massive walls of the Shanwarwada Palace are virtually all that remains of this 1736 fort. Across the river is the Aga Khan's Palace where Gandhi was imprisoned for a time – it is now maintained as a Gandhi memorial.

Places to Stay

When the Rajneesh Ashram was in full swing finding a place to stay in Pune could be difficult, now it is much easier. There is the usual collection of drab cheapies near the railway station. The *Green Hotel* in Wilson Garden is better at Rs 35 a double. Next door is the similarly priced *Semrat* and across the road is the cheaper *Central Lodge* (Rs 25 a double) and the more expensive *Alankar Hotel* (Rs 50 a double). Wilson Garden starts directly opposite the railway station, beside the *National Hotel* which is Rs 40 a double.

There are also *Railway Retiring Rooms* at Rs 15 a head or Rs 10 in the dorm or out at the Nehru Stadium (Rs 5 or 6 by auto-rickshaw from the railway station) the *Hotel Saras* is Rs 50/75 for singles/doubles and quite pleasant. Behind the Shivajinagar phone exchange the *Ashwamedh Hotel* is middle bracket at Rs 90 a double, but very good.

Places to Eat

There are a number of good, cheap places to eat by the railway station – like the *Neelam Restaurant* or the *Hotel Madhura* in the big Hotel Metro building. Excellent thalis and good lassi in the latter. A couple of doors down the *Savera Restaurant* also has good food. The expensive *Hotel Amir* (which is also very close to the railway station) has an air-con restaurant.

Getting There & Around

It's four or five hours by train from Bombay or you can take a bus – air-con buses are available at Rs 45 – or taxi. Pune has three main bus stations for towns in different directions. Pune is packed with bicycle rental shops and there are also lots of taxis and auto-rickshaws.

AROUND PUNE

Simhagad, the 'lion fort', is 25 km south-west, it was the site for more deeds of derring-do by Shivaji. Mahabaleshwar is another popular Maharashtra hill station and it was here that Shivaji met with General Afzal Khan, supposedly for a discussion on a peace treaty, but ended up disembowelling him with his 'tiger claws'. Further on is Panchgani, another hill station.

NASIK

An interesting little town with picturesque bathing ghats where the Kumbh Mela is held every 12 years. There are a series of Hinayana Buddhist Caves at Pandu Lena, eight km south-west.

AURANGABAD

Although Aurangabad's main function, for many travellers, is as a jumping off point for visits to the Ajanta and Ellora Caves there are also a number of places of interest in the town itself. The Bibika-Maqbara is a poor man's Taj Mahal; built in 1679 by Aurangzeb's son it looks remarkably like the Taj but without its architectural grace or its precision construction. The Panchakki is a water mill now used as cool and pleasant gardens. North of the city the Aurangabad Caves are usually forgotten when the more impressive caves of Ajanta and Ellora are so close by.

Near the railway station there's a state tourist office in the Holiday Camp and round the corner a Government of India Tourist Office on Station Rd.

Places to Stay

Most of Aurangabad's cheap accommodation is near the railway station – the exception being the excellent *Youth Hostel* which is midway between the station and the main part of town (where the bus station is also located). Dorm beds are Rs 8, a rupee less if you're a YHA member. The government *Holiday Camp*, about a hundred metres from the railway station, has doubles from Rs 35 to 45, excellent value.

There are a string of hotels between the camp (which isn't a camp at all, more like a motel) and the station or round the corner towards the national tourist office. The *Kathiawad Hotel* is beside the national tourist office – Rs 25 for doubles and a helpful manager. The *Tourist Home* is Rs 25, fair to reasonable. *Hotel Ashok* or *Ashok Lodging* is dirt cheap at Rs 15. The *Arnanda Lodge* is marginally more expensive.

Places to Eat

Good food, even cornflakes for breakfast, at the *Hotel Guru*. The *Holiday Camp* has a dining hall with the usual rest-house-style menu.

Getting There

Aurangabad is the main centre for both cave groups – Ajanta is 106 km away, Ellora is 30 km. It's quite easy to day trip to Ellora from Aurangabad but most travellers stay at Ajanta. Jalgaon, the other main centre, is 59 km beyond Ajanta. It's on the main broad gauge line from Bombay but to Aurangabad you have to change to metre gauge to get there. On the other hand Aurangabad is the obvious place to go from Pune (by road) or Hyderabad (by rail, metre gauge all the way). You can also fly to Aurangabad.

Buses depart every half hour to Ellora for Rs 4, to Ajanta it's Rs 10 and can take quite a time. Tours are operated by the state and national tourist offices and by the state system. A day tour to the Ellora Caves is Rs 20, to Ajanta it's Rs 40. If you're thoroughly fed up with the local buses it is worth enquiring about taking the tour bus to Ajanta even if you're planning to stay there and not return to Aurangabad.

AURANGABAD TO ELLORA

There are a number of places of interest between Aurangabad and the Ellora Caves. The magnificent hilltop fortress of Daulatabad is surrounded by five km of walls. It was built in the 14th century by a slightly crazy Delhi ruler who not only built the fortress as his new capital but attempted to transfer the whole population of Delhi as well. En route to the top of the fortress, from where there are superb views over the surrounding countryside, you pass through a complicated series of defences, gates, false corridors and moats.

Rauza, or Khuldabad, a walled town only three km from Ellora, is the final resting place of Aurangzeb, the last great Moghul. Aurangzeb's pious austerity extended even to his own tomb, a simple affair of bare earth.

ELLORA CAVES

Cut into a cliff face the Ellora Caves are noted for their superb sculptures and

Around Aurangabad

carvings, all cut from solid rock. There are 34 caves here, 12 Buddhist, 17 Hindu and five Jain, all either *viharas* or *chaityas* (temples).

Most fantastic of the caves is the Kailasa, a huge Hindu temple which covers an area twice as large as the Parthenon in Athens and is 1½ times as high. Remember all these temples were cut from the top down to the ground, it has been estimated that cutting the Kailasa involved removal of 200,000 tons of rock! The Ellora Caves are not as old as those at Ajanta; since the rock face they are cut into slopes gradually back many of them are much more 'open' and less cave-like than those at Ajanta.

Close to the Ellora caves the 18th century Shiva temple at Verul is one of the 12 Shiva *jyotorlingas* in India.

Places to Stay & Eat

It's possible to stay at Ellora at the *Hotel*

Kailasa where singles/doubles are Rs 40/60. There's a restaurant attached to the hotel and another, more expensive one, nearby.

AJANTA CAVES

The Ajanta Caves pre-date those of Ellora. They were mainly cut in the four centuries from about 200 BC, although the builders had a second go around the 6th century AD and a final session around the 7th century, before abruptly abandoning Ajanta for Ellora, to the south. This sudden change makes a very interesting contrast as the Ajanta caves are mainly in the aristocratic Hinayana style while at Ellora the more generally popular Mahayana style had come into vogue – but at this time Buddhism was already declining in India and at Ellora the caves are Hindu and Jain as well as Buddhist.

The Ajanta Caves were stumbled upon by a hunting party of British officers in 1819 – quite a find. The caves were overgrown and often covered over – they are cut into a spectacular horseshoe-shaped ravine. While the Ellora Caves are notable for their sculpture here it is the wall paintings that are of greatest interest. Some of them are marvellously preserved but the caves are kept deliberately darkened and to see them you must either pay for a 'lighting ticket' or try tagging along with a tour group.

Places to Stay & Eat

Right by the cave there is a small *Forestry Rest House* but most people stay at Fardapur, five km from the caves and on the main road – the caves are a couple of km off the road. The excellent *Holiday Camp* at Fardapur has pleasant rooms on an open verandah costing from Rs 30. It's a nice place to sit in the evening, sip a tepid beer and discuss the day's sightseeing. There's a simple restaurant at one end of the building and some food stalls just down the road. The *Fardapur Travellers Bungalow* is right behind the Holiday Camp.

A bus to the caves from Fardapur is less than a rupee although the cost seems to vary with each bus.

Goa

In 1510, just a year before he captured Melaka in Malaya, Alfonso de Albuquerque captured Goa for Portugal and the Portuguese HQ in India was transferred north from Cochin. It remained here for 450 years until the Indians chucked them out in 1961. Goa has a totally different atmosphere to the rest of India but it is also far more than just an ex-colony with a bit of interesting history to be seen. Goa also has some of the best tropical beaches to be found anywhere in the world, good swimming, cheap living – hardly surprisingly it has become a major freak centre and at Christmas each year it is the place in India to be.

PANJIM (Panaji)

The small and pleasant riverside capital of the state still has a very Portuguese feel to it. It's mainly used by travellers as a central place for getting things done and for visiting Old Goa. There is an Indian Airlines office, GPO with poste restante, tourist office and various travel agencies in Panjim.

Places to Stay

The government run *Tourist Hostel* (tel 2303), close to the river, is such good value that it is usually totally full. Singles/doubles are Rs 30/60, dorm beds Rs 8 and there is a restaurant on the first floor. Other better places include the *Hotel Aroma* (tel 3519) and the nearby *Safari Hotel*, both on Cunha Rivara Rd. Rooms are Rs 35/70 in the Aroma, only Rs 20/30 in the more basic Safari.

The *Hotel Republica* on José Falcao Rd has good rooms overlooking the river that cost Rs 12 to 15 for singles, Rs 20 to 25 for doubles. Right next door is the *Hotel*

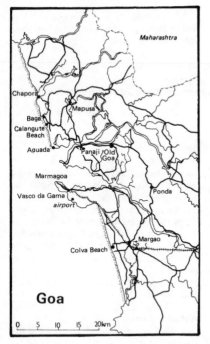

has excellent milkshakes, the *Tourist Hotel* good thalis, the *A Pasteria* cake shop is a good place for snacks. For a minor splurge try the *Shere Punjab Restaurant* on 18th June Rd, the *Shalimar* or the adjoining *Taj Mahal Restaurant* on Alfonso de Albuquerque Rd. Finally, for a big splurge, there's the elegant Portuguese *El Gazelle Restaurant* at Miramar.

Getting There

There is a daily (except Wednesdays from Panjim and Tuesdays from Bombay) ferry between Bombay and Panjim. It does not run during the monsoon. It departs Bombay at 10 am and arrives in Panjim 22 hours later. It's a fine trip with fares from Rs 48 to 72 for deck passage, Rs 220 to 300 for cabins. Lower deck is only for the hardy.

Air-con luxury buses between Bombay and Goa take about 16 hours and cost Rs 110 to 115. There are also ordinary state transport buses to Bombay and other centres. Trains operate through Vasco da Gama but take a long time.

Getting Around

The airport is at Dabolim, near Vasco da Gama, and the airport bus into town costs Rs 20, which is absurd when you can take a whole taxi for Rs 20. There are a number of ferries operating on the rivers in Goa, they're an enjoyable way of getting around. There are a variety of bus services from Panjim to other towns, they're quite civilised. It's easy to hire bicycles and even motorcycles in Goa.

Palace which has rooms from Rs 10 to Rs 35 but only the two rooms with balconies are pleasant – the others are all dingy little boxes. Really basic places tend to be a bit dreary. There are lots of them in the streets behind the GPO. The *Goa Tourist Lodge* is one of the few reasonable ones. There is a *Youth Hostel* three km out of town at Miramar Beach.

Places to Eat

Panjim has some great places to eat like the relatively new *Godinho* which offers Goan and other Indian dishes. The *Hotel Aroma* on the Municipal Park square is also good. Across the square from the Aroma the *New Punjab Restaurant* does excellent Punjabi and tandoor food.

In the narrow street behind the GPO the *Hotel Venite* has a limited menu but is a great place for a drink. The *Jesmal Cafe*

OLD GOA

Velha Goa, the old Portuguese capital, is nine km from the new capital of Panjim. It was deserted in favour of the new city because of its unhealthy malarial climate. The most important of the many Portuguese buildings in old Goa is the Basilica of the Bom Jesus, built between 1594 and 1603. It is a fine example of Portuguese architecture but is best known for its famous inmate – St Francis Xavier. St

Francis had a spell of converting the heathen in this area before moving on to fresh challenges. After his death his body, after several moves, eventually ended up back here and lies in an extravagantly decorated silver casket. Every 10 years the body is taken out to be shown to the faithful – minus both big toes (bitten off by zealous women!) and one arm (sent to Rome for a zealous Pope). Next big day is scheduled for 1994.

Other important buildings include the Se Cathedral, construction of which commenced in 1562. The main altar is dedicated to St Catherine. The Church of St Francis of Assisi has a floor paved with old gravestones and the convent behind it houses the Archaeological Museum. All that is left of the ruined Church of St Augustine is the huge bell tower. Then there is the Church of St Cajetan, the Church & Convent of St Monica, the Viceroy's Arch and a number of other points of interest.

Getting There

There are frequent buses from the Panjim bus stand or take any Ponda bus. The 20 to 30 minute trip costs Rs 1. During festivals ferries go there from the Panjim jetty.

MARGAO

The main town in the south of Goa has a good market and an interesting old church but is mainly used as a transport point for nearby Colva Beach. There is a tourist office and GPO with poste restante facilities nearby.

Places to Stay

Singles/doubles cost from Rs 30/40 at the *Goa Woodlands Hotel*, one of the better and cheaper hotels. Only Rs 15/20 at the *Milan Kamat Hotel* off Station Rd. *Centaur Lodging*, opposite the Milan Kemat, is also cheap. Or there is the *Sankit Hotel*, similarly priced, opposite the railway station. The *Rukrish Hotel* on Station Rd has good clean rooms – singles

with a balcony over the street are Rs 25, doubles Rs 30 to 40.

Places to Eat

Superb Goan-style food at the *Kandell* (or is is Icandeel?). Close to the Colva bus stand *La Marina Cafe* is also good but only really for the evenings. *Hotel Prasad* has typical vegetarian food. *Marliz*, beside the Municipal Gardens, is a very popular cafe for a quick snack.

Getting There

Buses run hourly (approximately) to Colva Beach, a 20 minute Rs 0.60 trip. Taxis are Rs 2 per person, or from beside the bus station you can get a ride to the beach on the back of a 'motorcycle taxi' for Rs 6.

A bus to Panjim takes about 1½ hours and costs Rs 3.50 to 4. This route is much faster since the completion of the Zuari River bridge. A taxi will cost about Rs 100 and since the drivers will hang around for a couple of hours if you have something to do there this can be a good way of getting to Panjim for a group of half a dozen.

MAPUSA

This is the northern centre and performs the same function for the northern beaches that Margao does for Colva. There is a good Friday market.

Places to Stay

The *Hotel Bardez* has singles/doubles at Rs 40/50 or there's the *Tourist Hostel* at Rs 20/30. Good food at the *Imperial Bar & Restaurant*.

THE BEACHES

The towns may be pleasant but it's the beaches people come to Goa for. Despite the 'hippies' Mecca' image they're actually great places to visit and a real breather from 'India'. Calangute is the best known beach and has the most development in terms of places to stay and eat. Baga, Anjuna and Chapora, to the north, are somewhat quieter. Colva, in the south of

Goa, is probably the finest beach though. Aguada and Bagmalo are jetsetters' beaches with expensive hotels.

COLVA

Colva has a superb beach, colourful fishermen and their boats, and just enough development to make it comfortable but not over-developed. It's quiet and unhassled, just the occasional party of Indian tourists come to see the naked hippies!

Places to Stay

For a long term stay you can rent rooms or houses or even build your own palm hut. Take care of your possessions though – Colva (and the other Goa resorts) have a lot of theft. More expensive places to stay include the pleasant *Whitesands Hotel* from Rs 65, more with air-con. The *Tourist Cottages* are excellent value but very popular and often full. The *Mare Sol Hotel* at the back of the Vincy Bar has doubles with fan and bath for Rs 45. The *Sukhsagar Beach Resort* is similar.

Otherwise you can try the rambling old *Tourist Nest* at Rs 20 to 30 or cheaper places like the *Lucky Star* or the *Sunset Restaurant*. Head two km south to Benaulim Beach for tranquil places like *L'Amour Beach Resort* for Rs 30 a double or the similar *O Palmar Beach Cottages*.

Places to Eat

Pedro's Bar & Restaurant at Benaulim Beach has excellent seafood, good music and pleasant surroundings. *L'Amour Beach Resort* has a good restaurant too. *Lucky Star* at the Colva end is good too or you could try the popular *Lactancia Restaurant*. The long running *Vincy's Bar* may have lost some of its early spirit but keeps on keeping on.

Getting There

See Margao for details of transport, this is the usual jumping off point for Colva.

CALANGUTE & BAGA

North of the river Calangute has been dubbed the 'Queen' of Goa's beaches by the tourist department although it's not really number one at all. In fact Baga, which you reach if you simply stroll north along Calangute, is really rather better and others are better still. Calangute is the beach which gave Goa its 'Hippie Mecca' image, however. And it's still a major gathering place each Christmas.

Places to Stay

Since this is the most popular beach there are all sorts of places to stay. The *Calangute Beach Guest House* is good value with doubles at Rs 35 or Rs 65 with bath. The *Tourist Hostel* is also good value, but ugly. Rooms cost Rs 40/55 with bath, there are dorm beds for Rs 8 or cottages for Rs 35/50. The *Souza Lobo Restaurant* also has good value rooms at Rs 35.

Behind the Tourist Hostel *Meena's Lodge* has rooms from Rs 40 (without bath) to Rs 100 (with). The *Tourist Dormitory & Annapurna Restaurant* is probably the cheapest place in Calangute – dorm beds at Rs 8.

Moving along the beach towards Baga the *Overseas Tourist Home* is a quiet, shady place with rooms for Rs 25 per person. The *Sunshine Beach Resort* has big, airy rooms for Rs 70 a double. *Vila Bomfim* is one of the best places at Calangute/Baga and has doubles at Rs 60. At Baga *Jack's Bar & Restaurant* has cottages at Rs 50 a double. The *Riverside* has cottages at Rs 70.

Places to Eat

There are lots of places to eat including the *Sea View Restaurant* which has good food but in small quantities. *Souza Lobo Restaurant* is similar but the setting is superb, a good place to watch the sunset. Mid-way between Calangute and Baga is the popular and friendly *Richdavy Restaurant*.

Getting There

Buses run to Calangute and Baga from Mapusa or Panjim. It's 30 minutes from Panjim at a cost of Rs 1.30.

ANJUNA

If Calangute was last year's 'in-place' then this is this year's.

Places to Stay & Eat

Anjuna is a major scene but there's not much by the way of accommodation apart from a few little hotels by the road junction. They're usually permanently full and you may have to opt for a primitive rented room at first. *Rose Garden Restaurant* on the beach has excellent, if slightly expensive, food.

Getting There

Buses run every couple of hours to Chapora and Mapusa or take a motorcycle-taxi for Rs 8.

CHAPORA

Like Anjuna this is a popular beach for a longer stay but it's more attractive, less spoilt than Anjuna.

Places to Stay & Eat

There's just one 'international' resort here and a couple of cheapies. *Dr Lobo's* has rooms for Rs 10 to 15 but the facilities are basic. Rooms are Rs 15/30 at the *Noble Nest Restaurant & Boarding*. Otherwise it's a question of renting a room. Ask around in the restaurants or on the beach. There are a number of restaurants along the main street of Chapora village, *Lobo's* (no connection to Dr Lobo's) is good.

Getting There

To get there take a bus from Mapusa (Rs 0.75) or there are three direct buses daily from Panjim. There are also motorcycles.

OTHER

Goa has the Bondla Wildlife Sanctuary in the foothills of the Western Ghats, a number of temples which somehow escaped Portuguese destruction or were rebuilt after they'd had their fling, plus several old Portuguese forts. The one at Chapora is particularly good. Most of the interesting temples and the Safe Masjid mosque are close to or in Ponda, about 22 km from Panjim.

Karnataka

Formerly known as Mysore the state of Karnataka is easy-going but full of contrasts from the modern city of Bangalore at one extreme to the rural farming areas at the other. The superb Chalukyan and Hoysala temples are major attractions of the state and many travellers find Mysore a pleasant and relaxed city to visit.

BANGALORE

The capital of the state is an industrial city and quite a pleasant place although not of great interest. At the northern end of Cubbon Park the Vidhana Soudha is a spectacular building which is floodlit on Sunday evenings. Cubbon Park is the 'lungs' of the city and the Government Museum and the Technological & Industrial Museum are located here.

The Lai Bagh Botanical Gardens in the south of the city were laid out by Hyder Ali and his son, Tipu Sultan. The old fort and Tipu Sultan's Palace are not of great interest. On Bugle Hill the Bull Temple has a huge Nandi, the bull 'vehicle' of Shiva.

Places to Stay

Cheap hotels are mainly around City Market. The *Sudha Lodge* on Cottonpet Bhashyam Rd has rooms at Rs 20/30 and is clean, friendly and popular. The *Sudarshan Hotel* is also good, it's down a side street diagonally opposite the elevated pedestrian walkway which goes through the Central Bus Station. Rooms here are Rs 15/30.

Two others in the same area are the

Hotel Venus at Rs 15/25 and the *Sri Shanthi Lodge* (tel 27114) at Rs 17/27. Other cheapies are located around the City Market on Sri Narsimharaja Rd. They include the *Bilal, Rainbow, Delhi Bhavan, Chandra Vihar, Nataraj* and *Isaquia Hotels*. There are two *YMCAs* – on Nrupatunga Rd (tel 24848) and on Infantry Rd but they both seem to be permanently full with local students.

Places to Eat

There are countless restaurants offering standard South Indian vegetarian fare in the Gandhi Nagar and Chickpet areas. A masala dosa and coffee will only be about Rs 2.50. The *Kamat Hotels*, there are several around town, offer good thalis for Rs 4. Or try *Hotel Blue Star* opposite the Tribhuvan Cinema at the back of Kempegowda Circle for an extensive vegetarian and non-vegetarian menu. For a minor splurge try the *Aishwarya Restaurant* on the 1st floor of Gupta Market, Kempegowda Rd.

Getting There

There are flights to Bangalore from other major cities and daily expresses to all the main cities in the south, in central India and to Delhi. Delhi is 38 hours by the twice-weekly express, Bombay takes from 24 hours, Madras only seven hours on the fast express and mail trains.

Bangalore has a well-organised central bus station for long distance buses. It's right in front of the City Railway Station. There are also many private bus companies around the road which circles the bus station. These have similar routes to the state buses but are more luxurious.

MYSORE

A very popular travellers' centre, Mysore is friendly, easy-going and full of interest yet small enough to make getting around very easy. It's also a centre for production of incense sticks! The Maharaja's Palace, a beautifully extravagant building dating from 1911-12, is certainly worth a visit.

It's open from 10.30 am to 5.30 pm and admission is Rs 2.

You can also devote a pleasant half day to climbing the thousand steps to the top of Chamundi Hill where you can visit the huge Sri Chamundeswari Temple. It's open from 9 am to 12 noon and 5 to 9 pm and non-Hindus are allowed inside. Two-thirds of the way up the steps you come to the huge stone image of Shiva's bull Nandi. There are buses from the central bus station about every half hour. Note that the hilltop is 13 km from the city by road but only four km by the steps.

Other places worth visiting include the Devaraja Fruit & Vegetable Market and the Kaveri Arts & Crafts Emporium.

Places to Stay

Mysore has a lot of places to stay, most of them along Dhanvantri Rd or around Gandhi Square. They include *New Gayathri Bhavan* (tel 21224) on Dhanvantri Rd from Rs 18/30 or the similarly priced *Agarwal Lodge* (tel 22730) on the same road. Still on Dhanvantri Rd the *Hotel Indra Bhavan* (tel 23933) has rooms for Rs 25/35. At all these places rooms have attached bathrooms.

On Gandhi Square *Hotel Satkar* has very reasonably priced rooms at Rs 20/35. Opposite is the huge *Hotel Dasaprakash* (tel 24444) with rooms from Rs 35 to 40 single or Rs 60 all the way to 125 double. All rooms have attached bathrooms but the top price ones also have air-con.

Close by is *Hotel Durbar* with rooms at Rs 15/25, more expensive with attached bathroom. On Ashoka Rd near Gandhi Square the *Balaji Lodge* is a friendly place with doubles for Rs 30. The *KTDC Hotel Mayura Hoysala* (tel 25349) on Jhansi Lakshmi Bai Rd is excellent value in the mid range with rooms for Rs 50/70. Indian Airlines have their office here. The *Ritz Hotel* is a real treat with good rooms and a great location for Rs 50 a single.

Places to Eat

There are lots of cheap south Indian

vegetarian places along Dhanvantri Rd or Gandhi Square – try the *New Gayathri Bhavan*, *Hotel Indra Bhavan*, *Bombay Indra Bhavan*, *Indra Cafe* or *Hotel Durbar*. The very popular *Punjabi Restaurant Bombay Juice Centre*, on Dhanvantri Rd near the junction with Sayaji Rd, has a wide menu of excellent food. *Shilpashtri Restaurant & Bar* on Gandhi Square also has good food and cold beer. The *Kwality Restaurant* on Dhanvantri Rd is not bad either.

Getting There
There are frequent express and passenger trains to Bangalore and further afield. The enquiry office at Mysore is very good. Long distance buses generally depart from the Central Bus Station. They include services to Arsikere (for the Hoysala temples at Belur and Halebid and for Sravanabelagola), to Bangalore, Calicut, Mangalore and Ooty.

To Somnathpur get a bus to Tirarasipura and a second bus to Somnathpur. There's a direct bus from Somnathpur to Srirangapatnam at 1 pm or you can do it at other times via Bannur. There are lots of direct buses between Mysore and Srirangapatnam, many of them continuing further on.

Getting Around
Local buses include the 1 and 1A to the sandalwood oil factory and the 4 and 5 to the silk weaving factory. To Chamundi Hill take a bus (every 30 minutes) from the Suburban Bus Stand at the east end of Gandhi Square. There are lots of auto-rickshaws around Mysore and the drivers use their meters.

AROUND MYSORE
Srirangapatnam
Situated 16 km from Bangalore this was the capital of Hyder Ali and Tipu Sultan from which they ruled much of southern India until Tipu Sultan's defeat by the British in 1799. Tipu's summer palace and his mausoleum stand in a well-maintained garden.

Somnathpur
The Sri Channakeshara Temple, 45 km east of Mysore, was built around 1260 AD at the height of the Hoysala period. The temple walls are superbly sculptured. Just outside the temple compound is the *Tourist Home & Restaurant* with good rooms at Rs 35.

Other
The Bandipur Wildlife Sanctuary adjoins another sanctuary in Tamil Nadu. The Ranganathittu Bird Sanctuary is just three km from Srirangapatnam. The ornamental Brindavan Gardens are 19 km from Mysore across the Cauvery River.

THE HOYSALA TEMPLES
Somnathpur is one of the great Hoysala temples, the others being at Belur and Halebid. The sculptural decorations of these temples rival Khajuraho or Konarak but they do not have the soaring size of other great temples – their scale is more human. The Hoysalas ruled this part of the Deccan from the 11th to 13th centuries. Both temples are open every day, admission is free at Halebid, Rs 0.50 at Belur. There's a small museum adjacent to the Halebid temple. The Channakeshara Temple at Belur is the only one of the three great Hoysala temples still used as a temple.

Places to Stay
Halebid is little more than a village now, Belur is a small town, but there are accommodation facilities at both centres. The *KSTDC Tourist Cottages* at Halebid adjoin the temple and cost Rs 20/24. It's only half a km from the centre of the village but there is no other accommodation here.

The *KSTDC Tourist Cottage* in Belur is 200 metres from the temple and is the same price as the one at Halebid but has no catering facilities. There is also a *Traveller's Bungalow* and a couple of basic hotels here. Many people use Hassan as a base for the whole area.

SRAVANABELAGOLA

This important Jain pilgrimage site is dominated by the huge 17-metre-high statue of Gomateshvara (Lord Bahubali). It's one of the world's tallest monolithic statues. You have to climb 614 steps up the rock face of the Indragiri Hill to the towering nude statue. There are several interesting temples nearby. Every 12 to 14 years a festival is held at Sravanabelagola and in 1981 the festival coincided with the 1000th anniversary of the statue's erection and over one million pilgrims flocked to the tiny town.

Places to Stay

There are two hotels in the town and a *Tourist Bungalow* at the foot of the hill. They're all usually permanently full. It's probably easier to use Hassan as a base.

Getting There

Belur and Halebid are 16 km apart but it's not possible to see both the Hoysala temples and Sravanabelagola in one day using public transport. If you want to do so take a KSTDC tour from Mysore.

HASSAN

There's no interest in this town, it's just a centre for visiting the Hoysala temples and Sravanabelagola. The tourist office in Hassan will book accommodation at the Tourist Cottages in Belur or Halebid.

Places to Stay & Eat

Hassan's accommodation is often permanently full. The *Hassan Ashok* is part of the ITDC chain and costs Rs 110/140, more with air-con. Much cheaper hotels include the very popular *Hotel Dwaraka* at Rs 9/17 or Rs 12/20 with attached bathroom. Similarly priced places include the *Sathyaprakash Hotel*, the *Prashanth Tourist Home* or the *Hotel Madhu Nivas*.

The *Shanbag Cafe*, next to the bus stand, is the place to eat – huge meals for just a few rupees. *Three Star Lodge* is good for a non-vegetarian meal and it stays open late.

Getting There

Hassan is 4½ hours by train from Mysore. You can do a loop from Hassan to Belur and Halebid, there are plenty of daily buses. There are only three buses to Sravanabelagola each day, however. The trip takes 1½ hours to Sravanabelagola, two hours to Halebid, just half an hour between Halebid and Belur. There are plenty of buses daily to Bangalore and Mysore.

ARSIKERE

Like Hassan this is a base for temple explorations of the area but Arsikere also has a Hoysala temple of its own, though much damaged.

Places to Stay & Eat

Accommodation facilities here are rather basic. There's a *Tourist Lodge* near the bus stand at Rs 10/15 which is probably the best place in Arsikere. Other places around are rather dismal.

Prasanna Hotel is probably the best vegetarian place in town but *Hotel Majestic* is also open late at night.

COORG & THE SOUTH-WEST

Until 1956 Coorg was a mini-state in its own right. On the edge of the Western Ghats, Mercara has an interesting fort and temple. The west coast railway line from Kerala terminates at the port of Mangalore, once a major seaport and shipbuilding centre. There are a number of interesting Jain pilgrimage centres near Mangalore.

HAMPI

In the Vijayanagar period Hampi was the capital of the whole of south India. In 1565 its period of power came to an abrupt end when the Deccan Sultans conspired to defeat and sack the city.

The ruins here are superb though widely scattered. Since the site does not attract great numbers of tourists it's poorly signposted and takes some time to get around. Important buildings include the Vittala Temple with its stone chariot, the riverside Purandara Desara Mandapa and a number of other temples and palaces. It's definitely worth hiring a bike in Hospet, 13 km away, to save a lot of walking.

Places to Stay

Many people stay in Hospet but there's the *Hampi Power Station Inspection Bungalow* with rooms for Rs 5. It's three km from Kamalapuram. There are a number of simple cafes around Kamalapuram, the village by the ruins, and the *Government Tourist Canteen* between the Hazarama Temple and the palace site. It has a *very* limited menu.

HOSPET

This is the usual base for visiting the Hampi ruins but it's an attraction in its own right during the Muslim festival of Moharam when fire-walking is one of the major events.

Places to Stay & Eat

Malligi Tourist Home (tel 8377) off Hampi Rd is good value at Rs 14/27 for rooms with attached bathrooms, fan and mosquito nets. It's very friendly and there's an excellent vegetarian restaurant attached. *Hotel Sandarshan* on Station Rd is Rs 15/25 and very convenient though not such good value.

Hotel Mayura on Gandhi Chowk has rooms at Rs 10/18 with bathroom plus some cheaper bathless singles. *Lokare Lodge* on Station Rd costs Rs 15/24 for rooms with bathroom. Moving down the price scale the *MRK Lodge*, opposite the Old Bus Stand, costs Rs 7/13.

There are quite a few other places in this accommodation-packed town. *Malligi Tourist Home* is the best place to eat but the *Nagarjuna Bar & Restaurant* has non-vegetarian food and ice-cold beer.

Getting There

The railway station is a 15-minute walk or a couple of rupees by rickshaw from the town centre. There are plenty of express trains from here to Bangalore. There's one bus daily to Badami and eight to Bangalore plus a daily tourist bus. Frequent buses run to Hampi from platform 10 at the New Bus Stand. Get down at Kamalapuram rather than the terminus at Hampi Bazaar.

THE CHALUKYAN CAVES & TEMPLES

From the 4th to 8th century AD the Chalukyas were the principal power in south India and you can trace their development at their cities of Badami, Pattadakal and Aihole. Aihole is oldest and from the 4th to 7th centuries the earliest Dravidian rock cut temples were constructed here. There are around 70 structures at Aihole, many of them prototypes for the later developments in Tamil Nadu. Badami was the capital from 540 to 757 and is famous for its five rock-cut temples. Pattadakal reached its height of power in the 7th and 8th centuries.

Places to Stay

You can stay at Badami or Aihole or use Bagalkot, where there is better accommodation, as a base. Badami has the *KSTDC Tourist Bungalow* and a *PWD Inspection Bungalow* with rooms at Rs 15/30 – both about a half km from the centre. There is also the pretty terrible *Sri Mahakuteshwar Lodge* by the bus stand and the inconvenient *Travellers' Bungalow* by the railway station.

There's good food at *Hotel Sanman* near the bus stand or the vegetarian places by the tonga stand. Aihole has a *KSTDC Tourist Bungalow* also costing Rs 15/30.

Getting There

Badami and Bagalkot are on the Gadag-Bijapur railway line. Buses connect the three Chalukyan sites but they're difficult to find – these sites get very few foreign visitors. If you can manage the 100 km bike ride it's fairly straightforward to hire a bike in Badami (Rs 5 from the shop by the tonga stand) and do it yourself. The

Badami railway station is five km out of town – Rs 2 to 3 for a tonga into town. All trains from Badami are passenger trains but the slow travel is balanced by a constant series of buskers to entertain you.

BIJAPUR

This Muslim capital is a clear contrast to the exuberant architecture of Karnataka's Chalukyan and Hoysala monuments. Bijapur was a Muslim capital which allied with the other 'Deccan Sultans' to over-throw the Hindu Vajayanagar kingdom in 1565.

The city's major attraction is the huge Golgumbaz mausoleum capped by a dome said to be the second largest in the world. Entry is Rs 0.50 except on Sundays when it is free. The Ibrahim Roza is as delicate and elegant as the Golgumbaz is massive. Bijapur also has the finely proportioned Jami-e-Masjid. The palace of Asar Mahal, the much ruined citadel, the 24-metre-high watchtower and the huge Malik-e-Maidan cannon.

Places to Stay & Eat

The *KSTDC Tourist Home* has rooms at Rs 25/35 with attached bathroom and a pleasant situation. It's better value than the nearby *ITDC Travellers' Lodge* at Rs 50/80 and offers very similar standards.

Others include the *Hotel Midland* on Station Rd with rooms from Rs 10 to 20, the *Hotel Tourist* on Gandhi Rd (further down Station Rd changes names) at Rs 20 to 35, or the *Mysore Lodge* which is adjacent to the Hotel Midland and very cheap and basic.

Hotel Tourist does excellent vegetarian meals. The *Tourist Home* does excellent breakfasts but tea here is absurdly expensive.

Getting There & Around

Train reservations out of Bijapur are generally no trouble. There are daily buses to Aurangabad, Bangalore, Bombay and other centres. Around town there are auto-rickshaws and tongas. Railway station to Tourist Home is about Rs 2 to 2.50 by auto-rickshaw, Tourist Home to Ibrahim Roza is about Rs 3.50 per person in a tonga.

HUBLI

This is another travel crossroads, useful if you're travelling from Bombay to Bangalore, Goa or north Karnataka. Everything you need is conveniently close to the railway station.

Places to Stay & Eat

Hotel Ajanta is a big place visible from the railway station. Rooms are Rs 16/30 and there's a good restaurant on the ground floor. Or there's the *Modern Lodge* which is cheaper and more basic and the similar *Udipi Hotel.*

The *Kamat Hotel*, close to the Modern Lodge, is fairly good for vegetarian food or there's the *Bombay Restaurant* next door.

Getting There

There are a lot of trains through Hubli but it takes persuasion, even a little baksheesh sometimes, to unlock the sleeper reservations! This is a major change point for trains to Goa.

Andhra Pradesh

Although its last ruler, the Nizam of Hyderabad, was reputed to be one of the richest men on earth, Andhra Pradesh is one of India's poorest and least developed states. Most of it stands on the Deccan plateau, sloping down to the Bay of Bengal.

HYDERABAD

The capital of the state is an important centre of Islamic culture but it's a dry, dusty place. The city is divided into two parts, Hyderabad and Secunderabad, by the Hussain Segar lake. The 1591 triumphal arch known as the Charminar is in the centre of the old walled city. There's a good view from the top. Completed in 1687 the adjoining Mecca Masjid is one of the largest mosques in the world. Other points of interest include the beautiful modern Birla Mandir Hindu temple, the extensive exhibits of the Salar Jang Museum and the small Archaeological Museum. The Nehru Zoological Park is one of the largest zoos in India.

The sprawling Golconda Fort, 11 km out of the city, deserves at least a half day's exploration. The fort had several periods of importance but after the Moghul era it was replaced by Hyderabad as the capital of the Nizams. You can get out to Golconda by a 119 or 142 bus from opposite the Hyderabad Railway Station or by taxi.

Places to Stay

Most of the better cheap hotels are in the area known as Abids, between the GPO and Hyderabad Railway Station. The *Super Lodge* on Nampally High Rd is relatively quiet and good value. Others on the same road include the *Royal Lodge* with singles at Rs 12 to 20, doubles for Rs 30 to 50.

The more expensive *Sri Brindavan Hotel* (tel 220820) on Station Rd has good rooms with fan and attached bathroom for Rs 40/60. It's a friendly, well run place. Other better hotels include the *Taj Mahal Hotel* (tel 221167) on King Kothi Rd at Rs 45/65. The *Hotel Jaya International* (tel 223444) in Abids is Rs 50 to 100 for singles, Rs 70 to 130 for doubles. The more expensive rooms in this pleasant, modern hotel have air-con.

The *Youth Hostel* is behind the Boat Club at the north-east end of Hussain Sagar, Secunderabad and has dorm beds for Rs 5. The YMCA and YWCA, also in Secunderabad, are both almost permanently full and so is the *Railway Retiring Room* (there's only one) at Secunderabad Station.

Places to Eat

Apart from the hotels there aren't many places to eat in Hyderabad. The *Kamat Hotel* chain (there are several of them around) does good vegetarian meals. One is opposite the public gardens between Nampally High Rd and the station. Other good places include the *Emerald Restaurant* with wonderful vegetarian food and the *Shalimar Bar & Restaurant* at the Sri Brindavan Hotel which has non-vegetarian food, welcome in very vegetarian Hyderabad.

Getting There

Hyderabad is a major air destination. Note that the main railway station is at Secunderabad, Hyderabad is only a branch line. It's about a 10-minute journey from Secunderabad to Hyderabad. If you're staying in Abids, however, and travelling to Bangalore or Madras you can board the train at Kacheguda station. To Delhi can take less than 24 hours, to Calcutta you have to change at Vijayawada, Bombay is 15 hours away, Bangalore 19. Secunderabad to Aurangabad is metre gauge and the line continues to Manmad on the Bombay-Delhi line. Secunderabad-Ajmer is also metre gauge.

Getting Around

Local buses in Hyderabad tend to be impossibly crowded. If you want to try it a 2 operates between Secunderabad station and Charminar, take a 7 from the station through Abids. Auto-rickshaws will use their meters.

OTHER PLACES

There is not a lot of interest elsewhere in the state but Nagarjunakonda is the site of some very early Buddhist excavations and there is a museum. Warangal is an important site for Chalukyan temples, they make an interesting comparison with the Chalukyan temples of Karnataka.

Kerala

The land of 'green magic' is a narrow coastal strip bordered by the Western Ghats. It has one of India's best beaches, an interesting wildlife sanctuary, a Christian community which may be the oldest in the world and you can make the unique 'backwater trip' through the coastal lagoons.

CALICUT

Although Calicut does not have a great deal to see this is the place where Vasco da Gama first landed in India in 1498. He was the first European to reach India via the sea route around Africa.

COCHIN & ERNAKULAM

Cochin, set on a group of islands, is both picturesque and historically interesting – a strange combination of Portuguese, Dutch and English colonial buildings in a tropical setting. It's also a busy port with a steady stream of ocean freighters coming in to dock.

Cochin consists of Ernakulam on the mainland and a series of islands in the harbour. The main places of interest are in Fort Cochin and Mattancherry but most of the accommodation is in Ernakulam. The Tourist Office, however, is on Willingdon Island, where the airport is also located. There is also a Tourist Reception Centre in Ernakulam.

Things to See

St Francis Church Located in Cochin this is the oldest European-constructed church in India; it contains Vasco da Gama's tomb. Despite its age, it was originally constructed in 1503, Cochin's Christian history goes back far longer – it's said that St Thomas the Apostle first brought Christianity here in 52 AD and there is certainly documentary evidence of Christian communities by the 6th century. The Portuguese were not at all amused to find that the heathen had already adopted Christianity long before they arrived toting their brand of the religion.

Mattancherry Palace Originally built by the Portuguese, but later substantially renovated by the Dutch, the palace is notable for its superb murals in the bed chambers. The palace is open daily from 9 am to 5 pm.

Other The Jewish Synagogue, in an area of Mattancherry known as 'Jewtown', dates from 1567. It is said that the first Jewish settlers arrived at the same time as St Thomas the Apostle. Of late their numbers have been steadily declining and there are now less than 50 left.

Look for the Chinese fishing nets at the northern tip of Fort Cochin, opposite Vypeen Island. You'll also see them along the backwater trip from Cochin to Kottayam. Ernakulam is a centre for the spectacular dance-drama known as Kathakali dancing. There are performances every evening at 7 pm at Gurukulam Kathakali Yogam off Chittoor Rd.

Places to Stay

You've got a choice of sleepy old Fort Cochin or modern Ernakulam. In Fort Cochin the small *PWD Bungalow* is the best budget accommodation with rooms at Rs 12/16. Close to St Francis Church the creaky old *Elite Hotel* has rooms at Rs 6/12. The small *YWCA* near the GPO is good value but often full. About half way between Fort Cochin and Mattancherry the *Port View Lodge* is run down but still full of character and has rooms from Rs 10.

In Ernakulam the small, simple and friendly *Basoto Lodge* on Press Club Rd has rooms from Rs 10/20. If it's full try the similarly priced *Hotel National* on Cannon Shed Rd, just up from the main boat jetty. The *Central Lodge* near the railway station is good value at Rs 12/18 or Rs 16/22 with attached bathroom.

The *Bolgatty Palace Hotel* (tel 35003) on Bolgatty Island was originally a Dutch palace and later the British Residency. Today it's run by the state tourist office and accommodation costs a bargain Rs 35/62 for rooms with bath. Book through the Tourist Reception Centre in Ernakulam who will supply details on the island ferry service.

Other good hotels include the *Hotel Blue Diamond* (tel 33221) on Market Rd with singles/doubles at Rs 30/58. The *Hakoba Hotel* on Shanmughan Rd by the waterfront is cheaper at Rs 20/30, more with air-con.

Places to Eat

A number of the hotels have restaurants or you can try the several *Indian Coffee Houses* – the one at the bottom of Canon Shed Rd is good and convenient. The *Bharat Coffee House*, next door to Indian Airlines on Broadway, is similar. The *Woodlands Hotel* on Mahatma Gandhi Rd is good or the *Ranjim Vegetarian Restaurant* which is part of the Sangeetha Hotel on Chittoor Rd. Near the Hakoba Hotel, *Arul Jyothi* has good masala dosa.

The *Elite Hotel* in Fort Cochin is very good for non-vegetarian food. Good Chinese food can be found at the *Golden Dragon Restaurant*, opposite the Park Hotel. There are lots of bars along Mahatma Gandhi Rd and Shanmughan Rd in Ernakulam – dimly lit and lively.

Getting There

You can fly from Bombay, Madras and other centres in the south. There are rail connections from Bangalore, Bombay and even Delhi. The Malabar Express makes a daily run from Mangalore to Trivandrum right along the Kerala coast. The 201 km trip to Trivandrum takes four to five hours and costs Rs 17 in 2nd, Rs 66 in 1st. The central bus station is in Ernakulam and there are connections all over the south.

Getting Around

Ferries are the main means of travel around the islands of Cochin. Since getting between Fort Cochin and Mattancherry on Cochin Island is not too convenient you may have to do some travelling back and forth. The Ernakulam-Fort Cochin ferry is somewhat chaotic and disorganised. There is no ferry between Fort Cochin and Willingdon Island but a row boat would only be Rs 2. Between Fort Cochin and Mattancherry an auto-rickshaw (say Rs 3) would be the easiest means of transport. In Ernakulam auto-rickshaws are convenient and they will use their meters.

AROUND COCHIN

There are regular ferry services through the lagoons between Kottayam and Alleppey. Kottayam is a good base for visiting the Periyar Wildlife Sanctuary close to the Tamil Nadu border. The sanctuary has bison, elephants and even a few tigers.

ALLEPPEY

Apart from the annual snakeboat race on the second Saturday in August there's no real reason to visit Alleppey – apart from it being the starting or finishing point for the backwater trip. It is, however, a quite pleasant market town.

Places to Stay

With rooms at Rs 12/20 *St George's Lodging* is superb value and far and away the best place to stay in Alleppey. Second best places include the *Raja Tourist Home*, the *Dhanalakshmi Lodge* and the *PWD Bungalow*, which is close to the beach but inconvenient for the town.

Places to Eat

The *Indian Coffee House*, opposite the Hindu temple, is a good place to eat – complete with Raj-style waiters in cummer-bunds and turbans. Or try the *Komala Hotel* on the other side of the canal bridge.

Getting There

If you don't take the backwater trip it is also possible to bus north or south from Alleppey.

QUILON

This lakeside town was tied up with Portuguese, Dutch and British commercial rivalry in the area. It's a pleasant market town to spend a day or two in but there is not much to see apart from the ruined fort at Thangasseri. It is, however, the jumping off point for the backwater trip, one of the nicest things to do while in Kerala.

Places to Stay

The *Tourist Bungalow*, formerly the British Residency, is pleasant and at Rs 15 per person pretty cheap but rather inconveniently located – an auto-rickshaw from town will be about Rs 10. More centrally located the large new *Hotel Karthika* (tel 3760, 3764) is excellent value at Rs 14/27 for rooms with bathroom, more with air-con. Also central, the *Hotel Sudarsan* is on Parameswar Nagar between the post office and boat jetty and has rooms from Rs 26/40. *Sika Lodge/Hotel Apsara* is close to the river bridge and slightly cheaper.

Places to Eat

Good places to eat include the restaurant on the ground floor of the inconveniently located *Iswarya Lodge*. There's excellent vegetarian food at the *Hotel Guru Prasad* on Main St. Opposite the bus station the *Mahalakshmi Lodge* does good south Indian vegetarian food, as does the *Hotel Apsara*.

Getting There

It takes three or four hours from Cochin to Quilon by rail. There are also trains to Madras and to Trivandrum but the latter route is very slow, although also very cheap. Buses to Trivandrum are much faster but most buses simply pass through Quilon, they do not originate there.

Backwater Trip The trip through the lagoons is a highlight of a Kerala visit as you travel along canals, through lagoons and across lakes from one tiny settlement to another. The 8½ hour trip costs just Rs

3 and departures from Quilon are at 10 am and 8.30 pm, from Alleppey at 7.30 am and 10.30 pm. There's always plenty to see along the way and the boat makes a couple of chai stops but make sure you get your tickets before departure.

TRIVANDRUM

Although it is the state capital Trivandrum does not have a great number of attractions and most travellers head rapidly through it to the greater joys of Kovalam Beach, 16 km south.

In the park at the north end of the city there is a museum, art gallery and zoo. They're all open 8 am to 6 pm daily except for Mondays and Wednesday mornings. Trivandrum's Sri Padmanabhaswamy Temple is no real attraction since non-Hindus are barred from entry. The Padmanabhapuram Palace is worth a visit though – it's 55 km south of Trivandrum on the way to Kanyakumari.

Places to Stay

Most travellers will head for Kovalam, only a half-hour bus ride away, but if you do want to stay here then *Nalada Tourist Home* on Mahatma Gandhi Rd between the railway bridge and bus stand costs Rs 25/30 and is good value. The *Streevas Tourist Home* on Station Rd has singles/doubles with attached bathroom at Rs 17.50/28. Opposite the GPO on Press Rd the *International Tourist Home* has rooms from Rs 12/20 and is also good value. Otherwise there are lots of rather basic cheapies from the station to the junction with Mahatma Gandhi Rd.

Places to Eat

Good vegetarian food can be found downstairs in the *Capri Hotel*, across the road from the municipal bus stand. The *Azad Restaurant* on Mahatma Gandhi Rd is more expensive if you're after a better class meal.

Getting There

You can fly to Trivandrum or get there by

bus or rail. The trains are rather slow, the buses rather reckless. There are about 25 buses daily between Trivandrum and Kovalam, they rapidly become less crowded after departure.

KOVALAM

With fine beaches, good places to stay, excellent food and even surf this is possibly India's best beach resort. Fortunately it's still sufficiently far off the beaten track to be quiet and unspoilt. It's a beach centre and travellers' resting place of sorts but still a long way from being the sort of 'scene' places like Goa have become. Take care of the tricky currents though.

Places to Stay & Eat

At Kovalam prices depend very much on demand – and how far you are from the beach. Places like *Sunshine House, Moon Cottage & Restaurant* and *Sea Rock Restaurant & Lodge* have good, clean doubles for around Rs 15. There are plenty of others around. If you're planning more than a few days' stay then it's worth making enquiries about renting a house.

All these places also do good food of the usual travellers' circuit variety – banana pancakes, fruit salad and so on. Lots of ganja available too.

More expensive places to stay, apart from the top bracket *Kovalam Beach Resort* (where you can even get yoga lessons!), include the *Raja Hotel* with doubles at Rs 60 or the cheaper *Hotel Blue Sea*.

Tamil Nadu

The southern state of Tamil Nadu is probably India's most 'Indian' state. It was an early centre of Hindu kingdoms with the Pallavas at Kanchipuram, the Cholas at Tanjore and the Pandyas at Madurai all ruling at some time. The later Muslim invaders never made more than fleeting incursions into the Dravidian south and even British influence here was not particularly strong.

Today it's a relaxed and easy-going state with prices generally lower than elsewhere in India. the temple hop through the state's many shrine-packed cities is interspersed with some excellent beaches and the famous hill station of Ooty. Food, so long as you like thalis, is generally excellent in Tamil Nadu although alcohol is not so readily available in this 'dry' state.

MADRAS

India's fourth largest city is much more relaxed than its northern counterparts. You can wander relatively easily around Madras and even the public transport works quite well. Although Madras was actually the East India Company's first major settlement in India it was later traded back and forth between France and England before firmly becoming a part of British India.

Orientation & Information

The older part of Madras is north of Poonamallee High Rd where you'll find most of the cheapest hotels and a number of important offices including the GPO. Parry's Corner/Popham's Broadway is the natural centre of this area and most of the bus stations are around it. Anna Salai, still generally known as Mount Rd, is the backbone of the other main part of the city and there you'll find the national and state tourist offices. The two main train stations are close to Poonamallee High Rd.

Things to See

Fort St George & St Mary's Church Built in 1653 but now much altered the old fort houses an interesting museum packed with reminders of the Raj era. The 1678 St Mary's Church is the oldest English church in India. Clive of India was married here.

Other Madras is not packed with things to see and do but you can visit the Government

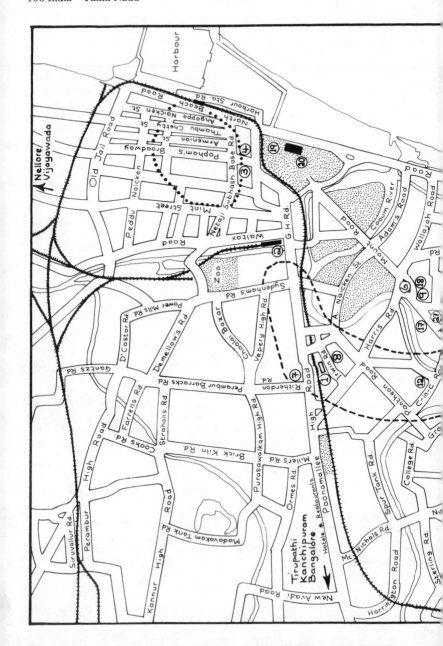

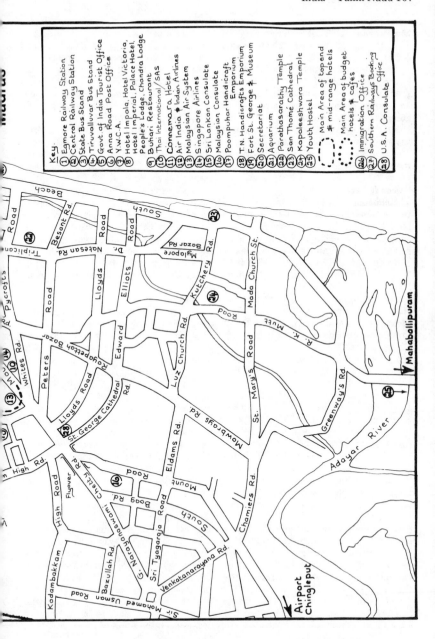

Madras

Key
1. Egmore Railway Station
2. Central Railway Station
3. State Bus Stand
4. Tiruvalluvar Bus Stand
5. Govt of India Tourist Office
6. Anna Road Post Office
7. Y.W.C.A.
8. Hotel Impala, Hotel Victoria, Hotel Imperial, Palace Hotel, People's Lodge, Chandra Lodge
9. Buhari Restaurant
10. Thai International/SAS
11. Connemara Hotel
12. Air India + Indian Airlines
13. Malaysian Air System
14. Singapore Airlines
15. Sri Lankan Consulate
16. Malaysian Consulate
17. Poompuhar Handicraft Emporium
18. T.N. Handicrafts Emporium
19. Fort St. George + Museum
20. Secretariat
21. Aquarium
22. Parathasarathy Temple
23. San Thome Cathedral
24. Kapaleeshwara Temple
25. Youth Hostel
26. Immigration Office
27. Southern Railways Booking Office
28. U.S.A. Consulate Office

⊙⊙ Main Area of topend & mid-range hotels
⋯ Main Area of budget hotels & cafes

Museum and Art Gallery on Pantheon Rd which is open daily except Friday, admission is free.

The 13-km-long beach known as the Marina is a natural focus for the city although swimming is not safe. There's an aquarium on the seafront. If you're not going to visit the great temple cities in the south then it's worth seeing the Kapaleeshwara Temple in the south of the city. The San Thome Cathedral is said to house the remains of St Thomas the Apostle.

Places to Stay

The cheapest places to stay are mainly in the old city area north of Poonamallee High Rd. slightly more expensive places are generally along that road, between the Egmore and Central Railway Stations.

Broadlands (tel 845573, 848131) at 16 Vallabha Agraharam St, off Triplican High Rd opposite the Star Cinema, is an extremely popular and pleasant place to stay with rooms for Rs 17/34. The *Malaysia Lodge* at 44 Armenian St off Popham's Broadway (Netaji Subhash Chandra Bose Rd) has been popular for years although it's extremely basic with rooms at just Rs 12/18 or with attached bathroom at Rs 15/22.

The central *Hotel Rolex* (tel 24236-9) at 190 Netaji Subhash Chandra Bose Rd has reasonable doubles at Rs 35 but it's often full. Away from the centre the *YWCA Guest House & Camping Ground* (tel 34945) at 1086 Poonamallee High Rd takes men and women and has a restaurant. Singles are Rs 23 to 30 plus a Rs 2 temporary membership fee. You can camp for Rs 3 per person and Rs 2 per tent.

Other possibilities include the *World University Service Centre* (tel 663991) on Spur Tank Rd west of Egmore Station and south of Poonamallee High Rd. For people with ISIC cards you can stay in the dorm for Rs 5 or rooms are Rs 8/15. Teachers (prove it) pay Rs 12/20, lesser mortals Rs 15/30. The *Youth Hostel* (tel 412882) at Indiranagar is on the southern outskirts of town and has dorm accommodation for Rs 5. At the TTC bus stand there's a 50-bed dorm which costs Rs 2. There are also *Retiring Rooms* at the Central Railway Station. The *Airport Inn* is just 1½ km from the airport and has rooms from Rs 15 per person up to Rs 100/120 with air-con.

Moving up a price notch the *Hotel Vagai* (tel 844031) at 3 Gandhi Irwin Rd is a new place with doubles for Rs 75. The *Tourist Home* (tel 844079) at 21 on the same street has rooms for Rs 38/60. A couple of doors up the *Hotel Ramprasad* has rooms at Rs 40 singles, Rs 50-70 double, all with attached bathroom. Directly opposite the station on Gandhi Irwin Rd the *Hotel Impala Continental* has rooms from Rs 20 to 40 but has become rather run down of late. There are plenty more middle category hotels around the station area.

Places to Eat

Air-con comfort and relatively high prices at the *Hotel Imperial* on Gandhi Irwin Rd. The *Impala*, opposite Egmore Station on Gandhi Irwin Rd, has excellent thalis and other south Indian vegetarian food. As does *Vega Vasanta Bhavan*.

The *Buhari* at 3/17 Mount Rd is again fiercely air-conditioned but the non-vegetarian food is excellent and the prices reasonable. Next door the *Godavasi* is equally good and cheaper. For a treat try the buffet lunch at the expensive *Connemara Hotel*. The *Fiesta Restaurant* on Anna Salai, diagonally opposite the tourist office, is good for moderately expensive snacks.

Getting There

Madras is an international arrival point by air and sea from Malaysia and also a major jumping off point for flights to Sri Lanka. Check with K P V Shaikh Mohammed Rowther, 202 Linghi Chetty St for details on the shipping service to Penang. Domestically there are connections to Calcutta, Delhi, Bombay and to a number of locations in the south of India.

The 2188 km rail journey from Delhi takes 40 hours and costs Rs 450 in 1st, Rs 114 in 2nd. Calcutta is 1162 km away, 33 hours at a cost of Rs 363 in 1st, Rs 93 in 2nd. Bombay is 1279 km and from 26 hours for Rs 300 in 1st, Rs 76 in 2nd. These trains all depart from Madras Central Station. Trains also run from Central to Ernakulam/Cochin in Kerala and to Mettupalayam for Ooty. Bangalore is just 356 km away, also from Central, as is Hyderabad, 794 km north.

From Egmore Station trains run to Trichy (337 km direct) and on to Madurai and finally (18 hours from Egmore Station) Rameswaram. For 2nd class reservations go to the Southern Railway Booking Office on Mount Rd.

The Tamil Nadu State Transport bus company and the private Tiruvalluvar Transport Corporation both have terminals off Esplanade Rd. There are bus services to all the main towns in the south.

Getting Around
You can get to Madras airport by commuter train from Egmore to the Ninambakkan station, 10 minutes walk from the airport. Or take the Rs 10 airport bus which coming from the airport stops at the main hotels and Egmore Station before terminating at the Indian Airlines office on Mount Rd. A taxi will be Rs 30-plus. There is a comprehensive bus network in Madras, taxis and bicycle rickshaws.

VELLORE
The well preserved 16th century Vijayanagar fort and the Jalakanteshwara Temple inside the fort are Vellore's attractions. It's the major fort of south India and the temple is a fine example of late Vijayanagar architecture.

Places to Stay & Eat
Hotel Sangeet (Rs 14/28) and the India Lodge (Rs 10/20) are cheap and central. There are many other similar lodges around and a number of good vegetarian restaurants including the India Lodge.

Try Hotel Paradise for non-vegetarian food. Good cold drinks and ice cream at the Simla Ice Cream Parlour.

Getting There
Plenty of buses make the 145 km trip from Madras. Or you can take a train to the nearby Katpadi station on the Madras-Bangalore line.

KANCHIPURAM
This is one of India's seven sacred cities and packed with temples, many of them the work of the Cholas and Vijayanagar kings. It takes at least a day to start seeing them all. Some of the most important temples include the Kailasenatha Temple dedicated to Shiva. It's one of the earliest and also has suffered less from later additions and alterations. The Ekambareshwara Temple is one of the largest in Kanchi and has a huge 59-metre-high gopuram. Others include the Kamakshiamman Temple, dedicated to Parvati and scene for an annual car festival; the Vishnu temple of Vaikuntaperumal; the huge Varadarajaperumal and many others.

Places to Stay & Eat
The ITDC Travellers' Lodge (tel 2561) is convenient for the bus and railway stations and has rooms for Rs 115/240 including meals. Other popular and cheaper places include the Municipal Rest House, Rama Lodge, Raja's Lodge and the Town Lodge. There are many cheap vegetarian restaurants around the bus stand. The New Madras Cafe has non-vegetarian food.

Getting There & Around
It's 2½ to three hours by bus from Madras. On to Mahabalipuram you have to change buses at Chingleput. You can also do the trip from Madras by train. The day tour from Madras through Kanchi and Mahabalipuram is extremely rushed; useless for more than just a cursory glance. A bicycle is probably the best way of exploring Kanchi. Have small change ready for the many temple hustlers.

MAHABALIPURAM (Mamallapuram)

On the coast south of Madras this was a capital and the major sea port of the Pallavas. It's famous for its shore temples. There is also a superb beach here and the small town is becoming quite a travellers' centre. The sights at Mahabalipuram include the magnificent rock carving known as Arjuna's Penance. The Rathas or 'temple cars' are a collection of small temples which are noted as prototypes of the whole Dravidian school of architecture. The late-7th-century Shore Temples, situated right on the beach, are probably the most romantic and beautiful temples in India.

Places to Stay

There are cheap places to stay in town while to the north there is a series of more expensive, but very pleasant, beachfront places. The new *TTDC Youth Hostel & Cottages* is off the road to the Shore Temples and has dorm beds for Rs 7.50 (be prepared for ravenous mosquitoes) or doubles with bath for Rs 30. *Mamalla Bhavan* (tel 50) at the bus stand is also popular at Rs 20 for a double. Next up is the *Mamalla Lodge* which is run by the same people and has rooms at Rs 10/20.

Other cheap lodges – although they're not so good as the above – are the *Merina Lodge, Pallava Lodge, Royal Lodge* and the *Chitra Lodge.*

Moving to the more expensive places along the beach the best value is the *TTDC Beach Resort Complex* (tel 35, 36) which has rooms at Rs 65/75 or Rs 85/100 with air-con. Last on the line is the small *Ideal Beach Resort* (tel 40) with rooms at Rs 50/70 or Rs 100/135 with air-con. Both these places have swimming pools.

Places to Eat

There's great food at the *Rose Garden Restaurant*, the *Village Restaurant*, the *Sea View Restaurant* or the *Bamboo Restaurant*. The latter is a currently popular meeting place. For superb lunchtime thalis try the *Mamalla Bhavan*.

Getting There

It's a 2½ hour journey from Madras for Rs 6 to 7 by bus. The trip further south to Pondicherry also takes 2½ hours. Chingleput buses depart hourly.

AROUND MADRAS

Other places around Madras include Chingleput with its ruined fort. Tirukkalikundram, between Kanchi and Mahabalipuram, has a hill-top temple where eagles come to be fed each day, supposedly flying all the way from Varanasi. At the base of the hill is a complex of superb temples. There is a crocodile farm 15 km north of Mahabalipuram. Vedanthangal is one of India's major bird sanctuaries, 80 km from Madras. Further south from Kanchi, Tiruvannamalai has many temples including the Temple of Arunachaleswar, said to be the largest in India.

PONDICHERRY

Until the early '50s Pondicherry was a French colony but there is little trace of the French today. The town's main attraction is Auroville, the ashram of Sri Aurobindo.

Places to Stay

The ashram's *Park Guest House* on Goubert Avenue is large enough to virtually guarantee a room at any time of year and is excellent value at Rs 40 to 50 for doubles with bath. The other ashram hotel, the *International Guest House* (tel 2200) on Gingy Salai St, has rooms at Rs 18 to 50.

Otherwise the *Government Tourist Home* (tel 694) on Uppalam Rd has rooms for Rs 10/20 or Rs 25/40 with air-con. It's very good value and has a restaurant serving south Indian vegetarian food. There's a wide range along Rangapillai St starting with the *Hotel Ellora* (tel 2111) at Rs 15 to 50 and up. *Hotel Seker* at 48 Rangapillai St has rooms with bath at Rs 25/40. *Ajantha Lodge* at 144 is good value at Rs 20/35 or the *Amala Lodge* at Rs 15/25, more for rooms with attached bath.

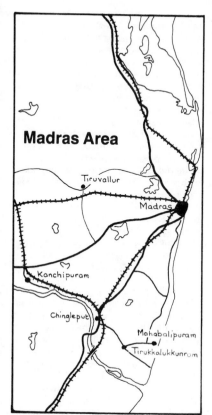

Madras Area

Tiruvallur

Madras

Kanchipuram

Chingleput

Mahabalipuram

Tirukkalukkunram

Pondicherry is actually on a branch line but there is a daily train direct to Madras; Villupuram is the usual changing point otherwise. Coming from the south Thiruppapuliyar station is more convenient. The bus station in Pondicherry is chaotic and if you're heading south it may well be easier to take a bus to Cuddalore (only an hour away and buses are frequent) then another bus from there. The best way to visit Auroville is by hiring a bicycle for the day.

TANJORE (Thanjavur)

Between 850 and 1270 AD the Chola empire included the whole south of India plus Sri Lanka and even parts of the Malay peninsula and Sumatra. Their capital was Tanjore and it was here that Dravidian culture and art reached its high point. The town is dominated by the huge Brihadeshwara Temple – the 63-metre-high gopuram is topped by a granite dome weighing 81 tons. To place this huge piece of stone required the construction of a ramp six-km long! The inner court also contains the second largest Nandi (Shiva's bull) in India, also carved from a single piece of rock.

The temple complex also encloses an archaeological museum. Tanjore has many other temples plus a sprawling, partially ruined palace, containing an art gallery and a library. They are closed on Wednesdays. Tanjore is an excellent place to buy wooden temple carvings, taken from dismantled temple chariots.

Finally the *Youth Hostel* (tel 3495) is the cheapest place in town at Rs 6 for a dorm bed. It's out in the northern suburbs at Solaithandavankuppam, OK if you've rented a bicycle.

Places to Eat

Hotel Aristo is probably the best restaurant in town although it's a bit expensive. On West Boulevard opposite the junction with Rangapillai St *Hotel Bilal* is a good, cheap, non-vegetarian cafe. On Rangapillai St the *Hotel Dhanalakshmi* is a good vegetarian restaurant.

Places to Stay

Ghandiji Rd, running between the bus and railway stations, is the locale for most of Tanjore's accommodation including the excellent *Hotel Tamil Nadu* (tel 57 or 601) with singles/doubles with bathroom for Rs 35/50. The *Ashok Travellers' Lodge* on Trichy Rd is rather more expensive Rs 50/100 but also very pleasant although a little inconveniently located.

Cheaper places include the large *Ashoka*

Lodge (tel 593-4) on Abraham Panjithar Rd at Rs 12/18 or with bath at Rs 18/30. Real cheapies include the *Hotel Bilal* on Gandhiji Rd where rooms are Rs 6/12 or with bath Rs 12/30. Others are the *Sri Rajeswari Lodge* at 17 Pillaiyar Koil St or the *Eswari Lodge* at 1338 South Rampart Rd near the bus station. Cheaper still are the *Sri Krishna Lodge*, the *Ajanta Lodge* at 1306 Soputh Main St, and *Raja's Rest House* behind the Hotel Tamil Nadu.

Places to Eat

The *Ananth Bhavan* on Gandhiji Rd has good vegetarian food but doesn't do food in the evening. *Sri Vasavi Cafe* at 1367 South Rampart does excellent thalis. The *Hotel Tamil Nadu's* restaurant has improved of late but in general in Tanjore it's thalis or nothing.

Getting There

Trains to Madras take 8½ hours, Madurai is seven hours away. It's only 1½ hours by train or even less by bus to Trichy. Buses depart every 10 minutes and many people day-trip between the two towns.

AROUND TANJORE

There are many other impressive Chola temples around Tanjore. Some of the more interesting include the Shiva temple of Panchanatheshwara at Thiruvaiyaru (13 km out) and the four huge temples at Kumbakonam (36 km). The largest of these is second only to the Meenakshi at Madurai.

At Gangakondacholapuram (71 km) the whole town is dominated by the temple's soaring gopuram. Chidambaram, south of Pondicherry, has one of the most famous Dravidian temples in Tamil Nadu – the great temple of Nataraja, the dancing Shiva.

TIRUCHIRAPPALLI

Trichy, as it's usually (thank goodness) referred to is dominated by the Rock Fort Temple which towers high over the town. A long, winding flight of steps leads to this hilltop temple. North of this is the Srirangam Temple which sprawls across 250 hectares on an island in the Cauvery River. The temple is ringed by seven walls with 21 gopurams. Nearby there is another large temple complex, the Sri Jambukeshwara.

Places to Stay

Accommodation is concentrated in the cantonment area, south of the Rock Fort. Popular places include the *Hotel Tamil Nadu* (tel 253383) opposite the bus stand with rooms at Rs 30/40, more with air-con. The tourist office is also here. The *Hotel Anand* (tel 26545) at 1 Racquet Court Lane is Rs 25/45 – a bit grubby but one of the best middle range places.

Opposite the bus stand at 13A Royal Rd the *Guru Hotel* (tel 25298) is a pleasant place at Rs 20/30. Just beyond it is the slightly more expensive, but also slightly better, *Hotel Lakshmi* (tel 25298) at 3A Alexander Rd. *Hotel Ajanta* (tel 24501) on Junction Rd is a huge place with rooms at Rs 25/40. Right next to the Guru Hotel at 13B the *Vijay Lodge* (tel 24511) has rooms at Rs 19/30.

There are a number of very cheap hotels along Junction Rd between the railway station and the bus stand. There's not much to choose between them although the *Selvam Lodge* (tel 23114) has rooms at Rs 12/20 and has been very popular for years. Alternatively near the Rock Fort the *City Lodge* (tel 23452) at 69 West Boulevard Rd has rooms at Rs 7/15.

Places to Eat

The *Guru Hotel* and the rooftop restaurant at the *Selvam Lodge* are both good places to eat. There are lots of thali places around the bus stand and along Junction Rd. Or try the *Vijay Lodge*, the *Hotel Anand* or the *Karitha*, almost opposite the Hotel Anand.

Getting There

Trichy is on the main Madras-Madurai railway line. Trains from Madras take five to eight hours, Madurai is 2½ to four hours away. The state bus company and the Tiruvalluvar buses have stands only a couple of minutes apart. It's generally easier to get state buses out of Trichy. Trichy is also an international airport with flights to Colombo in Sri Lanka as well as domestic flights to Madras.

Getting Around

Trichy is very spread out but the town bus system is, fortunately, pretty good and not too crowded. A number 1 bus runs between the cantonment area, the rock fort and Srirangam about every five minutes.

MADURAI

The busy city of Madurai is famed for the superb Shree Meenakshi Temple, generally agreed to be the 'best' temple in the south of India. The present temple dates from 1560 and it's a huge, sprawling, complex with a continually interesting confusion of corridors, courtyards, enclosures and towers. The soaring gopurams are a brightly painted Disneyland of Hindu figures and for Rs 0.50 you can climb to the top of the south tower. The temple is open between 5 am and 12.30 pm and between 4 and 10 pm. Photography, which costs an extra Rs 5, is only permitted from 12.30 to 4 pm. You have to leave your shoes outside. There's also a Temple Art Gallery within the complex – admission is another Rs 0.50 plus Rs 5 for taking pictures.

Other attractions in Madurai include the Tirumalai Naick Palace, now much ruined but still worth a visit. There's a Gandhi Museum in the old palace of the Rani Mangammal, open daily except Wednesdays. Madurai has several other temples, all in the late-Dravidian style, and the large Mariamman Teppakkulam Tank, site for an annual float festival in January and February.

Information & Orientation

The old city of Madurai is bounded by the four Veli Sts and almost everything of interest plus the bus station, GPO, tourist Office and hotels are within these boundaries.

Places to Stay

Real cheapies in Madurai tend to be rather too grotty for comfort but there are quite a few places just a small notch up market which are excellent value. They include the Hotel Apsara (tel 31444-5) at 137 West Masai St with doubles at Rs 34 with bathroom – it's very popular with travellers although it can be very noisy. New College House on Town Hall Rd is huge and also popular. Rooms cost from Rs 16 to 36. Opposite New College House is Hotel International, a modern hotel with good doubles at Rs 30.

Other good places include the Hotel Prem Nivas (tel 625001) at 102 West Perumal Maistry St with rooms from Rs 25/46. The new Hotel Aarathy (tel 31571) at 9 Perumalkoil West Mada St is similar in standard and costs from Rs 35/60. The state government's Hotel Tamil Nadu (tel 31435) on West Veli St has rooms from Rs 35/50.

Cheaper places include the TM Lodge on West Perumal Maistry St which is excellent value at Rs 25/45. Habitable bottom end places include the Hotel Krishna and the Santhanam Lodge, both on Town Hall Rd, cost Rs 10/25.

Places to Eat

There are lots of typical south Indian vegetarian places around the temple, along Town Hall Rd, Dindigul Rd and West Masai St. New Arya Bhavan on West Masai St is good, as is the restaurant at the junction of Dindigul Rd and West Masai St.

The Hotel Tamil Nadu's restaurant is a good place for non-vegetarian food, or try the Indo-Ceylon Restaurant on Town Hall Rd, near New College House, or the Taj Restaurant on the same street. Splash out at the Pandyan Hotel, Madurai's premier hotel.

Getting There

You can fly to Madurai or take the train from Madras – eight hours via Trichy at a cost of Rs 37 in 2nd, Rs 143 in 1st class. To Rameswaram is six hours for Rs 15 or Rs 57. If you're heading to Kerala then take the morning Madras-Quilon Mail, since the route goes through interesting scenery which it is best to see by daylight. It takes about six hours to Quilon so you have plenty of time to get to Trivandrum or Kovalam Beach in the afternoon.

The private and state bus stands are both on West Veli St – the Tourist Office is nearby on the same street.

Getting Around

Around Madurai take a 3 or 4 bus to the Gandhi Museum, 4 to the Mariamman Teppakkulam Tank, 5 to the Tiruparan-kundram rock-cut temple outside Madurai.

RAMESWARAM

Rameswaram is a major pilgrimage centre because of its huge Ramanathaswamy Temple, but it is also an important place for travellers as the ferry crosses to Talaimannar in Sri Lanka from here. Rameswaram is tied up in the Rama legends and the story of the Ramayana, hence the magnificent temple which boasts a corridor 1220-metres long!

Rameswaram is actually an island, connected by a causeway to the mainland. A road bridge is under construction but meanwhile the only way to get to the island is by rail. In 1964 a cyclone wiped out Dhanushkodi village at the tip of the island but left the Kothandaraswamy Temple standing.

Places to Stay & Eat

Accommodation can be a real problem at Rameswaram, particularly on the night before a ferry departure for Sri Lanka. The *Hotel Tamil Nadu* (tel 77) is probably the best place to stay but if at all possible make a reservation in advance from another bungalow or tourist office. Doubles with bath – Rs 77 and terrible food.

Alanka Lodge is a new place near the temple entrance with rooms at Rs 25. *Nadar Mahajana Sangam Lodge* on New St is also good value. There are *Railway Retiring Rooms* at the station and a host of very cheap lodges. You can get the usual thalis at a number of places around town.

Getting There

See the Sri Lanka section for ferry details. Trains come to Rameswaram from Madras and Madurai.

KANYAKUMARI (Cape Cormorin)

The southernmost tip of India is another important pilgrimage spot and a popular place to watch the sunset and sunrise. The Kanyakumari Temple overlooking the shore is the main temple but there is also the Vivekananda Memorial on two rocky islands about 200 metres off shore. Boats run out there from 7 to 11 am and 2 to 5 pm.

Places to Stay

There is a *Hotel Tamil Nadu* (tel 22, 57) with really pleasant rooms, some over-looking the sea, at Rs 50 for doubles. *Kerala House* (tel 29) also has a pleasant situation and doubles here are Rs 25. *Sankar's Guest House*, close to the railway station on the way into town, is one of the best places in town but costs just Rs 32/52.

There are a number of cheap hotels behind the bus stand close to Vinayakar Koil. They include the *Raja Tourist Lodge*, *Gopi Nivas Lodge* and the *Sri Bhagavathi Lodge*, all with rooms at around Rs 15/30. In the same area *Devi Cottage* is cheaper still.

Right in the centre of town the *Darsana Tourist Home* has doubles with bath for Rs 35. Also similarly priced is the *Parvathi Nivas Lodge*, close to the expensive Sangam Hotel.

Getting There

Buses run from Nagarcoil or Trivandrum.

You can take a day trip tour from Trivandrum.

KODAIKANAL
This quieter hill station is overshadowed by the more famous Ooty. There are a number of pleasant walks and a lake to go boating on.

Places to Stay
Hotel prices zoom in the high season. The *Hotel Tamil Nadu & Youth Hostel* (tel 481) on Fern Hill Rd costs Rs 60/110 in the high season. Dorm beds in the hostel are Rs 10.50 in the high season. Get off the bus at the hotel on your way into town, don't go all the way to the bus stand.

Many of the budget hotels are found along Bazaar Rd, downhill from the post office. They're all pretty good value – try the *Lodge Siraaj, Lodge Everest. Guru Lodge* or *Hotel Amar*, all at Rs 12/20. *Greenlands Youth Hostel* has dorm beds at Rs 7.50 and is very good. Right at the bottom of the price scale the *Zum Zum Lodge* is primitive but dirt cheap and friendly. It's at the top end of Bryant Park.

Places to Eat
Hospital Rd is a good centre for restaurants and taste treats – like the guy who does fantastic french fries. There's also the friendly *Tibetan Brothers Restaurant*, the *Silver Inn Restaurant* and the *Kodai Milk Bar*. Good Punjabi food at the *Shere-e-Punjab* just off Hospital Rd. For vegetarian thalis at lunchtime try the *Pakia Deepam*, opposite the bus stand between the Hotels Anjay and Jaya. *Manna Bakery & Restaurant* is also very good.

Getting There
Buses run from a number of towns in the south including Madurai, 125 km away.

OOTACAMUND (Ooty)
The best known southern hill station, Ooty is a pleasant escape from the heat of the plains but it's more a faded touch of the Raj (and a rather run down touch at that) than anything else. Ooty is not all the tourist literature makes it out to be. It is, however, a good place for quiet walks and lazy boating on the lake.

Places to Stay
Above the Tourist Office is the *Hotel Tamil Nadu* (tel 2543-4) with rooms at Rs 60/100 in the high season. It's not one of the best state government places, but OK. The seedy old *Hotel Dasaprakash* (tel 2460, 2680) still has moth-eaten reminders of its former glory and rooms from Rs 30/60 and up.

Opposite the Tourist Office on Commercial Rd the *Nahar Tourist Home* is a modern building with singles/doubles with bath at Rs 50/60. On Anandagiri Ettines Rd the *YWCA* (tel 2218) takes men and women and has doubles for Rs 55 in season. On the hill behind the railway station *Hotel Gaylord* (tel 2378) is Rs 18/32.

Down at the rock bottom end of the price scale *Sri K R Bhavan Boarding & Lodging* is a friendly little place with doubles for Rs 8, but you have to provide your own bedding. *Green Lands Hotel* is another small cheapie at Rs 6. Shop around the really cheap places, though. Standards vary considerably.

Places to Eat
Many of the hotels have restaurants or you could try the *Hotel Paradis* on Commercial Rd where the food is excellent and reasonably priced. *Nahar Tourist Home* has slightly expensive but very good thalis or there's the Chinese *Zodiac Room*, close to the GPO.

Getting There
You can get up to Ooty by its unique 'rack' train that engages a toothed central rail on the steeper sections. The views on this spectacular rail line are superb. the train starts from Mettupalayam where it connects with the Nilgiri Express from

Madras or Coimbatore. the 46 km journey up to Ooty takes 4¼ hours, only 3½ going down. You can also get to Ooty, less spectacularly, by bus.

COIMBATORE
This reasonably large town is useful only as a jumping off point for Ooty and the other hill stations of the Nilgiri Hills.

Places to Stay & Eat
Opposite the bus station the *Hotel Sree Shakti* (tel 34225, 34229) has rooms at Rs 30/45. The *Zakin Hotel* is just a few doors up the road and costs Rs 20/30. The *Hotel*

Tamil Nadu is across from the bus station on Dr Nanjappa Rd and here rooms are Rs 60/90, more with air-con. The *Zakin Hotel* does non-vegetarian food.

WILDLIFE SANCTUARIES
Tamil Nadu has a number of interesting wildlife sanctuaries including the Mudumalai Sanctuary where you might even see tigers. There is also the Vedanthangal Water Birds Sanctuary near Kanchi, the Calimere Sanctuary, the Mundanthurai Tiger Sanctuary, the Anamalai Sanctuary and the Guindy Deer Park within the Madras city boundaries.

Iran

Even before the revolution people tended to rush through Iran. If you were travelling west it was a case of in from Afghanistan, a short pause in Mashed, zap to Tehran, another short pause, zap to Tabriz, then out to Turkey. Or vice versa, with hardly a pause to see what it had to offer. It was a great mistake as those who made the effort to get off the beaten track – to head south to Isfahan, Shiraz and Persepolis, or simply to explore some of the less well known areas – found out. Iran was a much more interesting and even hospitable country than its detractors would admit.

Since the revolution things have been very different although, to the surprise of many people, the borders have not been shut. Most overland bus operators have continued to operate through Iran right through the hostage crisis and the Iran-Iraq conflict, with hardly a pause. Of course the number of travellers going through Iran today is a far fewer than in the heyday of the Asia overland trip, but some still do make it. In fact we have had a number of letters of late extolling the virtues of backpacking through Iran – the people are friendly, the costs are low, the black market rate on US dollars is terrific!

The usual route through Iran these days is – when entering from Turkey – Tabriz, Tehran, then south to Isfahan and Shiraz, then east to Zahedan and thus into Pakistan. Many travellers avoid Tehran, never a very interesting city and today the centre of the maelstrom as far as Iranian politics go. Since the Afghanistan route is closed off there is also no point in travelling east from Tehran to Mashed, the usual gateway to Herat in Afghanistan. In any case Mashed was always one of the centres for overheated Islamic fervour and is probably even worse today.

HISTORY

During the 6th century BC, Cyrus the Great appeared as the first notable Persian ruler. The Achaemenian Empire, which he founded, lasted from 558 to 330 BC and his successors, Darius I and Xerxes, expanded all the way to India in the east and the Aegean Sea in the west. Even Egypt came under Persian rule and the magnificent complex of Persepolis became the hub of the empire.

Xerxes's defeat by the Greeks at Marathon marked the end of the Achaemenians and this great period of Persian history. Soon it was Europe's turn to conquer and in the 4th century BC Alexander the Great invaded Persia and 'accidentally' burned down Persepolis. After Alexander's death the Greek influence rapidly declined, first with the breakaway region of north-east Iran ruled by the Parthians.

The Sassanids controlled Persia from 224 to 638 AD but through these centuries Persian history was a story of continuing conflict with the Roman and later Byzantine empires. Weakened by this interminable scrapping the Zoroastrian Persians fell easy prey to the spread of Islam and the Arabs. Between 637 and 642 AD all of Persia was taken by the Arabs and the country forsook Zoroaster for Mohammed. Muslim rule in Persia was confused by the great split between the Sunnites and the Shi'ites. Even today Iran is almost unique in the Muslim world for following the breakaway Shi'ite sect.

Arab power over Persia continued for nearly 600 years but towards the end of that period they were gradually supplanted by the Turkish Seljuk dynasty. At that time the Turks were still gradually absorbing the tattered remnants of the Byzantine Empire. The Seljuks heralded a new era of Persian art, literature and science, marked by men such as the mathematician-poet

Omar Khayyam. Then in 1220 the Seljuk period abruptly collapsed when Genghis Khan swept in and commenced a cold-blooded devastation that was to last for two centuries.

Another invasion by Tamurlane in 1380 did not help matters, but in 1502 the Safavid era commenced and heralded a Persian renaissance. Under Shah Abbas (1587-1629) foreign influences were once again purged from the country and he went on to perform his architectural miracles in Isfahan to leave a permanent reminder of this period. The decline of the Safavids was hastened by an invasion from Afghanistan but in 1736 Nadir Shah, a sort of Persian 'country boy', overthrew the impotent Safavids and proceeded to chuck out Afghanis, Russians and Turks in all directions. For an encore he then rushed off to do a little conquering himself, returning from India loaded with goodies, but virtually exhausting the country with his warring. It was a relief to all, both within Iran and without, when he was finally assassinated.

The following Zand and Qajar periods were not notable and in 1926 the father of the last Shah founded the Pahlavi dynasty. Foreign influence (and oil) then became an important element in Iran's story. In WW II Iran was officially neutral but Reza Khan was forced into exile in 1941, to South Africa, because he was felt to be too friendly with the Axis powers. His 20-year-old son took over after the war, the invading Russian forces were persuaded to depart (with difficulty and American conniving), the Shah assumed absolute power and Iran was aligned with the west.

The Shah's government was repressive, but forward looking, and Iran was rapidly modernised – at least in some ways and in some places. Illiteracy was reduced, women emancipated, land holdings redistributed, health services improved and a major programme of industrialisation embarked upon. At the same time the Shah's family and friends became very, very rich.

The oil price revolution turned out to be the Shah's undoing. Instead of channelling this new found wealth into development he allowed US arms merchants to persuade him to squander it on huge arsenals of inappropriate and utterly useless weapons. So the flood of petro-dollars ended up lining the pockets of a select few outside the military while galloping inflation made the majority of the country worse off than before. All through the reign of the Shah and that of his father there had been smouldering resistance to his dictatorial reign; resistance which the Shahs had stamped out with all the power and brutality available to the absolute ruler of an oil-rich country which enjoyed unquestioning backing from the major western powers.

As the economy went from bad to worse under the Shah's post oil-boom mismanagement the underlying opposition came out into the streets with acts of guerrilla war and massive street demonstrations. From his exile, first in Iraq and then in France, the Ayatollah Khomeini became the leader of the Shah's opponents. When the Shah's previously total US support began to weaken, then buckle, his days were numbered and the Ayatollah flew back to Iran in triumph. In exile the Shah was harried from country to country with America showing clearly how much their strong support means, even in a personal sense, when a dictatorial ruler finds himself on the losing side.

Once in control in Iran the Ayatollah was soon to prove the truth in that old adage that 'after the revolution comes the revolution'. His intention was to set up a clergy-dominated Islamic republic in place of the Shah's rule. In actual fact, however, the clergy and their followers had done little of the real leg work within the country in order to overthrow the Shah. It was groups like the Peoples' Fedayeen and the Islamic Peoples' Mujahedeen who took the real risks and created the situation in which the Shah could not continue. The Ayatollah's role

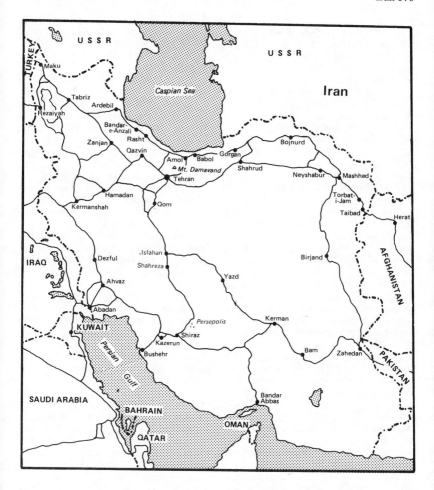

was simply as a central figure behind which all the opposition forces could rally – there might be no agreement on politics but they were all Muslims.

Government under the Ayatollah soon proved to be absolutely chaotic and the brutality and repression every bit as horrific as under the Shah. Just as in the Shah's era people disappeared from the streets, executions took place after brief and meaningless trials and minor officials took the law totally into their own hands. Naturally the opposition forces, temporarily united in their hatred for the Shah, soon started opposing the Ayatollah's hopeless Islamic government. Government officials and leaders of the clergy have been assassinated and to further complicate matters the Iranian government has had to struggle with breakaway revolts by the Kurds and an all-out, if half-hearted, war with neighbouring Iraq.

At present the forces in opposition to the Islamic government are varied, but probably spearheaded by the Marxist Islamic Peoples' Mujahedeen. The People's Fedayeen have been compromised by their unquestioning support of the clergy. The official communist party, Tudeh, has been even more compromised by trying to support both the clergy and Moscow. Then there are the various minority groups, principally the Kurds who fought the Shah long and hard for the establishment of a Kurdish state.

Waiting in the wings is yet another, and potentially one of the strongest forces, the military. The various military arms were the backbone of the Shah's power so it is hardly surprising that those officers not actually purged by the new government have kept a low profile. Yet some observers feel that in the event of a complete collapse of the clergy-led government the final struggle for power could come down to one between the Mujahedeen and the military. Despite all the bickering Iran seems to have regained a measure of internal stability although the country continues to drain itself away on the futile war with Iraq; a war that seems to have deteriorated to being a personal feud between the rulers of the two countries.

FACTS

Population The population of Iran is about 32 million. Although the vast majority are Shi'ite Muslims there is also a substantial Kurdish minority and smaller groups of Armenians and Jews. The Kurds, amongst the strongest opponents of the Islamic government, increased considerably in number during the '70s due to the failure of their revolt in Iraq. This had been strongly supported by Iran but finally failed when the Shah withdrew his support. Tehran, the capital of Iran, is also the largest city with a population of about four million. Mashed, Isfahan and Tabriz are other major cities.

Geography Iran covers 1,600,000 square km, most of it a great, dry plateau at between 1000 and 1500 metres altitude. In the north it is bordered by the Elburz Mountains where the highest peak in western Asia, Mt Damavand, towers to over 5500 metres only a short distance north from Tehran. In the west, towards Iraq and Turkey, and in the south, towards the Persian Gulf and the Indian Ocean, the plateau is bordered by the Zagros Mountains. A number of smaller ranges rise towards the Afghanistan border in the east. Much of the eastern part of the plateau is a practically uninhabited desert – the Dasht-i-Kavir (Great Salt Desert) in the north and the Dasht-i-Lut (Great Sand Desert) in the south. Apart from the green, fertile northern slopes of the Elburz mountains, running down to the Caspian Sea, most of Iran is a parched, arid country. The southern cities of Isfahan and Shiraz are oasis towns; the country running down to the Persian Gulf is oppressively hot and dry in the summer.

Economy Despite a considerable drop from its pre-revolution production levels oil is still far and away the mainstay of the Iranian economy. Were it not for Iran's oil wealth the path towards ultimate collapse would have been steep and fast. Oil was first discovered in Iran in 1908 but the country's proven reserves are much more limited than some of the other Gulf oil producers. The Shah had embarked upon a major programme of industrialisation intended to reduce the country's oil dependency. Although this has resulted in Iran becoming one of the major car manufacturers of western Asia the programme has slowed considerably since the revolution. Carpet manufacturing remains Iran's second biggest export activity and carpet weaving has continued apace right through the years of turmoil. There are large herds of goats and sheep (the latter providing wool for the carpets) while agriculture is extensively practised in the Caspian Sea region and in the other, more limited fertile areas.

Religion The Iranians are unique in the

Muslim world for predominantly following the Shi'ite division of Islam rather than the more common Sunnite sect. There are, however, Shi'ite minorities in other Islamic countries. See the introductory section on religions for a full explanation of Sunnites and Shi'ites. Minority religions include Christians, Jews and followers of the Baha'i faith. The latter have been particularly ruthlessly discriminated against by the Islamic government. Mazdaites, followers of Zoroaster, are found mainly in Shiraz, Tehran, Kerman and Yazd. Iran was once predominantly Zoroastrian, but many Zoroastrians fled east to India when the Arabs carried Islam east.

INFO

There used to be a tourist office in Tehran at 174 Elizabeth II Boulevard (surely that street has been renamed?) and others in Mashed, Isfahan, Shiraz and Tabriz. Some of them are still operating. There was also a booth at the Tehran airport.

BOOKS

Iran's mosques and religious buildings are, as you will soon realise, extremely photogenic so it is not surprising that there are some really beautiful (and often very expensive) coffee table photographic books on Iran's Islamic art. *Bridge of Turquoise* (published by Thames & Hudson) is one of the most spectacular and most expensive. There are many others on the development of Islamic art and architecture.

The downfall of the Shah has naturally inspired a number of books on the path to Iran's Islamic revolution and the reasons for the Shah's fall. Books that provide some interesting general insights include, as ever, Paul Theroux's *Great Railway Bazaar*. Recently re-published, *The Road to Oxiana* by Robert Byron is an interesting description of a visit to Iran in the '30s – and shows how little the Shah in the '70s had changed from his father, the Shah at that time.

VISAS

If you're an American you can currently forget it. At present almost all nationalities require a visa for a visit to Iran. Their availability varies widely from country to country although in general they're somewhat easier to get than a few years ago. They seem to be fairly readily obtainable in Asian countries in the region – so long as you have the patience and endurance! The process is considerably speeded up if you can get a 'recommendation' from your own embassy.

In New Delhi:

Iranian visas take four to five weeks for Australians, British and New Zealanders and the cost is nothing or purely nominal. With a letter of recommendation from your embassy they can be done in four days, but since New Zealand no longer has an embassy in India kiwis are out of luck. The Iranian embassy is open only on Tuesdays, Thursdays 'and Saturdays from 9 am to 12 noon. Only 20 people can visit it on each of those days so arrive early (8 am) and fight for your place in the queue. You must then fill in an application form and bring it back the next day the consulate is open and fight the queueing system again in order to submit it! Four weeks later, *if* your visa comes through, you must present your passport for stamping, which takes another four days. Apart from the time involved there is generally no problem getting transit visas.

Reportedly visas are now easier to obtain in London than in New Delhi. In Turkey and Pakistan, other popular places for obtaining Iranian visas:

Visas in Istanbul take five weeks and costs 3500 Tl. If you get a letter of recommendation from your embassy (the British embassy charges 1200 Tl!) visas can be issued in Ankara in just 24 hours. In Islamabad in Pakistan visas takes just two days and cost a nominal Rs 3 – if you have a recommendation. The British Embassy charges Rs 66 here. Quetta in Pakistan and Athens in Greece are other places travellers have tried.

Another traveller reported on the visa situation to the west of Iran:

Athens is the best place in the region. I tried to get a visa in Damascus, thinking that as Syria was on good terms with Iran the embassy here would be more free with issuing visas. No chance. My application form was passed from official to official (none of whom spoke English) and finally on to a mullah who glanced at it for a few few minutes and then told me (through some Pakistanis applying for visas) that I should return after 15 days. There was no guarantee that I would get my visa then so I I headed on to Ankara where I found that, with a note from the British embassy, I only had to wait two days for my visas.

I Krishnasamy – UK

Make sure your visa is clean and unaltered. One traveller reported major difficulties because his visa's validity had been changed, by the Iranian embassy, from 45 days to two months. At the Turkey-Iran border he was accused of having made the alteration himself and sent back to Erzurum to sort it out! Keep a tight grip on your passport in Iran. They're worth gold, particularly Swiss ones, and it's not unknown for unscrupulous officials to steal them.

MONEY

A$1	=	70 rials
US$1	=	100 rials
£1	=	140 rials

The official exchange rates above are highly unlikely to bear much reality to street levels. There is an extremely healthy black market for US dollars in Iran. So healthy, in fact, that many travellers have reported that Iran is currently one of the cheapest counties in Asia! Just don't get caught importing undeclared US currency. At latest report US dollars fetched around 400 to 500 rials, about five times the official rate of exchange. Other travellers have reported it is easier to bring rials in from Turkey or Pakistan, rather than change money on the black market in Iran. There are money changers with rials available at healthy rates on the Pakistan side of the Pakistan-

Iran border but coming from Turkey it's wise to change money in Dogubayazit rather than at the border.

It appears bringing in rials (up to 20,000) is no hassle, they just don't like you changing foreign currency within the country on the black market. Travellers' cheques (even American Express?) can be changed in banks in Iran. You have to declare all currency on arrival, it's written in to your passport and it's carefully checked when you depart. So if you want to play currency games in Iran make sure you surreptitiously bring in some excess currency. One traveller reported, however, that he and a friend cashed £50 between them officially but lost the bank form for £40 of it. The border official announced that 'you must be crazy' when told of this but let them through without a hassle!

It is important to learn your Arabic numerals in order to deal with Iranian currency – western numbers do not appear on the coins. Prices are often quoted in toman, which are equal to 10 rials. This can be very confusing. Iran has suffered rapid inflation since the revolution although it was also having that same problem during the latter years of the Shah's reign.

CLIMATE

Iran is a hot, dry, desert country in the summer and a cold, dry one in the winter. North of the Elburz Mountains, along the Caspian coast, there is reasonable rainfall, but in the rest of the country it is extremely dry even in the winter. The middle of the summer, July and August in particular, can get pretty mean down south. In the desert and along the Gulf summer temperatures way over 40°C are common and usually come in combination, with debilitating humidity.

Temperatures over 40°C are not uncommon in Tehran but the humidity is nowhere near as bad. All the main cities, Tabriz in particular, are a fair bit above sea-level which tends to moderate the temperatures. On the other hand it makes the winters that much colder. Tehran, Tabriz and Mashed are all fairly icy in January. There is good skiing only a short drive north of Tehran.

ACCOMMODATION
Pre-revolution there were plenty of cheap hotels throughout Iran although many of them refused to take westerners and some of the popular travellers' hotels were generally 100% full all the time. No doubt the reduced flow of travellers has prompted some price cutting! Travellers in Iran since the revolution report that while the most expensive hotels are still used by journalists and other foreign visitors those a notch down the scale had been taken over by students to replace their own 'inadequate' housing!

Iran had a number of government operated campsites which have long been popular with the overland companies. They can also be used by travellers not equipped for camping since they have pre-erected tents with camp beds. They do, however, tend to be some distance out from the town centres and may no longer be operating.

FOOD
There are a couple of important words if you want to eat regularly in Iran – *chelo kebab*. This concoction of a rather bland skewer of lamb on a heap of equally bland rice qualifies as the national dish. Knead a lump of butter into the dish and add side dishes of yoghurt, raw onions and cucumber to spice things up a bit. You'll find chelo kebab cafes all over Iran.

Other dishes to sample include *chelo khoresh*, the most popular dish after chelo kebab. It consists of rice with a heavy meat and vegetable sauce plus nuts. *Jujeh kebab* is marinated chicken on a skewer. *Fesunjun* is a real delicacy, chicken or duck in pomegranate juice with ground walnuts. *Kofte* are meatballs which come in several varieties as does *abgusht*, a blanket term for stews. *Dolmeh* are stuffed vegetables, as in Turkey. That all

sounds pretty hopeful but in practise you'll probably find that it is chelo kebab, chelo kebab, chelo kebab.

As in Afghanistan it is wise to be very careful with fresh vegetables; a salad I foolishly ate in Isfahan made that point very clear to me. Iranian melons are out of this world, they have an incredible variety of them, many of which I'm certain you'll never have tasted before – you'll find them unique and delicious. Melon stalls will offer you samples to help you make a decision which to buy. That well known overlander Marco Polo thought the melons in this part of the world were pretty hot stuff. Other fruit, grapes in particular, are also excellent.

The bread, *nan*, in Iran is probably the best all the way across Asia. Bread in Turkey is great but it is very similar to bread in the west – in Iran it is quite different in texture and shaped like an oval pancake. There are a number of varieties – *nan sangak* is the bread with the curiously dimpled look which comes from cooking it on a bed of small stones. Make sure there are no stones left before you take a bite! *Nan lavashe* is bread from the pit-type ovens. Bread is often sold by weight.

You can find good sandwiches – rolls stuffed with vegetables – at street stalls. Soup (*ash*) is an Iranian staple to such an extent that the word for cook is *ash-paz*. A bowl of soup with bread is a good, cheap fill up. The dividing line between a thick *ash* and a thin *abgusht* is a hazy one.

Iranians have notable sweet tooths which they indulge on sweet pastries and confectionery. You'll find bakeries dispensing the goodies in almost any reasonable town. Nuts and raisins are other popular Iranian snacks and nibbles.

Drink
The water is supposed to be drinkable in Tehran, but it is not recommended. Fruit juice is readily available from street stalls and, of course, Coca-Cola is still found throughout Iran, just like any other place

where civilisation has arrived. Canada Dry has such a monopoly on fizzy-orange that a bottle of orange was known simply as a 'Canada'. Iran used to be an important wine centre – didn't Omar Khayyam go on about 'a glass of wine and thou'? Shiraz grapes give their name to a type of red wine. Unhappily a thousand years of dry Muslim influence has done its work and although the wine industry made a modest comeback in recent years it has now, no doubt, been firmly crushed by the Ayatollah's spoilsport friends.

Doogh is a yoghurt and mineral water drink which is widely available and very popular, particularly in the summer when it is a real thirst quencher. *Palouden* is rose-flavoured ice drink with fresh lemon juice, a speciality of Shiraz. Nevertheless, tea is still the staple Iranian drink and you'll learn to love it. Drunk in tiny glasses it only costs a few rials a throw, depending on the quality of the establishment. Many tea houses also provide hookah pipes; in the bazaars small boys will rush in and out carrying them to stall holders.

Some current prices in Iran include soft drinks for around 25 rials, a meal of chelo kebab and a drink for around 350 rials in Tehran, tea for 20 rials. It's becoming more difficult to find specific restaurants in Iran because signs seem to be disappearing.

GETTING THERE
Air
Although Tehran is connected by Iran Air and other airlines with neighbouring Asian countries and with European capitals most travellers will probably arrive in Iran by more down-to-earth methods.

From/to Afghanistan
The traditional route across Asia involved crossing the border between Iran and Afghanistan at Islam Qala, between Mashed and Herat. Due to the impossible situation in Afghanistan this route is no longer usable.

From/to Pakistan
Until the Afghanistan route became no-go the route through Pakistan was only an alternative for overlanders. It was not much used in the summer, when the temperature often soared to thermometer bursting levels, but made a good winter alternative when the high passes in Afghanistan might be blocked by snow. From Zahedan in Iran you take a bus to the Iran-Pakistan border. The trip takes about 1½ hours and costs about 550 rials. The actual border is marked by barbed wire and two white buildings. If you have to stay in Zahedan there's a 300 rial hotel right above the Taavonia bus office. Mirjaweh is the Iranian border town and from here it is about six (12? 14?) km, by taxi (fare of Rs 10 to 15) or on foot, to Taftan station where the train to Quetta operates.

Taftan is the Pakistani immigration and customs point and from here trains operate once a week (eastbound on Monday, westbound on Saturday) and take about 45 hours for the 500 km trip to

Quetta at a cost of Rs 60 in 2nd class. Recent reports are that it now does the trip in less than 30 hours. It's cheap but slow and uncomfortable as the train stops at every little station on the route. You should bring food and water with you although there is now an expensive and fly-ridden restaurant car on the train.

Alternatively there are Baluchistan Road Transport Board buses three times daily between Taftan and Quetta, the trip takes about 24 hours and costs Rs 85. From Taftan to Nukundi the road is simply a desert track but the remaining two-thirds distance is on a sealed road. This road is being rapidly improved and may soon all be sealed. See the Pakistan section for more details.

One traveller's report of this route:

Zahedan is sprawling, and you get dumped on the edge of nowhere at the bus terminal. Buses from Zahedan to the border are at the very least daily. I joined an enormous queue for tickets at 6 am, and my bus was the ninth bus going from Zahedan to Mirjaweh that morning. Fare 50 rials for locals, 550 rials for the occasional foreigner. The bus goes right up to the border-post, having been stopped at about half a dozen army check-points where everyone except the privileged foreigner has to get off and stand in the unbearable heat for about 15 minutes while everything is searched for smuggled goods and currency.

The bus I was on broke down shortly before Mirjaweh, so after an hour or so we all decided to walk to the border. Unfortunately we met another army post, and had to wait there until the bus arrived, squatting or standing, because the ground was too hot to sit on. The shade temperature was 52°C, but there wasn't any. By the time the bus had caught us up and got us to the border, the customs officials were taking their siesta so we had one as well – until about 4 pm. Their only concern was that our money added up – baggage search was only a quick peep into the top of the rucksack. Coming the other way from Pakistan, my baggage wasn't searched at all, but on the road from Zahedan up to Mashed we were continually searched for hash – including opening your camera and taking out the film.

From/to Turkey

The train between Istanbul and Tehran no longer seems to operate, or no longer seems to connect straight through anyway. The train trip took about three days including a ferry crossing of Lake Van in eastern Turkey. Only 1st class passengers stayed in the same carriage, all others had to fight for a spot on the new carriage on the other side.

Buses are rather faster and there are direct services between Istanbul, Ankara or Erzurum and Tehran. From Istanbul you leave around 5 to 7 pm and stop the next night in Erzurum. There are also bus services from Tabriz to the Turkish border or right through to Erzurum. The Turks close their side of the border at noon on Saturdays. The congestion of trucks at the border can tail back for many km. You're supposed to have your luggage checked at a white office about three km inside the Iran border! Eastbound the first town inside the Iranian border is only a couple of km and from there local buses run to Maku. It is then a four or five-hour bus ride to Tabriz or there is a daily bus direct from the border to Tabriz. If you get stuck in Maku the *Alvan Hotel*, just down from the bus station, has rooms at 400 rials per person.

Turkish bus scams from Istanbul into Europe have been part of the travellers' lore for years. Now there seem to be rip offs on buses to Iran too. Don't buy tickets in Istanbul for buses operating Istanbul-Tehran-Zahedan. In Tehran you have to change from a Turkish bus to an Iranian one and by the time you find that the Iranian company won't accept the Turkish ticket for travel Tehran-Zahedan the Turkish bus will have disappeared! Get tickets to Tehran only. As well as Turkish buses there may also be Iranian buses operating between Istanbul and Tehran. They will probably be more comfortable.

The border point is a large compound more or less in the middle of nowhere. Money changing facilities are available at the border, but if you arrive too late to get a bus to Erzurum, or even to Doğubayazit or Ağri, you may have to spend the night here on the restaurant floor.

From/to the USSR

Foreigners can use the trains 93 and 94 of USSR Railways to travel to Jolfa (Djulfa) in Iran. The train originates in Moscow (Kurshi) one night, reaches Rostar-on-Dor nearly 24 hours later, Bahu on the third evening and Jolfa the morning after that. You arrive at the Soviet frontier at 7.50 am and it's 4½ *hours* later that it leaves the frontier post. Another three hours are spent at the Iranian frontier post. Everything gets searched. Because of the unsettled situation in north-west Iran you must board a train to Tabriz immediately.

ROUTES

The traditional route through Afghanistan has been written off by the situation there and the continuing turmoil. On that route eastbound travellers would cross the Turkish border, continue east through Tabriz to Tehran then either head directly east to Mashed or loop slightly north to the Caspian Sea then down to Mashed. From there it was a short trip to Herat in Afghanistan. Today the most popular route is from Tabriz to Tehran to Isfahan then continue south-east to Kerman and Zahedan and on into Pakistan. Many people try to avoid Tehran – the usual alternative is to turn south at Tabriz and go directly to Isfahan. It is also possible to continue south from Isfahan to Shiraz then U-turn back to Isfahan. Or intrepid travellers could try entering Iran from the Gulf or from the USSR.

Some travellers' tales of travel through Khomeini's Iran:

The journey from Zahedan to Mashed was the only time in my whole three weeks in Iran that I felt at all hassled by officials. There are plenty of government statements against the western powers, but they are at pains to show that they hate western governments, not western people.

I'm sure that any American travelling through the country would get as warm a welcome as I did. People everywhere were most friendly and helpful. In Tehran and Isfahan and at the border they're used to seeing the occasional foreign backpacker passing through, but elsewhere you're still something of a novelty.

Very few people visit Mashed now – and it was there that I came in for some of the best of Muslim hospitality. I must have been the first European to set foot in Gorgan since the revolution. One old man called me over to his shop doorway and shook both my hands very long and hard, and was absolutely overjoyed just to see me there. He kept repeating 'Inglisi', pointing to me, 'Iran', pointing to the ground, as if he was trying to convince himself that it was true.

Wherever I went I was in demand for conversation. People want to know what's going on in the outside world, often they just want a chat. They weren't at all afraid to express their opinions on the government, which were usually highly unfavourable. What they miss is the nightlife, the alcohol, the music, the discos, the films on TV, all the things Islam takes away from you. But no-one has a good word for the Shah, and it's surprising how many people agree that the new government will be good for Iran's economy in the long run. It's the westernised city-dwellers who are opposed to the government. In places where Islam still had a firm hold on culture and life even before the revolution, support for the new government is very strong. And there is a considerable number of university students and other young people who had turned back to Muslim fundamentalism in despair at the Shah's rapid westernisation.

They don't mind if you say you think the government is evil – a Muslim has a great respect for other people's beliefs – religious or political – and the principle of hospitality applies to infidels as well as to fellow Muslims. There's no danger now from riots in the streets – travelling through Iran is quite safe again from that point of view. Sometimes people in Tehran will say, 'two years ago there was fighting in this street – tanks and machine guns' – but they usually prefer to forget it.

'Disappearances' and summary execution of opponents of the government have ceased – Islamic law is enforced strictly and fairly – people agree there's much less corruption now than before the revolution. Swift Islamic justice can certainly commend itself to the unfortunate traveller in some circumstances – I had my camera stolen on the bus journey from Zahedan to Mashed. A couple of the other passengers suspected the driver, so we all went to the police headquarters in Mashed. The case was presented before a young police lieutenant who spoke quite good English. He took statements from everyone and spent about two hours questioning them individually and collectively. I just sat there bemused as to what exactly was going on. Whenever I asked him he changed the subject, such as saying how much he hated the Khomeini government. There was a steady stream through the room of people with minor grievances against their neighbours – right through to smugglers and thieves brought in in handcuffs. After about three hours, the lieutenant came to his verdict, took it next door for it to be signed and the bus driver handed over 10,000 rials compensation. Imagine how long it would take to prove the same case in England?

But then I was lucky to be on the right side. I don't think the driver would have had too many channels of appeal if he'd thought he'd been wronged. Sudden cries of pain down the corridor startled me – but no-one else batted an eyelid. Just someone taking too long over his confession. Islamic justice is quick, clean and harsh. I stumbled across a public flogging in one of Isfahan's shopping streets, which drew a small crowd of vaguely interested on-lookers. It's not a country to set a foot wrong. There's just no question of trying to take drugs through – although I saw no harm in accepting a joint offered to me in someone's house.

Decent dress is most important. Long trousers, of course, and preferably long-sleeved shirts, although some Iranians get away with short sleeves in Tehran. No-one wears T-shirts – they just brand you as an untidy anti-revolutionary. If you wander around dirty, smelly and untidy you'll notice a big change in people's attitudes. They won't want to be seen near you. The reason the overland companies' Bedford trucks have to rush through Iran still is because they carry loads of long-haired, patched-jeans, dirty-nailed hippies, looking as if they've just come from Athens or Kathmandu. (Not necessarily true! – Tony Wheeler) The 'hippy' concept might be 20 years out of date around here, but in Iran anyone with long hair is a hippy, the worst product of western materialism and decadence and a corrupting influence on Muslim society. Islamic hospitality is wonderful, but you have to do your bit. If you can't bear to

have your hair cut, fly straight to India – you'll hate Iran and it'll hate you. It really is a shame to spoil your chances of all those free meals and free nights' accommodation with the wonderful Iranian people.

I've been saying all this with male persons in mind – I don't see any reason why women shouldn't travel in Iran with male escort, providing they bear in mind that it's not something a Muslim woman would be allowed to do. Your slightest indiscretion – even your mere presence – would create suspicion. I'd imagine you'd have to stay in far more expensive hotels, and you'd enjoy a lot less hospitality because people would be afraid of giving it to you. Dresswise, you'd have to be completely covered, except for your face and hands. Not necessarily with one of those black things trailing the ground which you usually associate with Muslim women – a headscarf and ankle-length coat would do. But it must be loose. Anything which defines the shape of your chest or your waist or your hips will give an open invitation to any bloke who feels in the mood – and there'll be plenty!

Nicholas Pierce – UK

This is probably the best country on the overland route to visit these days. There is no hint of war except for the ever present posters of 'martyrs'. The people are very friendly, the standard of living is very high compared with Turkey and everywhere to the east and its ridiculously cheap. The people we met who complained of heavy Muslim and police hassles were without exception those who had transited non-stop in three or four days; not surprising with seven to 10 hour border crossings at each border and passport 'checks' every 50 kms or so along the way. The officials can be arseholes so it's no wonder travellers get negative views if officials are the only people they meet.

If you take your time and explore off the main route, the hassles become negligible (the police are only curious to discover where you come from, hence the passport 'checks', and they can't read English script anyway!) and you find that Iran has been really badly maligned as it really is a great place to visit. Iran is very much more western than we'd been led to believe. Perhaps that is a reason why Khomeini is trying to enforce a return to a more fundamental Islamic view but his regime is not popular. The people have had a taste of western (decadent?) life under the Shah and have no desire to exercise restraint. The women are much more liberated than in Pakistan – most wear only a token scarf instead of the full Muslim veil, they wear very fashionable clothing etc, but it's still death if you so much as glance at them!

Geoff Blundell – NZ

GETTING AROUND

Trains The railway network runs south, east and west from Tehran. Southwards the line runs to Kerman but travellers heading to Pakistan have to continue by bus to the Pakistan border before picking up the rails again. Heading east the line terminates at Mashed and there are no railways at all through Afghanistan. Westbound the line runs through Tabriz and all the way across Turkey to Istanbul, interrupted only by the ferry crossing of Lake Van, but at present there are no Iran-Turkey train services operating. Shortly after Tabriz there is a branch off northwest into the USSR. Cars can be transported into Russia on this route but you are not allowed to drive across the border.

Iran has ordinary trains with 2nd and 3rd class, expresses with 1st, 2nd and 3rd class and some more expensive night expresses. Tehran-Mashed takes from 14 to 18 hours, Tehran-Tabriz takes a similar time. Student reductions are available on the fares.

Buses Iran has an extensive bus network with a varied selection of bus companies like Mihantour, Iran Peyma, TBT and Levantour. Not all of them operate to all centres and fares do tend to vary a bit from company to company. Most bus operators have regular (de-luxe) and more expensive super services. Compared to Turkey the buses are comfortable, compared to Pakistan they're incredibly comfortable. Except in Tabriz and Tehran each bus company will usually have their own office and terminal.

It's wise to book your bus out as soon as you arrive in a town since most are fully booked for days ahead. Usually they'll find foreigners a seat if you insist that you have visa problems. Some approximate fares and travel times from Tehran are:

	rials	hours
Tabriz	800	9
Zahedan	1500-1800	24
Bandar Abbas	1400	25
Kerman	1100	18
Yazd	700	11
Shiraz	1000	14
Isfahan	550	7
Mashed	1000	20

Bus fares haven't increased much in the past couple of years but because of shortages of spare parts breakdowns are hard to repair and buses are often booked up. Private cars often operate a sort of long-distance private-taxi service. They're faster than the buses but about twice as expensive.

Driving Iran has some of the best roads on the overland route although there are also some pretty terrible desert roads. Fuel is still comparatively cheap. At present driving through Iran is considerably complicated by the customs problem. Iran will not, at the moment, recognise any carnet for importing a foreign registered car. Or perhaps the carnet is so expensive that nobody even considers it or they're simply unobtainable. Anyway the end result is that the only way you can bring any vehicle into Iran (including a motor-cycle) is to be accompanied by an Iranian customs official from arrival in Iran right through until you depart. This tends to be expensive, and in any case your time is limited, so overland companies pick up their customs official, zip down to Isfahan where they spend a couple of days, then head straight for the Pakistan border where they drop him off. People in their own vehicle have to wait at the border until there are enough vehicles assembled to form a convoy. They can then share one customs official between them. Fortunately the wait at the border does not, usually, seem to be too long and travellers have reported that their official was quite friendly and even doubled as a tourist guide on the trip across!

Air Iran Air has a comprehensive domestic route network using Boeing 737s and 727s. Now where do they get the spare parts from?

THINGS TO BUY

Travellers in Iran since the revolution report that with fewer customers bazaar merchants are often more willing to bargain and that prices may be lower than before. Carpets are, of course, the thing that springs to mind when you mention Persia. If you're in Tehran then it's worth looking at the state-owned Iran Carpet Company at 165 Ferdowsi Avenue where the carpets are of guaranteed quality and fixed, but not rock bottom, price. There are many other carpet dealers along Ferdowsi Avenue (carpet row in Tehran) and in the Tehran bazaar where there is a special carpet section. Bargain hard, even in the flashiest establishment.

If price is all important and you are sufficiently expert to know what you're about then you may do better in a regional centre such as Tabriz or Isfahan. Overall prices for Persian carpets seem to have fallen since the revolution – in the west as well as back at source.

The best pile will be wool (silk carpets are really for decoration rather than use) and the best wool will be Persian. A shortage of real Persian wool is said to be one reason for a decline in quality of Persian carpets. Another reason is said to be laws prohibiting children from working on them – their tiny fingers tied tiny knots. The old, and now rare, vegetable dyes were good but modern chrome dyes are equally suitable. Aniline dyes are no good. An ordinary carpet will have less than 30 knots per square cm, medium quality will be 30 to 50 and fine, 50 to 60. With superfine quality the sky is the limit but once again these will be mainly decorative. Look for false knots, tied around four rather than two warp threads. Lay any carpet you're considering on flat ground and look for bumps and wrinkles. A small bump may flatten with time and, after all, this is a hand made item so don't expect machine perfection.

The best advice for Persian carpets, though, is don't buy them in Persia unless you have a clear idea what a similar carpet would cost you back home. There are so many carpet dealers in the west who buy them in bulk, ship them in bulk and sell them in quantity that you may find it hard to buy one in Iran and get it home at a lower cost. Plus your local dealer, who knows you're just round the corner, may be less likely to rip you off than some faraway bazaar merchant.

There are many other things to consider buying in Iran. In Tehran there were government-run handicraft centres at 381 Takht-e-Jamshid Avenue and at 296 Villa Avenue. Isfahan brasswork or silver or copper objects are good value. Persian miniature paintings have a long history, but the really good, old ones are, not unexpectedly, very expensive and face various export restrictions. You can find some pleasant modern imitations. Enamelwork and inlaid woodwork are other regional finds. The bazaars have terrific hookah pipes and printed cloth you could use on a table. For your donkey or camel there are groovy donkey or camel accessories to doll him up. Or jazz up your tent with tent accessories.

Iran has also got one thing definitely not to buy – Mashed turquoises. Visitors to Mashed would inevitably get a very convincing sales pitch about how much more they are worth outside Iran and a lot of people fell for this racket. They weren't! Since Mashed is now generally off the route the Mashed turquoise racketeers must be having a hard time. Another Iranian purchase you can forget about is caviar, exporting it is a government monopoly.

LANGUAGE

Farsi, as the Persian language is known, is spoken throughout Iran and is the language of government in Afghanistan. It is also spoken by most people in Herat. English is beginning to supersede French and German as the second language in Iran. Since all translations from Persian are phonetic the spellings of the words below may differ from other sources.

hello	*shalam*
good-bye	*khoda hafez*
thank you	*teshekoor*
where?	*kochas?*
yes/no	*naleh/nakheyr*
do you have?	*darid?*
how much?	*chan dai?*
expensive	*na arzan*
cheap	*arzan*
please	*beformayd*
bread	*nan*
tea	*chai*
water	*ab*
butter	*karay*
yogurt	*mahst*
bus	*autobus*
house	*khane*
hotel	*mehmankhane*
restaurant	*restouran*
yesterday	*dirouz*
today	*emrouz*
tomorrow	*farda*

Merci, as in French, is often used for thank you. For finding your way round the towns – *maidan* is square, *khiaban* is street or avenue and *kuche* is alley or lane.

1	*yeg*	7	*haft*
2	*do*	8	*hasht*
3	*say*	9	*no*
4	*chahar*	10	*da*
5	*panj*	100	*sad*
6	*sheesh*	1000	*hezar*

1 \ 2 C 3 ⌐ 4 ⌐ 5 ○ 6 Ϋ 7 √ 8 Λ 9 ٩ 10 \○

TEHRAN

Never judge a country by its capital city is a frequently uttered platitude. It is worth remembering in Tehran because it really is a dreadful hole – about the only good thing you can say about it is that there is no reason to hang around for very long. The overall impression it will probably leave is one of dreadful, dreary, dull-grey tackiness. And since the revolution it has become not only expensive but also, sometimes, unsafe.

Tehran has only been the capital since 1783. Long ago it was just a small neighbour to a town called Rey. In 1197 Rey was wiped out and Tehran became the main city of the area. Tehran is at an altitude of over 1000 metres. It is hot and dry in the summer when the whole town is cloaked in a cloud of dust and in winter the temperature can hit freezing. Skiing is (or was) popular in the mountains only a short distance to the north.

Having said that there is not much reason to hang around in Tehran for very long I will now admit that there are a fair number of things to do, although many of them may be shut at present. These days Tehran pretty well closes up by 9 pm.

1	to Afghan Embassy	10	GPO
2	Indian Embassy	11	Masjid-e-Sepahsalar
3	American Express	12	Basgah-e-Ja'fari (Zurkaneh)
4	Youth Hostel	13	Bus 213 to Railway Station
5	Iran Peyma bus office	14	Golestan Palace
6	Bank-e-Meli (Zurkaneh)	15	Amir Kabir Hotel
7	Crown Jewels	16	Bazaar
8	Bus 108 to Afghan Embassy	17	Railway Station
9	Mihantour bus office		

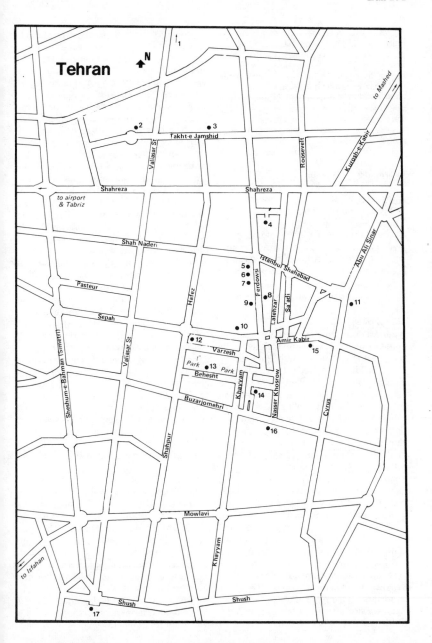

An interesting spectacle throughout Iran (but more especially in Tehran) are the propaganda posters, slogans and paintings on walls. A good number are headed in English so they seem to be for the benefit of tourists – when our taxi driver saw our interest in them, he took us on a guided tour of slogans around Tehran! Despite the hostile tone of the slogans, one doesn't feel threatened – people are very friendly by and large (even the officials) as long as one respects their code of dress.

I Krishnasamy – UK

Information & Orientation

Tehran is pancake flat and terribly sprawling. Getting from anywhere to anywhere entails long distance travel. There is no real 'centre' to speak of although there are a number of important main streets such as Ferdowsi Avenue and, of course, Amir Kabir Avenue. Discerning which way you are pointing is easy (on a reasonably clear day) as the Elburz Mountains tower to the north.

Things to See

Bank Markazi On Ferdowsi Avenue this houses the jewel collection claimed to be the finest in the world. Highlights are the Peacock Throne (carted off from Delhi by Nadir Shah), the jewelled globe (just to use up 51,366 spare precious stones) and the Darya-e-Nour (Sea of Light) diamond, claimed to be the largest uncut diamond in the world. Today about the only way to go see the collection is with a written invitation, which your embassy might be willing to help you obtain.

Shahyad Monument That strange-looking centrepiece (I think it has been renamed) you see on the road to the airport and Tabriz was built to mark the 2500th anniversary of the Persian empire in 1971. There's a museum on the 1st floor, an audio-visual history of Iran and a lift to the top for the view. Tehranis like to come here to be photographed at night.

Sepahshah Mosque This is the most important mosque in Tehran – it's on Baharestan Square, quite close to Amir Kabir Avenue. You used to be able to

wander around quite freely, even climb to the top of one of the minarets if the mood was good. There was also a marble-pillared room with an amazing echo. Today you'd better be a Muslim before you even think about it!

Golestan Palace This was the palace of the Qajars when Tehran first became the capital. It is now a museum with a fine carpet collection and is set in a formal Persian garden.

Museums There are quite a few – the Archaeological Museum houses a pre-Islamic as well as post-Islamic collection. The Ethnological Museum has waxwork models of early Persian life. The Pahlavi Museum has a beautiful dome and lovely gardens. The National Arts Museum has a crafts workshop as well as state exhibits. The Negarestan Museum houses an exhibit of more recent Iranian art.

The Covered Bazaar South of the centre this bazaar is a huge maze of shops and stalls, including a memorable carpet section, a spices section and the (noisy) metal craftsmen. The Shah Mosque, with excellent Qajar tilework, is in the bazaar.

The Zurkhaneh There are a couple of these traditional Persian 'Houses of Strength' where the local editions of Arnold Schwarzenegger go through their own 2500-year-old 'pumping iron' ritual. You used to be able to see the club swinging, iron chains and chanting at the Bank-e-Melli Zurkhaneh or the Ja'afari Athletic Club, Park-e-Shah, Varzesh Avenue.

Places to Stay & Eat

The cheap hotels in Tehran which take foreign visitors have dwindled down to one solitary survivor – the good old *Amir Kabir* on Amir Kabir Avenue. This was always the most popular place in Tehran, the flagship of the city's miserable collection of generally miserable places to stay, so it's fitting it should be the one that has carried on. The Amir Kabir is fairly big (60-plus rooms, 150 beds) and in the old days it was permanently full. Today it's often got just a half dozen people staying!

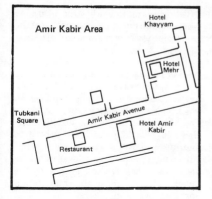

Amir Kabir Area

Hotel Khayyam

Hotel Mehr

Tubkani Square

Amir Kabir Avenue

Hotel Amir Kabir

Restaurant

and a swimming pool. A bus ran to it from Maidan-i-Gomrok, near the railway station. It was about 10 km out so rather expensive by taxi.

Getting There

Tehran is the travel centre of Iran for air, rail and bus travel. In Tehran there are big bus terminals where all the buses arrive and depart, unlike most other Iranian cities where each company will have their own office and terminal. The west terminal, out near the Shahyad monument, is where you come and go to Turkey, the south terminal is for Isfahan and Zahedan. The Iran Peyma bus office is on the corner of Sevom-e-Esfand and Ferdowsi Avenue. Mihantour is on Sevom-e-Esfand. Iran Peyma has a bus garage actually on Amir Kabir as does TBT. Levantour buses stop on Nasser Khosrow Avenue, just round the corner from Amir Kabir, but their station is at Villa Avenue. TBT's station is near the youth hostel.

Getting Around

Buses Routes and route numbers are only in Arabic script. Take a 213 bus to the train station from Tubkani Square, reasonably close to Amir Kabir Avenue. A 141 double-decker bus from almost across from the Amir Kabir will take you to the southern bus terminal. You have to buy tickets from a bus kiosk – standard fares for any trip within the city limits.

Taxis There are three types of taxis – all rather confusing in their operation and none particularly cheap. There are orange metered taxis, blue service taxis that run fixed routes picking up fares along the way and radio taxis. The orange ones often operate the same way as the blue ones – picking up people heading roughly the same way as you and darting all over town before arriving at your ultimate objective. On these the meter never gets switched on and you have to know roughly what you should be paying or agree the fare beforehand. No tipping is necessary.

Some approximate fares are 600 rials

At last report rooms are around 400 rials for a single, 250 rials for a dorm bed and it's very run down. Food, of a kind, is available at the Amir Kabir – bread and eggs for breakfast costs 20 rials.

There are a host of places around the Amir Kabir; perhaps they'll open their doors again although many of them would not take westerners even prior to the revolution. The *Tous*, directly across the road from the Amir Kabir, was similarly priced. Nearby was the slightly pricier *Mehr*. Also just off Amir Kabir Avenue was the *Khayyam* (or *Kaiam*) which was about twice the price (and twice the standard) of the Amir Kabir.

For food you could survive at the Amir Kabir or 100 metres along the road towards the Tubkani Square (formerly Maidan-i-Sepah) a large illuminated sign announced 'Restaurant' and you can get chelo kebab for around 400 rials. There are a number of places to eat along Amir Kabir Avenue and also around Tubkani Square.

Away from the Amir Kabir Avenue area there is a *Youth Hostel* which you could find by proceeding down Ferdowsi Avenue, past the British Council, turning right into Kushk Avenue and right again into Behdasht Kuche. Doubles are 1100 rials. Outside Tehran on the Isfahan road the *Gol-e-Shah campsite* had good facilities from the West Bus Terminal to Ferdowsi Square or 120-150 rials to the South Terminal. Or straight from one terminal to the other for around 500 rials. From Ferdowsi Square you can also take a bus then a share taxi to get there.

Airport There is no airport bus although a public bus reportedly runs to the Mehrabad airport. You can take a taxi and from the airport there is a fixed-price taxi service. For this you buy tickets from a kiosk to the right as you leave the terminal. Beware – it may be your first encounter with Iranian money if you've just flown in and the guys selling the tickets may try to take advantage of your unfamiliarity with the coins. On departure there is an airport tax. No photography is permitted at the airport.

AZERBAIJAN

The Azerbaijan area is the top north-west corner of Iran – squeezed up between Turkey, the USSR and the Caspian Sea. Tabriz is the main city in the region and for most people that is all they see of it. You can approach Tabriz from several routes apart from the straightforward Erzurum-Tehran road. It is possible to skirt around the Caspian Sea and turn down through Ardebil. Or you can approach from Kermanshah in the south. You can also exit Iran to the USSR by rail, crossing the border at Jolfa, north of Tabriz.

Tabriz

This large, industrial city had a short period as the Persian capital during the Safavid era. Tabriz has a very fine 15th-century covered bazaar which is worth exploring. The Ark, a huge and crumbling brick citadel in the centre of the city is a Tabriz landmark and is built on the site of a massive mosque which collapsed over 500 years ago. The Masjid-i-Kabud or Blue Mosque dates from 1465 and although much damaged by earthquakes it is still notable for its extremely good tilework. Tabriz also boasts a number of Armenian churches including one mentioned by Marco Polo on his travels.

Tabriz was particularly strife-torn after the revolution but appears to be one of the few Iranian towns with some sort of tourist office still functioning.

Places to Stay Cheap hotels in Tabriz are mainly in the small alleys off Ferdowsi Avenue. Many are not marked in English which makes finding them a little difficult! The Mihantour bus (which usually overnights here on the run from Tehran to Erzurum in Turkey) will drop you off at rather more expensive places like the *Grand* or *Jahan Nama*. To get to the cheaper places walk to the train station from the bus station (just a couple of hundred metres) and take a bus to the centre – cheaper than a taxi. The *Shah Goli* camping site, just out of town, was pleasant and well equipped but also tended to be rather noisy.

Ardebil

Situated 218 km north-east of Tabriz and only 70 km from the Caspian Sea, this small town is notable for its shrine of Sheikh Safieddin, who preceded the Safavid dynasty.

Other

South of Maku is the ancient Armenian church of St Thaddeus where services are held only once each year in August. Rezaiyeh, on the lake of the same name, is said to be the birthplace of Zoroaster. The area is noted for its wood carving and handicrafts. Maragheh, on the other side of the lake, has a number of interesting tomb towers and you can see many old pigeon towers around nearby Bonab.

ISFAHAN

The expression 'Isfahan is half the world' was coined in the 16th century to express the city's grandeur. You may well agree it has a ring of truth even today. Isfahan had long been an important trading centre, strategically situated in the south of modern Iran, but it came to its peak during the reign of Shah Abbas the Great.

Iran had been in a period of decline until in the early 1500s the first rulers of the Safavid dynasty chucked the Mongols out of the country. Shah Abbas came to power in 1587, extended his influence over rivals within the country then pushed out the Ottaman Turks, who had occupied a large part of Persia. With his country once more united and free of foreign influence Shah Abbas set out to make Isfahan a great and beautiful city. Its period of glory lasted for little over a hundred years – an invasion from Afghanistan hastened the decline and the capital was subsequently transferred to Shiraz and then to Tehran. The power and breadth of Shah Abbas' vision is still very much in evidence, for what remains in Isfahan today is just a small taste of what the city was at its height.

During the period of his rule Isfahan produced some of the more beautiful and inspiring architecture seen anywhere in the Islamic world. The cool blue tiles of Isfahan contrast perfectly with the hot, dry Iranian countryside around it – Isfahan is a sight you won't forget. It also appears to be relatively more free and easy than other towns in Iran.

Information

There's a tourist office on the corner of Chahar Bagh Avenue and Shah Abbas-i-Kabir Avenue, opposite the Madrasse-i-Madir-i-Shah. There is no sign for it. The street-name-changing urge has been particularly strong in Isfahan and, as in so many other places in the world, this is likely to cause confusion for some time.

Things to See

Maidan-i-Shah The centre of Isfahan is a huge open square, claimed to be one of the largest in the world. Many of the most interesting sights in Isfahan are clustered around the square.

Masjid-i-Shah The magnificent 'King's Mosque' marks one end of the square and is probably one of the most stunning buildings in the world. It is completely covered, inside and out, with the pale blue tiles which became an Isfahan trademark. The mosque is a particularly inspiring sight at night when the tiles glow with a soft sheen. The dome is double layered and although the entrance, with its twin towers, faces squarely out onto the square, the mosque itself is at an angle to face towards Mecca.

Masjid-i-Sheik Lotfollah The small mosque on the side of the square, covered in cream-coloured tiles, is notable for not having any minarets. This is because it was built purely for family worship so there was no need for the faithful to be called to prayer. Sheik Lotfollah was a sort of Billy Graham of the time.

Ali Kapu On the opposite side of the square is this palace with its huge pavilion from which the royal spectators could watch the activities in the square below. At one time a polo field was laid out in the centre.

Kaisarieh The royal bazaar dominates the other end of the square from the King's Mosque. It covers a simply enormous area and since Isfahan is the artistic and craft centre of Iran it is one of the best places to make a shopping trip. There are something like five km of paths to stroll so allow plenty of time! There are other shops, many specialising in the brasswork for which Isfahan is also famous, around the square.

Chechel Sooton Behind the Ali Kapu palace is a park with this interesting pavilion. The name means 40 columns, although there are actually only 20. A reflecting pool is provided to see the other 20! A more mundane explanation is that 40 is used synonymously with 'many' in Persian.

Masjid-i-Jami This older, Friday Mosque is located away from the Maidan-i-Shah area. It has a beautiful dome and some fascinating cellars – a helpful official will show you around.

Bridges A number of interesting bridges cross the Zayandeh Rud River, particularly the '33-Arch' bridge, which runs from the end of Chahar Bagh, the main street of

1 to Friday Mosque
2 Bazaar
3 Chehil Sotoon
4 Ali Qapu
5 Post Office
6 Sheikh Lotfollah Mosque
7 Royal Mosque
8 Citadel
9 Madresse of the Shah's Mother
10 33-Arch Bridge
11 Djoubi Bridge
12 Khwaju Bridge

Isfahan. A little downstream is the slightly smaller, but possibly even more attractive, Khwaju bridge. There is an aqueduct between the two bridges. There's a Turkish bath at the square next to the 33-arch bridge.

Madrasse-i-Madir-i-Shah The theological school of the Shah's mother, as the name translates, is just off Chahar Bagh Avenue and close to the splendid Shah Abbas Hotel. The courtyard is extraordinarily beautiful and restful but unfortunately the building appears to be closed to non-Muslims now. For some pleasant views of Isfahan try to see the Pasolini film *Arabian Nights*, which was partly filmed on location in Isfahan and some other equally exotic parts. One amusing scene takes place in this courtyard. The nearby Shah Abbas Hotel was elegantly converted from an old caravanserai and is worth a look around – even a stay if you can afford it.

Minarets Isfahan has a whole selection of minarets, many of which have outlasted the mosques they were once part of. A good number of the 43 in the city are of great architectural value, but they are equally interesting for the views from the top. From above the fact that Isfahan is a green, oasis town, becomes very clear.

Around Isfahan

Just across the river by the 33-arch bridge is Jolfa, once the Armenian quarter. The skills of these industrious Christians were coveted but it was preferred that they were kept in one area and away from the Islamic centres. There are some interesting churches and an intriguing old cemetery. Only seven km from the city are the Manar-i-Djonban or 'swaying minarets'. If you climb to the top of one of these twin minarets and lean hard against the wall it will start to sway back and forth. And so will its twin! A little further on the road is a fire altar and from the hillside you get a good view back to the city.

Places to Stay & Eat

Isfahan's popular *Youth Hostel*, where you could also camp, has become a *Young Tourists' Inn*. It's some distance from the centre, costs 500 rials a night and is clean and pleasant. You can get dull but edible meals for 80 rials.

Around the bus station there are places like the *Hotel Jamshid* at 1500 rials or on Chahar Bagh-i-Abbasi Avenue there's the *Hotel Golestan* at 750 rials for a double and the *Hotel Pars* at 1250 rials. On this same avenue the *Hotel Tous* is friendly and good.

On the corner of the avenue, near the corner of Masjid-i-Seyyed Avenue (it used to be Mohamed Reza Shah Avenue!) the *Amir Kabir Hotel* costs 800 rials for a double while just opposite is the *Mihantour Hotel* with doubles for 850 rials. *Restaurant Nobahor* is just up from the Amir Kabir and has good snacks and light meals. There's a gaudy but reasonably tolerable restaurant about 200 metres up Chahar Bagh from the 33-arch bridge.

Each room in the not-overwhelmingly-expensive *Shah Abbas Hotel* is individually decorated with gorgeous paintings and gilded ceilings. Unfortunately the garden tea room (and nightclub?) is now shut (surprise! surprise!) but the restaurant is excellent. For a minor splurge the Shah Abbas is an experience not to be forgotten. Doubles are around 3500 to 5000 rials including tax, not too bad in black market money. A first floor double has a balcony overlooking the courtyard, air-con, bath and shower, bidet and room service! Breakfast – eggs, bread and butter, coffee – is 250 rials.

Getting There

Bus offices are on Farughi Avenue. TBT buses go from Isfahan to Zahedan.

PERSEPOLIS & FARS

Fars is the southern region of Iran, where the great Persian empires were once centred and from which the name Persia was derived. Persepolis was the greatest city of this region and the principal attraction today – but it is far from the only reminder of Persia at its peak.

Persepolis

The earlier capital of the Achaemanians was at Pasargadae, further north, but in 521 BC Darius the Great started construction of this massive and magnificent palace complex. It sits on a plateau on the slopes of Koh-i-Rahmet and at one time was surrounded by a wall 18 metres high. In 323 BC Alexander the Great burnt it to the ground, fortunately after he had the enormous library translated into Greek. The ruins you see today are just a shadow of Persepolis' former glory. As you survey the barren land around it remember that this area was once far more fertile than it is today.

The only entrance to the palace was the four flights of steps of the Grand Stairway. At the top they led to Xerxes Gateway with three entrances – the western one flanked by two, seven-metre-high stone bulls while the eastern one is flanked by two winged bulls with human heads. The southern door leads to the immense Apadana where the kings once held audiences and received visitors. The roof was supported by 36 stone columns each 20-metres high but the main interest today is in the superb reliefs that decorate the stairways. Altogether they are over 300 metres long and when, in Persepolis' heyday, they were brightly coloured they must have been an amazing spectacle. The quality of the work is still astounding today. The 'Parade of Nations' shows people and animals bringing tribute to the Persian king while other reliefs show the 'Immortals', the 10,000 man palace guard.

Behind the Apadana are the smaller palaces of Darius and Xerxes and in one of the *anderouns* (harems), a small museum has been set up. The eastern door from Xerxes Gateway leads to the Hall of 32 Columns, behind which is the now totally demolished Treasury of Darius. Below Persepolis there used to be a tent city which was assembled for the 2500th anniversary of the Persian empire in 1971, a final swan song of the Shah's.

Persepolis is well worth the effort to visit – the lack of visitors is very pleasant as you have the site virtually to yourself. In summer it is wise to visit the area early in the morning or late in the afternoon – avoiding the intense mid-day heat.

Getting There Situated 57 km from Shiraz on the road to Isfahan, Persepolis (ask for Takht-e-Jamshid when asking the locals) takes about an hour to get to by bus from Shiraz. Mercedes minibuses depart every hour from Darvazeh-e-Isfahan in Shiraz.

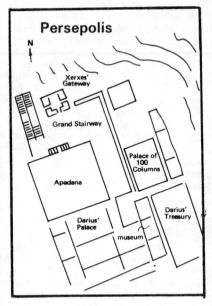

The bus trip is about 75 rials, entrance fee 30 rials, another 20 rials to the museum.

Other Places

Nakshi Rustam The four tombs of Nakshi Rustam are believed to be those of Darius I (the Great), Xerxes, Artaxerxes and Darius II, but only that of Darius I has been positively identified. There are also reliefs cut into the stone from the far later Sassanid dynasty and a fire-temple from Achaemenian time.

Pasargadae The capital of Cyrus the Great is 130 km from Shiraz and rather further off the main road. It is nowhere near as interesting as Persepolis and what remains is fairly widely scattered. Begun under Cyrus the Great, it was succeeded soon after his death by Darius I's magnificent palace and some historians feel that the construction of Persepolis may actually have started under Cyrus.

SHIRAZ

Nearly 500 km further south from Isfahan, Shiraz is the romantic and artistic soul of Iran. It's famed for nightingales, poetry, roses and, at one time, wine. Prior to the revolution it looked like the Shiraz wine business might be enjoying a modest revival but now it's back to the dark ages.

Close to Shiraz are the historic ruins of Persepolis – once capital of the Persian empire. Shiraz too had a spell as the Persian capital in the early years of the Islamic era and later, for a short spell, during the Zand dynasty from 1753 to 1794. Many of Shiraz's most beautiful buildings were built or restored in that period.

The two most famous Persian poets were born and lived in Shiraz – Hafez (1320-1389) and Saadi (1207-1291). Both have famous mausoleums. Omar Khayyam is not so highly rated by the Iranians, he's esteemed more as a mathematician than as a poet.

Things to See

Mausoleum of Hafezieyen His poetry made Shiraz famous so it is fitting that his tomb, with its beautiful gardens, is popular to this day.

Mausoleum of Saadi Situated north-east of the city, this tomb has gardens and a natural spring. Saadi's most famous book was the *Golestan* – 'garden of roses'.

Masjid-i-Jami The Friday Mosque was begun in 894 AD and is one of the oldest Islamic buildings in Shiraz. It has a 14th century turret derived from the Kaaba at Mecca.

Masjid Now The 13th century New Mosque is said to be the largest in Iran and has impressive barrel vaulting.

Vakil Bazaar The chief bazaar in Shiraz was built during the Zand dynasty and was part of a plan to make Shiraz a great trade centre. The lofty brick ceilings ensure that the interior is cool in the summer and warm in winter.

Other There are some very pleasant gardens, particularly the Bagh-i-Eram.

The *Masjid-i-Shah Cheragh*, which houses the tombs of the two younger sons of the Caliph Ali who were killed in Shiraz, is a must. The brilliance of the mirror-lined interiors is stunning and as one of the major places of Shi'ite pilgrimage it is fascinating to see the hordes of supplicants and the piles of money and gold they give every day. Be sure to ask permission before entering though, and have clean feet or socks, mine were smelled before I was allowed in!

Martin Powell – UK

Places to Stay & Eat

There are cheap hotels, like the *Hotel Shiraz*, on Darius Avenue. Shiraz also has an excellent campsite with good facilities.

YAZD

Situated on the Isfahan-Kerman road Yazd is particularly interesting for its relationship with its desert environment. It stands on the border between the northern salt desert and the southern sand desert. It has some of the best adobe architecture in the region. Look out for the tall wind towers designed to catch even the lightest breezes and direct them down to the below-ground-level living rooms. In a city where summer temperatures hit 42°C or more they are very necessary. The Yazd water reservoir has six of these towers.

Yazd has no less than 12 busy bazaars, a number of fine mosques and city walls from the 13th and 14th centuries which are said to be the most interesting in Iran. Yazd was also an important religious centre in the pre-Islamic days of Zoroastrianism and there is still a substantial minority of followers of Zoroaster in Yazd today.

KERMAN

Between Zahedan and Yazd this place is worth visiting for its Zoroastian temples. The people here don't speak Farsi and are much more Indian looking. There are lots of hotels near the railway terminus with prices of 300 rials or less.

CASPIAN SEA

The Caspian Sea is actually not a sea at all, it is the world's largest lake and particularly famous for its sturgeon from which comes that gourmet's delight – caviar. If you have a yen for high living you will find caviar is much cheaper here than elsewhere in the world. You can see it being processed at Bandar-e-Anzali or Babolsar. To Iranians the Caspian coast is a popular holiday resort, the 'Iranian Riviera'.

North of the Elburz Mountains is a green and lush countryside in total contrast to the arid and rocky Iranian plateau to the south. There are good roads all along the coast and you can easily stop off here between Mashed and Tehran or make a longer trip between Tehran and Tabriz via the coast. There are three main road routes from Tehran to the coast as well as the rail line that terminates at Gorgan, a good stretch of the way between Tehran and Mashed. The main resort towns of the coast are Babolsar, Ramsar and Bandar-e-Anzali.

In summer the water temperature hovers in the mid-20°Cs – very pleasant for swimming. It's a great place to visit if you like being a novelty.

Places to Stay

There are no hotels in Amol but in Rasht the *Hotel Iran Javan* is an excellent cheap hotel. Sari also has a good place to stay.

MASHED

Iran is a Shi'ite Muslim country and Mashed is their chief pilgrimage city. To Shi'ites only Mecca is of greater importance than Mashed. It was also the last major stopping point before Afghanistan for eastbound travellers so it was quite a bottleneck for visitors and pilgrims. Today, with Iran's smaller number of travellers all taking the southern route through Iran, it's right off the beaten track.

Things to See

Tomb of the Imam Reza The Imam Reza, 8th of the 12 Imams, was poisoned in 817 AD by his son and around his tomb a complex of mosques, seminaries, libraries, museums and a bazaar has sprung up. The tomb itself is marked by its golden dome – gilded during the rule of Shah Abbas the Great. Unfortunately your infidel presence is not wanted and any attempt to make your way through the bazaar to the courtyard of the shrine will be firmly turned back. Mashed can be a heavy place, especially during the late-June to mid-July pilgrimage period. A glimpse of the dome and the tops of the gold minarets is likely to be all you can manage.

Gaur Shad Mosque In the same complex, and therefore equally inaccessible, is this twin-minaretted mosque. Crowned with a blue-tiled dome, it was built in 1418.

The Museum This one is open to the public – it has pottery, antique carpets, metalwork and a gold bas-relief door from the tomb.

Other There are quite a few other interesting sites in the Khorosan area, of which Mashed is the main centre. Toos is just 30 km north-east of Mashed and here, beside the ruins of the ancient fortress, is the tomb of Ferdowsi, the great 11th century poet. Better known to westerners is Omar Khayyam and you can find his rather dull tomb in Neyshabur, 130 km west of Mashed on the southern road to Tehran. The tomb of Sheikh Attar, another renowned poet who also made his name as a scientist, is just a km from Neyshabur. Exploring other Khorosan attractions will require some effort and a sturdy vehicle.

Places to Stay & Eat

The Mashed camping site, a little distance from the centre of town towards the airport and the Afghan border, was particularly well equipped. There were permanently erected tents on concrete floors, camp beds, hot showers and a good bus service between the campsite and the town centre and also shared taxis.

In town you can find cheap hotels along Tehran Avenue such as the *Darbandin Hotel*. Particularly popular with travellers is the *Shahsavar Hotel*, opposite the Khavar bus office on Nakrisi St or the slightly more expensive *Tourist Hotel*. *Karoun Lodge* is also popular. Many of the real cheapies are for local pilgrims only, no travellers wanted. There are some more expensive places along Avenue Naderi – like *Hotel Blue Star* or *Hotel Jouharie*.

You can get good chelo kebab at the restaurant on the corner of Pahlavi and Jam Sts.

Maldives

The Maldives are a long string of tropical islands to the south-west of India and Sri Lanka. They're normally reached through Sri Lanka and have acquired something of a 'lost paradise' image over the past few years – with good reason, they're beautiful, virtually unspoilt and as far away from everything as you could possibly ask. People coming to the Maldives are mainly bound for the various resort islands in the archipelago although there are also dhoni trips which go around a number of islands.

Although the islands are so beautiful and the diving can be terrific the Maldives are essentially a place for watersport enthusiasts or for lying under a palm tree and doing nothing. To visit the Maldives you need to either be wealthy enough to afford the expensive resorts or hardy and enterprising enough to find your way around the islands on fishing boats.

HISTORY
The Maldives have almost always been an independent nation, although for the period from 1887 until independence in 1965 they were a British protectorate. For a short period from 1558 to 1575 the Portuguese conquered Male. There was a major British airbase at Gan, the furthest south of the islands, but it is now deserted. The Maldivians were always traders and their islands were strategically placed on the old Indian Ocean trading routes.

FACTS
Population The population of the Maldives is about 160,000, making it the smallest country in south Asia. Male, the capital and only town in the islands, has a population of 45,000. Only 200 of the two-thousand-odd islands are inhabited.

Economy Male is the only town in the country and the only place with any sort of 'industry', apart from fishing. The economy of the country was totally based on fishing until tourism began to develop from the early '70s. There are now more than 20 resorts in operation with more being planned. The Maldives are fairly affluent, despite the last president fleeing with half the national account.

Geography The Maldives stretch for 764 km from just north of the equator but the archipelago is only 128 km wide at its widest. The total land area is only 298 square km. Male, which is at the centre of the archipelago, is 670 km from Colombo in Sri Lanka. Officially there are 1196 islands but if you add tiny spits and bars the figure is probably over two thousand. The islands are almost uniform in their appearance – tiny spots in the ocean, ringed by a white sandy beach, a coral reef and crystal clear water. You can divide the islands into four groups – Male with its town, the resort islands (most resorts occupy an entire island), the fishing islands where the 'rural' population of the Maldives lives, and the many uninhabited islands. Most of the resorts are located in Male Atoll, close to the island of Male itself.

Religion The Maldives may originally have been Buddhist but in 1163 the ruler became Muslim and the population is now entirely Islamic. It's a low key, easy going brand of the religion, however.

INFORMATION
The Maldives Tourist Board is part of the Department of Information in Male. The various resorts are owned by government organisations – principally Crescent Tourist Agency on Marine Drive or Universal at 15 Chandani Rd. The tourist information counter at the airport has a list of all guest houses on the fishing islands.

Every island has an office which is in contact with Male daily. Cable & Wireless

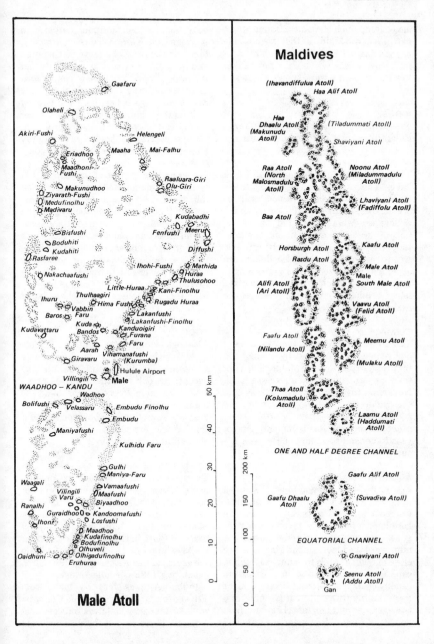

Maldives

(Ihavandiffulua Atoll)

Haa Alif Atoll

Haa Dhaalu Atoll (Makunudu Atoll)

(Tiladummati Atoll)

Shaviyani Atoll

Raa Atoll (North Malosmadulu Atoll)

Noonu Atoll (Miladummadulu Atoll)

Lhaviyani Atoll (Fadiffolu Atoll)

Baa Atoll

Horsburgh Atoll

Kaafu Atoll

Rasdu Atoll

Male Atoll

Male

South Male Atoll

Alifi Atoll (Ari Atoll)

Vaavu Atoll (Felid Atoll)

Faafu Atoll (Nilandu Atoll)

Meemu Atoll

(Mulaku Atoll)

Thaa Atoll (Kolumadulu Atoll)

Laamu Atoll (Haddumati Atoll)

ONE AND HALF DEGREE CHANNEL

Gaafu Alif Atoll

Gaafu Dhaalu Atoll

(Suvadiva Atoll)

EQUATORIAL CHANNEL

Gnaviyani Atoll

Seenu Atoll (Addu Atoll)

Gan

200 km
150
100
50
0

Male Atoll

Gaafaru

Olaheli

Akiri-Fushi

Helengeli

Eriadhoo

Maaha

Mai-Falhu

Maadhoni-Fushi

Makunudhoo

Raaluara-Giri

Olu-Giri

Ziyarath-Fushi

Medufinolhu

Madivaru

Kudabadhi

Bisfushi

Fenfushi

Meeru

Boduhiti

Diffushi

Kudahiti

Rasfaree

Ihohi-Fushi

Mathida

Nakachaafushi

Huraa

Thulusohoo

Thulhaagiri

Little-Huraa

Kani-Finolhu

Ihuru

Hima Fushi

Rugadu Huraa

Vabbin Faru

Lakanfushi

Baros

Lakanfushi-Finolhu

Kudavattaru

Kuda Bandos

Kanduoigiri

Furana

Aarah

Faru

Vihamanafushi (Kurumba)

Giravaru

Hulule Airport

Villingili

Male

WAADHOO – KANDU

Wadhoo

Bolifushi

Velassaru

Embudu Finolhu

Embudu

Maniyafushi

Kulhidu Faru

Gulhi

Maniya-Faru

Waagali

Vamaafushi

Vilingili Varu

Maafushi

Biyaadhoo

Ranalhi

Guraidhoo

Kandoomafushi

Ihoni

Losfushi

Maadhoo

Kudafinolhu

Bodufinolhu

Olhuveli

Oaidhuni

Olhigadufinolhu

Eruhuraa

50 km
40
30
20
10
0

have set up such a good communications network in the Maldives that it is possible to get a line to Europe from the Male post office in one minute! This also means that the government always knows where you are.

VISAS

No visas are required but a Rs 150 tax is charged for stays beyond one month.

MONEY

The Maldivian rupee is divided into 100 larees. The exchange rate is approximately Rs 9 to the US dollar. Although rupees are, of course, the everyday currency US dollars are usually required for airline ticket purchases and can be spent in tourist shops and for other such purposes. At the resort islands only US dollars are accepted. Every visitor has to pay a daily tax of US$3, which makes the Maldives fairly expensive, particularly since the exchange rate is rather poor.

CLIMATE

The tropical climate of the Maldives is almost always tempered by cooling sea breezes. No place on the Maldives is more than a couple of metres above sea level. November to March is the main season in the Maldives, from May to October the south-east monsoon usually brings some rain each day and this is the only time of year to consider avoiding. Otherwise it's sunny and dry most of the year.

ACCOMMODATION

Few visitors stay long in Male, it's only a jumping off point for the other islands. Indeed the Male airport is on nearby Hulule Island and most resorts pick their guests up straight from the airport. A number of the resorts in the Male atoll are close enough to Male to commute into the capital. Accommodation in the resorts usually costs from around US$50 a night for a double with full board. There are, however, a number of cheaper guest houses in Male. Most resort visitors will

have booked their accommodation as a package from Europe. You can, however, book through travel agents in Colombo and quite possibly pick up a good deal in this way. It's also possible to simply turn up at the airport and find something – the resort operators collect their pre-booked visitors there and also grab anybody else not already organised! If you want to change resorts you simply make your way back to the airport and see what's going that day.

You are not supposed to sleep on the beaches of uninhabited islands but can on inhabited ones that do not have guest houses. The best bet is probably to speak to any traveller you meet in Male and try to get an idea of an island you will like. Once you get there it is far cheaper to lie on the beach or snorkel than to island hop. Don't count on being able to find a guest house (or food, markets, toilets, etc) on just any island. Guest houses will probably start from around US$8 including food.

FOOD

Although some of the southern islands grow a little food most food, including vegetables, is imported. The obvious exception is fish and other seafoods. Some fruit – principally coconuts, bananas, mangoes, breadfruit, limes and papayas are also grown, but it's not surprising that things are expensive. No alcohol is allowed into the Maldives.

GETTING THERE

There are occasional ships from Colombo in Sri Lanka, the trip takes a couple of days, but apart from that the usual route to the Maldives is by air. Check with C V Soerensen (tel 93256, 98732) at 169 Stafford Place in Colombo 10 about their weekly shipping service to Male. In Male the agent is Imad's Agency (tel 2964), MA Javahiriya, 39/2 Chandani Magu.

Indian Airlines flies to Male from Trivandrum or you can fly from Colombo with Air Lanka or Maldives International Airlines. There are two flights a day from

Colombo almost every day of the week and the fare is Rs 1557. At present Maldives Airlines is simply an Indian Airlines flight operated in their name but there is talk of actually establishing an airline. Airport tax on departure is US$6.

If you're young and not in a resort group your baggage is likely to be thoroughly searched on arrival. Furthermore, reported one visitor, 'if you've not got a cholera vaccination certificate when coming from Sri Lanka you get vaccinated on arrival and then have to spend five days in Male, before you can visit the islands. Strangely this doesn't seem to apply if you're staying at a $100-a-day resort!'

GETTING AROUND

Ferries operate approximately hourly between Hulule airport and Male, the fare is Rs 0.50. Male is the only place in the Maldives with cars and all taxis operate from a stand outside the Government Hospital. The town is small enough to walk around or you can hire bicycles.

Before you can visit the islands you must get a permit from the Atolls Administration Office in Male. The permit is free but limited to three island. At the moment the government is having an Islamic-purity campaign and trying to limit contact between islanders and visitors. Island guest houses are being shut and regulations about carrying tourists on fishing boats are being tightened up. The resort islands have their own boats, of course, but individuals can hire *dhonis*, the local dhow-like fishing boats, by the day or for longer periods.

Ask around the fish market for a boat going to the island you want to get to. It costs US$5 per person to travel to any island – there are no ferries as such, all inter-island travel is done on fishing boats, always at US$5 per trip. Since boats are infrequent and irregular, once you get to an islands you're stuck – the 'boat is not working' or 'weather is too bad' syndrome will probably apply. This can be a problem if you don't like the island. Leave your island at least a day early and spend your last night in Male, so you can be certain you will catch your flight.

THINGS TO BUY

Hopefully the government is clamping down on the large scale export of turtle shell products – before the turtles are hunted to extinction. Apart from tourist souvenirs the main things to buy are seashells, woven grass mats and *felis* – local made sarongs.

LANGUAGE

The national language is Dhivehi, which is related to Sinhala. You can pick up a locally produced phrase book called *In Maldives* while you are in Male. English is widely spoken.

MALE

Male is the capital city and also the name of the island. Although most visitors merely pause here before heading out to the other islands you can happily spend some time looking at the market, the fishing boats, dhonis being built or repaired, the museum and the various mosques. The waterfront Marine Drive is the location for the GPO, the resort island offices and the bank. Chandani Magu and Orchid Magu are the main shopping streets.

Places to Stay

More expensive hotels in Male include the 18 room *Alia Hotel*, the smaller *Sosunge* and *Blue Haven*. There are many guest houses in Male such as the *Malam International Guest House* at 8 Majeed Magu, not far from where the airport ferry drops you. It's a pleasant place to stay with singles/doubles for US$5/10. Meals add another US$4 per person. There are usually a few room touts at the airport seeking solo travellers. If you go with one you do at least get a free ferry ride but their commission gets added to the bill.

Places to Eat

Rather expensive food is available at the *Alia Hotel* or at *Food City* on Chandani Magu. There are two cheap cafes on Orchid Magu, the *Moon* is the better of them. They serve up very sweet black tea and a table full of cakes and savouries. You pay for what you eat. At night before 8 pm it is just possible to get some rice and fish in these places.

For local food try the *Neon Hotel* on Chandani Magu, the *Crest Hotel* on January Magu or *Majeedee Ufaa* on Majeedee Magu. Cold drinks can be found at *Icege* on Orchid Magu, *Icecone* on Chandani Magu or *Beach Crescent* on Marine Drive.

RESORT ISLANDS

The Male Atoll extends for a little over 100 km from the southern end of South Male to the northern end of the main Male Atoll. Male itself and nearby Hulule, where the airport is located, are at the southern end of the main Male Atoll. Most of the resort islands are in the Male Atoll, many of them 10 km or less out of Male. The local word for island is *fushi*, thus Furana island might be referred to as Furanafushi.

Some of the island resorts include: Alimat (56 km from Male), Bandos (8), Baros (16), Boduhithi, Embodu, Farukolhu (7), Furana (10), Helengeli, Ihuru (19), Kanifinolhu (27), Kuramathi (64), Kuredu (131), Kurumba (4), Little Huraa (16), Loi Meerufen (43), Medufinolhu, Nakachcha, Nolhivaranfaru (210), Ranalhi (43), Vaadho (or Wadu) (8), Vabbinfaru (15), Velassaru (11) and Villingili (3). Farukolhu is the site of the Male Club Mediterranee.

At most of the resorts, nightly costs with meals run from around US$50 for a double. Resorts range from smaller places with just half a dozen rooms to resorts like Bandos or Villingili with over 100 rooms. Dhoni trips around the Maldives – from Australia they are operated by Australian Himalayan Expeditions and Peregrine Expeditions – usually camp on fishing-village islands or uninhabited islands. Solo travellers could, no doubt, do the same. Many of the uninhabited islands have wells so drinking water is available. A few island and boat trip reports from visitors:

Gulhi Island is very small with a nice beach. On Maafushi there is a German guest house costing US$8 each for half board. It is run by a German and his Maldivian wife and it's really a home from home although the beach here is not one of the best. There are masks, snorkels and even a dinghy which you can use.

Rannali is highly recommended. It's a small, oval island with a self-contained resort (capacity about 150 people), about 2½ hours by slow boat, south of Male. The reef here is the best I've ever seen, both in terms of coral and fish. Forget your swimsuit, people don't use such things there. Accommodation, about US$40 with meals, consists of pleasant huts ringing the island. They're comfortable, clean and each has beach frontage and shade trees. Rooms have a ceiling fan and bathrooms with saltwater (ugh!) showers. The restaurant is excellent, if you like seafood, with a different fresh fish each night. The island has a great open-air bar, cold beer and European ice cream. Plus good music, some entertainment and sports facilities including, of course, a diving shop.

There are several small dhonis for rent at very low rates which you can take out with or without a boatman. There are also powerboats which will take you to the neighbouring islands, of which there are many – some inhabited.

Dhoni trips are not for the soft. There's little fresh water for washing and the diet can be monotonous. You generally sleep on board or on a beach – there are no mosquitoes. The boats carry very little safety equipment and the water can get very rough, fortunately they're good sailors but in a mishap your chances would be slim. You rarely wear more than a swimsuit (at the most) so bring more than one.

Some of the islands we went to included Halaveli – an idyllic though very small island in a perfect atoll. Ukulhas you could walk right around in 20 minutes. Ten minutes was long enough to do a circuit of Rasdhu, very near Kuramathi, a German resort island. On Alifu Atoll there was actually a small town on Toddu, which took half an hour to walk right around. Giraavanu was a very small resort island.

Some islands have better food than others. The German resort islands generally bring their food straight from Germany via the charter airline Condor. On other islands the food may be much more limited in quantity and quality. There are German, French, Australian (Furana Island) and Maldivian-run resort islands.

Nepal

Nepal's image as a hippy haven almost overpowers the variety this lush, green, mountainous country can offer. If you just want to look and study it is a feast of temples, stupas and buildings. If you want to burn up energy it offers probably the best walking in the world. In Kathmandu every other building is a temple and every other day a festival. In the high Himalaya that make up half the country you can see the mightiest mountains on earth.

HISTORY

Nepalese history is really non-history. While things were happening elsewhere they weren't in Nepal, which accounts for the way the country is today. Although Nepal is related culturally and through religion to India it is also curiously isolated from it. The rise of the Muslim religion in India never climbed over the mountains into Nepal. The blend of Buddhism and Hinduism seen in Nepal is quite unlike their counterparts elsewhere. Nor did the later growth of the British empire extend into Nepal: Nepalese support of the British army during the Indian mutiny did lead to the long association of Gurkha regiments with the British, however.

The Nepalese certainly did not try to reduce their isolation. Even Marco Polo commented on the lack of desire to let foreigners into the country. It took a revolution and the building of the Rajpath road up from India in 1954 to open what is in many ways still a medieval country. Modern Nepalese history dates from the arrival of Indians forced out of their own country by Muslims in the 16th century.

For centuries Nepal consisted of many small, independent kingdoms. The Kathmandu Valley had separate kingdoms at each of its major towns. They reached their peak of power and artistic skills under the Malla kings. Then in 1768 King Prithvi Narayan Shah, ruler of the small principality of Gorkha, west of Kathmandu, conquered the valley and brought Nepal together in close to its present form.

During the last century real power was taken from the king by his prime minister, Jung Bahadur. From that date Nepal had an extraordinary succession of hereditary 'Rana' prime ministers. The king was a mere puppet of the repressive Ranas. Finally in 1951 a quiet revolution brought the king back to real power, although the Ranas still have much influence.

An indication of Nepal's recent emergence is that slavery was not abolished until 1926! Nor was *sati*, the practice of burning the (often reluctant) wife with her deceased husband, stopped until over a hundred years after the Indians prohibited it. Today Nepal is in the midst of a tourist boom and, at least in the Kathmandu Valley, things are changing rapidly. Its buffer position between India and China makes it important to both countries while the canny Nepalese also play the Russians off against the Americans in an often successful quest for foreign aid.

In the past few years Nepal has suffered a number of internal difficulties. The simmering opposition to the king's autocratic rule has boiled over on a number of occasions and the limited steps towards re-introducing a greater element of democracy to the country's government have also caused problems.

FACTS

Population Nepal's population is about 16 million and is composed of many different groupings. In the southern lowlands the people are closely related to those across the border in India, although there has also been much resettlement there from elsewhere in Nepal since malaria has been controlled. In the centre of the country are the heavily populated areas such as the

Kathmandu and Pokhara valleys. Kathmandu is the capital and largest city with a population of about 300,000. The people of the valley are Newars. Finally in the high hills are many different people some, such as the Sherpas, of Tibetan stock.

Economy Nepal is still a country engaged in subsistence agriculture although its many natural and man-made wonders have also made tourism very important. Rice and jute are the main exports and the earnings sent back by the Gurkha soldiers (long an important Nepalese export) continue to be important.

Geography The 142,000 square km of Nepal spreads over some of the most rugged country on earth including the highest mountain in the world, Mt Everest. Nepal is comprised of a series of narrow strips. Closest to the border with India is the low, jungle-covered Terai. From this rises the Siwalik Hills, then the higher Mahabharat Hills. A number of fertile valleys nestle north of these hills and north again rise the massive snow-covered Himalaya. The border with the Tibetan province of China runs along the range and they slope off into the high, barren Tibetan plateau.

Religion Nepal is predominantly Hindu, although there are distinct groups, such as the Sherpas of the Everest region, who follow Tibetan Buddhism and everywhere the religions are intermingled.

INFO

Kathmandu has a useful tourist office near the Durbar Square with some interesting brochures, leaflets and maps and it shows films from time to time.

BOOKS

If you want much more information about Nepal then the Lonely Planet guidebook *Kathmandu & the Kingdom of Nepal* covers everything you'll need to know about places to stay and eat, things to do and see, and how to get around. Its author, Prakash A Raj, is a western-educated Nepali who published earlier editions

himself in Kathmandu before it was taken over by Lonely Planet.

Trekking in the Nepal Himalaya by Stan Armington is a considerably revised new edition of his earlier trekking guide. It pays much more attention to the individual trekker with day-by-day route reports on all the major treks and up to the minute route maps. Stan is an American who has been living in Kathmandu since the early '70s.

If you're interested in the mountains or are trekking it is also worth reading accounts of some of the major mountaineering expeditions. Chris Bonnington's accounts of his recent climbs are particularly interesting – look for *Everest the Hard Way. The Snow Leopard* by Peter Matthiessen is a wonderful blend of trekking, wildlife, people and Buddhism.

There are a number of interesting locally produced books you'll find in Kathmandu bookshops – such as *Exploring Mysterious Kathmandu* by Katherine Hoag, which takes you on some fascinating walking tours around the city. Kathmandu has a surprising number of excellent bookshops.

VISAS

Visas are required by most nationalities and are available from embassies and consulates abroad, at the border from India or on arrival at Kathmandu airport. They cost from around US$5 to 10 depending on where you get them. If you obtain a visa abroad it is valid for 30 days while a visa obtained on arrival is only valid for seven days. A seven-day visa can be extended to 30 days and there is no additional cost but extending it is a hassle in as much as you have to queue up, fill in forms, stand around and generally waste a lot of time. It's worth getting your visa in advance if possible.

Visas for Nepal are only valid for the Kathmandu and Pokhara valleys, the Chitwan area and along the main roads. If you want to go outside these areas, ie to trek, you have to obtain a trekking permit

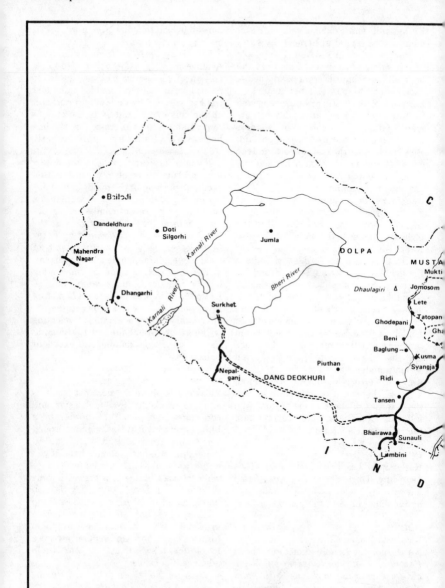

Nepal

international boundary
river
road
road under construction
trail
towns & villages

0 10 20 30 40 50 60 km

either in Kathmandu or Pokhara. A trekking permit costs Rs 75 per week but it also includes a visa extension, whereas a visa extension (beyond the 30 days) by itself costs Rs 60 a week. So if you're going to sightsee and trek do it in that order – otherwise you'll be paying Rs 75 a week to trek and (after 30 days) Rs 60 a week to extend your visas.

Visas are available for Nepal in Europe, the USA or Australia. In Asia the most popular places for Nepalese visas are Delhi in India, Bangkok in Thailand or in Singapore.

MONEY

A$1	=	Rs 14
US$1	=	Rs 18
£1	=	Rs 28

The rupee is divided into 100 paisa and is worth somewhat less than the Indian rupee. You can easily change Indian rupees at the border but watch the money changers there. Nepal has a thriving black market, particularly for cash dollars although travellers' cheques can also be changed. Indian rupees can also be bought in Nepal at a useful discount – of course it's illegal to bring Indian rupees into India.

CLIMATE

The cool season is the time to visit Nepal. After the monsoons end in October everything is green and beautiful, the days are warm, the nights cool to chilly. As the cool season continues it gets progressively colder at night although in the valley it is really chilly rather than cold. Up in the mountains it will be icy and you cannot make high altitude treks in January or February. Excellent-quality cold-weather gear for trekking can be rented in Kathmandu.

By the end of the dry season, April, May and early June, it gets very dry and dusty and mountain views are not so good. In compensation the wildflowers will be out in abundance. Then in June the rains arrive and you won't see the mountains for cloud until October rolls around again. During that time the unpleasant weather and equally unpleasant leeches make trekking impossible.

ACCOMMODATION

Good standards and low prices, the competition between the cheap hotels in Kathmandu is so intense that prices have hardly risen in years. Outside Kathmandu the only place with much choice of accommodation is Pokhara. There are also a few places to stay at the border towns and at some other major centres.

If you are trekking you can generally find a roof over your head at the tea shops known as *bhattis*. Often if will be free so long as you buy food there. So many small lodges and guest houses have sprung up along the most popular trekking routes that you can virtually trek from one to another although it's still wise to be prepared to camp out if necessary.

FOOD

Nepalese food is very simple; *dhal bhat tarkari* – a lentil soup, rice and curried vegetable concoction – is the national dish. Away from the few big towns it is very often all there is. But Kathmandu is a food trip to end all food trips. There are probably more of those 'international traveller' restaurants here than anywhere else on the route apart from Kuta Beach in Bali. You can find just about anything you want including mind-blowing pies – fruit, chocolate, lemon meringue, all your dreams materialised.

Kathmandu is also a good place to sample Tibetan food like *momos*. Of course since Nepal is Hindu, you won't find beef on the menu – plenty of buffburgers, buffsteaks and other buff(alo) dishes though. Try *chang* the locally brewed Tibetan-style beer too.

Hepatitis is not an uncommon affliction for the unwary in Nepal so be careful what and where you eat. The cleaner, more popular places should be OK.

GETTING THERE

Air People flying into Kathmandu generally come from either Bangkok or from New Delhi although there are also connections from Dacca in Bangladesh, from Calcutta, from Rangoon in Burma, and from Colombo in Sri Lanka. Coming from Bangkok it is possible to fly via Rangoon and include a visit to that fascinating country in your trip.

Airlines operating into Nepal are Bangladesh Biman, Burma Airways Corporation, Indian Airlines, Pakistan International Airlines, Royal Nepal Airlines Corporation and Thai International. Bangkok-Kathmandu costs around US$285 officially but in practice a little shopping around should find tickets around US$200. Delhi-Kathmandu is US$142. Unfortunately

the Kathmandu-Patna flights seem to have been dropped.

You'll have a superb view of the Himalaya as you fly into Kathmandu – if you choose the correct side of the aircraft. Coming from Bangkok or Calcutta try to sit on the right-hand side. Coming from Delhi it's the left-hand side you want. Although flying into or out of Kathmandu can be visually spectacular and is far more comfortable than slogging it out for a couple of days on public transport the bus trip up and over the foothills from the Indian plains to the Kathmandu valley is something everybody should do once.

Road It is strange that only a few years ago there was really only one land entry point to Nepal while now there are three in regular use. Of course there are many others but some are still off-limits while others are just inconvenient.

Raxaul-Kathmandu The old faithful entry point. Raxaul is the railhead in India from where a rupee or two will transport you by trishaw across the border to Birganj on the Nepalese side – including the necessary customs, immigration and money-change stops. You will probably have to overnight in Birganj as all the buses leave early in the morning. Book your seats the night before and avoid the uncomfortably bumpy back seats. Rs 40 for the normal buses (student discounts available), Rs 30 or even less (bargain) for a truck ride or Rs 44 for the faster and more comfortable minibuses. It is only 200 km from Birganj to Kathmandu, but the road wanders up, down and around endlessly and you will arrive tired out late in the afternoon. Many travellers come up from Patna in India to the Raxaul border crossing and that trip has become much simpler since the new bridge was completed at Patna.

Nautanwa-Pokhara or Kathmandu It is a similar process on this route, the Nepalese border town is Bhairawa and you may want to make a trip from here to Lumbini, the birthplace of Buddha, which is about 25 km away. Buses to Pokhara cost Rs 37, it is worth backtracking from Bhairawa to Sunauli right on the border to get the best choice of seats. This road is of rather better quality than the older Birganj-Kathmandu road.

You can also travel from the border directly to Kathmandu. The bus starts from Sunauli, just as for the Pokhara buses, then turns east at Butwal and travels along the flat, fast East-West Highway across the Terai. At Narayanghat, near the Chitwan National Park, you turn north and follow the Trisuli River to Mugling on the Kathmandu-Pokhara road. The fare is Rs 50.

Darjeeling-Kathmandu This is the longest route and uses the East-West Highway which runs through the Terai parallel to the Indian border. Eventually this road will run all the way to the western border with India but at present it peters out after the Pokhara-Nautanwa road. From Darjeeling you bus or jeep to Siliguri then cross the border to the Nepalese town of Kakarbitta. The buses from here cost Rs 98 (25% discount to student card holders). The trip takes at least two days including an overnight stop at Janakpur. The road eventually intersects the Birganj-Kathmandu road and you then follow that route to the capital. During the monsoon this route may be impossible due to the road being flooded.

If you're leaving Nepal this way note that you need a special permit for Darjeeling.

Kodari-Kathmandu You can now cross from Tibet into Nepal at Kodari, it's more difficult vice versa because of visa problems. Tibet was opened to independent travellers in China in September 1984 so you can now travel right across China and through Nepal into India.

GETTING AROUND
Air
If you want to fly there is a network of regular RNAC routes and also charter connections which are so frequent you can almost treat them like regular services.

They are mainly for the trekkers who want to get to remote places fast.

Bus
Apart from those three routes from India to Kathmandu there is very little road in Nepal – to get further afield you fly or walk. The few road stretches that do exist are:

Kathmandu-Pokhara There are plenty of buses every day, public buses cost Rs 35 while the more expensive private ones will be around Rs 40. The 'Swiss Bus' costs Rs 50 and is reckoned to be the flagship on the Kathmandu-Pokhara route but the only thing Swiss about it is the sign! It's worth the extra cost because of the comfortable, uncrowded seats and the less frequent stops. Get tickets the day before – early morning departure, mid-afternoon arrival and a meal stop on the way. Flying only takes about half an hour.

Kathmandu-Kodari There are no direct buses to Kodari on the Chinese border but you can get a ride on the early morning post office truck (Rs 24 round trip as far as Dhulikhel) or bus to Barabise (Rs 12) then hitch, or you may find an overland bus organising a day trip during its lay-up in Kathmandu.

Local Transport
Bus There is a network of bus routes around the valley and to places just outside such as Dhulikhel or Trisuli. Bhaktapur costs Rs 1.35, Dhulikhel outside the valley Rs 4.50. The minibuses or three-wheeler tempos are faster than the rickety buses.

Pushbikes Pushbikes are the transport to have, the valley is sufficiently compact and flat to make riding a pleasure. Get your bike early as the better ones tend to be snatched up leaving the old nails for the late risers. There are bike shops all over town and they cost just Rs 7 to 10 a day. You can also hire motorbikes, but only by the hour which makes them quite expensive. Trishaws are also available around town.

THINGS TO BUY

Tibetan carpets are beautiful even if they are rather heavy to transport. There are many Tibetan handicrafts such as prayer wheels, you whirl them round to say the prayer written inside. Just like in India there are lots of clothes, the yak wool 'yakets' are particularly popular. Or look for bulky and bright Tibetan jewellery. Block prints and drawings on rice paper are worth looking at in the Print Shop. Tankas, the Tibetan religious paintings, are popular but antique ones are often artificially aged and they have become very expensive if they are at all good.

LANGUAGE

Nepali is the major local language, but English is widely spoken in the touristed areas. *Nepal Phrasebook* is a handy introduction to Nepali, particularly useful for trekkers. It's one of the Lonely Planet Language Survival Kits. A few words:

how much?	*kati?*		
less/more	*kam/badhi*		
thank you	*dhanyabad*		
here/there	*yaha/tyaha*		
give me	*malai dinos*		
that's enough	*pugyo*		
I do not have	*chhaina*		
today	*aaja*		
yesterday	*hijo*		
tomorrow	*bholi*		
food	*khana*		
water	*pani*		
rice	*bhat*		
bread	*pauroti*		
1	९	*ek*	6	६	*chha*
2	२	*dui*	7	७	*sat*
3	३	*teen*	8	८	*sath*
4	४	*char*	9	९	*nau*
5	५	*panch*	10	९०	*das*

KATHMANDU

Kathmandu must rate as one of the dirtiest cities in Asia, but it is cheap and

fascinating and that can make up for a lot. It is a place of everlasting interest – every corner will take you to some new surprise whether it is another strange temple or just a colourful market. Your starting point should be the centre of the city, Durbar Square, around which many of the most interesting sights crowd. Kathmandu is the largest of the three cities in the Kathmandu Valley and the capital of the country.

Things to See

Durbar Square The Durbar or 'Palace' Square marks the centre of Kathmandu, just like the Durbar Squares of the other valley towns – Patan and Bhaktapur (or Bhadgaon). The square is packed with temples, monuments, statues and, of course, the palace. It is also the main meeting point for people in Kathmandu. It is a fascinating place just to sit on the steps of a temple and watch the world go by. There are so many things crammed into the square that a guide to them, available from bookshops in Kathmandu is a wise investment. Just a few:

Hanuman Dhoka This is the royal palace, so named because a statue of the monkey god Hanuman, cloaked in red, guards the door. The palace was built by King Pratap Malla in the 17th century. You can enter the palace courtyard for Rs 1 and climb to the top of the highest of the four towers – the Basantapur Tower. You get a marvellous view of the city from the topmost, ninth storey. A UNESCO restoration project is painstakingly restoring the palace.

Kumari Devi Looking out onto the main square is the house of the living goddess – the Kumari Devi. The young girl selected as the living goddess is paraded round Kathmandu once a year in a huge chariot kept behind the gate next to her house. She only remains a goddess until her first period; when that occurs she reverts to being a normal human and another goddess must be selected to replace her. Enter the courtyard and you may catch a

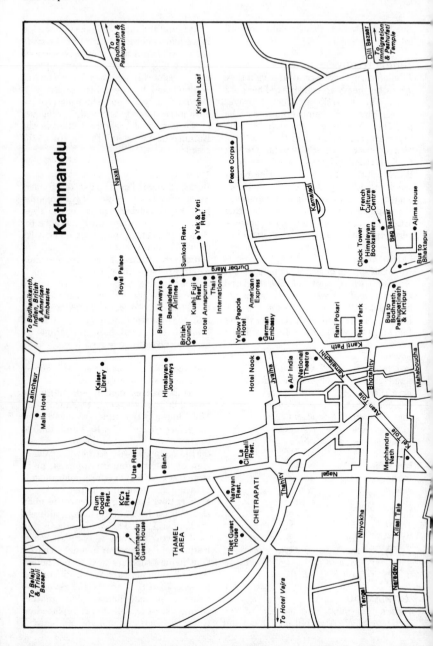

Kathmandu

glimpse of her on the upper balcony, a little baksheesh may help!

Black Bhairab The terrible figure of Kalo Bhairab, God of Terror, or Black Bhairab, stands close to the Hanuman Dhoka. Sweta Bhairab, White Bhairab, is shielded by a lattice gate behind Black Bhairab and is only revealed once a year.

Other At the top of 'Pig Alley', the rather dirty lane down to the river with all the pie shops, is the small and very popular Maru Ganesh temple. Across from it and a couple of paces down the alley is a Shiva temple with barbers squatting around it. Study the erotic carvings on the roof struts of the Jaganath Temple beside the Hanuman gate – a popular explanation for their presence is that it keeps the goddess of lightning, who is a bit of a prude, well away from the temple. Or encourages athletic procreation? The king seated on a column with his four sons is Pratap Malla the most famous of the Malla kings.

In the Durbar Square the temple of Shiva-Parvati is easily picked out by the figures of the god and his goddess looking out from the window. Don't miss the aptly named Big Drum and Big Bell. Best of all just wander round the town – watch out for the flute sellers, the passing freaks, the monks, the hill people in the big city on a shopping trip and all the bustling scenes that make Kathmandu so fascinating.

Places to Stay

Kathmandu has a very wide selection of places to stay. They're concentrated mainly around the Freak St area or in Thamel, a short walk north, with a few odd places dotted elsewhere. Freak St and the adjoining streets was the original travellers' accommodation centre in Kathmandu but now the centre of gravity has definitely moved to Thamel. It's also decisively moved up market! One very nice thing to have in Kathmandu is a hotel with some garden space. In winter buildings in Kathmandu tend to be somewhat gloomy and cold inside, while outside it can be very pleasant so long as you're in the sun.

A garden is definitely something to look for.

Thamel It's about 10-minutes walk from the central Freak St area to Thamel and here you will find the *Kathmandu Guest House* (tel 213628) which has rooms from as little as US$4 while better rooms, some with attached bathrooms, go up to US$10 or more. This popular guest house is quiet since it is a little off the beaten track and has a particularly pleasant garden for lazing around it. It's so popular that at peak times you really have to book ahead to get a room.

The *Star Hotel* (tel 412100) is right beside the Kathmandu Guest House and is also popular at US$2/4 although to some extent it just functions as an overflow place. The *Hotel Asia* (tel 216541) has rooms from US$3/6 and is another popular Thamel place. *Hotel Shakti* (tel 216121) with its pleasant garden is a good place with singles with bath for US$5.

Cheaper places around Thamel include the *Om Guest House* at Rs 50/60, the *Yeti Cottage* at Rs 25/50, *Earth House Lodge* at Rs 20/35 and so on. There are numerous others.

Freak St The real cheapies are in the central area – such as the *Oriental Lodge* and the *Century Lodge* on Freak St with rooms as cheap as Rs 15. Others in the same central area with equally cheap and basic rooms include the *Monumental Lodge*, *Annapurna Lodge* and *Everest Lodge*, all on Freak St.

Tourist Cottage is opposite the Mt Makalu Hotel just a block from New Rd. *Kathmandu Lodge* (tel 213868) is a bit more expensive (Rs 25/35 for singles/ doubles) but deservedly popular and it's also in the Durbar Square area. In fact there are far too many central places to make any specific recommendations – just wander into a few, if one doesn't suit you'll soon find another. Freak St, Durbar Square and to the north of Durbar Square and down Pig Alley are good hunting grounds. Some of the cheapest lodges are at the bottom of Pig Alley near the river. **Other Areas** Up the hill towards Swayambhunath the *Hotel Catnap* is a good place with rooms at Rs 35/45. Also on the way to Swayambhunath the *Hotel Vajra* is a good place with rooms from around Rs 100 to 125 or from Rs 125 to 150 with attached shower and toilet. There's a roof garden and the *Explorer's Restaurant*.

Ajima Guest House (tel 216088) is in Bag Bazaar near the clock tower. It's a different sort of location and has clean, well kept rooms at Rs 25/35 up to Rs 60 for the more expensive rooms. Nearby the *Capitol Restaurant* is quite popular.

In the central part of town the *Hotel Nook* (tel 13627) is a popular middle range place with rooms, all with attached bath, around US\$10 to 20. North of the palace area in Lazimpat the *Hotel Ambassador* (tel 14432) is a very pleasant middle range place with similarly priced rooms. It's got a good restaurant and very pleasant garden.

There are also some interesting possibilities around Kathmandu itself. At Jawlakhel, near the zoo and 15 minutes from the Patan bus stop, is the *Youth Hostel* (Mahendra Yuvalaya) (tel 521003) with rooms at under Rs 20, dorm beds at under Rs 10. You'll also find places across the river or towards the monkey temple. It's quiet and peaceful out here and places like the *Shampang Hotel* offer a garden and friendly atmosphere for Rs 20 a double. Longer stay visitors can rent rooms in private houses or even entire houses. Check the noticeboards in places like Aunt Jane's, the Kathmandu Guest House or the Peace Corps Office.

Places to Eat

Kathmandu is a real food trip – or at least it used to be in the days when people made the long trek across Asia and Kathmandu burst upon you like some sort of culinary fantasy after long weeks of dhal and rice in India or chelo kebab in Iran. Today, when people fly in to Kathmandu only hours from home, some of the old magic is gone but you can still recreate it by a month or two in India! The restaurants that follow are just a handful of favourites.

KC's Restaurant started life as a small Thamel snack bar, but grew to become the most popular restaurant in Kathmandu. It's well kept, imaginatively designed, the food is good and it's always full. You really need to book in the evening. Their breakfasts are great (muesli, porridge, yoghurt, you name it), dinner is fine, and don't miss the apple pie and ice cream. You think we've come a long way from the hippy-overland days of the '60s and early '70s? Well KC's takes Amex cards.

There are plenty of other popular restaurants around the Thamel area. Like the long running and down-to-earth *Utse* for Chinese and Tibetan food. *Jamaly's* is another long runner in the Thamel area. There's an old and a new branch on opposite sides of the road. The larger new one is upstairs and does pretty good food although not as classy as KC's.

Beside the Kathmandu Guest House the *Red Square* is great for those who'd like a hearty bortsch without forking out for one of the restaurants the legendary Boris has had a hand in. It's recently changed hands so standards may have changed. The Kathmandu Guest House itself has the *Astha Mangala Restaurant*, while just round the corner from KC's is *Rum Doodle*, named after that classic mountaineering book *The Ascent of Rum Doodle*. Rum Doodle, as if you didn't know, is the world's highest mountain; at 40,000½ feet towering a good 3000 metres above Everest. The menu and prices are similar to KC's and they've got a bar upstairs.

Across from KC's, *Govinda's* occupies his original building. *Namkha Ding* does Tibetan and Nepalese food. There's good pies and cakes at *Narayan's Restaurant*, run by the former owner of Jamaly's.

Moving away from the Thamel area, at *Kabab Corner*, right behind the Hotel Nook, you can find some of the best tandoori food I've had outside India (and London!). It's a little more expensive but worth it.

There are still numerous places around the Freak St and Durbar Square area. Some are really walking-wounded survivors of the '60s but others retain that old free-wheeling spirit. *Aunt Jane's* is one street over from Freak St and upstairs. Originally set up by the wife of the local peace corps' director it still has a bit of American influence. Just down from Durbar Square the *Blue Bird Restaurant* is still pretty good. If your budget is tight there are many real cheapies like *Hungry Eye*, *Eat at Joe's* or the *Om Restaurant*.

Eating in Kathmandu must include a visit to the pie shops – they are mainly on Pie (or Pig) Alley, the dirty lane from Durbar Square down to the river. The *Chi & Pie* is the oldest but many people recommend the *New Style Pie Shop* for the best selection and quality – lemon meringue, mixed fruit, apple, chocolate, you name it and they will probably have it. *Panchas Pastries* or the *Lunch Box* in Freak St, *Narayan's* in Thamel or *Baker's Cafe* on the way to Thamel from New Rd are also popular pie shop. The pie shops are good meeting places late in the evening. At the Crystal Hotel corner on New Rd *Sub Zero* is a good multi-flavour ice cream parlour with good Indian Kwality ice cream. There's another branch near the Nook Hotel.

If you want to splash out a bit try the waiter service and starched white tablecloths of the *Other Room* in the central Crystal Hotel. Or there's the *Kushi Fuji* with authentic and delicious Japanese food on Durbar Marg near the Hotel de l'Annapurna. Their fixed-price lunch is particularly good value. A little further up Durbar Marg towards the Royal Palace is *Sunkosi* with excellent Nepalese food although a complete meal will cost from Rs 100 per person. Finally you should at least look in and savour the atmosphere in the very expensive *Yak & Yeti*, originally established by the famous Boris.

AROUND THE VALLEY
Swayambhunath

The 'monkey temple', just across the river from the centre of Kathmandu, is quite the best place in the valley. Perched on top of the hill, visible almost anywhere in the valley, is the circular mound of the stupa, surmounted by a golden spire. It's claimed to be over 2000-years old, there are records of Ashoka, the Indian Buddhist-Emperor, having been there in 250 BC. Legend has it that the valley was once a lake and was drained from this spot.

Park your bike at the bottom of the hill near the seated Buddhas (please don't be so crass as to sit in their laps for a photo) and climb up the long flight of steps. You will soon see where the name 'monkey temple' comes from. Down the central handrail slide bands of primates; flying down one at a time, upside down, piggy back and in convoys. Great free entertainment.

At the top of the hill is the stupa, a colourful hodge podge of shops and temples and a superb view over Kathmandu. The eyes painted on the four sides of the spire are supposed to watch the valley for righteous behaviour, but from their look it is more likely to be the unrighteous they are on the watch for. Give the gigantic prayer wheel in the temple a couple of twirls for guaranteed Nirvana.

Pashupatinath

A couple of km on the other side of Kathmandu, this is the most holy Hindu temple in the valley. It stands on the banks of the Bagmati River, the Ganges of Nepal, and is dedicated to Shiva. Unfortunately non-believers are not allowed inside, but you can look down on it from the opposite river bank.

Bodhnath

A little further out, past the airport and still a pleasant bicycle ride, is Bodhnath, a huge Buddhist stupa surmounted by an eight-eyed spire like Swayambhunath.

Bodnath, Nepal.

Behave yourself! Around the stupa are shops selling handicrafts from the Tibetan refugees who fled to Nepal in large numbers after the Chinese takeover.

Gokarna & Sundarijal
If you continue on beyond Bodhnath you will come to the royal game reserve at Gokarna. Branch north and you will eventually reach the beautiful waterfalls of Sundarijal, right on the edge of the valley. Beyond this point you have to walk.

Changunarayan
The beautifully preserved temple of Changunarayan stands on a hilltop with an excellent view over the valley. Getting there means a bit of a walk but you can take a pleasant stroll from Bhaktapur to Bodhnath and visit the temple on the way. Or you can descend from Nagarkot via Changunarayan.

Kirtipur
Close to Kathmandu and also situated on a hilltop this small, somnolent, old village was the last hold out when King Prithvi Narayan Shan conquered the valley in 1768. Incensed at their desperate defence and to show he meant business the king had the nose chopped off every male over 12 years old – except those who played wind instruments of course.

Budhanilkantha
A statue of Vishnu lies on a bed of snakes in a pool here. The king of Nepal can never visit Budhanilkantha since he is an incarnation of Vishnu and to see himself would be disastrous.

Nagarkot
During the clear post-monsoon days you can see Himalayan peaks rising up north of the valley rim but it is worth a closer look. Nagarkot is a pleasant stroll up from Bhaktapur and from here you will get a spectacular view of the mountains, particularly at dawn as the sun rises over the whole jagged sweep. You will need a mountain profile, from the tourist office, to pick out Everest which is far to the east.

There is now a road running right up to Nagarkot but it's still a pleasant walk up from Bhaktapur, or you can walk up the ridge from Changunarayan. For something

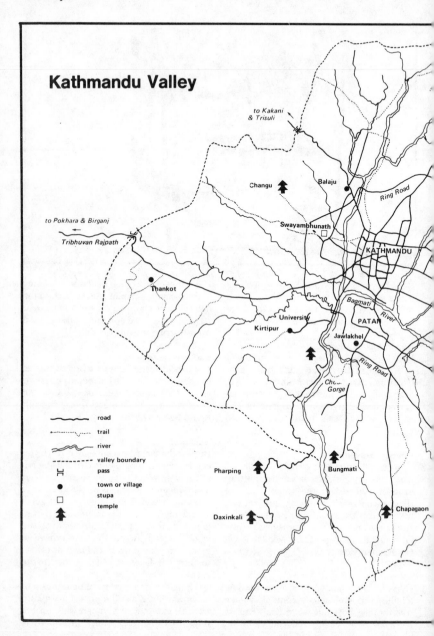

Kathmandu Valley

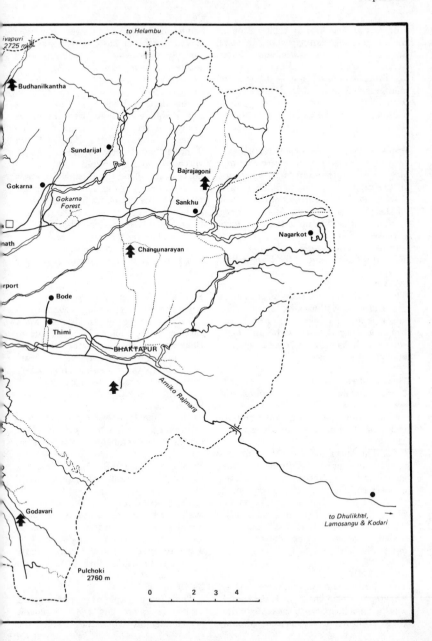

different you could walk right out of the valley from Nagarkot by walking downhill to Banepa on the Kathmandu-Kodari road. It takes about four hours and following a precise trail is difficult, no matter since they all lead there. From Banepa it's only a few minutes by bus to Dhulikhel and the delightful Dhulikhel Lodge.

Places to Stay There are several places to stay up at Nagarkot. The *Everest Cottage* has rooms for around Rs 70. Near the top of the ridge is the *Nagarkot Lodge* with doubles at Rs 40-50. Right at the bottom of the price range is the *Mount Everest Lodge*, right at the top is the *Taragaon-Nagarkot. Sun Rays & Moon Beams* is another cheap place. You can eat at the *Restaurant at the End of the Universe*!

PATAN

The second city of the valley is just across the river from Kathmandu, less than five km, it is an easy bike ride or there are frequent tempos. Grassy humps mark where Ashoka visited the town and erected four stupas.

Things to See
Durbar Square Like Kathmandu, the centre of Patan is Durbar Square with a wild assortment of temples and buildings including the fine, Indian-style, Krishna Mandir.
Other The Hiranya Varna Mahabihar is one of the most beautiful Buddhist monasteries in Nepal, it is situated between the bus stop and Durbar Square. Close to it is the Kumbeshwar Temple to Shiva. Beyond the Durbar Square is the temple of one thousand Buddhas, Mahabouddha – every brick has an image of Buddha.

BHAKTAPUR

The third major city of the valley, Bhaktapur is also known as Bhadgaon. It was the most primitive of the major cities, but in recent years it has been considerably

modernised – the main street has been paved and it even has a sewerage system now. In some ways it is still the most interesting valley town.

Things to See
Durbar Square Bhaktapur too has its palace square and here you will find the interesting art gallery, the great Golden Gate, a replica of the Pashupatinath Temple (with some energetic erotic carvings) and the 55-Window Palace.
Other Just beyond the Durbar Square is the Nyatapola Pagoda. This is the highest temple in the valley, its five-tier base is surmounted by a five-tier pagoda structure. Each of the base platforms has a pair of mythical beasts 10 times as strong as the pair below. On the bottom platform are two giants, said to be 10 times stronger than any mortal.

Continuing beyond the square the Pujahari Math monastery has a fine peacock window generally recognised as the finest piece of traditional wood carving in the valley. You can get to Bhaktapur by bus or by the trolleybus service. You can also ride there by bike. En route it's worth visiting Thimi where papier mache masks are made.

Places to Stay
Recently Bhaktapur has begun to develop as an alternative place to stay in the valley. On the Kathmandu side of the town the *Bhaktapur Guest House* has rooms at Rs 35/55 or with bath at Rs 65/100. There's a garden, a restaurant, a fireplace, bicycle hire and it's a popular place to stay. Right in the centre of town the *Nyatapola Inn* has a superb location overlooking Taumadhi Square where the Nyatapola Temple is located. It's a spartan and simple place with rooms at Rs 25, 35 and 50. Also fairly central, just north of Durbar Square, the *Bhaktapur City Guest House* has rooms at Rs 20 and 30.

There are a couple of places to eat at Taumadhi Square. The *Cafe Nyatapola* is in an old temple right in the middle of the square. You sit out around the balconies downstairs or upstairs with good views over the square. The *Restaurant Bhaktapur* is on the corner of the square and also has an open air balcony. Neither restaurant is really up to the standard of the better places in Kathmandu although the cafe is probably the better of the two.

AWAY FROM THE VALLEY
Mountain Flight

Nagarkot should just whet your appetite to see more of the mountains. If you can't spare the time to go trekking and see them for real a good second best is the daily mountain flight. This takes you on an hour-long trip along the whole eastern sweep of the Himalaya with a good opportunity for a close-up view plus a visit to the flight deck to see them from up front.

Kodari

This is the point where the 'Chinese Road' crosses into Tibet, a popular excursion so you can say you have been to China or at least as close as you are allowed to go. There is no regular public transport there, but you can get there by a mixture of public transport and hitching, on the morning mail bus, or on the occasionally arranged trips on overland buses.

Dhulikhel

This colourful little village is on the Chinese road not far outside the valley. Dhulikhel makes an excellent excursion from the valley and there's a very fine place to stay. The village is of interest in its own right, much more 'ancient' looking than Kathmandu and the other comparatively modernised cities of the valley. It's also a good place for dawn views of the Himalaya and there's a superb viewpoint in the village.

Dhulikhel also makes a very good centre for pleasant day walks or for some trekking acclimatisation. The favourite walk is the one-day trek to the temple of Namobuddha which takes you through a series of interesting Nepali villages. It's only an hour or two's walk from Dhulikhel to the expensive Mountain Resort further along the road – the trail loops back away from the road. Or take the interesting day walk to Panauti, a very pretty little village with some interesting old temples. From Panauti you can take a bus back to Banepa on the Chinese road.

To get to Dhulikhel take a Banepa bus from Kathmandu for Rs 3.25. From Banepa it's only another 50p to Dhulikhel, some of the buses run right there, after a short stop in Banepa.

Places to Stay The *Dhulikhel Lodge* is as much an attraction as Dhulikhel itself. It's a fine old building with an excellent restaurant and a pleasant grassy courtyard. Rooms are very simple but quite comfortable and in the front rooms you don't even have to climb out of bed to enjoy the Himalayan dawn! Nightly cost is Rs 15 per person and this is a wonderful place to just laze around and talk to people.

The people who run the lodge are also planning a slightly classier place in Dhulikhel to be called the *Sun & Snow*. If you're really counting the rupees there's also the cheaper *Sunrise Inn*. At the other extreme, a couple of km beyond the village of Dhulikhel the *Dhulikhel Mountain Resort* is a much more up-market place with singles/doubles at US$25/30.

Chitwan Valley

This game park in the southern Terai is best known for its famous (and expensive) Tiger Tops jungle camp. If you can't afford those sorts of costs there are other more budget-conscious camps or you can stay in villages outside the park and make day trips into the reserve. Unlike African game parks you can enter Chitwan on foot with a guide (which your hotel can often arrange). Entry to the park costs Rs 65 and February-April (when the grass is short) is the best time although October-December is not bad either. If you stay in the park you only pay the entry charge once, if you stay outside at Sauraha you must pay it each time you enter the park.

Some of the cheap lodges outside the park organise guided nature hikes into the park for Rs 25, they last about three hours. Shiva from Wendy's Lodge and Krishna from Cristobal Lodge are said to be good. You can also take early morning canoe trips down the Septi River (Rs 30) but the elephant rides are now very expensive (Rs 200 per person per hour). You do, however, have a very good chance of seeing rhinos from elephant back. Book canoes and elephants in advance.

You can get to Narayanghat from Pokhara or Kathmandu by bus for Rs 30. Some buses go right through Narayanghat to Tadi Bazaar at no additional cost. From Tadi Bazaar you can hitch or take an ox cart (Rs 5) to Sauraha at the park entrance.

Places to Stay There are a number of cheap lodges in Sauraha, or you can stay in park accommodation inside the park although you have to walk out to Sauraha to get food. In Sauraha *Wendy's Lodge* is Rs 15/20. *Sunset Lodge, Cristobal Lodge, Peacock Lodge* and *Crocodile Lodge* are others.

POKHARA

The second town of Nepal, Pokhara is a day's bus trip west of Kathmandu. It does not have the temples and historic interest of the Kathmandu Valley, but compensates with its scenic attractions. It is much closer to the mountains, particularly the Annapurnas and majestic Macchapuchhare, than Kathmandu. You can take some interesting short walks from Pokhara, use it as a base for some of the best treks in Nepal or simply laze around delightful Phewa Lake.

Gorkha, the small town from which King Prithvi Narayan Shah set out to conquer all of Nepal, is an interesting walk north of the Kathmandu-Pokhara road.

Places to Stay

Although there are also hotels in the bazaar area, most of the cheapies are strung out along the lakeside road, which is a couple of km south of the town centre.

Staying in the bazaar area is convenient if you want to make an early start on a trek. Here you'll find the *Hotel New Asia* with rooms from Rs 60 to 90, or the *Hotel Mandar* with rooms from Rs 60/95. There are many other hotels and restaurants in the town.

There are several cheaper hotels close to the dam at the end of the lake. The *Hotel Garden, Hotel Mount View* and *Hotel Peaceful* are all popular.

Or there's a whole string of places close to the lake with prices from Rs 15 and up. The *Kantipur Hotel* is a pleasant place with a nice garden for sitting out. Rooms range from Rs 50 to 120, the more expensive ones have toilet, shower and hot water. Other popular places include the *Yeti Guest House* with a garden and rooms at Rs 20/30. The *Monal Hotel* is a pleasant, well-furnished place with good views over the lake. It's more expensive at Rs 50/60. The *Tranquility Lodge* is a peaceful place with rooms at just Rs 15/25. There are countless others as well as a camping area by the lake.

Places to Eat

Although there is nowhere near the choice of Kathmandu you can still find some interesting places here. Most of them have an outside seating area. The *Kantipur Restaurant* has good food including excellent pizzas at Rs 15 to 20 and great minestrone soup. *Baba's Restaurant* is very good for breakfast, try their terrific muesli with curd and fruit.

Close to the boat harbour there's a cluster of restaurants including the *Hungry Eye* which does curry, not bad pizzas and a mind boggling selection of cakes and pies.

Getting There & Away

See the introductory Nepal Getting Around section for more details on Kathmandu-Pokhara buses. The private buses run right to the lake, much more convenient than arriving in the town area, several km away. The Swiss Bus arrives and departs from the Kantipur Hotel & Restaurant. You can hire bikes at Pokhara for Rs 2 an hour, Rs 10 per day. Some newer bikes are Rs 12. On the lake canoes can be hired for Rs 4 to 6 an hour. It's very pleasant to paddle out into the centre of the lake and go in for a swim.

OTHER PLACES

Few people pause at the Terai towns on their way up from the Indian plains to Kathmandu or Pokhara. Lumbini, the birthplace of Buddha, is the one place of great interest, it's just 22 km from Bhairawa, the border town for the route up to Pokhara. Buses run to Lumbini every two hours. There is an Ashoka pillar and a more modern temple and monastery here.

Places to Stay

Birganj There's not much to be said for the accommodation in Birganj, it's simply a place you have to stay since almost all the buses depart in the early morning for Kathmandu. The *Amrapali*, *Tourist* and *Delicious* are some of the better lodges – they're all around the bus station, fairly similar and cost about Rs 15 for a basic single. *Hotel Diyalo* is rather better and rather more expensive at Rs 40 or there's the similarly priced *Samjhana Hotel*, away from the centre of town.

Bhairawa Rooms are Rs 25/35 in the *Hotel Kailash* and *Shambhala Guest House*, both in the centre of town and popular with travellers. *Pashupati Lodge* is cheaper, *Hotel Himalayan Inn* is more expensive. At Lumbini there's the *Lumbini Guest House* with rooms at Rs 100 – they can be knocked down.

TREKS

Kathmandu's temples may be fascinating but it is the mighty mountains of the Himalaya that really inspire. The Himalaya start where the Swiss Alps leave off and if you want to get among them you have got to trek. Going on a trek is not mountaineering, it is taking a walk – perhaps just a day or maybe over a month – along tracks and trails used by the local people to get from place to place. Roads are still rare things in Nepal and the walking trails are still the main trade routes. Some are so steep that it is a good question if a road will ever be able to replace them.

Treks can either be organised or do-it-yourself. There are many trekking agencies in Nepal and they will fix you up on a trek that is so carefully organised all you need to do is carry your camera and walk. Food, tents, and everything else will be carried and fixed for you. Or you can just put your pack on your back and head off yourself, staying each night in the tea houses or occasional lodges that dot the trail. Even if you do opt to organise your own trek you may decide it is worth hiring a porter to carry the gear for you, the cost is remarkably low and a good porter will be a guide and organiser as well. Finding a porter for your party is usually fairly easy. At the altitudes Nepalese trekking trails often lead to you may find yourself in no shape for carrying much weight.

Before departing Kathmandu you will need gear and a trekking permit. Particularly if you are heading up to high altitudes during the colder months good warm clothing and high quality sleeping bags will be a must. The trekking shops in Kathmandu have a large variety of gear to rent although it is no longer as cheap as it used to be. Once upon a time mountaineering expeditions dumped their gear after they finished their climb and it found its way into the Kathmandu trekking shops. These days they're not so profligate and are equally likely to take it back with them. A trekking permit is necessary to leave the limited areas covered by your

Nepalese visas. They are available in Kathmandu and in Pokhara.

For much more detail on trekking see the two Lonely Planet guides mentioned in 'books'. If you want just a short taste of trekking you can make day or even shorter walks in and around the Kathmandu and Pokhara Valleys. The Nagarkot and Dhulikhel walks are just some possibilities. The following are some of the most popular longer treks:

Everest

This is a long trek, lasting over a month if you walk all the way, to the Solu Khumbu region where the Sherpas live. Very popular because everyone knows Everest. At the height of the winter it may be too cold to get to the Everest base camp itself. It is possible to fly part of the way from Kathmandu, but it is wisest to do this on the return trip rather than on the way up since you need the altitude acclimatisation on this trek.

Helambu

This is a week-long trek north of Kathmandu. It passes through interesting Sherpa villages, but offers poor views of the mountains. The trek starts from right in the Kathmandu Valley.

Langtang

A longer two-week trek north of Kathmandu to the Langtang peak in a Tibetan ethnic region. Like the Helambu trek an advantage of this trek is that it does not involve any complicated travel getting to or from the starting point since you start out at Trisuli, only 72 km from Kathmandu.

Annapurna Sanctuary

This two-week trek from Pokhara passes through Gurung villages to the base of the Annapurna mountains.

Jomosom & Muktinath

One of the most interesting treks in Nepal, it takes two weeks from Pokhara and passes right across the Himalaya to the Tibetan plateau to the north. The route follows the mighty Kali Gandaki gorge.

Warning There have been a number of cases of robbery and even attacks on trekkers over the past couple of years. It is recommended that you do not trek alone. Most of these incidents have occurred along the Pokhara-Jomosom trail or near Dhorpatan.

RAFTING

White water rafting has become very popular in Nepal in the past few years. There are agents in Kathmandu who can organise rafting trips – one of the cheapest is Encounter Overland who have an office in the Kathmandu Guest House. They charge from around US$25 per day. The Sun Kosi to the east and the Kali Gandaki to the west are the two main rivers used for rafting trips.

Pakistan

Pakistan was never the most popular place on the Asia overland trip. Eastbound, people left the excitements of Afghanistan and set out for India, the ultimate goal, at full speed. Westbound it was just a place to get across – India was behind and Afghanistan ahead. Since the Iranian revolution and the invasion of Afghanistan, the country has been right out on a limb and tales of Islamic excesses hardly endear the country to potential visitors. Yet if you pause to give it a little time Pakistan can show you some real surprises. The north – places like Swat, the Chitral Valley, Gilgit or Hunza – includes some of the most beautiful and unspoilt spots on earth. In the south is Moenjodaro, the ruined city of the ancient Indus civilisation. Even on the old route across the north there's Peshawar, capital of the swashbuckling Pathans, and Lahore, once one of the most beautiful cities of the mighty Moghul empire.

HISTORY

Pakistan only came into existence in 1947, prior to that it was just a part of the Indian sub-continent. About four thousand years ago Pakistan was the centre for the Indus civilisation which flourished from 2500 to 1500 BC. You can see the remains of ancient cities at Harappa and, more particularly, Moenjodaro, in the south of Pakistan. The Indus civilisation is still the subject of considerable study and its script has not yet been deciphered.

After this early civilisation abruptly collapsed Pakistan became just another part of Asia to be conquered or fought over by whoever was conquering things. The Greeks, the Persians, the Turks, all had a go but the rise of the Moghul Empire from Ghazni in Afghanistan once more put the region on top. As its power grew the Moghul empire gradually moved its centre eastward and for a long time Lahore was the capital of an empire that eventually spread from Afghanistan right across Pakistan and northern India.

The decline of the Moghuls coincided with the arrival of the British but when, after WW II, the British decided the time had come to cut India loose they were faced with a difficult problem. India was a predominantly Hindu country which had been ruled by Muslims for centuries before the British took over. What would happen when they pulled out? The solution was to carve it up into a central, predominantly Hindu, India, and two flanking, Muslim Pakistans. Hardly surprisingly this neat plan did not work exactly to schedule.

The major problem centred on the Punjab, the region encompassing Lahore and Amritsar. When the Sikhs on the Pakistan side of the border upped and shifted across to the Indian side serious rioting broke out and eventually six to seven million Muslims who found themselves in Hindu India moved west and a similar number of Hindus headed east. Much bloodshed accompanied this wholesale exchange of population.

Nor was a simple swap of people the only problem, for Pakistan ended up short of many of the commercial skills the Hindus had supplied. Worse, the borders were a subject of dispute and to this day both sides claim the predominantly Muslim region of Kashmir although it is the Indians who physically control most of it. Each time India and Pakistan find themselves at each other's throats, which over the last 30 years has been quite often, the Kashmir question is inevitably a central issue.

Long term, Pakistan's most serious problem was simply the fact that there were two Pakistans – east and west. The western half was always the dominant partner despite the fact that it was the

Bengalis in East Pakistan who supplied the majority of the country's export earnings. It is probably indicative that even the name Pakistan – P-Punjab, A-Afghan, K-Kashmir, I-Indus, STAN-Baluchistan – covered all the major regions of West Pakistan but never mentioned the Bengalis of the eastern half. The only real connection between the two halves was that they were both Muslim. Over a thousand km of hostile India was stretched between them.

After independence Pakistan had 11 years of inefficient and corrupt 'democratic' government before General Ayub Khan set up the first military government in 1958. He produced a number of excellent reforms, particularly with the perennial third-world land-holding problem, but in 1969 he handed over to another General – Yahya Khan. All this time discontent had been growing in the eastern half. Their standard of living was lower, their representation in the government, civil service and military was far smaller and their share of overseas aid and development projects was also disproportionately small.

In 1970 two events shook the country apart. A disastrous cyclone wreaked havoc on the eastern half and the assistance the Bengalis received from West Pakistan was shamefully indifferent. Then in December 1970 elections took place to return the country to civilian government. For the first time the elections were held on a one-man one-vote franchise. In West Pakistan Zulfikar Bhutto took 88 of the 144 seats but in East Pakistan Sheikh Mujibur Rahman took 167 of the 169 seats and was therefore entitled to govern both halves. The West Pakistanis were not going to stand for this and the Sheikh soon found himself imprisoned. Tension and incidents escalated and when the Pakistan Army stepped in during 1971 a full scale civil war erupted. The army's cruelty prompted a bitter guerrilla opposition and finally India, flooded with Bengali refugees, stepped in by declaring

war against Pakistan. The Pakistan army was soon defeated in the east and East Pakistan became the independent state of Bangladesh.

Back in the west, Yahya Khan was now nobody's favourite soldier and Bhutto came to power. He held that position until in 1977 the results of his re-election were violently debated. While the arguments on whether or not he had rigged the votes and whether or not there should be a re-run raged on, the military once more took over and Bhutto found himself at the receiving end of the military boot and eventually the military noose. Despite vague promises of a return to civilian government 'soon', it seems a remote possibility. The government has followed the general eastern swing to more fundamental Islamic rule with strict and conservative application of Muslim law. Prohibition of alcohol is one result.

Pakistan does, at least, appear to be reconciled to the loss of its eastern wing and relations with Bangladesh, while far from amicable, have been restored. The situation with India, however, continues to swing from hot to cold and Kashmir remains a constant friction point. The instability in Iran and the Russian invasion of Afghanistan have also caused great difficulties for the Pakistanis. It has been estimated that three million refugees have fled from Afghanistan into Pakistan's North-West Frontier Province, causing an immense problem for a country as poor as Pakistan.

FACTS

Population Pakistan is the ninth largest country in the world by population, which is currently estimated to be about 80 million. It is far from evenly distributed as the north of the country is mountainous and rugged and the far south dry and barren. Much of the population is concentrated in the central part or along the Indus and other rivers that run down from the northern mountains. The north, including Pakistan's part of Kashmir,

known as Gilgit, is inhabited by the Hunzas and in the Chitral Valley are the Kafirs. Around Peshawar are the Pathans who have much in common with their brothers across the border in Afghanistan. The Punjabis predominate around Rawalpindi, Lahore and Islamabad – the most heavily populated part of the country. Karachi (three million plus) is the largest city, Lahore (two million) the second largest.

Economy Pakistan is still predominantly agricultural and its industries are very much in their infancy. Prior to the Bangladesh split the majority of the country's exports were jute, all from the eastern half. Pakistan has made a remarkable recovery from the loss of this important export but the economic situation is still precarious. Pakistan was probably worse affected by the 1947 partition than India since its population loss included a large part of the country's skilled workers, civil servants and businessmen while the population gain was to a

large extent peasants, most of whom had no knowledge of the irrigated agriculture upon which Pakistan is dependent.

Geography The area of Pakistan is 790,000 square km. In the north the country is very mountainous as the Hindu Kush, western extremity of the Himalaya, extends across Pakistan and into Afghanistan. Here are some of the world's highest mountains including K2, at 8611 metres the second highest in the world. Further south the fertile central region deteriorates into the dry south – virtually uninhabited and searingly hot Baluchistan in the west and the equally unpleasant Thar Desert in the east.

Religion Islamic religion has a central importance to Pakistan. It was the reason for the country's creation in the partition from India and it remains an important influence on the country's government and politics. It is a 'heavy' Muslim country where western women can expect to be hassled and annoyed by men who suffer from that weird Muslim sexual segregation.

There are still a number of Hindus in the country, mainly in the southern Sind; their number (less than a million) is far smaller than the proportion of Muslims remaining in India (more than 50 million). Pakistan also has a Christian minority and an influential group of followers of Zoroaster in Karachi. They form an important channel of communication with India via their fellow fire worshippers in Bombay.

INFO

The head office of the Pakistan Tourist Development Corporation is in the Hotel Metropole, Club Rd, Karachi 4. They have the usual collection of pretty brochures and pamphlets, some of them quite informative. Other offices are at:

Lahore – Transport House, Egerton Rd
Rawalpindi – InterContinental Hotel & Flashman's Hotel, The Mall
Peshawar – Dean's Hotel, Shahrah-e-Reza Rd
Abbottabad – Club Annex
Saidu Sharif, Swat – Swat Hotel, Saidu Sharif Rd

BOOKS

Yes we have a guide to Pakistan – *Pakistan – a travel survival kit* covers all of the country in as much detail as most travellers will require. Most other books with any useful information on Pakistan will be of the 'India and' variety.

VISAS

Commonwealth citizens, except Indians and Bangladeshis, do not need visas to visit Pakistan. For most western European countries a visa is not required, or if it is only for stays longer than three months. Americans need a visa if they are staying longer than one month and it is advisable to get it before you enter if you do intend to stay that long. Non-Commonwealth citizens must register with the police after the first month.

It is now relatively easy to get Indian visas in Islamabad, they take a day or two to issue. It does require a visit to

Islamabad, however, and there's the inevitable sub-continent hassles so if you can get it earlier it's worth doing.

MONEY

A$1	=	Rs 11
US$1	=	Rs 16
£1	=	Rs 22

The rupee (Rs) is divided into 100 paise but you may occasionally hear prices quoted in annas – once upon a time a rupee was divided into 16 annas. You can bring up to Rs 100 into the country with you and upon departure you can reconvert Rs 500 into hard currency. As in India getting money transferred to you from abroad can sometimes be a fraught process.

CLIMATE

Pakistan has some real climatic extremes from the broiling heat of the southern deserts to the freezing cold of the northern mountains. Mid-April to mid-July is the hottest period and the southern route to Iran can be very uncomfortable at that time. The monsoons come from mid-July to mid-September, but are not as severe as in India or South-East Asia. From December through February it ranges from cool to cold.

ACCOMMODATION

Places to stay in Pakistan are very similar to India. There are railway retiring rooms at major railway stations although these generally only supply beds – you must have your own bedding or sleeping bag. There are YMCAs in Karachi and Lahore, open to non-members, plus there are still some youth hostels left although many of these have closed down. The Pakistan Tourist Development Corporation operates rest houses in some major tourist areas.

At the bottom end of the price scale are the *muzzaffar khanas* or *sarais*, local inns, and the cheaper hotels. Some of the bottom bracket hotels, particularly in Lahore, are notorious for their rip-offs so

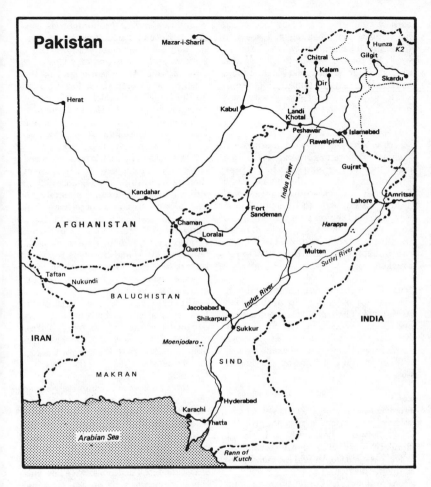

take care and remember that simply locking your room means nothing at all. It is possible to camp in the gardens of Dak Bungalows, rest houses, youth hostels and many hotels.

FOOD

Pakistani food is very similar to Indian – curries and so on. If anything it doesn't aspire to the same extremes of fieriness that Indian curry can. Around the Lahore area Moghul food, from the days of the great Moghul empire, is a speciality. Tandoori chicken and other food cooked in the tandoor oven is especially good here.

Around Peshawar the food is more closely related to the Pathan food of Afghanistan – kebabs and other Middle Eastern food. In Karachi the sea food has a good reputation, I spent the first few years of my life in Karachi and one of my earliest memories is of being threatened by a lobster in the kitchen, I seem to remember it being about twice as large as I was! Like the Indians the Pakistanis also do a good job of mangling English food; cooking English-style is pretty hopeless to start with so you can guess how it tastes here.

GETTING THERE

Air Although there are some international flights to Lahore or Rawalpindi the vast majority of them are into Karachi. Pakistan International Airlines are the Pakistani flag carriers and many other international airlines also operate to Karachi. A one-way ticket London-Karachi will cost something around £200 while a ticket from the Australian east coast to Karachi can probably be found in the A$600 to 700 bracket.

Ship There are a number of shipping services operating from the Arabian Gulf to Karachi. The trip takes about a week and services are regular, particularly from Kuwait. There used to be boats between Karachi and Bombay but it would be very difficult to find one taking passengers now.

Land

From/to Afghanistan There is still a once-weekly bus service across the Khyber Pass between Peshawar and Kabul. Similarly it is also technically feasible to travel between Quetta and Kandahar. Not many people do.

From/to India The border crossing point for India is between Lahore in Pakistan and Amritsar in India. There's a road crossing point at Wagah and a rail crossing point at Attari but these are the only places where you can travel between the two countries by land. Prior to partition there were many roads and railway lines which led across the area where the border now runs.

Because of the upheavals in the Indian Punjab, particularly after the assassination of Indira Gandhi, the border was completely closed for some time and recently has only been open on the 2nd, 12th and 22nd of each month and only between 9 am and 1 pm. At present it appears that westerners are only allowed to cross the border in their own vehicles or some other foreign vehicle. In the *Hotel International* in Lahore or at the Tourist Camp in Islamabad it's possible to hook up with an overland group – like Top Deck.

If the border situation is back to normal, which appears unlikely at the moment, then the daily train leaves Lahore at 2 pm after clearing customs and immigration at the railway station. Lahore-Attari and Attari-Amritsar each cost about Rs 5. Supposedly the train arrives around 6 pm. It takes a long, tedious time to cross the border at Attari and travellers report all sorts of hassles, dope searches and so on. Change some money in Attari for your initial expenses in Amritsar.

Although many more travellers take the train it is also possible, under normal circumstances, to cross by road. Take a minibus from near the General Bus Station in Lahore to Wagah, walk across the border then take another bus into Amritsar.

If the land border is completely closed you can still fly between India and Pakistan – Delhi-Lahore (a surprisingly reasonable US$45) or Bombay-Karachi.

From/to Iran See the Iran section for more information on the train or bus service from Quetta to the Pakistan/Iran border near Zahedan. The train service now only operates once a week on Saturday and takes about 30 hours. Fares are Rs 60 in 2nd class, Rs 150 in 1st, Rs 250 for sleepers. It actually stops about six km before the border from where you can walk or take a taxi (Rs 10) to Mirjaweh, the border town. A truck or bus will then take you into Zahedan. The Pakistani immigration and customs point is at Taftan.

On the other hand buses are now much more regular, the road is much improved and the trip only takes about 24 hours (a very uncomfortable 24 hours) depending on how many customs and security stops take place and how often your bus breaks down. A rest stop is made in the middle of the night. The fare is Rs 85. The first two-thirds of the 720 km trip, as far as Yarmach, has been sealed for some time and reportedly the desert road is now sealed on from there as far as Nukundi.

From/to China If you were allowed to take the Karakoram Highway on its 2500 km trip from Islamabad to China's Sinkiang Province it would certainly be interesting! Actually things are so much more open in China these days that it's quite probable people are getting across the border and making that trip.

GETTING AROUND

Air PIA is the only domestic airline. Some of their routes in the north are not only much faster and less wearing than land travel they are also, due to heavy subsidies, cheaper. There is an airport tax of Rs 5 on domestic flights.

Rail The main railway routes are Karachi-Lahore, Rawalpindi and Peshawar and Karachi-Sukkur, Quetta and the Iranian border. There are a variety of classes from air-con, down through 1st and 2nd class and there are also faster mail and express trains and slower ordinary trains. Student card holders are eligible for a 50% discount. Trains tend to be crowded so make reservations as early as possible. In 2nd class you can spend 24 hours standing up or squatting on your pack on some routes.

The ticket process in Pakistan is very similar to India but considerably less hassle. If you are after student concessions, the programme is to get a student concession form, fill it in and get an authorisation then get your ticket and then make a seat reservation. It is always easier if you do this the day before the train departs. Laying out the money for a seat reservation may or may not prove anything, a rupee or two to the porter who

offers to find you a seat may (or may not!) help as well. At night you can reserve a sleeper which considerably increases your chance of a space of your own.

Bus There is a fairly extensive bus network. On some of the main bus routes, Lahore-Peshawar in particular, the buses run at night to avoid the heavy daytime traffic.

Driving As in India driving is pretty hard going due to the heavy traffic (pedestrians and animals, not just motor vehicles). The roads themselves are generally OK. Petrol is pretty expensive and you need a carnet to bring a vehicle into Pakistan.

THINGS TO BUY

Pakistani carpets can be of very high quality although they lack the 'name' appeal of the Persian variety. Local handicrafts and expensive cashmere shawls are other Pakistani buys. Toilet paper is much cheaper (and better) than in India. If you need a new cricket bat, this is the place to buy it.

LANGUAGE

English is widely spoken throughout Pakistan although there are a plethora of local languages most common of which are Punjabi and Urdu. Urdu is also spoken in parts of northern India. Close to the Afghanistan border, Pushtu is spoken. The following words are in Urdu:

hello	*salaam*
please	*janab*
thank you	*choukria*
yes/no	*hen/mehi*
how much?	*kytna?*
expensive	*mahnga*
where?	*kehan*
that	*voh*
bread	*roti*
water	*pani*
tea	*chai*
bus	*motor*

1	ek	6	che
2	do	7	sat
3	thin	8	ath
4	char	9	no
5	panch	10	das

Sind

This region in the south of the country takes its name from the Indus River – the Sindhu as it is known in Pakistan. Until the completion of a huge dam at Sukkur in 1932 it was a barren desert but careful irrigation has restored a large area of it. At Sukkur the road branches off north-west through Jacobabad, the hottest place in Pakistan, to Quetta.

KARACHI

Although Karachi is the only large port in Pakistan and the largest city, it is comparatively new and of little real interest. It has grown so rapidly since independence partly because of the flood of refugees who arrived here after partition. If you are there for some reason it is worth wandering around Karachi's interesting bazaars and keep an eye out for the unique camel-carts.

Karachi also has a good National Museum and the mausoleum of Jinnah (Tomb of Quaid-i-Azam), founder of modern Pakistan. His birthplace and a small museum are here too. Karachi has some good beaches – Clifton (bus No 20) is the nearest and there is an aquarium here, further out are Hawkes Bay and Sandspit. Rent sailboats from Keamari, the main harbour for Karachi, or take a 61A bus 12 km out to Korangi, the old fashioned village for sailboats.

Like Bombay, Karachi is a centre for the Pharsis and there are some of their burial 'Towers of Silence' on the Korangi Rd. Karachi is surrounded by inhospitable desert, but if you care to venture out a few km there are some things to be seen – Manghophir (15 km out) with its mausoleum, hot spring and crocodile pool or Chaukandi (30 km out) a strange tomb complex.

Information

There are Tourist Information Centres at Karachi Airport and in the Hotel Inter-Continental and the Hotel Metropole.

Places to Stay

Karachi's youth hostel is known as *Amin House* and is located on Maulvi Tamizuddin Khan Rd, about Rs 3 to 5 by auto-rickshaw from the Cantonment Railway Station. The dorm is Rs 15 or a single with shower costs Rs 20. The *YMCA Hostel* (tel 51 6927) is opposite the PIA office on Statchen Rd and there's a Rs 20 temporary membership charge. Singles/doubles are Rs 50/60. There's also a *YWCA* (tel 7 1662) on M A Jinnah Rd and *Railway Retiring Rooms* at both the city and the cantonment stations.

Cheap hotels include the *Estate Hotel* on Rajagazanfar Ali Rd, south of Empress Market in the central Saddar area. It's a popular travellers' centre and reasonably clean with rooms at Rs 25/45. The *Asia Hotel* is similarly priced for doubles (no singles) and is also in the Saddar area on Zaibunissa St. The *Hotel Shalimar* is new, pleasant and good value at Rs 50 for a double with bath. It's in an alley off Rajagazanfar Ali Rd.

Slightly more expensive at Rs 30/50 you'll find the *Khyber Hotel* on M A Jinnah Rd, also in Saddar. The *United Hotel*, Dr Daud Pota Rd is Rs 40/70 and once again it's in Saddar. Down the road you'll find the similarly priced *Salatin Hotel* and across the street is the cheaper *International Hotel*.

More expensive places include the *North-Western* (tel 51 0843) at 26

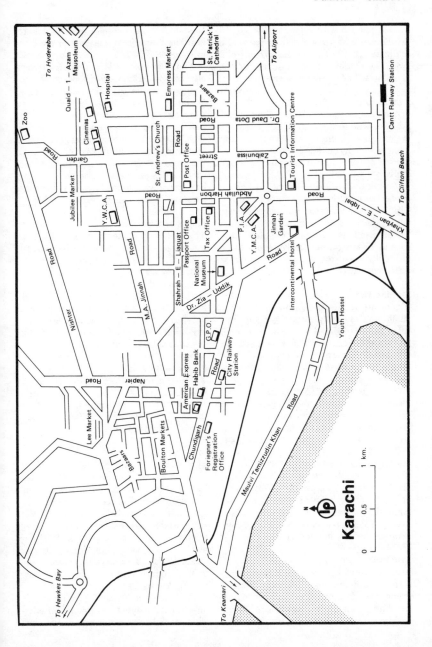

Karachi

Beaumont Rd with rooms at Rs 70/115 which are better than their price would indicate. Or there's the *Al-Farooq* (tel 2 2811-2) off Zaibunissa St at Rs 60/100. The latter has a renowned restaurant.

Places to Eat

Cheap eating places can be found in Lee Market around the bus station. There are a number of Chinese restaurants around Empress Market. The *South China Restaurant* on Shahrah-i-Iraq Rd is often open only in the evening.

Farooq's Restaurant in the Al-Farooq Hotel is noted for its Pakistani specialties. Opposite the Sheraton Hotel, *Le Cafe* has tasty snacks and burgers. You can get cheap fried fish at stalls out at Clifton Beach. Getting a beer in Karachi can be difficult, start by asking for a tourist certificate at the tourist office.

Getting There

There are flights from Karachi to other major centres in Pakistan. By train it Rs 87 in 2nd, Rs 145 in 1st for a seat on a mail or express to Lahore. The trip takes 19 to 21 hours but there is also the daily Shalimar Express which takes 16 hours and costs Rs 264.

Trains to Rawalpindi take 28 hours, to Peshawar 32 hours. Apply to the tourist office for information on rail concessions. Buses depart hourly for the two-hour trip to Thatta or three-hour trip to Hyderabad.

Getting Around

The airport is Rs 2.25 away by minibus, Rs 30 by taxi. It's only Rs 0.75 by bus or Rs 3 to 5 by auto-rickshaw from the Cantonment Railway Station into the city centre. Taxi meters never 'work' so always arrange the fare in advance.

THATTA

Situated 100 km from Karachi the town of Thatta is dominated by Shah Jahan's great mosque with superb acoustics and fine blue ceramic tiles. Just before Thatta is Makli Hill with exotic and beautiful sandstone tombs spread over 15 square km. They are said to contain over a million graves.

Thatta was once a large and prosperous city but when the course of the Indus changed and left it high and dry it soon declined. After his long march east Alexander the Great rested his men here before sailing back west to the Persian Gulf. Look for the wind collectors on rooftops – for about 40 days of each year the wind blows from one direction and these wind catchers funnel the cooling breezes down into the houses. During the summer Thatta can get extremely hot.

Places to Stay

The PTDC erects tents at Makli Hill and there's a a *Dak Bungalow* for Rs 30/50.

HYDERABAD

The second largest city of the Sind, Hyderabad is 180 km north of Karachi. It's of little interest apart from a couple of old forts and water barrages for local irrigation projects although you can also see the roof top wind catchers here.

Places to Stay

Try the *Yasrab* or the *Firdaus Hotel* in the Ghari Khatta area. The cheaper hotels around Shahi Bazaar will not take foreigners. There are other more epensive hotels around the city.

MOENJODARO

The ruined 'mound of the dead' is the greatest city of the ancient Indus civilisation. Moenjodaro, which has a small museum, was only discovered in 1922 and is thought to date back to 2500 BC. For some reason the site was abruptly deserted a couple of thousand years later. Whether due to an invasion or some climatic change, for the area was much more fertile in Moenjodaro's heyday than it is today, nobody knows.

The ruins are interesting for the highly developed lifestyle they appear to imply – wide, straight streets; even private toilets and garbage chutes out into the street for the better houses. The ruins of a later Buddhist stupa provides a good overall view of the whole area and the 'Great Bath', which is thought to have been used for religious ceremonies. Outside the winter months Moenjodaro is very hot and uncomfortable to visit.

Places to Stay

There is a PTDC operated *Rest House* on the site or an *Archaeological Dak Bungalow*. If you arrive early in the morning it's quite possible to see the site and continue on by evening.

Getting There

Travelling north get off at the Moenjodaro station near Dokri village. It's a Rs 10 to 15 tonga trip to the site. Southbound you get off at Larkana from where it is a 28 km taxi trip to the site or a Rs 3 bus ride.

Punjab

The fertile northern area of the Indus plain is the core of Pakistan. Since the distant past this has been the traditional route to the sub-continent from central Asia and it's still the main route across the region today. Strung along what the British knew as the Grand Trunk Road and what is today the Asian Highway are the important towns of Rawalpindi and Lahore with the capital of Pakistan, Islamabad, just north of Rawalpindi. This has long been a centre for great kingdoms, as the ruins of Taxila indicate. The Moghuls also made Lahore their capital for some time.

MULTAN

One of Pakistan's most 'undiscovered' cities Multan is noted for its beautiful mausoleums in the old fort but it is situated in one of the hottest and driest parts of the country.

Places to Stay

The *Mahmood Hotel* on Sher Shah Rd between the GTS Bus Stand and the Cantonment Railway Station is very cheap. There's also a *Youth Hostel*, opposite the Muslim High School, about 2½ km from the station.

HARAPPA

Situated between Multan and Lahore, the ruins of Harappa were discovered in 1920. Although this was the first city of the Indus civilisation to be unearthed it is of little interest compared to Moenjodaro. If you're heading south you can forget about visiting Harappa. To get there leave the train at Sahiwal (which used to be called Montgomery) and take a taxi the 10 km to Harappa Road.

LAHORE

Lahore is the second largest city in Pakistan and probably the most visited by foreigners. Back in the heady days of the Moghul Empire this was one of the most important places in their region. On the old overland route from Europe this was often the first place where you felt that incredible Indian crush – the almost impossibly tightly packed, jostling crowds of humanity that seem to characterise city life on the sub-continent. It is a very hassling feeling at first.

At its Moghul peak under Shah Jahan (of Taj fame) and Aurangzeb, Lahore acquired some beautiful buildings. Later they were neglected during a period of Sikh dominance and more or less forgotten while the British ruled but since independence they have been restored.

Information

There are Tourist Information Centres at the airport and at Transport House on Egerton Rd. PIA, Amex and the GPO are all close to The Mall.

Things to See

The Mall Your first view of Lahore will probably be the decidedly British Mall. At

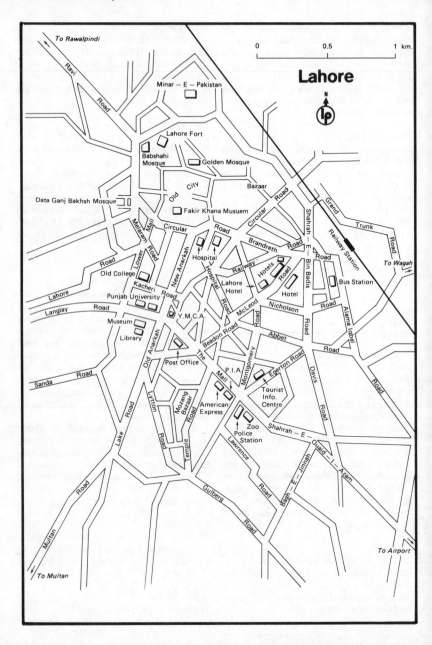

the bottom end of The Mall, where it ends on Lower Mall, is a huge cannon known as Kim's Gun since it featured in Kipling's book *Kim*. It is also known as the Zamzama Gun (or loud roar). Rudyard Kipling's father was for many years the curator of the Lahore museum which is across the road from the gun. It is a fine museum with exhibits connected with many of the cultures of the sub-continent, particularly the Indus Valley. Alongside the Upper Mall are the pleasant Jinnah Gardens and the rather poor Lahore zoo.

Lahore Fort The fort was built, destroyed, damaged, demolished, rebuilt and restored several times before being built in its current form by Akbar in 1566. It was later modified by his successors and considerably damaged by the British although it has now been partially restored. Highpoint of the fort is the magnificent 'decorated wall' covered in mosaic tiles in a Moghul interpretation of the Persian style. There are also gardens, palaces and halls in the fort and a fine view across to the Badshahi Mosque. There are son et lumiere performances here at night.

Badshahi Mosque Completed in 1676 under Aurangzeb, this is the largest mosque in the world and said to be the final architectural fling of the Moghuls. It is supposed to hold 60,000 people on major occasions. Although it was somewhat damaged by the British, they later restored it. It is possible to climb to the top of one of the minarets – 204 steps up to a magnificent view.

Other Also in the old walled city you can find the cenotaph of Ranjit Singh, one of Lahore's Sikh rulers, which looks out onto the same Hazuri Bagh square as the Badshahi Mosque and the fort. Behind the fort is the tiled Mosque of Wazir Khan. The Shalimar Gardens, 10 km outside the city (bus 3, 12 or 17), were one of three gardens of that name built by Shah Jahan. The Shalimar Gardens in Delhi have now completely disappeared but you can still see the ones in Srinagar, Kashmir. The gardens in Lahore are beautiful and peaceful – a strange contrast to the hustle and hassle of life in Pakistan.

Places to Stay

There are a wide variety of cheap hotels around the railway station area, particularly along McLeod Rd and Railway Rd. Lahore has been notorious for rip-offs for a number of years and travellers should take great care in some of these cheap hotels. In particular places at 55 or 57 McLeod Rd should be avoided whatever their name might be – they've changed the names on a number of occasions. All the usual rackets take place – stealing things from your room, planting dope and notifying the police and then getting a share of the pay-offs. Despite warning people over and over again we still continue to get a steady stream of letters from people ripped off in these places. Since the last edition they've included one guy who had his gear stolen from his locked room while taking a shower. And a couple who discovered that travellers' cheques had been stolen from their room – but not all of them. The hotel manager had removed just some of them, counting on them not noticing until they were well down the road from his hotel. Take care at any of the cheaper McLeod Rd or Badrenath Rd hotels.

Hotels in that questionable station area are Rs 20 or even less but it's really difficult to make any recommendations when we get so many warnings about so many places in that area. If you do stay there check windows, doors and ceiling for possible ways of breaking in. Never leave anything of value in your room at any time for even a moment. Don't deposit it with the hotel either. And don't accept offers of a cup of tea or a smoke from anybody.

Safer alternatives include the *Railway Retiring Rooms* where singles/doubles are Rs 20/30. Or outside Lahore at the Wagha border there's a *PTDC Motel* with dorm beds for Rs 30.

Lahore's *Youth Hostel* (tel 8 3145) is at

110B Firdous Market, Gulberg III and has beds at Rs 8 to 10. It's a long way out from the centre, take a bus 25 or wagon 15 south from the terminus at the railway station end of McLeod Rd. The *YMCA Hostel* (tel 5 4433) is just beyond the GPO on the right side of The Mall. It's easy to miss so look carefully for the entrance. There are other beds at Rs 10, singles at Rs 20, doubles at Rs 30. It's a popular place with travellers, some rooms also have bathrooms attached and breakfast is available. At 14 Fatimah Jinnah Rd the *YWCA Hostel* will only take women, unlike the YMCA which accepts either sex. At number 35 on the same road there is a *Salvation Army Hostel* which is also Rs 20 for a single – all rooms have showers and toilets.

Middle price hotels include the *Orient* and the *Lahore Hotel*, adjacent to each other on McLeod Rd, where rooms with fans and attached toilets and showers are Rs 60/100 for singles/doubles. The *Asia Hotel*, near the station, is cheap for a hotel with air-con. If you've got a vehicle and want to camp there are gardens at the YWCA and the Sally Army Hostel. Camping is also possible, but not so good, at the youth hostel.

Places to Eat

Cheap food can be found near the railway station or along alleys off The Mall. Good local and western food in the slightly more expensive *Shishan Restaurant*. On Jail Rd the *Kebana Restaurant* has probably the best Pakistani food in town for Rs 20-30 for a meal. Excellent Chinese food can be found at the *Cathay Restaurant*, opposite American Express on The Mall. For spiced and grilled chicken tikka try the Mozang Bazaar area.

Getting There

PIA fly from Lahore to Quetta, Karachi and Peshawar. There are four trains daily to Karachi – the 19 to 21 hour trip costs Rs 87 in 2nd class, Rs 145 in 1st (on mail or express trains). There's also a faster 16-hour express service each morning at 6 am which costs Rs 264.

Buses run regularly to Rawalpindi and on to Peshawar. Lahore-Rawalpindi costs Rs 20 by bus (five hours), Rs 25 by minibus (four hours) and there are also de-luxe buses for Rs 50. There are also two daily shuttle trains between Lahore and Rawalpindi which are faster and more comfortable than the buses although slightly more expensive. For details on getting to India from Lahore see the Pakistan 'Getting There' section.

Getting Around

A taxi to the airport costs about Rs 10, by bus it's Rs 1. Within the city a taxi costs Rs 5, an auto-rickshaw is Rs 2 to 3 but agree the fare first.

RAWALPINDI & ISLAMABAD

The two cities, old and new, are less than 20 km apart and situated approximately midway between Lahore and Peshawar. They are not of sufficient interest to require a special visit but if you are branching off from Rawalpindi to the northern mountains or to see Taxila you might as well have a glance.

When Pakistan became independent in 1947 it faced the usual problem of nominating a capital. If either of the two major cities, Karachi or Lahore, were made the capital there would be the inevitable city-to-city rivalry and additionally Karachi was far from the centre of the country while Lahore was uncomfortably close to the Indian border and too heavily influenced by its religious nature. Karachi eventually got the nod temporarily but in 1959 the capital was transferred to Rawalpindi while a new capital was built at Islamabad.

Construction of Islamabad only started in 1961 and it is still far from complete. It is a completely planned city like Canberra or Brasilia. Eventually it will overlap Rawalpindi – which has always been an important stopping point on the Grand Trunk Road but is of no real interest.

Information

There are Tourist Information Centres in Rawalpindi in the Hotel InterContinental and in Flashman's Hotel, both on The Mall. American Express is on Shahrah-e-Reza Pelhvi Rd, three blocks from The Mall. Islamabad's Tourist Information Centre is in the Islamabad Hotel on Municipal Rd, Ramma 6. American Express is at Aabphara on the Grand Trunk Rd.

The Ministry of Tourism is on College Rd, F-7/2. You get trekking and mountaineering permits there but it appears a Karakoram Highway Permit is no longer necessary should you intend to visit Gilgit – check. Take a 1A minibus from near the General Bus Terminal behind Aabphara Market.

Places to Stay

There is a *Tourist Camp* opposite Aabphara near the Rose & Jasmine Gardens but this is the only cheap place to stay in Islamabad. If you have a tent it costs Rs 6 per person and it's convenient for the GTS bus stand but has become rather run down – if you stay here take great care of your gear.

Rawalpindi, on the other hand, has plenty of places to stay although these days many of them are permanently full of Afghanis. As usual there are lots of places around the railway station with prices around Rs 20 to 30. Try the *Shalimar* (Al-Shams), about half a km to the left. It's good value at Rs 25/45 but tends to be noisy. Don't confuse it with the expensive Hotel Shalimar near The Mall.

Along Hatti Chowk, Massey Gate and off Kashmiri Rd are slightly more expensive places with fans and attached bathrooms. The *Shah Taj Hotel* or the *Al Hamra Hotel* have reasonably clean doubles from Rs 30, Rs 40 with bath. In the old city, along College Rd in the Rajah Bazaar area, the *Majesty* and *Royal Hotels* are cheap places from Rs 15/25 for singles/doubles.

In Satellite Town the *Arosha Guest House* is fairly clean with fans and attached bathrooms for Rs 25/45. Take a minibus and get off at the Rahmadabad bus stop. In Pir Wadhai the *Al-Aziz Hotel* has rooms at Rs 25/33 and dorm beds. The *Corner Hotel* is new and clean and has rooms with fans and attached bathrooms for Rs 20/40.

There are *Railway Retiring Rooms* at Rs 10/20 but you have to supply your own bedding. Rawalpindi has a *Youth Hostel* but it's too far out to be worthwhile. Find it in the boy scouts building at 25 Gulistan Colony near the Ayub National Park. From the Grand Trunk Road you walk right through the park, keeping a little to the right and then ask around. Or take a 10 bus from the GPO and walk back from the Garden Restaurant. The *YWCA Hostel* (not YMCA as tourist literature indicates) is run down and takes women only. It's at 65A Satellite Town.

Places to Eat

In Rawalpindi the Saddar Bazaar area is the place to hunt for cheap food but you'll find excellent Pakistani food around Rajah Bazaar in the old city. Chinese restaurants with good food for around Rs 25-30 per meal can be found on Murree Rd and Khyber Rd. The *Pakeeza Restaurant* is a traditional Pathan eating place on Liaquat Rd near the Savoy Hotel. Try the *Kamran Restaurant* on Bank St, just behind London Books on Saddar St, for snacks. It's a bit pricey but good.

In Islamabad you'll find cheap food behind Aabphara. With a liquor permit you can have a beer in the *Holiday Inn* or the *Islamabad Hotel*.

Getting There

Rawalpindi is 274 km west of Lahore, 166 km east of Peshawar. Trains through Rawalpindi tend to be slow and crowded so it's faster and more comfortable to travel in either direction by bus. Peshawar is Rs 15 by bus, Rs 17 by minibus, three hours. Lahore is Rs 20 to 25, four to five hours. There's a Rs 50 de-luxe bus.

It takes 17 to 20 hours to Gilgit and costs Rs 86 by bus. They depart from Pir Wadhai. Minibus departures are more erratic but are faster and cleaner. They do the trip in two or three hours less time and cost Rs 110. Try Speedway Buses at the Inter-Pak Hotel or Rakaposhi Buses at the Modern Hotel. If you're flying there are one or two flights daily (see the Northern Territory for more details) at a cost of Rs 150 to Skardu or to Gilgit.

Getting Around

Taxis cost Rs 10 within the city limits of Rawalpindi, Rs 3 to 5 for an auto-rickshaw or a tonga, Rs 2 to 3 for rickshaws. A government bus to Islamabad costs Rs 1.25, private buses Rs 1.75, minibuses Rs 2.25.

MURREE

One of Pakistan's most popular hill resorts, Murree is 59 km north-east of Islamabad in the foothills of the Kashmiri Himalaya. Murree is small and still has a distinctly British atmosphere, particularly in the upper town area. It's a good place for bracing walks in the cooler mountain air.

Places to Stay

The *Abbasi Restaurant* at Jhika Gali, three km north of Murree, has a Rs 10 dormitory. At Bhurban, seven km further on, there is a *Youth Hostel*. Most hotels and guest houses in Murree tend to be relatively expensive although prices drop in the off-season.

ABBOTTABAD

Further north this is another popular hill station and a crossroads for trips to a number of other northern destinations including Muzzaffarabad in Pakistani Kashmir.

Places to Stay & Eat

There is a very good *Youth Hostel* about five km north of the town on the main road to Balakot. It's near Burn Hall Senior School and you can get there by Suzuki for around Rs 1. The *Pine View Hotel* in the town itself costs Rs 25/35.

The *Modern Bakery*, opposite the post office, has a fantastic selection of cakes and pastries.

TAXILA

The ruins of the ancient city of Taxila are only 30 km from Rawalpindi and on the railway line to Peshawar so you can reach them by rail or bus. Unfortunately when you get there the ruins are very scattered so if you want to visit parts of the site remote from the museum you will have to hire a rickshaw or tonga.

The city was once under the control of the Persian Achaemenian empire which built Persepolis. The remains of this earliest period can be seen at Bhir Mound, easy walking distance. It is also possible to walk to the later remains at Sirkap which date from the 2nd century BC when Taxila was in its Greek period following the arrival of Alexander the Great. The museum is noted for its collection of Gandharan art – that fascinating cross between Greek and Buddhist styles.

Places to Stay

The *Youth Hostel*, on the left as you arrive in Taxila, accepts YHA members only and costs Rs 8 in the dorm or Rs 12/20 for singles/doubles. The *PTDC Motel* is beyond the youth hostel and costs from Rs 100 plus 15% tax. The Tourist Information Centre is there.

Getting There

Taxila is about three km north of the Grand Trunk Rd, beyond the railway station. A tonga should cost about Rs 1.50 each between six people.

North-West Frontier Province

Composed of a number of autonomous tribal areas and political agencies it is only along the Khyber Valley that the central government has real control in the NWFP. This is the land of the Pathans who still treat the border between Pakistan and Afghanistan, also inhabited by Pathans, with traditional disdain. Neither the Moghuls nor the British were able to control the Pathans and the Pakistanis have simply continued the British system of allowing them local autonomy. There are many refugees from the Russian invasion of Afghanistan who have fled into the province.

PESHAWAR

Only 160 km north-west of Rawalpindi, Peshawar has long marked the dividing line between the sub-continent and central Asia. It is still a fascinating city today and the capital of the swaggering Pathans. This tribal link to Afghanistan has caused considerable friction since there have been occasional moves to push for an independent 'Pushtanistan'. The word Pathan is a recent term invented by Rudyard Kipling; they refer to themselves as Pushtus. Because of its strategic location, just 15 km from the eastern end of the Khyber Pass, every conqueror passing through has had to pause to take the town. The British built their own separate Peshawar so today it is still in two parts – the spacious cantonment and the old town with its narrow, winding streets.

Information

There are Tourist Information Centres at the airport and at Dean's Hotel on Shahrah-e-Reza Pelhvi. Talk to them if you want to visit tribal areas. The Afghan Consulate is on Sahibzada A Qayyum Rd.

Things to See

Old Town This is the most interesting area of course. The old city walls have 20 gates and the Kabul Gate leads to the Qissa Khwani or 'street of story-tellers'. Unhappily the story-tellers have long gone but it is still a fascinating bazaar to wander around. Everywhere you will see the tall, proud Pathans – usually armed to the teeth. Other bazaars are the Bater Bazen or 'street of partridge lovers', which was once a bird market, and the Mochilara or 'shoe-makers street'.

Bala Hissar Fort Overlooking the city from a rise to the north-west the fort was built by Babar and later reconstructed by the Sikhs.

Other The museum has an interesting if haphazard collection. The Mosque of Mahabat Khan is the finest in the city. There are a number of Buddhist sites around Peshawar. If you head south from Peshawar towards Kohat you will come to Darra, 40 km out, where blacksmiths manufacture by hand perfect replicas of military rifles.

Places to Stay

In the Khyber Bazaar area of the old city the *Rainbow Hotel* or the *National Hotel* are typical of Peshawar's cheaper hotels. Dorm-like rooms cost Rs 12.50 for a bed or singles/doubles are Rs 15/25. Down a bit from the Rainbow and across the road the *Kamran Hotel* is a bit higher standard. In the cantonment area (more or less across from the GPO on Saddar Bazaar) are the similarly cheap *Khyber Hotel* and *Green Hotel* – both popular with travellers as is the *Al Kharim*.

A little up-market you could try places like *Jan's Hotel* (tel 7 3006), on Islamia Rd near the corner with Saddar Bazaar, where singles/doubles are Rs 60/85. In Khyber Bazaar, more or less next door to the Rainbow, the *Habib Hotel* is similarly priced to Jan's but higher standard. The *Park Hotel* is almost next door again.

The 50-bed *Youth Hostel* is on the university campus on Jamrud Rd, some

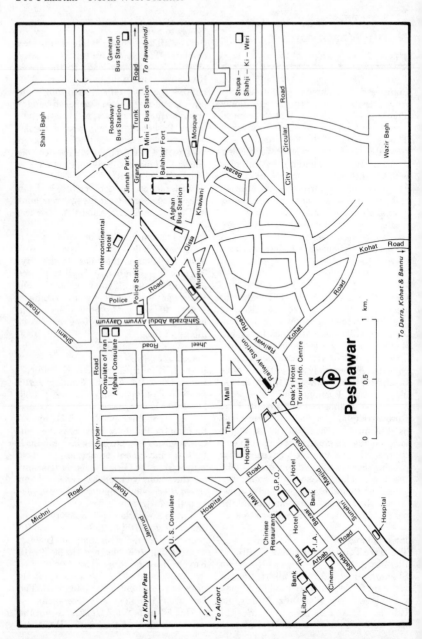

Peshawar

distance out of the city towards Torkham. You can camp at the site near Jan's Hotel.

Places to Eat
Cheap places to eat can be found around Saddar Bazaar and in the old city. For a fancier meal try *Dean's Hotel* or splurge at the *Salatin Hotel* in the old city where the Pakistani food is excellent. On The Mall there are a couple of Chinese restaurants, the *Nanking* and the *Hong Kong*, and there's a pleasant ice cream parlour on Arbab Rd near the cinema.

Getting There
You can fly to Chitral for Rs 130 or to Saidu Sharif for Rs 95 if you're heading north. The trains to Rawalpindi tend to be crowded and they're slow although you may want to opt for rail if you're heading right through to Lahore. Otherwise take a bus – it's faster, less crowded and more comfortable.

Peshawar has a number of bus stands: Soekarna Chowk for Landi Kotal, Torkham, Jallalabad and Kabul; Broadway House on the Grand Trunk Road for Darra, Kohat, Bannu and Dera Ismail Khan. There is a minibus station near the Bala Hissar fort which has services to Mardan, Swat and Dir, while the Central Bus Terminal on the Grand Trunk Road opposite the Royal Hotel is the place for Attock, Hasanabdal, Taxila and Rawalpindi. Departures are frequent and Rawalpindi costs about Rs 15, Torkham Rs 8 or Dir Rs 20.

Getting Around
Taxis cost Rs 7 around town while autorickshaws are generally Rs 5. Tongas are a bit cheaper. It shouldn't be more than a couple of rupees from the cantonment to the bazaar area. Numerous buses operate between Saddar Bazaar, the Old City bazaars and the bus stations on the Grand Trunk Road. Fares are Rs 0.75 to 1.25.

KHYBER PASS
The fort at Jamrud marks the start of the pass – it's a jumble of towers and turrets and at this point you will see signs warning you that you are entering tribal territory. In other words the government has not got too much control over what goes down from here on. The actual border is at Torkham but shortly before the border is Landi Kotal, a market town where the bazaar is packed with all those western items impossible to obtain in Pakistan or if they are obtainable only at great price. The Pathans smuggle them in and sell them here, the government realises that if they tried to stop them they would have an armed (heavily armed!) insurrection on their hands so in this one small location they get away with it. Over the Khyber Pass a separate trail parallels the main road – signs clearly indicate that it's for camels only.

ELSEWHERE IN THE REGION
The town of Darra, with its weapons' manufacturing business, can be a day trip from Peshawar or simply a pause on your way south. Although you can continue south through Kohat and Bannu all the way to Dera Ismail Khan you need special permission to take the direct route to Quetta from there. This trip, through the barren and jagged Salt Range, crosses desolate and bleak country for great distances.

Heading north from Peshawar there are interesting archaeological sites from the Gandhara period at Charsada, Shahbaz Ghari near Mardan and Chanaka Dheri. Routes continue north to the Swat Valley or to Chitral via Dir. You can also loop north of the Grand Trunk Road through some other interesting sites and finally rejoin the road at Nowshera, about a third of the way to Rawalpindi.

Baluchistan

Baluchistan is the remote, desolate south-west region of Pakistan – bounded by Afghanistan to the north, Iran to the west and the Arabian Sea to the south. It is a dry, dusty, barren area with the lowest population density in the country. The inhabitants are mainly nomadic shepherds and since they don't get on too well with the Pakistan government the security situation is often a little fraught – armed guards on the train between Quetta and the Iran border for example. Few people used to travel through this region unless they were taking the southern route into Iran but now, with Afghanistan shut off, this is the main overland route.

QUETTA

The principal town in Baluchistan, Quetta is a fertile oasis in the dry mountains of the province. It was virtually wiped out by a huge earthquake in 1935 and is of no particular interest today although it does have a pleasant bazaar and is a reasonably relaxing place to pause on your travels. The summers here are relatively cool, due to the 1700-metre altitude, but the road west to Zahedan can be very hot and heavy going. In the winter it gets extremely cold in Quetta and it is often snowed in.

Information

There are Tourist Information Centres at the airport and on Jinnah Rd. The Afghan Consulate is on The Mall, the Iranian Consulate is on Hali Rd.

Places to Stay

You can find cheap hotels with fans and attached bathrooms along Jinnah Rd, near the station – Rs 30/50 at the *Allah-Wallah Hotel* or Rs 25/45 for the fairly clean, modern *Muslim Hotel & Restaurant*. With a quiet garden and beds for Rs 15 the *Hotel tourist* is also popular with travellers. Other more expensive hotels can also be found along this road. The *Osmani Hotel* is close to the New Adda bus station. It has a cheap Rs 15 dormitory but also has lots of mosquitoes. On Shirki Rd, also near the Taftan bus terminal, the *Mohammed Tanzabee Hotel* has dorm beds for Rs 10, rooms for Rs 15 to 30. The nearby bazaar is interesting and little visited by tourists.

Middle range places include the *Shabistan Hotel* on Shahrah-e-Adalat St or the clean *Asia Hotel* with singles at Rs 25 or doubles with bath at Rs 40. The expensive *Lourdes Hotel* has a camping ground. Only the better cheapies have hot water (a real necessity in winter) and in the middle of summer accommodation can be hard to find since many people come here from the heat of the plains to enjoy Quetta's cooler climate.

Places to Eat

There are cheap restaurants along Jinnah Rd from the station to the city centre and also in the bazaar. The food stalls in the alley next to the tourist information centre are good – Rs 25 for a roast leg of lamb. The *China Cafe*, near the PIA office and the Pakistan National Bank, is a good place for a better quality though more expensive meal.

Getting There

There are flights from Quetta to Karachi, Lahore and Rawalpindi. See the introductory section on getting to Pakistan for details on the train or bus trip to Taftan and on to Zahedan in Iran. There are four trains daily to Karachi and the 16 to 18 hour trip costs Rs 64 for a 2nd class seat, Rs 121 in 1st. Three trains daily make the 22-hour trip to Lahore. It's Rs 8 by bus to Chaman, Rs 16 to Ziarat.

Getting Around

Auto-rickshaws are the usual means of transport around town, the fare is usually Rs 2 or less.

AROUND QUETTA

Much of the area around Quetta is off

limits without special permission. The trip to Kandahar in Afghanistan is not a wise idea these days. You require a special pass to make the direct trip from Quetta to Peshawar via Fort Sandeman. Similarly it requires special permission to head directly for Dera Ghazi Khan.

The Chutair Valley, near Quetta, is a pleasant high altitude retreat and Ziarat, where there is a youth hostel, is a good base for walking trips. The Makran area, the barren sandy region bordering the Arabian Sea in the south of Baluchistan, is also off-limits for foreigners.

The Northern Territory

North of the Grand Trunk Road is some of the most interesting country in Pakistan. It is still relatively untouristed and offers magnificent scenery, interesting people and fine trekking. The main routes north into this Himalayan region are from Rawalpindi in the east and Peshawar in the west but there are cross-connections between the various valleys and centres so you can, for example, head north from Peshawar to Swat and Chitral then loop east and return south to Rawalpindi through Gilgit-Hunza and the Kaghan Valley.

The northern region can be roughly divided into the lower north and the upper north. In the east you head north through the Hazara and Kaghan Valley to Dardistan and then the Gilgit region and the Hunza Valley. To the east is the remote trans-Himalayan region of Baltistan, closely related to Ladakh in India. This towering Himalayan region includes some of the highest mountains on earth. The alternative route north from Peshawar takes you through the lower and upper Swat Valleys or to Chitral, an area of unique culture close to the border with Afghanistan.

MUZZAFFARABAD
This is the major town in the Pakistani held portion of Kashmir. Muzzaffarabad used to be on the main road to Srinagar but the route has been closed since partition.

Places to Stay
The cheap *Rainbow Hotel & Restaurant* with rooms at Rs 10/20 and other medium-class hotels can be found around the bus station and the main bazaar. The *Galani Hotel* is Rs 15/30, the *Rest House* is Rs 25/50.

Getting There
A bus from Rawalpindi takes five to six hours and costs Rs 15. From Jhelum to Muzzaffarabad takes eight to 10 hours.

HAZARA & THE KAGHAN VALLEY
This region extends from the hill stations of the Punjab right up to the Gilgit area which is entered over the Babusar Pass. From Rawalpindi you enter Hazara either through Haripur or Murree. Only 29 km beyond Murree at Ayubia you have already entered the Hazara region. The small villages here are popular hot season retreats for people on the Punjab plains. Balakot forms the entry point into the Kaghan Valley. Beyond Balakot at Mahandri the surfaced road becomes a dirt one and the valley gets narrower and narrower to Kaghan and then Naran, from where the road is only suitable for jeeps.

Naran is a good trekking base although it is relatively expensive. The beautiful Lake Saiful Muluk is only eight km from the village and from Lalazar, a village 11 km further on, you can see Nanga Parbat, one of the mightiest Himalayan peaks. The jeep road north is only open for four months of the year. It usually opens in mid-July although trekkers can use the route by late-June. Occasional cargo jeeps take this route to Gilgit over the 4067 metre Babusar Pass but they're infrequent and unreliable as well as expensive so trekking is a wise alternative to waiting for a vehicle.

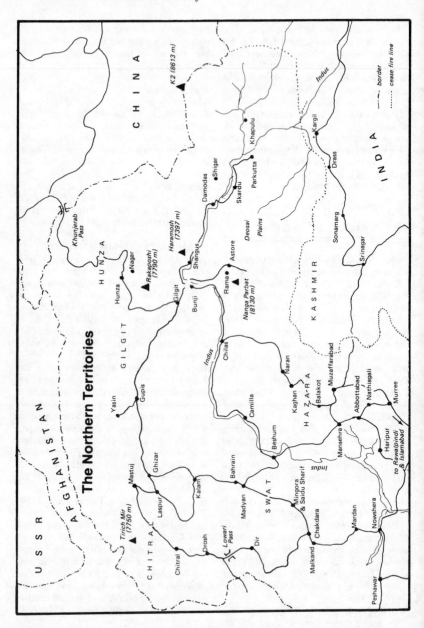

The Northern Territories

Places to Stay

Balakot There is a *Youth Hostel* on the right side before the Tourist Lodge. Dorm beds cost Rs 10. The *PTDC Tourist Lodge* is modern and clean but costs from Rs 50/75 plus tax. There are a number of small hotels in the village with singles from Rs 15.

Naran There is also a *Youth Hostel* here, about three km before the village, with beds at Rs 10. Again there is a *PTDC Tourist Inn* at Rs 100/160 or a *Government Rest House* at Rs 40 per bed. In front of the bus stop there's a reasonably clean hotel at Rs 15/25 for singles/doubles and there are other cheaper, and much more primitive, hotels in the village.

Getting There

There are two buses daily between Balakot and Naran, the trip takes six hours and costs Rs 14. Balakot to Abbottabad takes two hours at a cost of Rs 8 and there are regular departures. Minibuses are Rs 9 to Abbottabad or Manshera. From Abbottabad to Rawalpindi takes four hours for Rs 14.

In Naran jeeps can be hired by the km, a jeep from Naran to the Babusar Pass will cost around Rs 1200 return. You can also hire horses here. A round trip to Saiful Muluk Lake costs about Rs 80.

GILGIT & HUNZA

The upper northern region is barren and dry, much of it climatically and culturally similar to the Tibetan regions of India and China. The main towns of the northern region are Chitral in the west, Gilgit in the centre and Skardu, in Baltistan, in the east. The year round life-line to Gilgit and Hunza is the Chinese-constructed Karakoram Highway. This winds its way north from Rawalpindi, following the Indus River through Beshum and Chilas to Gilgit. The Kaghan Valley route joins the highway at Chilas. From Gilgit the highway continues north to Hunza and eventually crosses the Khunjerab Pass into China. Two other roads lead from Gilgit, one heading west to the Chitral region while the other goes south-east to Skardu in Baltistan.

Gilgit is the centre of the whole upper northern region including Hunza and Dardistan. The town has a beautiful garden, the Chinar Bagh, on the banks of the Gilgit River, while eight km south you can visit the 700-year-old Taj Mughal victory monument. On the Punial road in the Kargah Valley, a similar distance west, a Tibetan Buddha is carved into a rock face. Gilgit is also a good base for trekking trips in the surrounding area. There are some interesting trekking routes from Gilgit to Hunza or you can take the Karakoram Highway – this stretch was the most difficult and costly to construct of the entire highway. The 600-year-old Baltit Fort rises above the village of Hunza and a km-long aqueduct connects it to Altit where there is another, smaller, fort.

From Hunza you can trek up the Nagar Valley to the Hospar and Hispar glaciers at the foot of Mt Rakaposhi. Although a Karakoram Highway Permit is no longer required there are still a couple of police checkpoints along the road. The people of Hunza are chiefly Ismailis, followers of the Aga Khan, and are reputed to live to a very venerable age due to their excellent diet.

Places to Stay & Eat

In Gilgit the *Jubilee Hotel & Restaurant* on Cinema Bazaar is reasonably clean and cheap at Rs 25. Down an alley off Jamaat Khana Bazaar the *Firdaus Hotel* is cheaper. The *Hunza Inn* is slightly more expensive at Rs 30/50 for singles/doubles with attached bathrooms. The *Chinar Inn* is next door and costs Rs 100 plus tax.

In the Jutial area, a km from the centre, the *Tourist Cottage* is excellent value at Rs 15/25 – you can also camp there. Good food can be found at the *Hunza Inn*, the *Chinar Inn* or the *Rakaposhi Inn* – the latter is the most expensive hotel in town. The *Tourist Cottage* offers probably the best eating value in town – Rs 12 gets you a complete and filling three-course meal and in summer the tables are set up outside on the lawn.

Hunza consists of the small villages of Ali-Abad, Ganesh and Karimabad. The newish *Prince Hotel* in Ali-Abad is cheap at Rs 10 for dorm style beds and there's also a PTDC campsite there. In Karimabad there's the clean and reasonably priced *Tourist Inn* with rooms from Rs 25 to 45 and good views over the valley from the balcony. The nearby *Hunza Hotel* is similar. Along the Nagar Valley there are rest houses in Nagar, Hospar and Hispar.

Getting There

There are flights twice daily from Rawalpindi to Gilgit for Rs 160 but the spectacular flight is often cancelled due to weather conditions. January-February and the monsoon season from June-July through to mid-October is very uncertain.

There are twice daily buses operating along the Karakoram Highway to Beshum (Rs 50) and Rawalpindi (Rs 75). Faster minibuses (14 to 16 hours against 16 to 18) cost Rs 100. There is supposedly a daily bus to Skardu but it's rather irregular. A cargo jeep to Chitral will cost around Rs 150 but they're very scarce for most of the year. A bus to Hunza will be Rs 12, a minibus Rs 14. Go to Cinema Bazaar for Rawalpindi or Astor-Rama buses, Saddar Bazaar for the Chitral route, Jamaat Khana Bazaar for Hunza.

BALTISTAN

The most isolated region of Pakistan's Northern Territory, Baltistan is the area where the Indus River enters Pakistan. It's similar to Ladakh in climate and land form although the people here are predominantly Shi'ite Muslims, like the people of nearby Kargil in India. The major town in Baltistan is Skardu and it is reached via Gilgit. There is a more direct route from Muzzaffarabad but this is through the tense region bordering Indian-held Kashmir and is closed to foreigners.

Skardu is a dusty little town on the banks of the Indus, overlooked by an aqueduct and the Askandria Fort high above on the 'Rock of Skardu'. One-day trekking trips can be made to a number of places around Skardu. They include the trip to Shigar, gateway to mighty K2, the second highest mountain on earth at 8611 metres. A number of other great Himalayan peaks and glaciers can also be reached via this route. Other places around Skardu include Khapulu (102 km to the east), the Satpara Lake (a day trip from Skardu) and the Deosai Plains.

Places to Stay

There are *Rest Houses* in Skardu, Shigar and Khapulu which cost Rs 30 per bed but the Skardu one is usually fully booked. The *K2 Motel* in Skardu is only open in the spring and summer tourist season. Economy singles are Rs 50 or doubles are Rs 100, plus tax. The food here is good and there's also free camping, down by the Indus.

Other possibilities in Skardu include the *Shangrilla Hotel* which costs Rs 25 to 40 or the *Masherbrum Hotel* at the same price. Both are in New Bazaar. There are various other very cheap hotels around New Bazaar near the PIA office and around the war memorial.

Getting There

It costs Rs 165 for the Rawalpindi-Skardu flight which is far less than it would cost to travel here by road. The flight is extremely spectacular since the tiny F27 flies past mountains like Nanga Parbat which tower far above its maximum altitude. The flights, which supposedly operate twice daily, are subject to frequent cancellation and are often turned back by inclement weather even as they approach Skardu. From Skardu airport into the town you can either take a minibus for Rs 7 to 10, a bus for Rs 3 or wait for the free PIA jeep at 2 pm – it's 15 km away.

Cargo-jeep services from Skardu to places around are irregular and indefinite. There is, however, an almost daily bus service for Gilgit which costs Rs 50 to 60 against Rs 80 to 100 for a jeep. There are no longer any flights to Gilgit. Skardu-Gilgit is 240 km and takes about 12 hours by jeep. The road is now supposed to be open year round but it is frequently closed by landslides or the almost constant erosion. Straight-through jeeps are pretty rare, you'll probably have to change at Damodas, 80 km from Skardu.

DARDISTAN

Astore and Rama are the main villages in Dardistan which lies south-west of Baltistan and south-east of Gilgit. It's an interesting trekking region dominated by the towering peak of Nanga Parbat, the 'Naked Mountain' which at 8216 metres is the eighth highest in the world.

SWAT & UPPER SWAT VALLEY

The scenically beautiful Swat Valley was also a major centre of the Buddhist Gandhara culture of over 2000 years ago. Lower Swat extends from Mardan to Bahrain and the archaeological ruins of the Gandhara period are chiefly found around Mingora in this region. Mingora and neighbouring Saidu Sharif is the main centre in Lower Swat. Further up the valley the scenery becomes wilder but more scenic through the small towns of Madyan and Bahrain. The valley then widens out into the region known as Kohistan but the road terminates at Kalem and to continue further to Chitral or Gilgit is possible only by trekking. The Swat Valley is a relaxed and easy-going area, some travellers say it is even more pleasant than Kashmir.

Places to Stay

In Mingora and Saidu Sharif foreigners are not welcome in the cheapest inns. The *Park Hotel* on Saidu Sharif Rd is fairly clean and has rooms with attached bathrooms at Rs 25. The *Malik Hotel* is similar while the *Holiday Hotel* is a bit more expensive at Rs 40/75. Also on Saidu Sharif Rd the *Ilam Hotel* is cheaper

at Rs 12.50/20 for reasonably clean singles/doubles. or there's the *Mingora Hotel* at Rs 20/30 on Madyan Rd and the more expensive *Al Basin Hotel* on the same road which has rooms from Rs 50.

Madyan has the cheap but somewhat run down *Summer Hill Hotel* and the similarly priced and recently renovated *Hunza Inn*. There are also a number of better hotels with rooms from Rs 40 and up. Only 10 km further up the valley Bahrain tends to be rather more expensive – try the *Paris Hotel* on the river bank with rooms at Rs 15/25 or the similarly priced *Darol Hotel*. Better hotels usually have rooms with attached bathrooms. At Kalam the *Khaled Hotel* in front of the bus stop is cheap with doubles at Rs 20. Higher up the hillside the *Heaven Breeze Hotel* is Rs 25/40 for singles/doubles with bath and the restaurant has good food. Still higher up the hill there are PTDC cabins and other more expensive hotels. The PTDC have a dining hall up here.

Getting There

Mingora has two bus stations – the General Bus Station on the Grand Trunk Road is for points south. A bus to Peshawar costs Rs 16 and you can also get buses from here to Khwazakhela (Rs 2) from where buses operate to Beshum (Rs 11) and then to Gilgit. The New Road Bus Station is mainly for Upper Swat and buses here tend to be cheaper although also slower, dirtier, less comfortable and less reliable. From Mingora through Bahrain to Kalam will be about Rs 8 by bus or Rs 10 by minibus.

Heading to Gilgit from Swat the daily Beshum-Gilgit bus departs at 6 am so you have to overnight there. Later buses originate in Abbottabad or Rawalpindi so seats will probably be scarce. Buses also go from Beshum in the afternoon to Abbottabad or Manshera in the Kaghan Valley.

Getting Around

A variety of transport including tongas,

auto-rickshaws and Suzukis operate between Mingora and Saidu Sharif, or around the town. Auto-rickshaws cost Rs 2 within the town limits.

CHITRAL

The region bordering Afghanistan in the north-west of Pakistan is the home of the 'Kafirs' or non-believers. They resisted the advance of Islam longer than any other people in the region and indeed it is only since WW II that they have finally abandoned their colourful and often drunken festivals. Travelling to Chitral from the south you pass through Dir, only 115 km south of Chitral but it's a hard 10 to 12-hour trip and the road is only open for a few months of each year.

Chitral is the main town in the region and a good base for trekking trips. Garam Chasma, 45 km north-west of Chitral, is a small village with a natural hot spring. The tiny fort of Birmughlast is 14 km from Garam Chasma, a steep four-hour climb. The Kalash Valleys, where the final remnants of the Kafirs live, are west and south-west of Chitral. There are only about 5000 of them left and they are found mainly in the Birer, Bumburet and Rumbur valleys. It's possible to walk from valley to valley.

Places to Stay

Dir has a number of reasonably priced hotels near the bus station if you overnight there. The *Al Hayat Hotel*, at the extreme end of town near the bridge, is a pleasant place to relax although rather far from transport if you have to leave early.

Popular cheaper hotels in Chitral include the *Garden Hotel* (with a lovely garden) after the Attalique Bridge towards the Deputy Commissioner's office and the *Tirich Mir Hotel* near the mosque.

There's also a *PTDC Tourist Lodge* at Rs 75 plus tax. The restaurant there is fairly good. Good food used to be found at the *YZ Hotel & Restaurant* but it's now operated by Afghans for Afghans only. Right at the bottom of the price scale for accommodation and for food is the *Shabnam Hotel & Restaurant* on the right side heading towards the polo ground.

Getting There

Cargo-jeeps operate to various places around Chitral. It's Rs 75 in the front seats, Rs 60 in the back over the Lowari Pass to Dir. There are supposedly two flights daily from Peshawar at Rs 150, but as usual these northern flights are highly dependent upon weather conditions.

GILGIT-CHITRAL

Even by jeep it's very hard going on the 400 km route between Gilgit and Chitral. Without your own vehicle making the trip would probably consist of a series of treks interspersed by cargo-jeep rides. There are rest houses in many of the villages along the route but food can often be scarce.

Sri Lanka

The island hung off the southern end of India is not, as many people think, just another part of that country. Known until 1972 as Ceylon, Sri Lanka is a Buddhist country with a lengthy and interesting history. For the traveller it also offers some of the best beaches you will find anywhere in the world.

HISTORY

Sri Lanka first pops up in the epic of the *Ramayana*. It was the evil Rawana, King of Lanka, who abducted Sita, the beautiful wife of Rama, and carted her off to this island lair. With help from his faithful ally Hanuman, the monkey god, Rama eventually managed to rescue her.

Although it is not known if this legend has any historical basis, the arrival of Buddhism is firmly dated. One of the great Emperor Ashoka's sons brought Buddhism to the island in 247 BC. Buddhism spread throughout the country and later on to South-East Asia.

Sri Lanka had a period of international adventuring including invasions of Burma, but generally it was on the other side of that game. There were various incursions from southern India before the Portuguese arrived in search of those highly desirable spices. It was only a hundred years later in 1656 when the Dutch turned up and kicked them out. In 1795 the British started moving in and by 1802 had shoved the Dutch out. They eventually incorporated Kandy – the final Sri Lankan hold-out which had outlasted the Portuguese and Dutch – and Sri Lanka remained British until after WW II.

Post-independence Sri Lanka has had a series of remarkably unstable governments. The first one took nepotism to previously unheard of heights as the first three prime ministers were father, son then uncle. They were succeeded by a coalition party led by one of the few members of the first cabinet who was not a relation. He was later assassinated and the government went back to the son then to the widow of the assassinated PM and after a few more gyrations appears to have entered a period of relative stability under J R Jayewardene. The previous wilder socialist excesses appear to be curbed and a real effort has been made to attract foreign investment and get the economy moving.

Political instability and poor economic performance may have been a large part of Sri Lanka's problems but the most visible one is, in part, a legacy of the British. When the Sri Lankans proved reluctant to work for the British, large numbers of Tamil workers were brought in from India. There has always been friction between the hard working Tamils and the relatively easy going Sinhalese and from time to time there have been outbursts of racial violence, spurred on by the activities of Tamil extremists promoting the idea of a separate Tamil state in the north of the island.

In 1983 the country was plunged into complete anarchy after Tamil extremists massacred an army patrol. For days mobs rampaged around the country burning down Tamil businesses and slaughtering any Tamils unwise enough to show their faces on the streets. The army and police completely lost control and as a result the barrier between the two sides has now become a gaping chasm. There have been sporadic flare-ups ever since but finding a solution to the 'Tamil problem' now looks to be nearly impossible. Since the Tamils constitute more than 20% of the population and many have been in Sri Lanka since long before the British, having come with the earlier Tamil invasions, ideas of 'repatriating' them to India are hardly likely to be possible. In late-85 a conference was held in Bhutan between the two sides but no resolution was reached.

Although tourism dropped dramatically after the '83 explosion there has actually been little effect on foreign visitors. Unfortunately, although it's basically one side versus the other, recently purely random acts of violence have also begun to occur. Although the violence is generally restricted to the Tamil regions of the north, particularly around Jaffna and Mannar, there have also been sporadic outbreaks around Trincomalee and a violent massacre in Anuradhapura.

FACTS

Population Sri Lanka's population is around 14 million, resulting in one of the highest population densities in Asia. The Sinhalese make up about 70% of the population with Tamils, who comprise about 20% and live principally in the north around Jaffna and on the great tea plantations, the second largest group. The remaining 10% is made up of a variety of elements including the Burghers, Eurasian descendants of the early Dutch and Portuguese colonists.

Geography Teardrop shaped, Sri Lanka has an area of 66,000 square km and is just 353 km from north to south and 183 km wide at its widest point. The central hill country is surrounded by a coastal plain which is much more extensive and much drier in the north. The highest mountain is Pidurutalagala at 2524 metres, but Adam's Peak (Sri Pada) is much more spectacular at 2224 metres. Sri Lanka is almost connected to India by the chain of sandbanks known as Adam's Bridge.

Economy Sri Lanka's economy is still overwhelmingly based on tea, rubber and coconuts although the government is making major efforts to develop an industrial sector, principally through the free trade zone they have established near Colombo. Tourism has also become very important over the past 10 years.

Religion The country is overwhelmingly Buddhist although the Tamils are principally Hindu while there are also smaller minorities of Christians and Muslims.

INFO

The Ceylon Tourist Board has their main office in Colombo, there is also a counter at the airport and an office in Kandy. Pick up a copy of their *Sri Lanka Tourist Information* booklet which has a great deal of information including train schedules. They also put out a separate *Accommodation Guide* which is rather haphazardly organised but still useful.

Admission Charges One somewhat unpleasant aspect about Sri Lanka is that at many attractions foreigners have to pay a higher entry charge than Sri Lankans – sometimes it can be 10 to 15 times as high or there may be no charge at all for the locals. Get a permit (which also include permission to take photographs) for Rs 225 which covers Polonnaruwa, Sigiriya, Anuradhapura and Dambulla. It's more convenient than paying as you go along. Entry charges are also made for the zoo in Colombo, botanical gardens at Peradeniya (Kandy) and Hakgala (Nuwara Eliya) and camera fees are charged at various places.

BOOKS

For much more extensive information on Sri Lanka pick up a copy of *Sri Lanka - a travel survival kit*. There are various locally produced guidebooks to the ancient cities or the whole country. SF author Arthur C Clarke is one of Sri Lanka's best known foreign residents and one of his novels, *The Fountains of Paradise*, is set in an island remarkably like Sri Lanka – right down to an Adam's Peak and a Sigiriya! In an earlier era Leonard Woolf, Virginia's husband, also lived in Sri Lanka for a time and his novel *The Village in the Jungle* is a readable, but depressing, tale of village life around the turn of the century.

VISAS

For most western nationalities no visa is required for entry to Sri Lanka and an initial stay of one month is permitted. Extension of stay is not now as easy as it

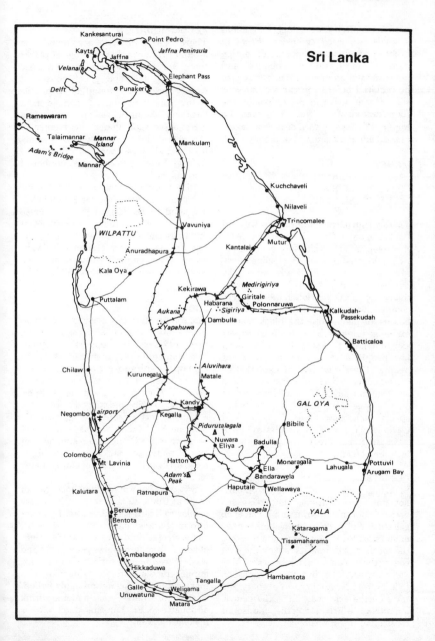

Sri Lanka

Kankesanturai
Point Pedro
Kayts
Jaffna
Jaffna Peninsula
Velanai
Elephant Pass
Delft
o Punakeri
Rameswaram
Talaimannar
Mannar Island
Adam's Bridge
Mannar
Mankulam
Kuchchaveli
Nilaveli
Vavuniya
Trincomalee
WILPATTU
Anuradhapura
Kantalai
Mutur
Kala Oya
Kekirawa
Medirigiriya
Giritale
Puttalam
Habarana
Polonnaruwa
Aukana
Sigiriya
Kalkudah-Passekudah
Yapahuwa
Dambulla
Batticaloa
Chilaw
Aluvihara
Matale
Kurunegala
GAL OYA
Kandy
Kegalla
Pidurutalagala
Bibile
Negombo *airport*
Nuwara Eliya
Badulla
Colombo
Mt Lavinia
Hatton
Ella
Monaragala
Lahugala
Pottuvil
Adam's Peak
Bandarawela
Arugam Bay
Kalutara
Haputale
Wellawaya
Ratnapura
Beruwela
Buduruvagala
YALA
Bentota
Kataragama
Tissamaharama
Ambalangoda
Hikkaduwa
Tangalla
Hambantota
Galle
Weligama
Unuwatuna
Matara

used to be, often you may only be granted a single two week extension. Proof of exchanging adequate amounts of foreign currency or travellers' cheques and possession of an onward ticket may also be required before you can extend your stay. If you arrive in Sri Lanka by the Rameswaram ferry you may well be required to have onward or return tickets plus an adequate amount of money.

MONEY

A$1	=	SL Rs 21
US$1	=	SL Rs 30
£1	=	SL Rs 42

There are no particular problems with Sri Lankan money. Over the past few years the steep inflation rate has been somewhat mitigated by a steady decline in the exchange rate. Additionally since the number of visitors to Sri Lanka is lower than prior to the '83 riots hotels are very competitive with their prices. In Colombo beware of people offering black market exchange rates – some of them are expert sleight of hand tricksters and more than a few people have lost money to these people. There's no real blackmarket of consequence in Sri Lanka. Banking hours are 9 am to 1 pm on Mondays, to 1.30 pm on other weekdays. In Colombo there is a special exchange counter of the Bank of Ceylon in York St, Fort, which stays open 8 am to 8 pm every day of the week including holidays.

CLIMATE

Sri Lanka's climate is typically tropical – hot and sticky. Along the coast sea breezes cool things down and it can even get a little chilly at night in the high central mountains. Sri Lanka has two monsoons, the south-west dumps its rain on the west coast (the Colombo side) between May and August. The north-east monsoon follows from November to February and rains on the east coast. It is the central mountains which stop the monsoons crossing to the opposite coast.

ACCOMMODATION

There's a wide variety of accommodation around Sri Lanka. In a number of places there are youth hostels and YMCAs/ YWCAs. Hotels and guest houses at varying prices are found all over the country and a number of them in main locations have been brought together in a loose association under the banner of 'Travellers' Halts'. They produce a guidebook which lists them all. There are Railway Retiring Rooms at a number of stations too.

Nicest accommodation in Sri Lanka, although the usual price for a double has escalated to Rs 250, is the rest house chain. They're often very pleasant buildings and almost invariably have the finest setting in town. Rest houses always seem to have superb views of beaches, islands, ravines, hills or whatever is locally available!

FOOD

The food picture is somewhat similar to India – lots of curries, which can often be very hot. Look for 'hoppers' a popular local snack either as a plain pancake, as an egg hopper with an egg fried into the top of the pancake or as a tangled circle of noodles known as a string hopper. 'Lamprai' is a rice and curry dish baked in a banana leaf wrapper. A particularly pleasant Sri Lankan meal is 'short eats'. Somewhat like Chinese dim sum you get lots of plates of snacks and your bill is toted up from the number of empty plates left.

Sri Lanka has a marvellous collection of tropical fruits, in that respect it is very similar to South-East Asia. So if you are into rambutans, mangosteens, avocados, custard apples and so on you will feel right at home. Take care to always peel fruit and wash it well before eating. Caution also applies to the water, outside Colombo make sure it has been thoroughly boiled. Tea is, of course, the national drink although the Sri Lankans don't always make it too well.

'Jaggery', a sweet fudge-like substance made from kitul palm sap is eaten as a dessert, snack and even used as a substitute for sugar. A favourite, and very delicious, dessert or snack is Sri Lanka's superb curd (yoghurt) which often comes with treacle (really just kitul palm sap) – often spelt 'curd & tricle'. Sri Lanka has reasonable beer and a variety of soft drinks including Coca-Cola and the cheaper local Elephant House brands.

GETTING THERE

Air From Europe you can get tickets to Sri Lanka for around £250 one-way or from around £500 you can find through tickets to Australia with a Sri Lankan stop-over. Cheap tickets from Australia will be around A$600. Main Asian jumping off points to Sri Lanka are Singapore, Bangkok or Madras. Count on around US$200 from Singapore or similar prices from Bangkok. You can also fly Kathmandu-Colombo direct.

Flights between India and Sri Lanka used to be rather fraught but there are now many more flights and the story is much better. Madras (about US$60) is the main centre for flights to Sri Lanka but there are also flights to and from Trivandrum and Trichy. Sri Lanka is also the usual stepping stone for getting to Male in the Maldives.

Colombo has become a good place for getting airline tickets – examples include Colombo-London with Pakistan International for US$315 with a stop-over somewhere along the way. Even more interesting are flights to Africa such as Colombo-Nairobi with Ethiopian Airlines or British Airways for US$400 or Colombo-Johannesburg with British Airways for US$595 – again with interesting stop-over possibilities.

There is a Rs 100 departure tax at the airport.

Ferry If you don't fly then the usual route to Sri Lanka is the three-times-weekly ferry between Rameswaram in India and Talaimannar in Sri Lanka. The old problem with the ferry used to be it simply did not have enough capacity for the number of passengers who wanted to use it and at peak times you could get stranded for days on end. That's no longer a hassle (there are lots more flights these days) but a new problem is that Mannar in Sri Lanka is a Tamil trouble zone and it's wise to enquire about local conditions before deciding to take the ferry.

It is possible to get rail-ferry-rail tickets all the way from Madras to Colombo. Otherwise a ferry ticket will be I Rs 89 upper deck, I Rs 65 lower deck. From Sri Lanka it's SL Rs 220 and 165 respectively. Ferry departures from Rameswaram are on Mondays, Wednesdays and Fridays; from Talaimannar on Tuesdays, Thursdays and Saturdays. The service is suspended during the worst of the monsoon, usually November and December.

Official departure times are 2 pm (arriving 5 pm) from India and 10 am (arriving 1 pm) from Sri Lanka but delays are not at all uncommon. The whole process is a bit of a bore and there are hours of bureaucratic hassles to go through at each end. Plus the pier at Rameswaram is not deep enough for the ferry to dock, meaning you have to transfer in small boats. Worst of all you've got lengthy train journeys at each end of the ferry trip.

There's not much comfort difference between upper and lower deck but the extra cost is money well spent on arrival since upper deck gets off the boat first and can avoid a lot of crush and scramble. At the Sri Lanka end you also get first chance at the limited number of sleepers on the train. There is accommodation, of sorts, available at Mannar at the Sri Lankan end. Otherwise you've got a long overnight train journey to Colombo or the option of disembarking in the middle of the night at Anuradhapura. In India accommodation in Rameswaram is often unable to cope with the crush on a pre-ferry departure night.

GETTING AROUND

Rail Train travel in Sri Lanka is not too bad. The trains are often (but not always) much less crowded than in India, the bureaucratic hassles of ticketing and reservations are much simpler and the distances are (mercifully) far shorter. Life certainly doesn't revolve around the railways to anywhere near the same extent in Sri Lanka as India. Trains have three classes, 2nd is twice as expensive as 3rd, 1st is three times as expensive. In 1st class there is always a supplementary charge – either for air-conditioning, for the observation coach in the hill country or for a sleeper at night. On 2nd and 3rd class supplementary charges are made at night for sleepers (Rs 30 in 2nd) or for sleeperettes (sleeping chairs) (Rs 15 in 2nd, Rs 10 in 3rd). Sleeper reservations should be made as far in advance as possible.

Bus & Minibus The terrible bus system operated by the CTB (Ceylon Transport Board) has been considerably improved by the addition of private minibus services. These not only give you a faster and more comfortable (but also more expensive and more dangerous) alternative to the public buses but they have also taken the pressure off the CTB buses. End result is that bus transport, once the biggest drawback to visiting Sri Lanka, is now much easier.

Other Transport You can rent motorcycles fairly readily, particularly in Hikkaduwa. Cars can also be rented although they are fairly expensive.

THINGS TO BUY

Sri Lanka has all sorts of handicrafts including the colourful and attractive dance masks – somewhat similar to those from Bali. Batik making is a relatively new development but already widespread. Sri Lanka is famous for its gemstones although jewellery is not of very high quality. Leatherwork can be quite good. Lots of interesting clothes although again the quality is pretty miserable. Check the big Laksala handicrafts store for an overall view of what is available. It's in Colombo Fort.

LANGUAGE

Sinhala is the national language although about a third of the population speak Tamil. English is widely spoken.

Colombo

The capital doesn't have as much to see as its long history might indicate. It was already an important spice trading centre when the Portuguese turned up in 1505. They lasted for about 150 years before the Dutch took over and the British then moved in in 1796. The 'Fort' is the central business area and here you will find the old clocktower/lighthouse which is a Colombo landmark. Nearby is the Pettah, a busy bazaar area although badly damaged in the '83 riots. Colombo has an excellent museum and a number of interesting temples and mosques. Colombo's zoo, in the south of the city at Dehiwala, is particularly popular for its late-afternoon elephant show.

Information & Orientation

Colombo is basically a long coastal strip from Fort to Mt Lavinia, about 10 or 12 km south. The Galle Rd is the spine of the coastal strip, but finding your way along the Galle Rd is slightly complicated by the numbers reverting to zero in each new district. Thus you can have 147 Galle Rd in Colombo 3 and again in Colombo 4 and Colombo 6. The Fort is the main business centre where you'll find banks, airline offices and the excellent Laksala handicraft centre. The Tourist Office is semi-temporarily located at 41 Glen Aber Place, just off the Galle Rd in Colombo 4. There are left-luggage facilities at the Fort Railway Station.

Places to Stay

Although you'll find some of the cheaper hotels and the popular YMCA in and around the centre, Colombo's guest house bargains are mainly further out. As you move down Galle Rd from Colombo Fort you'll find cheaper places in Bambalapitiya (Colombo 4) and especially Dehiwala (Colombo 6 – more or less). Prices generally go down as you get further out, Dehiwala is about eight km (five miles) straight out the Galle Rd from the centre. After Dehiwala they climb again as you move into the beach resort of Mt Lavinia, although still fairly reasonably priced.

There are a few cheap places smack in the middle of Colombo, but some of them tend to be perpetually full. The *Central YMCA* is at 39 Bristol St, only a short stroll from the Fort Railway Station. There are 58 beds here with fanless doubles at Rs 102, singles/doubles with fan at Rs 106/157 or doubles with bathroom for Rs 232. The rooms with fan are up on the top floor and tend to get hot. If you're sharing a room make sure your locker can be locked. There is an additional Rs 1 daily or Rs 2.50 weekly temporary membership charge. The Y also has a cafeteria; it's a good place for breakfast if you arrive in Colombo by an early morning train.

Virtually next door at 29 Bristol St, the *Sri Lankan Ex-Servicemen's Institute* has eight rooms at Rs 78/162.50 for singles/doubles. The bar has the cheapest beer in town. There are a couple of other cheap hotels in town along Mudalige Mawatha, beside the Nectar Cafe. The *Globe Hotel*, with doubles from around Rs 125, is typical but one angry woman wrote recently that the rooms have all been 'peepholed' so unless you like putting on a free show for the staff don't stay there.

The *Lodgings*, at 41 1/1 Mahavidyalaya Mawatha (formerly Barber St), Colombo 13, has 18 rooms with doubles and attached bath, prices from Rs 75. It's 1½ km from the Fort Railway Station and close to the Central Bus Station and Pettah area. Rooms are reasonably clean and comfortable. To get there take a bus from Jayatilaka Mawatha to St Anthony's Church in Kochikade from where you take the road opposite the church, then third turn on the right, straight up to the top of the hill and left at the clock tower. It's next to the Bank of Ceylon. There are some good restaurants (like the Moslem *Iqbal*), a bakery (*Lion's Bakery*) and a milk outlet nearby.

There are some cheap hotels right across from the Fort Railway Station, but this area was badly hit during the 1983 riots. Look for the *Maliban Hotel* (tel 21973) at 850 Olcott Mawatha for basic but reasonable rooms. Some of the hotels along here were really for emergencies only.

The *Scout Hostel* (tel 33131) at 131 Baladaksha Mawatha, Colombo 3 has just eight dorm beds but they also have camping facilities. There is a *Girl Guide Hostel* (tel 97720) for women only at 10 Sir Marcus Fernando Mawatha, Colombo 7. A bit further out at 50 Haig Rd, Bambalapitiya, Colombo 4 the *Youth Council Hostel* has 30 beds at Rs 20 for YHA members, Rs 25 for non-members. The *Horton Youth Hostel* has moved to Station Rd, Wellawatta.

There are a number of base price places further out along the Galle Rd in Dehiwala, the last Colombo suburb along the Galle Rd, although Mt Lavinia is really just another suburb of the city. It will cost you a couple of rupees for a bus this far out – take a 100, 101, 102, 105, 106, 133 or 134. Not all buses go this far along the Galle Rd. A three-wheeler will cost you Rs 30 to 50. Get off at St Mary's Church, the cheap accommodation here is all on the coast side of the Galle Rd. *Big John's* (tel 715027), at 47 Albert Place, is the mainstay of the Travellers' Halt network in Sri Lanka. Dorm beds here cost Rs 25 or there are singles from Rs 30, doubles from Rs 70. They have various overflow places in the locality.

The next street along is Campbell Place

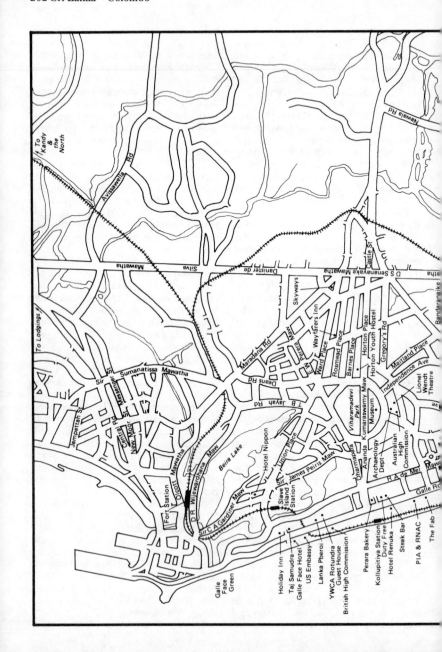

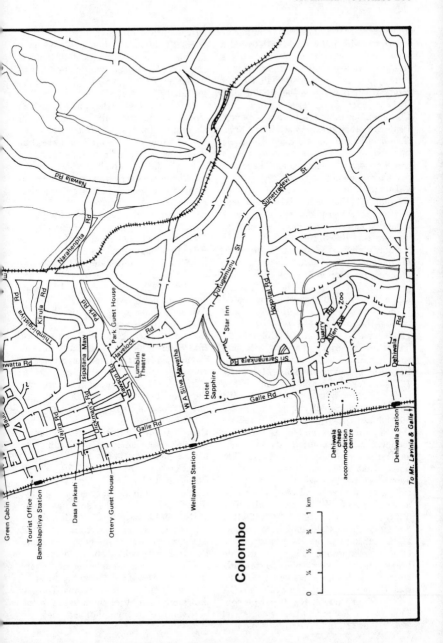

Colombo

0   ¼   ½   ¾   1 km

To Mt. Lavinia & Galle →

and *Seabreeze* (tel 717996) at number 37 has rooms with and without bath from Rs 25 to Rs 75 plus a small dorm. It's a friendly, well-run place. Right by the railway line at 55 Vanderworth Place, four more streets down from Campbell Place, is the *Beach Spot*. The *Surf-In* at 2 Campbell Place and *Sea View* at 34 Albert Place are other guest houses in the area. *Gehan Villa* at 9 Second Lane, Dehiwala has had several recommendations from travellers who thought the food here was particularly good.

Tourist Rest (tel 714521) at 7 Park Avenue, off Waidya Rd, Dehiwala, near the zoo, is a nice place with a spacious verandah and bicycles for hire. Singles/ doubles cost Rs 75/100. From Dehiwala it's only a short stroll along the beach to Mt Lavinia.

Moving up a notch in price there are a great number of places in the middle range including many guest houses listed in the Tourist Office's booklet. A popular place is the *Hotel Nippon* (tel 31887-8) at 123 Kumaran Ratnam Rd, Colombo 2. There are a variety of rooms with and without bathrooms, balconies and air-con. Prices, all including breakfast, start at Rs 125/175 for the bathless, non air-con rooms upstairs. With bath they're Rs 150/ 200 then with air-con as well they're Rs 200/250. Although most travellers reckon the Nippon is OK and good value for money, some have pointed out that it's not as clean as it could be and it can get rather noisy. Take a 138 bus from Fort or its about Rs 8 by three-wheeler.

Apart from the central YMCA there are also a couple of YWCAs in Colombo. The *YWCA International* (tel 24181, 24694) at 393 Union Place, Colombo 2 has 20 rooms at Rs 115/230 or at Rs 124/250 with attached bathroom, all rates include breakfast. This is a good place to stay – it's clean and well kept and since it's off the road it's fairly quiet. Meals at the YWCA are excellent value at Rs 30 per person. The *YWCA Rotunda Guest Rooms* (tel 23489) is at 7 Rotunda Gardens, Colombo

3 (Kollupitiya), off the Galle Rd just along from the Lanka Oberoi. They have doubles with bath at Rs 250 to 300, singles at Rs 90 and two five-bed dormitories at Rs 65 per person. All rates include breakfast.

Also fairly close to the centre at 15 Sea View Avenue, just off the Galle Rd in Colombo 3, the *Sea View Hotel* (tel 26516) certainly doesn't have a view of the sea but does have 23 rooms with doubles at Rs 275. Also in Colombo 3 at 265 Galle Rd the *Chinese Lotus Hotel* (see the Places to Eat section · below) has large, spacious rooms with fan from around Rs 250. It's next door to the Duty Free Shopping Centre.

Continue a little further along the Galle Rd to Bambalapitiya, where the *Ottery Inn* (tel 83727) at 29 Melbourne Avenue has eight rooms with singles/doubles at Rs 150/200 including breakfast. It's quiet and reasonably well kept. Melbourne Avenue is almost directly across the Galle Rd from Dickman's Rd. Down Dickman's Rd and to the right, the *Tourist Guest House* (tel 84005) at 8/1 Elibank Rd, has rooms from Rs 40 and 'apartments' for Rs 100.

In Dehiwala, almost out at the zoo, the *Star Inn* (tel 714030, 716999, 717523) has 22 rooms at Rs 150/175. It's at 73/22 Sri Saranankera Rd; to find it turn off at Canal Bank Rd or Hospital Rd, just after the Dehiwala Canal and a half km or so before the zoo turn-off.

Back towards the centre at 77 Rosemead Place in Colombo 7, the Cinnamon Gardens diplomatic quarter of the city, the *Wayfarer's Inn* (tel 93936) has rooms at Rs 250/325 or at Rs 350/425 with air-con. It has a pleasant garden and is located in a peaceful area of the city. A taxi into Fort from here will be about Rs 25.

There are a great number of private guest houses around Colombo, most of them with only one or two rooms. You can find more than 50 of them listed in the tourist office accommodation guide!

Places to Eat

Colombo has a better selection of restaurants than anywhere else in Sri Lanka and is also one of the better places for finding real Sri Lankan food. A Colombo favourite (mine and nearly everybody else's it would appear) is the genteel *Pagoda Tea Room* on Chatham St in Fort. It's a big, old fashioned, crowded place – definitely a mile away from your average run-of-the-mill Asian cheapie. White tablecloths (if they aren't at the wash) and hovering waiters are all part of the scene, but the food is of excellent quality and remarkably low in price. They have one of the best selection of short eats in Sri Lanka or for Rs 25 you could indulge yourself on fillet steak and vegetables. On hot days their Rs 4 lemon squash is knockout and so is their Rs 5 ice cream, but the Pagoda is mainly a lunchtime place as it shuts at 6 pm. Incidentally, rock music fans may have seen the Pagoda in a Duran Duran video film clip!

For a quick, cheap snack try the *Nectar Cafe* on the corner of York St and Mudalige Mawatha in Fort. It's a self-service cafe with very reasonably priced food and snacks. Their low-priced ice cream is just one dish that packs in the travellers. There are a number of very cheap places along Mudalige Mawatha offering vegetarian food, like south Indian thalis, for just a few rupees.

In this same central area *Cargill's* have good cold drinks and the *YMCA* on Bristol St has a cheap self-service cafeteria and is a good place for an early breakfast when most of Colombo is still asleep. Western-style fast food outlets are springing up around Fort – like *The Picnic* or *Gillo's*.

On the corner of Chatham St and Janadhipathi Mawatha the *Nanking Hotel* is a popular Chinese restaurant that has the commendable virtue of staying open late at night – well late by early-to-bed Colombo standards anyway. The menu is Chinese standard (including delicious crab) and the prices are quite reasonable. At 70 Chatham St there is also the *Peony Restaurant*. On the north side of Upper Chatham St the *Taj Restaurant* is cheap and OK and seems to stay open later than most other restaurants around.

Out of the central Fort area there are a number of other Chinese restaurants including the *Hotel Nippon* at 123 Kumaran Ratnam Rd, Colombo 2 which does excellent Chinese food and also specialises in Japanese food. Ten to 15 minutes walk from the Nippon is the *Seafish*, behind the cinema on Kumaran Ratnam Rd. The seafood grill or beachcomber special is very good, as are desserts.

At 199 Union Place the *Fountain Cafe* is owned by Ceylon Cold Stores (bottlers of Elephant House soft drinks) and is something of a showcase. They do western and Sri Lankan meals from Rs 20 to 60 plus terrific ice cream and iced coffee. It's open 11 am to 11 pm daily plus there's a snack bar out back from 4.30 to 6.30 pm. Located midway between the Hotel Nippon and the YWCA this real find is cool, peaceful and surrounded by a garden.

More restaurants can be found along the Galle Rd. If you like the Pagoda then the *Green Cabin* at 453 Galle Rd, Colombo 3 will appeal just as much – because it's run by the same people. It's rather smaller than the Pagoda, but the food is of equally high quality and you can also eat outside. Don't miss their excellent lamprai if it's available. The Green Cabin has one big advantage over the Pagoda in that it's open in the evenings.

Perera & Sons (Bakers) at 217 Galle Rd, Kollupitiya, Colombo 3, does cheap short eats but although there are a few chairs it's basically a take-away place. They have cold drinks and cakes too. The *Steak Bar*, on the Galle Rd in Colombo 3, is an air-con hamburger joint – good milkshakes but their hamburgers are not too exciting. Back up by the Galle Face Green the *Courtyard Restaurant* is in the Galle Face Courtyard, across from the Galle Face Hotel, and is a pretty reasonable sort of place.

There are also a number of Chinese restaurants along the Galle Rd. The *Chinese Lotus Hotel*, at 265 Galle Rd, Colombo 3, does good fresh crab; you can choose your crab in the kitchen. Opposite Dickman's Rd in Colombo 4, the *Chinese Dragon Hotel* at 231 Galle Rd has good, cheap food. The *Park View Lodge Restaurant*, at 70 Park St, Colombo 7, has good Chinese, western and Sri Lankan food.

Unfortunately the popular Greenlands Hotel was burnt out in the riots but you can get excellent Indian vegetarian food at *Dasaprakash* at 237 Galle Rd, Colombo 4, just before Dickman's Rd. It's a clean, modern place and the food, although not super-cheap, is excellent and their ice cream a real taste treat.

Getting There

Colombo is not only the main gateway to Sri Lanka it's also the centre of the bus and rail network. See the relevant regional sections for details of getting to or from Colombo by bus or rail. Trains go from the station in Fort. Minibuses depart from the bus park or road in front of the station or from the open area beside the CTB bus station which is just a short distance further along Olcott Mawatha from the station.

Getting Around

Airport Transport to the airport is not the easiest thing to do. A taxi will cost Rs 250 approximately. The public bus or minibus costs Rs 5, it doesn't run later than 9 or 10 pm. There is a railway station right at the airport but train departures are infrequent and usually at inconvenient times. There is, however, a Rs 75 bus service which operates beside the Taprobane Hotel and connects to all international flights. See Negombo for an alternative place for airport transport.

City Transport The main railway station, Colombo Fort, is within easy walking distance of the city centre. The bus station is just the other side of the Pettah from the centre, as is the minibus station. Buses are cheap and very crowded, keep a tight grip on your valuables, pickpockets are rife. Taxis, all old British Morris Minors, are metered but expensive. The Indian-made three-wheeler auto-rickshaws are somewhat cheaper.

West Coast Beaches

This is the major sea-sand-sun tourist strip with beach after beautiful beach. The best beaches start south of Colombo and run right around to Hambantota where the coast road turns inland and runs north to the hill country.

NEGOMBO

Situated 30 km north of Colombo the fishing villages around here are Catholic, a hangover from the Portuguese days. Although there are some interesting canals to wander along, the beach itself is not very special – use Negombo as a base for the airport, nothing else. The beach road, Negombo's main artery, is Lewis Place.

Places to Stay

The places to stay are mainly along the shoreline, about a km north of town. Several shoestring places have rooms under Rs 100 including the *Negombo Guest House* at 2 Lewis Place which is the cheapest of the cheapies. Rooms are very bare and basic but it's clean. Continue about a km further along Lewis Place, the beachfront road, and turn off to *Travellers' Halt* at 26 Perera Place. Rooms cost from Rs 50 to 80 and it's friendly and well kept. Over beside the canal at 47 Anderson Rd, *Dillwood* has seven well kept rooms, all with fans and at prices from Rs 80 to 200. There are countless other places around Negombo, particularly in the Rs 150 to 250 price bracket.

Negombo also has two rest houses. The pleasant *Lagoon View Rest House* is by the lagoon bridge and costs Rs 250/350 for singles/doubles including all meals. The *Sea View Rest House* is more expensive at Rs 220/250 room only.

Places to Eat

There are a number of good seafood places along Lewis Place like the small group opposite Brown's Beach Hotel. Further north the *Windmill Hotel's* restaurant has great food including an all-you-can-eat smorgasbord. *Joy's Restaurant* on Lewis Place by Carron Place does good and reasonably priced food. In town you'll find quite a selection of the standard rice and curry places plus the *Coronation Hotel* which also has good short eats.

Getting There

Negombo is a popular jumping off point for the airport as it's conveniently close and there are frequent buses and taxis. A minibus to the airport costs just Rs 3, a taxi about Rs 80 from the bus stand, Rs 125 from the hotel strip. Colombo is 35 km away and by minibus it costs Rs 4.50. Trains are Rs 5.50 in 3rd class but they're rather slower than the buses.

A taxi between the minibus station and Lewis Place should be around Rs 25 – it's quite a distance from the centre to Lewis Place. You can hire bicycles to explore Negombo – ride along the canal bank – from places along Lewis Place.

MT LAVINIA

Only 11 km from the centre of Colombo, Mt Lavinia is very popular on weekends, too popular in fact. It's within walking distance of the cheap accommodation centre at Dehiwala.

Places to Stay & Eat

There are lots of private rooms and guest houses here although none of them are really dirt cheap. *Joe Silvas* at 27C De Saram Rd has rooms at Rs 100. *Mrs A H Seeladasa* at 10/3 Lillian Avenue, near the Mt Lavinia Hotel, has three immaculate rooms at Rs 150. The *Thilanka Beach*

Bungalows at 26/2 Sri Dharmapala Rd have cabanas with attached bathroom at Rs 100.

The *Mount Grill* on the Galle Rd has good food at reasonable prices.

BERUWELA & BENTOTA

Continuing south from Colombo these adjoining towns are the site for a lot of top end hotels, but not too much for the shoestring traveller. Alutgama serves as the railway station and bus terminus for both centres.

Places to Stay

There are a few cheap places just to the south of the Bentota National Holiday Resort – you could try the *Susanta Guest House* close to the Bentota railway station or the *Thewalauwa Guest House*, about 100 metres south down the main road. On the south edge of town the *Silkoga Inn* is a friendly and moderately priced place not too far from the beach. The *Tharanga Hopper Bar* in the resort shopping centre has good food at fairly reasonable prices.

Eight km south of Bentota the small fishing village of Induruwa has a pleasant little guest house known as *Ripples Tourist Inn*.

AMBALANGODA

Only 13 km north of Hikkaduwa this small town is chiefly known for the many mask carvers who work here. It's worth a pause to visit a few of the carvers and see their work. Mettananda's Mask Centre at 142 Patabendimulla (the main road) is one of the best, in my opinion. Ambalangoda is only a couple of rupees from Hikkaduwa by bus.

Places to Stay

The *Rest House*, right by the seashore, overlooking a pleasant little bay, is particularly good – rooms are Rs 250/275 and it has good food. Otherwise there are guest houses like the *Blue Horizon Tour Inn* at 129 High Beach Rd which has rooms at Rs 125/1775. *Darshana* at 14/1

Sea Beach Rd has been recommended as cheap, clean and friendly. Or there's the *Randomba Inn* at 738-740 Galle Rd, *Brooklyn* on New Galle Rd and many others. Ambalangoda also has lots of terrible touts.

You can also find a number of places to stay between Ambalangoda and Hikkaduwa in small centres like Akurala (11 km north of Hikkaduwa) or Kahawa (six km north).

HIKKADUWA

This is the travellers' centre of Sri Lanka, 100 km south of Colombo. There's brilliant coral and clear water around the rocky island sanctuary which you can swim out to from the beach. Plus an untold number of places to stay and eat – this is definitely not a place to come to if you want to get away from it all! Beware also of the heavy traffic which hurtles through Hikkaduwa at great risk to life and limb. Snorkelling gear can be rented from shops in Hikkaduwa as can surfboards – the beach a little further south, which is not sheltered by the reef, has quite good surf.

The downside of Hikkaduwa is that like Kuta Beach in Bali it has suffered from heedless and unplanned over development. There are simply too many hotels crammed in together with too little forethought. Many of them are pure and simple eyesores. Hikkaduwa now sprawls a considerable distance south towards Galle.

Places to Stay

There are an enormous number of places to stay although prices depend very much on when you are there and how many rooms are already full. It's another of those places where you just wander along until you find something that suits. During the off-season the prices of the more expensive places tumble – Rs 500 places fall to Rs 100. Even in season you can find places for Rs 100 but when you want extras like a fan, mosquito net or attached toilet the price starts to climb.

Starting in the centre of things, on the beach side the more expensive *Poseidon Diving Adventures* (tel 09-3294) is at the top end of the guest house price scale. Across the road and back over the railway tracks the *Lovely Guest House* has pleasant doubles with fans and bathrooms, but again at the top of the guest house scale. Back on the sea side of the road, and still in the more expensive category, the *Dharshana Guest House* has had a number of good reports from travellers.

Prices rapidly start to drop with the *Pink House*, back over the railway tracks. This very popular travellers' centre is a good place for a long stay. Up the road opposite the big Coral Reef Hotel is the *White House*, a friendly and well run place with a beautiful garden and similarly low prices. Two other popular cheapies are side by side a little further down – the *Hotel Seashells* and the *Sun Sea Sand Hotel*. Both have pleasant verandahs and are at the upper end of the cheap scale with rooms in the Rs 100 to 150 bracket. The *Coral Front Inn*, still on the railway side of the road, has a variety of rooms, the better ones open out onto the verandah and garden.

At the *Coral View Hotel* rather bare doubles are Rs 125. There are a series of places back around the creek. The *Rising Sun Guest House* is pretty good value and well away from the noise of the road – but right by the noise of the railway! Comfortable doubles with bathroom and mosquito net, looking out onto a cool, shady verandah, cost Rs 100 at the *Udula Guest House*. Across the road and right on the beach the *Lotus Guest House* has nice rooms but again more expensive – Rs 250 for a bed and breakfast double.

Prices go down as you move further along the beach. At places like the *Surfers' Rest Guest House* rooms are as cheap as you'll find them. *Hotel Francis* is a notch up market from these places with doubles around Rs 150. The relatively new *Blue Note Cabanas* are pleasant at Rs 150. The *Homeley Guest House* is a fine-looking old building run by a very friendly lady. Rooms cost from Rs 70 for doubles and it's lovely inside and has lots of space and pleasant gardens. Then there's the *Wekunagoda Guest House* with rooms from Rs 50, the *Lakmal Hotel*, where doubles cost Rs 150 with their own bathroom, and quite a few others further along the road.

In fact these days you'll find places to stay almost all the way to Galle including a number of good places in Dodanduwa, four km south of Hikkaduwa. They include the friendly *Anoma Guest House* and the *Kusum Tourist Inn*.

Apart from the many guest houses it is also quite easy to get cheaper rooms in village houses. Just wander along looking hopeful and somebody will descend on you! Of course you may have to do without mod cons like running water but if the well is OK by you then you can get very good accommodation. Down at the southern end of the strip, or on the many little lanes that run inland, are the places to look.

Places to Eat

The selection of places to eat is as varied as the places to stay. You'll find all the usual travellers' menu items from banana pancakes to fruit salad.

Places to try include the *Farm House*, *Udula's*, the *Sydney Country Spot*, the excellent *Shyan's Living Kitchen*, the more expensive but popular *Restaurant Paradiso*, *Restaurant Francis* with some of the best food along the beach or the *Catamaran Curry Centre*. Opposite the big Coral Gardens Hotel the tiny *Reef Coldspot* is a favourite which is crowded at any time of day, particularly breakfast.

Down at the southern end of the strip *Rangith's Snacks* has the best ice cream and milkshakes along the beach and is always crowded in the evenings. On the beach side of the road *Big Budde* has excellent food and fast service. Still further south *Brother's Spot* is a pleasant beachfront place while next door *Silta's* is good, friendly and not too expensive.

Getting There

Trains from Colombo start from Rs 12.50 in 2nd and the trip takes two to three hours. This route can be very crowded. The new one class Inter-City Express service is more than twice as expensive but it's very fast, taking less than two hours. Buses range from Rs 13 to 18, there are buses from Hikkaduwa to nearby Galle and Ambalangoda. There are also daily minibuses direct to Colombo Airport for Rs 100. Bicycles (Rs 20 a day) and motorcycles can easily be hired from Hikkaduwa.

GALLE

Thought to be the biblical city of Tarshish. Galle is 115 km south of Colombo and very close to Hikkaduwa. It's an easygoing, old walled city with a real feeling of history. There is some interesting architecture and a stroll around the city walls is a fine early evening activity. Within the walled fort area look for the old Dutch gates, the Groote Kerk or Great Church which was built in 1752 on the site of an even older church and the old Dutch Government House, now used as offices by Walker & Sons.

Places to Stay

Beach Haven is a very popular little guest house at 65 Lighthouse St, rooms cost around Rs 150 for an excellent double and there are also some cheaper doubles at Rs 50, room only. Food here is good also. A few doors down at 61 the *Orchard Holiday Home* is a popular small hotel with rooms with bathroom at Rs 100/150 for singles/doubles.

On the corner of Rampart and Church Sts, near the lighthouse, the *Sea View Lodge & Restaurant* is a rather decrepit looking place with rooms from Rs 40 to 100, the higher priced rooms with attached bathroom. On Rampart St the *New Hotel Aquamarine* is basic and nothing special with singles at Rs 50 to 90, doubles at Rs 75 to 125.

There are also lots of guest houses in

Galle such as *R K Kodikara's* at 29 Rampart St which is friendly and cheap though perhaps not as well kept as it could be. Others include *Mrs Mashoor's* at 8 Parawa St, *Mrs Khalid's* at 106 Pedlar St and *Mrs Saheed's Guest House* at 79 Lighthouse St.

Finally beside the bus station, outside the fort, the *Sydney Hotel* is dirt cheap but also as dull and dingy as it's Rs 50 price would indicate. Or at the other extreme you can stay in real luxury at the delightful old world *New Oriental Hotel* which has fine rooms from Rs 290/375. Wherever you intend to stay beware of Galle's hotel touts who are as persistent as ever – and as likely to lead you to places you didn't want to go to.

Places to Eat

The *New Oriental* is a great place for a meal, worth the cost for the colonial splendour. Next door the *New Oriental Hotel Bakery* does short eats or rice and curry. You can also eat in the *Sea View Hotel*.

Otherwise almost all the places to eat are outside the fort. Near the grubby Sydney Hotel, across from the fort and by the CTB bus stand, the *South Ceylon Restaurant* has excellent food – cheap too. Around the corner at 30 Havelock Place, the road parallel to the railway line and canal, the *Chinese Globe Restaurant* is also excellent value. Or a couple of doors down the *Snackbar* is a clean, quiet place for a cold drink.

Getting There

Trains from Colombo run through Galle and right on to Matara where the coast line terminates. Fare in 2nd class is Rs 14.90 and the trip usually takes about three hours. There's also a new one class Inter-City Express which takes just two hours – the fare to Galle is Rs 40. There are also plenty of minibuses, from Colombo private buses to Galle cost Rs 18.

It's only 20 to 40 minutes by bus from Hikkaduwa to Galle at a cost of just a couple of rupees. Unawatuna, the next popular beach centre along the coast, is only 15 minutes away.

UNAWATUNA

Only a few km south of Galle the beach at Unawatuna is a picturebook sweep of golden sand. Hotels and restaurants are springing up and although it's a long way (a pleasantly long way) short of being another Hikkaduwa it's more of the same totally unplanned development which has spoilt other beaches in Sri Lanka.

Places to Stay

The *Sunny Beach Hotel* has pleasantly comfortable rooms from Rs 100 to 250. The *Rumassala Hotel*, between the more expensive Unawatuna Beach Resort and the Sunny Beach, is similarly priced. Other places further along the beach include the *Full Moon Inn* at Rs 150 or the *Saliya Beach Residence* and, on the road back from the beach, the *Unawatuna Beach Cabanas* and the *Strand Guest House*. There are also lots of rooms available in homes back here.

Along the main road from Galle, where it meets the coast, *Greenlodge Guest House* has nice doubles with bath at Rs 150. On the beach side of the road the *Sun 'n Sea Beach Cottages* are similarly priced. Recently opened *Nooit Gedacht* is a guest house in an elegant 17th century Dutch administrator's residence, 10 minutes walk from the beach. Singles/doubles, all with bath and verandah, are Rs 100/175 in season.

Places to Eat

There are a number of very pleasant places to eat right on the beach at Unawatuna. In front of the Sunny Beach Hotel the *Chinese Restaurant* has terrific food, some of the best I've had in Sri Lanka. Just beyond it is *Happy Bananas*, again with very good seafood. There are a number of others strung along the beach while back from the beach is the Rajneesh *Zorba's Wholemeal Restaurant* with pricier but excellent food in very neat and tidy surroundings.

WELIGAMA

About 30 km beyond Galle there's a fine sandy sweep of beach with a little island within wading distance of the shore – it used to be the home of an artist and certainly looks like an ideal retreat. Just by the railway crossing on the road that runs slightly inland from the coast there's a fine rock-carved statue known as the Kustaraja figure.

Places to Stay

Try *Sam's Holiday Cabanas* at 484 New By Pass Rd at the Matara end of town. Rooms cost Rs 100/150 in this pleasant and unhurried place. Close to the Weligama Bay Inn there are several small guest houses such as the *Holiday Rest* at 245 Main St or *Raja's Guest House* at Paranakade. The *Ruhunu Guest House* on D M Samaraweera Mawatha is more expensive at around Rs 200 including breakfast.

The very attractive *Weligama Bay Inn* is, despite it's name, another of Sri Lanka's excellent rest houses. Rooms are Rs 150/200 and there's a fine view across the bay. There's a second and slightly cheaper *Rest House* on the Galle side of the Bay Inn.

MATARA

This is the end of the south coast railway line. The town has two Dutch forts, the larger one contains a large part of the town, the other is the tiny Star Fort of 1763. Matara is famous for its curd and treacle so don't miss trying it. The best beach is a few km north of the town at Polhena.

Places to Stay

There are a lot of cheap places to stay here. The *Matara Rest House* is as beautifully situated as they all are, it's by the beach inside the fort. Rooms cost from Rs 60 to 130 and the food in the reasonably priced restaurant is good.

There are also some cheap doubles in the old building which are excellent value.

Further inside the fort is the the *River Inn Guest House* by the river at 96A Wilfred Gunasekera with singles/doubles at Rs 125/150. At number 38 the *Blue Ripples Guest House* is a very pleasant place with just two rooms at Rs 60. There are several other guest houses in the fort area and also places along the coast road towards Tangalla – not the main road which runs a block inland. The *Jez Look Beach Lodge* at 47 Beach Rd has dorm beds at Rs 25 and singles/doubles at Rs 75/150. There are other Matara cheapies on the way out of town towards Galle. A block beyond the railway station turnoff the *Chamin Restaurant & Guest House* has clean, functional rooms at Rs 60.

At Polhena, the popular beach three km west of Matara, the *TK Travellers' Halt* has dorm beds and also rooms from Rs 50 to 125. There are other small guest houses here.

Places to Eat

The *Chamin Restaurant* has a long menu of the Chinese regulars plus good fish and chips. Further back towards the bus station and the fort entrance there's the *GOB Restaurant* and right by the bridge you can get good short eats or cakes at the *Richcurd Bakery*. The fruit stalls by the bridge in Matara have a wide variety of excellent tropical fruit.

Getting There

Matara is the end of the railway line from Colombo and fares in 2nd class are Rs 20.50. From Galle a minibus costs Rs 6. Take a 350, 356 or 460 bus from the Matara bus stand to Polhena Beach.

MATARA TO TANGALLA

Soon after you leave Matara a turn inland will take you to the Weherehena temple with its underground 'cave' decorated in comic-book style. At Dikwella a turn inland takes you to the huge 50-metre-high seated Buddha figure at the Wewurukannala Vihara. It's about 1½ km inland and you can climb up inside the figure to look out over the shoulder or peer inside his head.

TANGALLA

This is a fine place to laze around and do very little. There's a nice little town and some delightful beaches. The rest house is one of the oldest in the country, dating back to the Dutch days.

North of Tangalla the Mulkirigala rock temple has a little of Dambulla and Sigiriya about it. Steps lead up to a series of cleft-like caves in the huge rock and at the very top is a dagoba, from where there are fine views over the surrounding country. You can get to Mulkirigala on a Middeniya bus but check it will go via Beliatta. Or take a bus just to Beliatta and a minibus from there. It's even possible to ride there by bicycle, if you have plenty of energy.

Places to Stay

Tangalla, like Matara, has a wide range of cheap places to stay as well as plenty of very persuasive hotel touts waiting in hiding around the bus station for travellers to arrive.

About a half km out of town on the Matara side the *Tangalla Beach Hotel* is basic and cheap with dorm beds or rooms with prices up to Rs 100. Negotiate here, it's a long way from luxurious and the first price asked is only a starting point. A little further along towards the expensive Tangalla Bay Hotel is the *Seaview Tourist Inn* which is somewhat more comfortable but not much more expensive. Next door is the friendly *Tourist Guest House* with rooms with attached bathrooms and mosquito nets.

Back in the centre the *Diana Travellers Lodge* is a popular member of the Travellers' Halt Chain. It's about seven-minutes walk uphill (the only hill) from the bus station, back towards Colombo. There's a big garden and kitchen facilities; good doubles are just Rs 50. Along Beach

Rd, towards the rest house from the bus station, there are a string of guest houses and more can be found on Samuel Mawatha off Beach Rd. Examples are the *Beach Inn Guest House*, the *Sethsiri Tourist Rest House*, the *Deepa Tourist Inn* and the *Santana Guest House*, all of which have been recommended by travellers. There are lots of others in this area or on the Hambantota side of town.

Moving up a notch in price the *Tangalla Rest House* is pleasantly situated on the promontory at the start of the beach stretching to the east. It's one of the oldest rest houses in the country, originally constructed by the Dutch in 1774, and has rooms at Rs 150/250. On the Matara side of town the pleasant *Peace Haven Guest House* has rooms from Rs 200 to 350 and a couple of superb little beaches just down below it. The cheapest rooms are bare and fanless. Also sharing these beaches are the delightful *Palm Paradise Cabanas* with quite beautiful individual cabanas, each with a verandah and bathroom, for Rs 400 in season.

Places to Eat

Southern Bakeries, just beyond the Diana Lodge from the bus station, has good snacks and short eats. In the centre *Gamini's Hotel* is a good curry and rice specialist. In the market you can get excellent curd and honey. *Maxim's Harbour Inn* is a pleasantly breezy little open air restaurant on the way down to the rest house. The *Rest House* itself has an excellent reputation for its seafood. Finally *Turtle Landing Restaurant* is another small snack bar by the beach out of town towards the Tangalla Bay Hotel.

HAMBANTOTA

This is where the road turns inland from the coast and skirts around the Yala park before rejoining the coast at Arugam Bay. The long stretch of beach is lined with picturesque fishing boats. Just out of town on the road north are a string of curd and treacle stalls.

Places to Stay

Just on the Tangalla side of town the small *Joy Rest Home* has a handful of rooms from Rs 30 to 75. Next door is the *Hambantota Guest House* or there's *Mrs M S M Nihar's Guest House* at 9 Terrace St. In Galwala, about a km from the bus stand on the Tissa side of town, the *Sea Spray Guest House* is a well maintained place with rooms at around Rs 200.

The *Hambantota Rest House* is nicely situated on top of the promontory and costs Rs 100 per person including breakfast.

TISSAMAHARAMA & KATARAGAMA

A little north of Hambantota a road turns off to these towns, Tissamaharama has an interesting dagoba and is a jumping off point for trips to the Yala park while Kataragama is the site for a major Hindu pilgrimage in July and August with fire walking and other acts of ritual masochism! South of Tissamaharama, which also has a large and beautiful tank, is the small coastal village of Kirinda with a fine beach.

Wirawila, between Hambantota and the Tissa turn-off, is on the large Wirawila Wewa, an extensive tank with much birdlife. There is also some accommodation here.

Places to Stay

Anumpa Guest House in Tissa is Rs 50/75 and there are quite a few other places to stay although most of them are more expensive. In Kataragama you can try the reasonably priced *Kataragama Rest House* or the *Bank of Ceylon* has an excellent guest house with rooms for Rs 75, although you're supposed to book it ahead in Colombo.

The Hill Country

Sri Lanka's hill country offers plenty of interest as well as an escape from the heat of the lowlands. It's also a good opportunity to get away from the tourist hype of so many of the coastal resorts.

KANDY

This is the best known of Sri Lanka's hill stations, 115 km from Colombo. It's famous for the Temple of the Tooth or Dalada Maligawa which is said to contain one of the Buddha's pearlies. For 10 nights around full moon each year in late-July or early August a spectacular festival takes place here, culminating in a parade where a replica of the tooth is carried through the town on an elephant. The festival, Esala Perahera, is said to be one of the most magnificent sights in Asia. The Portuguese, incidentally, claim they destroyed the tooth in the process of making Ceylon fit for Christians. The Sinhalese say they were fobbed off with a fake one.

Kandy also has an excellent botanical garden a few km out at Peradeniya. There are numerous temples around Kandy or you can see traditional Kandyan dancing (nightly performances). Elephant bath time at nearby Katugastota is a bit of a tourist rip-off. A more interesting excursion is to the Pinnewala Elephant Orphanage, three km south of Rambukkana Station, back towards Colombo. Get there by taking a 662 bus to Kegalle and another bus from there.

Information & Orientation

The town clusters around the lake and is surrounded by hills with many fine views. The main part of the town is to the north of the lake where you will also find the Temple of the Tooth. The Tourist Office is at the Kandy Arts Centre, a short distance round the lake. This may only be a temporary location. The office is only open on weekdays. The Wheel, further around the lake, is a Buddhist information centre with a wide variety of books, brochures and pamphlets on Buddhism.

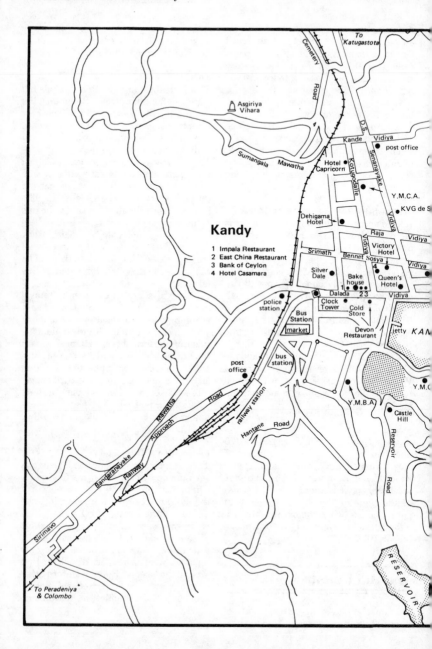

Kandy

1 Impala Restaurant
2 East China Restaurant
3 Bank of Ceylon
4 Hotel Casamara

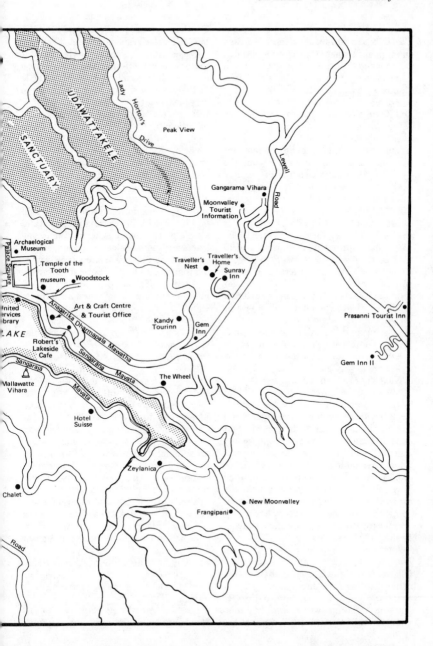

Places to Stay

Two things to beware of in Kandy – during the annual Perahera the prices go through the roof and even finding a place to stay in Kandy can be hard. The other problem is Kandy's terrible touts, it's one of the worst places in Sri Lanka for hotel touts and if you allow yourself to be taken to a place you'll be pushing prices up for everybody else.

Three of the most popular cheapies are in a small cluster about a km beyond the town centre – only a couple of minutes walk off the road to the left, down in the rice paddies. Here you'll find the *Travellers' Nest* (tel 08-22633) at 117/4 Anagarika Dharmapala Mawatha, which is so popular that a host of imitators with 'nest-like' names have sprung up. They now have 26 rooms – the basic rooms cost Rs 30/50 for singles/doubles, then there are rooms with fan and bath for Rs 75/100, fancier rooms at Rs 125 to 150 and upstairs larger doubles with attached bath and hot water for Rs 250 including breakfast. There's also a second building of 'economic' rooms. There's a pleasant balcony where you can sit and watch the monkeys and the food here is very good.

Next door is *Traveller's Home* (tel 08-22800) with similar sorts of prices. Third in this group is the *Sunray Inn* (tel 08-23322) with 18 double rooms from Rs 60 to 300. All three of these places are just far enough off the beaten track to be pleasantly quiet yet not too far from the town centre. Food is available at all of them too. A 654 or 655 bus will take you to them from the town but if you're lightly laden it's just a pleasant stroll uphill from the lakeside. If you phone from the station they'll probably arrange transport or pay for a taxi, to avoid dealing with the touts.

Another very popular place is the *Gem Inn* (tel 08-24239) at 39 Anagarika Dharmapala Mawatha just before the turn-off to the first three places. Rooms cost Rs 50 and 75 with common bath or Rs 100 for a double with bath. It's five-minutes' walk beyond the Temple of the Tooth, or you can get there on a 654 or 655 bus, as for the Travellers' Nest. There are only a handful of rooms at the Gem Inn but there is a second Gem Inn which is superb if you're planning a longer stay. It's a little further out of town but the *Gem Inn II* is a very pleasant, spacious and relaxed house with excellent doubles with attached bathroom for Rs 150. You can walk down along the ridge to the town or a taxi will cost you Rs 30 to 40. Check in at the original Gem Inn.

Take the steep road up behind the Kandy Museum and the Temple of the Tooth, veer left up the steep dirt path and at the top of the path and some steps you'll find *Woodstock*. It's a straightforward and simple place which has, according to one traveller, 'the best location in town, you get a wonderful breeze and a nice view of the temple and lake'. There are a variety of rooms with prices of Rs 30, 50 and 60 plus an octagonal room at the front for Rs 100. There are common bathrooms and toilets.

A place which has become very popular in the last year or so is the *Prasanna Guest House* (tel 08-24365) at 53/29 Hewaketa Rd. To find it continue on beyond the Travellers' Nest group until you see the steep downhill turn off to the left of the road. Basic rooms are Rs 40, no bath, or rooms with bath cost Rs 50 to 75. It's clean, neat and well equipped and several travellers have written to comment on the exceptional helpfulness of the owner. Further down the steep road at the river is a good swimming spot and also a non-commercial elephant bathing place.

Kandy has a great number of other places to stay and the tourist office by the lakeside will provide you with more information on smaller hotels and guest houses. Many of these small guest houses will only have a couple of rooms. Those that follow are just a limited selection, most of which have been recommended by travellers:

Mrs De Silva's guest house at 15 Malabar St (sometimes known as 'Doctor's

House') is pleasant and friendly with rooms from Rs 75. The *Mawilmada Tourist Rest* (tel 08-23250) at 16 Mawilmada Rd has five rooms from Rs 30 to 75. The *New Moonvalley* has rooms at Rs 75 with bath – it's plain but OK, quite a way up the road from the lake and opposite the Frangipani Guest House.

Several people have written to recommend *Lucktissme* (tel 08-22725) at 125 Pitakanda Rd, Mahayaya where singles/doubles are Rs 75/150. It's up the hill from the Katugastota road, near the elephant baths, but they'll pick you up from the station. 'A lovely place to stay, nice people and good food'. Several letters have also recommended *Jingle Bells* at 26 Sangamitta Mawatha. 'I checked it out because of the silly name', said one visitor, 'but the rooms (from Rs 60 to 125) were good and the family very friendly and helpful. The cooking was the best I had in Sri Lanka'.

Other places which have been recommended include *Lakshmi*, uphill (follow the Lake Inn signs) just before the Suisse. It's spotlessly clean and has rooms from Rs 50 to 100. Right in the centre, at 31 King St, the *Charlton Guest House* (no sign but the Charlton Shopping Centre is next door) is Rs 50 to 75 for a double. Also conveniently central *Mrs Wadugodapitiya's* guest house is at 74 Peradeniya Rd, about due west of the market across the foot bridge. The large rooms cost from Rs 50 – modern bathrooms and pleasantly run.

Next to the YMCA at the lake, *Victoria Cottage* at 6 Victoria Drive is a beautiful house with doubles with bathroom for Rs 50 to 70. Somewhat more expensive, the *Sunrock Holiday Home* (tel 08-24137) is at 195 Heerassagala Rd and has rooms at Rs 150/200. At 30/61 Bangalawatta, Lewella Rd the *Linton Lodge* is on the edge of town, a 15-minute walk to the temple. You can get there on a 655 bus. The rooms cost from Rs 35 and are very clean, the food is OK. *St Michael's Guest House* at Ampitiya is easy going and has good music – rooms are Rs 75/150 including breakfast.

There are *Railway Retiring Rooms* (tel 08-22271) at the Kandy station with rooms at Rs 143 and 163. Close to the Temple of the Tooth, the *Olde Empire* (tel 08-24284) is one of the cheapest hotels in Kandy and it's a pretty good place. Rooms cost Rs 80 to 100, cheaper at the back although the singles there are a little cramped and dingy. There are fine views from the balconies and the place has a 'wonderful colonial feel'. A number of travellers have written to recommend it.

Kandy also has a number of Ys. Probably the best value of the lot is the *YMBA* (Young Men's Buddhist Association) at 5 Rajapihilla Mawatha – overlooking the lake and close to the Royal Palace Park. Costs here range from Rs 25 per person. Also on this side of the lake is the *YMCA* at 4 and 4a Sangaraja Mawatha. It has 10 rooms and is similarly priced but is only open to men and is rather run down.

There is a second *YMCA* (tel 08-23529) on Kotugodella Vidiya, very close to the town centre. There are singles at Rs 23, fancier doubles with bath at Rs 84.50, share rooms (men only) are Rs 17.50 each or a dorm (again men only) at Rs 9.25.

Also centrally located, the *Kandy City Mission* is at 125 Trincomalee St, a few blocks up from the Queen's Hotel. It's very reasonable, clean and comfortable with rooms around Rs 75 to 150. The food here, both Sri Lankan and western, is good.

There's a small *Boy Scout Youth Hostel* at the Boy Scout Headquarters, back across the lake again and further up the hill on Keppetipola Rd. At Katugastota the *Travellers' Halt* is 'one of the nicest youth hostels in Asia' according to a traveller. Ask directions for the railway bridge at Katugastota, cross the bridge and the hostel (which has no sign) is the second house on the left.

Places to Eat

Kandy's cheaper restaurants all seem to get mixed reports. None of them would rate culinary raves but they seem to yo-yo between acceptable and awful! Two of them are on the main road, virtually opposite each other. The *Bake House* is a big, two-level place with good short eats and a comprehensive menu although it's now quite expensive and a number of travellers have reported the food here can be very variable.

The *Ceylon Cold Store*, across the road, is not open in the evenings but is good for lunch and popular for quick snacks, drinks or ice cream ('delicious strawberry ice cream' reported one traveller). Good take-aways and ice cream from out front too. Like the Bake House it's now moderately expensive; meals generally cost from Rs 20 or 30 and up.

The rather scruffy *Impala Restaurant* (biriyanis a speciality) also does a really refreshing mixed-fruit drink. On the left side of the Peradeniya road, just past the main roundabout in Kandy, the *Lyons Cafe* is clean, has quick service and good, cheap food.

Other cheaper restaurants include the *East China* (painfully slow service and the food is not very good when it finally arrives) on the Bake House side; the very popular *Devon* ('good and cheap') on the Cold Store side and the *Silver Dale* round the corner. At the latter the food can be very variable – some people find it terrible, others excellent.

The *Olde Empire*, between the Queen's Hotel and the Tooth Temple, may look a little grey and dreary, but the food here is surprisingly good. Come here for a good rice and curry and try their excellent ice cream. The *Kandy City Mission* at 125 Trincomalee St has good short eats plus their own cheese and brown bread. The *Jayananda Hotel*, nearly opposite the mission, has good rice and curry and also cheap western food.

The newly opened *Robert's Lakeside Cafe* is a pleasant outdoor snack place. Drinks are Rs 7.50 to 10, sandwiches Rs 15 to 30. And each table comes with a bell to ring for service! The *Victory Hotel* on

Srimath Bennet Sosya Vidiya has a good variety of food and you can get a beer at the *Sosya Irdeega* (loose beer shop!), just down from it.

Good food, pleasant surroundings but rather higher prices can be found at the *Royal Park Cafeteria* in the Botanic Gardens – lunch times only of course. The Rs 55 set lunch is good but here too the service can be slow. There is also a cheaper employees' cafeteria in the gardens.

Getting There

From Colombo by train it's about three hours and costs Rs 15.80 in 3rd class, Rs 38.70 in 2nd. There's also a new one-class Inter-City Express which takes just two hours and costs Rs 40. Superb views on the way up. By CTB bus it's Rs 16, minibus is Rs 20. Buses run from here to Trincomalee, Anuradhapura, Polonnaruwa and to other hill country centres.

Getting Around

Around Kandy most buses go from the Torrington Bus Stand close to the market. CTB buses depart from the Central Bus Stand in front of the market. Buses to Hatton go from close to the Temple of the Tooth. The Lakeside Cafe rents out bicycles and motorcycles.

ADAM'S PEAK

This beautifully symmetrical mountain is where Adam is said to have first set foot to earth having been cast out of Eden. Or perhaps that's Buddha's giant footprint on the top? Whichever legend you care to believe pilgrims have been making a pre-dawn ascent for over a thousand years.

The pilgrimage season runs from December to April and every night thousands of people climb the endless stairs to the top of the 2224 metre peak and watch for the spectacular sunrise as the shadow of the peak is reflected on the morning clouds far below. It takes about three hours to climb to the top and come prepared for the pre-dawn chill – you work up quite a sweat on the climb and it's very cold waiting for the sun to rise.

The usual ascent route is from Dalhousie, a 33 km, two-hour trip from Hatton which is on the Kandy-Nuwara Eliya bus route. You can leave your gear at the bottom or take a room at the *Wijitha Hotel* until you want to leave. It's also possible to climb the peak from the Ratnapura side but this takes much longer and is much harder work.

NUWARA ELIYA

This terribly English hill station is a great place for a rest-and-relax visit although you can also climb Pidurutalagala from here. At 2524 metres it's the highest in Sri Lanka and has Sri Lanka's TV transmitter mounted on the top. Near to Nuwara Eliya is the small, but very pleasant, Hakgala Botanic Gardens. It features in the Ramayana legend. Nuwara Eliya was badly damaged in the 1983 riots.

Places to Stay

Nuwara Eliya is not a great place for cheap accommodation and it's plagued by hotel touts. *Molesworth* is part of the travellers' halt network and close to the Grand Hotel. According to some visitors it's damp, musty and none too special – which doesn't stop it from being the main travellers' locale. There are dorm beds, singles/doubles at Rs 50/75 and a nice lounge and gardens.

There are a number of guest houses in the vicinity which may be worth investigating if Molesworth does not appeal. The nearby *Nuwara Eliya Inn* has rooms at Rs 125, 150 and up. It gets mixed reviews – 'pretty reasonable' reported one visitor; 'one of the worst places we stayed' said another. *Wattles Inn* on St Andrew's Drive has rooms at Rs 125/150 but also gets distinctly mixed reports.

The *Ascot Guest House*, opposite the race track, has doubles at Rs 125 – they're good value including breakfast and with hot water and extra sheets. On Badulla Rd, *Collingwood* is an amazing old mock-Tudor house originally built by a Scottish planter with just one room at Rs 150 including breakfast.

Behind the Fancy Market on Old Bazaar St the *Hemamala Guest House* is pleasant with singles at Rs 50, doubles with hot shower at Rs 125. *Mrs Weeramanthy* on Lebana Rd has rooms for Rs 80 and 'she's a superb cook'. Other guest houses are *Lyndhurst* (tel 0522-347) on Waterfield Drive, and the *Alpen Guest house* by the Grosvenor Hotel. The rooms at the Alpen are good, the staff friendly and doubles are Rs 175; for Rs 20 extra you can have the fire lit in your room.

Mr Cader's *Pink House* has also been recommended – continue past the round-about to the new town hall and cinema (10 to 15 minutes walk), then turn right up the hill on the track. Ask directions from here, it's hard to find but when you get there rooms cost from just Rs 50.

Note that Nuwara Eliya can get pretty cold at night – impecunious travellers without coats and sweaters can pick up second hand ones from the street stalls.

Places to Eat

If you're not eating in your hotel or guest house, Nuwara Eliya has a rather disreputable looking collection of restaurants along the main street. None of them are terribly appetising and their numbers were reduced by the '83 violence. You could always try the *Star Hotel & Bakery* and the *Dale West* at the end of the road by the roundabout. The Dale West is probably the better of the two. The *New Royal Hotel*, next to the Star Hotel, makes excellent tea and short eats although you are not encouraged to linger if it's busy. There's a 'loose beer shop' on Lawson St.

At the other end of the price scale, or at least the Sri Lankan price scale, a meal at the *Hill Club* is an experience not to be missed. Dinner is served at 8 pm and costs Rs 125; lunch is Rs 100. You get a full five-course meal – soup, fish course, main course, dessert, tea or coffee. If you're going to have just one splurge in all of Sri Lanka make it here! You must be properly dressed – no jeans allowed in this august establishment. Men must wear ties. If, like most travellers, you do not possess such an arcane piece of attire they'll loan you one for a Rs 50 deposit and Rs 5 fee. One traveller wrote of the embarrassment of having to return his tie, to get back his deposit, before he could pay the bill!

The Rest has had a reputation of being a sort of Sri Lankan, government-run version of Fawlty Towers but recently it seems to aspired to rather better food. Finally, just beyond the Hakgala Botanical Gardens entrance, *Humbugs* is a pleasant small restaurant/snack bar with very fine views out from its hillside location. In season they even have strawberries and cream and in any season they have a most amusing sign out front.

Getting There

Trains don't actually run through Nuwara Eliya, the station is at Nanu Oya, a few km away. From Kandy it's five or six hours by train with great views all the way. If you can run to it take the 1st class 'observation coach' and enjoy the view in real comfort. From Colombo the fare is Rs 27.10 in 3rd, Rs 66.60 in 2nd, Rs 104 in 1st – plus Rs 25 for the observation coach on top of the 1st class fare. From Nanu Oya to Nuwara Eliya costs Rs 3 by bus or Rs 50 by taxi.

You can break the trip at Hatton to climb Adam's Peak. A minibus from Kandy is Rs 18.

WORLD'S END

South of Nuwara Eliya and west of Haputale this high and windy plateau is notable for the sheer drop off the edge to the coastal plain below. It's a stunning sight but cloud and mist often obscure the view.

BANDARAWELA

This pleasant hill country town is a good base for walks in the area. See the Dowa Temple with its fine four-metre-high rock-cut Buddha figure, just off the road on the way to Badulla.

Places to Stay

The *Rest House* here is well signposted from the centre and costs Rs 150/275 including breakfast. The *Chinese Union Hotel*, next to the big Orient Hotel at 8 Mt Pleasant, has rooms from Rs 60. Couples only can use the *YWCA Holiday Home* or next door to the post office and across from the bus station, smack in the middle of town, there is *Justin Fernando's*.

The *Riverside Inn* on the way out to Haputale at 114 Ellatota Rd has rooms at Rs 100/150. Just out of town on the Welimada side the *Ventnor Guest House* at 23 Welimada Rd has singles/doubles at just Rs 30/40.

ELLA

This is another pleasant hill town with a very fine view from the front of the Rest House. Below your feet the Ella Gap falls away to the coastal plain 1000 metres lower down. You can walk or bus down the road five km from Ella to the spectacular Rawana Ella Falls.

Places to Stay

Rooms cost Rs 250 in the *Rest House*; the spectacular view comes for free. There are a couple of places right beside it – the *Rock View Rest House* has rooms from Rs 125 to 175, the simple *Ella Rest Inn* costs Rs 25 to 75.

Just round the corner the *Ella Gap Tourist Inn* costs from Rs 75 to 150, up to Rs 200 with attached bath. The food here is very good and there's a pleasant patio. Going down the hill towards the railway station you come to *Lizzie's Villa Rest House* and the *SK Tourist Rest House* across the road from it. Both have rooms down to around Rs 50. Unfortunately the very popular Sunnyside Lodge was burnt out in the '83 riots.

BADULLA

Badulla marks the south-eastern extremity

of the hill country and the gateway to the east coast. The hill country railway line terminates here too. From here you can visit the Dunhinda Falls, a 2½ km walk to reach them.

Places to Stay

Right in the centre of town the *Badulla Rest House* has rooms at Rs 60/100 for singles/doubles. Centrally located, five minutes walk from the railway and bus stations to the east of the centre, the *Castle Hotel* (tel 055-2334) is at 134 Lower St and has doubles at Rs 60.

A little further down the street is the very simple *Uva Hotel* with rooms at Rs 60 to 100. The *Riverside Holiday Inn* (tel 055-2090) is at 27 Lower King St, 300 metres from the bus stand, and has doubles all the way from Rs 30 to 150. The *Myura Tourinn* is 100 metres past the bus stand on the top road away from the clocktower. Doubles are Rs 60 to 100 and the food here is good.

Mrs Mala Jayakody's guest house at 7 Race Course Rd has also been recommended; rooms cost Rs 20 to 50. *Richard & Astrid Fernandez* have a small guest house at 26 Old Bede's Rd, just out of town. Ask directions at the YMCA, where Richard works. Rooms are cheap and the food is plentiful – 'enough leftovers to feed your pet elephant'.

Getting There

There are frequent buses from Nuwara Eliya, you change at Welimada or Bandarawela – the trip takes about two hours in either case and costs Rs 12.50. Badulla is the end of the railway line from Colombo – a nine-hour trip. It's a lovely journey between Ella and Haputale.

HAPUTALE

Perched right at the southern edge of the hill country Haputale also has spectacular views, right down to the south coast in clear weather. It's another good base for walking trips such as to Adisham, a Benedictine monastery about an hour

away. Down towards Wellawaya is the Diyaluma Falls where you can climb to the top for a secluded swim in the rock pool above the falls.

Places to Stay

Highcliffe is one of the nicest cheap places to stay in Sri Lanka. It's right by the railway line and has rooms at Rs 15/30. Food here is also good and cheap and there's a visitor's book with useful recommendations on local walks. Other good places include the *Amerasinghe Guest House* although it can be difficult to find since the owner's shop was burnt out in the '83 riots. Or there's *Hyacinth Cottage* on Temple Rd, the *Friendly Place Guest House* (it is indeed friendly and has very good food) next door to Highcliffe, and the *Bawa Inn* with a fine view from the ridge down to the south coast.

Haputale now has two rest houses. The old *Rest House* is across the railway tracks from Highcliffe. It's a bit bleak and bare at Rs 87.50/175. The new *Rest House* is a km or two out of town on the Bandarawela side and costs Rs 100/200.

RATNAPURA

The 'city of gems' is a mining centre for semi-precious stones and has an interesting little gem museum. Otherwise there's not a lot of interest although you could visit the town's small museum.

Places to Stay

The Ratnapura bus station is just off the centre of town, on the rise that culminates in the rest house. Half way up the hill you will find *Travellers' Rest* at 66 Inner Circular Rd (or Rest House Rd). It's simple and very basic with rooms from just Rs 30. Right beside it at number 60 is the similar standard *Star Light Tourist Rest*.

A third possibility is the *Travellers' Halt* at 30 Outer Circular Rd. It's about 15 minutes brisk walk from the bus station (which is the old, and now disused, railway station). Walk away from the town, when you pass the Ratnapura convent number 30 is about 100 metres beyond it. There are some slightly hidden signs along the way, follow the signs for Polhengoda village. Dorm beds are Rs 10, doubles from Rs 40. In Polhengoda the *Hotel Kalawathie* 'is a beautiful hotel, like a museum and surrounded by herb gardens'.

Right at the top of the central hill the pleasant *Rest House* has rooms at Rs 110/210 with bath, some basic rooms downstairs and a superb view.

Places to Eat

The *Ratnaloka Hotel* (no relation to the expensive Ratnaloka Tour Inn) is a good place for a cheap curry and rice. Or try the cool, clean and rather more expensive *Nilani Tourist Restaurant*. The *Rest House* also has good food with that usual graciously old fashioned service.

Getting There

Buses from Colombo cost Rs 10.50 for the CTB buses, Rs 12 for minibuses. Trains no longer run to Ratnapura. There is a direct, but roundabout, bus from Ratnapura to Matara and Tangalla twice daily.

BUDURUVAGALA

About five km south of Wellawaya on the road towards Hambantota (and thus really down on the coastal plain and out of the hill country), it's worth the several km stroll to this isolated cliff face with its fine rock-cut figures of the Buddha and disciples. The main figure stands 15 metres high.

Places to Stay

In Wellawaya the *Old Rest House* was out of commission for renovations. It's very close to the central crossroads on the Old Ella Rd. A little way out towards Ella, just after the old road merges with the New Ella Rd, is the shiny new *Wellawaya Inn Rest House* with doubles at Rs 150. Between these two rest houses, close to the old one, is the *Wellawaya Rest Inn* with doubles at Rs 40.

The Ancient Cities

North of the hill country in the dry plains of the northern region stand the deserted ruins of Sri Lanka's ancient capitals. They're magnificent reminders of the strength of Buddhist culture and definitely worth a visit.

ANURADHAPURA

The most extensive and important of Sri Lanka's ancient cities, Anuradhapura first became a capital in 380 BC but rose to great importance when Buddhism came to Sri Lanka. Despite the Tamil invasions from south India the city reached its height around 300 AD and survived for another 500 years before being abandoned in favour of Polonnaruwa. Like Angkor Wat in Cambodia it disappeared into the jungle and was not rediscovered until 1845. Although the ruins are fairly widely spread and some of them have been poorly restored it's a superb place to visit.

Things to See

Around the Bo-Tree The sacred Bo-tree is the centrepiece of the city. It was grown from a sapling brought from Bodh Gaya in India, from the very tree under which the Buddha attained enlightenment. It's over two thousand years old, the oldest historically authenticated tree in the world. Nearby is the Brazen Palace, only the remains of its 1600 columns indicate its position. The Anuradhapura Museum is open from 8 am to 4 pm except on Tuesdays and is also in this area. North of the museum and the Brazen Palace is the fine Ruvanvelisaya Dagoba. Further north again is the Thuparama Dagoba, the oldest in Anuradhapura and possibly in Sri Lanka.

Northern Ruins The other main group of ruins are some distance to the north of the Bo-tree group. They include the Royal Palace and the huge Abhayagiri Dagoba. Mahasen's Palace has one of the finest 'moonstone' doorsteps in Sri Lanka. The Samadhi Buddha statue is said to be the finest Buddha image in Sri Lanka while a little beyond that is the Kuttam Pokuna or 'twin ponds'. Looping back to the south you pass the Jetavanarama Dagoba, rivalling the Abhayagiri in size.

Beside the Tissawewa More interesting ruins can be seen close to the huge Tissawewa tank. They include the fine Isurumuniya temple with some particularly renowned rock bas reliefs. Right beside the tank and the Pleasure Garden ruins and a little further round you come to another huge dagoba, the Mirisavatiya.

Places to Stay

Most places in Anuradhapura are rather inconveniently far from the old city area. The sole exception is the beautifully situated old *Tissawewa Rest House* which is rather expensive at Rs 300/400.

Popular travellers' centres include the *Shanthi Guest House* (tel 025-2515) at 891 Mailagas Junction. It's about two km from the new town centre and a fair stroll from the new bus terminal. It's got rooms ranging from Rs 50 for the simplest economy rooms up to Rs 100 for doubles, Rs 150 with bath, even Rs 250 for deluxe doubles. If you phone up they'll collect you or pay for a taxi from the bus or train station to avoid the terrible touts. The food at Shanthi is very good.

The *Tourist Holiday Home* is a relatively recent addition close to the post office and centre of town. Rooms cost Rs 75/100 downstairs, Rs 100/125 upstairs – all with mosquito net, fan and attached bathroom. Right across the road from it the grubby *Paramount Hotel* is an emergencies only dive at Rs 50 per person.

On the other side of town, at the junction where the Jaffna road joins the Mihintale road, is the *Travellers' Halt* at 15 Jaffna Junction. Rooms are Rs 25/50. About a hundred metres along the Mihintale road from the junction, and well back from the road, is *King's Dale* with singles/doubles at Rs 30/50 and good food. If you're coming by bus from Trincomalee get off at the junction for either of these places, don't take it all the way into town.

Others places include the *Dilkushi Holiday Home* on the Kandy road with rooms at Rs 150/250. Or the *Hotel Monara* at 63 Freeman Mawatha near the bus stop. Or the rather anonymous *Number 5*, about a hundred metres beyond the Tissawewa Rest House, a rock bottom local place. Or the *Railway Retiring Rooms* at the station which cost Rs 110 for a double with bath – choose a room on the road rather than the railway side.

Places to Eat

There's little choice of places to eat apart from at the places you stay. The *Paramount Hotel* has a reasonable, if sometimes terribly slow, restaurant. Just east of the Isurumuniya the *Madhura Cool Hut & Coffee Centre* is a nice place for a cool drink or simple snacks. In general the shops along the roads between the ruins are cheaper for soft drinks than the vendors on the sites.

Getting There

Anuradhapura is on the Colombo-Jaffna and Colombo-Talaimannar railway lines. It takes about four to five hours from Colombo by train and costs from Rs 26.70 in 3rd class, Rs 65.60 in 2nd. The one class Inter-City Express runs three times weekly and takes 3¼ hours from Colombo to Anuradhapura at a fare of Rs 51. It's a further three hours on from there to Jaffna for another Rs 48.

By bus from Colombo is Rs 23 with CTB, Rs 28 in a minibus. About a dozen buses a day make the five-hour trip to Kandy with fares from Rs 18 to 23. Other services include Dambulla, Jaffna, Polonnaruwa or Trincomalee. Minibuses go from the New Town centre, CTB Colombo buses from the station there, other CTB buses from the new bus station.

Getting Around
Hire a bicycle to get around but, as usual in Sri Lanka, check it over carefully first. Daily rates are Rs 25 to 30. The Shanthi Guest House, amongst others, rents them out. It's only a few rupees by bus to nearby Mihintale. Unless you have an all-in ancient cities pass there's a Rs 75 admission charge to the ancient sites for foreigners.

MIHINTALE
Off the Trincomalee road, 11 km from Anuradhapura, this site marks the spot where Mahinda, the son of India's Buddhist Emperor Ashoka, met King Devanampiya Tissa and introduced Buddhism to Sri Lanka. There is a superb stairway up the hill and a series of temples, dagobas and other points of interest.

POLONNARUWA
When Anuradhapura proved too vulnerable to invasion from India the decision was made to shift to this new city. It reached its height in the 12th century AD but after only two centuries it too proved susceptible to invasion and in its turn Polonnaruwa was abandoned. The ruins here are in somewhat better shape than Anuradhapura and are more compactly situated.

Things to See
Rest House Group These ruins are not the most interesting here but the museum is worth a visit.
Royal Palace Group Across the main road from the Rest House Group this group includes the massive ruins of the palace plus other palace building ruins.
Quadrangle Only a short stroll north of the palace group the quadrangle is a compact group of fascinating ruins. They include the Vatadage, a typical 'circular relic house' with fine guardstones, moonstones and Buddha images. There are several other interesting buildings here plus the massive Gal-Potha, a nine-metre-long stone 'book'.

Northern Group The structures in the northern group are much more spread out. They include the Rankot Vihara, largest dagoba in Sri Lanka after the three huge ones at Anuradhapura. Nearby is the Lankatilaka, a huge 'gedige' with cathedral-like walls and the Kiri Vihara, a fine unrestored dagoba. Across the road are four rock-cut images of the Buddha known as the Gal Vihara, they're certainly the high point of Polonnaruwa and amongst the finest Buddha images in the country. Further up the road you come to the Lotus Pond and the Tivanka Image House with a frieze of dwarves cavorting around the outside.
Southern Group Close to the complex of deluxe hotels, reached by a road that runs along the bund of the Topawewa tank, this group contains the unusual Potgul Vihara and the controversial Potgul statue – there is much speculation as to whom it represents.

Places to Stay
In the old town the *Chinese Rest House* has rooms from Rs 50 to 150 and is pretty fair value. Nearby is the *Orchid Rest House* which is similarly priced. Next door the *Samudra Hotel* has rooms from Rs 30 to 75 and has had several recommendations. The *Wijaya Hotel* costs Rs 40 a doubles – big clean rooms. Near the old town post office the *Free Tourist Resort* has clean rooms from Rs 75.

There are a couple of places just off the road to New Town, a half km from the old town. The *Jenica Guest House* is cheap but dirty, *Devi Tourist Home* is similarly priced, it may be better. On the road out of town towards the railway station is the new *Ranketha Guest House* with rooms at Rs 150 to 200. There are a couple of others out this way. Expensive at Rs 275, but as beautifully situated as ever, the *Rest House* is on a promontory by the tank.

Out at No 2 Channel, New Town the *Nimalia Guest House* has doubles from Rs 150 but it's a long way from anywhere.

Right next door is the *Sri Lankan Inns* with rooms at Rs 150/200 and back towards the New Town bus stop is the *Neela Tourist Lodge* at Rs 150/175. Take an 847 bus from the railway station or the bus stop in the old town.

Places to Eat
There's not much choice of places to eat apart from the hotels and guest houses. The Rest House or the Ranketha Guest House are probably your best bets.

Getting There
Polonnaruwa is on the Colombo-Batticaloa road shortly after the junction to Trincomalee. It's about six hours by the day express from Colombo, fares are from Rs 33.80 in 3rd class, Rs 85.20 in 2nd. It's only about an hour and a half from Polonnaruwa to Batticaloa. Buses from Colombo operate via Dambulla. From Kandy the bus fare is Rs 28.

Getting Around
Bikes are the best way of getting around the ancient city ruins. Several paces hire them in the old town area. the bus and train stations are both some distance out of the old town, even further from the new town. Get to them on an 847 local bus. Solo women should be careful when wandering the more remote ruins. Unless you've got an all-in ancient cities pass there is a Rs 75 admission charge for foreigners at Polonnaruwa.

MEDIRIGIRIYA
About 40 km from Polonnaruwa the vatadage here is identical in design and size to the one at Polonnaruwa but is isolated and remote in its location. Getting to Medirigiriya, some distance north of the Polonnaruwa-Anuradhapura road, is a little difficult and time consuming.

DAMBULLA
High in a rock face overlooking the small town of Dambulla are a series of rock-cut temples packed with colourful frescoes and Buddha images. Artistically they are not that special but the view from the caves is very fine, you can see Sigiriya to the north.

Places to Stay
There are a string of places along the road at the base of the hill and more further north at the junction. The *Dambulla Rest House* is pleasant but pricey at Rs 220 for a double. Nearby the *Oasis Tourist Welfare Centre* is very basic (no electricity) but very cheap.

Other low priced places include the *Heley Tourist Inn*, the *Chamara Tourist Inn* and the pink-painted *Number 97*. The *Travellers' Inn* is simple, clean and neat with doubles from Rs 50. Close to the bus stop the *Sena Tourist Inn* is similarly priced and has good food.

Take the turn off towards the police station and directly below the rock, about 400 metres off the main road, is *Freddy's Holiday Inn* – a fine little place with rooms from Rs 50 to 150. Next door is the *Ceylonica Tourist Rest*. If you continue up the main road to the junction the *Rangiri Rest House* is plain and spartan with doubles at Rs 50. The *Sayanora Lodge* is further down, behind the cinema, and is well kept but a little far from anywhere. Rooms cost from Rs 100. Right up at the end of this stretch, at the Mirigoniyama Junction, *The Colony* has cabana-style rooms from Rs 60 and a restaurant.

Getting There
Dambulla is on the main road from Kandy to Anuradhapura, Polonnaruwa or Trincomalee so there are plenty of buses.

SIGIRIYA
This magnificent rock fortress is one of Sri Lanka's 'not to be missed' attractions. At one time it must have been something like a European chateau plonked atop a Sinhalese Ayer's Rock. There are only ruins on top now but the situation is superb and the idea is mind boggling. It

was built 1500 years ago by Kasyapa, as a hideaway from his vengeful half-brother after Kasyapa buried their father alive! The rock is famous for its magnificent wall paintings of the 'Sigiriya damsels'.

Places to Stay

Once again the *Rest House* has a superb location but is pricey at Rs 225 to 275 for a double. The *Nilmini Lodge*, on the right hand side of the road by the ruin's entrance, is very basic but cheap at just Rs 30 to 50 for a double. The *Sigiri Guest House* is equally cheap.

Beyond the rock is the *Ajantha Guest House* with good food and rooms from Rs 50 or the *Susantha Guest House*. At the rather isolated *Apsara Holiday Resort* you can camp or rent a cabin or cabana for Rs 150.

Getting There

Sigiriya is about 10 km off the main Dambulla-Habarana road. There are buses approximately hourly in the morning from Dambulla for Rs 2.50, they are less frequent in the afternoon. There's a bus direct to Sigiriya from Kandy once daily.

OTHER PLACES

Habarana is a central town for all the ancient cities. There's a *Rest House* with rooms at Rs 175/200 and also the pleasant little *Habarana Inn* at Rs 175/250 including breakfast.

The huge standing-Buddha image at Aukana is a bit difficult to get to although there should be a direct bus from Dambulla at 10 am via Kekirawa. You should visit Aukana at dawn as the statue was designed to be illuminated by the first rays of the sun – the name means 'sun eating'.

Yapahuwa and Padnuvasnavara are other lesser-known ancient cities. Aluvihara, between Kandy and Dambulla, is a small complex of cave temples.

East Coast Beaches

The east coast has not been as developed as the west but that is rapidly changing as more resorts open and the number of hotels and guest houses multiply.

TRINCOMALEE

The major east coast port of Trinco was traded back and forth between the European powers before eventually ending with the British and being developed as a major naval base. Fort Frederick occupies a peninsula with Swami Rock at the end of it. It's quite a pleasant town just to stroll around.

Places to Stay

Almost next door to the rest house on Dockyard Rd is the *Beach Paradise* where reasonably clean, if rather spartan and drab, doubles cost from Rs 50. The engagingly named, if very unspecial, *Guest 'Ome* (it used to be the Tourist 'Ome) is a little back off the main road here.

If you carry on another hundred or so metres, keeping close to the waterfront on Dyke St, you come to a string of popular cheap places. They include the *Rainbow Beach Hotel* (tel 026-2365) at 322 Dyke St, a more expensive place (by Dyke St standards) with rooms from Rs 100 to 250, they all have attached bathrooms. There's an open air dining area looking out on to the beach and the food here is very good. Across the road, and with the same owners, is the *Kitsinn Tourist Inn* (tel 026-2568) at 255 – doubles Rs 150.

At 312 the *Chinese Rest House* (tel 026-2455) has a variety of rooms – fairly spartan doubles cost from Rs 60. Almost next door, and also backing on to the beach, is the rather dingy *Travellers' Halt* at 300 Dyke St. There are dorm beds or rooms from Rs 50. Then there's the *Mehila Beach Place*, a travellers' halt place with dorm beds and rooms, at 224. Finally at 210/1 Dyke St you come to *Dyke Corner* with rooms from Rs 80.

More cheapies can be found scattered around town. *Votre Maison* at 45 Green Rd (behind the Nelson Cinema) is signposted from both ends of the road. It's a spartan, basic, sort of place but popular with shoestring travellers. There are dorm beds for Rs 10, singles from Rs 25, doubles from Rs 50 to 60. They do good food, especially seafood, and delicious curd too.

Bavan's Pension, close to the Dyke St places, is another simple place with rooms at Rs 35. They have bicycles to rent and it has been recommended by several people. Also down at this end of town *Mohamed's Place*, opposite the general hospital, has rooms from Rs 30. There's a good little beach nearby.

Back in the centre, close to the bus stand, *Newlands* (tel 026-2668) at 87 Rajavarothayam Rd has rooms from Rs 40 to 75, from Rs 100 to 150 with bathroom. The manager and owner are pleasant people and food, particularly the seafood, at this well run and clean place is particularly good. Several travellers have written to speak highly of Newlands.

The beach places at Uppuveli are no great distance from town – it would be no hardship staying out there and getting into town when necessary.

Places to Eat

There is not a great choice of food places although the *Beach Paradise Hotel* has surprisingly good food in their restaurant including boiled crab which is a real taste treat and an economical one too. There are several Chinese restaurants along Ehamparam Rd; the *Chinese Eastern Restaurant* by the clocktower is cheap and OK.

You can get Chinese food at the *ABCD Chinese Restaurant* or the *Sunlaing Restaurant*. A couple of other places are good for a snack – ice cream and milk shakes in a duo of snack bars on Dockyard Rd towards the bus station (the *Flora Fountain* is the better of the two); good curd and honey at the *Sirasara* store just down from

the ABCD. And plenty of local 'boutiques' for a cheap rice and curry, near the bus station. On the Dockyard Rd side of the junction with Dyke St, near the ABCD, *Miranda's* sells cheap, cold beer.

Getting There

Trains take six to seven hours from Colombo by day, nine hours by night. Fares range from Rs 48.70 in 3rd, Rs 95.10 in 2nd. You can also travel by bus from Colombo, Jaffna, Anuradhapura, Polonnaruwa and Kandy.

Getting Around

It's only a few rupees for the short trip up the coast to Nilaveli. You can rent bicycles to get around Trinco or to ride out to Kanniyai or Uppuveli.

UPPUVELI

The beach stretching from three to six km north of Trinco is a good alternative to staying in the town itself.

Places to Stay

The *Pragash Guest House* at French Gardens has rooms from Rs 100 to 200 and is very close to the beach. The *Shangri La Tourist Beach Inn* is a very pleasant place at the 3rd milepost. The rooms have fans, mosquito nets and bathrooms and there's good seafood available. There are a number of other pleasant guest houses here such as the *Sandpiper* at 16 Murugapuri Avenue, the *Son Tourist Lodge* at 692 Ahambarum Rd or the *TF Tourist Beach House* at 686 Ehamparam Rd.

Getting There

Take an 867 or 900 bus from Trinco – or just walk there along the beach.

NILAVELI

The beautiful beach of Nilaveli stretches for quite a distance, north of Trinco. The village of Nilaveli is around the 9th milepost but the cheaper accommodation is mainly around the 13th. A stay here is mainly for a spell of lazing around and suntan collecting. A little further up the coast at Kuchchaveli there is a small archaeological museum beside the foundations of an ancient temple.

Places to Stay

If you travel right down to the end of Nilaveli and crossed the lagoon bridge, about a hundred metres on your right you come to the two real cheapies – *Trails End* and *Travellers' Halt*. They're both basic and spartan places – no glass in the windows, water from the well, that sort of thing. If you can face that then they are pleasant and relaxed places to drop out for a while. Double rooms are Rs 40. When you cross the bridge you move from Nilaveli to Kumburupiddy although the village of that name is actually a couple of km inland.

There are several more expensive guest houses. The *Isola Bella* is close to the lagoon mouth and has singles/doubles at Rs 150/175. Between here and the more expensive hotel group the *Mauro Inn* (tel Nilaveli 802) has singles/doubles at Rs 250/350. Right by the two large top end hotels the *Nilaveli Surf Club* is pleasant and has good food and attractive rooms.

There are also a handful of places to stay around the 9th and 10th milepost, at this point the road is about a km back from the beach. They include the *Hotel Sea Yard*, the *Beach Retreat*, the *Ann-Marie Lodge*, the *Sunny Sand Beach Inn*, the rather basic *Sea Breeze Inn* and the more expensive *Shahira Hotel*.

At the lagoon mouth, beside the Isola Bella, the *Blue Lagoon Hotel* (tel Nilaveli 26) is more expensive but a great place to stay. There are a few basic economy rooms at Rs 50 or 100 and a number of very comfortable bungalows with shared verandahs at Rs 260. The food here is excellent – big, filling, appetising meals.

Up the coast you can stay at the rock bottom *Shanty* at the 21st milepost or at the *Pirates Roost* beyond the 23rd.

Places to Eat

There are a number of small food stalls and snack bars near the bridge in Nilaveli where you can get delicious vegetable and egg rotis, curd, baked goodies and fruit.

KALKUDAH-PASSEKUDAH

South of Trinco towards Batticaloa this is the major east coast resort development with a fine sweep of sheltered bay and some expensive resort hotels plus a whole string of cheapies. Valachchenai is the nearby bus station and railway station centre for both Passekudah and Kalkudah.

Places to Stay

The cheap places are mainly at Kalkudah rather than Passekudah and are not so conveniently situated for the beach as the Passekudah de-luxe hotels. Prices are very variable with demand and season; from November to March the prices plummet.

Starting from the rest house junction and moving along the main road to Valachchenai places to stay include the *Mala Guest House*, with new rooms at Rs 100 and 125 with attached shower. The *Kalkudah Holiday Resort* is a more expensive place with rooms with attached bathroom at Rs 250 to 300. There are a great number of other guest houses and lodges along the Valachchenai road including the *Shamila*, the *Nanthang Tea Room*, the *Kalkudah Guest House*, the *Yoga Centre*, the *Green Wood Guest House*, *Kalkudah Holiday Homes* and the *Sunnyland Pensione*. The Yoga Centre has been recommended by travelling yoga enthusiasts – there are morning and afternoon yoga sessions and you can join for week courses or go there just for individual sessions.

A dirt road leads off the main road and eventually reaches the *Sun Rise Bay Bungalow* on the riverside – rooms with toilet and shower for Rs 150 for those who want to get away from it all.

Starting from the rest house junction once again, but now following the road towards Batticaloa, you come to another collection of places including *Sandyland*, one of the longest established places at Kalkudah. The cabanas here are good value at Rs 150 to 200 in season. Further along, the *Blue Land Tour Inn* is another pleasant place with rooms as low as Rs 50 and up to Rs 150 with attached bathroom. The atmosphere here is relaxed and the food very good.

The *Seaview Guesthouse* has rooms at Rs 75 to 100. Behind the post office *Mahadevi's Cabanas* is basic (no electricity, water from the well) but friendly, cheap and the food is not only good 'but it's the two-chili tourist variety as opposed to the 20-chili Tamil type'! The *Siloam Guest House* has rooms from Rs 100 to 150 in season – all with fan and attached bathroom. They serve an interesting variety of genuine Sri Lankan food as well as western food. There are numerous other places along the Batticaloa road or there's the *Leguana Club*, down towards the beach.

A paved road leads off the Batticaloa road towards the beach, where you'll find the *Fishing Village – Madawala's Place* with rooms in the Rs 100 to 150 bracket again. In the afternoon you can see the fishermen bring in the catch on the beach here.

There are also several places around the rest house junction – like the *Ashok Land* and *Hotel Flamboyant* with rooms at Rs 150 to 200. The Flamboyant has a shady courtyard/dining area, friendly people run it and produce good food.

Places to Eat

There are a number of good places to eat in Kalkudah including the popular *Goat in the Gutter*, near the rest house junction, which does good breakfasts, snacks and ice cream. On the beach near the rest house *Vitha's* has good food.

Along the road towards Batticaloa, just along from the junction, there are a string of restaurants including *Gopaluta's Hut*, another of Kalkudah's more popular

eating places. The *Seaview Restaurant* in this stretch is also good although the service can be excruciatingly slow.

Getting There

The railway line from Colombo runs through Polonnaruwa and Valachchenai down to Batticaloa, only an hour to the south. From Trincomalee the normal route by bus is inland towards Polonnaruwa, then turning and heading back towards the coast. The seemingly more direct route down the coast is interrupted by a number of ferry crossings. It is a much more interesting route, however. From Trinco you have a 1½ hour ferry crossing to Mutur from where it takes three to four hours by bus (which is ferried across the remaining rivers) to Valachchenai.

If you're coming to Kalkudah by train there is also a small Kalkudah train station which is closer to most of the accommodation than the station in Valachchenai. Similarly if you're travelling from Batticaloa by bus it's worth getting off before you get right into Valachchenai.

BATTICALOA

Midway down the east coast Batticaloa was the first Dutch foothold on the island and in late 1978 bore the brunt of the cyclone that devastated the east coast. Most of the damage has now been repaired although it will be many years before the plantations are regrown. Batticaloa has a local mystery in the form of the 'singing fish' who can be heard in the lagoon on full moon nights.

Places to Stay

Few travellers pause for long in Batti, the greater attractions of Kalkudah and Passekudah are too close to hand. The *Orient Hotel* has rooms from Rs 60 to 100. Directly across from the bus halt, across the river, the small *Jothi's Tour Inn* has very basic roms from Rs 50. Ditto the *Wijayaweena Hotel*. Close to Jothi's, behind the Subaraj Cinema, the *Subaraj Guest House* is similarly priced.

There are *Railway Retiring Rooms* at the station for Rs 110 or cross the railway tracks towards town and turn left away from town to the pleasant *Sunshine Inn* at 118 Bar Rd. Singles are Rs 25, doubles Rs 50 to 100. If you take an 884 bus to the end of Bar Rd, about five km from town, the *Beach House* is a pleasant guest house by the lighthouse. Next door is *East Winds* with similar prices of Rs 50 to 75 for a double with fan.

Getting There

The train trip from Colombo takes 7½ to nine hours. Fares are from Rs 45.50 in 3rd, Rs 112 in 2nd. Buses run north and south of Batticaloa, it's only a couple of hours to Polonnaruwa.

ARUGAM BAY & POTTUVIL

Further south from Batti this is where the road turns inland for the hill country or skirts around the Yala wildlife reserve to rejoin the coast at Hambantota. Pottuvil is a dreary little town where the buses halt and Arugam Bay, with its beautiful beach, is a couple of km south. All the accommodation is down at Arugam Bay.

Places to Stay

There are a handful of places to stay on the Pottuvil side of the Arugam lagoon mouth and great number on the other side. Starting on the Pottuvil side there's the *Cuckoo's Nest Rest House* with basic cabana-style accommodation at Rs 15 and rooms with bath at Rs 150. Right next door is the very comfortable *Arugam Bay Rest House* which has doubles at Rs 150. Another hundred metres down towards the lagoon mouth is *Sea Sands* (tel 067-7372), right by the beach with rooms in the Rs 125 to 200 range.

Still on the Pottuvil side of the lagoon mouth, but on the lagoon side of the road rather than the sea side, is *Crystal Isle*, by the bridge. Here rooms cost Rs 100 or Rs 150 with attached bathroom. Meals are also available. A bit further back towards Pottuvil is the friendly *Crosswinds Tourist Inn*, where rooms are also Rs 150. Good meals here.

Cross the bridge over the lagoon mouth to the Arugam Bay fishing village and you'll come to a whole series of accommodation possibilities – many of them very cheap. A couple of years ago you could rent rooms off the fishermen and many of the places to stay are still of that nature – basic little *kachan* (palm leaf) cabanas with prices down to less than Rs 50 a night. An example is the *Golden Beach Hotel*, at the northern end, with spartan cabanas, good food and rock bottom prices.

Other places include the beachfront *Meezan Beach Hotel* where reasonable doubles with bath are Rs 150. Also on the beachfront the *Mermaid Village* has rooms at Rs 75. On the lagoon side of the road the attractive *Hideaway* has rooms upstairs at Rs 150 or a series of very pleasant little cottages with bathroom and verandah for Rs 200. On the same side is *Sooriya's Beach Hut*, basic little cabanas but a number of travellers have spoken very highly of this place. It's run by brothers and is very well kept.

Continuing along the road you'll find the *Jez Look Holiday Cottages*, related to the popular Jez Look in Matara on the east coast. The comfortable rooms here cost Rs 150/225 for singles/doubles including all meals. Right up at the north end of the village, and rather a long way back from the beach, the *Palm Groove Holiday Inn* has pleasant rooms, each with bathroom and verandah, at Rs 200.

Places to Eat

Sooriya's is said to have very good vegetarian food and the *Beach Hut* has good food including muesli with curd. *Fishing Net* is a popular new place with a three-course meal for Rs 30 or there's *Golden Sands* or the rather fly-ridden *Rupa's Restaurant*.

Getting There

It's 107 km from Batticaloa to Pottuvil

and a fair number of buses make the trip each day. From Pottuvil you can catch buses to Badulla in the hill country or to Wellawaya from where you turn south to Hambantota. There are local buses running from Pottuvil to Arugam Bay and on to Panama.

Jaffna & the North

The least visited region of Sri Lanka, the north is much drier than the rest of the country and is also the centre for much of the country's Tamil population. People visiting the north generally either go to the Jaffna peninsula or to the island of Mannar, from where the ferries run to India. Because of the continuing unrest in this region few people take the risk.

JAFFNA

The Jaffna region is low-lying and dotted with lagoons. There are a number of interesting islands off shore. Once the site of an independent Tamil kingdom, Jaffna was the last stronghold of the Portuguese and fell to the Dutch in 1658. There are the remains of two Portuguese and three Dutch forts to be seen in and around Jaffna. The main one is in Jaffna itself, built by the Dutch in 1680 the Jaffna Fort is particularly well preserved. The old Dutch church inside the fort is open Monday to Friday and there is an interesting little archaeological museum.

Places to Stay

There are *Railway Retiring Rooms*, the somewhat mosquito-infested *Grand Hotel* (which is very cheap) and other cheap hotels like the *Paradaise Hotel* in the middle of town or the *Kumaran Tourist Inn* at 67 Stanley Rd. The *YMCA* is open to men only. The *Rest House* is not very good. The *Brodie Guest House*, at 4 Brodie Lane, near the 317 km post on the main road, is a little pricier at Rs 75 for a single but an excellent place to stay.

Places to Eat

There are quite a few places to eat, particularly around the market and bus station area. Try the *Subhas Cafe* which also has good ice cream. Or *Ricoh*, a couple of doors down. In the market look for Jaffna's famous mangoes.

Getting There

The regular trains take 7½ to 11 hours from Colombo with fares from Rs 51.50 in 3rd, Rs 126.80 in 2nd. The three times weekly Inter-City Express takes just 6½ hours and costs Rs 51 from Colombo. There are also buses including from Colombo and Trincomalee. The trains go via Anuradhapura.

AROUND THE PENINSULA

The Jaffna peninsula is notable for its tidal wells which rise and fall, though out of harmony with the tides. The beaches here are undeveloped in the resort sense. Three of the main islands are joined to the mainland by peninsula and you can take ferries out to other islands like Delft.

Wildlife Parks

Sri Lanka has a number of interesting wildlife parks where you can see much local animal and birdlife – particularly elephants and leopards. The two main parks are Wilpattu and Yala.

Close to Anuradhapura, the Wilpattu park is the one where you have the best chance of spotting a leopard. You want to get there as close to dawn as possible. There is a Rs 50 admission charge to the park and then you can either travel by minibus for Rs 150 per person (6.30 am and 2.30 to 3 pm departures) or rent a jeep at Rs 125 per person but with a minimum charge of Rs 500. There is a bus to the park twice daily from Anuradhapura.

Yala is down at the south-east corner of the island and visits are usually made from Tissamaharama, 25 km away. Again there's an admission charge to the park and you have a choice of a seat in the government safari bus or getting a group together for a jeep.

There are a number of other parks including Gal Oya and Lahugala, near Pottuvil, which often has a very large elephant population.

Turkey

Some people love Turkey, some people hate it – it is undeniably the go-either-way country on the overland trip. I'm willing to bet that the travellers who dislike it most are the ones who spend the shortest time there. It is far more than Istanbul and a long haul across Anatolia to or from Iran. Spend some time in Cappadocia in the south, explore the beautiful Mediterranean coast, get into the delicious Turkish food and you too will be looking forward to your next visit. The Turks can be a little heavy at times, particularly in the east, but if you have a smooth trip this is one country you can't get enough of.

HISTORY

Traces of early Turkish people have been dated right back to the 6th millenium BC but the earliest known Turkish civilisation was that of the Hittites. Long believed to be a purely mythical people they actually had power over much of Anatolia, Asian Turkey, from 2000 to 1200 BC. You can gauge the power of their culture from the stupendous size of their ruined capital city of Hattuşaş. It is only a short distance off the road between Ankara and Samsun on the Black Sea coast.

After the collapse of the Hittites, Turkey broke up into a number of small states and not until the Graeco-Roman period were parts of the country reunited. Later Christianity spread through Turkey, carried by people such as Paul the Apostle, who operated from Tarsus in southern Turkey.

In 330 AD the Emperor Constantine transferred the capital of the Roman Empire to Byzantium, modern Istanbul. He renamed this strategic city Constantinople and for a thousand years it was the centre of the Byzantine Empire. During the European dark ages, as Greece and its culture became just a memory and as Rome was overrun by the barbarians, Byzantine kept alive the flame of their culture. At times it was threatened by the same barbarian hordes and on one occasion the Crusaders, looking for easier prey than Jerusalem, took and sacked the city, but still Byzantine stumbled on as the government became increasingly confused and entangled in webs of intrigue.

The end of the now decrepit empire was spelt by the rise of the Muslim Arab states and the arrival of the Turkish people from the east. Adopting Islam as they moved west the first great Turkish empire of the Seljuks soon pressed the Byzantines back until they were little more than a city-state. The Seljuks were followed by the Ottoman Turks and in 1452 Constantinople fell to Mehmet the Conqueror. It's strange to consider that this last outpost of the Roman Empire lasted until little more than 500 years ago, only 40 years before Columbus sailed to America.

Constantinople, once more the capital of a mighty empire, went through a new golden period as magnificent mosques and palaces were constructed. Less than 200 years later, under Süleyman the Magnificent, the Ottoman Empire had spread far into Europe. The Janissaries, the first modern standing army, gave the Turks a military power unknown amongst the European nations who had to raise an army from scratch each time a war started. The Turks also treated minority groups, including Christians and Jews, with some consideration, but decline soon set it.

The Ottoman success was based on expansion – not industry or agriculture. When their march westwards was abruptly halted at Vienna in 1683 the rot started and Turkey quickly became the 'sick man' of Europe. A procession of incompetent and ineffective sultans hardly helped matters; especially when combined with scheming in the harem and discontent

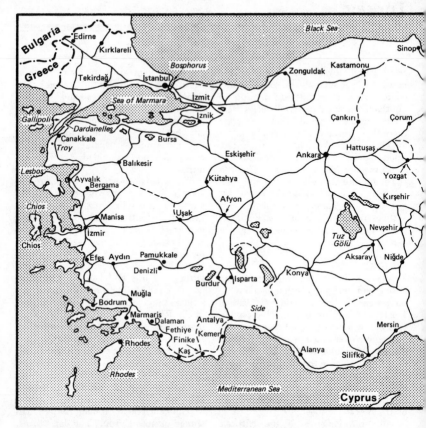

amongst the now totally unreliable Janissaries.

As the nationalist ideal swept through Europe, after the French revolution, Turkey found itself with unruly possessions in the Balkans and Greece. Harsh attempts to crush the popular risings with cruelty only hastened the decline. In 1829 the Greeks won their independence followed by the Serbians, Rumanians and Bulgarians in 1878. Italy took Tripolitania in North Africa from Turkey in 1911 and Albania and Macedonia escaped after the 1912-13 Balkan War. Finally the unfortunate Turks picked the wrong side in WW I and emerged stripped of their final possessions – Syria, Palestine, Mesopotamia (Iraq) and Arabia.

At this low point of Turkish history Mustafa Kemal, the father of modern Turkey, came to the fore. Atatürk, as he chose to be called, had made his name by repelling the Anzacs in their futile and wasteful attempt to capture Gallipoli. Turkey at this time was about to be chopped up and parcelled out amongst the victorious allies, but when it was suggested that even the Greeks should get a slice things had gone too far. Rallying the tattered remnants of the army he pushed the final weak Ottoman rulers to one side and out-manoeuvred the allied forces.

Unhappily the conflict with the Greek invaders was a bloody affair and after a massacre at Smyrna – a predominantly Greek city on the Mediterranean coast of Turkey, today known as İzmir – an exchange of populations took place similar to that in India at the time of the India-Pakistan partition. Well over a million Greeks left Turkey and nearly a half million Turks returned. Relations with Greece have never been good since that time.

With Turkey reduced to smaller, but secure, boundaries Atatürk then proceeded on a rapid modernisation programme, the essence of which was the separation of

religion from politics, introduction of the western alphabet and western dress, and moving the capital from European Istanbul (the name change from Constantinople was another Atatürk innovation) to Asian Ankara. Naturally such sweeping changes did not come easily, progress has been slow and much of the country is still desperately poor although Atatürk remains very much the symbol of modern Turkey.

Turkey is also hampered by its strategic position and importance to both the major powers. Periodic confrontations with Greece, most recently over the still stalemated Cyprus conflict, also have their cost. Turkey also made a very poor recovery from the oil crisis of the early '70s and at times teetered on the brink of bankruptcy. As the '70s wore on Turkey became more and more unstable politically and was wracked by left-right conflict, mob violence and terrorism, all spurred on by the shocking economic situation with high unemployment and galloping inflation. Finally, to almost nobody's surprise, the often reluctant military kicked out the hopelessly inept civilian government in 1980. Strong government and less internal conflict does seem to have got the country back on the straight and narrow and Turkey is once more a popular destination for travellers.

FACTS

Population The population of Turkey is approximately 45 million. The four major cities are Istanbul (2.5 million), Ankara (1.7 million), Adana (.47 million) and Bursa (.35 million). Ankara, centrally located in Asian Turkey, is the capital.

Geography Turkey is divided into Asian and European parts by the Dardanelles, the Sea of Marmara and the Bosphorus. Thrace, European Turkey, comprises only 3% of the total 780,000 square km land area. The remaining 97% is Anatolia, a vast plateau rising towards the Russian steppes in the east. The coastline of Turkey is over 7000 km long and rapidly becoming a popular resort area.

Economy Turkey is still primarily an agricultural country although chrome is an important export and there is some other mining. Sheep are the main livestock and Turkey is the biggest wool producer in Europe. There is still a large Turkish work force in the industries of Europe, particularly Germany.

Religion Turkey is almost 100% Muslim, but due to the efforts of Atatürk, religion and government is not so tightly intertwined as in other Muslim states and the religious attitudes are not so oppressive.

INFO

There are a number of tourist offices in Istanbul, none of which are particularly knockout. They do have excellent regional brochures though. The local offices around the country are often rather more helpful. In Istanbul the main one is in the Hilton Hotel arcade in Taksim. You can find other, lesser, ones at the Sirkeci Railway Station, across from the Pudding Shop in Sultanahmet and at the airport.

BOOKS

Our much delayed *Turkey – a travel survival kit* is finally available. For an absolutely gripping account of the decline of the Ottoman Empire from its peak under Süleyman the Magnificent read *Lords of the Golden Horn* by Noel Barber. Originally published in 1973 it is available now in paperback. Full of sexual high jinks in the harem, mad bravery on the battlefield and dirty deeds in the palace – a very readable intro to Turkish history.

It's worth getting a guide book to Istanbul if you're going to spend any time and energy exploring the many sights. You'll find *A Guide to Istanbul* by Çelik Gülersoy in many bookshops – also available in French and German. Lots of sly digs at the Greeks! The best map of Istanbul is put out by Hallwag but there are other good ones available if you can't find that.

VISAS

Not required for most nationalities.

MONEY

A\$1	=	350 lirasi (Tl)
US\$1	=	500 lirasi (Tl)
£1	=	700 lirasi (Tl)

Turkish currency is the lira (plural lirasi) which is abbreviated to Tl and divided into 100 kuruş. For the visitor the effect of Turkey's galloping inflation has been tempered by frequent devaluations so you get more Tl for your dollar, pound or whatever. The lira is still falling rapidly despite the firm military rule. In '78 the exchange rate was only around 20 Tl to the

dollar, in '81 it went through the 100 Tl barrier, it's still dropping. Prices are generally quoted in this section in US dollars since that is likely to give you a more stable idea of the real price.

There's no blackmarket to speak of – dealing with those 'change money?' gentlemen is not recommended. It's highly probable to be a rip-off or, even worse, land you in trouble. Changing money can be a hassle since only a certain few banks will exchange travellers' cheques – particularly away from Istanbul. The process can be rather slow and laborious. Greek drachma are practically untouchable so dispose of them first if you're entering from Greece.

CLIMATE

In the west Turkey has a southern European climate and in the east a central Asian one. The weather there comes direct from Siberia; combine it with the altitude and you will know what cold means. Look out for mountains getting snowed under. In Istanbul the summer temperatures average around 28 to 30°C while the winters are not too cold in general – usually above freezing. In Ankara the climate is more extreme – warm and dry in the summer (not as hot as Istanbul) but much colder in the winter. Summer never gets as hot as further east but spring (April & May) and Autumn (September & October) are the pleasant times for a Turkish visit.

ACCOMMODATION

Turkey is well equipped with cheap hotels although the bottom end of the cheap rung is probably too basic for a lot of peoples'

tastes – mine included. The Turkish tourist office puts out a guide to hotels and campsites all over the country. It does indeed cover the whole country but the bottom end of their scale – H4 hotels – is still a bit above the top of mine. You probably won't find any of the places in this book in their brochure. Local tourist offices are helpful though, so make use of them if you can't find anything else.

The very cheap hotels, particularly in eastern Turkey, are simply dormitories where you just get crammed into a room with whoever else fronts up. If you intend to avoid this negotiate a price where you (and yours) have the whole room. Make your point clear or some peasant with a flock of sheep may arrive in your room unexpectedly! Most places are much more civilised and there are also quite a few student hostels or youth hostel places. Along the Mediterranean coast look for pensions (pansiyons) as well as cheap hotels.

If you are travelling east Turkey will be the first placed you consistently run into Asian toilets. Of course you will probably have seen them already, there are still some in France and as you head further and further east, you see more and more Asian-style, fewer and fewer European. After Istanbul they are almost all Asian-style. West bound travellers hit them in Indonesia as soon as they depart from Australia. For the uninitiated an Asian toilet is two footrests with a hole – aim at the hole! You will soon find that squatting to perform your bodily functions is much more natural than our western habit of sitting up and these toilets have another advantage. In countries where facilities (like running water) are not so readily available and the inclination to keep things clean is also somewhat lower than westerners are used to, the Asian toilet is much more sensible. Anyway, when in Rome. From Turkey onwards toilets are often not designed with toilet paper in mind. Rather than chop down trees and process them into toilet paper most

Asians use a jug of water and their left hand. If you are unable to adapt to life in the east to this extent at least use the paper sparingly. There may often be a box in the toilet for dumping used paper – it may look unhealthy but it is better than blocking the loo with paper it wasn't designed to digest.

If you are travelling in a vehicle you will find good camping facilities throughout Turkey. The European-style, well-equipped camp site caught on and even if there should not be one available many garages are only too happy to have you camp on their grounds – if you want that feeling of security. BP petrol stations have a string of BP mocamps throughout the country. The facilities are generally excellent but the prices are often absurdly high – much more than equivalent sites in Europe. If there is an alternative to a BP mocamp, check it out. BP also have some lower standard camps which don't rate their mocamp label and are also lower priced.

FOOD

Turkish food has often been called the French cuisine of Asia and there is more than a little truth in that idle comparison. The food really is knockout. If you've developed a taste for the better known delights of Greek cooking you may find Turkish food rather familiar – and with good reason the Turks will tell you, we taught the Greeks to cook. Ever ready for putting down Greeks they'll go on to tell you how Turkish cooking is much like Greek cooking only less greasy and more refined. I'll let you decide since I like both. But take my word for it, Turkish food is really great and away from the big cities one of the nicest parts of a Turkish meal is the inevitable invitation to pop in to the kitchen and see what's cooking. If you don't know how to ask for what you want, a look really helps.

For plain, ordinary, down to earth Turkish food the basic is *kebap* (kebab). *Shish (şiş) kebap*, lamb grilled on a skewer, is a Turkish invention and still a very popular dish. You'll find *kebapçi*, cafes that specialise in kebaps, almost everywhere and they are very cheap. Also try *döner kebap* – lamb packed onto a vertical revolving spit. Turkish sandwiches are also excellent – meat, salad (especially those tricky little fire-hot green peppers) and shoved into half a loaf of bread!

That's Turkish food plain and simple, but at some point you should try a proper meal which consists of a long procession of small dishes. Known as *meze*, hors d'oeuvres, it usually starts with *soğuk meme* – cold hors d'oeuvres. Such as:

cacık – yoghurt, cucumber & garlic
taramasalata – Turkish caviar, fish roe
piláki – beans vinaigrette
patlıcan tava – fried aubergines
beyaz peynir – white sheep's milk cheese
kabak dolması – stuffed squash or marrow
patlıcan salatası – pureed aubergine salad
yaprak dolma – stuffed grape leaves
fasulye – beans

Dolma are a very popular hors d'oeuvre – all sorts of vegetables (aubergine, peppers, cabbage leaves) are stuffed with rice, currants or pine nuts. Stuffed peppers are very popular but the aubergine (eggplant) is the number one vegetable to the Turks. It can be stuffed (*patlıcan dolması*), served pureed with lamb casserole (*hunkarbegendi*), stuffed with mince meat (*karhiyank*) or appear with exotic names like *imam bayıldı* – 'the priest fainted'. Which means stuffed with tomatoes, onions and garlic. Well might he!

The cold hors d'oeuvres are followed by the hot – the *sıcak meze*. Like:

börek – thin pastry stuffed with meat or cheese
köfte – spiced meatballs
graviyer kroket – fried cheese balls

That's just the starters – now comes the kebaps or fish (in Turkey they are fresh and delicious) or *pilav* – pilafs of cracked wheat (*bulgur*) or rice. Yoghurt is another Turkish specialty which accompanies many dishes or mixed with water makes a refreshing drink known as *ayran*.

At this point I'd be working up my sweet tooth for dessert where the Turks really pull out all the stops. If you've made a few visits to the Pudding Shop in Istanbul you'll soon get the message. Try *sütlaç* – rice pudding, *kazandibi* – baked pudding, *aşure* – fruit & nut pudding (knockout). Or the super sweet pastries like *baklava* – pastry stuffed with nuts and floating in syrup, *tel kadayıf* – shredded wheat with nuts in syrup. Or risk a taste of *kadin göbeği* – lady's navel – or *dilber dudagi* – lips of a beauty!

To wash it down? The best and one of the cheapest beers in Asia – Tuborg. Or good Turkish wine, red or white. Or fierce aniseed *rakı*, like Greek ouzo. Turkish coffee is legendary, a cm of coffee followed by two of sediment. Tea is served in tiny glasses, sweet and without milk. Finally Turkish fruit – terrific again, particularly the melons.

GETTING THERE

There are all sorts of routes and means of getting through Europe to Turkey – you can bus or train it or even stick out your thumb and hitch. Coming from Iran you've got a bus or train choice. Or you can fly – a number of airlines, including Turkish Airlines of course, fly to Turkey from European cities or from Turkey's Asian neighbours.

There's also one out-of-the-ordinary means of getting to Turkey – aboard the Turkish Maritime Lines' Mediterranean services. TML are great value around the Turkish coast and there are other companies who operate Mediterranean routes such as – Brindisi-Patras-Piraeus (Athens)-İzmir or Ancona-İzmir.

GETTING AROUND

With a student card you're eligible for a variety of student discounts in Turkey. On trains it's 10%, THY flights within Turkey

get 10%, On THY flights overseas you can get an amazing 60% discount on flights to Europe (but you must also be under 22). To the Middle East you can get 50% off so long as you're under 25. Turkish Maritime Lines may also have student discounts.

Rail There used to be a three day/four night Istanbul-Tehran train service but that is suspended at present. Fares on Turkish railways are generally somewhat less than by bus but the buses are much faster.

Istanbul has two main stations – Sirkeci on the European side and Haydarpaşa on the Asian side. Take a ferry across the Bosphorus from the Galata Bridge to Haydarpaşa. Student discounts are available on Turkish railways and you do not need a Turkish Student Card. It has been a long term rip-off getting Turkish Student Cards – an international one is all that is required. There are three classes on Turkish railways (TCDD – TC Devlet Demiryolları) and 3rd class is definitely a bit heavy. Unless you are penniless consider investing in 2nd. 1st class seats are booked but on 2nd and 3rd it is first come, first served. The old Istanbul-Tehran service ran to Ankara and then due east to Lake Van where you crossed on a ferry.

From Istanbul to Ankara there are frequent departures and the trip takes from seven hours (express) to 12 hours for the slower services. The *Mari Tren* or 'blue train' is the pride of Turkish railways and very good on the Ankara line. Istanbul-Erzurum takes about 40 hours, even longer if snow delays the train in winter. There is a dining car on the train but food is expensive. There are also services from Ankara south to Adana on the Mediterranean coast or on to Aleppo in Syria or Baghdad in Iraq.

Air Turkish Airlines (THY – Turk Hava Yollari) connect internationally and have a fairly extensive network centred on Istanbul and Ankara. Flights tend to be fairly crowded, sometimes overbooked – so be prepared to use your elbows. Safety isn't something THY is renowned for.

Bus Bus services around Turkey are very comprehensive, pretty cheap, fairly frequent and in many ways the best means of getting around the country. The drivers are not all A1 as the sight of the odd upside down bus by the roadside will soon confirm. From Istanbul you can get buses all over the country from the bus station just outside the Topkapı gate – that is the city wall entrance on the road out of Istanbul to Europe.

It's equally easy to get buses for other sectors along the route or, if speed is the name of your game, you can get buses direct between Istanbul and Tehran. In Istanbul there are many bus offices around the Sultanahmet-Pudding Shop area. Heading the other direction, Istanbul to Europe, be cautious. There has been quite a racket going on selling travellers tickets on buses from Istanbul to Munich or even further west when in actual fact the buses do not have licences to cross the German border – the irate passengers get dropped off at the border with no possibility of a refund. The bus companies now claim that they have the necessary paperwork to enter Germany but *caveat emptor*, buyer beware!

If you're crossing Turkey by stages the only place with any complication is around the Iran border. Ağri is the last major town before the border and you can get a bus direct to the border twice a day from Ağri or from Erzurum. Be careful you don't find yourself on a bus which terminates at Doğubayazit, the last small town in Turkey. From the Iran side there are two buses a day direct to Tabriz and Tehran. Alternatively you can walk the couple of km to Bazargan and then bus to Maku and again to Tabriz. The Iranian bus company Mihantour has direct bus services between Erzurum and Tehran.

The weather in the eastern part of Turkey is very cold in winter and it is not unusual for the road to be blocked by snow – particularly the stretch from Erzurum to the border. This also applies to the route through eastern Syria to the Iran border.

Turkish buses are far faster than the trains, often they take only half the time. Since there are no student discounts available they tend to be rather more expensive. They also make their rest stops at fairly expensive cafes so take your own food and drink if you're on a tight budget. In Erzurum the bus station is on the outskirts of town but the ticket offices will provide you with free transport to the station.

Car European insurance companies treat Turkey as part of Europe so if you're heading east your European policy will cover you. There is no requirement for carnets in Turkey but details of your car are stamped in your passport to ensure it leaves the country with you. Mechanical service is reasonably adept in Turkey, particularly in Istanbul where a large variety of different vehicles crowd the streets. Don't have accidents in Turkey – or anywhere else in Asia for that matter.

Boat Turkish Maritime Lines is the great Turkish travel bargain. They operate a number of ships on some really interesting routes. Two routes connect to other European centres – see Getting There. There are two routes to look for around Turkey. The first is the Black Sea route which runs back and forth from Istanbul to Samsun and Trabzon and a number of other Black Sea Ports. It provides an interesting alternative way of travelling between Erzurum in eastern Turkey and Istanbul.

The other route is the Mediterranean coastal line – from Istanbul it runs to İzmir and beyond with a whole procession of stops at ports which include Bodrum, Marmaris, Antalya, Alanya and İskenderun. At most ports the stops are long enough to have a look around, buy food, stretch your legs. There is also a service between

Mersin and Magosa on Cyprus and through the Sea of Marmara.

There are a wide variety of fares depending on the cabin (or lack of it). Meals are generally extra. Students are eligible for a 15% discount as are groups of five or more people. You can score an additional 10% discount for round trips. Most people rate the boats as fairly well kept and comfortable although there seem to be occasions when the standards fall down. Deck class is called *guverte*. Tourist A is the most expensive tourist class, generally two or three times the cheapest tourist class. First class is about half as much again.

Sea of Marmara If you are travelling around the Turkish Mediterranean coast the TML services through the Sea of Marmara are a convenient way to travel between Istanbul and the Dardanelles where the Sea of Marmara enters the Mediterranean. Boats run from Istanbul to Gallipoli (Gelibolu) and Çanakkale, near the site of Troy. There are also ferries across the straits between Eceabat on the European side and Çanakkale on the Asian side.

Greek Islands & Cyprus It's indicative of the state of relations between Turkey and Greece that the fares out from the coast to the Greek islands are much more expensive than TML's coastal fares or the fares from Athens to the islands, even though the distances are far far shorter. From Mersin to Magosa on Cyprus there are overnight ferries twice a week in winter, three times in summer. There are also other services to Cyprus from Taşucu and Alanya to Girne. Other Greek island services include Marmaris-Rhodes daily, Dikili-Mytileni (Lesbos), Çeşme-Chios daily, Kuşadasi-Samos is also daily, Bodrum-Kos is weekly.

Mediterranean Route The Mediterranean service departs Istanbul on Wednesdays, arrives at İskenderun on the following Monday then leaves the same day for Istanbul where it arrives on Sunday.

Sailing is almost all by night with days spent in port.

Black Sea Route Don't take this trip in winter when it can get very cold. There is a tourist service and also an express service which stops at fewer ports. Departures are Tuesdays and Saturdays from Istanbul, arriving in Trabzon on Thursday and Monday respectively. Returning the ships depart Trabzon on Fridays and Tuesdays and arrive Istanbul on Sunday or Thursday.

ROUTES

There are three main routes across Turkey – north, central and south. The central is the simplest, most direct, fastest and possibly least interesting. From Istanbul you head south-east to Ankara on good modern roads all the way. From Ankara the route runs more or less directly east. Although there are some bad stretches the worst part is between Erzurum and Ağri – shortly before the Iranian border. The road winds up and over a high mountain pass which can be snowbound in winter.

The northern route is a little more interesting and not very much further. From Istanbul it takes the same path to Ankara, then turns up to the Black Sea Coast at Samsun, runs along the coast to Trabzon and then turns south again to intersect the central route before Erzurum. Although there is some unsurfaced road heading out from Trabzon it is quite OK. Going this way you can visit the Hittite capital of Hattuşaş, see the Black Sea coast and explore the cliff face monastery of Sumela.

The southern route is a less well-beaten track and offers much more off the route possibilities. A possible path is to head south from Ankara to Kayseri and the Göreme area then east through Eláziğ to Van. Here you can turn north and meet the other routes at Ağri or south to a smaller crossing into Iran. Or you could take a still further south route through Turkey which runs east all the way from Adana on the coast. You can also go south into Syria and travel through the Middle East down to the Gulf.

Whichever route you take across Turkey, there are two parts of the country not to be missed. One is Göreme in the Cappadocia region south of Ankara. If you travel on the northern or central route divert to this fascinating area. The second part is, of course, the Mediterranean coast with its delightful little ports and engrossing Greek and Roman ruins. It is a long trip from Istanbul to Ankara via the coast but if you can invest the time you won't regret it.

The Turkey-Iran border crossing is a long and often rather hassling experience. Relations between the Turks and Iranians here are none too good and Iranians have to put up with particularly long waits at the border. Make sure your cholera shots, etc are up to date or you'll get more on the spot!

THINGS TO BUY

The covered bazaar in Istanbul may have become a bit of a tourist trap and a number of rebuilds following fires has more or less completely taken away the old eastern flavour, but it remains one of the largest and most varied bazaars in Asia. You'll get a good impression of what is available from all over Turkey in this one location but you may find it worth looking in the various regional centres. Strenuous bargaining is, of course, the order of the day. Clothes, jewellery, handicrafts, leatherware, some good carpets from the Konya area, even brassware, are all Turkish buys.

LANGUAGE

Until Atatürk embarked on his modernisation programme Turkish was written in Arabic script. Conversion to western script was sensibly done phonetically so it is reasonably easy to pronounce Turkish words, once you've learnt a few important differences!

cedillas – those little bottom strokes of a 5 often appear under c or s – it means pronounce it like a ch or sh – thus ç is like church or ş is like shoe
i can be dotted (pronounced ee) or undotted (pronounced uh), a dotted capital I is written Í
c is pronounced like a j or a soft g
g is pronounced hard, gun not gem
ğ this is the soft g which is not pronounced but it lengthens the preceding vowel
ö and ü are pronounced like similar German letters with pursed lips

In main centres English is fairly widely spoken and due to the many Turks who work in Europe you'll also find German and some French. A few words:

hello	*merhabah*
good morning	*günaydín*
goodbye (to one going)	*güle güle*
goodbye (to one staying)	*allaha ısmarladik*
thank you	*teşekkür ederim*
how much?	*kaç?*
where/when?	*nerede/ne zaman?*
expensive	*pahalı*
this/that	*bu/şu*
yes/no	*evet/hayir*
bread	*ekmek*
butter	*terayağí*
water	*su*
tea	*çay*
bus	*otobüs*
hotel	*otel*
train	*tren*
station	*ístasyon*
I don't understand	*anlamiyorun*

1	*bir*	8	*sekiz*
2	*iki*	9	*dokuz*
3	*üç*	10	*on*
4	*dort*	20	*yirmi*
5	*beş*	30	*otuz*
6	*alti*	100	*yüz*
7	*yedi*		

Istanbul

Istanbul is a treasure trove of places and things to see – after a day of wandering around mosques, ruins, walls, aqueducts and tangled streets where empires have risen and fallen, you'll realise how the description 'Byzantine' came about. Istanbul is undoubtedly one of the most historic cities in the world – simply listing its changing names sounds like a history lesson – Constantinople, Byzantium, Stamboul, Istanbul. Nor should it be forgotten that it was here, little over 500 years ago, that the final fragment of the Roman Empire eventually crumbled. Or that through the European dark ages this was the city which carried European civilisation on from its Greek and Roman origins.

In the centuries before Christ, Byzantium had already been a thriving city, perched as it was on the contact point between Asia and Europe. Already it was a city in a state of continuous flux – pushed from one side by the Persians then from another by the Greeks. In the late 2nd century AD Rome conquered Byzantium and in 325 AD the Emperor Constantine began to turn it into his capital – in 330 the capital of the empire was transferred from Rome. For the next thousand year it was the site of an almost continuous struggle both with the enemy without and between factions within. The city walls, extended time after time as the city grew, kept out barbarians for century after century as the western part of the Roman Empire collapsed before Goths, Vandals and Huns.

When Byzantium did first fall it was not to the infidel hordes but to the 4th Crusade. The Crusaders had always been more intent on pillage than liberation and when Jerusalem proved too hard a task their attention was turned to easier prey. The city fell in 1204 after a prolonged siege and the Crusaders ravaged the churches, shipped out the art, melted down the silver and gold. Prior to this invasion Byzantium had enjoyed four relatively peaceful centuries but when the Byzantines regained the city in 1261 it was only a shadow of its former glory. The next two centuries were a story of decline and decay. Indeed the city was sometimes overshadowed by the Venetian and Genoese trading colonies which operated from the Golden Horn and were often far more powerful and rich. Their own squabbles only added to the general instability.

Now Byzantium was besieged by the Ottoman Turks who had been gaining strength from the east for centuries. In 1314 they actually reached the walls of the city but withdrew. In the 1400s the Ottomans were delayed in their conquest for another 50 years by the threat from Timur and his Mongols in the east. Finally in 1453, after a long and bitter siege, the walls were breached and Mehmet II, the Conqueror, marched to St Sophia and converted the church to a mosque. The Byzantine era had ended.

As capital of the Ottoman Empire the city entered a new golden age with many new buildings and mosques. Although it was no longer besieged by hostile neighbours, the city once again started to decline as the Ottoman Empire became the 'sick man' of Europe. After WW I it seemed certain that the Turkish state would collapse until Atatürk rallied support. In 1923 the capital of the new Turkey was transferred to Ankara and in 1930 the city's name was changed from Constantinople to Istanbul.

Information

The tourist office opposite the Pudding Shop in Sultanahmet is open from 9 am to 9 pm daily. There are a number of other offices including one in the Hilton Hotel Arcade and one at the airport. The student office is on the 7th floor, Halaskargazi Caddesi 219/3. Apart from travel discounts your student card also gets you reduced admission charges to some museums and archaeological sites in Turkey.

Orientation

Istanbul is divided into three parts. It straddles the Bosphorus which separates Europe from Asia so first there is Asian Istanbul and European Istanbul. European Istanbul is further divided by the historic inlet known as the Golden Horn into new Istanbul and old Stamboul. It is in this old part of town where you will find many of the historic attractions and most of the cheap hotels and good restaurants.

Old Stamboul is a neatly packaged area – bounded on three sides by water (the Golden Horn, the Bosphorus and the Sea of Marmara), the fourth boundary is the old wall which runs from the Golden Horn clear across to the Sea of Marmara.

It is worth learning the locations of the major regions of Istanbul since most of the transport (taxis and minibuses) operate by simply shouting out the destinations. Millet Caddesi which runs through the centre of old Stamboul like a spine is the entrance for most travellers from Europe. It passes through the city wall at a place known as Topkapi (not to be confused with the Topkapi Palace). There is a major bus marshalling area just outside the Topkapi gates. Half-way into town the road passes through a major interchange known as Aksaray – the road to the left runs across the Atatürk bridge into new Istanbul. Further on the name changes to Divan Yolu Caddesi and it passes by the covered bazaar (Kapali Çarşi) and ends at Sultanahmet – the cheap hotel and restaurant area and location of many of the interesting sights. North of Sultanahmet is Sirkeci, where the rail line terminates close to the Galata Bridge across the Golden Horn to new Istanbul. Many of the Bosphorus ferries run from around the Galata Bridge.

By most standards Istanbul is pretty old but the new shops and buildings can be found here, especially along İstiklal Caddesi which terminates in Taksim Square in the big hotel and airline office area known as Taksim. The Şişhane air terminal is back from Taksim towards the old town. The Bosphorus Straits bridge is further north.

Things to See

Dotted along the side of the Bosphorus, north from Istanbul towards the Black Sea, are many small villages that act as dormitory suburbs. There are also a number of islands in the Sea of Marmara – popular as weekend holiday spots. Asian Istanbul is not of particular interest except for watching the sun set over the minaretted skyline of the European side.

Many of the most interesting places in Istanbul are concentrated in the Sultanahmet area, only a short walk from the cheap hotels. But first it is worth visiting the city walls; on both sides of which so much of the city's history took place:

City Walls Stretching for over six km from the Golden Horn to the Sea of Marmara, the walls in their present form date back to about 420 AD. They are still in remarkably good shape considering the goings-on they've witnessed. The inner wall was about 10-metres high and separated from the lower, outer wall by a 20-metre-wide ditch. You can walk along the outer wall and muse on the armies with their battering rams down below and the defenders pouring the old boiling oil on them. Or the terrible effects of 'Greek Fire', an early version of napalm.

Aya Sophia The church of St Sophia was commenced under the Emperor Justinian in 532 AD with the intention of building the finest church in the world. Five years later when the Emperor first entered his completed masterpiece, stunned by his own work, he spoke the immortal words, 'Oh Solomon, I have surpassed thee!'

It was indeed a pretty fine piece of work and on a colossal scale. Today only the far newer St Paul's in London, St Peter's in Rome and the Milan Duomo are larger cathedrals. The interior is the building's true magnificence – stunning even today, it must have been overwhelming centuries

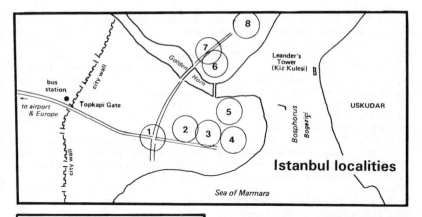

Istanbul localities

1	Aksaray
2	Beyazit
3	Cağoloğlu
4	Sultanahmet
5	Sirkeci
6	Galata
7	Sishane
8	Taksim

ago when it was covered in gilded mosaics. St Sophia has survived but the centuries have not always been kind to it. Earthquakes have damaged it and subsidence has rippled the floor and tilted the columns. If you look up at the huge dome, its perimeter is marked on the floor by metal crosses, you'll see that it is no longer perfectly circular – one side is of greater diameter than the other.

Climb up to the gallery and look down at the scene below. You will also find some of the finest mosaics up there. After the Turkish conquest many of the mosaics were covered over and not revealed again until Atatürk had the building converted into a museum in the 1930s. The minarets were, of course, added after St Sophia's conversion to a mosque.

Overlooking the main entrance to St Sophia is a fine mosaic showing the Virgin and Child with Constantine on one side holding his city, Justinian on the other holding the church. To me the most

'shiver up the spine' part of St Sophia is a simple thing. The central nave is reached by seven doors, the central and largest one was reserved for the emperor. On each side of this door you can see depressions in this stone – worn down by the guards. Somehow stone worn away by centuries of pilgrims and later tourists' feet seems quite probable and acceptable. But two guards!

The Blue Mosque The Sultanahmet or Blue Mosque was built between 1609 and 1619 and stands across the square from St Sophia. It is somehow light and delicate in comparison to the squat massiveness of St Sophia. The exterior is notable for having six slender minarets but it is inside where you will find the blue – a luminous overall impression created by the tiled walls. You're expected to make a small donation to visit the mosque – and leave your shoes outside. One of Istanbul's finest views can be seen from the park in front of the Blue Mosque. Each evening it looms in black silhouette as the sun sinks down behind it. There is a 'son et lumiere' in the evenings – different nights, different languages.

The Hippodrome Beside the Blue Mosque is the site of the Hippodrome where the chariot races and all those other Roman activities took place. Construction started in 203 AD, it was later enlarged by Constantine but only three columns remain.

The obelisk of Theodosius is an Egyptian column from the temple of Karnak, resting on a Byzantine base. The perfectly clear hieroglyphs are nearly 3500 years old. The 10-metre-high column of Constantine Porphyrogenetus was once covered in bronze (the Crusaders stole the bronze) – the base rests at the former level of the Hippodrome, now several metres below the ground line. Between these two columns is the remains of a column of intertwined snakes. Erected at Delphi by the Greeks to celebrate their victory over the Persians it was later transported to the Hippodrome.

These few traces in no way indicate the size and splendour of this arena. The Imperial Box of the emperor once looked out on the track from close to the Egyptian column. He had a passage back to his palace for use when the unruly mob became too unruly. Which from time to time they did in a fashion which would make a British soccer riot look passe. In 532 a rebellion against the emperor broke out in the stadium and 40,000 spectators were 'put to the sword'.

The Mosaic Museum If you admired the mosaics in St Sophia then pop round behind the Blue Mosque and visit the mosaics museum with its old bazaar street and fine mosaic palace floors. The stones are all naturally coloured.

Cistern Basilica Just round the corner from the Pudding Shop is a small building which is the entrance to the underground cistern known as Yerebatan. Built by Constantine and later enlarged by Justinian this vast, columned water tank held water not only for regular summer use but also for times of siege. When the revolting Janissaries revolted once too often and a sultan decided to have done with them for once and all their last survivors took refuge here but were overpowered and slaughtered.

Topkapi Seraglio Situated behind St Sophia and bordered by the Bosphorus, this was the palace of the sultans from 1462 until they transferred to the Dol-

mabahçe Palace, across the Golden Horn, during the last century. Topkapi is not just a palace but a whole collection of gardens, houses, libraries and, of course, the harem. You enter through the Imperial Gate and on the left is St Irene – the first church built in the city by the Byzantines. On the right in the central courtyard is a map indicating the main parts of the complex.

Amongst the things to be seen is the jewel collection in the treasury where you'll also find a not unexpected footprint and hair from the beard of the prophet and the perhaps less expected right arm (well most of it) of John the Baptist. Out front there's a spectacular view of the Bosphorus. If you know where to look you can also find the executioners block and the place where those unlucky heads were hung for public inspection (and warning).

Not to be missed is the tour of the harem, which you'll probably find a rather dull, cold place – not at all like the fantasy picture we tend to have. Life was pretty boring for the odalisques (ladies of the harem) sitting around waiting for the sultan to 'pleasure' them. They were strictly guarded by the harem eunuchs and, as a visitor from Venice reported:

it is not lawful for any one to bring ought in unto them, with which they may commit deeds of beastly uncleanesse; so that if they have a will to eate Cucumbers, they are sent in unto them sliced, so to deprive them of the meanes of playing the wantons.

There are three museums in the old palace gardens. The Archaeological Museum has a collection of classical art work and the sarcophagus (stone coffin) of Alexander the Great. The Museum of the Ancient Orient is dedicated to the pre-Islamic and pre-Byzantine civilisations. The Cinili Kiosk or tiled pavilion has an exhibition of tilework and mementoes of Sultan Mehmet the Conqueror.

The Burnt Column If you walk up Divan Yolu Caddesi from Sultanahmet towards the bazaar you pass the column of

Theodosius II. During a storm in 1105 his statue toppled off the top, killing several people sheltering below. In 1779 the column was badly damaged by a fire and subsequently strengthened with the iron hoops you can see today.

The Grand Bazaar The bazaar (Kepali Çarşi) is a labyrinth of passages and paths but compared to bazaars further east it's a relatively tame, antiseptic place. Most of the old stalls have been converted into modern, glassed-in shops. Still it is an enjoyable place to wander around and get lost in. Which you certainly will. The bazaar is divided into areas – carpets, jewellery, clothing, silverware and so on. At one place in the bazaar you can find a small shop with a spiral staircase to the roof from which you can get an aerial view of a small part of the bazaar.

Beyazıt Square Between the bazaar and the Beyazıt Square in front of the university is the old book market with many stalls selling secondhand books. Beyazıt was the son of Mehmet the Conqueror and his graceful mosque looks out on to the square. The university also has its imposing entrance on the square, it has frequently been the site of violent student protests. Inside the university grounds is the Tower of Beyazıt which, if it is open, you can climb to the top of for a fine view over the city. Like the Galata Tower across the Golden Horn it has been used as a fire lookout point. Many of Istanbul's buildings were once wooden and fires were frequent and disastrous although you can still find many old streets of wooden buildings.

Süleymaniye Mosque Behind the university is the mosque which many consider to be the finest in Istanbul. Construction was completed in 1557 and its designer, Sinan, was rated the architectural genius of his century. He personally thought his Selimiye mosque in Edirne was an even greater achievement. The terrace of the mosque provides another good viewpoint over the city because regulations have been passed prohibiting buildings blocking the view of the mosque. Sinan's mausoleum can be found close to the mosque – 'he wished to sign his great work humbly, in the margin'. The Museum of Turkish & Islamic Art is close to the mosque.

The Aqueduct of Valens This huge Roman-style aqueduct was built in 368 AD to bring water into the city – it straddles the road from Aksaray to the Atatürk Bridge.

Other Old Istanbul has many other attractions and fine mosques. If you wander down the narrow, winding streets behind the Süleymaniye Mosque you'll eventually find the small, fragrant spice bazaar, the Yeni Mosque and then the Golden Horn. This historic stretch of water is a constant hive of activity with ferries and boats churning back and forth. The Eyüp Mosque, Istanbul's most religiously significant, is on the old city side of the Horn, outside the walls.

The Galata Bridge The floating bridge crossing the Golden Horn only dates back to 1912 although there were earlier wooden bridges in the last century. It carries a constant stream of vehicular and pedestrian traffic and serves as the landing point for many ferries. Around the bridge, fishermen sell fresh fish and on the lower level are cafes where you can sip tea and watch the activity.

The Galata Tower It's uncertain when the tower was first built although its present form probably dates back to 1216 when this area was a Genoese trading colony. Later it served as a prison, an observatory, then a fire-lookout tower before it was burnt out itself in 1835. In 1967 it was completely restored and turned into a restaurant and night club. Find the straightfaced sign which announces that during the 17th century an intrepid local birdman launched himself from the top and made the first inter-continental flight clear across to Asian Istanbul.

Taksim This is the modern centre of Istanbul close to the big hotels and airline offices. It's also a major dolmuş and bus station. İstiklal Caddesi is the main shopping street in this area.

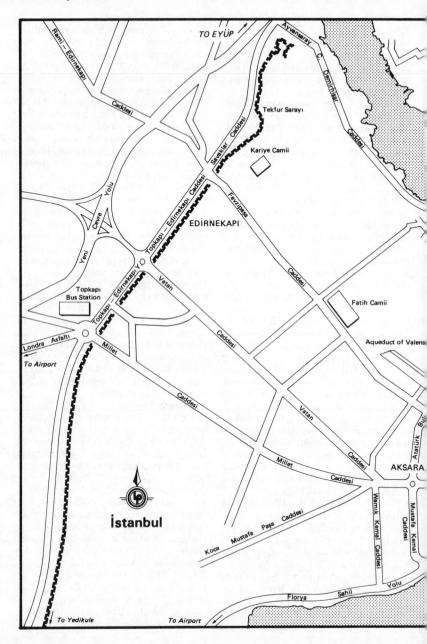

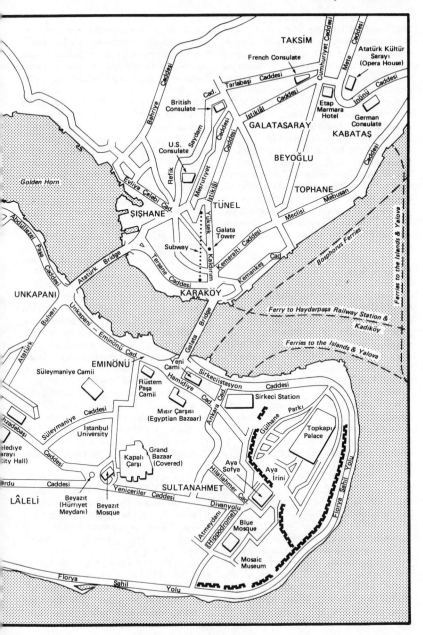

The Tower of Leander The tower in the Bosphorus close to the Asian side is known to the Turks as the Kız Kulesi, 'tower of the virgin'. The accompanying legend tells that a sultan kept his daughter there to prevent her predicted death from a snake bite. The snake duly arrived at the tower in a basket of grapes.

Üsküdar The Asian part of Istanbul is interesting for its many old wooden buildings and for the fine views back to European Istanbul, particularly at sunset.

The Islands Once the site of monasteries and a haven for pirates, the string of islands known as the Princes Isles are a popular weekend and summer getaway for local residents. They make a pleasant escape from the noise and hustle of Istanbul.

Places to Stay

Istanbul's real cheapies are mainly clustered around the Sultanahmet area of the old city. Since this is also the location for most of the interesting sights and for a good selection of economical eating places there is no real reason to head elsewhere. If you want to find slightly better accommodation you could try around Laleli or a notch up from that at Taksim.

With inflation in Turkey still high and the lira still gradually devaluing it doesn't make much sense to quote prices in local currency. All hotel prices are quoted in US dollars, which are likely to be a more stable indication of the actual price. Dorm beds in the typical Sultanahmet places cost around US$2, bathless doubles about US$8. You can also get triples and four-bed rooms.

Sultanahmet Area The road running right beside Aya Sofya from the square is called Caferiye Sokak (say 'Jiya-ferry Esso-kak') and down there you'll find two of the better value hotels although neither of them are especially clean. The *Yücelt Tourist Hotel* at number 6 (tel 522 4790) has dorm beds for around US$2.50,

double rooms for around US$8. Showers are included – something which is worth checking in most Istanbul cheapies since they often charge extra each time you take a shower. There's a good cafeteria on the outside terrace and it is often full.

Almost next door there's the *Hotel Büyük Ayasofya* which is similar in standards and price. It's at number 5 (tel 522 2981). Another pleasant place at slightly higher prices is the *Hotel Ayasofya Palace* at 33 Yerebatan Caddesi. That's the street which runs beside the underground cistern away from Aya Sofya. There is a pleasant small garden. Down a bit in price and quality is the *Hotel Stop*, right across the road. On Yerebatan Caddesi behind the Pudding Shop the *Sultan Tourist Hotel* has an excellent dorm at US$2.50 or good rooms at around US$8 a double.

All these places are within a couple of minutes walk of the Pudding Shop. *Hotel Gungor* is right next door at 44 Divan Yolu Caddesi. It's also in the same price bracket as the Yücelt and is fairly clean and well kept. Down the road a bit, past the Pudding Shop from the Gungor, is the *Hotel Pirlanta* which is marginally more expensive and has attached bathrooms. There are many other hotels around this area so if none of those suit you could just wander around. Try the *Hotel Nur* at Peykhane Caddesi 3, the *Hotel Yeni Topkapi* at Ipcili Cavus Sokak (behind the Pudding Shop) and the old *Hotel Gulhane Sinar*.

There is a youth hostel place run by the student organisation – the *TMGT Istanbul Youth Hostel* is at Cerrahpaşa Caddesi 63, Aksaray. It's not terribly special but it is cheap. There is another hostel down behind the Blue Mosque on Kucuk Ayasofya Caddesi.

If you'd like to pay a bit more there is no shortage of places to do so. Try the *Hotel Liz*, Kucuk Ayasofya Caddesi 42 which is down behind the Blue Mosque. It's modern, clean and only a little more expensive than the Sultanahmet places.

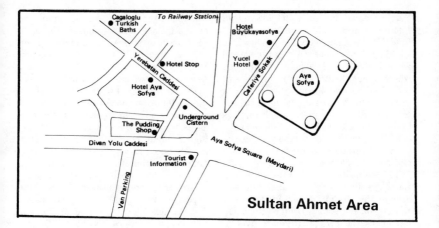

Sultan Ahmet Area

Laleli Area This area is just to the east of Aksaray and merges into the S'ehzadebaşı area. The streets here are relatively quiet and peaceful and you can find rooms from US$6 to 7 for singles, US$9 to 11 for doubles. There are a number of reasonable places along Harikzadeler Sokak such as the *Hotel Oran* (tel 528 5813 or 527 0572) at number 40; the *Hotel Ayda* (tel 526 7867) at number 11 or the *Hotel Surmalı* (tel 520 7642) at number 45.

Other Areas In Aksaray there's the *Hotel Bende*, Laleli Caddesi 34 or the *Hotel Batı*, Namik Kemal Caddesi 32. The Sirkeci railway station area tends to be a bit noisy but there are some good places along Orhaniye Caddesi. At number 12 the *Küçük Karadeniz Oteli* (tel 522 6300) has doubles from US$5 to 7. At number 9, right at the end of the street, the *Hotel İpek Palas* (tel 520 9724) is an old place with doubles with bath at US$10.

Camping If you're in a Kombi or campervan you can stay right in Sultanahmet. On the road opposite the Pudding Shop – where the Hippodrome used to be – there is a semi-official van park. No facilities, but for a small payment to the attendant you get your wheels guarded 24 hours a day. If you want a real site there are plenty available but they tend to be some

distance out from the city. There are two side by side out near Yeşilköy airport. The *BP Mocamp* is better equipped but more expensive than the *London Mocamp*.

Places to Eat
There are a number of popular eating places in the same Sultanahmet area as the cheap hotels. Best known is undoubtedly the famous *Pudding Shop*. It's one of those Asian 'bottlenecks' where eventually anybody who is kicking around Asia is bound to walk through the door. As a result the Pudding Shop is crowded from morning to night and, despite self-service and other modern 'improvements', it's certainly not cheap by Asian standards. Still you can't go to Istanbul and not eat there so give it a try even though these days it's just a pale shadow of its former glory. The Pudding Shop also has a useful noticeboard but beware of the various touts, rip-off merchants and other untrustworthy souls who ply their trade here.

The Pudding Shop is only one of a string of pudding shops and kebapçi along Divan Yolu Caddesi. One of the most popular is *Halk Kebapçi* – it looks good and it is. Since all the food is there on view, getting what you want is absolutely no problem.

Further down the road the *Restaurant Pilanta* is good value and serves tasty food. *Yenner's*, almost directly behind the Pudding Shop, was for a long time a real freak hangout with a famous notebook where people wrote the (far-out) tales of their travels and ideas. Ah those '60s dreams! On the corner just up from the Pudding Shop is a place which rejoices under the name of *The Pub*. You can get a cold Tuborg here of course. Or on the corner of Yerebatan Caddesi the pleasant *Cafeteria Yerebatan*.

There are also numerous restaurants in Laleli, around Sirkeci Station, in and around the Grand Bazaar, in the Spice Bazaar, on the Galata Bridge (great fish but check the prices). If you're over in Taksim there are some reasonably priced places close to Taksim Square. Such as the self-service *Selvi Kafeterya* at Sıraselviler Caddesi 38/40. All over town there'll be places where you can hop in for a baklava or something similar to fill the odd space. Might as well indulge yourself while you are here. If your cash situation will run to it try to splash out on a full meal with meze and so on, particularly in the lovely little places along the Bosphorus. Some of them are right on the waterfront, the setting is beautiful, the fish fresh, the food delicious.

Turkish Baths

When in Rome do as the Romans do, so while in Turkey have a Turkish bath. It's easy to do as there will be a bath (hamam) in almost every town. They're still social centres, particularly for men in the evenings. Istanbul has one rather touristy Turkish bath which is only a short stroll from the Sultan Ahmet area. You can find this one, the Cağaloğlu Hamami, at Yerebatan Caddesi 34 – there are separate entrances for men (on the main street) and women (around the corner). The men's section is open from 7 am to 10 pm daily, the women's only from 8 am to 7 pm. The prices here are also a little touristy.

Getting There

Istanbul-Ankara There are a variety of trains between Istanbul and Ankara daily.

The trip takes up to 12 hours, depending on the train – generally buses are faster than trains in Turkey. A 1st-class sleeper will be about US$20, 2nd-class sleeper US$14, seats much less. It's 578 km between the two cities by train.

By bus it is only 446 km and the trip is quite a bit faster than by rail. If you're in a real hurry you can fly between the two cities in about 45 minutes. There are flights about hourly but they're often heavily booked.

Istanbul-Erzurum It's 1728 km by train to Erzurum, one of the Ankara trains continues straight on to eastern Turkey. You depart Istanbul late one night, arrive Ankara next morning and Erzurum the following morning. So it's about a 36-hour trip. Avoid anything but the expresses on long trips in Turkey. The slower trains take a long long time.

Buses make the through trip in about 24 harrowing hours. You can also get to Erzurum by ship from Istanbul through the Black Sea to Trabzon and then a bus from there. Or you can fly Istanbul-Ankara-Erzurum.

Istanbul-Iran & Further Afield You can still get buses direct from Istanbul to Iran or alternatively from Ankara or Erzurum. In fact you can even get a bus ticket all the way from Istanbul to Zahedan although some travellers find this doesn't always work beyond Tehran. Check round the agents in Sultanahmet or Laleli. The rail service to Iran is suspended at present. There is an Iranian consulate in Istanbul but the embassy in Ankara is much better at issuing visas. You need a letter of introduction from your embassy plus two passport photographs. Incidentally Ankara is also a much better place for Indian visas than further east. Istanbul is a good place for buying Iranian rials cheaply.

Istanbul used to be a major staging post for the old India-bound magic buses. They're no longer so common although you may still find the occasional bus heading east – look for notices or listen for news at travellers' hangouts like the

Pudding Shop in Sultanahmet. Turkish buses heading west into Europe have a bad reputation for not getting you there. At various times lots of travellers have had problems with buses operators who have suddenly discovered they are not licenced to go as far as the tickets they have sold you.

You can also fly from Istanbul to points further east but Istanbul is not a great place for travel bargains – in this region Athens is the place to go for cheap flights.

Getting Around
Airport Transport There are several ways of travelling the 23 km between Yeşilköy airport and Istanbul. A taxi costs a fixed US$10 – you buy a coupon in the arrivals area and outside the waiting mob of taxi drivers will include a particular one whom you are assigned to.

For shoestringers an alternative is the airport bus service which costs US$1.50 and departs from the domestic terminal, not the international one, about every half hour. It runs from the airport to Aksaray (get off here for hotels in Laleli or to take a dolmuş on to Sultanahmet) and then across to the Turkish Airlines city terminal in the Şişhane quarter, near the Galata Tower. The small Turkish Airlines office in Aksaray is about 100 metres from the main drag, Millet Caddesi, on the left if you're coming from Sultanahmet. It's about a 20-minute walk between Sultanahmet and Aksaray. There is no left luggage facility at the Turkish Airlines terminal so don't go there planning to leave bags.

There are also regular public buses out to the airport but they're infrequent, as crowded as ever and impossible with any baggage.

Bus Stations If you arrive by bus from Europe the main station is the Topkapı Otogar which is just outside the city walls, about half way between the airport and Sultanahmet. Better bus companies may have a minibus service between the

station and their city office. You can probably arrange to be dropped off at intermediate points along the way. Alternatively if you walk from the station to the Cannon Gate, in the city wall, there's a city bus station just inside the wall. From here you can get a bus or dolmuş to Aksaray in the city, transfer there for Sultanahmet. There are also taxis, of course.

For getting around Istanbul the buses are frantically crowded but fairly easy to find your way around on, if you can only get on board. Ultimate destinations and intermediate stops are indicated. The Tourist Office put out a one-sheet guide to the numbers of the main routes. If you just want to get from Sultanahmet to Taksim Square take a M4, K4, OK2, G2, L2, 44 or 68. The standard fare is about 15c.

Dolmuş These are taxis that run fixed routes picking up passengers along the way like buses. They're faster and somewhat less crowded and although you have got to know where you are going the routes are generally pretty straightforward and are usually posted in the vehicle. You also need to have a reasonable idea of the fare although these too are generally posted or you can watch what other passengers pay. Make sure a dolmuş does not become a taxi just for you by picking one with passengers already aboard.

The main dolmuş terminals from the visitor's point of view are Taksim, Karaköy, Eminönü, Sirkeci and Beyazıt. Apart from dolmuş from Aksaray and Beyazıt it's not easy to get to Sultanahmet by dolmuş but a few blocks west dolmuş run to Cağaloğlu.

Taxis Taxis are pretty expensive due to the cost of fuel and the lengthy traffic jams. Meters usually don't work so you will have to bargain first. In taxis and dolmuş you must be prepared to pay extra for your baggage.

Train Station European trains arrive at Sirkeci, conveniently central for Sultanahmet and with frequent dolmuş services to Laleli, Aksaray and Taksim. Trains for Asian Turkey, Anatolia, arrive and depart from the Haydarpaşa station on the Asian

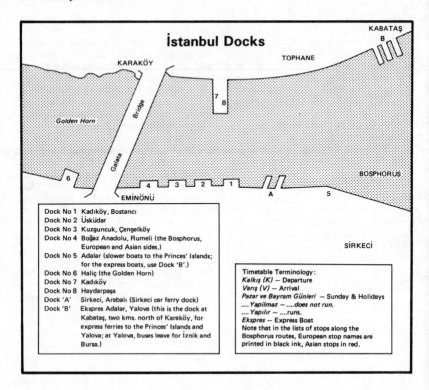

İstanbul Docks

KABATAŞ
B

KARAKÖY

TOPHANE

Golden Horn

Galata Bridge

BOSPHORUS

EMİNÖNÜ

A   5

SİRKECİ

Dock No 1 Kadıköy, Bostancı
Dock No 2 Üsküdar
Dock No 3 Kuzguncuk, Çengelköy
Dock No 4 Boğaz Anadolu, Rumeli (the Bosphorus,
           European and Asian sides.)
Dock No 5 Adalar (slower boats to the Princes' Islands;
           for the express boats, use Dock 'B'.)
Dock No 6 Haliç (the Golden Horn)
Dock No 7 Kadıköy
Dock No 8 Haydarpaşa
Dock 'A'   Sirkeci, Arabalı (Sirkeci car ferry dock)
Dock 'B'   Ekspres Adalar, Yalova (this is the dock at
           Kabataş, two kms. north of Karaköy, for
           express ferries to the Princes' Islands and
           Yalova; at Yalova, buses leave for İznik and
           Bursa.)

Timetable Terminology:
Kalkış (K) – Departure
Varış (V) – Arrival
Pazar ve Bayram Günleri – Sunday & Holidays
....Yapilmaz – *....does not run.*
.... Yapılır – *....runs.*
Ekspres – Express Boat
Note that in the lists of stops along the
Bosphorus routes, European stop names are
printed in black ink, Asian stops in red.

side. To get there take a ferry from Karaköy but make sure it's a Haydarpaşa ferry, some go to Haydarpaşa and Kadıköy, some only to Kadıköy. Ferry departures are every 15 to 30 minutes.

Ferries There are many ferries from around the Galata Bridge. They run up the Bosphorus stopping at the many villages on both sides, across to Asian Istanbul, out to the islands in the Sea of Marmara and up the Golden Horn. There are also car ferries as a more romantic alternative to the Bosphorus bridge. You can make an all day trip up the Bosphorus getting off and on at the various villages, all on the same ticket. There's a 'Special Tourist Excursion' boat which makes a 2½ hour

trip (one way) twice a day. The map shows where the various ferries depart from, around the Galata Bridge.

Other Transport Istanbul has a mini-subway system, the Tünel, which runs between Karaköy and İstiklal Caddesi. There is much discussion about constructing a proper mass transit system but it's likely to be a long way off. Much of the time walking is one of the best ways of getting around Istanbul's narrow, crowded, winding and hilly streets.

THRACE (Trakya)

The small (3%) portion of Turkey which is physically part of Europe is known as Thrace – heading either way, people are usually in a rush to get through this part of

Turkey; en route to Istanbul and their first taste of the east; or goodbye to Asia, Europe here they come. It is worth a pause in Edirne to see the Selimiye Mosque which is claimed to be one of the true masterpieces of Ottoman architecture.

Mediterranean Coast

There are two routes between Istanbul and the Mediterranean coast of Turkey. One heads from Istanbul back towards Europe, skirting the northern edge of the Sea of Marmara and crossing the Dardanelles to Asian Turkey at Çanakkale. This way you can get a look at Gallipoli (Gelibolu) on the northern side of the narrow Dardanelles and the site of Troy on the south. The alternative route crosses directly into Asia from Istanbul and then continues inland through Bursa to the coast.

BURSA
This was the Ottoman capital prior to the capture of Istanbul and it ranks second only to Istanbul in architectural elegance. It's a very traditional town with thermal springs and some fine mosques. The beautifully tiled Yeşil Cami or Green Mosque is across the road from the Yeşil Türbe or Green Tomb where Mehmet I lies.

Places to Stay
Although there are some hotels in the centre the best choice is in Çekirge. Get there by bus or dolmus from Heykel or along Atatürk Caddesi. The *Hüsnügüzel Oteli* (tel 11 640) is past the final bus stop in Çekirge and has very simple rooms for US$6 a double. The *Şifa Oteli* (tel 11 483) is across from the Ada Palas hotel in the centre of Cekirge and is similarly priced.

The *Temizel Oteli* (tel 11 682) or the *Yıldız Oteli* (tel 23 200 & 201) are near the Hüsnügüzel and are a bit more expensive at around US$9 but also rather better.

The *Otel Kılınç* (tel 12 536) is behind the Ada Palas at Birinci Murat Caddesi Arka Sokak 13 and is also around US$9. Up a notch again with doubles at US$12 the old but very popular *Hotel Ada Palas* (tel 19 200) is right on Çekirge Caddesi and has doubles at US$12.

Right in the centre the *Hotel Artıc* is on Atatürk Caddesi right next to the post office. It's conveniently central but can be a bit noisy; rooms are around the same price as the Ada Palas.

Places to Eat
Bursa is renowned for its roast meat dishes *Bursa kebap* and *İskender kebap* – look for restaurants called *Bursa kebapçısı*. *Inegöl köftesi*, a ground meat type of rissole, is another local speciality. Fresh fruit is also very good in Bursa.

ÇANAKKALE
Çanakkale is nothing special apart from being the Asian side of the Dardanelles where during WW I an awful lot of Anzacs and British troops proved that yes, indeed it was impossible to take the straits and yes, their leaders were pretty dumb to try it. The war graves are a moving experience and you can still see old, discarded equipment and trenches. It was here that Leander swam the Hellespont (names change) to his lover Hero and here too Lord Byron did his romantic bit and duplicated the feat. The old castle at Çanakkale, built by Sultan Mehmet II in 1452, is now a museum of WW I weaponry. It's interesting and sufficiently untouristed that you may get an army tour.

Places to Stay
Cheap hotels can be found around the clock tower where you will also find the tourist office. The *Küçük Truva Oteli* (tel 1552) has rooms at US$2 per person, US$2.60 with shower. The *Hotel Efes* is similar. The *Hotel Konak* is just behind the clock tower and has singles/doubles at US$2.60/3.50 or at US$4.60/6 with shower. The water here is hot!

Places to Eat

There are good cheap places to eat along the quay, to the right of the car ferry docks. If you walk inland along the main street you'll find even cheaper places.

TROY

There's not much of the historic 'Trojan Horse' Troy to be seen because it is estimated that nine successive cities have been built on this same site. Troy 1 goes right back to the bronze age. The history book Troy is thought to be Troy 6. Most of the ruins you see are Roman ones from Troy 9. Still it's nice to say you've been there and there are three buses a day from Çanakkale (the tourist office will tell you when) or you can go by dolmus. Take the Karakas bus from Çanakkale; from İzmir get off at Gokcali. There's an entry fee to the site and museum.

ASSOS

Now known as Behramkale, this was once the site for a Temple of Athena built by the Greeks and was said to be one of the most beautiful cities of the time. Aristotle is said to have lived there and it is still a very beautiful, delightfully laid back place today. If you just want to lie back, unwind and gaze across the narrow stretch of water to the Greek island of Lesbos (where the lesbians used to live you know) then this is the place. Continuing on to Ayvalık you can take a ferry across to Lesbos.

AYVALIK

Ferries run to Mytileni on the island of Lesbos from this small fishing port and beach resort. The short trip costs a hefty US\$20, an indicator of the state of relations between Turkey and Greece.

Places to Stay & Eat

There are cheap hotels in the town centre and others at Sarmisakh Plaj, the beach several km south. The *Ayvalık Palas* (tel 1064) is just off the main square by the harbour and has rooms at US\$2.50/4 for singles/doubles. On Talat Paşa Caddesi, also near the main square, the *El Otel* (tel 1604) is OK and a bit cheaper. The *Şehir Oteli* on the same street as the Ayvalik Palas is another possibility.

There are plenty of places to eat right on the main square or on the small streets around the Ayvalik Palas.

BERGAMA

Close to this city are the ruins of Pergamum, capital of a kingdom from the 3rd to the 1st century BC. There is an extensive series of Roman ruins in the lower city and three km above the town Greek ruins with an Acropolis, a theatre, temples and the Altar of Zeus.

Places to Stay

The *Park Oteli* (tel 246) is close to the central garage and has plain rooms for US\$3 and 4. The *Şehir Oteli* and the *Balar Oteli*, side by side on Hükümet Caddesi, are similarly priced.

There are a number of good restaurants between the central garage and the middle of town. You will also find good food in the little restaurants along Uzun Çarşi Caddesi.

İZMIR

There's more to see along the route south – Genoese fortresses and castles, Byzantine citadels, Greek and Roman ruins – but İzmir is nothing special apart from a very pleasant bayside location. Turkish tourist literature regrets that there is not much to see here due to the great fire of 1922. In actual fact Smyrna, as it was then known, was inhabited by Greeks and the town was fairly well wiped out (along with the Greeks) by the Turkish army. Visit the archaeological museum, the 2nd century AD Roman agora and the reasonably interesting and genuine bazaar. Homer was born in Smyrna.

Places to Stay

İzmir is not a good place for cheap accommodation, there aren't even so many around the Basmane railway station runs right up to the Kultur Park.

There's a *Youth Hostel* (Ogrenci Yurdu in Turkish) at Gazi Osman Paşa Bulvari 50. *Aksaz Oteli* at 42 is a reasonably cheap hotel. The *Pansiyon Fa* at Kizilay Caddesi, 1375 Sokak No 24/2 is good value at US$6 for doubles but it's small and usually full up.

Places to Eat

There are some excellent, atmospheric and moderately priced restaurants on the waterfront between Konak and Cumhuriyet Meydanı. Try the *Express, Mangal* and *Kazan* between 110 to 112 Birinci Kordon for good seafood and sidewalk tables. *Kordon Kebap Salonu* at 150 is cheap too. For rock-bottom prices try the places along Anafartalar Caddesi from Basmane in the bazaar.

Getting There & Around

The bus station is some distance north-east of the centre. Better bus lines provide a minibus shuttle from there into the centre, otherwise you can take a taxi, dolmuş or local bus. Konak is the central area although you'll find some of the cheapest hotels in Basmane, near the railway station.

EFES

Ephesus, as it was once named, is an easy 76-km bus trip south from İzmir. During its Greek heyday only Athens was more magnificent and the ruins of Efes are pretty amazing even today. The Arcadian Way through the town to the port was the main street. The immense amphitheatre held 24,000 people. The Temple of Hadrian, the Celsus Library, the Marble Way (on which the richies lived) and the Fountain of Trajan, should all be seen. The brothels, with their descriptive floor mosaics, are not up to the standard of Pompeii. Nor are the mosaics very well preserved.

Efes later became a Christian religious centre. In the nearby town of Selçuk is the Basilica of St John, said to be built over his tomb. To get to Efes from İzmir take a bus to Selçuk then a dolmus to the site where there is an entry fee. You can walk back to Selçuk afterwards as it is all downhill. The foundations of the Temple of Artemis, between Efes and Selçuk, are all that is left of one of the Seven Wonders of the World.

Places to Stay & Eat

Many people day-trip from İzmir but if you want to stay there are a few places in Selçuk, four km from the ruins. An alternative is the coastal resort of Kuşadasi, 17 km distance. Small pensions in Selçuk cost US$2 to 3 for doubles. Try the *Pension Kirhan* behind the museum, the *Pension Baykal* next to the museum, the *Pension Artemis* or several others.

Along Cengiz Topal Caddesi between the highway and the railway station there are several restaurants such as the *Yildiz Restaurant* with its outdoor eating section.

KUŞADASI

Slightly south again, this resort town is linked by a causeway to a castle once used by pirates, it's now a club. It's a popular stop for cruise ships.

Places to Stay & Eat

There are lots of cheap pensions with prices from US$3/5 for singles/doubles. Just look down the side streets, the further you get from the beach the cheaper they are. The tourist office in Kuşadasi can advise you. Kuşadasi also has several campsites including a BP Mocamp.

There are some good seafood places along the waterfront – the more expensive ones are close to the wharf, prices (but not quality) drop as you move north or south. If you move back from the waterfront places get much cheaper – try the *Konya Restoran* on Kahramanlar Caddesi.

MORE RUINS

If you're still in the mood for poking

around the antiquities you can continue south to Miletus, Priene or Didyma. Known as *Didim* in Turkish, Didyma was once the site of a huge, but never completed, Temple of Apollo. The great columns here are very impressive. Get off your dolmuş at the ruins, there's no point in going the extra couple of km to the dolmuş station at the nearby village.

Still more ruins – well you can continue inland from Denizli to Geyre which used to be known as Aphrodisias and was a centre for the worship of Aphrodite. Karacasu is an alternative approach to the ruins. There's nowhere to stay at the ruins but the museum is worth the detour.

If you want to change from ruins to beaches, head west from İzmir to Çesme, a pleasant port with a Genoese fortress. It's only 1¼ hours by bus and this is also a pleasant resort, a good place to arrive in Turkey from the Greek island of Chios. A couple of km away Ilica has great sandy beaches.

MORE BEACHES

Two popular resorts are Bodrum, opposite the Greek island of Kos, and Marmaris, opposite Rhodes. In fact, during summer both are probably a little too popular. Bodrum was the site of Halicarnassus and here was the Mausoleum of King Mausolus, another of the Seven Wonders of the ancient world. Again there's nothing left. The gothic castle, built by the Crusaders, overlooks the town and used stones from the tomb. There's good swimming at the bays a few km out of town.

Marmaris is not quite so pretty as Bodrum although swimming in the surrounding bays is probably better. From Marmaris it costs US$12 one-way to Rhodes, US$18 return. Further down the peninsula from Marmaris it's interesting to visit Datça and, right at the tip, the ruins of the ancient port of Cnidus.

Places to Stay & Eat

Apart from hotels there are also many pensions in both Bodrum and Marmaris.

In Bodrum look along the streets inland from Cumhuriyet Caddesi. Bodrum also has several campsites including *Ayaz Camping* at Gümbet beach. The best places to eat in Bodrum are close to the centre, around the market area.

In Marmaris it's again pensions which are the cheapest deal – prices range from around US$4/6 and the tourist office can make recommendations. Prices are similar at the small central hotels such as the *Kalyon, İmbat* or *Sema*. There are campsites near the Hotel Lidya. There are some pleasant, and not too pricey, restaurants around the yacht harbour or, once again, cheaper places close to the market.

LYCIA

The area from here to Antalya at the start of the Turquoise Coast was immortalised by Homer as 'Lycia'. There are ruins at Phaselis (near Kemer), Xanthos, Fethiye and at Termessos only 30 km from Antalya. Fethiye has a superb beach and cheap campsites although they're a bit crowded in summer – worth the diversion off the road. Outside Fethiye the lagoon of Ölüdeniz ('dead sea') is beautiful and there's a marked hiking trail to an abandoned village. There's good camping at the beach.

Kaş, between Fethiye and Antalya, is a picturesque little place with a good range of restaurants. The small town of Demre (also called Kale) is interesting because the one time Bishop of Demre was your actual St Nicholas who was gradually modified until he became Santa Claus. Nearby are the ruins of Myra.

The coast road on this stretch is very poor until you reach Antalya. There is much to be said for heading inland from Efes through Pamukkale and then turning south to Antalya. If you want to continue on the coast consider taking the Turkish Maritime Lines boat and giving your bottom a rest.

PAMUKKALE

Due east of Efes, this fascinating site has

hot thermal waters which flow down over a plateau edge to form a series of brilliant white steps. Behind this natural wonder are the extensive ruins of the Roman city of Hierapolis.

Places to Stay & Eat
There are cheap pensions at the base of the cliff like the pleasant *Konak Sade* pension. The *Anatolia Pension*, beyond the village and a km or so from the main pools, is also good. For food try the *Özel İdare* or places around the bus terminal in nearby Denizli.

The Turquoise Coast

South on the coast from İzmir and Efes, the coast starts to bend and run east. This southern stretch of the Mediterranean coast is known as the Turquoise Coast and is studded with beautiful beaches, washed by clear water ideal for scuba diving and liberally sprinkled with all sorts of of ruins.

ANTALYA
The main town of the coast, Antalya has one of the most attractive settings in the Mediterranean but apart from the beautiful location and the pleasant harbour area it is not of great interest. There is a nice bazaar, some mosques, an archaeological museum and, of course, some very fine beaches.

Places to Stay
Cheap hotels include the *Yesilova*, close to the bus station, and the *Pension King Hossein* (very good) just a bit further away on Cumhuriyet Caddesi. The *Öncel Pansiyon* (tel 12199) at Karaalioğlu Sokak 6 and nearby *Gönen Pansiyon* are pretty good places at US$6 a double. On Güllük Caddesi the *Atlas Pansiyon* (tel 12431) or the *Olimpiyat Pansiyon* (tel 12890) are a bit pricier at US$9.

The *Otel Tatoğlu* (tel 12119) is on Şarampol/Kazım Ozalp Caddesi 91, near the bus terminal, and is clean and comfortable. The rooms have bathrooms and balconies and cost US$8 for a double.

Places to Eat
There's good food (particularly kebaps) and outdoor tables at the little street parallel to Atatürk Caddesi from the intersection of that street and Cumhuriyet Caddesi. Its name, Eski Sebzeciler İçi Sokak, translates as 'The Old Inner Street of the Greengrocers' Market'! *Bozkurt Kebap Salonu* on that same street in the bazaar area is cheap and good. Or try the *Ankara Restaurant* at Hastahane Caddesi 38. The bars around the yacht harbour are pretty good too.

YET MORE RUINS
You may have had your fill of Greek and Roman ruins if you've been travelling south but this stretch of coast has plenty more if you can take them. Perge is a short distance from Antalya and includes a 12,000-seat stadium and a theatre for 15,000. Aspendos has the best preserved ancient theatre in Turkey, dating from the 2nd century AD. It is the site for performances in the Antalya festival each June. Side has more fine ruins including a Roman bath which is now a small museum and an amphitheatre. It was once the main slave market at this end of the Mediterranean. There are good beaches here.

Places to Stay & Eat
There are a number of pensions in Side including the excellent *Hermes Pansiyon*, ask at the boutique of that name in the main square. There are many other small pensions around the village – look for signs announcing *boş oda var* which means 'empty rooms here'.

Preparing your own food in a pension is the cheapest and best way to eat here. The *Enişte'nin Yeri* is about the only reasonably priced restaurant which also has reasonably good food.

ALANYA

The second major city of the coast, Alanya is dominated by the ruins of a magnificent Seljuk fortress perched high on a promontory. The town was a popular resort for Seljuk sultans. The Ulas beach, a bit out of town on the way to Manavgat, is good but take your own refreshments.

Places to Stay & Eat

Cheap hotels in Alanya are downtown, the more expensive places are out at the beach. You can find doubles for around US$4 at places like the *Yayla Palas Otel* on İskele Caddesi or at the nearby *Alanya Palas*.

Pricier places include the *Hotel Kent* at number 12 on the same street with doubles with shower for US$9. The *Hotel Riviera Plaj* on Gazi Paşa Caddesi has pleasant rooms, some of them with balconies. There are a number of small pensions where you can use the kitchen, about 20-minutes walk from the centre along the highway to the east. Camping areas can be found to the east and, to a lesser extent, to the west of the town along the beach.

There are a number of very pleasant waterfront restaurants along Gazi Paşa Caddesi. *Meydan Kebap Salonu*, on the other end of the street from the Riviera Plaj, is particularly cheap and good. Alanya is noted for its locally produced ice cream.

ANAMUR

The coast gets less touristy after Alanya and Anamur has a magnificent castle virtually on the beach. It was built by the Emirs of Karaman in 1230.

SİLİFKE

One of the finest and most imposing Crusader castles on the coast overlooks this small town. Inland there are more castles and ruins off the road to Konya.

MERSİN

This modern port town is of no great interest apart from being an exit point for ferries to Cyprus.

TARSUS

Tarsus was the birthplace of St Paul and the place where Anthony first ran into Cleopatra – it's a short distance beyond Mersin.

ADANA

This is the fourth largest city in Turkey and an important industrial centre.

İSKENDERUN

Alexander the Great beat the Persians here and founded the port. Johan is said to have been coughed up by a whale here too. The road onwards to Antakya is very exciting. Terrifying?

ANTAKYA

The Biblical Antioch, where St Peter did a spell of converting, was said to be the most depraved city in the Roman Empire. You can see his church just outside the town, magnificent Roman mosaics in the archaeological museum and (of course) more ruins. It is only a short trip from here to the Syrian border.

Central Anatolia

Anatolia is the heartland of Turkey – the Mediterranean coast may be pretty and relaxing, Istanbul may be exotic and intriguing, but it is Anatolia which is Turkey's core. Atatürk clearly saw this in his decision to move the capital east from Istanbul to Ankara in the centre of Turkey. Don't think of this area as a great central nothingness – put some effort into reaching the Hittite sites and you'll be knocked out by the strength of a civilisation you may not even have heard of. Head south to Cappadocia and you'll be equally amazed by a region that looks as if it belongs in another world.

ANKARA

The capital of Turkey since 1923, Ankara's site was a Hittite settlement nearly 4000 years ago. Apart from a couple of interesting things to see it is not of special interest but due to its central location there is a good chance you'll at least pass through it. The tourist office is at Gazi Mustafa Kemal Bulvari 33.

Things to See

Mausoleum of Atatürk A massive tomb and memorial to the father of modern Turkey. His house in Cankaya is now a museum.

Museum of Anatolian Civilisation If you are going or have been to the Hittite sites you'll find this museum, with the biggest collection of Hittite artifacts in the world, an essential visit. Closed on Mondays.

Other The old part of Ankara is mainly Byzantine – known as the Citadel. Nearby are some old mosques and some Roman ruins including the baths. There is an Ethnographical Museum (closed Monday) on Talatpaşa Bulvarı.

Places to Stay

The hunting ground for cheap accommodation in Ankara is the Ulus area. A typical reasonable value place is the *Erzurum Hotel* with rooms at around US$4. There is also a *TMGT student hostel* here. Other places to try include the *Yenisehir Saglik* at Kolejti Tuna Caddesi 41 or the similarly priced *Hotel Avrupa* on Susam Sokak.

There are many other hotels around Gençlik Park, beside Ulus, like the *Opera Oteli* at Kosova Sokak 5 or the *Ucler* and the *Tarabya* on the same street. Doubles are US$7, more with shower or bath, in the *Otel Devran* at Opera Meydanı Tavus Sokak 8. Look for the Gazi Lisesi high school on Sanayi Caddesi, across Atatürk Bulvari from the Opera House and Gençlik Park. *Vatan Oteli* (a good cheap hotel) and *Anadolu Oteli* are both on Aztat Sokak. The big *Terminal Oteli* is opposite the bus station.

You can also camp by the municipal swimming pool, just outside of Ankara, or at the very pleasant dam camping site about eight km from town on the Sivas road. There is a *BP Mocamp* on the Istanbul side of town.

Places to Eat

There are lots of good, cheap places to eat around Ulus such as the *Özel Urfa Aile Kebap Salonu* on Tavus Sokak where you can get a whole delicious meal for about US$1. In the same area *Hacı Bey* at Devren Sokak 1/B is a good kebap place. The *Akman Boza ve Pasta Salonu* at Atatürk Bulvari 3 is a good place for breakfast and lunch. Upstairs and behind it on Yenice Sokak is *9 Kebab Salonu*, a good place for a cheap and substantial meal.

Getting There

Ankara is very much the transportation centre for Asian Turkey.

Air Flights tend to be heavily booked although there are flights about hourly between Ankara and Istanbul.

Bus There are buses between Ankara and Istanbul every 15 minutes or so for much of the day. The trip takes about eight hours and costs US$6 to 8 depending on the bus company. The main bus station (*Otogar*) is a block north-west of the railway station just over a km from Ulus. There are rows of ticket kiosks for buses to towns all over the country.

Rail Only take *ekspres* or *mototren*, anything else will be painfully slow. Even the expresses are generally slower than buses – Istanbul-Ankara takes about 12 hours. There are a variety of trains between Istanbul and Ankara, some of them 1st class only. Some continue beyond Ankara (or start beyond Ankara) as far as Van or Kars. The service to Tehran in Iran is not currently operating. Other trains include a day and a night service Ankara-Izmir and daily expresses to Kayseri (slow!) or Adana.

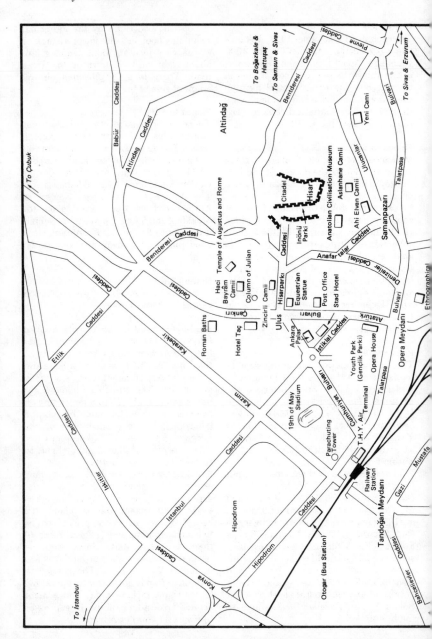

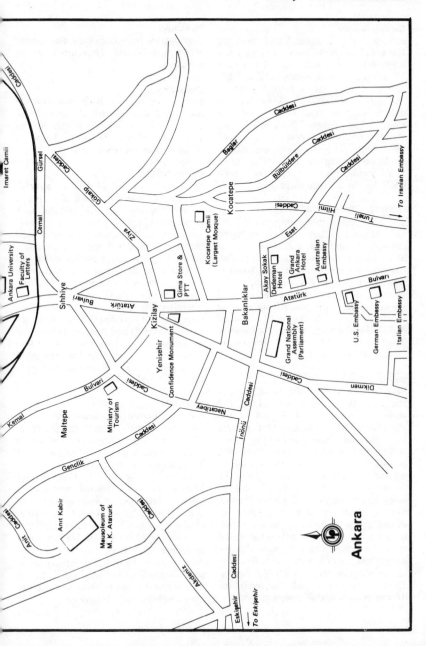

Getting Around

Ankara airport is about 30 km from the city but Turkish Airlines operates a bus for their flights. The Turkish Airlines Air Terminal is at the railway station, which is only a half km from the main bus station and on the same street. Ankara's bus and dolmuş services tend to be frantically crowded. The Çankaya-Ulus dolmuş service along Atatürk Caddesi is probably the most useful, since most cheap accommodation is centred in the Ulus area. Taxis around town generally cost about US$1 for the average short trip.

HITTITE & PHRYGIAN SITES

The Phrygians dated from around 1000 BC and most of their sites can be found between Ankara and Eskisehir – about mid-way between Ankara and Istanbul. Gordion, 93 km from Ankara, was the capital and where Alexander the Great was said to have cut the Gordion knot. Of greater interest are the Hittite sites, a short distance off the road between Ankara and the Black Sea port of Samsun. The Hittites ruled central Anatolia from about 2000 to 1180 BC.

Boğazkale

Situated 29 km off the main road is Hattuşaş the ancient capital of the Hittites until it was destroyed by the Phrygians. There is little left today apart from the walls and foundations of the buildings. But what walls – crumbling though they are they stretch for over 10 km and have five entrances including the Royal Gate, the Lion Gate (flanked by stone lions) and the underground tunnel Yer Kapi. And what foundations – massive, imposing and visited only by the occasional curious sheep. Largest is the site of the Great Temple of the Storm God which has no less than 70 storerooms. Near the village of Boğazköy is a small museum. The locals do a good trade flogging bits of 'Hittite' pottery to the infrequent visitor.

Yazılıkaya

Just two km from Boğazkale this natural rock temple has bas reliefs carved into the rock face.

Alaca Höyük

Situated 36 km from Boğazkale near the main road was the site of a pre-Hittite culture. The remains, including the Sphinx Gate, are Hittite however. There is another small museum here.

CAPPADOCIA

Situated south-east of Ankara, approximately half way to Adana, this area is notable for the fantastic natural rock formations of the Göreme Valley. The soft stone can easily be carved into rooms and chambers – you'll find churches, fortresses, even complete underground cities, all hollowed out of the other-worldly rock outcrops. There are two routes south from Ankara to this area. One runs more or less directly south by the salt lake, Tuz Gölü, then turns off east. On this stretch of the Konya-Kayseri road you pass three medieval caravanserai. One of them is still well preserved, camel stalls and all. The other route heads more south-east and goes through Kirşehir.

KAYSERI

Kayseri, known in Roman times as Caesarea, is the capital of the province. The city has an interesting covered bazaar – this is a major carpet weaving area and Turkish carpets are highly rated

The 1136 Seljuk Ulu Cami (Great Mosque) is only a hundred or so metres from an Ottoman mosque dating from 1580. They make an interesting architectural comparison. There is also a Byzantine fortress, the Mongol Kosk Madresse and an archaeological museum, but pride of place goes to the fine decorations of the small Döner Kümbet. At Kültepe, 21 km from Kayseri towards Sivas, you can see the foundations of a Hittite city.

Places to Stay

There is a good selection of hotels in Kayseri including the *Hotel Seyhan* (tel 23 489) at Mimar Sinan Caddesi, Seyhan Sokak 6/D. It's conveniently located on a quiet back street and has doubles for about US$4. The *Hotel Sur* (tel 19 545) at Cumhuriyet Mahallesi, Uğur Sokak 12 is a relatively new place and just a little more expensive. It's close to the citadel. The *Hotel Kent* near Düvenönü Meydanı is similar. Another reasonable place, with good food in its restaurant, is the *Divan Oteli* at 27 Mayis Caddesi 6.

Places to Eat

Cheap and filling food can be found at the *Hacı Usta Lokanta ve Kebap Salonu* (there are two of them) on Serdar Caddesi 3 and 7. The *Divan Pastanesi* is a good place for breakfast at 27 Mayis Caddesi. Kayseri has a number of tasty local specialities.

GÖREME

The Göreme valley is one of the most amazing sights in Turkey. Over the centuries the strange outcrops of rock have eroded into fantastic, eerie shapes. Into these soft rocks early Christians built their churches and homes; hollowing them into chambers, vaults and winding labyrinths. Painted frescoes, unlit for many centuries, have hardly eroded at all. Unhappily the effects of vandalism have been more severe.

Most of these chapels are from the 10th and 11th century and follow a similar cross-shaped pattern. Some of the best known are named after their fresco paintings – such as the Yilanli Kilise (Church with Snakes), the Elmalı Kilise (Church with an Apple), Karanlık Kilise (Dark Church) or Çarıklı Kilise (Church with Sandals). Altogether there are several dozen churches, a monastery and a nunnery in the small valley.

Avcılar A nearby village with houses carved into the rocks or perched precar-

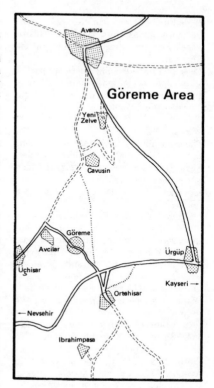

Göreme Area

iously on top of cones.

Avanos Another small village, famous for its pottery and onyx.

Ortahisar There is a particularly large peak here with an enormous citadel carved into it. A long scramble from room to room leads to a view over the surrounding country from the summit. There is a similar complex at Üçhisar.

Kaymaklı & Derinkuyu These sites, south of Nevşehir, are just two of the many underground cities used by your persecuted Christians in times of persecution. There is another of these amazing complexes of interconnected rooms at Ozkonok – it has a tunnel leading to it which is claimed to be several km long.

Aksaray Here there is a whole palace carved out of the same soft stone.

Niğde Further south from Nevşehir there are more monasteries, churches, Hittite traces and interesting mosques in the Nigde area.

Zelve The rock-dwellings here are particularly spectacular and there are many unlit tunnels. If you're exploring a torch (flashlight) is essential.

Places to Stay

There are many small hotels and pensions all around the area – in Ortahisar, Avcilar, Nevşehir and particularly in Ürgüp which is the most central place for the area, especially if you don't have your own vehicle.

Ürgüp has lots of small pensions (*pansiyons*) where you can get a basic but clean room for around US$2 per person. There are quite a few places along the main street like the old and extremely basic *Kayseri Otel*. The school next door to the big Büyük Otel becomes a student hostel at knock down prices during the summer months.

In Ortahisar the *Hotel Göreme* is not bad at US$5 to 6 for a double. You can also find a handful of pensions at Üçhisar or there are a number close to the river in Avanos. There are several camp sites in the Göreme area. Right at the turning to Göreme *Motel Paris/Camping* has room for 600 people, a swimming pool and motel rooms at US$12 a double. The nearby *Kaya Camping* has good views of the valley. Near Urgup the *Çimenli Motel/Camping* is another possibility for people with tents.

Places to Eat

The restaurant possibilities are not too exciting in the Göreme area. You could try the *Ossiana* near the Büyük Otel and the tourist office in Ürgüp or the small restaurants near the main square. Avanos also has some fairly basic eating places.

Getting There & Around

There are several buses daily from Ankara either to Nevşehir or Kayseri. Buses also run there from Konya. Ürgüp is the most central base for the Göreme region. You can get to Ürgüp by dolmuş from Nevşehir or Kayseri. Since Kayseri is 70 km from the Göreme region it doesn't make a good base.

There are frequent dolmuş services between Nevşehir and Ürgüp and you can get off at the Göreme turn-off, from where the site is only 15-minutes' walk. Dolmuşes also run from Nevşehir to the underground cities at Derinkuyu and Kaymaklı but otherwise you'll either have to walk, hitch or hire a taxi. The tourist office in Ürgüp will help you get a group together to hire a taxi.

KONYA

Known as Iconium in Roman times, the city of Konya later became the capital of the Seljuk Turks. Mevlana Rumi founded the Whirling Dervish sect here during that time. His green-tiled mausoleum is the most interesting building in the city although there are many other fine Seljuk buildings including the Karatay Müzesu, once a madresse but now a museum of Seljuk ceramics.

Places to Stay & Eat

There are lots of cheap hotels around Konya. The *Otel Saadat* on Mevlana Caddesi is reasonably cheap. *Hotel Fatih* on Hatuniye Sokak is rather better. *Otel Mevlana* on Mevlana Caddesi is popular with Turkish students, clean and good.

The *Köşem Restaurant* at Alaettin Bulvari 26/8 is a popular restaurant in Konya. On the same street the *Kenanlar Pasta Salonu* is good for breakfasts and light meals. Just behind the tourist office the *Çatal Lokantası* is a solid, simple kebap place.

ÇATAL HÖYÜK

Less than 50 km south-east of Konya, near Çumra, this is the site of Neolithic centres dating back to 7000 BC where mud houses had holes in the roof for entrances. There's little to see though.

CENTRAL TURKEY

Sivas on the central route through Turkey was the starting point for Atatürk's liberation movement after WW I. Far earlier it had been an important crossroads on the caravan route to Persia and Baghdad. Tokat, north of Sivas, has many interesting old buildings and so does Amasya, further north and close to the Ankara-Samsun road.

The Black Sea

The Black Sea coast has always been a little different from the rest of Turkey, partially due to the isolation imposed on it by the Pontic Mountain chain that runs parallel to the coast. There is a good road running most of the way along the coast but it peters out after Sinop so following the coastline all the way west to Istanbul is not possible.

SAMSUN

There is little of interest in Samsun although if you like hazel nuts this area is the largest producer of them in the world.

Places to Stay

There's the usual choice of cheap hotels, particularly around Kazım Paşa Caddesi. At the bus station the *Terminal Oteli* has doubles for US$12.

ALONG THE COAST

There are many interesting little villages and fine beaches along the coast from Samsun to Trabzon but the water is a little chilly except at the height of summer. Ünye and Ordu are two pleasant resort towns. Giresun is overlooked by a Byzantine fortress and it was from here that the first cherry tree was taken back to Europe by a Roman general.

Places to Stay

Along the Black Sea coast there are quite a number of pleasant places to stay. The *Belediye Çamlık Motel* is particularly nice with doubles at US$8, a restaurant and you can camp on the beach. The *Otel Ürer* in town is also good.

TRABZON

Known as Trebizond in Byzantine times this was the last town to fall to the Ottoman Turks, it held out for eight years after the fall of Constantinople. It held out for so long partially due to its importance as a trade centre and partially due to its very effective fortifications.

Places to Stay

Otel Benli, behind the İskander Paşa Cami off the west end of the square, is a good cheap place with doubles at US$6. Just outside of town on the road inland to Erzurum there is a Shell station which you can camp behind. Try the *Gaziantep Kebapçısı & Baklavaçısı* for good, cheap kebabs.

SUMELA

Heading inland from Trabzon the road winds up (and up) into the mountains. The monastery of Sumela is off the road 54 km south of Trabzon. Set into a sheer rock face the monastery was inhabited right up to this century and has many fine frescoes (much damaged by vandals) and some amazing views.

Eastern Turkey

The eastern part of Turkey is the harshest, hardest part of the country. It's also the area where the opium poppies used to grow and it's the area where the kids, if not egged on by their parents certainly not restrained, specialised in hurling stones through car windscreens. In the winter, which is very cold, the weather is imported direct from the Russian steppes.

ERZURUM

The rather drab town of Erzurum has Mongol and Seljuk buildings including the interesting twin-minaretted Çifte Minare Madresse. The Tourist Office is on Cemal Gürsel Caddesi and is open from 8 am to 5.30 pm daily.

Places to Stay

There are many hotels around the bus station. *Hotel Kervan Saray* and *Hotel Yesil Bayburt* are very similar and there are a number of other places of similar standard. Showers and heating in winter are often extra. *Hotel Tehran Palace* is a bit more luxurious and expensive, the *Polat Oteli* and the *San* still more so with rooms for US$9. The Polat is on Kazım Karabekir Caddesi. At Ayazpaşa Caddesi 18 the *Hotel Çinar* has rooms from US$5, with shower they are US$7. *Hotel Tahran* is pretty good too, there's a reasonable local restaurant opposite. The dirt cheap places are kind of dismal.

At the BP station just out of town on the road west you can camp although it is not a proper mocamp.

Getting There

Erzurum is a travel centre for people going to or from Iran. Buses run regularly to Tabriz and Tehran in Iran as well as to Ankara and other centres in Turkey. The Arat Travel Bureau on Kazım Karabekir Caddesi is the place for buses to Iran. Or try the Otel Hittit.

There are night and day trains from Erzurum to Ankara, the trip takes about 24 hours and the night departure continues on from Ankara overnight again to Istanbul, arriving about 36 hours after leaving Erzurum.

AROUND ERZURUM

Kars

North-east of Erzurum and under the shadow of Mt Ararat, this frontier town was much fought over and has a suitably massive fortress.

Mt Ararat (Ağri Dağı)

When the 40 days and 40 nights finally dried up this is where Noah and his flock are said to have come down to earth. Nice theory but you won't get to test it since the mountain is on the politically sensitive Turkey-USSR border and climbing is only allowed with permission from Ankara. Rising sheer from a level plain the snow capped mountain makes an impressive view from the main road between Erzurum and the Iran border. Throughout the east 40 is used either synonymously with many or as a lucky number. See the 40-column palace in Isfahan and the 40 steps at Kandahar. So perhaps Noah, if he did go for his long float, didn't really last 40 days at all.

DOĞUBAYAZIT

A miserable little town which is the last place before the Iran border. Overlooking it is the old Sultan's palace called the Işak Paşa Sarayı, you can look around and climb the claustrophobic minaret for the view.

Places to Stay

Accommodation is none too hot in this somewhat dreary place. There are a couple of rather flashy hotels (people with vans can negotiate the use of the *Hotel Ararat's* facilities). Cheaper places include the *Hotel Erzurum*, a popular travellers' centre on the main street, the *Hotel Gül* and the *Hotel Beyazıt*. After that the rest are pretty dismal.

There are several kebapçi along the main street. Take care after dark – this is eastern Turkey.

LAKE VAN

The railway between Istanbul and Tehran crosses the huge expanse of Lake Van by ferry. The city of Van has an interesting museum and a three-thousand-year-old citadel. There is a 10th century church on Akdamar Island in the lake. It's a really fascinating piece of early Christian architecture in a beautiful setting. There are frescoes in and reliefs outside, depicting Biblical scenes.

Places to Stay & Eat

Try the *Hotel Ferah* near the bus station or the equally cheap *Cihan Palas Hotel*. More expensive places include the *Beşkardeşler Oteli* at Cumhuriyet Caddesi 34 at US$9 a double. There are numerous kebapçi along Cumhuriyet Caddesi.

THE DEEP SOUTH

Right in the south of east Turkey is the region once known as upper-Mesopotamia – drained by the historic Tigris (Dicle) and Euphrates (Firat) rivers. The cities of Urfa, Mardin and Diyarbakır were all centres for the Hurri-Mitanni civilisation of 4000 years ago.

NEMRUT DAĞI

North of here, and pretty much in the middle of nowhere, is Nemrut Daği with huge stone-carved heads scattered indiscriminately on the ground.

Middle East

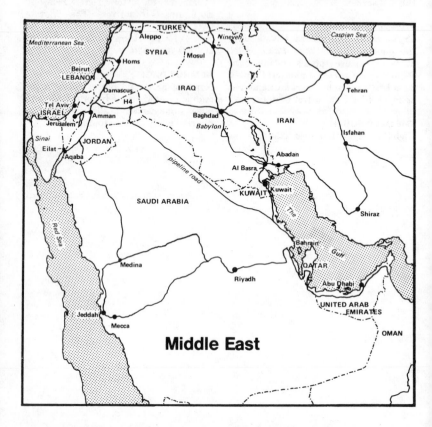

Middle East

In the past few years the Middle East region has made two steps forward and two back as a popular area for travellers. On one hand the troubles in Iran and Afghanistan have pushed people to consider these countries as an alternative. For a time more people did take routes down through the Middle Eastern countries to the Gulf, skirting around the areas in turmoil. Furthermore it seemed that countries which had once been very unwelcoming to visitors were loosening up.

But then there were the two steps back. The Lebanon civil war continues to bubble and boil and today shows no sign whatsoever of reaching any sort of resolution. Iraq's conflict with Iran has shut the door between those two interesting countries just when Iraq was showing signs of opening up. And the normalisation of relations between Israel and Egypt has been counter-balanced by the worsening of relations between Israel and everybody else. Final result? Stalemate.

Still you can visit some of these

countries and the effort is often well spent. Jordan and Israel are both wide open. The Lebanon is sort of open, but not a very wise place to visit. Syria is open but uneasy. Iraq is difficult due to the Iran conflict and Saudi Arabia is all but impossible as a matter of internal policy. If you can visit the Middle East you will find it interesting and worthwhile. The people are friendly and, compared to further east, there is a refreshing lack of touts, rip-offs, conniving and the general level of hassles which travellers always have to be wary of.

Costs are reasonable – they're high compared to further east but low compared to Europe in Jordan and Syria, high compared to anywhere around the Gulf. Standards of cleanliness are high, food quality and variety good. Furthermore you can reach the region easily overland through Turkey and get around equally easily by bus, service (shared) taxis and even hitch-hiking. Syria, Lebanon and Jordan at least are not in the staunchly conservative Muslim mould so you don't get those heavy hassles which some countries load upon you. Remember too that it is quite simple to travel between the Arab nations and Israel, so long as you follow the rules of the game.

Iraq

During the final years of the Shah of Iran's rule, relations with Iraq became much smoother and, partly as a result, a visit to Iraq became much easier. Now, with the long running war with the Ayatollah's Iran still smouldering, Iraq is once again an inaccessible country. You might still manage to visit Baghdad, but forget about crossing the border to Abadan in Iran!

HISTORY

Iraq was historically the 'land between the rivers', the ancient region of Mesopotamia lying between the Tigris and Euphrates Rivers. Under Nebuchadnezzar the kingdom of Babylonia reached its peak and was renowned for the 'Hanging Gardens of Babylon', one of the seven wonders of the ancient world. Then domination from the east (the Persians) and later the west (the Ottoman Turks) followed and it was not until the 1930s that Iraq once more became an independent entity. After the collapse of the Turkish empire there was a short, and unpopular, interlude of British rule.

Independent Iraq was ruled as a kingdom until 1958 when the king was killed in an army coup. A number of unstable and increasingly radical regimes followed – outright hatred of Iran and Israel was the one common theme. A long running internal war with the Kurds, who make up 15% of the population, further soured relations with Iran. When Iran abruptly withdrew their support of the Kurdish rebels, and their hopes for an independent Kurdistan evaporated, relations became somewhat more amicable. At the same time Iraq bounced back from its extreme views on all and sundry and became a slightly more stable country. Then with the fall of the Shah events about-turned and Iraq is once more an implacable foe of Iran and the war has undoubtedly made the Iraqi government's grasp on power more tenuous as well.

FACTS

Iraq has a population of about 10 million and a total area of about 434,000 square km. The capital is Baghdad. The northern Kurdish region is a high and rugged area while the centre is mainly desert. Only in the south, in the region between the two great rivers, is there much agricultural potential and then only with irrigation. Iraq has a very reasonable slice of the Gulf oil reserves and is also the world's largest producer of dates.

VISAS

Iraqi visas are difficult to obtain and if you do get one there will probably be at least several weeks' wait wherever you apply. It is impossible to get a visa at the border or on arrival. Visas cost about US$7 and are valid for 30 days. Don't plan on getting any visas for onward travel while in Iraq, collect them before you arrive there.

MONEY

A$1 = 0.2 dinar
US$1 = 0.3 dinar
£1 = 0.4 dinar

The approximate rates quoted above are official ones, on the free market your dollar or pound would buy about three times as many dinar. There are 1000 fils to the dinar.

CLIMATE

Hot in the summer and cold in the winter. In the south the summer also brings some very high humidity while in the centre you will have dust storms to contend with.

ACCOMMODATION & FOOD

There are youth hostels in Baghdad and Basra and a government camping site in Baghdad.

GETTING THERE & AROUND

It is possible to hitch to Baghdad from Syria or Jordan but in summer, particularly, it is a long, hot, dusty trip. Bus services run from Damascus to Baghdad for less than US$10, also trains from Turkey. Buses and trains, both cheap, run south from Baghdad to Basra, near the Gulf. It is only 30 km from Basra to the Iran border near Abadan where the fighting is taking place. It's possible to continue south from Baghdad to Kuwait.

THINGS TO SEE

Some of the places of interest are close to Baghdad. The city itself has some old mosques, interesting bazaars and good museums. The site of Babylon and the hanging gardens is about 100 km south.

In the north is Mosul, near the ruins of ancient Nineveh. At Nimrud you can see the remains of the seven-storey ziggurat which may be the real 'Tower of Babel'. In the south the Marsh Arabs live in the swampy basin of the Tigris and Euphrates. Basra, where Sinbad the Sailor is said to have sailed from, is near Al-Qurna, the supposed location of the Garden of Eden.

Israel

The mood may not be as unquenchably enthusiastic as it was a few years ago but Israel is still a fascinating country to visit. Say what you will the Israelis have performed the odd little miracle and the country is also a treasure trove of places and things to see.

HISTORY

The strategic position of Israel, or Palestine as it was once known, long made it a much fought over prize. Jewish kingdoms existed here over 2500 years ago but after conquest by the Assyrians, the Babylonians and the Greeks, it finally fell prey to the Romans in 63 BC and despite several Jewish rebellions did not re-emerge as an independent Jewish state until after WW II.

Along with all the other middle eastern countries, Israel was absorbed into the Ottoman empire and abruptly cut loose when the Ottomans collapsed after WW I. Under a British mandate Jewish immigration was encouraged and the idea of a 'Jewish national homeland' was first brought up. The region progressed despite conflict between the Arabs and the Jewish newcomers, but following WW II Britain had a serious change of heart about their 1917 Balfour Declaration as vast numbers of Jews were now desperate to move there from the ruins of war-torn Europe. In 1948 Britain washed its hands of the whole mess and cleared out, leaving an independent Jewish state to fight it out with its new Arab neighbours.

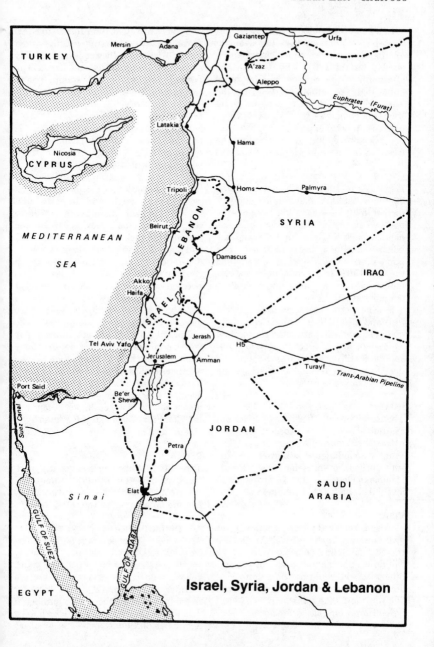

Israel, Syria, Jordan & Lebanon

Israel emerged victorious from that first Arab-Israeli bout, as they did again in 1956 and even more convincingly in the six-day war of 1967. But in 1973 the aftermath of the conflict had far more effect than the actual war itself, for the west – only too happy to support Israel when the going was good – was nowhere near so happy to support it when the Arab countries proved just how dependent the west was on oil – and who had it.

FACTS

Prior to the 1967 war Israel occupied 20,000 square km, that conflict added a further 67,000 square km, mainly the barren Sinai desert. Half of the Sinai was handed back to Egypt in 1979 and the balance has now been returned. The population of a little over three million in the pre-1967 Israel now has another million odd in the 'area under military administration'.

Israel exports large quantities of citrus fruit and also produces much high technology equipment, particularly weaponry. Tourism is also of great importance, but support is still necessary from Europe and the USA since Israel has a staggering military budget to cover.

INFO

The Israel tourist office really pushes out the information for visitors. There is a network of tourist offices around the country including at the border crossing with Jordan, in Jerusalem at 24 Rehov Hamelekh George and at Jaffa Gate, and in Tel Aviv at 7 Rehov Mendele.

VISAS

No visa is required for most nationalities or it is issued free on arrival. Make sure they do not stamp your passport – they will do it on a separate sheet of paper – otherwise you would not be able to visit any Arab country on the same passport. If you stay more than three months you will have to apply for a visa extension and your passport will then be stamped.

If you're travelling from Jordan to Israel to Egypt it's worth getting your Egyptian visa in Amman as they're issued quickly and easily there. If you get the visa in Israel you'll have Tel Aviv stamped on it. Not good in Syria!

MONEY

Quoting exchange rates in Israel is hopeless because the rate changes so fast – in mid-82 US$1 bought you I£16, three years later in mid-85 a dollar was worth about I£800. For years now Israel has had skyrocketing inflation to cope with, as well as unfriendly neighbours. In early 1980 the 100% annual inflation rate had got so out of hand that they renamed the currency the shekel (previously the pound) and started all over again. It's made little difference to the inflation rate which continues to zoom along. In fact it has become so much a fact of life that elaborate systems have been designed to make life liveable – savings in the bank are indexed to inflation for example. For the visitor the answers are not to bring any Israeli currency in with you, not to change more than you have to at one time (it'll be worth less tomorrow) and not to take any out with you (changing Israeli money overseas is virtually impossible). Jordanian dinars can be changed in Jerusalem but Israeli currency is a bad thing to have on you in the Arab countries.

CLIMATE

Typically Mediterranean – hot dry summers, mild wetter winters – along the coast. Further south it is dry and arid, very hot and humid around the Dead Sea.

ACCOMMODATION

Accommodation is generally fairly expensive in hotels, but Israel also has many youth hostels and camp sites. The youth hostels tend to be expensive, there are cheaper places around if you look for them. In Jerusalem there are a number of 'hostels' which are in reality cheap hotels. A number of kibbutz have guest houses where you can see how a kibbutz works without actually working . . . . If you do want to work on a kibbutz try to plan a stay of a reasonable length, they don't appreciate people just passing through or trying to make use of them as cheap accommodation. In summer there are many students there on working holidays, it's easier to find places in winter. One traveller's thoughts on kibbutz and moshav:

I highly recommend a moshav rather than kibbutz, I stayed on both; the moshav provides much better work, more responsibility, more contact with Israelis, still a lot of contact with others travellers, and pay! Kibbutzim have seen so many volunteers over the years and are not very satisfactory for the long-term traveller. They tend to be full of students on a two-month attempt to find a good-looking Israeli lover. They are interesting for observations of the life style and, if you make the effort to learn some Hebrew and talk to the kibbutzniks can be worthwhile.

FOOD

Food in Israel is much like the other countries of the Middle East. Good fruit juices available. To really eat cheaply patronise the take-aways.

GETTING THERE

You can fly to Tel Aviv from Cyprus, Athens or from Cairo now that relations between Egypt and Israel are on a formal basis. From the UK and USA there are lots of cheap flights and charters to Israel. By land you can enter Israel from either Egypt or Jordan. See *Africa on a Shoestring* for more information about Egypt-Israel travel. In brief you can go by shared taxi (*sherut*) or bus. By taxi the total cost is about US$15 per person between Tel Aviv and Cairo. You take one taxi from Jaffa clocktower to the border, another to the Suez Canal, crossing the canal is free and then another taxi takes you into Cairo. By bus you take an Egged bus 362 from Tel Aviv to the border then a sherut taxi to Cairo. Or there is a bus that connects straight through for around US$40.

For travel from Jordan to Israel (west bank) see the Jordan section. Once you have crossed the Jordan River to the west bank take a sherut to Damascus Gate in the old city of Jerusalem. Returning to Amman you again take a sherut from there. They're expensive but you can also take the daily Arab public bus which leaves Damascus Gate about 6.30 am and returns from the bridge about noon. There is a US$10 Israeli departure tax when you cross the Allenby Bridge.

At one time you could only travel from Israel to Jordan if you had first arrived in Israel from Jordan. In other words the polite fiction applied that you had been in 'occupied Jordan' the whole time. This no longer seems to apply and apparently you can now even enter Israel from a non-Arab country and continue to Jordan so long as you have a Jordanian visa and no Israeli stamps in your passport.

GETTING AROUND

The tourist office has extensive information on travelling around Israel. The public bus services are comfortable and on longer trips are air-con. They're also frequent, punctual, fast and cheap. Bus services (and a lot of other things) shut down from Friday sundown to Saturday sundown for the Jewish Sabbath. The main bus company is Egged. Hitching is reasonably easy, stand by a soldier, they're never left hitching for long. Share taxis or sheruts are very popular for inter-city trips, only 15 to 20% more than buses. Sherut taxis also operate on the regular bus routes within the cities. Regular city taxis have meters but you may sometimes have to insist that the drivers use them. There are trains in Israel but the routes are limited. There is also a domestic flight network.

THINGS TO BUY

Old Jerusalem has street after street of covered bazaars offering temptations for tourists. Sheepskin products – sheepskin coats, floor rugs, mittens – are known for their quality and good workmanship, not for their cheap price. Naturally there are plenty of religious souvenirs.

LANGUAGE

Hebrew and Arabic are the two official languages but English is a third unofficial one. Since Israel has such a cosmopolitan mix of races you'll usually find somebody who can speak almost any language.

JERUSALEM

The capital of Israel, Jerusalem is of great historic and religious significance to Jews and Arabs alike. The three thousand year old western wall of Solomon's Temple, the Wailing Wall, is the most sacred Jewish shrine. For Muslims the Mosque of Omar, which includes the Dome of the Rock, is their third most important shrine and also important to Jews and Christians. The Via Dolorosa is the route taken by Christ, carrying the cross, from the scene of his sentencing by Pontius Pilate to the crucifixion site. The Church of the Sepulchre stands over that supposed site. Around the city you'll find the Gardens of Gethsemene, the Mount of Olives and other familiarly religious places.

If you're not interested in religion Jerusalem also has its almost intact ancient city where donkeys and pushcarts are still the usual means of transport. Extensive excavations show ruins under the present city of Crusader, Roman and biblical origin. Just outside the walls is the Me'a She'arim quarter inhabited by strict Jews, many in the black European Hassidic garb and with their hair close cropped except for a long lock over each ear.

Places to Stay & Eat

Hotels are expensive but there are camping grounds and youth hostels. The streets leading out from the Damascus gate have cheap 'hotels' like the *Cairo Youth Hostel* in Derekh Shekhem at just a few dollars a night for a single with hot showers and plenty of mosquitoes. Still it's quiet and friendly and there always

seems to be a pleasant bunch of travellers there. There are many other such places within the walls.

The *King George Hostel* at 15 King George is cheap, clean and has cooking facilities. Around Damascus Gate in the Arab quarter there's the *Faisal* or the more expensive *Ramsis Student Hostel*. The *Swedish Youth Hostel*, near Jaffa Gate in the old city, is also good. Or try the *New Raghadan* at 10 Hanavim St or the large *Louise Waterman-Wise Hostel* at 8 Pisha Rd. Good food in *Hassan Effendi* on 3 Al Rashid St.

AKKO (Acre)

An old and historically important seaport with relics of both Crusader and Islamic influence.

Places to Stay & Eat

Try the *Palm Beach Youth Hostel* on Hof Hatmarin or the government hostel in the old city near Khan el Umdan. Good food in the *Abu Christos* cafe in the old city.

ELAT

This is a seaport and tourist resort at the northern end of the Gulf of Aqaba, very close to the Jordanian port of Aqaba.

Places to Stay & Eat

The government *Youth Hostel* is to the south, a hundred metres further down the road is the *Nophit Youth Hostel*. Other hostels include the *Beth Eschel Hostel* and the *Eilot Hostel*. There is also a camping ground here. There's good food in the *New Tourist Centre*, the self-service restaurant in the Egged bus station or in the *Orient Restaurant* in the business centre.

HAIFA

This large seaport is 100 km north of Tel Aviv. It's a beautifully situated town.

Places to Stay

The *Carmel Youth Hostel* in the south of the town is huge. There are other hostels about 20 km out of the city.

TEL AVIV

This is Israel's major commercial centre and the old city, Jaffa, is of historic interest.

Places to Stay

The *Youth Hostel* is south of the Yarkon in the northern part of the town. There are also a number of simple hotels like the *Migdal David* at 8 Allenby (several others down this same street) or the *Nes Ziona* at 10 Nes Ziona St.

SINAI

You can still make excursions down the Sinai coast of the Gulf of Aqaba and to St Catherine's Monastery from Israel although going further into the Sinai now requires an Egyptian visa. Try not to change too much money at the border at the official rates as there's a good black market in Egypt. There's a compulsory money change requirement but it can be got around with persistence. You'll need some money though, money changing facilities are few and far between. US dollars are the best currency to have.

All the beaches down the Gulf of Aqaba are fantastic and empty. The Egyptians and Bedouins are all very friendly and extremely hospitable, probably due to the lack of tourists.

Places to Stay & Eat

You can stay at the various townships but they are now almost deserted. Dahab is very pleasant and there's a small cafe at Nuweiba. Sharm-el-Sheik is the biggest town (although still very small) and has a youth hostel. You can get a beer at the UN base there.

Getting There

There's a bus once a day from Taba, south of Elat, to Sharm-el-Sheik and another in the morning from there to Cairo. If you miss the bus you wait until the next day. It's an all day trip to Cairo, the roads soon deteriorate into traces through the desert and it's rather dusty. Towns along the Gulf of Suez are much more developed and less appealing than those on the Gulf of Aqaba.

OTHER PLACES

Israel is, of course, full of places of historic, archaeological and religious interest. For Christians the whole country is of biblical interest and Bethlehem, Nazareth, the Sea of Galilee and the River Jordan are just a few of the names that pop up. Megiddo is of great archaeological interest and Massada is the fortress ruins of an heroic Jewish resistance to Roman rule.

Jordan

Despite being badly chopped up as a result of the 1967 Arab-Israeli conflict, Jordan is one of the most interesting and friendly of the Middle East countries and also the easiest to visit.

HISTORY

Jordan was another country which escaped from a long period of Turkish rule when the Ottoman Empire collapsed after WW I. A period of semi-independence followed with the British pulling the strings from above. After WW II Jordan became completely independent, but almost immediately was embroiled in the first Arab-Israeli war of 1948 and ended up with a large swag of Palestinian refugees.

Despite Jordan's relatively amenable attitude towards Israel its front line position has meant it has continued to bear the brunt of the following conflicts and in 1967 Jordan lost the west bank of the Jordan river, the most fertile and densely populated part of the country, and the Jordanian half of the city of Jerusalem. Jordan has enjoyed relatively stable government under King Hussein who has ruled the country since the 1951 assassination of his grandfather. He has kept Jordan aligned with the west.

FACTS

Jordan's population is about three million and the country occupies an area of approximately 97,000 square km, much of it uninhabited desert. Jordan shares none of its southern neighbours' oil wealth and is mainly agricultural although there are some mineral resources.

INFO

City maps and brochures of major places of interest are available at the Ministry of Tourism & Antiquities, Al Mutanabbi St, Amman, near the 3rd Circle.

VISAS

Visas are obtainable in neighbouring countries. For some nationalities they may be available at the border or at the airport on arrival but check carefully first. They cost from nothing to US$8 depending on your nationality and are issued same day. The embassy in Ankara is unfriendly and unhelpful, the embassy in Damascus is much better.

MONEY

A$1 = 0.3 dinar
US$1 = 0.4 dinar
£1 = 0.6 dinar

The dinar is divided into 1000 fils. Jordan is much more expensive than Turkey or Syria.

CLIMATE

The climate is pleasant on the west bank of the Jordan, now occupied by Israel, with some rain in winter and spring. The east bank is hot, dry and barren and the country eventually shades into the Syrian desert.

ACCOMMODATION

There is a wide range of hotels in the main towns of Jordan although costs tend to be fairly high by Asian standards.

FOOD

Take-aways from small cafes and street stalls are the cheapest way to eat. You'll find spiced lamb cut from revolving spits, chick-pea and salad sandwiches, yoghurt, round flat bread and syrupy nut-and-pastry cakes. In fact you'll find the food very similar not only to the other countries of the region (Lebanon, Israel, Syria) but also to Greece and Turkey. Meat is fairly expensive but houmos, foule, yoghurt (especially) are all cheap and good. Overall, however, food is rather more expensive than in Syria.

GETTING THERE

You can fly to Amman from Beirut, Damascus, Cairo or further afield. Jordan is the one Arab country which still has air links with Egypt. Alia is the Jordanian airline and they are relatively good with student discounts or cheap tickets. There are buses or service taxis to the Lebanon and Syria and it's possible to hitch from Jordan through Saudi Arabia to the Gulf – if you can get a visa. It is quite straightforward to cross from Jordan into Israel.

To Egypt Apart from flying between Amman and Cairo there is also a boat service between Suez and Aqaba departing at least once every two days. It costs about 20 dinars for a deck-class ticket – and that's all you need to buy – since they will give you a free cabin to 'welcome' you as a foreigner, even if you have only paid for deck-class. Many people even get a free first-class cabin. It's worth buying some Jordanian dinars in Suez before you leave – most of the moneychangers there gave better rates changing hard currency into dinars than anywhere in Jordan.

To Israel Well not to Israel, to the 'Occupied West Bank'. If you want to visit Israel don't, whatever you do, mention Israel. It's the 'occupied west bank' or 'Palestine' and if you cross the Jordan River to the west bank you're certainly not intending to go any further than that – certainly not into western Palestine, or whatever they call it! Of course once you're across the Jordan River you're in

Israel (at least according to the Israelis) and you can then go wherever you please – including to Egypt or back to Jordan.

There are certain rules to follow when crossing from the Arab world into Israel although it's actually very straightforward. First of all don't let on that you've been there – ask to have any immigration stamps put on a separate piece of paper in your passport. Once you have evidence that you've been into Israel your passport is useless back in the Arab world. You can enter Israel from two Arab countries – Egypt or Jordan. At one time you could not travel Israel-Jordan unless you had first travelled Jordan-Israel but now it appears you can go in either direction. The tricky question of how you managed to arrive from 'occupied Jordan' without first having been to 'unoccupied Jordan' seems to be ignored. Just make sure you have a visa for Jordan before you arrive in Israel.

To visit Israel from Jordan you need a permit to cross the Allenby Bridge – except while you are in Jordan it's the King Hussein Bridge. To get this you have to go to the Ministry of the Interior at the far end of King Hussein St in Amman. Take a service taxi to Nagra Circle and get there before 1 pm. You need a 50 fil stamp (from the post office or from a couple of Arabs sitting under an umbrella by the building), a photograph and 1.50 dinar fee. There is a form to be filled in then the pass takes from one to three days to issue. Some people reckon it's easier to get a travel agent to apply for the pass for you but the general consensus is that it's quite easy to do it yourself. The pass is only valid for a month so your stay is limited unless you're willing to go to Egypt and get a new passport.

Having got your pass you then have to get to the river. Easiest is to take a JETT air-con bus which will take you from Amman to the Jordan checkpoint, across the border and right through to the Israeli immigration point for 3 dinar – no hassles. With a little hassle you can take a service

taxi from Al Abduli station on King Hussein St in Amman to the Jordanian check-point for 1 dinar then take a bus from there to the Israeli immigration point for another 1.50 dinar. Most difficult of all would be to take a public bus from Amman to Salt, another to the Jordanian border. Or to hitch. Note that you cannot walk across the bridge, you must be driven. The bridge is closed on Saturdays, the Jewish Sabbath.

On your way to the bridge look out for Palestinian refugee camps. It is all but impossible to get Israeli currency before you arrive, but you can get some at the Israeli border check-point where you can also pick up Israeli tourist information. It's wise to keep some Jordanian money for your return journey as there is no place to get dinars at the Jordanian side of the border. Leaving Amman on the bus at 6.30 am it will take you all day to reach Jerusalem, only 80 km away. The 1.50 dinar bus across the border is a bit of a rip-off since it is only a km, but you've got no choice.

To Syria JETT buses or Karnak buses, the Syrian equivalent, operate twice a day. From Damascus the fare is expensive, around S£40. There's also a railway line, but at present there is no passenger service. There are service taxis though. You get to Beirut in Lebanon via Damascus.

To Saudi Arabia & the Gulf There is a road branching off south from Ma'an to Mecca and Riyadh and another continues on south from Aqaba, but most people will be following the oil pipeline to Kuwait through Saudi Arabia or into Iraq. The line road runs east from a point north of Amman to H5, which is the Jordanian customs point where you make the Saudi Arabia or Iraq decision. With so many trucks heading down to the Gulf these days there is a reasonable possibility of hitching a ride – see Saudi Arabia for more details.

There is a daily bus from Amman to Baghdad and this is a good way to get to

H5 as hitching to that point can be pretty difficult. There is a rest house where you can stay and many truckies will be heading east. A Saudi Arabian transit visa only allows entry at Turayf on the pipeline road.

GETTING AROUND

There are lots of service taxis (shared taxis), public buses (rather erratic schedules), a limited train service and luxury buses like those of JETT (Jordan Express Tourist Travel). They operate on all the main routes including to the King Hussein/Allenby Bridge. Many of their routes use air-con buses. Hitch-hiking is relatively easy although traffic is light on some routes and you have to compete with soldiers for rides.

THINGS TO BUY

What else but an Arab head-dress for a dinar or less. Look for the ones with a woven pattern – the poorer quality ones have a cheap, printed pattern.

LANGUAGE

The Jordanians are proud of their relatively high literacy rate and many people speak English, so communication is no problem. The English-language newspaper in Amman has Omar Sharif as its bridge columnist. The people in general are very helpful and friendly, some travellers say the most hospitable on the entire Asia overland route.

AMMAN

Amman is quite an interesting city and one of the most ancient in the world, dating back to 300 BC. Set amongst seven hills it is now a fast growing, modern city but also has well restored Roman ruins including a 6000-seat amphitheatre, a forum and a street of columns. There are two small museums in the amphitheatre – a folklore museum and a costume and jewellery museum. To the north, across from the amphitheatre on a hill, is the citadel – an old Roman garrison. The citadel is an unimpressive jumble of old stones but the hill gives a good view of Aman. There's also an Archaeological Museum up there.

Jerash is the most popular day trip from Amman but you can also visit Madaba where there are some good mosaics but little else of interest.

Places to Stay & Eat

Amman is expensive for accommodation, count on around 1.50 dinar for a dorm bed, 3 dinar for a double room. Sleeping on the roof of some cheap hotels is OK. The cheapest hotels include the *Al Farouq* and the *Cliff Hotel*, both on side lanes off the top end of King Faisal St. The *Cleopatra Hotel* is very conveniently situated at Al Abdali and has dorm beds for 1.50 dinars. *Lords*, on an extension of King Hussein St, is similarly priced. The *Quasar Abdeen Hotel* on Hashemi St is seven to 10 minutes from the city centre near the Roman amphitheatre, it's pretty good although it's worth haggling over the price. There are other similar hotels along the same street. The *Hotel Venice* is close to the centre and has hot showers and an English-speaking manager. Bargain diplomatically.

There's a great place to eat about two thirds of the way along King Tatal St, walking north.

Getting Around

A taxi into town from the airport is about a dinar. There is no airport bus but if you go 400 metres out of the terminal to the roundabout you can get a public bus. Get off at the bottom of King Faisal St – Amman is very confusing, it's built on seven hills and they're real hills!

The Al Abdali bus/taxi station is the important transport location. It's on King Hussein St before the branch to Abdali St. Buses go from here to Salt and on to the west bank or the Dead Sea; service taxis go to Jerash and direct to the west bank. Get to Al Abdali by a 15 to 20 minute walk down King Hussein St from the centre or get a service taxi from King Ghazi St (50 fils). The JETT bus station is about a km from Abdali towards Nagra Circle, just past the Alia office.

There are a number of government registered travel agencies, mainly on King Hussein St, which can arrange tours to Jerash, Aqaba, the Dead Sea and Petra by bus or taxi – but they're all very expensive.

JERASH

This beautifully preserved Graeco-Roman city was abandoned after an earthquake in 726 AD and disappeared into the desert. It was finally rediscovered in 1806 but not excavated until the 1920s. There are temples, churches, three theatres, Roman baths and an avenue of magnificent columns over a km long.

Getting There

Take a service taxi from Al Abdali (450 fils) to the ruins which are about a km from the present day town of Jerash. A bus is about 100 fils. Returning to Amman get a service taxi from the township. There are no hotels in Jerash.

PETRA

Like Jerash this lost city was forgotten by the outside world for a thousand years. Rediscovered in 1812 excavations only commenced in 1929 and the central city was not uncovered until after 1958. The spectacular city was commenced in the 3rd century BC by the Nabateans who carved palaces, temples, tombs, store-rooms and stables from the rocky cliffs. From here they commanded the trade route from Damascus to Arabia and through here the great spice, silk and slave caravans passed. The city is marvellously preserved and the effort and/or expense required to get here should not dissuade you from going. Admission fee to Petra is 1 dinar for foreigners.

Places to Stay

There is a *Rest House* but it is rather expensive. You can also get on-the-floor accommodation with local people in Wadi Musa. It's definitely worth spending longer at Petra than just a day trip. If you're going to walk along the gorge into Petra do it very early in the day – it gets very hot.

Getting There

It is a three hour, 262 km drive south from Amman to Petra. You'd have to be hardy to hitch there along the deserted desert road. There's a JETT bus but there is also a cheaper, although hard to find, minibus from Amman. The tourist office may deny it! Another cheap way is to take a minibus from Amman to Ma'an and from Ma'an to Wadi Musa, a km from Petra. The other alternative, though comfortable, is pricey. An air-con JETT tour bus does an all inclusive round trip – including two coffees, lunch, horses to travel the winding gorge into the city plus a guide. You can make the same trip with other tour companies by taxi at even greater cost. Minibuses also operate on from Petra to Aqaba at about half the cost of the JETT bus.

It's a common misconception that the only entrance to Petra is through the narrow, twisting, three km long Siq gorge, flanked by 70 metre high cliffs. There are, in actual fact, roads to the north and south. Wadi Musa, near the main road at the start of the gorge is the village nearest Petra.

AQABA

Aqaba was just a small fishing village until it was acquired from Saudi Arabia in 1955, giving Jordan access to the Red Sea. It was a port even before Roman times and today is important both as a deep water port and as a tourist centre. During WW I it was a locale for Lawrence of Arabia's activities.

There's good snorkelling around Aqaba – go south towards the Saudi Arabian border to Zubelin, near the phosphate factory and solar research centre. Be

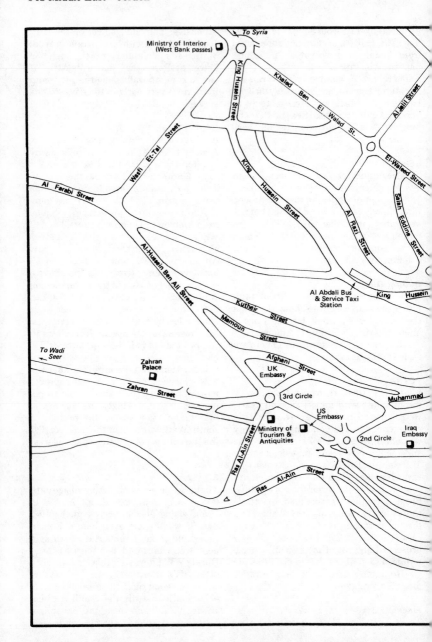

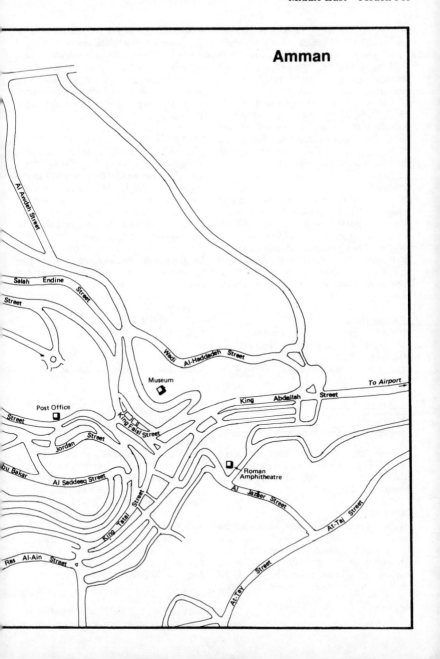

Amman

careful of coral cuts, poisonous fish and sea urchins – of which there are plenty. And if you hitch don't hitch rides with cars with Saudi Arabian plates – they may have designs on your body reported one traveller!

You can make a trip from Aqaba to Wadi Rum, a romantic desert valley with soaring cliffs carved into fantastic shapes by the wind and a crenellated desert fort. It's a superb place where you can stay with bedouin, there's not much else here.

Places to Stay
The *Jerusalem Hotel* is OK, you can also sleep on the roof. Similar 500 fil prices at the *Al Samarka Fish Restaurant*, which is on the waterfront, across from the JETT station. They have snorkelling equipment here. Other hotels include the *Aqaba* and the *Petra* and there is a *Rest House* near the port. Lots of good little places to eat.

Getting There
It's a five hour trip from Amman. There are two roads – the Desert Highway and the King's Highway which goes to Petra, closer to the border. A JETT bus from Amman is 4 dinar.

Kuwait

An oil-rich, super free-port, the lucky residents of Kuwait have cradle to grave care to such an extent that they hardly need raise a finger.

HISTORY
Kuwait's rapid progress to becoming the wealthiest country in the world (in terms of per capita income) only started with the discovery of oil in 1946. It was under British protection from 1914 until its independence was recognised in 1961.

FACTS
The population doubled in the 10 years from 1965 and is now 1.5 million. Most of the growth is due to the massive influx of foreign workers. The land area of this tiny state is just 24,000 square km, most of it desert. Kuwait is also a free port, appealing mainly to the richies from neighbouring Gulf states who fly in on shopping trips. It's a good place to sell blood.

VISAS
A transit visa, available in a few hours in Amman, is initially only valid for three days but can easily be extended at the office near the Hilton Hotel. If you are travelling through Saudi Arabia you must have a visa for the next country before applying for the Saudi one. In Tehran (if anyone is still getting visas in Tehran!) the Kuwait embassy would only issue a limited number of visas a day and you had to arrive early in the morning if you wanted one.

MONEY
A$1	=	0.2 dinar
US$1	=	0.3 dinar
£1	=	0.4 dinar

There are 1000 fils to the dinar.

CLIMATE
Hot, humid and dusty in summer. Not bad in winter.

GETTING THERE
See Saudi Arabia for details of getting there through that country. Ditto for Iraq. Travelling across the Gulf by dhow is kind of romantic but will involve some strong bargaining if you don't want to end up paying more than the airfare. There are also hydrofoils to/from Abadan – or at least there were prior to the Iraq-Iran conflict. There are regular ships from Kuwait to Karachi and on to Bombay. A 101 bus takes you to Kuwait airport.

THINGS TO SEE
Lots of rich people? Dhow building still goes on to some extent, visit the dhow port

near the Sief Palace. From there regular dhows sail the 30-odd km to Failake Island where there are three sites of archaeological interest – one dates back to the bronze age, one to the Persian Seleucid Empire and one is Greek. There is a small museum here and another in Kuwait.

PLACES TO STAY & EAT

Kuwait has a number of very expensive, very heavily booked 'international' hotels and not much else. In Salmieh there is a *Boy Scouts Hostel* open to men only, if they are in possession of a YHA card. You can only stay for a few days. Get there on a 14 bus, it may also be possible to camp there. Cheap meals are available at the university.

Lebanon

Prior to the civil war, the Lebanon was easily the most touristed and, therefore, the most expensive, of the Mediterranean Arab states. It looks like being a long while before visiting the Lebanon is easy once again although, surprisingly, travellers are going there and reporting no great difficulties.

HISTORY

The Lebanon was another country which emerged from the break-up of the Ottoman Empire after WW I. Between the wars it was under a French mandate and it became fully independent during WW II. Its strategic Middle Eastern location and relatively stable and west-leaning government made it a major trade and banking centre. Many western multi-nationals had their Middle Eastern or Arab nation head offices in Beirut.

But the Lebanon had a fatal flaw in its national make-up – power and control rested with the right wing Christian part of the population while the Muslim part (the population is almost exactly split 50:50)

felt they were excluded from real government. Add a liberal measure of displaced and unstable Palestinians and you have a recipe for disaster. The Americans waded in to help put down a Muslim rebellion in 1958 but in the mid-70s the all-out civil war tore the country apart. An uneasy peace was forced upon the two sides by the Syrians then the Israelis marched in, only to march out again leaving a worse mess than before. In the meantime the business emphasis has shifted from the Mediterranean to the Gulf and it is highly unlikely that Beirut will ever regain its pre-eminent commercial position.

FACTS

The Lebanon has a population of about 2½ million and an area of 8700 square km. The economy was principally agricultural but much of the country's income derived from its importance as a trade centre and from its touristic appeal.

VISAS

Required for most nationalities, cost depends on where you are from. Lebanese visas are easy to get outside the Middle East but can be terrible actually in the region.

MONEY

A$1	=	L£ 6.70
US$1	=	L£ 9.50
£1	=	L£13.40

CLIMATE

The Lebanon has a Mediterranean climate – hot and dry in the summer, cool and rainy in the winter.

GETTING THERE

You can fly to Beirut from neighbouring Arab states. MEA (Middle East Airlines), the Lebanon airline, had a reputation for being particularly liberal with student discounts and youth fares.

GETTING AROUND

There are buses and service taxis.

BEIRUT

This was the Paris of the Middle East and despite the fighting the shops managed to stay stocked with the latest fashions and an international selection of cosmetics, appliances and foods. In its prime Beirut was very cosmopolitan. Today most of the interesting tourist sites are off-limits – as is most of Beirut. The Dead Sea Scrolls are in the Beirut National Museum.

Places to Stay & Eat

No hostel card is needed at the *Club House Youth Hostel* in the central Al Hamra district. Otherwise accommodation is expensive. Clean street stalls and cafes sell delicious take-away shish kebabs, spiced lamb & salad, yoghurt, gooey syrup cakes and fresh fruit juices.

OTHER PLACES

There are impressive ruins at Byblos, believed to be where the word 'Bible' came from. More interesting ruins and temples at Baalbeck, this is also the centre of Lebanese hash production! There is a music and drama festival here every year. The Lebanon has many fine crusader castles including a particularly good one at Sidon.

Saudi Arabia

Saudi Arabia – the site of Mecca – is a vast, empty, desert land which, due to having lots of oil, is also one of the richest countries in the world. It's also very hard to visit. Saudi Arabia is a long way from almost anywhere, hard to get permission to enter and expensive to travel in. Since it is also an extremely conservative Muslim country there are a few additional hassles in that line. The one exception to the no-entry rules is that it is possible to get a three-day transit visa to pass through the country to the Gulf along the oil pipeline road.

HISTORY

Saudi Arabia is the site of Mecca and Medina and is thus of prime importance to the Islamic religion. It was from these holy cities that the Arabs swept out to carry Islam to the world and Arab power right across North Africa and into Spain to the west and all the way to India in the east. Later the region fell under the Ottoman shadow and for centuries was a prized possession of the mighty Turkish empire.

For the last hundred years of the Ottomans the rise of the fervent Wahabis, who were determined to restore Islam to its original purity, created havoc for the Turks. At times they snatched large parts of Saudi Arabia in episodes of romantic bravery. But it was not until the final collapse of the Ottomans that the state of Saudi Arabia came into existence. It was this colourful but deeply conservative history which led to Saudi Arabia's painfully puritanical stance today. The enormous wealth created by the country's massive oil reserves has caused a bizarre collision between the various attitudes in the country.

FACTS

The population of Saudi Arabia is estimated to be about nine million but could well be a lot less since many people are still nomadic and hard to keep track of. The land area is approximately 2,200,000 square km but much of this area is totally inhospitable desert. Only around the oases and in the south-west towards the Yemen is there land with agricultural possibilities. Small matter, for Saudi Arabia has vast oil reserves around the Gulf. Oil production is limited mainly by how fast they can process the flood of petro-dollars. It is virtually impossible to spend anything like the country's annual income and even finding ways of investing it has proved difficult. Amazingly Saudi Arabia's oil wealth did not start to be exploited until after WW II. Prior to that the country had a purely subsistence economy and oil was actually imported!

As a factor of its history Saudi Arabia is quite amazingly conservative – only recently have women been allowed any education at all and this aroused a storm of protest from religious leaders. They have managed to ban cinemas completely and tried to prevent the introduction of radio and TV. Alcohol is, of course, totally banned and taking photographs (making representations of human beings) is frowned on. Saudi Arabians don't pray towards Mecca just because they want to – they are required to by law! Women may not appear outside unveiled, are not allowed to drive nor may they work except in all-women working places. Female visitors (who are only allowed into the country if chaperoned by a male) should ensure they are well covered. This attitude is bound to be altered and not just by increased contact with the west. The country's pressing shortage of skilled labour has brought in many Egyptian and Palestinian workers who have brought with them much more enlightened inter-pretations of Islamic life.

VISAS

Difficult – three-day transit visas or business visas are all they normally issue and tickets out may be required. Always say you are travelling by car, not by bus or hitching, when applying for a visa. You also need a letter from your embassy saying you're a fine person and you must already have a visa for your next port of call. Thus if you're travelling on the pipeline road from Jordan you should get a Kuwait visa first.

You rarely meet travellers who've managed to spend any time in Saudi Arabia so I was interested to share a taxi into the city from Colombo's airport in Sri Lanka with someone who'd recently been there. He'd had the usual visa kickback but got around it with a little ingenuity and chutzpah. In Amman he'd gone to an international truck compound, copied down the licence plate details, truck owner's name, etc, from the side of a truck, then borrowed a typewriter at his embassy and typed up an official looking letter listing himself as passenger/co-driver for the truck. With this he managed to get a Saudi visa, though only a transit one for three days. He spent two weeks in Saudi Arabia, however, and no comment was made on departure – 'I don't think the officials can read their own language' was his comment.

He hitched across Saudi Arabia, a relatively easy task given the volume of truck traffic passing through but he warned that it's wise to stick to European, Lebanese or other Arab, but non-Saudi, trucks. He formed this opinion after fighting off the advances of amorous Saudi truck drivers on a couple of occasions. He spent a week in Riyadh, sleeping most nights beside a wall on a quiet and unfrequented area of garden beside the InterContinental Hotel. Towards the end of his stay he met a Lebanese who put him up for a couple of nights.

We hear from time to time from workers in Saudi Arabia but I wish we heard more often from intrepid travellers who manage to breach the barriers the Saudis put up to keep visitors out.

MONEY

A$1	=	2.70 SR
US$1	=	3.80 SR
£1	=	5.40 SR

The unit of currency is the Saudi Riyal (SR) divided into 100 halalah.

CLIMATE

The winter climate is quite pleasant, it can actually get cold at times, but in summer (April to September) the temperature can be searing. On both the east (Gulf) and west (Red Sea) coasts the high temper-atures are made worse by the extremely high humidity.

GETTING THERE

There are boats available across the Red Sea from Jeddah to the Sudan and Ethiopia (when that country is accessible) but it is generally as cheap to fly. You can transport cars across to Africa this way. There are three roads entering Saudi Arabia from Jordan. One follows the oil pipeline from the Gulf. This pipeline was laid in a remarkably short period of time after WW II. Another road follows the old pilgrim and caravan trade route south to Jeddah and Mecca while the third runs south from Aqaba along the coast. The roads are of good standard and are rapidly being extended but the distances are very great. Further south to the most interesting parts of the country and on into the Yemen the roads deteriorate.

If you are hitching along the pipeline road, across that long stretch of desert, a tent is a useful article since trucks often don't have sleeping room for more than the driver. The trucks usually travel in convoy so it doesn't hurt to split up with a hitching partner. The pipeline road runs right down to the Gulf where you can head south to Bahrain and Qatar or turn north to Kuwait. You can be pushed to cross Saudi Arabia in the time allowed by your transit visa.

THINGS TO SEE

The only really interesting places to see in Saudi Arabia – Mecca and Medina, are completely off-limits to non-believers although a million or more Muslims make the pilgrimage every year. On your transit visa, which only allows you to enter on the pipeline road, all you'll see is desert.

Syria

Syria remains one of the hardest-line Arab countries although visiting it or passing through it is no problem for visitors. The civil strife in the Lebanon and continuing friction with Israel have recently taken their toll in Syria and the internal situation, always a little uneasy, is now very fraught. Syria has lots of secret police so keep your mouth shut! And try to ignore the gunfire.

If you go with an open mind you can find it a surprisingly easy country to visit:

We spent two weeks in Syria and had a really fantastic time. Yes, there are lots of soldiers in Damascus, lots of police road blocks and secret police everywhere, but we (two females) met nothing but hospitality, kindness and consideration all the way. We were plied with tea, food, bus tickets and meals everywhere we went. In fact, the bus ticket situation was ludicrous – when we asked where to buy city bus tickets (in Damascus and Tartus) people just said 'Forget it – you're a tourist. Welcome,' and ushered us on board.

As seasoned travellers, we're used to the bum pinching and it took us a couple of days to realise that Syria's not like that. After growling and snarling our way round Damascus, we realised we were making a big mistake!

Anne Robinson & Jane Nineham

HISTORY

Historically Syria included the whole Mediterranean Arab world – Jordan, Israel, Lebanon and modern Syria. It was an important Phoenician trading post and later an equally important part of the Roman, Persian, Egyptian and Babylonian Empires – and for that matter anywhere else which was in the empire-building business. Finally it ended up as part of Ottoman Turkey and got dished out to France (along with the Lebanon) when it broke up after WW I. This event caused considerable local anger as the region had been independent for two years from the close of WW I until it was unilaterally handed over to France in 1920.

The French never had much luck with their Syria-Lebanon mandate and during WW II agreed that it should become independent. Typically they proved reluctant to actually grant that promised independence after the war but Syria finally did achieve it in 1946. A period of some political instability and a brief flirtation with the idea of a United Arab Republic followed and Syria remains at the front line of anti-Israeli attitudes.

FACTS

The Syrian population of approximately six million occupies an area of 182,000 square km. The economy is principally agricultural as the land bordering the Mediterranean is fertile – it becomes progressively less so inland, eventually sloping off into a barren desert. Syria also has some limited oil resources.

INFO

The country is not well set up for do-it-yourself tourism so information is hard to come by and limited in its scope. Try the Tourist Information Office in Boulevard Port Said, opposite the Aeroflot offices in Damascus. There is also the Ministry of Tourism on Fourat St near Ramy St in Damascus. The tourist police also lurk in this building somewhere. There is a tourist office at the Damascus airport but it is not always manned.

VISAS

Syrian visas are obtainable at consulates and embassies abroad. They can be tricky, people have reported being told in Ankara to go back to London for a visa! Insistence usually wins through although nobody seems to have much good to say about the embassy and consulate officials in Istanbul or Ankara. With a letter of recommendation from your embassy the visa should be issued in the same day and will cost anything from nothing to US$8 depending on your nationality. You should always check the latest visa situation before blithely turning up at the border. You are given 15 days on arrival and that can be extended. It's best not to admit plans to go any further than Syria or they may require you to get a visa for the next country – Jordanian visas are easier to get in Syria than in Turkey for example.

The Syrians are very touchy about Israel – any slight evidence of having been there is sufficient to get you kicked out. Even possession of Israeli money is enough. People have been handed over to the police and deported because a youth hostel manager spotted an Israeli YH stamp on their card. Damascus is a bad place for Kuwaiti or Saudi Arabian visas, better to get them in Amman.

MONEY

A$1	=	S£ 7.50
US$1	=	S£10.50
£1	=	S£15.00

The approximate rates quoted above are free market, the official rate is less than half the above. You're required to change US$100 into Syrian currency on arrival in Syria irrespective of your length of stay. They will try to get it out of you in cash but if you insist you only have travellers' cheques will accept that. There's a small black market in Syria, try shopkeepers. Syria is much cheaper than Jordan, about the same level as Turkey.

CLIMATE

Syria has a Mediterranean climate with hot, dry summers and mild, wet winters close to the coast. Inland it gets progressively drier and more inhospitable.

ACCOMMODATION

Syria has a number of youth hostels and reasonably priced hotels in Damascus, Hama, Homs, Aleppo and Palmyra.

FOOD

As in other Middle East countries.

GETTING THERE

There are regular flights to and from neighbouring Arab countries. Service taxis operate daily to Beirut (three hours when the route is possible) and to Amman. The station in Damascus is just two minutes up the road from the post office – ask, the people are very friendly and will show you where to go. Buses to Amman operate several times daily and cost S£30. There are trains to Amman twice a week. Although it's no great distance the border formalities take so long that the trip takes about six hours. So try to leave early.

It's easy to arrive in or depart from Syria overland through Turkey. Either up the coast through Latakia, from Aleppo to Antakya in Turkey or directly north from Aleppo through A'zaz.

GETTING AROUND

Hitching is fairly easy, long distance service taxis run between the main cities and there is an extensive bus network. Karnak is the Syrian equivalent of JETT in Jordan. They offer a comprehensive network and their services are fast, comfortable and reliable. It is advisable to book a day in advance. The bus office is usually in the town centre and therefore convenient (the 'garage' for other long distance buses is often on the edge of town). The office staff are harassed but helpful and Syrian hospitality extends to cold water and bonbons on board!

Other long distance buses tend to be slower and cheaper than Karnak and are often less comfortable. They have the advantage of going to places off the beaten track. Overall transport is about the same price as in Turkey and quite efficient.

City buses are cheap but it's necessary to buy tickets in advance. There are kiosks scattered around town for this purpose.

THINGS TO BUY

There are good buys in leather, brass and copperware or silver and gold. Damascus is the production centre for traditional Arab head-dresses, they are plentiful and cheap. Damascus has a large market or souk but the one in Aleppo is superb.

DAMASCUS

Damascus is probably the oldest continuously inhabited city in the world. It was a centre as long ago as 5000 BC. Later it was a Persian capital, fell to Alexander the Great, became a Greek centre and then a major Roman city. In 635 AD, with Byzantine power on the decline, Damascus fell to the Muslims and became an important Arab city. In 1400 it was sacked by the Mongols and then had centuries of slow decline under the Mamelukes and the Ottomans before eventually passing to French mandate and finally independence. Today Damascus has regained some of its former glory and has a population of about a million.

Most of the city walls and gates are still standing in the old biblical part of the city. Souk el Hamidiyeh is the foremost bazaar with a covered walkway of shops and stalls. Right at the back of the souk you come out at the Omayyade Mosque, the most important Muslim shrine. Next to this is the Kasr el Aazemn, an old palace which has been converted into a folk museum. Further into the old city is the Byzantine church of St Marie (in Kannisat el Mariamyeh) and further still the Chapel of St Paul (according to the Bible Paul was cured of blindness on the Damascus road). The tomb of John the Baptist is also supposed to be in the old city. Others things to see include the street called Straight (Madhat Bacha), the National Museum and the Craft Bazaar (Artisanat) which occupies part of an old caravanserai, the courtyards of which make nice resting places from which to watch the world go by. The Western (Hijaz) Railway Station has an interesting ceiling.

Damascus is a very pretty city (especially compared to the rest of the Middle East) with lots of trees and parks. The heavy Syrian atmosphere is always there, though. Gunfire is often in the background.

Information

Damascus has a tourist office which is open at least from 9 am to 8 pm. The staff are generally extremely helpful and speak good English. It's worth having a map of Damascus before you arrive there.

There are English language books in the big hotel bookshops (eg Sheraton, Meridian). There is an English/French bookshop on a street which connects Boulevard Port Said with Boulevard Youssef El Azmeh, just north of the expensive Hotel Venise. There's another in Sharia Fourat (the street north of the Central Post Office), almost opposite the Hotel Al Hambra.

Places to Stay

Accommodation is generally not that cheap – count on S£40-60 for a double, places cheaper than that are usually really bad. Cheap hotels are often crowded with the military. Look for places around the Central Post Office and in the small streets around the monument of the place of martyrs. El Wahde El Arabie is typical.

Hotel (Fondok) Said, just off Place Merge (Place of the Martyrs, Saahat El Chouhadaa) is S£50 for a triple room (the smallest they have) with sink. There is a communal toilet and shower, tea is served (free) ad infinitum and the people are friendly, although it's a bit noisy. The *Al Afamia* in the block behind the Central Post Office is a bit up-market at S£63 for a double with bath. The *Siaha,* opposite the Said (or Al-Sayeed) is also S£63 for a double.

There's a good *Youth Hostel* in Damascus at 66 Mazra Square, up the road from the Tourist Office. You absolutely have to have a YHA card to use the hostel, which costs S£8 a night. Maximum stay is three nights although how long you are allowed to stay basically depends on the old man who looks after the hostel. There is a strictly enforced 10 pm curfew which can be a real hassle.

Places to Eat

The *Najmeh Restaurant* on Ramy St does chicken and kebabs – a filling selection will cost about S£10-20. There is an excellent cafe on Sharia Fourat immediately next to the Arabic bookshop on the corner of Boulevard el Jabry. It serves mainly stews – with vegetables, kebab, beans, peas, macaroni. A plate of stew with salad is about S£10. There are lots of shawerma and juice shops around Place Merge.

Getting There

Microbuses to Palmyra run from a station known simply as 'Garage' (near Faressal Khoury). The fare is S£15.

Getting Around

Airport tax is S£10. The airport bus costs S£1 and drops you off at the side of the Central Post Office. It departs from there for the airport every hour on the hour. City bus tickets must be bought in advance. You can get them opposite the Hotel Venise or on Chouky Kouwatly, near Boulevard Port Said. Each ticket is good for two journeys by one person, or one journey for two people.

QUNAITRA

On the border with Israel this was the capital of the Golan Heights. It was occupied by Israel in 1967 and as they withdrew from it – under the terms of an armistice agreement in 1974 – they systematically destroyed the town. It's now a ghost town and fascinating to walk around, which you can do quite freely. You can visit the tombs the Israelis are claimed to have looted and the former Israeli army camp.

At Checkpoint Alpha, the sole border crossing between Israel and Syria which is only open to UN soldiers, the Syrian officers speak good English and are very friendly. They may well find you a lift back to Damascus with a UN soldier.

Getting There

To visit Qunaitra you need a special permit which is issued in five minutes or so at the office on Adnan Malki Bas near the American cultural centre and the Libyan Peoples' Bureau, in Damascus. The Damascus tourist office will send you to the wrong office if you ask them where to go. With your permit catch a microbus to Khan Arnabe from next to the Karnak bus station. Then walk to the United Nations checkpoint and hitch the few km into Qunaitra.

HOMS

Homs is a pleasant town with a *Youth Hostel* costing S£8 in the scout hall near the Karnak bus stop.

Getting There

Damascus to Homs is S£10, a further S£16 to Latakia. Buses go to Crac Des

Chevaliers (Qalaat Al-Hosn) a couple of times daily and cost S£3.

HAMA

Hama is reputed to be the most conservative and fundamental of Syria's towns, the women tend to veil more often than in other places. It's a good stopping off point and is scenic and restful. There are lots of gardens for lazing around in.

The town has lots of *norias* (water wheels) to watch – they are incredibly noisy (a creaking groan) and the local kids use them as diving boards. These huge constructions are 20 metres in diameter and two thousand years old. The best ones are about a km east of the town centre and there is a cafe on the opposite bank for tea and expensive food.

Hama's Great Mosque was spectacular, but was razed to the ground a few years ago. There are huge bombed or bulldozed areas, the remains of the government's brutal suppression of a Muslim revolt in 1982 when up to 30,000 people died.

The upstairs was the best part of Hama's good, small museum but it too was reduced to ruins during the revolt. Don't ask the tourist office about this. There are nice views over the river valley from the citadel.

Information

There's a helpful tourist office although their town map isn't accurate.

Places to Stay

The *Cairo Hotel* has good bathless doubles for S£40. Also on Boulevard Koutli there's the *Riad Hotel*.

Getting There

The daily Karnak bus from Aleppo cost S£11 and takes two hours. Buses to Damascus cost about S£15.

ALEPPO (Halab)

North of Damascus and Homs and near the border with Turkey, there are a lot of things to do in this interesting town.

There's a good museum, the souk is superb and there are many caravanserai. It's easy to spend days wandering around the souk. You can also have tea in the Baron Hotel of Lawrence of Arabia fame.

Places to Stay

Hotel Claridge in the Babel Forage district or the *Al Ma'ari Hotel* near the tourist office are cheap. The *Al Boustan/Heliopolis Hotel* in Bab al Faraj has doubles with bath for S£63.

Getting There

Buses, taxis and, twice a week, trains run from Damascus to Aleppo. From Hama the daily Karnak bus takes two hours and costs S£11.

Continuing to Turkey a service taxi to the border point for Antakya is S£10. There is a bus between the border points for S£5 and from there you can take a service taxi to Antakya. From Aleppo north to the Turkish border you can bus to A'zaz and then hitch or taxi the few km to the actual border. Or you can get a taxi straight from Aleppo – but coming from Turkey a taxi directly to Aleppo will probably be a rip-off, cheaper just to go to A'zaz and bus or taxi from there. Twice weekly there's a train from Adana to Aleppo which is very cheap compared to the daily bus from Antakya.

TARTUS

This Mediterranean port and resort has a small but interesting museum in the old cathedral. While it is possible for men to swim freely on the beach in town, women must cover up although bikinis are acceptable on the beaches south of town (10 minutes by bus) beside the chalets. You can use the beach belonging to the Chatel Achlem Restaurant for S£5 per day. The office is in a low round building immediately south of the restaurant and there are showers, changing rooms and chatty lifeguards.

Places to Stay & Eat

The *Grand Hotel* on the Corniche is pricey. *Hotel Baher* (Beach) on the Corniche costs S£63 for a double with bath. The *Tourism Hotel* is cheap and there are other hotels by Arwad Port. The beach chalets out of town are expensive.

Beside the falafel shops is a place with *wonderful* macaroons!

Getting There

Karnak buses from Damascus operate twice daily, take four hours and cost S£16. From Aleppo via Homs there's an early morning departure for the 4½ hour, S£19 bus. The trip from Homs to Tartus is really nice but if you're continuing from Homs to Latakia it may be worth buying a Damascus-Latakia ticket and throwing away the Damascus-Homs part. From Latakia to Aleppo is another S£8, a rather weird bus ride where you've got to fight for a seat. The Latakia-Antakya route is a pleasant way to or from Turkey. From the border to Latakia is S£15.

PALMYRA (Tadmor)

On the route across the desert from Damascus to the Euphrates (Furat), Palmyra was at one time a Greek outpost of considerable importance. It was an Assyrian caravan town over a thousand years BC but only enjoyed its later Greek period of glory for two centuries. In 106 AD it was annexed by the Roman empire and became a centre of unsurpassed wealth. In 226 the Romans lost it and in 241, following its recapture, it was sacked and subsequently has been deserted. The ruins are superb and don't miss the Wally (Valley) of the Tombs. Climb to the (modern) 17th century Arab castle for a splendid view over the ruins in the evening. The museum in Tadmor sells an interesting guide book titled *Welcome to Palmyra*.

Places to Stay & Eat

The *Orient Hotel* is S£58 for a double with bath and is very good. *Hotel Zenobia* is S£65 for a similarly equipped room. The *Tourist Hotel* is also in the same bracket.

The *Green Oasis Cafe* is good but pricey – a plate of kebab and grilled tomato, salad and tea for two costs S£42.

Getting There

There are Karnak buses twice daily from Damascus and the four hour trip costs S£25. Homs is 2½ hours away, there's one Karnak bus a day for S£11.

Onward Travel

Having got to the end of the line in Turkey or one of the Middle East countries that border the Med you've got to decide where next – Europe or Africa? Or alternatively you've got to get across Europe to your Asian starting point.

EUROPE

From London you can fly, bus, train or hitch-hike to Asia. From London bucket shop travel agents count on around £200 or less for a flight to Istanbul. A flight to Cairo, Tel Aviv or Damascus would be fairly similar – perhaps a bit more or less. Athens is a major travel centre for the eastern Mediterranean – lots of cheap tickets and other travel possibilities can be found here. You can also get 'magic buses' to Athens or even Istanbul. They hammer straight through in several days of non-stop travel – it's hard work. Much the same story applies in the opposite direction but be wary of bus tickets in Istanbul – they're notorious for not taking people to where they have paid for.

If you're not flying or going directly by bus across Europe then a variety of possible routes are open to you. From London hitching is fairly reasonable until you get to Yugoslavia, from where it is hard going. Coming from Turkey you can find a hitching partner or look for rides from Istanbul (check the Pudding Shop noticeboard) or in Greece the youth hostel in Thessaloniki is a popular bottleneck with many travellers passing through. If you want to cut through Bulgaria get a visa beforehand as at the border they're much more expensive. That country has a bad case of the long hair and beard phobia. The fast central route through Yugoslavia is a real bore, it's much more interesting to travel up the beautiful Adriatic coast.

An alternative to the Yugoslavia route is to go through Greece and then ferry across to Italy. You can take the conventional route from Istanbul to Thessaloniki and then Athens or cross over to one of the Greek islands and Athens and although the costs are not so low, the distances are very short between the Turkish mainland and the closer islands. Athens is a real travel centre – the Bangkok of south-east Europe. From Greece there are plenty of ferries from Igoumenitsa to Italy. The one to and from Otranto, right down on the heel of Italy, is the cheapest.

In Greece and Yugoslavia there are cheap hotels and pensions and everywhere in Europe reasonable accommodation can be found in youth hostels, camping sites or, during the university vacations, in student hostels. Take full advantage of the excellent tourist offices in every European country. They all have free maps and booklets listing their campsites. Greece even has 'Tourist Police' who are there simply to help visitors find accommodation or get over any problems – they'll even recommend the best beaches to sleep on. For information on travelling through Europe I recommend *Let's Go Europe*.

AFRICA

The alternative to Europe is Africa. It's quite easy to get across from the Middle East to Egypt either from one of the Arab nations by air or from Israel by land. Or you can go to Athens from where it's easy to fly to Cairo. You could then head south down the Nile and into darkest Africa or hop across Libya to the more hospitable parts of North Africa. There are a variety of options once you get to Tunisia, Algeria and Morocco. One is to ferry across from Tunisia to Sicily and Italy. A second is to continue to Morocco and ferry across to Spain. Or you could turn south and start out across the Sahara into Africa. For more information see Lonely Planet's *Africa on a Shoestring*.

SOUTH-EAST & NORTH-EAST ASIA

There's a lot more Asia to the east of the sub-continent. For full information on South-East Asia look for *South-East Asia on a Shoestring*. Travelling in this region is more expensive than in west Asia because of the stretches of sea you have to cross by boat or air. Accommodation and food are also generally a bit more pricey, but in compensation the standards are higher. Generally the South-East Asian countries are more affluent and westernised than the west Asian ones.

Travelling from Australia to Asia (read this backwards if you're going in the opposite direction) you have a choice of shipping or flying. There are regular ship departures from Perth in Western Australia to Singapore but this is really no cheaper than flying. You can fly direct from Perth, Darwin or the east coast capital cities to Indonesia, Singapore, Malaysia or Thailand and then start your South-East Asia travels from there. Most people travel around Indonesia, up through Malaysia, through Thailand and then across to the sub-continent.

Apart from the regular Penang (Malaysia) to Madras (India) ship service there is no alternative to flying from South-East Asia and flying will be the cheapest way. You cannot cross Burma by land. Flight possibilities include Singapore or Kuala Lumpur to Sri Lanka or India or from Bangkok to Bangladesh, India or Nepal. The Bangkok flights are the cheapest way to make the leap from South-East Asia to the sub-continent. Take advantage of going via Burma, seven days in that country (that's all they'll allow you) is an experience not to be missed.

Naturally there are variations on the straightforward routes – like going from Australia to Papua New Guinea then Indonesia. Or slotting in the Philippines and Hong Kong. Forgetting about Australia, if you're continuing on to the US from Asia you've got all of North-East Asia to consider as well as South-East Asia. From Bangkok it's easy to get tickets that take you to Hong Kong, Taiwan, Korea and Japan before the US west coast. For full details on travelling in those countries see our third Asia shoestring guide *North-East Asia on a Shoestring* – it's been long delayed but is finally available. Now that China has even opened up Tibet to independent travellers it's even possible to make an overland trip all the way from Hong Kong to London, now there's something to dream about!

Index

362 Index

Update Supplement

BANGLADESH
If you're flying through Bangladesh with Biman and have to make an overnight stopover in Dacca make certain your ticket is marked that Biman is supplying accommodation. Otherwise you will find you have the option of an uncomfortable night in the transit lounge or else going into Dacca at your own expense, paying for a hotel and paying the hefty departure tax the next day. Just because Biman tells you that accommodation will be supplied makes no difference if the ticket does not actually say so.

INDIA
Getting Around
Indian Airlines' youth fare is, it appears, a bit of a scam. The 25% reduction is only off the US dollar fare and at present 75% of the US dollar fare is more than 100% of the rupee fare!

Money
We've had several letters recently from people experiencing difficulties cashing American Express travellers' cheques in India. It seems to be fairly random but it might be an idea not to be 100% dependent on one brand of cheques in India.

Visas
Kuala Lumpur appears to be another bad place for obtaining Indian visas. Bangkok gets good and bad reports – one traveller said it was quick and easy there, another thought the Bangkok embassy was chaotic but got a visa quickly and easily in Chiang Mai.

IRAN
Tehran
The *Amir Kabir* is not the world's finest hostelry – a recent letter movingly commented that, 'I wouldn't lodge my worst friend's teddy bear in that dump.' The *Youth Hostel*, however, was recommended – cheap meals, friendly people and a maid cleans out your room and makes the bed every morning!

Isfahan
Cheap places are hard to come by but the *Shahzad Inn* on the main road near the major bus terminals is OK (just) at 400 rials per person.

364 Credits

Bos (Nl), Joan Brown (Aus), Craig Bullock (UK), Tony Bullock, Asim Butt (UK), Sylvia Caras (USA), Annie Caswell (C), Mickie Chronister (USA), Tim Clark, Jane Coburn & Phil Barnes (Aus), G Cockey (UK) Diana M Cohen (Nw), Gabriele & Brett Collins (USA), Paul Cooper (UK), Hugh Corbett (UK), Tim Court (UK), Simon Crivicich (UK), Peter Culross (Aus), Rod Cunningham (Aus), S Currie (Aus), Richard Davies (UK), Desh Deepak (I), H Deng-Hausen Jr (USA), Cathy Doherty & John Adams (Aus), A Drayton (Aus), Mark Dwyer (Aus), Roger Edmunds (UK), Jim Ellison (USA), Hilary English & Geoffrey Leigh (Aus), Bob Fisher (Aus), Nick Fisher (Aus), Pete & Gill Flegg (UK), Akviazili Fuson (B), Roslyn Garavaglia, P & M Girdler (Aus), Emily Goldfarb (USA), Rae Goldstein, Roni Goldstein (I), Richard Graves (UK), Jim Greenblatt (USA), G S Grimson (UK), Josh Groves (USA), Heleen Guizt (Nl), Nils Gustafsson, Tom Harriman & Jan King (USA), Nerida & Robert Hall (Aus), Bryan Hanson (UK), Suzanne Harris (Aus), Felicity Harvest (UK), David Hipgrave (Aus), Dorothy Hirschland (USA), Liam Hoey (Irl), Christopher Hogan (Aus), Josh & Charmy Holehouse (USA), Heather Julian & Lyndie Howard (Aus), Steve & Mandy Jones (Aus), Mark Kalish (USA), Wolfgang Kasper (Aus), Brian Kearns (UK), Donna Kirkland (USA), Judith Klenninan (UK), I Krishnasamy (UK), Peders Larsen (Dk), Anette Larsin (Dk), Robyn & Peter Lather (Aus), Steve Leathers (USA), Tom Lesisko (USA), Vivienne Linder (NZ), Linus & Sharon (Aus), Garth Martin (Aus), Pauly & Iain Maclean (NZ), Charlie & H John Maier (USA), Annie & Gerry Marcucci, Geoffrey J Martyn (USA), Mikkel Mcalinden, E J McGuinniety (UK), Fiona McRae (UK), Elan Melamid (USA), Chrissy Merton (UK), Roger G Michaud, H J Miller & G W Bowyer (UK), Catherine Mooney (D), G Morgan (Aus), Shirley Morris (Aus), Rosenzveig Moshe (Aus), Margit & Beat Muller (CH), William Munsey (Isr), Fraser Murdoch (UK), Bernadette Murphy (Irl), Simon Murry (UK), Meredith & Mark Neeson (Aus), Vicky & Kerry Nichols (Aus), Anders Nielsen (Dk), T O'Gorman (C), Jan Oprins (Nl), P J Pearson, Robert Peel (UK), Nicholas Pierce (UK), Peter Pimm (UK), Bruce Pink, P Pomarede (C), Martin Powell (UK), Jenny Pratt (Aus), Jim Priest (USA), Amy Prince (USA), Jean Rannie & Joe Hatz, Andy Rees, Tammy & Peter Reeves (UK), G & Z Reynish (Aus), Anne Robinson & Jane Nineham, Jean Robinson (UK), Marlene Roeder (USA), Lisa Roscoe, Mrs B Rose (UK), Michael Ross (Aus), Peter Ross (UK), Darren Russell (Aus), Catherine Saalfield (USA), Peter Saunders & Jane Appleton (Aus), Rian & Aleks Scheffer (Nl), Anya Schiffrin (USA), Dennis Schulz (Aus), Robert Sebes (Aus), Steve Sharp & Angie Finney, Paddy Sheehan (Irl), Dave & Angie Shiress (NZ), Gary Siegel (USA), Kevin Silva (USA), Matt Simmonds (UK), Bruce T Singer (USA), Fred & Sheila Smart (Aus), Peder Steffensen (Dk), Sally Stibbard (UK), Glenn Strachan (USA), John Stubbs (NZ), Sita Stuhlmiller (USA), Eugen Sobka (USA), Paul Suhler (USA), Richard Tanner (F), Keith Taylor (UK), Stephen Thomas (UK), Judith Tregear & David Murry-Smith (Aus), A J Truelove, David Teagle & Helen Turner (UK), Peter Tenenbaum (Aus), Syb Terwee (Nl), Mike Urlocker (C), Wim Voerman & Jela de Horst, Heinz Vohma (Aus), T B Wahl (D), Freida Wachsmann (Aus), Paul Wagner (Aus), Tim Walker (CH), W Wardrop (UK), Sheldon Weeks (PNG), Kathryn Wells & Gary Anderson (Aus), Alan W Welsh (UK), Peter Wettig (Aus), Rick Wicks (USA), Roz & Stephen Willis (Aus), George Wood (Sw), Michael Woodhouse (Aus), Coralie Younger (Aus)

A – Austria, Aus – Australia, B – Belgium, C – Canada, CH – Switzerland, D – Germany, Dk – Denmark, F – France, I – India, Irl – Ireland, Isr – Israel, Nl – Netherlands, Nw – Norway, NZ – New Zealand, Sp – Spain, Sw – Sweden, UK – UK, USA – USA, Z – Zambia

A Warning & a Request

Things change – prices go up, good places go bad, bad places go bankrupt and nothing stays the same. So if you find things better, worse, cheaper, more expensive, recently opened or long ago closed please don't blame me but please do write and tell me. The letters we get from 'our' travellers out there on the road are some of the nicest things about doing these guides for a living. As usual the best letters will score a free copy of the next edition (or any other LP guide if you prefer) (and your information is good enough!).

LONELY PLANET NEWSLETTER

We collect an enormous amount of information here at Lonely Planet. Apart from our research we also get a steady stream of letters from people out on the road – some of them are just one line on a postcard, others go on for pages. Plus we always have an ear to the ground for the latest on cheap airfares, new visa regulations, borders opening and closing. A lot of this information goes into our new editions or 'update supplements' in reprints. But we want to make better use of this information so, we also produce a quarterly newsletter packed full of the latest news from out on the road. It appears in January, April, July and October of each year. If you'd like an airmailed copy of the most recent newsletter just send us $7.50 for a years subscription, or for $2 each for single issues. That's US$ in the US or A$ for Australia, write to:

Lonely Planet Publications

PO Box 88, Sth Yarra, VIC., 3141 Australia

    or

Lonely Planet Publications

PO Box 2001A, Berkeley, CA 94702 USA